Lecture Notes in Computer Science 15841

Founding Editors

Gerhard Goos
Juris Hartmanis

Series Editors

Elisa Bertino, *Purdue University, West Lafayette, IN, USA*
Wen Gao, *Peking University, Beijing, China*
Bernhard Steffen , *TU Dortmund University, Dortmund, Germany*
Moti Yung, *Columbia University, New York, NY, USA*

The series Lecture Notes in Computer Science (LNCS), including its subseries Lecture Notes in Artificial Intelligence (LNAI) and Lecture Notes in Bioinformatics (LNBI), has established itself as a medium for the publication of new developments in computer science and information technology research, teaching, and education.

LNCS enjoys close cooperation with the computer science R & D community, the series counts many renowned academics among its volume editors and paper authors, and collaborates with prestigious societies. Its mission is to serve this international community by providing an invaluable service, mainly focused on the publication of conference and workshop proceedings and postproceedings. LNCS commenced publication in 1973.

Philipp Rümmer · Zhilin Wu

Editors

Theoretical Aspects of Software Engineering

19th International Symposium, TASE 2025
Limassol, Cyprus, July 14–16, 2025
Proceedings

 Springer

Editors
Philipp Rümmer ⓘ
University of Regensburg
Regensburg, Germany

Zhilin Wu ⓘ
Institute of Software, Chinese Academy
of Sciences
Beijing, China

ISSN 0302-9743   ISSN 1611-3349 (electronic)
Lecture Notes in Computer Science
ISBN 978-3-031-98207-1   ISBN 978-3-031-98208-8 (eBook)
https://doi.org/10.1007/978-3-031-98208-8

© The Editor(s) (if applicable) and The Author(s), under exclusive license
to Springer Nature Switzerland AG 2026

This work is subject to copyright. All rights are solely and exclusively licensed by the Publisher, whether
the whole or part of the material is concerned, specifically the rights of translation, reprinting, reuse of
illustrations, recitation, broadcasting, reproduction on microfilms or in any other physical way, and transmission
or information storage and retrieval, electronic adaptation, computer software, or by similar or dissimilar
methodology now known or hereafter developed.
The use of general descriptive names, registered names, trademarks, service marks, etc. in this publication
does not imply, even in the absence of a specific statement, that such names are exempt from the relevant
protective laws and regulations and therefore free for general use.
The publisher, the authors and the editors are safe to assume that the advice and information in this book
are believed to be true and accurate at the date of publication. Neither the publisher nor the authors or the
editors give a warranty, expressed or implied, with respect to the material contained herein or for any errors
or omissions that may have been made. The publisher remains neutral with regard to jurisdictional claims in
published maps and institutional affiliations.

This Springer imprint is published by the registered company Springer Nature Switzerland AG
The registered company address is: Gewerbestrasse 11, 6330 Cham, Switzerland

If disposing of this product, please recycle the paper.

Preface

The International Symposium on Theoretical Aspects of Software Engineering (TASE) brings together researchers and practitioners interested in new results and innovative advances in software engineering. It records the latest developments in formal and theoretical software engineering methods and techniques.

TASE 2025 was the 19th International Symposium on Theoretical Aspects of Software Engineering, a series of symposia started in 2007 with the aim to bring together researchers and developers from academia and industry with interest in the theoretical aspects of software engineering. In past years, TASE took place in Shanghai (2007), Nanjing (2008), Tianjing (2009), Taipei (2010), Xi'an (2011), Beijing (2012), Birmingham (2013), Changsha (2014), Nanjing (2015), Shanghai (2016), Sophia Antipolis (2017), Guangzhou (2018), Guilin (2019), Hangzhou (2020), Shanghai (2021), Cluj-Napoca (2022), Bristol (2023), and Guiyang (2024).

TASE 2025 was held in Limassol, Cyprus during July 14–16, 2025. This year we received 66 submissions covering different areas of theoretical software engineering. Each paper was single-blindly reviewed by at least three reviewers and the Program Committee accepted 20 regular long papers and 1 short paper leading to an attractive scientific program. This edition of TASE was enhanced by the presence of 2 keynote speakers, Konstantinos Sagonas (Uppsala University and National Technical University of Athens), and Min Zhang (East China Normal University).

TASE 2025 would not have succeeded without the deep investment and involvement of the Program Committee members and the external reviewers who evaluated and selected the best contributions. This event would not exist without the authors and contributors who submitted their papers. We address our thanks to everyone—reviewers, authors, Program Committee members, and organization committee members—involved in the success of TASE 2025.

The EasyChair system was set up for the management of TASE 2025, supporting submission, review, and volume preparation processes. It proved to be a powerful framework. We thank Springer for the smooth cooperation in the production of this proceedings volume.

TASE 2025 was hosted by the University of Cyprus, Cyprus, and sponsored by AWS, Amazon. The local organization committee offered all the facilities to run the event in a lovely and friendly atmosphere. Many thanks to all the local organizers, in particular, the general and local organization chair, George A. Papadopoulos.

Lastly, we wish to express our special thanks to the steering committee members, in particular Shengchao Qin and Huibiao Zhu, for their valuable support.

May 2025

Philipp Rümmer
Zhilin Wu

Organization

Program Committee

Jie An	Institute of Software, Chinese Academy of Sciences, China
Peter Backeman	Mälardalen University, Sweden
Guangdong Bai	The University of Queensland, Australia
Nikolaj Bjørner	Microsoft, USA
Marcello Bonsangue	Leiden University, Netherlands
Julie Cailler	LORIA, University of Lorraine, France
Mingshuai Chen	Zhejiang University, China
Lucas Cordeiro	The University of Manchester, UK
Mohammed Erradi	ENSIAS Rabat, Morocco
Grigory Fedyukovich	Florida State University, USA
Marc Frappier	Université de Sherbrooke, Canada
Hongfei Fu	Shanghai Jiao Tong University, China
Zoltán Horváth	Eötvös Loránd University, Hungary
Zhe Hou	Griffith University, Australia
Andreas Katis	KBR Inc. at NASA Ames Research Center, USA
Jyun-Ao Lin	National Taipei University of Technology, Taiwan
Shaoying Liu	East China Normal University, China
Wanwei Liu	National University of Defense Technology, China
Eric Mercer	Brigham Young University, USA
Dominique Mery	LORIA, Université de Lorraine, France
Mizuhito Ogawa	NPO "Old Teachers Network", Japan
Jun Pang	University of Luxembourg, Luxembourg
Andrei Paskevich	Université Paris-Saclay, LMF, France
Anna Philippou	University of Cyprus, Cyprus
Kristin Yvonne Rozier	Iowa State University, USA
Philipp Rümmer (PC Co-chair)	University of Regensburg, Germany and Uppsala University, Sweden
Daniel Stan	LRE EPITA, ICube, University of Strasbourg, France
Jun Sun	Singapore Management University, Singapore
Ramanathan Thinniyam Srinivasan	Uppsala University, Sweden
Aaron Tomb	Amazon Web Services, USA

Zhilin Wu (PC Co-chair)   Institute of Software, Chinese Academy of
                                     Sciences, China
Zhiwu Xu   Shenzhen University, China
Yedi Zhang   National University of Singapore, Singapore
Zhenya Zhang   Kyushu University, Japan

Additional Reviewers

Baskar, A.   Phan, Viet-Anh
Bense, Viktor   Rebii, Jamal
Bereczky, Péter   Riley, Daniel
Bouharoun, Mouad   Sa Menezes, Rafael
Britikov, Konstantin   Shang, Yuxiang
Cai, Shiyu   Somfai, Ellák
Chakir, El Mostapha   Stutz, Felix
Charalambous, Yiannis   Sun, Xinyu
Dantas, Pierre   Sun, Yutao
El-Yahyaoui, Abdeslam   Szalontai, Balázs
Farias, Bruno   Tawari, Anuj
Filliâtre, Jean-Christophe   Tejfel, Máté
Gamboa Guzman, Laura P.   Wang, Zhongyi
Hamza, Ameer   Wang, Zili
Huang, Lei   Wei, Chenfeng
Jerbi, Manel   Xiao, Yuan
Li, Shiyu   Yang, Linyu
Marmanis, Iason   Zhong, Zhiqiang
Mercha, El Mahdi

Optimal Algorithms for Stateless Model Checking (Invited Talk)

Konstantinos Sagonas[1,2] (ORCID)

[1] Uppsala University, Uppsala, Sweden
[2] National Technical University of Athens, Athens, Greece

Abstract. Stateless model checking (SMC) [9] is a fully automatic testing and verification technique with low memory requirements. It checks concurrent programs for safety errors (e.g. program crashes, assertion violations, etc.) by systematically exploring all possible thread schedulings. SMC becomes effective when coupled with Dynamic Partial Order Reduction (DPOR) [8,1], a runtime technique which introduces an equivalence on schedulings and reduces the amount of exploration. DPOR algorithms that are *optimal* [1] are particularly effective in that they guarantee to *explore* exactly one execution from each equivalence class, thereby avoiding redundant work and managing to achieve sometimes exponential reduction over non-optimal techniques.

This invited talk will present a variety of recently proposed techniques for stateless model checking, focussing on DPOR algorithms that provide (different kinds of) optimality guarantees [3,7,5,11,6,4]. We will review the challenges that are involved in designing such algorithms, and the time and space guarantees that some of these algorithms provide. Last, but not least, we will present SMC tools implementing these algorithms [2,10,12], and some results from code bases that these tools have been applied.

References

1. Abdulla, P., Aronis, S., Jonsson, B., Sagonas, K.: Optimal dynamic partial order reduction. In: Symposium on Principles of Programming Languages, pp. 373–384. POPL 2014, ACM, New York, NY, USA (2014). https://doi.org/10.1145/2535838.2535845
2. Abdulla, P.A., Aronis, S., Atig, M.F., Jonsson, B., Leonardsson, C., Sagonas, K.: Stateless model checking for TSO and PSO. In: Tools and Algorithms for the Construction and Analysis of Systems. LNCS, vol. 9035, pp. 353–367. Springer, Berlin, Heidelberg (2015). https://doi.org/10.1007/978-3-662-46681-0_28
3. Abdulla, P.A., Aronis, S., Jonsson, B., Sagonas, K.: Source sets: a foundation for optimal dynamic partial order reduction. J. ACM 64(4), 25:1–25:49 (2017). https://doi.org/10.1145/3073408
4. Abdulla, P.A., Atig, M.F., Das, S., Jonsson, B., Sagonas, K.: Parsimonious optimal dynamic partial order reduction. In: Sagonas, K. (ed.) Computer Aided Verification

- 36th International Conference, CAV 2024, Proceedings, Part II. LNCS, vol. 14682, pp. 2 19–43. Springer (2024). https://doi.org/10.1007/978-3-031-65630-9_2

5. Abdulla, P.A., Atig, M.F., Jonsson, B., Lång, M., Ngo, T.P., Sagonas, K.: Optimal stateless model checking for reads-from equivalence under sequential consistency. Proc. ACM Program. Lang. 3(OOPSLA), 150:1–150:29 (2019). https://doi.org/10.1145/3360576

6. Albert, E., de la Banda, M.G., Gómez-Zamalloa, M., Isabel, M., Stuckey, P.J.: Optimal dynamic partial order reduction with context-sensitive independence and observers. J. Syst. Softw. 202, 111730 (2023). https://doi.org/10.1016/J.JSS.2023.111730

7. Aronis, S., Jonsson, B., Lång, M., Sagonas, K.: Optimal dynamic partial order reduction with observers. In: Tools and Algorithms for the Construction and Analysis of Systems - 24th International Conference. LNCS, vol. 10806, pp. 229–248. Springer, Cham (2018). https://doi.org/10.1007/978-3-319-89963-3_14

8. Flanagan, C., Godefroid, P.: Dynamic partial-order reduction for model checking software. In: Principles of Programming Languages, (POPL), pp. 110–121. ACM, New York, NY, USA (2005). https://doi.org/10.1145/1040305.1040315

9. Godefroid, P.: Model checking for programming languages using VeriSoft. In: Principles of Programming Languages, (POPL), pp. 174–186. ACM Press, New York, NY, USA (1997). https://doi.org/10.1145/263699.263717

10. Kokologiannakis, M., Lahav, O., Sagonas, K., Vafeiadis, V.: Effective stateless model checking for C/C++ concurrency. Proc. ACM on Program. Lang. 2(POPL), 17:1–17:32 (2018). https://doi.org/10.1145/3158105

11. Kokologiannakis, M., Marmanis, I., Gladstein, V., Vafeiadis, V.: Truly stateless, optimal dynamic partial order reduction. Proc. ACM Program. Lang. 6(POPL), 1–28 (2022). https://doi.org/10.1145/3498711

12. Kokologiannakis, M., Vafeiadis, V.: GenMC: a model checker for weak memory models. In: Computer Aided Verification - 33rd International Conference, CAV 2021, Proceedings, Part I. LNCS, vol. 12759, pp. 427–440. Springer (2021). https://doi.org/10.1007/978-3-030-81685-8_20

Contents

Trustworthy AI and System Software

Program Analysis using Machine Learning

Security

Dynamic Analysis

of neural networks that first abstract an input concrete state and then map it to a corresponding symbolic state for both training and prediction. Crucially, this allows for the enumeration of all state-action relations for formal verification, even without knowledge of the network's internal structure, parameters, or activation functions. Experimental results on a wide range of benchmarks demonstrate that neural networks trained using this approach exhibit comparable performance, while the reachability analysis of the corresponding systems becomes significantly more amenable, showing improved tightness and efficiency over state-of-the-art white-box approaches.

Extending this abstraction-based methodology, our another approach involves training a linear constraint over all concrete states represented by the same symbolic state, alongside the action space [18]. Intuitively, this approximates a non-linear neural network controller using a set of piecewise linear ones, which are demonstrably more amenable to formal verification than complex neural networks. Since linear constraints offer greater expressiveness than constants, this method achieves an optimal balance between abstraction granularity and verification scalability.

Counterexample-Guided Verification-in-the-Loop Certifiably Safe Training. The level of abstraction granularity can be determined under the guidance of counterexamples, analogous to the CEGAR (CounterExample-Guided Abstraction and Refinement) approach in model checking [6]. A provably safe controller can be trained by repeatedly refining abstracted symbolic states. This refinement is guided by the counterexamples that witness how neural network controllers violate predefined safety properties. These counterexamples are typically obtained by model-checking the system's specified safety properties against the currently trained symbolic state space. When safety properties are violated by the controller under training within certain abstract states, these states are refined, and training continues on the enhanced state space. This iterative process persists until all predefined properties are formally verified against the trained model [12].

Integrating verification directly into the training loop offers multifold benefits. First, this *train-verify-refine* learning paradigm inherently provides a provable safety guarantee for the trained controller. Second, the timely feedback from verification results guides both state space refinement and subsequent training, leading to quicker convergence of learning. This contrasts sharply with conventional ex post facto bug detection after training, which significantly increases both the time and financial costs of development and deployment. Third, this new learning paradigm enables the elimination of neural network controllers during the verification phase, thus making it orthogonal to mainstream verification techniques such as reachability analysis [2], model checking [1], and barrier certificates [17].

Qualitative and Quantitative Verification of NNCSs under Environmental Uncertainties. Although qualitative verification can establish basic safety, it often falls short in dynamic, open environments where NNCSs are subject to various uncertainties. To build full confidence and enable broader adoption in safety-critical applications, it is essential to quantify the likelihood of unsafe events, even under adverse conditions. We further extend our approach to quantitatively verifying probabilistic DRL policies [24]. The abstract training enables the direct, black-box computation of probabilistic decision outputs for a set of states, significantly simplifying the complexity of reasoning about neural network outputs. We then abstract the execution of the trained neural network policy as a Markov Decision Process (MDP) and perform probabilistic model checking. This yields two types of upper bounds on the probability of unsafe behavior. During MDP construction, we incorporate the reuse of abstract states based on decision units, which significantly alleviates the state explosion problem. Experiments demonstrate that the proposed probabilistic quantitative verification method can yield tighter upper bounds on unsafe probabilities over longer time horizons more efficiently than the state-of-the-art methods, achieving up to a 90x speedup.

Besides probabilistic model checking, Barrier Certificates (BCs) [8] present another effective approach for the qualitative verification of NNCSs. By extending the constraints on traditional barrier certificates, we define various BC variants applicable to both qualitative and quantitative safety verification problems for NNCSs. Our methodology initially aims to establish almost-sure safety guarantees through qualitative verification. If qualitative verification fails, our quantitative verification method is invoked, providing precise lower and upper bounds on probabilistic safety across both infinite and finite time horizons. To facilitate the synthesis of Neural Barrier Certificates (NBCs), we introduce their k-inductive variants, whose conditions are relaxed compared to one-step cases. BCs can be implemented as neural networks and synthesized under the guidance of counterexamples, a process known as CounterExample-Guided Inductive Synthesis (CEGIS) [16]. Building upon CEGIS, we devise a simulation-guided approach for training NBCs, specifically aiming to achieve tightness in computing precise certified lower and upper bounds. We have prototyped our approach into a tool called UniQQ and demonstrate its efficacy on four classic NNCSs [31].

Under environmental perturbations, NNCSs can be modeled as stochastic processes. When such a stochastic process can be proven to be a martingale, several important system properties, such as robustness, can be quantitatively verified. The quantitative properties include: (i) guaranteed bounds for expected cumulative rewards, and (ii) tail bounds for cumulative rewards. For the first time, we introduce the notion of *reward martingales* for the quantitative robustness verification of NNCSs. A reward martingale offers a rigorous mathematical foundation to characterize the impact of state perturbations on system performance in terms of cumulative rewards. The verified results serve as provably quantitative certificates for these two aspects. Similar to neural barrier certificates, reward martingales can be implemented and trained via neural networks, adaptable to different types of control policies. Experimental results demonstrate that our certified bounds tightly enclose simulation outcomes on various NNCSs, indicating the effectiveness and generality of the proposed approach [30].

Barrier Certificate as Runtime Safeguarding Monitor. The aforementioned verification approaches are inherently *offline*, performed prior to system deployment.

These offline results typically rely on the assumption of a predefined fixed set of initial states. However, in many real-world applications, system initial states are often unknown or only partially known due to their inherent reliance on surrounding environments. Therefore, to ensure system safety, a crucial complementary solution involves monitoring the actions predicted by the decision-making neural network at runtime, verifying their safety, and correcting any unsafe actions before they are executed. We term this approach *runtime safeguarding*.

We propose a novel Barrier Certificate (BC)-based approach for the runtime safeguarding of NNCSs under state perturbations [29]. Specifically, for a given NNCS, we first establish an appropriate BC to ensure its offline safety. Subsequently, we transform the runtime safety verification problem into checking the satisfaction of these BC constraints. If these constraints are violated, the corresponding actions are deemed unsafe. In such instances, our method computes alternative safe actions based on the same BC constraints and selects an optimal one for execution. Our approach comprises two essential steps: (1) defining appropriate BCs tailored for specific systems, and (2) efficiently computing alternative safe actions. For the former, we introduce a new type of BCs specifically designed for reach-avoid tasks, in addition to leveraging existing BCs for pure safety tasks. For the latter, we uniformly reduce the safe action computation to a constraint satisfaction problem defined by the BCs. To enhance computational efficiency, we exploit the Lipschitz continuity of both the BCs and the system dynamics [21]. This enables the design of efficient binary search and action-space compression algorithms. Our experimental results demonstrate that, even under various perturbations, our method ensures 100% safety for both safety and reach-avoid tasks, while simultaneously maximizing the achievement of task objectives for reach-avoid scenarios. The average time overhead for safety verification is remarkably low, at only 0.002 s. Furthermore, by combining binary search with action space compression, facilitated by Lipschitz continuity properties, our safe action computation method achieves up to a 70.2% improvement in efficiency compared with random search over the entire action space.

3   Concluding Remarks

We briefly addressed the safety challenges in NN-controlled systems (NNCSs) by integrating formal methods to achieve robust and certifiable neural network controllers in both qualitative and quantitative ways, covering their entire design, training and execution lifecycle. A core idea underlying the introduced methods is to eliminate the black-box neural network controllers from formal models by transforming them into equivalent but verifiable alternatives. Our proposed abstraction-based verification-in-the-loop training paradigm ensures provable safety by design, accelerates safe learning, and is orthogonal to existing verification techniques by eliminating neural networks from formal models. Recognizing real-world uncertainties, we extended our approach to quantitative verification, providing tighter and more efficient probabilistic safety bounds through state space abstraction and Markov Decision Processes (MDPs). Finally, we introduced Barrier Certificates (BCs) as a runtime safeguarding monitor for scenarios with unknown or partially known initial states, ensuring 100% safety via continuous action monitoring and correction. Additionally, we developed reward martingales for quantitative robustness verification under perturbations. Together, our contributions provide a comprehensive framework for designing and deploying certifiably safe and reliable NNCSs in critical applications.

Building upon this established framework, several promising avenues for future research emerge towards developing and managing safe intelligent systems controlled neural networks. First, we plan to investigate the scalability of our abstraction and refinement techniques to even higher-dimensional and more complex industrial systems, potentially integrating adaptive abstraction mechanisms. Second, while our quantitative verification shows significant improvements, exploring methods for computing tighter lower bounds on safety probabilities remains crucial for more comprehensive risk assessment. Third, we aim to extend the application of reward martingales to dynamic and adaptive control policies, where system parameters or environmental conditions evolve over time. Finally, a critical next step involves real-world deployment and validation of our runtime safeguarding monitors on diverse hardware platforms, coupled with rigorous empirical evaluations in highly dynamic and unpredictable environments to further solidify their efficacy and generalizability.

References

1. Abate, A., Katoen, J.P., Lygeros, J., Prandini, M.: Approximate model checking of stochastic hybrid systems. Eur. J. Control. **16**(6), 624–641 (2010)
2. Althoff, M., Stursberg, O., Buss, M.: Reachability analysis of nonlinear systems with uncertain parameters using conservative linearization. In: IEEE Conference on Decision and Control (ICDC 2008), pp. 4042–4048. IEEE (2008)
3. Arulkumaran, K., Deisenroth, M.P., Brundage, M., Bharath, A.A.: Deep reinforcement learning: a brief survey. IEEE Signal Process. Mag. **34**(6), 26–38 (2017)
4. Baier, C., Katoen, J.P.: Principles of Model Checking. MIT Press (2008)
5. Chen, C., et al.: Toward a thousand lights: decentralized deep reinforcement learning for large-scale traffic signal control. In: Proceedings of the AAAI Conference on Artificial Intelligence (AAAI 2020), pp. 3414–3421 (2020)
6. Clarke, E., Grumberg, O., Jha, S., Lu, Y., Veith, H.: Counterexample-guided abstraction refinement. In: Computer Aided Verification: 12th International Conference (CAV 2000), pp. 154–169. Springer (2000)
7. Cousot, P.: Abstract interpretation based formal methods and future challenges. In: Informatics: 10 Years Back, 10 Years Ahead, pp. 138–156. Springer (2001)
8. Dawson, C., Gao, S., Fan, C.: Safe control with learned certificates: a survey of neural lyapunov, barrier, and contraction methods. arXiv:2202.11762 (2022)
9. Hobbs, J.R.: Granularity. In: International Joint Conference on Artificial Intelligence (IJCAI 1985), pp. 432–435 (1985)
10. Huang, C., Fan, J., Chen, X., Li, W., Zhu, Q.: Polar: a polynomial arithmetic framework for verifying neural-network controlled systems. In: ATVA, pp. 414–430 (2022)

11. Huang, C., Fan, J., Li, W., Chen, X., Zhu, Q.: Reachnn: reachability analysis of neural-network controlled systems. ACM Trans. Embed. Comput. Syst. (TECS) **18**(5s), 1–22 (2019)
12. Jin, P., Tian, J., Zhi, D., Wen, X., Zhang, M.: Trainify: a cegar-driven training and verification framework for safe deep reinforcement learning. In: International Conference on Computer Aided Verification (CAV 2022), pp. 193–218. Springer (2022)
13. Jin, P., Wang, Y., Zhang, M.: Efficient LTL model checking of deep reinforcement learning systems using policy extraction. In: International Conference on Software Engineering and Knowledge Engineering (SEKE 2022), pp. 357–362 (2022)
14. Kumar, N., Rahman, S.S., Dhakad, N.: Fuzzy inference enabled deep reinforcement learning-based traffic light control for intelligent transportation system. IEEE Trans. Intell. Transp. Syst. **22**(8), 4919–4928 (2021)
15. Landers, M., Doryab, A.: Deep reinforcement learning verification: a survey. ACM Comput. Surv. **55**(14s), 1–31 (2023)
16. Peruffo, A., Ahmed, D., Abate, A.: Automated and formal synthesis of neural barrier certificates for dynamical models. In: International Conference on Tools and Algorithms for the Construction and Analysis of Systems (TACAS 2021), pp. 370–388. Springer (2021)
17. Prajna, S., Jadbabaie, A.: Safety verification of hybrid systems using barrier certificates. In: International Workshop on Hybrid Systems: Computation and Control, pp. 477–492. Springer (2004)
18. Tian, J., Zhi, D., Liu, S., Wang, P., Chen, C., Zhang, M.: Boosting verification of deep reinforcement learning via piece-wise linear decision neural networks. In: Advances in Neural Information Processing Systems (NeurIPS 2023), vol. 36, pp. 10022–10037 (2023)
19. Tian, J., Zhi, D., Liu, S., Wang, P., Katz, G., Zhang, M.: Taming reachability analysis of DNN-controlled systems via abstraction-based training. In: International Conference on Verification, Model Checking, and Abstract Interpretation (VMCAI 2023), pp. 73–97. Springer (2023)
20. Wan, X., Zeng, L., Sun, M.: Exploring the vulnerability of deep reinforcement learning-based emergency control for low carbon power systems. In: International Joint Conference on Artificial Intelligence (IJCAI 2022), pp. 3954–3961 (2022)
21. Wang, L., Theodorou, E.A., Egerstedt, M.: Safe learning of quadrotor dynamics using barrier certificates. In: IEEE International Conference on Robotics and Automation (ICRA 2018), pp. 2460–2465 (2018)
22. Watanabe, K., Kang, E., Lin, C.W., Shiraishi, S.: Runtime monitoring for safety of intelligent vehicles. In: Annual Design Automation Conference (DAC 2018), pp. 1–6 (2018)
23. Woodlief, T., Toledo, F., Elbaum, S.G., Dwyer, M.B.: The SGSM framework: enabling the specification and monitor synthesis of safe driving properties through scene graphs. Sci. Comput. Program. **242**, 103252 (2025)
24. Yang, J., Zhang, M., Chen, X., Li, Q.: Formal verification of probabilistic deep reinforcement learning policies with abstract training. In: International Conference on Verification, Model Checking, and Abstract Interpretation (VMCAI 2025), pp. 125–147. Springer (2025)
25. Zhang, H., Gu, J., Zhang, Z., Du, L., et al.: Backdoor attacks against deep reinforcement learning based traffic signal control systems. Peer Peer Netw. Appl. **16**(1), 466–474 (2023)

26. Zhang, H., Chen, H., Boning, D.S., Hsieh, C.: Robust reinforcement learning on state observations with learned optimal adversary. In: International Conference on Learning Representations (ICLR 2021) (2021)

27. Zhang, H., et al.: Robust deep reinforcement learning against adversarial perturbations on state observations. In: Annual Conference on Neural Information Processing Systems (NeurIPS 2020), pp. 21024–21037 (2020)

28. Zhang, W., Tu, Z., Liu, W.: Optimal charging control of energy storage systems for pulse power load using deep reinforcement learning in shipboard integrated power systems. IEEE Trans. Ind. Inform. **19**(5), 6349–6363 (2023)

29. Zhi, D., Peixin, W., Zhang, M.: Runtime safeguarding of neural network-controlled systems without backup safety controllers (2025)

30. Zhi, D., Wang, P., Chen, C., Zhang, M.: Robustness verification of deep reinforcement learning based control systems using reward martingales. In: Proceedings of the AAAI Conference on Artificial Intelligence (AAAI 2024), vol. 38, pp. 19992–20000 (2024)

31. Zhi, D., Wang, P., Liu, S., Ong, C.H.L., Zhang, M.: Unifying qualitative and quantitative safety verification of DNN-controlled systems. In: International Conference on Computer Aided Verification (CAV 2024), pp. 401–426. Springer (2024)

Testing-Based Formal Verification with Program Slicing on Functional Soundness and Completeness

Ai Liu[1], Yang Liu[1], Shaoying Liu[2(✉)], and Zhibin Yang[1]

[1] College of Computer Science and Technology, Nanjing University of Aeronautics and Astronautics, Nanjing, China
shaoai@nuaa.edu.cn
[2] Software Engineering Institute, East China Normal University, Shanghai, China
syliu@sei.ecnu.edu.cn

Abstract. Soundness and completeness are two sides of the same coin, used in program analysis to balance between catching all errors and avoiding false positives. Testing-based formal verification has been proposed to reduce test costs and improve software reliability by automatically ensuring the correctness of a program execution path with regard to the functional scenario form of a specification. In this paper, we propose the notions of functional soundness and functional completeness with regard to a functional scenario and develop the corresponding analysis techniques by integrating testing-based formal verification with program slicing. Moreover, we implement tool support for the Java language and conduct an experiment.

Keywords: Functional scenario · Functional soundness · Functional completeness · Testing-based formal verification · Program slicing

1 Introduction

The essence of software engineering is to transform ideas (which are often vague and subjective) into programs. However, since a program is a formal entity with a precise functional implementation, the transition from ideas to programs should involve a formalisation at some point. The earlier this point is, the more benefits there are, such as formal concepts on an abstract level, unambiguous communication of ideas, and improving user trust. Formal methods for software engineering are a way to deal with this in a rigorous process [22].

Formal methods provide a structured approach to software development, with formal specification describing the software's expected behavior and properties, and verification ensuring that these specifications are satisfied, thus guaranteeing the software's reliability and safety [19]. The verification techniques mainly include model checking [2] and theorem proving [23]. Model checking can be

© The Author(s), under exclusive license to Springer Nature Switzerland AG 2026
P. Rümmer and Z. Wu (Eds.): TASE 2025, LNCS 15841, pp. 11–29, 2026.
https://doi.org/10.1007/978-3-031-98208-8_2

computationally expensive and limited to smaller models, while theorem proving can be complex, time-consuming, and may not always provide a conclusive answer due to the undecidability of some logical systems.

Testing-based formal verification (TBFV) combines specification-based testing and formal verification to reduce test costs as well as increase automation of the verification process. The initial idea of TBFV, proposed by [12], adopts Hoare logic [6] to ensure the correctness of program paths (unfolding loop structures) derived by test cases. The idea is further developed to combine with program inspection [16]. A collection of prototype tools to illustrate how to support the method is presented in [14]. The TBFV approach is applied to the verification of SysML activity diagrams [30]. The original framework of TBFV is extended in [9] to deal with operations, which may involve complex data structures and side effects. Replacing the application of Hoare logic with symbolic execution, testing-based formal verification with symbolic execution (TBFV-SE) is proposed in [25]. Branch sequence coverage (BSC) for TBFV-SE is considered in [26] and a fault localization approach is proposed to further pinpoint the problematic positions in the incorrect program paths given by TBFV-SE in [27]. Moreover, the idea is also applied to improve the verification of neural networks, resulting in TBFV-NN, a framework for verifying and improving neural networks [10, 11].

Functional scenario form (FSF), a transformation of formal specification, is used for formal specification animation [13] and test case generation in TBFV [17]. An FSF is a disjunction of functional scenarios, any of which consists of a testing condition and a defining condition. A testing condition is a constraint on some input variables and is used to generate test cases. A defining condition is a constraint that should involve at least one output variable to specify the expected function. In short, functional soundness ensures that the function is correctly implemented for all possible inputs (avoiding false positives) while functional completeness guarantees that all possible outputs can be generated (avoiding false negatives).

When we focus on a functional scenario with a defining condition which does not involve all output variables, there is no need to analyze the whole program and only the statements influencing the related output variables are worth analyzing. Program slicing is an effective technique to extract the part of the program that can affect the values computed at a given program point (a.k.a. slicing criterion) [5, 28]. An integral solution merging together the current program slicing extensions used to slice programs with exception-handling is proposed in [4]. Program slicing has been applied in many disciplines. For instance, an integration of program slicing with cognitive complexity for defect prediction is proposed in [1]. An empirical analysis on locating faults with program slicing is depicted in [24]. A debugging approach for runtime exceptions based on program slicing and stack traces is proposed in [8]. A fault localization approach for null pointer exceptions based on stack trace and program slicing is developed in [7]. A novel program segment testing technique for detecting potential occurrences

of runtime exceptions during the program construction process is described in
[21].

In this paper, we develop a methodology to analyze the program implementation corresponding to a functional scenario with the notions of functional soundness and functional completeness by integrating testing-based formal verification and program slicing. Our main contributions are as follows:

– We propose the notions of functional scenario, functional soundness and completeness.
– We develop a general methodology to verify functional soundness and completeness of a functional scenario by integrating program slicing and testing-based formal verification.
– We implement a tool support for the Java language and conduct an experiment with it.

The remainder of the document is organized as follows. Section 2 explains the motivation for this work. Section 3 defines the notions of functional soundness and functional completeness. Section 4 proposes our methodology. Section 5 conducts an experiment with tool support for the Java language. Section 6 concludes this document and discusses future work.

2 Motivation

Incorrectness logic [18], a formalism similar to Hoare logic, provides a principled logical system to reason about the presence of bugs and also needs to deal with loop structures manually. Although incorrectness logic was proposed in 2020, it has attracted many researchers' attention (more than 57 citations) and derived many variants, such as incorrectness logic for graph programs [20] and quantum programs [3, 29].

Hoare logic is based on specifications of the over-approximated triple

$$\{pre\text{-}condition\} \; program \; \{post\text{-}condition\}$$

which states that the *post-condition* over-approximates (describes a superset of) the set of states reachable upon program termination from states that satisfy the *pre-condition*. Conversely, incorrectness logic uses the under-approximated triple

$$[presumption] \; program \; [result]$$

which states that the *result* under-approximates (describes a subset of) the set of final states that can be reached starting from states satisfying the *presumption*. Example 1 shows that Hoare logic with over-approximated triples may result in false positives, reports of bugs that cannot happen. Example 2 illustrates that incorrectness logic with under-approximated triples may lead to false negatives (missed bugs).

Example 1. Consider the over-approximated triple of a method

$$\{x \in \mathbb{Z}\}$$
```
int f(int x){ return x*x+1;}
```
$$\{f(x) \geq 0\}$$

where $\mathbb{Z}$ is the domain of int type and the statement invoking the method int y=10000/f(x). Obviously, the triple meets Hoare logic. If we analyze the statement with it, it seems possible to trigger an arithmetic exception since $f(x)$ can be 0 in the post-condition. However, this exception will never happen.

Example 2. Consider the under-approximated triple of a method

$$[x \in \mathbb{Z}]$$
```
int g(int x){ return x*x;}
```
$$[g(x) > 0 \land g(x) \in \{n^2 \mid n \in \mathbb{Z}\}]$$

and the statement invoking the method int y=10000/g(x). Obviously, the triple meets incorrectness logic. If we analyze the statement with it, it can be proved that the arithmetic exception will not occur since $g(x)$ cannot be 0 in the result. However, this exception may occur when the input x is 0. Note that if we remove $g(x) \in \{n^2 \mid n \in \mathbb{Z}\}$ from the result, the triple will be neither under-approximated nor over-approximated.

However, reasoning with loop structures in both Hoare logic and incorrectness logic is difficult to be fully automated and requires experts in logic to manually handle. Moreover, the final pre-condition or result will be complex due to the loop invariants. Testing-based formal verification is an alternative approach proposed to unfold loop structures when executing the program with concrete test cases to automatically verify over-approximated triples to some extent. Over-approximated and under-approximated triples correspond to the notions of soundness and completeness, respectively. In this paper, we consider the notions of soundness and completeness for a functional scenario with regard to a program and further explore the utilization of TBFV for automatic verification on them.

3   Functional Soundness and Completeness

Our methodology is based on the notion of functional scenario. Given a functional specification, we should firstly transform it to functional scenarios in our methodology. However, this step is not considered in this document, and there already exists an automatic transformation from VDM operation specifications to functional scenarios in [15]. In this section, we firstly introduce the notions of functional scenario, functional soundness, and functional completeness. Note that the notion of functional scenario in Definition 1 is different from the one in [9,12], since our methodology considers both functional soundness and completeness, as in Definition 2.

Definition 1 (functional scenario). *A functional scenario is a pair of a testing condition T, a constraint restricted only on input variables in the specification and a definition condition D, restricted on at least one output variable, denoted by (T, D).*

A testing condition T represents a part of inputs and the corresponding D describes the expected behavior by restricting some output variables. The functional scenario only describes the functional behavior, but ignores to what extent it has been implemented, which is captured by the notions of functional soundness and completeness.

Definition 2 (functional soundness and completeness). *Given a functional scenario (T, D), where T is restricted on the input variables $x_1, \cdots, x_n$ and the output variables in D are $y_1, \cdots, y_m$, let $\boldsymbol{x} = (x_1, \cdots, x_n)$ and $\boldsymbol{y} = (y_1, \cdots, y_m)$. Given a program P, let $P(\boldsymbol{x})$ be the result of the output variables by executing P with $\boldsymbol{x}$ and $D(P(\boldsymbol{x})/\boldsymbol{y})$ the result by replacing $\boldsymbol{y}$ with $P(\boldsymbol{x})$ in D. Then,*

- *(T, D) is called sound with regard to P if the implication*

$$T \Rightarrow D(P(\boldsymbol{x})/\boldsymbol{y})$$

is a tautology;
- *(T, D) is called complete with regard to P if the implication*

$$\exists \boldsymbol{x} \, (T \wedge D) \Rightarrow \exists \boldsymbol{x} \, (T \wedge \boldsymbol{y} = P(\boldsymbol{x}))$$

is a tautology.

One may be confused about why the premise of completeness is $\exists \boldsymbol{x} \, T \wedge D$ rather than D. Since the definition of D does not have a restriction on input variables, D may contain some input variables. Using $\exists \boldsymbol{x} \, T \wedge D$, the free variables of the implication will only be the output variables.

The notions of functional soundness and completeness correspond to the over-approximated and under-approximated triples, respectively, as described in Theorem 1.

Theorem 1. *Given a functional scenario (T, D) and a program P, the followings hold:*

- *the functional scenario (T, D) is sound with regard to P if and only if $\{T\}P\{D\}$ is an over-approximated triple;*
- *the functional scenario (T, D) is complete with regard to P if and only if $[T]P[D]$ is an under-approximated triple.*

As we mentioned earlier, a specification should be transformed into a functional scenario family in our methodology. Note that two functional scenarios (T, D_1) and (T, D_2) are equivalent to $(T, D_1 \vee D_2)$ since they describe the same functional behavior, i.e., if the input validates the testing condition T, the output is expected to validate either D_1 or D_2. Obviously, the functional soundness (completeness) of (T, D_i) $(i = 1, 2)$ may be different from $(T, D_1 \vee D_2)$. Therefore, we should explore the relation among functional scenarios further, resulting in Definition 3.

Definition 3 (functional scenario family). *A functional scenario family is a set of functional scenarios, denoted by* $\{(T_1, D_1), \cdots, (T_l, D_l)\}$. *Specifically,*

- *it is called a functional scenario family with mutually exclusive input if* $T_i \wedge T_j$ *is a contradiction when* $i \neq j$;
- *it is called a functional scenario family with mutually exclusive output if* $D_i \wedge D_j$ *is a contradiction when* D_i *and* D_j *have the same variables and* $i \neq j$.

Theorem 1 demonstrates the correspondence between functional soundness (completeness) and over-(under-)approximated triples. As an over-approximated triple strictly requires that the post-condition should hold after the program is executed if the pre-condition is validated, if there are other possible outputs for the inputs validating the testing condition, the functional soundness of the functional scenario does not make sense, as demonstrated in Example 3. Therefore, when we consider the functional soundness of a functional scenario belonging to a functional scenario family, we should ensure the functional scenario is with mutually exclusive input at first.

Example 3. Continuing Example 2, it is obvious that

$$(x \in \mathbb{Z}, g(x) > 0 \wedge g(x) \in \{n^2 \mid n \in \mathbb{Z}\})$$

is unsound with regard to the program `int g(int x){ return x*x;}` and $(x \in \mathbb{Z}, g(x) = 0)$ is unsound with regard to the same program. However, if the specification derives the two functional scenarios, the functional behavior should describe that the program should return the square of the integer input. Therefore, to separately verify the functional soundness of the two functional scenarios does not make sense. The functional scenario to be considered should be

$$(x \in \mathbb{Z}, g(x) \geq 0 \wedge g(x) \in \{n^2 \mid n \in \mathbb{Z}\})$$

which is sound with regard to the program.

As for the functional completeness, considering a functional scenario family $\{(T_1, D), (T_2, D)\}$ induced by a certain specification, the corresponding functional behavior requires that the inputs validate T_1 or T_2 and the outputs validate D. Naturally, when it comes to completeness, we should find at least one input validating $T_1 \vee T_2$ for each output validating D so the functional scenario to be verified should be $(T_1 \vee T_2, D)$. Therefore, when we consider the functional completeness of a functional scenario belonging to a functional scenario family, we should ensure the functional scenario is with mutually exclusive outputs in advance.

4   Methodology

As introduced in Sect. 3, the prerequisite of our methodology is a functional specification–functional scenario family $\{(T_1, D_1), \cdots, (T_l, D_l)\}$ with mutually exclusive input and output, where T_i is the constraint restricted only on input variables and D_i the constraint restricted on at least one output variable. Given a functional scenario (T, D), we use a vector $\boldsymbol{x} = (x_1, \cdots, x_n)$ as an input to denote all input variables $x_1, \cdots, x_n$ in T and a vector $\boldsymbol{y} = (y_1, \cdots, y_m)$ as an output to denote all output variables $y_1, \cdots, y_m$ in D.

4.1   An Overview

Given a functional scenario, we intend to analyze its soundness and completeness by integrating testing-based formal verification with program slicing. An overview of our methodology is depicted in Fig. 1. There are three stages: slicing stage, testing stage, and verification stage.

- In the slicing stage, with the program slicing technique, we will obtain a program slice, which is the part of the program that can affect the values of the output variables $y_1, \cdots, y_m$ and also a new executable program. This stage aims to reduce the program scale and thus reduce the cost of testing-based formal verification.
- In the testing stage, based on the obtained program slice, we will generate test cases $t_1, \cdots, t_k$, resulting in different program execution paths $path_1, \cdots, path_k$. For each $path_i$, we will derive the corresponding path condition C_i, which is a constraint restricted only on input variables and represents the inputs resulting in the same path $path_i$, and the corresponding state representation of the output variables $f_i : C_i \wedge T \rightarrow Y_1 \times \cdots \times Y_m$ (Y_i is the domain of y_i), which maps an input $\boldsymbol{x}$ to the output of executing the program slice with it, denoted by $\boldsymbol{y} = f_i(\boldsymbol{x})$.
- In the verification stage, with the above ingredients, we can verify functional soundness and completeness, respectively. For functional soundness, the subsequent steps are as follows.
  - Let $D(f_i(\boldsymbol{x})/\boldsymbol{y})$ be the result by replacing the output $\boldsymbol{y}$ with $f_i(\boldsymbol{x})$ in D and thus its free variables will only include $x_1, \cdots, x_n$.
  - If the implication $\bigwedge_{i=1}^{k}(T \wedge C_i \Rightarrow D(f_i(\boldsymbol{x})/\boldsymbol{y}))$ is not a tautology, it means that there exists at least one input such that the output is not as expected, i.e., the program implementation is unsound with regard to the functional scenario (T, D).

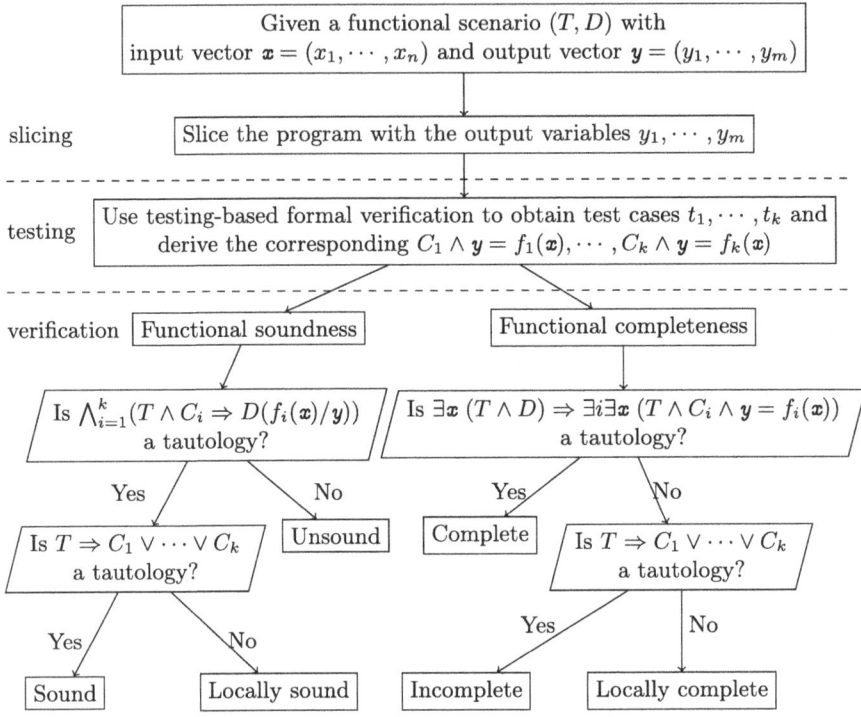

Fig. 1. The overview of our methodology

- If the above implication is a tautology, the other implication $T \Rightarrow C_1 \vee \cdots \vee C_k$ is to be considered: if it is a tautology, the program implementation is sound with regard to the functional scenario (T, D); otherwise, the program implementation is locally sound for inputs validating $(C_1 \vee \cdots \vee C_k) \wedge T$.

For functional completeness, the subsequent steps are as follows.

- The free variables of the implication $\exists x\, (T \wedge D) \Rightarrow \exists i \exists x\, (T \wedge C_i \wedge y = f_i(x))$ will only include $y_1, \cdots, y_m$. If it is a tautology, the program implementation is complete with regard to the functional scenario (T, D).
- If the above implication is not a tautology, the other implication $T \Rightarrow C_1 \vee \cdots \vee C_k$ is to be considered: if it is not a tautology, there exists at least one output which validates D but can not be obtained by executing the program with any input validating T, i.e., the program implementation is incomplete with regard to the functional scenario (T, D); otherwise, the program implementation is locally complete for the outputs that can be obtained by executing the program from some input validating $(C_1 \vee \cdots \vee C_k) \wedge T$.

4.2   Slicing Stage

Program slicing is a sophisticated program analysis technique aimed at extracting relevant parts of a program that pertain to a particular computation or point of interest, known as the slicing criterion. This method is widely utilized in debugging, understanding, testing, and optimizing code by isolating segments that directly influence specific variables or output. The complexity and vastness of modern software systems require such techniques to streamline the process of program comprehension and fault isolation. In this section, we will adapt program slicing to obtain an expected program slice in our methodology.

A critical component in program slicing is program dependency graph (PDG). A PDG is a directed graph representing both data and control dependencies between the statements and predicates within a program. It serves as a comprehensive model to visualize how data flows and how control decisions are made in the program. The basis of PDG is a control flow graph (CFG) of a program, which is a graph $\langle N, E \rangle$ ($E \subseteq N \times N$) which can derive all possible execution paths of a program. Each statement is represented by a node $n \in N$, and two nodes are connected, i.e., $(m, n) \in E$ if they may be executed sequentially. Besides, two nodes *Enter* and *Exit* are added to, respectively, represent the initial and final nodes of the program execution. There are some definitions based on CFG.

Definition 4. *Given a CFG $\langle N, E \rangle$ and a node $n \in N$, the sct of all the program variables that are defined (assigned with values) in n is denoted by $DEF(n)$.*

Definition 5. *Given a CFG $\langle N, E \rangle$ and a node $n \in N$, the set of all the program variables that are used (accessed with values) at n is denoted by $USE(n)$.*

Definition 6. *Given a CFG $\langle N, E \rangle$ and two nodes $m, n \in N$, we say that n post-dominates m if every directed path from m to the Exit node passes through n. We say that n is control dependent on m if and only if n post-dominates one but not all of m's successors, denoted by $m \rightarrow n$.*

Definition 7. *Given a CFG $\langle N, E \rangle$ and two nodes $m, n \in N$, we say that n is data dependent on m if there exists a variable v satisfying:*

- $v \in DEF(m)$;
- $v \in USE(n)$;
- *there exists a path in $\langle N, E \rangle$ from m to n where v is not redefined. In particular, this case is denoted by $m \xrightarrow{v} n$.*

With the above definitions, we can define the notion of PDG and calculate a program slice for a slice criterion.

Definition 8. *Given a CFG $\langle N, E \rangle$ and a program P with $Var(P)$ denoting the set of variables in P, the corresponding PDG is a graph $\langle N', E', \phi \rangle$ where*

- $N' = N - \{Exit\}$;

- $(m, n) \in E'$ if n is data dependent on m (the edge is called data arc) or n is control dependent on m (the edge is called control arc).
- $\phi : E' \to \mathcal{P}(Var(P))$ is a function such that

$$\phi((m, n)) = \begin{cases} \emptyset & n \text{ is control dependent on } m \\ \{v \mid m \xrightarrow{v} n\} & otherwise \end{cases}$$

Definition 9. *Given a PDG for a program P and slicing criterion (k, V) where $V \subseteq DEF(k) \cup USE(k)$, the program slice denoted by $PS(P, (k, V))$ is defined as*

$$PS(P, (k, V)) = \{m \mid (m \xrightarrow{*}{\xrightarrow{v}} k \wedge v \in V) \vee (m \xrightarrow{*} k)\}$$

where $m \to^*$ represents the set of all descendant nodes of m (including itself).

As illustrated in Fig. 1, the desired program slice in our methodology is the relevant parts which will influence some output variables. Therefore, we need find the locations which are the exports of output variables at first. Then, we obtain a program slice for each location with the corresponding output variables. Finally, we should integrate these program slices to be an executable program. It is concluded in Definition 10.

Definition 10. *Given a PDG for a program P and output variables $\{y_1, \cdots, y_m\}$ in P, denote the exports of each y_i as $l_i^1, \cdots, l_i^{k_i}$ and the program slice denoted by $PS(P, \{y_1, \cdots, y_m\})$ is defined as the integration of*

$$\bigcup_{i=1}^{m} \bigcup_{j=1}^{k_i} PS(P, (l_i^j, \{y_i\}))$$

and appropriate braces to make it an executable program. When there's no ambiguity, $PS(P, \{y_1, \cdots, y_m\})$ is abbreviated as $PS(y_1, \cdots, y_m)$.

Example 4. Consider the Java program which calculates and outputs the smallest integer n such that the sum of the cubes of natural numbers from 1 to n is greater than or equal to the user-inputted integer x. Moreover, if x is non-positive, the output should be $error = -1$. The corresponding functional scenario form should have two functional scenarios $(T_1 \wedge D_1) \vee (T_2 \wedge D_2)$ where

$$T_1 := x \leq 0, D_1 := error = -1$$
$$T_2 := x > 0, D_2 := \frac{(n-1)^2 n^2}{4} < x \leq \frac{n^2(n+1)^2}{4}$$

When considering the first functional scenario, the output variable is $error$ and its export is at Line 8. The corresponding program slice $PS(error)$ is obtained by deleting Lines 8–16. Note that Line 8 is also removed since it will change the value of $error$. For the second functional scenario, the output variable is n and its export is at Line 16. The corresponding program slice $PS(n)$ is obtained by deleting Lines 7, 8 and 16.

```
public class UserInputProgram {
    public static void main(String[] args) {
        Scanner scanner = new Scanner(System.in);
        System.out.print("Enter a number: ");
        int x = scanner.nextInt();
        if (x <= 0) {
            int error = -1;
            System.out.println("error = " + error);
        } else {
            int sum = 0;
            int n = 0;
            while (sum < x) {
                n = n + 1;
                sum = sum + (n * n * n);
            }
            System.out.println("n = " + n);
        }
    }
}
```

4.3   Testing Stage

After slicing the program with all output variables $\{y_1, \cdots, y_m\}$ in D to obtain a program slice, we should generate test cases, obtain the traversed paths, and derive the corresponding path conditions and state representations in the testing stage. The detailed steps are depicted in Fig. 2 and explained as follows.

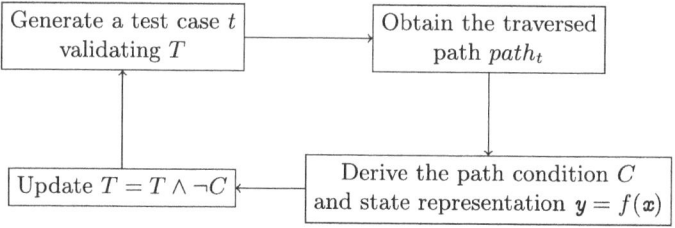

Fig. 2. Testing stage

- Step 1: Generate a test case t validating T.
- Step 2: Execute the program slice with the test case t and record the execution path, consisting of assignment statements, judgments of conditions, and other statements which do not change the program state (e.g. print statements).

- Step 3: Derive the path condition C and state representation $y = f(x)$ according to the following axioms.

$$\frac{}{\{Q(E/x)\}\ x = E\ \{Q\}} \qquad \text{(Assignment)}$$

$$\frac{}{\{Q\}\ S\ \{Q\}} \qquad \text{(Identity)}$$

$$\frac{}{\{B \wedge Q\}\ B\ \{Q\}} \qquad \text{(Branch-T)}$$

$$\frac{}{\{\neg B \wedge Q\}\ \neg B\ \{Q\}} \qquad \text{(Branch-F)}$$

$$\frac{\{Q_1\}\ S_1\ \{Q_2\},\ \{Q_2\}\ S_2\ \{Q_3\}}{\{Q_1\}\ S_1; S_2\ \{Q_3\}} \qquad \text{(Composition)}$$

The Assignment axiom states that the assignment $x = E$ correctly assigns the result of evaluating expression E to variable x with respect to the given post-condition Q and the pre-condition $Q(E/x)$, a predicate resulting from substituting E for all of the free occurrences of x in Q. Note that if x does not appear in Q, $Q(E/x)$ will be equal to Q. The Identity axiom is applied to the statements that do not change the program state, such as *printing statement* and *break statement*. It describes that the pre-condition and post-condition for any of such statements are the same because none of them changes the state. A judgement statement B is a Boolean expression that may be used in $\text{if}(B)\{\cdots\}$ or $\textbf{while}(B)\{\cdots\}$. The Branch-T and Branch-F axioms correspond to the two situations whether the branch is valid or not, respectively. The Composition axiom allows for the sequential composition of program fragments. Finally, C is a constraint on input variables $x_1, \cdots, x_n$ and $y = f(x)$ records a substitution where the output variable $y_1, \cdots, y_m$ are expressions of $x_1, \cdots, x_n$.

- Step 4: Since all test cases validating C will induce the same execution path, to generate any such test case makes no sense. Therefore, we update T as $T \wedge \neg C$ and repeat Step 1.

Example 5. Continuing Example 4, for the program slice $PS(n)$, the first case is generated randomly from the testing condition $x > 0$ and assume that it is 6. Then, we will obtain the following execution path and the corresponding backward derivation process.

$\{1 < x \leq 9, n = 2\}$

¬(x<=0)

$\{0 < x \wedge 1 < x \wedge \neg 9 < x, \hat{n} = 2\}$

sum=0

$\{sum < x \wedge sum + 1 < x \wedge \neg sum + 9 < x, \hat{n} = 2\}$

n=0

$\{sum < x \wedge sum + (n+1)^3 < x \wedge \neg sum + (n+1)^3 + (n+2)^3, \hat{n} = n+2\}$

sum<x

$\{sum + (n+1)^3 \wedge \neg sum + (n+1)^3 + (n+2)^3, \hat{n} = n+1+1)\}$

n=n+1

$\{sum + n^3 \wedge \neg sum + n^3 + (n+1)^3, \hat{n} = n+1\}$

sum=sum+(n*n*n)

$\{sum < x \wedge \neg sum + (n+1)^3 < x, \hat{n} = n+1\}$

sum<x

$\{\neg sum + (n+1)^3 < x, \hat{n} = n+1\}$

n=n+1

$\{\neg sum + n^3 < x, \hat{n} = n\}$

sum=sum+(n*n*n)

$\{\neg sum < x, \hat{n} = n\}$

¬sum<x

$\{\hat{n} = n\}$

In the state representation $\hat{n} = n$ (the start point of the derivation process), $\hat{n}$ represents the final value of the output variable n and thus it could not be substituted in the derivation process while n (on the right side) should be substituted according to the axioms. At the end of the derivation process, the hat of $\hat{n}$ will be removed. Finally, we obtain the path condition $1 < x \leq 9$, representing all inputs inducing the same path, and the corresponding state representation $n = 2$, representing the corresponding output value of n is 2 for this path. For brevity, the statements satisfying the Identity axiom are ignored. Then, a new test case will be randomly generated from the expression $x > 0 \wedge \neg 1 < x \leq 9$. Assume it is 120, the corresponding path condition and state representation will be $64 < x \leq 225$ and $n = 5$. Repeat these processes to obtain more test cases.

4.4   Verification Stage

Since the steps are carried out iteratively in Fig. 2, a natural question is when the process should be stopped. An intuitive termination is achieved if the finally updated T is a contradiction, which means that all execution paths of all test cases validating T have been generated. In this case, functional soundness and functional completeness are two decidable issues, as stated in Theorem 2.

Theorem 2. *Given a functional scenario (T, D) and a program P, assume that for the program slice by slicing P with the output variables $y_1, \cdots, y_m$, the generated test cases are $t_1, \cdots, t_k$ with the corresponding $C_1 \wedge y = f_1(x), \cdots, C_k \wedge y = f_k(x)$ such that $T \Rightarrow C_1 \vee \cdots \vee C_k$ is a tautology. Then, the following hold*

- *(T, D) is sound with regard to P if and only if $\bigwedge_{i=1}^{k}(T \wedge C_i \Rightarrow D(f_i(x)/y))$ is a tautology;*
- *(T, D) is complete with regard to P if and only if $\exists x \, (T \wedge D) \Rightarrow \exists i \exists x \, (T \wedge C_i \wedge y = f_i(x))$ is a tautology.*

In some cases, to make $T \Rightarrow C_1 \vee \cdots \vee C_k$ a tautology may need a huge k, so we may stop early and obtain weaker notions, as in Definition 11. Note that the early stop may depend on the value of k or some coverage criterion, which will be studied in the future.

Definition 11. *Given a functional scenario (T, D) and a program P, assume that for the program slice by slicing P with the output variables $y_1, \cdots, y_m$, the generated test cases are $t_1, \cdots, t_k$ with the corresponding $C_1 \wedge y = f_1(x), \cdots, C_k \wedge y = f_k(x)$. Then, we say that*

- *(T, D) is locally sound with regard to P on $\bigvee_{i=1}^{k} C_i$ if $\bigwedge_{i=1}^{k}(T \wedge C_i \Rightarrow D(f_i(x)/y))$ is a tautology;*
- *(T, D) is locally complete with regard to P on $\bigvee_{i=1}^{k} C_i$ if $\exists x \, (T \wedge D) \Rightarrow \exists i \exists x \, (T \wedge C_i \wedge y = f_i(x))$ is a tautology.*

5 Experiment

5.1 Experiment Setup

Although our methodology is a universal technique, we develop a tool support for the Java language to exemplify its efficiency and accuracy. Since the program slicing is a mature technique, we focus on the efficiency and accuracy of the testing and verification stages in this paper. The tool consists of modules for code parsing, test case generation, dynamic execution, iterative execution, and a verification engine. The workflow is as follows: After users input the target code and the functional scenario, the tool automatically parses the program, generates constraint-based test cases, executes the program, obtains the corresponding path conditions and state representations, and verifies the functional correctness and completeness of the program using the Z3 solver. The tool is developed on IntelliJ IDEA 2024.3.4 and is deployed in a Linux cluster environment (Ubuntu 22.04 LTS). The core logic of the tool consists of 1250 lines of Java code, while an auxiliary module, comprising 500 lines of code, handles dynamic execution and verification functionalities. Key dependencies include Z3 (4.12.2), JavaParser (3.25.4), and Subprocess (3.10.9), which together enable automatic parsing, execution, and verification of Java code within the tool.

The experiment recruited 4 graduate students with intermediate Java programming skills (1–3 years of development experience) to manually analyze 20 open source Java programs and derive the corresponding functional scenarios. The selected programs address typical computational problems, such as cube sum calculation and quadratic equation solving. The authors then use the tool to automatically verify their functional soundness and completeness, respectively.

5.2   An Illustrative Example

Continuing Examples 4 and 5, after the program slice $PS(n)$ and the first functional scenario (T_1, D_1) were given to the tool, only one test case ($x = -10$ in the experiment) was generated and the updated testing condition is a contradiction in the second iteration, since all test cases $x \leq 0$ induce the same path. The tool execution time was 0.980829 s. When considering the second functional scenario, we replaced $0 < x \leq 500$ with $T_2 : x > 0$ as the initial testing condition to avoid the endless generation of test cases. Upon completion of program execution, 7 test cases were generated within the interval $(0, 500]$, in order: $x = 4$ (corresponding to $n = 2$), $x = 365$ (corresponding to $n = 6$), $x = 58$ (corresponding to $n = 4$), $x = 1$ (corresponding to $n = 1$), $x = 470$ (corresponding to $n = 7$), $x = 215$ (corresponding to $n = 5$), $x = 23$ (corresponding to $n = 3$). The tool execution time was 7.205893 s. In summary, there were 10 iterations and the total execution time was 8.186722 s. Therefore, we can calculate an average iteration execution time as $8.186722/10 = 0.818672$ seconds. In the experiment, the average time is used as the efficiency index.

Table 1. Verification Results of D_2 and Its Mutants

No.	D_2	Soundness	Completeness
1	$\frac{(n-1)^2 n^2}{4} < x \leq \frac{n^2(n+1)^2}{4}$	Sound	Complete
2	$\frac{(n-1)^2 n^2}{4} \leq x \leq \frac{n^2(n+1)^2}{4}$	Sound	Incomplete
3	$\frac{(n-1)^2 n^2}{4} < x < \frac{n^2(n+1)^2}{4}$	Unsound	Complete
4	$\frac{(n-1)^2 n^2}{4} \leq x < \frac{n^2(n+1)^2}{4}$	Unsound	Incomplete

To evaluate the accuracy of our methodology, we made three mutants of D_2 and the verification results are shown in Table 1. The experimental results show that the original functional scenario is both sound and complete with regard to the program. It is worth noting that when the lower bound constraint of D_2 is relaxed (No.2), the program still maintains functional soundness, but due to the lack of coverage for some values of output variables, completeness fails. Conversely, when the upper bound constraint is strengthened (No.3), the program maintains output completeness, but due to incorrect functional implementation, soundness fails. It should be mentioned that the test cases generated for No.2, No.3 and No.4 were mutually distinct, as well as different from the previous values, due to the random generation, but the amounts were still 7 since the 7 traversed paths have covered the condition $0 < x \leq 500$ and the execution times were very close.

Table 2. Experiment Results

No.	Name	No. of Iterations	Time(s)	Average Time(s)	Soundness	Completeness
1	CubeSumCalculator	10	8.186722	0.818672	Sound	Complete
2	SquareSumCalculator	13	14.010357	1.000739	UnSound	InComplete
3	NatureSumCalculator	34	68.572322	2.016833	Sound	Complete
4	SetSwitch	6	3.55248	0.59208	Sound	Complete
5	SecantSqrt	23	61.16298	2.659260	Sound	Complete
6	PyramidLayers	37	23.586057	0.637461	Sound	Complete
7	NewtonSqrt	36	35.893584	0.997044	Sound	InComplete
8	NaturalSequence	29	25.441149	0.877281	UnSound	InComplete
9	IsGetTempTime	26	16.443128	0.632428	Sound	Complete
10	PerfectNumber	7	6.207411	0.886773	Sound	Complete
11	Fibonacci	34	53.590494	1.576191	Sound	Complete
12	DigitalRoot	14	7.101598	0.507257	Sound	Complete
13	BisectionSqrt	28	30.839872	1.101424	Sound	Complete
14	FreeFall	29	18.873374	0.650806	Sound	Complete
15	NandGate	5	4.386405	0.877281	Sound	Complete
16	Mormon	9	6.579486	0.731054	Sound	Complete
17	Snowflake	28	22.213352	0.793334	Sound	Complete
18	Inequlity	42	46.921182	1.117171	UnSound	InComplete
19	CubicNumber	27	29.784753	1.103139	Sound	Complete
20	AbsolyteDriver	20	12.28986	0.614693	Sound	Complete

5.3   Experiment Results

As illustrated in the previous example, we use the average iteration execution time to evaluate the efficiency. For convenience in statistics, we just verified the 20 functional scenarios derived by the students, and the results of the experiment are summarized in Table 2. Note that we also limited the values of input variables between the interval $[-500, 500]$. The results demonstrate that the average execution time is close to 1 s in most cases and that four functional scenarios are not consistent with the corresponding programs. All authors have checked and agreed that the four functional scenarios did have problems. Therefore, the experiment results exemplify that our methodology could be used to automatically verify functional soundness and completeness without derivation of loop invariants.

Although the experiment results validate our methodology, we have also learned some lessons from the experiment. The testing condition

$$T \wedge \neg C_{t_1} \wedge \neg C_{t_2} \wedge \neg C_{t_3} \wedge \cdots$$

will become more and more tedious and complex as test cases $t_1, t_2, t_3, \cdots$ are continuously generated. If the number of possible paths is huge, such updating process does not have a termination condition, and the randomness may be ignorant of some representative paths until termination, resulting in low code coverage (e.g. branch coverage and condition coverage). Moreover, the derivation of path conditions and state representations cannot deal with complex data structures and method invocations.

6   Conclusion

In this paper, we introduce the notions of functional soundness and completeness based on the notion of functional scenario. We develop a general methodology to verify the functional soundness and completeness of a functional scenario. In the methodology, program slicing is used to reduce the complexity of the problem and test costs, and testing-based formal verification is used to avoid the difficulty of deriving loop invariants and then enhance the degree of automation of our methodology. We also implement tool support for our methodology for the Java language and conduct an experiment with it.

According to the previous lessons from the experiment, there are two topics that are worth exploring further. A test case coverage criterion is in demand and a corresponding strategy to automatically achieve the criterion would be best. The current methodology cannot be applied directly to programs that have complex data structures and method invocations, since the axioms cannot handle such cases. Taking this into account will greatly enhance the ability of our methodology.

Acknowledgments. The research work is supported by the supporting funds for talents of Nanjing University of Aeronautics and Astronautics. This work is also supported by the Joint Fund of the National Natural Science Foundation of China (Grant No. U2241216).

References

1. Alqadi, B.S., Maletic, J.I.: Integration of program slicing with cognitive complexity for defect prediction. In: Proceedings of ICSME 2020, Adelaide, Australia, pp. 839–843. IEEE (2020). https://doi.org/10.1109/ICSME46990.2020.00106
2. Baier, C., Katoen, J.: Principles of Model Checking. MIT Press, Cambridge (2008)

3. Feng, Y., Li, S.: Abstract interpretation, hoare logic, and incorrectness logic for quantum programs. Inf. Comput. **294**, 105077 (2023). https://doi.org/10.1016/J. IC.2023.105077
4. Galindo, C., Pérez, S., Silva, J.: Exception-sensitive program slicing. J. Log. Algebraic Methods Program. **130**, 100832 (2023). https://doi.org/10.1016/j.jlamp. 2022.100832
5. Galindo, C., Pérez, S., Silva, J.: Program slicing of Java programs. J. Log. Algebraic Methods Program. **130**, 100826 (2023). https://doi.org/10.1016/j.jlamp. 2022.100826
6. Hoare, C., Wirth, N.: An axiomatic definition of the programming language PASCAL. Acta Informatica **2**, 335–355 (1973)
7. Jiang, S., Li, W., Li, H., Zhang, Y., Zhang, H., Liu, Y.: Fault localization for null pointer exception based on stack trace and program slicing. In: Proceedings of QSIC 2012, Xi'an, Shaanxi, China, pp. 9–12. IEEE (2012). https://doi.org/10. 1109/QSIC.2012.36
8. Jiang, S., Zhang, H., Wang, Q., Zhang, Y.: A debugging approach for Java runtime exceptions based on program slicing and stack traces. In: Proceedings of QSIC 2010, Zhangjiajie, China, pp. 393–398. IEEE Computer Society (2010). https://doi.org/ 10.1109/QSIC.2010.23
9. Liu, A., Liu, S.: Enhancing the capability of testing-based formal verification by handling operations in software packages. IEEE Trans. Softw. Eng. **49**(1), 304–324 (2023). https://doi.org/10.1109/TSE.2022.3150333
10. Liu, H., Liu, S., Liu, A., Fang, D., Xu, G.: Verifying and improving neural networks using testing-based formal verification. In: Proceedings of SOFL+MSVL 2022, Madrid, Spain. Lecture Notes in Computer Science, vol. 13854, pp. 126–141. Springer, Cham (2022). https://doi.org/10.1007/978-3-031-29476-1_11
11. Liu, H., Liu, S., Xu, G., Liu, A., Fang, D.: NNTBFV: simplifying and verifying neural networks using testing-based formal verification. Int. J. Softw. Eng. Knowl. Eng. **34**(2), 273–300 (2024). https://doi.org/10.1142/S0218194023500523
12. Liu, S.: Utilizing Hoare logic to strengthen testing for error detection in programs. In: Turing-100 - The Alan Turing Centenary, Manchester, UK. EPiC Series in Computing, vol. 10, pp. 229–238. EasyChair (2012). https://easychair. org/publications/paper/476
13. Liu, S.: Automatic selection of system functional scenarios for formal specification animation. In: Proceedings of APSEC 2015, New Delhi, India, pp. 72–79. IEEE Computer Society (2015). https://doi.org/10.1109/APSEC.2015.15
14. Liu, S.: A tool supported testing method for reducing cost and improving quality. In: Proceedings of QRS 2016, Vienna, Austria, pp. 448–455. IEEE (2016). https:// doi.org/10.1109/QRS.2016.56
15. Liu, S., Hayashi, T., Takahashi, K., Kimura, K., Nakayama, T., Nakajima, S.: Automatic transformation from formal specifications to functional scenario forms for automatic test case generation. In: Proceedings of the 9th SoMeT_10, Yokohama City, Japan. Frontiers in Artificial Intelligence and Applications, vol. 217, pp. 383–397. IOS Press (2010). https://doi.org/10.3233/978-1-60750-629-4-383
16. Liu, S., Nakajima, S.: Combining specification-based testing, correctness proof, and inspection for program verification in practice. In: Liu, S., Duan, Z. (eds.) SOFL+MSVL 2013. LNCS, vol. 8332, pp. 3–16. Springer, Cham (2014). https:// doi.org/10.1007/978-3-319-04915-1_1
17. Liu, S., Nakajima, S.: Automatic test case and test oracle generation based on functional scenarios in formal specifications for conformance testing. IEEE Trans. Softw. Eng. **48**(2), 691–712 (2022). https://doi.org/10.1109/TSE.2020.2999884

18. O'Hearn, P.W.: Incorrectness logic. Proc. ACM Program. Lang. **4**(POPL), 10:1–10:32 (2020). https://doi.org/10.1145/3371078

19. Peled, D.A.: Software Reliability Methods. Texts in Computer Science. Springer, Cham (2001). https://doi.org/10.1007/978-1-4757-3540-6

20. Poskitt, C.M.: Incorrectness logic for graph programs. In: Gadducci, F., Kehrer, T. (eds.) ICGT 2021. LNCS, vol. 12741, pp. 81–101. Springer, Cham (2021). https://doi.org/10.1007/978-3-030-78946-6_5

21. Rao, L., Liu, S., Liu, A.: Testing program segments to detect runtime exceptions in Java. In: Proceedings of SOFL+MSVL 2022, Madrid, Spain. Lecture Notes in Computer Science, vol. 13854, pp. 93–105. Springer, Cham (2022). https://doi.org/10.1007/978-3-031-29476-1_8

22. Roggenbach, M., Cerone, A., Schlingloff, B., Schneider, G., Shaikh, S.A.: Formal Methods for Software Engineering - Languages, Methods, Application Domains. Texts in Theoretical Computer Science. An EATCS Series. Springer, Cham (2022). https://doi.org/10.1007/978-3-030-38800-3

23. Schumann, J.: Automated Theorem Proving in Software Engineering. Springer, Cham (2001). http://www.springer.com/computer/swe/book/978-3-540-67989-9

24. Soremekun, E., Kirschner, L., Böhme, M., Zeller, A.: Locating faults with program slicing: an empirical analysis. Empir. Softw. Eng. **26**(3), 1–45 (2021). https://doi.org/10.1007/s10664-020-09931-7

25. Wang, R., Liu, S.: TBFV-SE: testing-based formal verification with symbolic execution. In: Proceedings of QRS 2018, Lisbon, Portugal, pp. 59–66. IEEE (2018). https://doi.org/10.1109/QRS.2018.00019

26. Wang, R., Liu, S.: Branch sequence coverage criterion for testing-based formal verification with symbolic execution. In: Proceedings of QRS Companion 2019, Sofia, Bulgaria, pp. 205–212. IEEE (2019). https://doi.org/10.1109/QRS-C.2019.00049

27. Wang, R., Liu, S., Sato, Y.: A fault localization approach derived from testing-based formal verification. In: Proceedings of ICECCS 2020, Singapore, pp. 165–170. IEEE (2020). https://doi.org/10.1109/ICECCS51672.2020.00026

28. Weiser, M.D.: Program slicing. IEEE Trans. Softw. Eng. **10**(4), 352–357 (1984). https://doi.org/10.1109/TSE.1984.5010248

29. Yan, P., Jiang, H., Yu, N.: On incorrectness logic for quantum programs. Proc. ACM Program. Lang. **6**(OOPSLA1), 1–28 (2022). https://doi.org/10.1145/3527316

30. Yin, Y., Liu, S., Chen, Y.: Verification of SysML activity diagrams using Hoare logic and SOFL. In: Duan, Z., Liu, S., Tian, C., Nagoya, F. (eds.) SOFL+MSVL 2018. LNCS, vol. 11392, pp. 71–88. Springer, Cham (2019). https://doi.org/10.1007/978-3-030-13651-2_5

Dependent Assertion Logic for Modular Software Verification

Lukas Grätz$^{(\boxtimes)}$ (iD)

Technical University of Darmstadt, Darmstadt, Germany
`lukas.graetz@tu-darmstadt.de`

Abstract. Software is often not designed for formal specification using method contracts (without source refactoring). As solution, we propose dependent assertions, a generalization of method contracts. Our formalization uses the propositional dynamic logic PDL but with Dijkstra's dynamic indices instead of programs inside modal operators. For deductive verification based on a new symbolic execution approach, we outline a sequent calculus to prove basic dependent assertions, including loop invariants. Finally, we can use any (D)PDL solver to prove modular contracts from basic dependencies and other contracts.

1 Introduction

There is a famous quotation from Dijkstra [8]: "Program testing can be used to show the presence of bugs, but never to show their absence!" So instead of testing, it is advisable to formally verify essential and non-trivial parts of the software. However, there is a serious bottleneck [4]: A human needs to provide a formal software specification. Usually, a specification consists of method/function contracts (pre- and post-conditions for each called method) and loop invariants. This provides modularization for called methods/functions, abstracting away their implementation. Modularization/reusability is the cornerstone of Design by Contract [19].

Nevertheless, method contracts place a heavy constraint on the implementation. Implemented (legacy) software systems might not be structured to support post-hoc modular specification [14] and would need source code refactoring prior to formal specification and verification, as it was the case for the verification of Java's standard sorting implementation, Dual Pivot Quicksort [5].

In this paper, we propose *dependent assertions* to position pre- and post-conditions anywhere in the source code *without refactoring*. We also show a translation from pre- and post-conditions of method contracts as well as from loop invariants. Hence, dependent assertions are a generalization from method contracts, retaining features such as modularization.

Example 1. The left part of Listing 1 contains the implementation of a dice game written in Rust. The method `game()` is called with a number of `count` times a dice is rolled by calling `roll_dice()`. The game is won if `game()` returns `true`.

© The Author(s), under exclusive license to Springer Nature Switzerland AG 2026
P. Rümmer and Z. Wu (Eds.): TASE 2025, LNCS 15841, pp. 30–48, 2026.
https://doi.org/10.1007/978-3-031-98208-8_3

Listing 1: Example software for a dice rolled `count` times, written in Rust. Left: Original. Right: Refactored with a JML-like contract.

```
1    /* dice game */
2
3    fn game (self, count: usize) -> bool {
4        // seen[0] has no use, hence length 7
5        let mut seen = [false; 7];
6
7
8        for i in 0..count {
9            let dice_num = self.roll_dice();
10           seen[dice_num] = true;
11       }
12       return seen[6];
13   }
```

```
1    /*@ ensures \result
2    @    == ∃k in 0..count: nums[k] == 6; */
3    fn game (self, count: usize) -> bool {
4        let mut nums = vec![0; count];
5        let mut seen = [false; 7];
6        /*@ invariant seen[6]
7        @    == ∃k in 0..i: nums[k] == 6; */
8        for i in 0..count {
9            nums[i] = self.roll_dice();
10           seen[nums[i]] = true;
11       }
12       return seen[6];
13   }
```

The intended winning condition (result `true`) *should* be met iff the 6 matches one of the dice results. So to formally verify the `game()` with a method contract, either a pre-condition or the post-condition needs access to `dice_num`. However, when using classical method contracts, pre-conditions are evaluated only in the pre-state when the method was called and post-conditions after the method returned. Thus, a method contract cannot access individual `dice_num` values without adding ghost-code or source refactoring.

One such refactoring is on the right of Listing 1: Here the vector `nums` saves the rolled dice outcomes. This might seem harmless, but such refactoring cannot be done automatically; and, in our case, additional memory is needed for the vector (although optimized away by a good compiler). After refactoring, the method contract is a simple exercise. There is no pre-condition but a post-condition (the `ensures` clause) that the returned `\result` is true iff one of the rolled dices showed the number 6. The method contract can be proven, provided that the loop invariant (with the keyword `invariant` in Line 6) is valid.

Our new approach is—without the need to refactor—to place pre- and post-conditions at deliberate positions without restrictions. Instead of the loop invariant, we add a pre-condition `dice_num==6` after Line 9. Then we formulate a post-condition that the result is true iff the pre-condition holds for at least one loop iteration. We see the full specification of the unmodified code in Sect. 4.

We have the following main contributions: (1) a novel usage and semantics of dynamic logic to formulate assertion dependencies, orthogonal to the classical use of dynamic logic, (2) a translation of method contracts and loop invariants into assertion dependencies, (3) the verification of basic assertion dependencies with a sequent calculus based on a novel symbolic execution approach.

The Paper's Structure: Section 2 describes the intermediate language with examples, Sect. 3 describes dynamic logic and how we use it, Sect. 4 describes modular contracts in the logic, Sect. 5 describes the sequent calculus for symbolic execution, and Sect. 6 concludes and discusses related work.

2   The REPEAT Language

It is common for verification tools to use intermediate languages such as Boogie [3], Viper [20] or Why3 [10]. Our intermediate language should fulfill the following requirements:

1. We use Dijkstra's *structured programming* assumption that every state in the program execution can be uniquely described by a *dynamic index* [8,9]—in modern terms, the call stack augmented by loop iteration numbers. This assumption holds in all programming languages without a `goto` statement. Our assertion dependencies formalize the relationship between assertions at different dynamic indices.
2. Changes to the memory may only happen in *primitive assignments*. They assign a value to a variable/field without conditional execution, loops or calls. Other variables should not be affected, so assigned variables must not alias. Assertions can then be placed anywhere in the source code where the memory state changes—so before and after any primitive assignment.
3. Assertion conditions must be *side-effect free* and *deterministic*, so that their evaluation alone does not affect the memory state or control flow. This is an often-used assumption in software verification. In our intermediate language, all expressions will be deterministic and side-effect free, in particular, they do not cause a run-time exception or panic.
4. For *modular verification*, we assume that there are contracts for library methods. The reason is that library methods such as `v.sort()` or even arithmetic expressions in Rust like `v + w` have multiple implementations. Showing those contracts valid is the responsibility of the library.

Higher programming languages have statements with multiple side-effects, even in branching conditions (`if`- or `while`-conditions). We get the desired assumptions if we *automatically* translate the source code into an intermediate programming language with primitive assignments as primitive statements, while retaining the source code structure with method calls and loops. Since we also automatically translate higher language specification such as method contracts into the intermediate language, we lose nothing.

To satisfy our constraints, we use a simple language REPEAT as an intermediate language. There are only three language constructs: Assignments, (self-repeating) methods and conditional breaks/returns. The syntax is given in Listing 2.

A (self-repeating) method can use (recursive) calls but can also loop, when it has the `repeat` keyword at the end. Without a `repeat`, a method returns at the end. The statement `if expr return` is a conditional return when the expression `expr` evaluates to `true`. Self-repeating methods are equivalent to Ω_k-structures [7, 17].

For an example translation see Listing 3. In the translation, control structures like `if` and `loop` become separate (repeated) methods like `\foo_loop` and `\foo_loop_if`. To avoid namespace pollution, new names added by the translation

Listing 2: BNF syntax of the REPEAT language

$\langle declaration \rangle$:=   'fn' name '(' $\langle param \rangle$* ')' '{' $\langle statement \rangle$* | 'repeat' | '}'
$\langle statement \rangle$:= $\langle call \rangle$ | $\langle return \rangle$ | $\langle assignment \rangle$
$\langle call \rangle$:=   expression '(' $\langle argument \rangle$* ')'   // with restricted aliasing
$\langle return \rangle$:=   'if' expression 'return'
$\langle assignment \rangle$:=   variable $\langle field \rangle$* '=' expression
$\langle field \rangle$:=   '[' expression ']' | '.' name
$\langle param \rangle$:=   'mut' variable | immutable
$\langle argument \rangle$:=   'mut' variable | variable | immutable

Listing 3: Rust code with control structures (in box) and translation (outside).

```
fn foo() -> i32 {
    let mut num = 3;
    'label: loop {
        if num == 3 {
            num = 4;
        } else if num == 4 {
            break 'label;
        }
        print("next");
    }
    return num;
}
```

```
  fn foo (mut \result) {
0     num = 3
1     \foo_loop (mut num)
2     \result = num
  }
```

```
fn \foo_loop (mut num) {
0    \break = \nobreak
1    \foo_loop_if (mut num, mut \ifcond, mut \break)
2    \foo_loop_elif (num, mut \ifcond, mut \break)
3    if \break != \nobreak return // break propagation
4    print("next")
$    repeat
 }
fn \foo_loop_elif (num, mut \ifcond, mut \break) {
0    if \ifcond return // else check
1    \ifcond = num == 4
2    if ! \ifcond return // if check
3    \break = 'label
 }
fn \foo_loop_if (mut num, mut \ifcond, mut \break) {
0    \ifcond = num == 3
1    if ! \ifcond return // if check
2    num = 4
 }
```

start with a backslash \. There are special variables introduced by the translation: \ifcond, \break and \result. During execution, they are treated exactly like any other variable. For the translation of a break, the variable \break is initially set to a constant \nobreak and then to a break label constant 'label. The translation sets \result to the result/return value, if any.

Types of variables are the same as in the original programming language (Rust). Like in Java and other object-oriented languages, all variables are either parameters or local variables (we do not support global variables). To simplify the presentation, local variable declarations are implicit: Any undeclared variable is a mutable, local variable by default.

For arguments, we use aliasing restrictions as in Rust: A variable cannot be modified when there exists another reference to it. Thus, when passing a variable as mutable mut argument in a call, we cannot use the same variable for another argument in the same call. Only unmodified parameters without `mut` can be aliased. This is needed for soundness of the replacement rules we see in Sect. 5.

Unlike in Rust, there is no distinction between method parameters and returned results. `mut` arguments take the parameter's value when the method returns. In the translation, the result (if any) becomes the last parameter `mut \result`.

In theory, there should never be a read access from an unassigned variable, because the code is a translation from Rust, and Rust's type checker prevents it. Nevertheless, we model unassigned variables as follows: When executing code, an unassigned variable has a *fresh, random value* that remains during execution until an assignment. This is needed for Definition 4 further below and also eases verification, see Sect. 5. For the execution of translated, type-checked Rust, nothing changes.

An expression is either an access to (a field in) a variable or it is composed by operators from other expressions. We allow all (arithmetic, logic, ...) operators languages usually have, only that we assume that expressions cannot cause runtime exceptions or panics. Instead, underspecified operations result in values that seem to be random (there are no "default values"). To translate Rust expressions that can panic (like the division `i/0`, the sum `MAX+1` due to an overflow, or an access `a[i]` due to an array index out of bounds), we add extra method calls, like `\check_div()`, `\check_add()` or `\check_bounds()`.

Line numbers inside the repeated methods will be used to define the *dynamic index*, the unique counter to describe the state of the current execution.

Definition 1. When executing a REPEAT method, the *dynamic index* is a string composed of the dynamic index in the calling method, postfixed with $\$$ for each passed iteration, postfixed with the current line number $0, 1, 2, \ldots$ in the method. After a return, there is a special state marked by the postfix #. We use a point . as separation. The initial state before the first call has the *empty index* ϵ.

Examples of dynamic indices: ϵ, $2.\$.\$$, $2.\$.\#$, 3. By the next definition, they are ordered as: $\epsilon \preccurlyeq 2.\$.\$.0 \preccurlyeq 2.\$.\$.\# \preccurlyeq 3$.

Definition 2. The relation $\preccurlyeq$ is the *lexicographic order* between dynamic indices, corresponding to the order of execution, with $\epsilon \preccurlyeq 0 \preccurlyeq 1 \preccurlyeq 2 \preccurlyeq \cdots \preccurlyeq \$ \preccurlyeq$ #.

˙   The final step is to access a state within the execution using a dynamic index, which is handled by the following definitions for state expressions and program executions.

Definition 3. The set *Expr* of *state expressions* consists of all (side-effect free) expressions of the language. In addition to all variables (assigned or unassigned), state expressions can further use *state properties*. State properties are preceded by the symbol @.

State properties are not allowed in REPEAT, so state expressions clearly extend REPEAT expressions. The state property @fn refers to the current method.

We plan to introduce further state properties like @line for the current line, @location for the original source code location (of the Rust program). A property @old() could work like in JML to evaluate sub-expressions at other states.

Definition 4. A *program execution* is a tuple $E = (\mathcal{S}, eval)$, where the set $\mathcal{S}$ contains the dynamic indices for all states of the execution and the evaluation function $eval \colon \mathcal{S} \times Expr \to Value$ maps a state $s \in \mathcal{S}$, given by its dynamic index, and a state expression $e \in Expr$ to a value $v \in Value$.

Note that the definition is language-independent.

Example 2. For the execution $E_1 = (\mathcal{S}_1, eval_1)$ of Listing 3, we have the set of dynamic indices $\mathcal{S}_1$:

```
ϵ // initial state    1.2                  1.$.0 // 2nd loop iter  1.$.2.3
0 // foo()            1.2.0 // else if     1.$.1                   1.$.2.#
1                     1.2.#                1.$.1.0 // if           1.$.3
1.0 // loop           1.3                  1.$.1.1                 1.$.#
1.1                   1.4                  1.$.1.#                 1.# // loop end
1.1.0 // if           1.4.0 // print       1.$.2                   2
1.1.1                 // (internal states) 1.$.2.0 // else if      # // foo() return
1.1.2                 1.4.#                1.$.2.1
1.1.#                 1.$                  1.$.2.2
```

The same in a more compact notation, where $\frown$ indicates a direct succession of states and $\frown^*$ when states might be omitted, see Definition 13 in Sect. 5:

$$\mathcal{S}_1 = \epsilon.\{0 \frown 1.\{0 \frown 1.\{0 \frown 1 \frown 2 \frown \#\} \frown 2.\{0 \frown \#\} \frown 3 \frown 4.\{0 \frown^* \#\} \frown$$
$$\$.\{0 \frown 1.\{0 \frown 1 \frown \#\} \frown 2.\{0 \frown 1 \frown 2 \frown 3 \frown \#\} \frown 3 \frown \#\} \frown \#\} \frown 2 \frown \#\}$$

Some evaluations at states of execution E_1:

$$eval_1(1, \quad\quad num \quad\quad) = 3 \quad\quad eval_1(0, \quad num \quad) = 42$$
$$eval_1(1.3, \quad\quad \backslash break \quad) = \backslash nobreak \quad eval_1(0, \quad \backslash break) = 17$$
$$eval_1(1.\$.2.1, \backslash ifcond \quad) = false \quad eval_1(1.0, \backslash break) = 9$$
$$eval_1(1.\$.2.1, num == 4) = true \quad eval_1(1.\#, \backslash break) = \text{'label}$$
$$eval_1(1.\$.2.2, \backslash ifcond \quad) = true \quad eval_1(\#, \quad \backslash break) = 17$$

The left side should be clear. On the right side, the variable num is unassigned at state 0, so $eval_1(0, num)$ results in a random value, which is 42 in this example. With this value, $eval_1(0, num == 3) = false$. Likewise, \break is unassigned at state 0 and has a random value 17. State 1.0 is in another method \foo_loop() so there is a new unassigned value \break, here 9, that later gets assigned the values \nobreak and 'label. But \break is not returned (not an argument of \foo_loop()), so the final evaluation of \break at state # is again 17.

3   Logic: Semantics

In this section, dynamic logic is combined with the dynamic index. On this basis, we can express dependent assertions.

First, to avoid any confusion: Our logic is based on dynamic logic [11, 21, 22], but for its usage, we take a different, orthogonal approach. Classical contracts for a method $m(\dots)$ with pre-condition *pre* and post-condition *post* are usually translated into dynamic logic like this: $pre \rightarrow \langle m(\dots)\rangle post$ (when the pre-condition holds in the pre-state, then we can execute $m(\dots)$ such that it terminates and the post-condition holds afterward). In this paper, however, the contract is translated into $\langle 0\rangle pre \rightarrow \langle \#\rangle post$ (when, for a method, the call-state 0 is reached and the pre-condition holds in 0, then the return-state $\#$ is reached and the post-condition holds in $\#$). We see more about method contracts in Sect. 4.

We start with *propositional dynamic logic* (PDL), as defined in [11]. There are two kinds of variables, *propositional variables* $\mathcal{F}_0 = \{p, q, r, \dots\}$ and *atomic transitions* $\mathcal{T}_0 = \{a, b, c, \dots\}$. Classically, transitions in PDL were called "programs". However, in our use case, they do not correspond to programs but to dynamic indices, as we see later. We believe the name "transition" makes sense from a formal perspective, because in the semantics, to anticipate Definition 7, transitions are interpreted as binary relations between states.

Definition 5. The set of *transitions* is the smallest set $\mathcal{T}$, containing all atomic transitions $\mathcal{T}_0$, the *wildcard* $\bullet$, the *composition* $\alpha.\beta$ (originally $\alpha;\beta$), the *union* $\alpha \cup \beta$ and the *iteration/recursion* α^* for all transitions $\alpha, \beta \in \mathcal{T}$.

Note that we added the wildcard $\bullet$ that is not part of original PDL. On the other hand, we have no use or intuition for the *test A?*, so we removed it here.

Definition 6. The set of *PDL formulas* is the smallest set $\mathcal{F} \supseteq \mathcal{F}_0$, containing the propositional variables $\mathcal{F}_0$ and when $A, B \in \mathcal{F}$, then also $\neg A \in \mathcal{F}$, $A \rightarrow B \in \mathcal{F}$ and $\langle \alpha \rangle A \in \mathcal{F}$ for all $\alpha \in \mathcal{T}$.

Abbreviations `true`, `false`, $A \wedge B$, $A \vee B$ and $[\alpha]A$ are defined as $A \rightarrow A$, $\neg(A \rightarrow A)$, $\neg(A \rightarrow \neg B)$, $A \rightarrow \neg B$ and $\neg\langle \alpha \rangle\neg A$, respectively. The *box* $[\alpha]$ and *diamond* $\langle \alpha \rangle$ are known as *modal operators*.

We mostly follow [15], see there for mathematical preliminaries, including the *relation composition* $R \circ V$: For binary relations R, V, we have $R \circ V = \{(r_1, v_2) \mid (r_1, x) \in R, (x, v_2) \in V\}$. Since a set X is also a unary relation, we have $R \circ X = \{r_1 \mid (r_1, x) \in R, x \in X\}$ and $X \circ R = \{r_2 \mid x \in X, (x, r_2) \in R\}$. For sets X, Y, we have $X \circ Y = \{() \mid x \in X, x \in Y\}$—so either $\emptyset$ or $\{()\}$, with a length-0-tuple $()$. For a binary relation R and $n \geq 1$, we have $R^n = R \circ \cdots \circ R$ (n times R). A binary relation R is *right-unique* or a *partial function*, iff $(s, r) \in R$ and $(s, r') \in R$ implies $r = r'$.

Definition 7. A *Kripke model* $\mathcal{K} = (\mathcal{S}, v, \rho)$ is a set $\mathcal{S}$ of states, a function $\rho : \mathcal{T}_0 \rightarrow 2^{\mathcal{S} \times \mathcal{S}}$ to assign a relation $\rho(a) \subseteq \mathcal{S} \times \mathcal{S}$ to each atomic transition $a \in \mathcal{T}_0$ and a valuation $v : \mathcal{F}_0 \rightarrow 2^{\mathcal{S}}$ to assign a subset $v(p) \subseteq \mathcal{S}$ to each propositional variable $p \in \mathcal{F}_0$. Valuations and relations are inductively extended to $v : \mathcal{F} \rightarrow 2^{\mathcal{S}}$ for PDL formulas $A, B \in \mathcal{F}$ and $\rho : \mathcal{T} \rightarrow 2^{\mathcal{S} \times \mathcal{S}}$ for transitions $\alpha, \beta \in \mathcal{T}$ as follows:

$$v(\neg A) = \mathcal{S} \setminus v(A)$$

$$v(A \to B) = (\mathcal{S} \setminus v(A)) \cup v(B)$$

$$v(\langle \alpha \rangle A) = \rho(\alpha) \circ v(A)$$

$$\rho(\alpha \cup \beta) = \rho(\alpha) \cup \rho(\beta)$$

$$\rho(\alpha.\beta) = \rho(\alpha) \circ \rho(\beta)$$

$$\rho(\alpha^*) = \{(u,u) \mid u \in \mathcal{S}\} \cup \bigcup_{n \geq 1} \rho(\alpha)^n$$

$$\rho(\bullet) = \bigcup_{a \in \mathcal{T}_0} \rho(a)$$

The Kripke model $\mathcal{K} = (\mathcal{S}, v, \rho)$ is *right-unique*, iff for all atomic transitions $a \in \mathcal{T}_0$, the relation $\rho(a)$ is right-unique.

This is a formal definition that could be used in different situations, not just for programs or executions. How to apply it to the REPEAT language defined in the last section? The next definition shows how to connect program executions to Kripke models in our sense:

Definition 8. Let $E = (\mathcal{S}_E, \mathit{eval}_E)$ be a program execution. Then $\mathcal{K}_E = (\mathcal{S}_E, v, \rho)$ is the *Kripke model for* E, where the states are $\mathcal{S}_E$ with initial state $\epsilon \in \mathcal{S}_E$, atomic transitions are $\mathcal{T}_0 = \{\$, \#, 0, 1, 2, \dots\}$, propositional variables are all boolean state expressions $\mathcal{F}_0 = \{'\text{expr}' \mid \text{expr}: \text{bool} \in \mathit{Expr}\}$ and ρ, v are defined by:

$$\rho(a) = \{(u, u.a) \in \mathcal{S}_E \times \mathcal{S}_E\} \sqcup \{(\epsilon, a) \in \mathcal{S}_E \times \mathcal{S}_E\} \qquad \text{for all } u \in \mathcal{T}_0$$

$$v(p) = \{u \in \mathcal{S}_E \mid \mathit{eval}_E(u, p) = \text{true}\} \qquad \text{for all } p \in \mathcal{F}_0$$

This definition brings together multiple concepts at once, so we take some time to disentangle it. First, it makes sense to describe the set of states $\mathcal{S}$ by a set of dynamic indices $\mathcal{S}_E$, because each index uniquely describes a state in the execution E.

Classically, transitions in PDL are programs, but not here. In fact, it might be best to forget the semantics for the moment. Instead, we can just think of transitions as regular expressions over dynamic indices. As atomic transitions we have $\mathcal{T}_0 = \{0, 1, 2, \dots, \$, \#\}$, which is the infinite set of line numbers plus $\$$ and $\#$. In other words, $\mathcal{T}_0$ is the set of symbols appearing in dynamic indices (compare Definition 1). And by using the composition . as concatenation of these symbols, we can build any dynamic index. The union $\cup$ and the iteration/recursion $*$ complete this picture, you can see them as alternation and Kleene star of regular expressions over dynamic indices. The wildcard $\bullet$ matches any symbol. Intuitively, the iterated transition $\$^*.0$ describes all dynamic indices for line 0 in all iterations, so $\$^*.0 = 0 \cup \$.0 \cup \$.\$.0 \cup \cdots$. By using i^* in a method recursively calling itself in line number i, we describe all recursive calls.

Coming back to the semantics, $\rho(\alpha)$ for $\alpha \in \mathcal{T}$ is not a set of dynamic indices but a relation between them. The idea is that the regular expression is appended to the state we begin with. So starting with ϵ, the set $\{\epsilon\} \circ \rho(\alpha)$ is the set of dynamic indices of the execution E matching the regular expression α. And when starting with some state $u \in \mathcal{S}_E$, we get $\{u\} \circ \rho(\alpha) = \{\epsilon\} \circ \rho(u) \circ \rho(\alpha) = \{\epsilon\} \circ \rho(u.\alpha)$ by Definition 7 backwards.

For a propositional variable $p = \texttt{'expr'} \in \mathcal{F}_0$, the set $v(p)$ are all states in which the state expression $\texttt{expr}$ evaluates to $\texttt{true}$. We use ticks around $\texttt{'expr'}$ for a clear separation between our propositional language and state expressions with their own inner structure. Intuitively, the set $v(\langle \alpha \rangle A) = \rho(\alpha) \circ v(A)$ are all states, from which we can access a state via α, such that A holds there.

Definition 9. Given a Kripke model $\mathcal{K} = (\mathcal{S}, v, \rho)$ and a state $s \in \mathcal{S}$, we define the *semantic satisfaction* $\mathcal{K}, s \vDash A$ for a formula $A \in \mathcal{F}$ as follows:

$$\mathcal{K}, s \vDash A \quad :\Longleftrightarrow \quad s \in v(A)$$

Example 3. We continue Example 2 from Sect. 2 (Listing 3) with the Kripke model $\mathcal{K} = \mathcal{K}_{E_1}$ for the given execution E_1 and play with the semantics a bit:

$$v(\texttt{'@fn==foo'}) = \{0, \ 1, \ 2, \ \#\}$$

$$v(\texttt{'num==3'}) = \{1, \ 1.0, \ 1.1, \ 1.1.0, \ 1.1.1, \ 1.1.2\}$$

Since $\{1.1\} \circ \rho(0) = \{1.1.0\}$ and $1.1.0 \in v(\texttt{'num==3'})$, we get $1.1 \in v(\langle 0 \rangle \texttt{'num==3'})$.

$$\mathcal{K}, 1.1 \vDash \langle 0 \rangle \texttt{'num==3'} \quad \text{since } 1.1 \in v(\langle 0 \rangle \texttt{'num==3'}).$$

One would expect $\{2\} \circ \rho(1)$ to yield $\{2.1\}$, but $\{2\} \circ \rho(1) = \emptyset$ since $2.1 \notin \mathcal{S}$ (a dynamic index 2.1 does simply not exist for execution E_1). Therefore, $2 \notin \rho(1) \circ v(\texttt{'num==3'})$, hence $2 \in \mathcal{S} \setminus (\rho(1) \circ v(\texttt{'num==3'})) = v(\neg \langle 1 \rangle \texttt{'num==3'})$ and

$$\mathcal{K}, 2 \vDash \neg \langle 1 \rangle \texttt{'num==3'} \quad \text{since } 2 \in v(\neg \langle 1 \rangle \texttt{'num==3'}).$$

Corollary 1. For any execution E, the Kripke model $\mathcal{K}_E$ is right-unique.

Deterministic propositional dynamic logic DPDL is based on right-unique Kripke models [6,22]. Right-unique models are called *deterministic* in the literature [15,22]. However, for our logic, there is no connection between deterministic execution and right-uniqueness *at all*. A non-deterministic program just has multiple executions E for all combinations of non-deterministic choices. All executions have a corresponding Kripke model $\mathcal{K}_E$. And all of these Kripke models are right-unique by the corollary above. In the following definition, DA is our new *dependent assertion logic*.

Definition 10. A formula A is *valid* in PDL/DPDL/DA:

$$\text{PDL} \vDash A \quad :\Longleftrightarrow \quad \mathcal{K}, s \vDash A \text{ for all } \mathcal{K} = (\mathcal{S}, v, \rho) \text{ and all } s \in \mathcal{S}$$

$$\text{DPDL} \vDash A \quad :\Longleftrightarrow \quad \mathcal{K}, s \vDash A \text{ for all right-unique } \mathcal{K} = (\mathcal{S}, v, \rho) \text{ and } s \in \mathcal{S}$$

$$\text{DA} \vDash A \quad :\Longleftrightarrow \quad \mathcal{K}_E, s_E \vDash A \text{ for all } E = (\mathcal{S}_E, eval_E) \text{ and all } s_E \in \mathcal{S}_E$$

Corollary 2. Since DA models are right-unique Kripke models:

$$\text{PDL} \vDash A \quad \Longrightarrow \quad \text{DA} \vDash A \qquad \text{and} \qquad \text{DPDL} \vDash A \quad \Longrightarrow \quad \text{DA} \vDash A$$

Whether $\rho(\alpha)$ is right-unique, depends on how the transition α is composed of. If $\rho(\alpha)$ and $\rho(\beta)$ are right-unique, then $\rho(\alpha.\beta)$ is also right-unique. In most cases, $\rho(\bullet)$, $\rho(\alpha^*)$ and $\rho(\alpha \cup \beta)$ are not right-unique.

Listing 4: Code to test if a vector/array `arr` contains an element `el`.

```
fn contains (arr, el, mut \result) {          fn contains_loop(arr, el, i, mut \result) {
0    i = 0                                    0    if arr.len == i return
1    \result = false                         1    \result = \result || arr[i] == el
2    contains_loop(arr, el, i, mut \result)   2    i = i+1
}                                            3    repeat
                                             }
```

4   Method Contracts, Invariants and Meta Reasoning

With our logic in place, we can now define dependent assertions. We explain the translation of method contracts, loop invariants and similar into dependent assertions. Finally, we specify Example 1 using dependent assertions.

Definition 11. A *dependent assertion* is any PDL formula $A \in \mathcal{F}$ as defined in the previous section. An *assertion* is a boolean state expression `expr` occurring in A as propositional variable $'\texttt{expr}' \in \mathcal{F}_0$.

Note that we do not exclude formulas A that contain only trivial or no assertions, to keep the definition simple.

A contract for a method `foo` consists of two assertions: A pre-condition *pre* to hold in line 0 and a post-condition *post* to hold in the return state `#`. We can express this as $\text{DA} \vDash \langle 0 \rangle pre \rightarrow \langle\texttt{\#}\rangle post$. An important part of the pre-condition is $'\texttt{@fn==foo}'$, expressing that we are in method `foo`. In contrast, in classical dynamic logic, the program code of `foo` would be inside a modal operator.

Example 4. For the code in Listing 3 (Sect. 2), we want to prove the following method contract (1) that `foo` terminates normally with `num==4`. To prove `foo`'s contract, we do not need a loop invariant, because the loop has a bounded number of just two iterations. But we need a contract (2) that `print` also terminates normally. To use the contract (2) for a specific state in the proof of `foo`, we precede it with the corresponding dynamic index—or with the wildcard $[\bullet^*]$. Dependent assertion (3) can be proven with the sequent calculus we see in the next section. We use PDL to show that the contract (1) follows from (2) and (3).

$$\text{DA} \vDash \langle 0 \rangle'\texttt{@fn==foo}' \rightarrow \langle\texttt{\#}\rangle'\texttt{num==4}' \tag{1}$$

$$\text{DA} \vDash \langle 0 \rangle'\texttt{@fn==print}' \rightarrow \langle\texttt{\#}\rangle\texttt{true} \tag{2}$$

$$\text{DA} \vDash [\bullet^*](\langle 0 \rangle'\texttt{@fn==print}' \rightarrow \langle\texttt{\#}\rangle\texttt{true}) \rightarrow (\langle 0 \rangle'\texttt{@fn==foo}' \rightarrow \langle\texttt{\#}\rangle'\texttt{num==4}') \tag{3}$$

Example 5. The method `contains()` in Listing 4 checks whether the array `arr` (in Rust called vector) contains an element `el`. Thus, the contract of `contains()` has the post-condition:

$$post := \texttt{\textbackslash result}==\exists k \in \{0, \ldots, \texttt{arr.len}-1\}: \texttt{arr[k]}==\texttt{el}$$

To prove that the post-condition holds, we need a loop-invariant to hold before and after each loop iteration. For `contains_loop`, the invariant is similar to *post*, only that `arr.len` is replaced by the variable `i`. Additionally, we have $0 \leq i \leq$ `arr.len` and that the current method is `contains_loop`. So the final loop-invariant is:

$$inv := {}'\texttt{@fn==contains\_loop} \land 0 \leq \texttt{i} \leq \texttt{arr.len} \land$$
$$\texttt{\textbackslash result==}\exists \texttt{k} \in \{0, \ldots, \texttt{i-1}\}: \texttt{arr[k]==el}'$$

Now we can prove (for example, with the sequent calculus in Sect. 5) the following three dependent assertions: When the pre-condition of `contains` holds, then the invariant holds at the beginning of `contains_loop` (4). When the invariant holds at the beginning of one loop iteration, then `contains_loop` either finishes and the invariant holds for the last state or the invariant holds in the next iteration (5). When the invariant holds in the last state of the loop, the post-condition holds in the return state of `contains` (6).

$$\text{DA} \models \langle 0 \rangle \, '\texttt{@fn==contains}' \rightarrow \langle 2.0 \rangle inv \tag{4}$$

$$\text{DA} \models \langle 0 \rangle inv \rightarrow (\langle \texttt{\#} \rangle inv \lor \langle \$.0 \rangle inv) \tag{5}$$

$$\text{DA} \models (\langle 0 \rangle '\texttt{@fn==contains}' \land \langle 2.\texttt{\#} \rangle inv) \rightarrow \langle \texttt{\#} \rangle post \tag{6}$$

We need to show an additional dependent assertion, that the loop terminates: (4) If the invariant holds for `contains_loop`, then there is one last iteration without a following iteration:

$$\text{DA} \models \langle 0 \rangle inv \rightarrow \langle \$^* \rangle \neg \langle \$ \rangle \texttt{true} \tag{7}$$

This is known as the termination property and is usually shown using a variant. Our sequent calculus in Sect. 5 cannot prove variants yet—but we can rely on existing frameworks.

Traditionally, we would be done with stating that the method contract follows intuitively from the facts we have shown around loop-invariants. Here we go a step further.

Corollary 3. For any propositional variable $inv \in \mathcal{F}_0$, the following holds:

$$\text{DA} \models \langle \$.\texttt{\#} \rangle inv \rightarrow \langle \texttt{\#} \rangle inv$$

Theorem 1 (Basic Loop-Invariant Pattern). For propositional variables $pre, inv, post \in \mathcal{F}_0$ and a line number $\texttt{i} \in \mathcal{T}_0$, the following holds:

$$\text{DA} \models \begin{pmatrix} (\langle 0 \rangle pre \rightarrow \langle \texttt{i}.0 \rangle inv) \\ \land \quad [\bullet^*](\langle 0 \rangle inv \rightarrow \langle \texttt{\#} \rangle inv \lor \langle \$.0 \rangle inv) \\ \land \, (\langle 0 \rangle pre \land \langle \texttt{i}.\texttt{\#} \rangle inv \rightarrow \langle \texttt{\#} \rangle post) \\ \land \quad [\bullet^*](\langle 0 \rangle inv \rightarrow \langle \$^* \rangle \neg \langle \$ \rangle \texttt{true}) \end{pmatrix} \rightarrow \left(\langle 0 \rangle pre \rightarrow \langle \texttt{\#} \rangle post \right)$$

Listing 5: Translation of the introductory example (left of Listing 1)

```
  fn game (self, cnt: usize, mut \result) {      fn \game_for (self, cnt, mut seen, mut i) {
0   seen = [false; 7]                          0   \break = \nobreak
1   \i: usize = 0                              1   if i == cnt return
2   \game_for (self, cnt, mut seen, mut \i)    2   self.roll_dice (self, mut dice_num)
3   \result = seen[6]                          3   \check_bounds(seen, dice_num)
  }                                            4   seen[dice_num] = true
                                               5   i = i + 1
                                               $   repeat
                                                 }
```

Proof. To use a PDL solver, we added two assumptions $[\bullet^*](\langle\#\rangle\langle 0\rangle inv \rightarrow [\#]\langle 0\rangle inv)$, which is valid in DPDL, and $[\bullet^*](\langle \$.\#\rangle inv \rightarrow \langle\#\rangle inv)$, which holds by Corollary 3. We also replaced $\bullet$, which is not part of original PDL, by $(\mathtt{i} \cup \$)$ for a stronger version of the theorem. We used the tool *mlsolver* [12] to prove that version. Our DA version follows from the PDL version.

Example 6. The intermediate language translation of the dice game from the introduction is in Listing 5. The `for` loop gets extracted as method `\game_for()`. That method repeats itself until `i == cnt` is true in Statement 0. The loop variable `i` is initialized in `game()`, but using the name `\i`, because `i` is technically out of scope outside the `for` loop.

The dependent assertion (8) specifies that the `\result` is `true`, iff one of the `roll_dice()` results is 6. There is one called method `\check_bounds` with contract (9). We can show dependent assertion for `game` in the sequent calculus, using the contract for `\check_bounds` (9) and using a loop invariant (10).

$$\mathrm{DA} \vDash \langle 0\rangle'\texttt{@fn==game}' \rightarrow (\langle 2.\$^*.3\rangle'\texttt{dice\_num==6}' \leftrightarrow \langle\#\rangle'\texttt{\textbackslash result==true}') \qquad (8)$$

$$\mathrm{DA} \vDash \langle 0\rangle('\texttt{@fn==\textbackslash check\_bounds}' \wedge '0 \le \texttt{i} < \texttt{array.len}') \rightarrow \langle\#\rangle\texttt{true} \qquad (9)$$

$$\mathrm{DA} \vDash \langle 0\rangle'\texttt{@fn==\textbackslash game\_for}' \rightarrow [\$^*](\langle 0\rangle'\texttt{seen[6]}' \rightarrow \langle\# \cup \$.0\rangle'\texttt{seen[6]}') \qquad (10)$$

Note that dependent assertions refer to line numbers in the translated code of the intermediate language. However, we think that specifications should be done in the original code, not in the translation. We believe dependent assertions can be ultimately formulated without line numbers using the code's structure in the original language (Rust) and then we translate these high-level dependent assertions. But this is future work, so in the meantime, we only translate conventional method contracts, loop invariants and similar.

5 Deductive Verification

After the last two sections, we can create a Kripke model from a single, concrete execution of a software written in a common programming language like Rust. Using a Kripke model, we can do model checking with PDL formulas as done in

Example 3. This worked well for Listing 3, because the deterministic control-flow resulted in exactly one execution. In general, checking all concrete executions is not feasible, so in this section, we introduce a sequent calculus for *deductive verification* based on symbolic execution.

Based on Definition 4 for *program execution*, we see a *symbolic execution* as a notational challenge to describe only a part of the execution while treating the rest symbolic. Usually, symbolic execution describes the constraints from symbolic execution in a path condition—instead, we go a bit further and include the path itself.

Definition 12. *Free dynamic indices* extend dynamic indices by allowing symbolic numbers $k, l, \ldots$ for the number of recursions/iterations. Every dynamic index s is a free dynamic index. When r, s, t are free dynamic indices and k is a symbolic number, then $r.s^k.t$ is also a free dynamic index.

For example, the free dynamic index $1.\$^k.2.0$ could either stand for dynamic indices of the first iteration $1.2.0$ when $k = 0$, of the second iteration $1.\$.2.0$ when $k = 1$, of the third iteration $1.\$.\$.2.0$ when $k = 2$ and so on. The free dynamic index $1.(\$.\$)^k.3$ describes an even iteration, and $2^k.3.\$^l.1$ describes an iteration of the method from line 3 in a recursive call from line 2.

Definition 13. A *free execution path* $\mathcal{S}$ is partially described as a list of successions between free dynamic indices $s, t \in \mathcal{S}$. A *direct succession* $s \curvearrowright t$ of corresponding states in the execution means that $s \neq t$ and that t follows after s with no states in between. A *free succession* $s \curvearrowright^* t$ means either that $s = t$ or that t follows after s but there might be states in between.

Note that we used the same $\mathcal{S}$ for a set of dynamic indices and a free execution path. This is because we see a free execution path as a partial description of a set of dynamic indices. For a set of dynamic indices $\mathcal{S}$, the succession $s \curvearrowright^* t$ is implicit by the order $s \preccurlyeq t$ for all $s, t \in \mathcal{S}$. On the other hand, the description of a free execution path could leave both $s \in \mathcal{S}$ or $s \notin \mathcal{S}$ possible. Only if the free execution path $\mathcal{S}$ contains a direct succession $r \curvearrowright t$ and the indices are ordered as $r \prec s \prec t$, we definitely know that $s \notin \mathcal{S}$. Furthermore, for *free* dynamic indices, we would not know whether $\$^k \preccurlyeq \$^l$ or $\$^l \preccurlyeq \$^k$.

Definition 14. If (a part of) a free execution path $s \curvearrowright s.\alpha_1 \curvearrowright^* s.\alpha_2 \curvearrowright^* \ldots \curvearrowright^* s.\alpha_n$ shares the same prefix s, we may also use a *compact notation* $s.\{\alpha_1 \curvearrowright^* \alpha_2 \curvearrowright^* \ldots \curvearrowright^* \alpha_n\}$. Analog for direct successions $\curvearrowright$ instead of $\curvearrowright^*$.

Example 7. We already used the compact notation for $\mathcal{S}_1$ in Example 2. By abstracting away the paths inside if/else, we get the following free path:

$$\mathcal{S}_2 = \epsilon.\{0 \curvearrowright 1.\{0 \curvearrowright 1.\{0 \curvearrowright^* \#\} \curvearrowright 2.\{0 \curvearrowright^* \#\} \curvearrowright 3 \curvearrowright 4.\{0 \curvearrowright^* \#\} \curvearrowright$$
$$\$.\{0 \curvearrowright 1.\{0 \curvearrowright^* \#\} \curvearrowright 2.\{0 \curvearrowright^* \#\} \curvearrowright 3 \curvearrowright \#\} \curvearrowright \#\} \curvearrowright 2 \curvearrowright \#\}$$

Note that there are multiple nestings of the compact notation. The beginning of S_2 without compact notation:

$$S_3 = \epsilon \curvearrowright 0 \curvearrowright 1 \curvearrowright 1.0 \curvearrowright 1.1 \curvearrowright 1.1.0 \curvearrowright^* 1.1.\# \curvearrowright 1.2 \curvearrowright 1.2.0 \curvearrowright^* 1.2.\#$$

Both free paths S_2 and S_3 are partial descriptions and can be concretized to the same set of dynamic indices from execution E_1 in Example 2.

In contrast to the literature [1], a free execution path is part of each sequent.

Definition 15. A *sequent* has the form

$$S \mid {}_{s_1}A_1, \ldots, {}_{s_m}A_m \Rightarrow {}_{r_1}B_1, \ldots, {}_{r_n}B_n$$

where S is a free execution path and $A_1, \ldots, A_m, B_1, \ldots, B_n \in \mathcal{F}$ are PDL formulas with free dynamic indices $s_1, \ldots, s_m, r_1, \ldots, r_n \in S$ as left subscripts.

Definition 16. The sequent calculus for our logic is *sound*, when a proof of

$$\epsilon \mid {}_\epsilon A_1, \ldots, {}_\epsilon A_n \Rightarrow {}_\epsilon B$$

exists only when $\mathrm{DA} \models A_1 \wedge \cdots A_n \rightarrow B$.

5.1 Rules for the Sequent Calculus

In contrast to Sects. 3 and 4, our sequent calculus is not restricted to PDL and its propositions, so rules are allowed to manipulate the inner structure of expressions. The rules of our calculus are the rules of the standard sequent calculus, plus rules for the modal operators, plus rules for symbolic execution, plus rules for computing/replacing expressions of the programming language. In the following, the usual $S \mid \Gamma \Rightarrow \Delta$ is omitted to improve readability. Note that we leave soundness and the full presentation of all rules as future work.

Logic Rules. The rules of the standard sequent calculus can be imported by adding indices to the formulas. As example, the rules $\rightarrow$*left* and $\rightarrow$*right*:

$$\rightarrow\!\textit{left} \; \frac{\mid \Rightarrow {}_sA \qquad \mid {}_sB \Rightarrow}{\mid {}_sA \rightarrow B \Rightarrow} \qquad\qquad \rightarrow\!\textit{right} \; \frac{\mid {}_sA \Rightarrow {}_sB}{\mid \Rightarrow {}_sA \rightarrow B}$$

For modal operators $\langle \alpha \rangle$ the following rules $\langle \alpha \rangle$*empty* and $\langle \alpha \rangle$*unique* can be applied both on the left and right side when the respective side-condition follows from the free path S. The condition $\{s\} \circ \rho_S(r) = \{s.r\}$ is fulfilled when the description of the free path S contains $s.r$. On the other hand, we get $\{s\} \circ \rho_S(r) = \emptyset$ if the free path S does not contain $s.r$ but contains a direct succession $u \curvearrowright x$ and the order is $u \prec s.r \prec x$. For non right-unique α, the rule $\langle \alpha \rangle$*inst* can be used only on the right side—or we can use the rules $\langle \alpha^* \rangle$*skolem* on the left side. Technically, rules for $[\alpha]$ are not needed, as it is just an abbreviation for $\neg\langle \alpha \rangle\neg$. To avoid applications of $\neg$*left* and $\neg$*right*, we will still use, for example $[\alpha]$*inst*.

$$\langle\alpha\rangle empty \ \frac{\epsilon\texttt{false}}{s\langle\alpha\rangle A} \ \{s\} \circ \rho_S(\alpha) = \emptyset \qquad\qquad \langle\alpha\rangle unique \ \frac{xA}{s\langle\alpha\rangle A} \ \{s\} \circ \rho_S(\alpha) = \{x\}$$

$$\langle\alpha^*\rangle skolem \ \frac{\mid s\langle\alpha^k\rangle A \Rightarrow}{\mid s\langle\alpha^*\rangle A \Rightarrow} \ k \ \text{fresh} \qquad\qquad \langle\alpha\rangle inst \ \frac{\mid \Rightarrow xA}{\mid \Rightarrow s\langle\alpha\rangle A} \ \{s\} \circ \rho_S(\alpha) \ni x$$

$$\langle\alpha.\beta\rangle conc \ \frac{s\langle\alpha\rangle\langle\beta\rangle A}{s\langle\alpha.\beta\rangle A} \qquad\qquad [\alpha] inst \ \frac{\mid xA \Rightarrow}{\mid s[\alpha]A \Rightarrow} \ \{s\} \circ \rho_S(\alpha) \ni x$$

Symbolic Execution Rules. The rules for symbolic execution act mostly on the free execution path S. There are no symbolic variable updates, so the *assign* rule does not do the actual assignment and looks similar to the *return* rule. Instead, the replacement rules further below depend both on S and the code. In the following, $n(\texttt{i})$ stands for the respective next line $\texttt{i+1}$, #, or $.

$$assign \ \frac{s.\texttt{i} \curvearrowright s.n(\texttt{i}) \mid \Rightarrow}{s.\texttt{i} \mid \Rightarrow} \ s.\texttt{i} \ \text{line: } \texttt{lhs=rhs} \qquad\qquad return \ \frac{s.\texttt{i.\#} \curvearrowright s.n(\texttt{i}) \mid \Rightarrow}{s.\texttt{i.\#} \mid \Rightarrow}$$

$$repeat \ \frac{s.\$ \curvearrowright s.\$.0 \mid \Rightarrow}{s.\$ \mid \Rightarrow} \ s.\$ \ \text{line: } \texttt{repeat}$$

The *if* rule has the usual two cases depending on $s.\texttt{i}'\texttt{e}'$:

$$if \ \frac{s.\texttt{i} \curvearrowright s.n(\texttt{i}) \mid \Rightarrow_{s.\texttt{i}}'\texttt{e}' \qquad s.\texttt{i} \curvearrowright s.\texttt{\#} \mid s.\texttt{i}'\texttt{e}' \Rightarrow}{s.\texttt{i} \mid \Rightarrow} \ s.\texttt{i} \ \text{line: } \texttt{if e return}$$

The *call* rule takes care of resolving the method from $s'\texttt{expr}'$:

$$call \ \frac{s \curvearrowright s.0 \mid s.0'\texttt{@fn}' = s'\texttt{expr}' \Rightarrow}{s \mid \Rightarrow} \ s \ \text{line: } \texttt{expr(...)}$$

Finally, the $\langle r\rangle free$ rule skips execution steps when a formula $s\langle u\rangle A$ is on the left, usually from a loop-invariant or from a post-condition of a called method. The rule is needed for modularity.

$$\langle r\rangle free \ \frac{s.u \curvearrowright^* s.r \mid \Rightarrow}{s.u \mid s\langle r\rangle A \Rightarrow} \ s.u \preccurlyeq s.r$$

Language Expression Rules. Language expression rules can be applied on both sides of the sequent. They include rules to *compute* or *simplify* expressions, not shown here. We only show *replacement rules* connected to symbolic execution:

$$replace\text{-}assign \ \frac{s.\texttt{i}'\texttt{rhs}'}{s.n(\texttt{i})'\texttt{lhs}'} \ s.\texttt{i} \ \text{line: } \texttt{lhs=rhs}$$

$$replace\text{-}keep \ \frac{s'\texttt{expr}'}{r'\texttt{expr}'} \ \text{execution from } s \text{ to } r \text{ does not modify } \texttt{expr}$$

When the line $s.\mathtt{i}$ is a call with argument $\mathtt{arg}$ for parameter $\mathtt{param}$:

$$replace\text{-}param \ \frac{s.\mathtt{i}\,'\mathtt{arg}'}{s.\mathtt{i}.0\,'\mathtt{param}'} \qquad replace\text{-}arg \ \frac{s.\mathtt{i}.\#\,'\mathtt{param}'}{s.n(\mathtt{i})\,'\mathtt{arg}'}$$

Example 8. We show the contract of a very simple program in the calculus:

```
fn f (mut r) {
0    r = 3
1    b(r)
     }
```

The contract is $\langle 0\rangle'\mathtt{@fn}{=}{=}\mathtt{f}' \to \langle \#\rangle'\mathtt{r}{=}{=}3'$, or in words: Method $\mathtt{f}$ terminates normally with $\mathtt{r}$ equals 3. This depends on the contract that $\mathtt{b}$ terminates normally, $\langle 0\rangle'\mathtt{@fn}{=}{=}\mathtt{b}' \to \langle \#\rangle\mathtt{true}$. In contrast to $\mathtt{b(mut\ r)}$, $\mathtt{b(r)}$ does not modify $\mathtt{r}$. Subscript ϵ is omitted to improve readability, so A instead of $_\epsilon A$. Here is the proof:

$$
\begin{array}{l}
close \ \dfrac{}{\epsilon \curvearrowright 0 \curvearrowright 1 \curvearrowright 1.0 \mid {}_0'\mathtt{@fn}'{=}'\mathtt{f}', {}_{1.0}'\mathtt{@fn}'{=}_1'\mathtt{b}' \Rightarrow {}_{1.0}'\mathtt{@fn}'{=}_1'\mathtt{b}'} \\[4pt]
replace\text{-}keep \ \dfrac{}{\epsilon \curvearrowright 0 \curvearrowright 1 \curvearrowright 1.0 \mid {}_0'\mathtt{@fn}'{=}'\mathtt{f}', {}_{1.0}'\mathtt{@fn}'{=}_1'\mathtt{b}' \Rightarrow {}_{1.0}'\mathtt{@fn}'{=}_{1.0}'\mathtt{b}'} \\[4pt]
== \\[4pt]
\langle 0\rangle\,unique \ \dfrac{}{\epsilon \curvearrowright 0 \curvearrowright 1 \curvearrowright 1.0 \mid {}_0'\mathtt{@fn}'{=}'\mathtt{f}', {}_{1.0}'\mathtt{@fn}'{=}_1'\mathtt{b}' \Rightarrow {}_{1.0}'\mathtt{@fn}{=}{=}\mathtt{b}'} \\[4pt]
call \ \dfrac{}{\epsilon \curvearrowright 0 \curvearrowright 1 \curvearrowright 1.0 \mid {}_0'\mathtt{@fn}'{=}'\mathtt{f}', {}_{1.0}'\mathtt{@fn}'{=}_1'\mathtt{b}' \Rightarrow {}_1\langle 0\rangle'\mathtt{@fn}{=}{=}\mathtt{b}'} \\[4pt]
\dfrac{}{\epsilon \curvearrowright 0 \curvearrowright 1 \mid {}_0'\mathtt{@fn}'{=}'\mathtt{f}' \Rightarrow {}_1\langle 0\rangle'\mathtt{@fn}{=}{=}\mathtt{b}'}
\end{array}
$$

(continues ✂)

$$
\begin{array}{l}
{=}close \ \dfrac{}{\epsilon \curvearrowright 0 \curvearrowright 1 \curvearrowright^* 1.\# \curvearrowright \# \mid {}_0'\mathtt{@fn}'{=}'\mathtt{f}' \Rightarrow {}_0'3'{=}_0'3'} \\[4pt]
replace\text{-}assign \ \dfrac{}{\epsilon \curvearrowright 0 \curvearrowright 1 \curvearrowright^* 1.\# \curvearrowright \# \mid {}_0'\mathtt{@fn}'{=}'\mathtt{f}' \Rightarrow {}_1'\mathtt{r}'{=}_0'3'} \\[4pt]
replace\text{-}keep\ (2\mathrm{x}) \ \dfrac{}{\epsilon \curvearrowright 0 \curvearrowright 1 \curvearrowright^* 1.\# \curvearrowright \# \mid {}_0'\mathtt{@fn}'{=}'\mathtt{f}' \Rightarrow {}_\#'\mathtt{r}'{=}_\#'3'} \\[4pt]
== \\[4pt]
return,\ \langle \#\rangle\,unique \ \dfrac{}{\epsilon \curvearrowright 0 \curvearrowright 1 \curvearrowright^* 1.\# \curvearrowright \# \mid {}_0'\mathtt{@fn}'{=}'\mathtt{f}' \Rightarrow {}_\#'\mathtt{r}{=}{=}3'} \\[4pt]
\langle \#\rangle\,free \ \dfrac{}{\epsilon \curvearrowright 0 \curvearrowright 1 \curvearrowright^* 1.\# \mid {}_0'\mathtt{@fn}'{=}'\mathtt{f}' \Rightarrow \langle \#\rangle'\mathtt{r}{=}{=}3'} \\[4pt]
\dfrac{}{\epsilon \curvearrowright 0 \curvearrowright 1 \mid {}_1\langle \#\rangle\mathtt{true}, {}_0'\mathtt{@fn}'{=}'\mathtt{f}' \Rightarrow \langle \#\rangle'\mathtt{r}{=}{=}3'}
\end{array}
$$

$$
\begin{array}{l}
\to left \quad ✂ \\[4pt]
[\bullet^*]inst \ \dfrac{}{\epsilon \curvearrowright 0 \curvearrowright 1 \mid {}_1(\langle 0\rangle'\mathtt{@fn}{=}{=}\mathtt{b}' \to \langle \#\rangle\mathtt{true}), {}_0'\mathtt{@fn}'{=}'\mathtt{f}' \Rightarrow \langle \#\rangle'\mathtt{r}{=}{=}3'} \\[4pt]
assign \ \dfrac{}{\epsilon \curvearrowright 0 \curvearrowright 1 \mid [\bullet^*](\langle 0\rangle'\mathtt{@fn}{=}{=}\mathtt{b}' \to \langle \#\rangle\mathtt{true}), {}_0'\mathtt{@fn}'{=}'\mathtt{f}' \Rightarrow \langle \#\rangle'\mathtt{r}{=}{=}3'} \\[4pt]
replace\text{-}keep \ \dfrac{}{\epsilon \curvearrowright 0 \mid [\bullet^*](\langle 0\rangle'\mathtt{@fn}{=}{=}\mathtt{b}' \to \langle \#\rangle\mathtt{true}), {}_0'\mathtt{@fn}'{=}'\mathtt{f}' \Rightarrow \langle \#\rangle'\mathtt{r}{=}{=}3'} \\[4pt]
== \\[4pt]
\dfrac{}{\epsilon \curvearrowright 0 \mid [\bullet^*](\langle 0\rangle'\mathtt{@fn}{=}{=}\mathtt{b}' \to \langle \#\rangle\mathtt{true}), {}_0'\mathtt{@fn}'{=}_0'\mathtt{f}' \Rightarrow \langle \#\rangle'\mathtt{r}{=}{=}3'} \\[4pt]
\langle 0\rangle\,unique \ \dfrac{}{\epsilon \curvearrowright 0 \mid [\bullet^*](\langle 0\rangle'\mathtt{@fn}{=}{=}\mathtt{b}' \to \langle \#\rangle\mathtt{true}), {}_0'\mathtt{@fn}{=}{=}\mathtt{f}' \Rightarrow \langle \#\rangle'\mathtt{r}{=}{=}3'} \\[4pt]
call,\ \to right \ \dfrac{}{\epsilon \mid [\bullet^*](\langle 0\rangle'\mathtt{@fn}{=}{=}\mathtt{b}' \to \langle \#\rangle\mathtt{true}), \langle 0\rangle'\mathtt{@fn}{=}{=}\mathtt{f}' \Rightarrow \langle \#\rangle'\mathtt{r}{=}{=}3'} \\[4pt]
\dfrac{}{\epsilon \mid [\bullet^*](\langle 0\rangle'\mathtt{@fn}{=}{=}\mathtt{b}' \to \langle \#\rangle\mathtt{true}) \Rightarrow \langle 0\rangle'\mathtt{@fn}{=}{=}\mathtt{f}' \to \langle \#\rangle'\mathtt{r}{=}{=}3'}
\end{array}
$$

We used the computation rule $==$, which replaces $s'\mathtt{x}{=}{=}\mathtt{y}'$ by $s'\mathtt{x}'{=}s'\mathtt{y}'$. At the very bottom, we started with the rule *call* to append $\curvearrowright 0$ to the free path, needed by the next rule $\langle 0\rangle$ *unique*. The left branch of $\to left$ (shown at the top) proves the pre-condition of $\mathtt{b}$'s contract, while the right branch uses the post-condition of that contract. The right branch is closed with the $=close$ rule, since $_0'3'{=}_0'3'$. We got that equation from $_\#'\mathtt{r}'{=}_\#'3'$ by applications of the *replace-keep* and *replace-assign* rules. The *assign* rule further below just added the $\curvearrowright 1$.

6   Related Work and Conclusion

The initial goal was to formalize dependent assertions but we ended up with much more. We formalized the dynamic index, only described in words by Dijkstra [8,9]. Recently, another work [13] used a similar approach but for a single function with loops and if/else. In [13] first-order-logic is used, while we use (deterministic) propositional dynamic logic—as a result, implementation-independent entailments, like in Theorem 1, are decidable [6].

Unlike classical DL, we allow recursive calls. One conventional solution was to use more general grammars instead of regular expressions in the modal operators [16,18]. Our solution is that the regular expressions describe dynamic indices, not programs. Another solution by the deductive verifier KeY, based on the dynamic logic *JavaDL*, extends the calculus at run-time to generate use-contract and use-loop-invariant rules for called methods and loops [1]. In our sequent calculus, assumed contracts are simply on the left side of the sequent.

In our calculus, we use a free execution path instead the symbolic execution's usual path constraint [2]. Expressions can be replaced later by replacement rules if needed—using a no-aliasing property from Sect. 2.

For future work, we have yet to show formally the soundness of the calculus. We also plan to implement our framework and to develop high-level dependent assertions as mentioned in Sect. 4.

Acknowledgements. I would like to thank Daniel Drodt, Niklas Heidler, Marco Scaletta, Richard Bubel, Hans-Dieter Hiep and Reiner Hähnle for useful suggestions.

References

1. Ahrendt, W., Beckert, B., Bubel, R., Hähnle, R., Schmitt, P.H., Ulbrich, M. (eds.): Deductive Software Verification, The KeY Book, From Theory to Practice, LNCS, vol. 10001. Springer, Heidelberg (2016). https://doi.org/10.1007/978-3-319-49812-6
2. Baldoni, R., Coppa, E., D'Elia, D.C., Demetrescu, C., Finocchi, I.: A survey of symbolic execution techniques. ACM Comput. Surv. **51**(3), 50:1–50:39 (2018). https://doi.org/10.1145/3182657
3. Barnett, M., Chang, B.-Y.E., DeLine, R., Jacobs, B., Leino, K.: Boogie: a modular reusable verifier for object-oriented programs. In: de Boer, F.S., Bonsangue, M.M., Graf, S., de Roever, W.-P. (eds.) FMCO 2005. LNCS, vol. 4111, pp. 364–387. Springer, Heidelberg (2006). https://doi.org/10.1007/11804192_17
4. Baumann, C., Beckert, B., Blasum, H., Bormer, T.: Lessons learned from micro-kernel verification—specification is the new bottleneck. In: Cassez, F., Huuck, R., Klein, G., Schlich, B. (eds.) SSV 2012. EPTCS, vol. 102, pp. 18–32 (2012). https://doi.org/10.4204/EPTCS.102.4
5. Beckert, B., Schiffl, J., Schmitt, P.H., Ulbrich, M.: Proving JDK's dual pivot quicksort correct. In: Paskevich, A., Wies, T. (eds.) VSTTE 2017. LNCS, vol. 10712, pp. 35–48. Springer, Cham (2017). https://doi.org/10.1007/978-3-319-72308-2_3

6. Ben-Ari, M., Halpern, J.Y., Pnueli, A.: Deterministic propositional dynamic logic: finite models, complexity, and completeness. J. Comput. Syst. Sci. **25**(3), 402–417 (1982). https://doi.org/10.1016/0022-0000(82)90018-6

7. Böhm, C., Jacopini, G.: Flow diagrams, Turing machines and languages with only two formation rules. Commun. ACM **9**(5), 366–371 (1966). https://doi.org/10.1145/355592.365646

8. Dijkstra, E.W.: Notes on structured programming. Technical Report 70-WSK-03, Technological University Eindhoven, Department of Mathematics, EWD249 (1969)

9. Dijkstra, E.W.: Letters to the editor: go to statement considered harmful. Commun. ACM **11**(3), 147–148 (1968). https://doi.org/10.1145/362929.362947

10. Filliâtre, J.-C., Paskevich, A.: Why3—where programs meet provers. In: Felleisen, M., Gardner, P. (eds.) ESOP 2013. LNCS, vol. 7792, pp. 125–128. Springer, Heidelberg (2013). https://doi.org/10.1007/978-3-642-37036-6_8

11. Fischer, M.J., Ladner, R.E.: Propositional dynamic logic of regular programs. J. Comput. Syst. Sci. **18**(2), 194–211 (1979). https://doi.org/10.1016/0022-0000(79)90046-1

12. Friedmann, O., Lange, M.: A solver for modal fixpoint logics. In: Bolander, T., Braüner, T. (eds.) M4M 2009. Electronic Notes in Theoretical Computer Science, vol. 262, pp. 99–111. Elsevier (2009). https://doi.org/10.1016/J.ENTCS.2010.04.008

13. Georgiou, P., Gleiss, B., Kovács, L.: Trace logic for inductive loop reasoning. In: Ivrii, A., Strichman, O. (eds.) FMCAD 2020, pp. 255–263. IEEE (2020). https://doi.org/10.34727/2020/ISBN.978-3-85448-042-6_33

14. Hähnle, R., Huisman, M.: Deductive software verification: from pen-and-paper proofs to industrial tools. In: Steffen, B., Woeginger, G. (eds.) Computing and Software Science. LNCS, vol. 10000, pp. 345–373. Springer, Cham (2019). https://doi.org/10.1007/978-3-319-91908-9_18

15. Harel, D., Kozen, D., Tiuryn, J.: Dynamic Logic. MIT Press, Cambridge (2000)

16. Harel, D., Pnueli, A., Stavi, J.: Propositional dynamic logic of nonregular programs. J. Comput. Syst. Sci. **26**(2), 222–243 (1983). https://doi.org/10.1016/0022-0000(83)90014-4

17. Ledgard, H.F., Marcotty, M.: A genealogy of control structures. Commun. ACM **18**(11), 629–639 (1975). https://doi.org/10.1145/361219.361222

18. Löding, C., Lutz, C., Serre, O.: Propositional dynamic logic with recursive programs. J. Log. Algebraic Methods Program. **73**(1–2), 51–69 (2007). https://doi.org/10.1016/J.JLAP.2006.11.003

19. Meyer, B.: Applying "design by contract". Computer **25**(10), 40–51 (1992). https://doi.org/10.1109/2.161279

20. Müller, P., Schwerhoff, M., Summers, A.J.: Viper: a verification infrastructure for permission-based reasoning. In: Jobstmann, B., Leino, K. (eds.) VMCAI 2016. LNCS, vol. 9583, pp. 41–62. Springer, Heidelberg (2016). https://doi.org/10.1007/978-3-662-49122-5_2

21. Pratt, V.R.: Semantical considerations on Floyd-Hoare logic. In: SFCS 1976, pp. 109–121. IEEE Computer Society (1976). https://doi.org/10.1109/SFCS.1976.27
22. Valiev, M.K.: On axiomatization of deterministic propositional dynamic logic. In: Bečvář, J. (ed.) MFCS 1979. LNCS, vol. 74, pp. 482–491. Springer, Heidelberg (1979). https://doi.org/10.1007/3-540-09526-8_48

A Formal Framework for Naturally Specifying and Verifying Sequential Algorithms

Chengxi Yang[1], Shushu Wu[2], and Qinxiang Cao[2(✉)]

[1] Zhiyuan College, Shanghai Jiao Tong University, Shanghai, China
arcadia-y@sjtu.edu.cn
[2] Shanghai Jiao Tong University, Shanghai, China
{Ciel77,caoqinxiang}@sjtu.edu.cn

Abstract. Current approaches for formal verification of algorithms face important limitations. For specification, they cannot express algorithms naturally and concisely, especially for algorithms with states and flexible control flow. For verification, formal proof based on Hoare logic cannot reflect the logical structure of natural proof. To address these challenges, we introduce a formal framework for naturally specifying and verifying sequential algorithms in Coq. We use the state relation monad to integrate Coq's expressive type system with the flexible control flow of imperative languages. It supports nondeterministic operations and customizable program states, enabling specifying algorithms at an appropriate level of abstraction. For verification, we build a Hoare logic for the monad and propose a novel two-stage proof approach that separates natural logical reasoning from mechanical composition. It reflects the logical structure of natural proof, enhancing modularity and readability. We evaluate the framework by formalizing the Depth-First Search (DFS) algorithm and verifying the Knuth-Morris-Pratt (KMP) algorithm.

Keywords: Formal Verification · Monad · Hoare Logic · Coq

1 Introduction

The formal verification of algorithms aims to formally specify algorithms and mathematically state and prove their functional correctness. It is canonical to formalize sequential algorithms in proof assistants like Coq[1] [17] and Isabelle/HOL [13], and there have been various approaches.

A common approach is to define algorithms as pure functions and prove their correctness using proof assistants' built-in logic, such as Verified Functional

---

C. Yang and S. Wu—These authors contributed equally to this work.

[1] Currently Coq was recently renamed to "Rocq", see https://rocq-prover.org/about# Name. However, we still use the name "Coq" in this paper since we adopt an older version (8.15.2) for formalization.

ⓒ The Author(s), under exclusive license to Springer Nature Switzerland AG 2026
P. Rümmer and Z. Wu (Eds.): TASE 2025, LNCS 15841, pp. 49–66, 2026.
https://doi.org/10.1007/978-3-031-98208-8_4

Algorithms [2]. Still, many algorithms are naturally expressed in an imperative sequential form rather than pure functional form. Moreover, the restriction to structural recursion in Coq further complicates the task of specifying algorithms. For instance, even simple graph algorithms like Depth-First Search (DFS) become cumbersome to define under these constraints.

Another approach involves defining a simple imperative language, such as Imp [15], and formalizing algorithms within it. While this method allows for imperative constructs, it fails to leverage Coq's powerful type system, limiting its expressiveness for abstract operations like selecting an arbitrary element from a set.

In addition, the Isabelle Refinement Framework [8] enables users to formulate nondeterministic algorithms in a monadic style. Nevertheless, since it only supports functional and stateless programs, it is not convenient when formulating stateful algorithms (e.g. algorithms with a working set or state machine).

Beyond formalization, current verification approaches face additional limitations. Most frameworks for imperative algorithm verification rely on Hoare logic [5], which structures proofs according to the program's syntactic structure. This often requires grouping all propositions about the current program state into a conjunction and applying Hoare rules corresponding to the current statement. In contrast, natural proofs tend to organize propositions based on their logical relationships, following the proof's natural structure rather than the program's. This discrepancy becomes particularly evident when propositions span different program segments or loops, which Hoare logic struggles to handle elegantly.

Consider, for example, the *match* procedure in the Knuth–Morris–Pratt (KMP) algorithm [7], which finds the first occurrence of a pattern string in a text string. The procedure is shown in Algorithm 1.

Algorithm 1. Match procedure in the KMP algorithm

1: **procedure** MATCH($patn$, $text$, $next$)
2:     $j = 0$
3:     **for** i **from** 0 **to** $text.len$ **do**
4:         $ch = text[i]$
5:         **loop**
6:             **if** $patn[j] = ch$ **then**
7:                 $j \leftarrow j + 1$
8:                 **break**
9:             **if** $j = 0$ **then**
10:                 **break**
11:             $j \leftarrow next[j - 1]$
12:         **if** $j = patn.len$ **then**
13:             **return** $i - patn.len + 1$
14:     **return** -1

In Algorithm 1, *patn* represents the pattern string to be located within the text string *text*, while *next* is an array containing shift information critical to the algorithm's efficiency. It is precomputed by the table-building procedure in the KMP algorithm, and it represents the prefix function[2] of *patn*, which stores for each position j in *patn* the length of the longest proper prefix of $patn[0..j]$ that is also a suffix. *a.len* denotes the length of an array a.

To verify the procedure using the Hoare logic, one usually first provides a loop invariant I for the for-loop such as $jrange \wedge partial\_match \wedge partial\_bound \wedge no\_occur$, where

- *jrange* means that $0 \leq j < next.len$ so j is a valid index for *next* and *patn*.
- *partial_match* means that j is a partial match result for $text[0..i]$[3], i.e. $patn[0..j] = text[i - j..i]$.
- *partial_bound* asserts that j is an upperbound for the partial match result for $text[0..i]$. This with *partial_match* ensures j is the best result.
- *no_occur* states that there's no occurrence of *patn* in $text[0..i]$.

Then she aims to prove the for-loop body preserves I if the loop continues. To do so, she may assert another invariant I' for the inner loop such as $jrange \wedge partial\_match \wedge presuffix\_inv$, where *presuffix_inv* states some proposition that any partial match result k for $text[0..i + 1]$ must obey. Next she proves that the inner loop body preserves I', I' can derive some propositions P when the inner loop breaks, and with P the for-loop body preserves I. Finally she can prove some postconditions with I when the procedure returns.

In contrast, a natural proof might proceed as follows: *jrange* trivially holds throughout the for-loop due to preconditions. Based on *jrange*, the inner loop preserves *partial_match* and hence outer loop preserves *partial_match*. Furthermore, we can prove the inner loop also preserves *presuffix_inv*. As a consequence, *partial_bound* and *no_occur* are invariants of the for-loop. These invariants collectively lead to the desired postconditions.

As shown in the example, a natural proof tends to incrementally assert and prove properties of the program according to their logical relevance and relations. In the process, the logical dependency between propositions (e.g. *no_occur* depends on *jrange*) is also naturally presented. This reveals the gap between the natural proof and the Hoare logic-based formal proof.

To address these challenges, we present a formal framework for naturally specifying and verifying sequential algorithms in Coq. Our approach introduces a state relation monad for algorithm specification based on the denotational semantics. The monad, defined over the ternary relation of initial state, return value, and resulting state, supports imperative constructs such as general recursion and loops break. It also integrates Coq's powerful type system with non-deterministic operations, enabling users to specify algorithms at an appropriate level of abstraction and customize program states as needed. We also provide stateless and errorful variants of the monad for different needs.

---

[2] More details of the prefix function can be found in classic algorithm textbooks [4].

[3] $array[s..t]$ refers to the 0-indexed segment of *array* ranging from s (included) to t (excluded).

For verification, we develop a proof framework for partial correctness tailored to our monad. It includes Hoare rules for various statements and introduces a novel approach to organizing proofs. This approach divides proofs into two parts: *essential proof* that captures the key logical implications in each basic block, and *mechanized proof* that combines propositions to establish end-to-end correctness. The latter can be highly automated. This results in proof that is more natural, modular, and readable.

We evaluate our framework by formalizing the DFS algorithm, and specifying and verifying the KMP algorithm. In another work [20], we further prove the correctness of a C program by proving it refines the KMP algorithm we specify in our framework. This highlights the real-world applicability and versatility of our framework.

The source code of our framework is available at https://github.com/Arcadia-Y/TASE25-Artifact.

Outline. The rest of the paper is organized as follows: Sect. 2 introduces the state relation monad used for defining algorithms and uses it to formalize the DFS algorithm. Section 3 presents the Hoare logic and our proof approach, with the KMP algorithm as a case study. In Sect. 4, we discuss related work, and in Sect. 5, we conclude with a summary and directions for future work.

2   State Relation Monad

2.1   Monad Design

Our framework is based on the monad, a well-established abstraction in functional programming for structuring computations with effects [10]. Its definition contains a type constructor M: `Type` $\rightarrow$ `Type` and two operators:

- `return`: A $\rightarrow$ M A (abbreviated as `ret`), which takes a value of type A and wraps it as a value of type M A.
- `bind`: (M A) $\rightarrow$ (A $\rightarrow$ M B) $\rightarrow$ (M B), which takes a monadic value m of type M A and a function f of type A $\rightarrow$ M B. It tries to somehow unwrap m, applies f to it and returns the result as another monadic value.

In our framework, we model a program as a *state relation monad*, defined as a ternary relation over $\Sigma \times A \times \Sigma$, where Σ is the type of the program state and A is the type of the return value. This relation encodes the denotational semantics of a nondeterministic program c : $(s_1, r, s_2) \in c$ means that, starting from the state s_1, program c may terminate at s_2 and return r. We use the `unit` type with only one value `tt` to represent cases of no return value.

Our framework is based on a Coq library of sets [3], where sets and relations are represented as curried functions, such as A $\rightarrow$ `Prop` and A $\rightarrow$ B $\rightarrow$ `Prop`. The definition of a monadic program is as follows[4]:

---

[4] For simplicity and readability, some tedious portions of Coq code (e.g., implicit type parameters) are omitted in this paper.

```
Definition program (Σ A: Type): Type := Σ → A → Σ → Prop.
```

For any type Σ, `program` Σ is the type constructor for the state relation monad. The definitions of the two basic monad operators follow directly from the denotational semantics:

– For any a of type `A`, $\text{ret}(a)$ is value of type `program` Σ `A` defined as

$$(s_1, r, s_2) \in \text{ret}(a) \iff r = a \wedge s_1 = s_2$$

– For any c of type `program` Σ `A` and f of type `A` $\to$ `program` Σ `B`, $\text{bind}(c, f)$ is a value of type `program` Σ `B` defined as

$$(s_1, b, s_3) \in \text{bind}(c, f) \iff \exists\, a\ s_2,\ (s_1, a, s_2) \in c \wedge (s_2, b, s_3) \in f(a)$$

Intuitively, `ret` returns a value without changing the state, and `bind` composes two programs by passing the return value and terminal state of the first program to the second program. They satisfy the standard monad laws[5]:

1. `ret` is the left identity for `bind`: $\text{bind}(\text{ret}(x), f) = f(x)$.
2. `ret` is the right identity for `bind`: $\text{bind}(c, \text{ret}) = c$.
3. `bind` is associative: $\text{bind}(\text{bind}(c, f), g) = \text{bind}(c, \lambda x.\text{bind}(f(x), g))$.

To achieve an imperative-style syntax, we adopt a notation similar to Haskell's do-notation:

```
Notation "x ← c1 ;; c2" := (bind c1 (fun x ⇒ c2)) ...
Notation "e1 ;; e2" := (bind e1 (fun _: unit ⇒ e2)) ...
```

The expressiveness of the state relation monad stems from the fact that defining a program is equivalent to defining a ternary relation in Coq's logical system. Combined with customizable states, this allows users to define program statements at an appropriate level of abstraction, providing high extensibility and flexibility.

In addition to user-defined statements, we provide several operators for convenient program construction:

– `choice` stands for nondeterministic choice between two programs.
– `assume` adds a logical proposition regarding the program state as an assumption. `assume'` is the notation for assumptions independent of the state.
– `any` returns an arbitrary value of a given type without changing the state.
– `update` modifies the state according to a binary relation over program states.

$$\text{choice}(f, g) := f \cup g$$
$$\forall P : \Sigma \to \text{Prop},\ (s_1, \text{tt}, s_2) \in \text{assume}(P) \iff P(s_1) \wedge s_1 = s_2$$
$$\forall A : \text{Type},\ (s_1, a, s_2) \in \text{any}(A) \iff s_1 = s_2$$
$$\forall R : \Sigma \to \Sigma \to \text{Prop},\ (s_1, \text{tt}, s_2) \in \text{update}(R) \iff R(s_1, s_2)$$

---

[5] Here, equality (=) denotes program equivalence, which corresponds to the equality of the underlying ternary relations, i.e. double inclusion.

By combining `choice` and `assume`, we can easily express common branching statements in imperative programs. For example, the following program computes the absolute value of an integer:

```
Example compute_abs: program unit Z :=
  choice (assume' (z >= 0);; ret z)
         (assume' (z < 0);; ret (-z)).
```

We can also use `any` and `assume` to define nondeterministic abstract operations. For instance, the following program returns an arbitrary prime number:

```
Example any_prime: program unit nat :=
  x ← any nat;;
  assume' (¬ exists (m n: nat), m > 1 ∧ n > 1 ∧ x = m * n);;
  ret x.
```

To express recursions and loops, we follow the standard approach in the denotational semantics by using the least fixed point in the Kleene fixed-point theorem [19]. For any directed-complete partial order A with a least element $\bot$ and any function $f : A \to A$, we define $\texttt{Lfix}$[6] as the supremum of the set produced by iterating f on $\bot$.

$$\texttt{Lfix}(f) := \sup(\{f^n(\bot) \mid n \in \mathbf{N}\})$$

Recursion can then be expressed directly using `Lfix`. For example, the following program computes the Fibonacci number:

```
Example Fibonacci: nat → program unit nat :=
  Lfix
  (fun (W: nat → program unit nat) (n: nat) ⇒
    choice
      (assume' (n <= 1);; ret n)
      (assume' (n > 1);;
        x ← W (n - 1);;
        y ← W (n - 2);;
        ret (x + y))).
```

We also define various loops using the least fixed point. For instance, we define loops with break to express flexible control flows. We first define an inductive type `ContinueOrBreak` similar to a sum type to represent results with control flow annotation, and then formalize loops using `Lfix`.

```
Inductive ContinueOrBreak (A B: Type): Type :=
| by_continue (a: A)
| by_break (b: B).
```

---

[6] It is defined for any f, although to apply the Kleene fixed-point theorem, f should be monotone and continuous.

```
Definition repeat_break_f
  (body: A → program Σ (ContinueOrBreak A B)) :=
  fun (W: A → program Σ B) (a: A) ⇒
      x ← body a;;
      match x with
      | by_continue a' ⇒ W a'
      | by_break b ⇒ ret b
      end.
Definition repeat_break
  (body: A → program Σ (ContinueOrBreak A B)): A → program Σ B :=
  Lfix (repeat_break_f body).
Definition continue (a: A): program Σ (ContinueOrBreak A B) :=
  ret (by_continue a).
Definition break (b: B): program Σ (ContinueOrBreak A B) :=
  ret (by_break b).
```

Using `continue` and `break`, we can construct loops with break. Below is an example of a loop that computes hailstone numbers.

```
Example hailstone: Z → program unit Z :=
  repeat_break
  (fun (x: Z) ⇒
    choice
      (assume' (x <= 1);; break x)
      (assume' (x > 1);;
       choice
         (assume' (exists k, x = 2 * k);;
         continue (x / 2))
         (assume' (exists k, x = 2 * k + 1);;
         continue (3 * x + 1)))).
```

For some algorithms, it is unnecessary to involve states; for some other algorithms, we need to model errorful computations. To address these cases, we provide stateless and errorful variants of our state relation monad: the set monad and state relation monad with error. Their syntax is very similar to the original monad. More details can be found in appendix A of the extended version [21].

2.2 Case Study: Formulating the DFS Algorithm

We formalize the Depth-First Search (DFS) algorithm in its imperative form using the state relation monad. Our definition of directed graphs and the step relation is based on a library of formalized graph theory [18].

```
Record PreGraph (Vertex Edge: Type) := {
  vvalid : Vertex → Prop; (* vertex set *)
  evalid : Edge → Prop; (* edge set*)
  src : Edge → Vertex; (* source of an edge *)
  dst : Edge → Vertex  (* destination of an edge *)
}.
```

```
Record step_aux (pg: PreGraph V E) (e: E) (x y: V): Prop := {
  step_evalid: pg.(evalid) e;
  step_src_valid: pg.(vvalid) x;
  step_dst_valid: pg.(vvalid) y;
  step_src: pg.(src) e = x;
  step_dst: pg.(dst) e = y;
}.
Definition step (pg: PreGraph V E) (x y: V): Prop :=
  exists e, step_aux pg e x y.
```

The program state for the DFS algorithm consists of a visited set that stores visited vertices and a stack that maintains the search path.

```
Record state (V: Type): Type := {
  stack: list V;
  visited: V → Prop;
}.
```

We also define several basic operations required for DFS:

visit(v) :=
　　update$(\lambda s_1 s_2.\ s_2.\text{visited} = s_1.\text{visited} \cup \{v\} \ \wedge\ s_2.\text{stack} = s_1.\text{stack})$
push_stack(v) :=
　　update$(\lambda s_1 s_2.\ s_2.\text{stack} = v :: s_1.\text{stack} \ \wedge\ s_2.\text{visited} = s_1.\text{visited})$
pop_stack :=
　　$\lambda s_1 v s_2.\ s_1.\text{stack} = v :: s_2.\text{stack} \ \wedge\ s_2.\text{visited} = s_1.\text{visited}$
if_all_neighbor_visited(pg, u) :=
　　assume$(\lambda s.\ \forall v,\ \text{step}(u, v) \rightarrow v \in s.\text{visited})$

- visit(v) marks vertex v as visited and leaves the stack unchanged.
- push_stack(v) pushes vertex v onto the stack without modifying the visited set.
- pop_stack pops the top vertex from the stack and returns it. Note how relation enables us to define the action of modifying the stack and returning the popped value concisely.
- if_all_neighbor_visited(pg, u) assumes that all neighbors of vertex u have been visited.

The DFS algorithm is then defined as follows:

```
Definition DFS_body (pg: PreGraph V E): V → program (state V) unit :=
  fun u ⇒
    choice
    (if_all_neighbor_visited pg u;;
      choice
      (assume (fun s ⇒ s.(stack) = nil);; break tt)
      (v ← pop_stack;; continue v))
```

```
      (v ← any V;;
       assume (fun s ⇒ ¬ v ∈ s.(visited));;
       assume' (step pg u v);;
       push_stack u;;
       visit v;;
       continue v).
Definition DFS (pg: PreGraph V E): V → program (state V) unit :=
  fun u ⇒
    visit u;; repeat_break (DFS_body pg) u.
```

The algorithm works as follows:

1. It visits the first vertex and begins to search from it.
2. If all neighbors of the current vertex u have been visited, it either terminates (if the stack is empty) or backtracks by popping the stack.
3. Otherwise, it nondeterministically selects an unvisited neighbor v, pushes u onto the stack, marks v as visited, and continues the search from v.

This formulation is concise and appropriately abstract, as it specifies neither the order in which vertices are visited, nor the concrete data structures used, aligning with the nondeterministic nature of DFS. We proved that a vertex is visited after the DFS if and only if it is reachable from the starting vertex based on the formulation.

3   Proof Framework

3.1   Hoare Logic

We develop a Hoare logic for our state relation monad to prove the partial correctness of algorithms. Drawing inspiration from Hoare Type Theory (HTT) [11], which integrates dependent types with Hoare triples, our logic adapts HTT's principles to a relational semantics while addressing imperative and nondeterministic constructs.

In our framework, a Hoare triple `Hoare P c Q` asserts that, for any initial state satisfying P, if the program c terminates, then resulting state and return value satisfy Q.

```
Definition Hoare (P: Σ → Prop) (c: program Σ A) (Q: A → Σ → Prop) :=
  forall s1 a s2, P s1 → (s1, a, s2) ∈ c → Q a s2.
```

We prove the following core Hoare rules[7]. Basic rules including bind, return and consequence are adapted from HTT's typing judgements. Choice rule enables compositional proof for branching programs. Assume, any and update rules provide strongest postcondition for our program constructs. For user-defined statements, step rule offers a general strongest postcondition. Pre-exist rule is useful

---

[7] We use the canonical notation $\{P\}c\{Q\}$ to denote a Hoare triple. Besides, for simplicity, some propositions may require lifting (e.g. $P \wedge Q$ may mean $\lambda s.P(s) \wedge Q(s)$).

for extracting existential variables in the precondition, which are often introduced by previous rules. We also adapt the conjunction rule into our logic to modularize proof for complicated postconditions, which is fundamental to our two-stage proof approach.

$$\text{BIND} \ \frac{\{P\}f\{Q\} \qquad \forall a, \ \{Q(a)\}g(a)\{R\}}{\{P\}\texttt{bind}(f,g)\{R\}} \qquad \qquad \text{RET} \ \frac{P : \texttt{A} \to \Sigma \to \texttt{Prop}}{\{P(a)\}\texttt{ret}(a)\{P\}}$$

$$\text{CHOICE} \ \frac{\{P\}f\{Q\} \qquad \{P\}g\{Q\}}{\{P\}\texttt{choice}(f,g)\{Q\}} \qquad \qquad \text{ASSUME} \ \frac{}{\{P\}\texttt{assume}(Q)\{P \wedge Q\}}$$

$$\text{ANY} \ \frac{}{\{P\}\texttt{any}(A)\{P\}} \qquad \text{UPDATE} \ \frac{f : \Sigma \to \Sigma \to \texttt{Prop}}{\{P\}\texttt{update}(f)\{\lambda a s_2. \ \exists s_1, f(s_1, s_2) \wedge P(s_1)\}}$$

$$\text{STEP} \ \frac{f : \Sigma \to \texttt{A} \to \Sigma \to \texttt{Prop}}{\{P\}f\{\lambda a s_2. \ \exists s_1, f(s_1, a, s_2) \wedge P(s_1)\}}$$

$$\text{CONSEQ} \ \frac{P_1 \to P_2 \qquad \{P_2\}f\{Q_2\} \qquad Q_2 \to Q_1}{\{P_1\}f\{Q_1\}}$$

$$\text{PREEX} \ \frac{\forall x, \ \{P(x)\}f\{Q\}}{\{\lambda s. \ \exists x, P(x,s)\}f\{Q\}} \qquad \qquad \text{CONJ} \ \frac{\{P\}f\{Q_1\} \qquad \{P\}f\{Q_2\}}{\{P\}f\{Q_1 \wedge Q_2\}}$$

We also prove rules for recursions and loops with break. The fixed-point rule for recursions formalizes the induction principle for the iterated function in their denotational semantics.

$$\text{FIX} \ \frac{\forall W, \ (\forall a, \ \{P(a)\}W(a)\{Q\}) \to (\forall a, \ \{P(a)\}F(W,a)\{Q\})}{\forall a, \ \{P(a)\}\texttt{Lfix}(F,a)\{Q\}}$$

For loops with break, we introduce two auxiliary operators to modularize proof. One operator continue_case assumes that x has the form by_continue a and unwraps it to return a. The other one break_case is analogous. These lead to a more modular repeat-break rule.

$$\text{REPEATBREAK} \ \frac{\begin{array}{c} \forall a, \ \{P(a)\}x \leftarrow f(a); ; \texttt{continue\_case}(x)\{P\} \\ \forall a, \ \{P(a)\}x \leftarrow f(a); ; \texttt{break\_case}(x)\{Q\} \end{array}}{\forall a, \ \{P(a)\}\texttt{repeat\_break}(f,a)\{Q\}}$$

For set monad and state relation monad with errors, we build a similar Hoare logic as well. See appendix A of the extended version [21] for more details.

3.2   The Two-Stage Proof Approach

Our framework introduces a two-stage proof approach to bridge the gap between natural reasoning and formal verification. This approach separates natural logical reasoning from mechanical composition, enhancing modularity and readability.

Consider for example, the *match* procedure in the KMP algorithm shown in Algorithm 1. We formalize it using the set monad as follows. A is the character type, and `range_iter_break`(l, h, f, j_0) is a for-loop with loop body being f, i ranging from l (included) to h (excluded) and j initialized as j_0.

```
Context {A: Type} (default: A)
         (patn text: list A) (next: list nat).
Definition inner_body(ch: A): nat → program (ContinueOrBreak nat nat) :=
  fun j ⇒
    choice
      (assume(ch = nth j patn default);; break (j+1))
      (assume(ch <> nth j patn default);;
      choice
        (assume(j = 0);; break 0)
        (assume(j <> 0);; continue (nth (j-1) next 0))).
Definition inner_loop(ch: A): nat → program nat :=
  repeat_break (inner_body ch).
Definition match_body:
  nat → nat → program (ContinueOrBreak nat nat) :=
  fun i j ⇒
      let ch := nth i text default in
      j' ← inner_loop ch j;;
      choice
        (assume (j' = length patn);;
        break (i - length patn + 1))
        (assume (j' < length patn);;
        continue (j')).
Definition match_loop: program (ContinueOrBreak nat nat) :=
  range_iter_break 0 (length text) match_body 0.
```

The correctness of *match* can be stated as follows: if *patn* is nonempty, *patn* and *next* has the same length and *next* is a prefix function of *patn*, then the return value r is either $by\_break(i)$ representing the first occurrence of *patn* in *text*, or $by\_continue(i)$ meaning there's no occurrence of *patn* in *text*. We formalize it as the following Hoare triple:

$$\{patn \neq nil \land patn.len = next.len \land prefix\_func(next)\}$$

$$\texttt{match\_loop}$$

$$\left\{ \lambda r. \begin{cases} first\_occur(i) & \text{if } r = by\_break(i) \\ no\_occur(text.len) & \text{if } r = by\_continue(i) \end{cases} \right\}$$

The formal definition of these logical predicates and those introduced in Sect. 1 can be found in appendix C of the extended version [21].

The first stage of our two-stage proof is the **essential proof** that captures the logical structure of the algorithm proof. In this stage, the proof proceeds by

logical groups, each of which focuses on a logical topic and contains propositions relevant to the topic. For each group, we propose and prove **basic block propositions**, Hoare triples of relevant basic blocks. Tactics like `hoare_auto` could facilitate the basic block verification. Between adjacent basic blocks, we prove **logical implications** connecting their preconditions and postconditions. These also include implications between pre/post-conditions of the procedure and pre/post-condition of some basic blocks.

We provide tactical support for decomposing programs into individual basic blocks and verifying them conveniently (see appendix B of the extended version [21] for more details). Luckily, for the *match* example, the program is already well-structured so we do not need to transform it. Then following the natural proof, our proof proceeds as follows:

Group 1: range. In this group we prove *jrange* holds throughout the for-loop as a foundation for other propositions. Since *patn* is non-empty and *next* has the same length as *patn*, *jrange* holds when entering the match loop:

$$patn \neq nil \land patn.len = next.len \rightarrow jrange(0)$$

next is a prefix function implies that its elements are within certain range.

$$prefix\_func(next) \rightarrow \forall k : jrange(k), next[k] \in [0, k]$$

By definition, basic block is a program segment without control flow transfer like loops and branches [1]. However, in our framework, it can contain `choice` or even loops that have been verified previously, depending on the user's needs. Since *jrange* is a simple proposition, we treat `inner_body` as a basic block in this group. When it continues, *jrange* is preserved.

$$\{jrange(j) \land (\forall k : jrange(k), next[k] \in [0, k])\}$$
$$x \leftarrow \texttt{inner\_body}(ch, j); ; \texttt{continue\_case}(x)$$
$$\{\lambda j'.\ jrange(j')\}$$

When it breaks, *jrange* no longer holds and the range of j is as follows.

$$\{jrange(j)\}\ x \leftarrow \texttt{inner\_body}(ch, j); ; \texttt{break\_case}(x)\ \{\lambda j'.\ j' \in [0, patn.len]\}$$

After exiting the inner loop, when outer loop continues, *jrange* is back again.

$$\{j' \in [0, patn.len]\}\ \texttt{assume}(j' < patn.len); ; \texttt{ret}(j')\ \{\lambda j''.\ jrange(j'')\}$$

Some reader may point out that in the original program it ends with $continue(j')$ instead of $ret(j')$. This does not matter since $x \leftarrow continue(j'); ; continue\_case(x)$ is equivalent to $ret(j')$. When applying the repeat-break rule in the second stage, the original basic block will become just like this.

Group 2: partial match. In this group we prove that $partial\_match(i,j)$ is an invariant of the for-loop, but we do not care about whether j is the best result. Obviously, it holds when the outer loop begins: $partial\_match(0,0)$. Based on *jrange* and preconditions, $partial\_match(i,j)$ is preserved by the continue branch of the inner body.

$$\{next.len \leq patn.len \wedge prefix\_func(next) \wedge jrange(j) \wedge partial\_match(i,j)\}$$
$$\texttt{assume}(j \neq 0); ; \texttt{ret}(next[j-1])$$
$$\{\lambda j'. \ partial\_match(i,j')\}$$

When inner loop breaks, we aim to prove the original $partial\_match(i,j)$ is extended to next i and current j, i.e. $partial\_match(i+1,j')$. The first case where $text[i] = patn[j]$ needs preconditions and the range of i in the for-loop.

$$\{next.len \leq patn.len \wedge i \in [0, text.len) \wedge jrange(j) \wedge partial\_match(i,j)\}$$
$$\texttt{assume}(text[i] = patn[j]); ; \texttt{ret}(j+1)$$
$$\{\lambda j'. \ partial\_match(i+1,j')\}$$

The second case where $j = 0$ is trivial.

$$\{\} \ \texttt{assume}(j=0); ; \texttt{ret}(0) \ \{\lambda j'. \ partial\_match(i+1,j')\}$$

$partial\_match(i+1,j')$ is preserved when the for-loop continues because j' is not changed.

Group 3: partial bound. In this group, to prepare for the two *no_occur* in the postcondition, we prove that $partial\_bound$ is an invariant of the for-loop. It holds when the for-loop starts: $partial\_bound(0,0)$. For inner loop, we propose a new invariant $presuffix\_inv(i,j)$. The two invariants of the for-loop, $partial\_match(i,j)$ and $partial\_bound(i,j)$, ensure $presuffix\_inv(i,j)$ when entering the inner loop.

$$next.len \leq patn.len \wedge i \in [0, text.len) \wedge partial\_match(i,j) \wedge$$
$$partial\_bound(i,j) \rightarrow presuffix\_inv(i,j)$$

When the inner loop continues, $presuffix\_inv(i,j)$ is preserved.

$$\{next.len \leq patn.len \wedge prefix\_func(next) \wedge jrange(j) \wedge$$
$$presuffix\_inv(i,j) \wedge text[i] \neq patn[j]\}$$
$$\texttt{assume}(j \neq 0); ; \texttt{ret}(next[j-1])$$
$$\{\lambda j'. \ presuffix\_inv(i,j')\}$$

When inner loop breaks, we leverage $presuffix\_inv(i,j)$ to prove $partial\_bound(i+1,j')$. The first case is $text[i] = patn[j]$:

$$\{next.len \leq patn.len \wedge jrange(j) \wedge presuffix\_inv(i,j)\}$$
$$\texttt{assume}(text[i] = patn[j]); ; \texttt{ret}(j+1)$$
$$\{\lambda j'. \ partial\_bound(i+1,j')\}$$

The second case is $text[i] \neq patn[j]$:

$$\{text[i] \neq patn[j] \wedge presuffix\_inv(i,j)\}$$
$$\mathtt{assume}(j = 0);;\mathtt{ret}(0)$$
$$\{\lambda j'.\ partial\_bound(i+1,j')\}$$

Similar to group 2, it is preserved when for-loop continues.

Group 4: post loop. In this group we prove the postcondition using the previous results. Firstly, we prove that $no\_occur(i)$ is an invariant of for-loop. Obviously $no\_occur(0)$. Based on $partial\_bound(i+1,j')$ and $jrange(j')$, we can prove it is preserved.

$$i \in [0, text.len) \wedge jrange(j') \wedge partial\_bound(i+1,j') \wedge no\_occur(i) \rightarrow$$
$$no\_occur(i+1)$$

If the for-loop terminates because i reaches the upperbound, then we have $no\_occur(text.len)$, which is half of our postcondition. On the other hand, if the for-loop terminates because it breaks, we can prove the no_occur part of *first_occur*.

$$\{no\_occur(i)\}$$
$$\mathtt{assume}(j' = patn.len);;\mathtt{ret}(i - patn.len + 1)$$
$$\{\lambda r.\ no\_occur(r + patn.len - 1)\}$$

Using $partial\_match(i+1,j')$, we can prove the other part of *first_occur*.

$$\{partial\_match(i+1,j')\}$$
$$\mathtt{assume}(j' = patn.len);;\mathtt{ret}(i - patn.len + 1)$$
$$\{\lambda r.\ text[r..r + patn.len] = patn\}$$

Although the proof is complete from natural understanding, the formal proof needs to establish an end-to-end correctness theorem. Therefore, the second stage is the **mechanized proof**, which composes the essential proof's results into a complete formal argument using Hoare rules. In this stage, by repeatedly using conjunction rule and consequence rule, we can merge grouped propositions of the same basic block into a single Hoare triple. Then we can use choice rules to combine two branches' Hoare triples, use loop rules to transform the loop body's Hoare triple into the loop's Hoare triple, and use bind rule to combine them altogether.

In our example, combining results from the essential proof, the inner body satisfy following Hoare triples:

$$\{next.len \leq patn.len \wedge prefix\_func(next) \wedge (\forall k : jrange(k), next[k] \in [0,k]) \wedge$$
$$jrange(j) \wedge partial\_match(i,j) \wedge presuffix\_inv(i,j)\}$$
$$x \leftarrow \mathtt{inner\_body}(text[i],j);;\mathtt{continue\_case}(x)$$
$$\{\lambda j'.\ jrange(j') \wedge partial\_match(i+1,j') \wedge presuffix\_inv(i+1,j')\}$$

$$\{next.len \leq patn.len \wedge prefix\_func(next) \wedge i \in [0, text.len) \wedge$$
$$jrange(j) \wedge partial\_match(i, j) \wedge presuffix\_inv(i, j)\}$$
$$x \leftarrow \texttt{inner\_body}(text[i], j); ; \texttt{break\_case}(x)$$
$$\{\lambda j'. \ j' \in [0, patn.len] \wedge partial\_match(i+1, j') \wedge partial\_bound(i+1, j')\}$$

Using the repeat-break rule and the consequence rule, we further obtain the Hoare triple of the inner loop:

$$\{next.len \leq patn.len \wedge prefix\_func(next) \wedge i \in [0, text.len) \wedge$$
$$jrange(j) \wedge partial\_match(i, j) \wedge partial\_bound(i, j) \wedge no\_occur(i)\}$$
$$\texttt{inner\_loop}(text[i], j)$$
$$\{\lambda j'. \ j' \in [0, patn.len] \wedge partial\_match(i+1, j') \wedge$$
$$partial\_bound(i+1, j') \wedge no\_occur(i+1)\}$$

Then similarly we can obtain Hoare triples for the match body and the match loop, finishing the proof.

This two-stage proof approach improves modularity by splitting complicated propositions of complex programs into simple propositions of basic blocks. Besides, it enhances readability by ensuring that proofs reflect the natural logical structure of the correctness argument rather than the program's syntactic structure. Moreover, the approach achieves generality, as it can be applied to almost all formal frameworks based on Hoare logic.

In addition, we also formalize and prove the table-building procedure in the KMP algorithm, further showcasing the usability of our framework.

4   Related Work

The Isabelle Refinement Framework [8] provides a monadic approach to program verification, enabling users to specify and refine nondeterministic algorithms in a functional style. While it supports abstract specifications and stepwise refinement, it is primarily designed for functional and stateless programs, making it less suitable for imperative algorithms with complex state transitions. In contrast, our framework introduces customizable states and more flexible control flow constructs such as loops with break, which are convenient for naturally specifying algorithms like DFS and KMP. Additionally, it focuses on the data refinement and program refinement, but our work focuses more on specifying and verifying abstract algorithms.

Separation Logic [16] provides a foundation for reasoning about programs with mutable state and pointers, focusing on local reasoning about memory. Frameworks like the Iris [6] build upon Separation Logic to verify concrete programs, often involving complex memory manipulations. While these frameworks excel at verifying low-level implementation details, our approach focuses on specifying and verifying algorithms at a higher level of abstraction using a state relation monad, aiming to separate the core algorithmic logic from more concrete implementation concerns like memory management.

Nigron et al. also developed a framework with a Hoare logic for monadic programs in Coq [12]. While their work, like ours, utilizes monads and builds a corresponding Hoare logic, the motivations and resulting logics differ significantly. They aimed to reason about identifier freshness generated by monadic programs. To achieve this, they employed separation logic principles, tailoring their Hoare logic to enable local reasoning about freshness, notably featuring the frame rule. In contrast, our framework uses the state relation monad primarily to specify algorithms naturally and concisely. Consequently, our Hoare logic is designed to mirror the structure of natural proofs, featuring rules for various monadic operators, loop constructs, and recursion, alongside structural rules like the conjunction rule to facilitate modular natural reasoning about algorithm correctness.

Lammich and Neumann's framework for verifying DFS algorithms [9] provides a structured approach to specifying and proving the correctness of DFS using a combination of refinement techniques and modular proof components. Since it is built on the Isabelle Refinement Framework, it represents program states as explicit arguments. In contrast, our framework abstracts away the state using a state relation monad, enabling more concise and elegant formulations of algorithms. Besides, while the DFS framework features the design principle and technique of incrementally establishing invariants, our two-stage proof approach can not only achieve the same effect, but also handle more complex structures, such as multiple layers of loops and intricate branches. This makes our framework suitable for a wider range of algorithms.

There has been formal proof of the KMP algorithm, such as Paulson's [14]. It describes the table-building and matching procedures as single-layer loops and uses traditional Hoare logic for verification. In contrast, we model both procedures as two-layer loops that share the same inner loop, aligning more closely with common practices. Our proof framework allows us to provide a modular and readable proof for such formulation.

5   Conclusion

In this paper, we introduced a formal framework for naturally specifying and verifying sequential algorithms in Coq. Our approach leverages a state relation monad to integrate Coq's expressive type system with the flexible control flow of imperative languages. This allows for the specification of algorithms at an appropriate level of abstraction, supporting nondeterministic operations and customizable program states. We provided stateless and errorful variants of the monad. We also developed a proof framework for partial correctness tailored to our monad, which includes Hoare rules for various statements and a novel two-stage proof approach. This approach separates natural logical reasoning from mechanical composition, enhancing modularity and readability. We demonstrated the versatility and applicability of our framework through practical evaluations, including the formalization of the DFS algorithm and the verification of the KMP algorithm.

Acknowledgments. This material is based upon work supported by NSF China 62472274 and 92370201.

Disclosure of Interests. The authors have no competing interests to declare that are relevant to the content of this article.

References

1. Aho, A.V., Lam, M.S., Sethi, R., Ullman, J.D.: Compilers: Principles, Techniques, and Tools, 2nd edn. Addison-Wesley (2007)
2. Appel, A.W.: Verified Functional Algorithms, Software Foundations, vol. 3. Electronic textbook (2024), version 1.5.5. http://softwarefoundations.cis.upenn.edu
3. Cao, Q., Wu, X., Liang, Y.: A Coq library of sets for teaching denotational semantics. Electron. Proc. Theor. Comput. Sci. **400**, 79–95 (2024). https://doi.org/10.4204/EPTCS.400.6
4. Cormen, T.H., Leiserson, C.E., Rivest, R.L., Stein, C.: Introduction to Algorithms, 3rd edn. The MIT Press (2009)
5. Hoare, C.: An axiomatic basis for computer programming. Commun. ACM **12**(10), 576–580 (1969). https://doi.org/10.1145/363235.363259
6. Jung, R., Krebbers, R., Jourdan, J.H., Bizjak, A., Birkedal, L., Dreyer, D.: Iris from the ground up: a modular foundation for higher-order concurrent separation logic. J. Funct. Program. **28**, e20 (2018). https://doi.org/10.1017/S095679681800014X
7. Knuth, D.E., Morris, J.H., Pratt, V.R.: Fast pattern matching in strings. SIAM J. Comput. **6**, 323–350 (1977). https://api.semanticscholar.org/CorpusID:11697579
8. Lammich, P.: Refinement for monadic programs. Archive of Formal Proofs (2012). https://isa-afp.org/entries/Refine_Monadic.html, Formal proof development
9. Lammich, P., Neumann, R.: A framework for verifying depth-first search algorithms. In: CPP 2015, pp. 137–146. Association for Computing Machinery, New York (2015). https://doi.org/10.1145/2676724.2693165
10. Moggi, E.: Notions of computation and monads. Inf. Comput. **93**(1), 55–92 (1991). https://doi.org/10.1016/0890-5401(91)90052-4
11. Nanevski, A., Morrisett, J., Birkedal, L.: Hoare type theory, polymorphism and separation. J. Funct. Program. **18**, 865–911 (2008). https://doi.org/10.1017/S0956796808006953
12. Nigron, P., Dagand, P.E.: Reaching for the star: tale of a monad in Coq. In: Cohen, L., Kaliszyk, C. (eds.) 12th International Conference on Interactive Theorem Proving (ITP 2021). Leibniz International Proceedings in Informatics (LIPIcs), vol. 193, pp. 29:1–29:19. Schloss Dagstuhl – Leibniz-Zentrum für Informatik, Dagstuhl, Germany (2021). https://doi.org/10.4230/LIPIcs.ITP.2021.29
13. Nipkow, T., Wenzel, M., Paulson, L.C.: Isabelle/HOL: A Proof Assistant for Higher-Order Logic. Springer, Heidelberg (2002)
14. Paulson, L.C.: Knuth–Morris–Pratt string search. Archive of Formal Proofs (2023). https://isa-afp.org/entries/KnuthMorrisPratt.html, Formal proof development
15. Pierce, B.C., et al.: Programming Language Foundations, Software Foundations, vol. 2. Electronic Textbook (2024)
16. Reynolds, J.C.: Separation logic: a logic for shared mutable data structures. In: Proceedings of the 17th Annual IEEE Symposium on Logic in Computer Science (LICS 2002), pp. 59–78. IEEE Computer Society (2002). https://doi.org/10.1109/LICS.2002.1029817

17. The Coq Development Team: The Coq reference manual – release 8.19.0 (2024). https://coq.inria.fr/doc/V8.19.0/refman

18. Wang, S., Cao, Q., Mohan, A., Hobor, A.: Certifying graph-manipulating C programs via localizations within data structures. Proc. ACM Program. Lang. **3**(OOPSLA) (2019). https://doi.org/10.1145/3360597

19. Winskel, G.: The Formal Semantics of Programming Languages: An Introduction. MIT Press, Cambridge (1993)

20. Wu, S., Wu, X., Cao, Q.: Encode the ∀∃ relational Hoare logic into standard Hoare logic (2025). https://arxiv.org/abs/2504.17444

21. Yang, C., Wu, S., Cao, Q.: A formal framework for naturally specifying and verifying sequential algorithms (2025). https://arxiv.org/abs/2504.19852

Machine-Checked Compositional Specification and Proofs for Embedded Systems

Karl Palmskog[1]([⊠]), Mattias Nyberg[2], and Dilian Gurov[1]

[1] KTH Royal Institute of Technology, Stockholm, Sweden
{palmskog,dilian}@kth.se
[2] Scania CV AB, Södertälje, Sweden
mattias.nyberg@scania.com

Abstract. The effort of formal verification of large heterogeneous systems needs to scale linearly with the number of interacting components, to be feasible in industrial practice. This is made possible by compositional specification methods and proof systems. In this paper, we demonstrate how trustworthy verified decomposition can be performed for an industry-relevant embedded system: a fuel level display. We first formalize the underlying theory in the HOL4 theorem prover, and augment this theory to allow specifications using Metric Interval Temporal Logic (MITL) We then state a top-level specification for our system using MITL and decompose it down to the system components. Our HOL4 formalization provides a corrected and extended restatement of a general specification language and proof system from previous work and showcases its usefulness for verified decomposition of systems.

Keywords: Compositional proof · formal verification · embedded systems · HOL4

1 Introduction

A fundamental problem in applying formal verification to large-scale, heterogeneous industrial systems is the complexity of performing reasoning across many independent interacting components [11]. If the complexity grows with the size of the global state space, e.g., as defined by a product of many automata, then such verification quickly becomes unfeasible. The promise of *compositional* specification methods and proof systems is that the complexity of reasoning may instead grow only linearly with the number of components in the system, thanks to contract-based reasoning at each individual component, e.g., in the assume-guarantee style.

To this end, Nyberg et al. proposed a theory for compositional specification and proof, based on first-order logic [9]. Although motivated by industrial requirements, the theory is general and abstract, even eliding commitment to

© The Author(s), under exclusive license to Springer Nature Switzerland AG 2026
P. Rümmer and Z. Wu (Eds.): TASE 2025, LNCS 15841, pp. 67–82, 2026.
https://doi.org/10.1007/978-3-031-98208-8_5

logical formulas for describing the behavior of individual components. However, this also means that there is a significant gap between the theory as initially presented and its application to specify and verify concrete systems relevant to industrial practice. Moreover, the theory is only demonstrated on small running examples, which may be insufficient to guide application to real systems.

In this paper we consider decomposition of formal verification for an industry-relevant embedded system: a vehicle fuel-level display (FLD). To enable trust-worthy decomposition of a correctness proof, we first formalize the theory of Nyberg et al. in the HOL4 theorem prover [13] and instantiate it with a notion of *timed words* in place of its abstract set of (unstructured) system *runs*. This enables us to provide a natural top-level specification of the system using Metric Interval Temporal Logic (MITL) [1,8] that can be soundly decomposed. Besides paving the way for more automated tools for compositional specification and verification, our HOL4 formalization corrects several issues in the original account of the specification and proof theory and puts its connection to first-order logic on firm ground.

In summary, we make the following *contributions*:

(i) We formalize the abstract compositional specification theory and proof system of Nyberg et al. in the HOL4 theorem prover, including its interpretation in (sorted) first-order logic and soundness of the proof system.
(ii) We instantiate the theory and proof system for timed words, and augment specifications to allow occurrences of MITL formulas.
(iii) We further instantiate the theory of timed words for an embedded fuel level display system, and demonstrate how its verification can be soundly decomposed. The system design and structure is derived from a real industrial system implemented in Scania trucks.

We provide the code that comprises the HOL4 formalization (around 6000 lines) as supplementary material to the paper [10].

2 Fuel Level Display System Description

We apply the theory of Nyberg et al. [9] for compositional specification and verification of a cyber-physical embedded system that measures, processes, and displays the fuel level in a vehicle, as illustrated in Fig. 1.

The system consists of a fuel *tank* equipped with a sensor (left), a digital *controller* (top), and an analog fuel level *meter* (right). The tank sensor has a slider connected to a "floater" that measures the fuel (sensed) level Sl, trailing the (actual) level Al in the tank. The position of the slider maps to an analog voltage Av_{in}. This voltage is converted to a digital representation Dv_{in} by an Analog-to-Digital Converter (ADC) inside the controller. The digital voltage is processed by the *program* in the controller, which consists of *infrastructure software* and *application software*. Periodically, Dv_{in} is transformed by the program into Dv_{out}, which is then converted to an analog voltage Av_{out} by a Digital-to-Analog Converter (DAC). This analog voltage then maps to a (displayed) level Dl, shown by the meter.

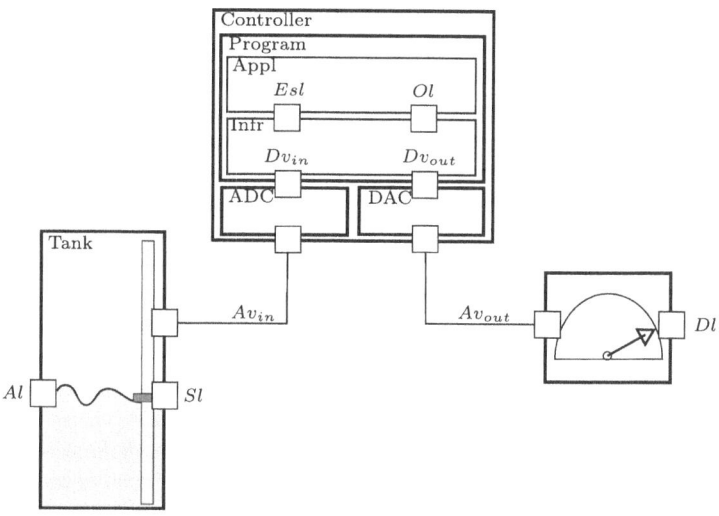

Fig. 1. Fuel level display (FLD) system architecture, diagram by Jonas Westman

In summary, the relevant variables of the fuel level display (FLD) system and their ranges and kinds are as follows:

Al, actual level, range 0–100, percentage.
Sl, sensed level (position of floater), range 0–100, percentage.
Av_{in}, analog voltage (w.r.t. ground), range ≥ 0, volts.
Dv_{in}, digital voltage, non-negative decimal number.
Esl, estimated sensed level, range 0–100, percentage.
Ol, output level, range 0–100, percentage.
Dv_{out}, digital voltage, non-negative decimal number.
Av_{out}, analog voltage out (w.r.t. ground), range ≥ 0, volts.
Dl, displayed level, range 0–100, percentage.

3   Specification Language and Proof System

In this section, we informally present our reformulation of the compositional specification language and proof system of Nyberg et al. [9], which we have formalized in HOL4, while highlighting some changes compared to the original presentation.

3.1   Syntax

The specification language syntax is divided into *components c, specifications S,* and *predicates P*, as shown in Fig. 2. To enable translation to a first-order logic theory (signature), components and specifications may be represented using both constants and variables. Intuitively, constants and their meaning depend on the system and context we are trying to describe, while variables are used when predicates about components and specifications contain quantification.

Component and Specification Syntax. A component is either a constant name $\mathbf{c}$, a variable q, or a composition $c_1 \times c_2$ of two components c_1 and c_2. A specification is either a constant $\mathbb{S}$, a variable V, or a combination of two specifications S_1 and S_2 in the form of a conjunction $S_1 \sqcap S_2$, an assume-guarantee pair (S_1, S_2), also referred to as *contract*, or a parallel composition $S_1 \parallel S_2$. Special specification constants include $\copyright$ for "compatibility" and $T_\parallel$ for "top", whose meaning is elaborated below. Finally, Assertional(S) is meant to capture when the implementation of S is monotonic with respect to component composition.

Predicate Syntax. The predicate syntax expresses assertions about components and specifications. A component c may implement ("satisfy") a specification S, written $c : S$, and a specification S_1 may refine another specification S_2, written $S_1 \sqsubseteq S_2$. In contrast to the initial presentation [9], we distinguish quantification over components from quantification over specifications by writing $\forall_C$ and $\forall_S$, respectively. Moreover, we explicitly allow predicates expressing equality between two components $(=_C)$ or two specifications $(=_S)$.

$\mathbf{c}$: component constant name $\mathbf{S}$: specification constant name
q: component variable V: specification variable

$$
\begin{aligned}
c &::= \mathbf{c} \mid c \times c \mid q & &\text{component} \\
\mathbb{S} &::= \mathbf{S} \mid \copyright \mid T_\parallel & &\text{specification constant} \\
S &::= \mathbb{S} \mid S \sqcap S \mid (S, S) \mid S \parallel S \mid V & &\text{specification} \\
P &::= c : S \mid S \sqsubseteq S \mid \mathsf{Assertional}(S) \mid \forall_C q.\, P & &\text{predicate} \\
&\quad \mid \forall_S V.\, P \mid P \wedge P \mid \neg P \mid c =_C c \mid S =_S S
\end{aligned}
$$

Fig. 2. Component, specification, and predicate syntax

Example 1. Consider the predicate $c_1 \times c_2 : (A \sqcap \copyright, G \sqcap \copyright)$ in the specification language. This predicate expresses that the composition of the components c_1 and c_2 implements an assume-guarantee pair, where $A \sqcap \copyright$ is the assumption and $G \sqcap \copyright$ is the corresponding guarantee. The occurrences of the compatibility specification $\copyright$ ensure, intuitively, that the contract is not vacuously satisfied, i.e., that there exist corresponding system runs that are consistent with the (allowed) behaviors of both components.

3.2   Semantics

We define the semantics of the specification language from Fig. 2 in terms of an abstract set Ω, whose elements are not given an explicit structure, but intuitively represent *runs* (or *executions*) of the system we are considering. For example, the elements of Ω may be (finite or infinite) sequences of system states, where each adjacent pair is connected by a label describing a state transition, or *timed words*, as described in Sect. 4. To give meaning to constants, we use models $\mathcal{M}$ that map *component* constants to subsets of Ω, and map *specification* constants to sets of subsets of Ω. Analogously, we use substitutions σ to assign meaning to variables.

Semantics of Components. Following our definition of models, we define the semantics of components by mapping them to subsets of Ω, as shown in Fig. 3. Intuitively, the set of runs of a component describes its possible runtime behaviors. As hinted at in Example 1, the set may be empty for two composed components when they are incompatible.

$$[\![\mathbf{c}]\!]_{\mathcal{M}}^{\sigma} = \mathcal{M}(\mathbf{c})$$
$$[\![c_1 \times c_2]\!]_{\mathcal{M}}^{\sigma} = [\![c_1]\!]_{\mathcal{M}}^{\sigma} \cap [\![c_2]\!]_{\mathcal{M}}^{\sigma}$$
$$[\![q]\!]_{\mathcal{M}}^{\sigma} = \sigma(q)$$

Fig. 3. Semantics of components

Semantics of Specifications. We define the semantics of specifications by mapping them to subsets of the powerset $\mathcal{P}(\Omega)$ of Ω, as shown in Fig. 4. Intuitively, describing specifications as sets of sets of runs (as opposed to simply sets of runs) means that we can capture relational properties over runs, e.g., security properties such as noninterference. We use the auxiliary definition below for the parallel operator $||$.

Definition 1. *The* double intersection *of the two sets of sets s_1 and s_2, written $s_1 \between s_2$, is the set $\{a \cap b \mid a \in s_1, b \in s_2\}$.*

$$[\![\mathbf{S}]\!]_{\mathcal{M}}^{\sigma} = \mathcal{M}(\mathbf{S})$$
$$[\![\text{\textcircled{C}}]\!]_{\mathcal{M}}^{\sigma} = \{B \in \Omega \mid B \neq \emptyset\}$$
$$[\![T_{||}]\!]_{\mathcal{M}}^{\sigma} = \{\Omega\}$$
$$[\![S_1 \sqcap S_2]\!]_{\mathcal{M}}^{\sigma} = [\![S_1]\!]_{\mathcal{M}}^{\sigma} \cap [\![S_2]\!]_{\mathcal{M}}^{\sigma}$$
$$[\![S_1 || S_2]\!]_{\mathcal{M}}^{\sigma} = [\![S_1]\!]_{\mathcal{M}}^{\sigma} \between [\![S_2]\!]_{\mathcal{M}}^{\sigma}$$
$$[\![(S_1, S_2)]\!]_{\mathcal{M}}^{\sigma} = \{B \mid \forall B' \in [\![S_1]\!]_{\mathcal{M}}^{\sigma}. B \cap B' \in [\![S_2]\!]_{\mathcal{M}}^{\sigma}\}$$
$$[\![V]\!]_{\mathcal{M}}^{\sigma} = \sigma(V)$$

Fig. 4. Semantics of specifications

Semantics of Predicates. We define the semantics of predicates in Fig. 5 by mapping them to propositions in the metalanguage (bool in HOL4). We use the notation $\sigma[x \mapsto s]$ for the substitution σ updated with a mapping from the variable x to the set s. The translation uses the following auxiliary definition to define predicates of the form $\mathsf{Assertional}(S)$.

Definition 2. *A set s is* downward closed *when for every $e \in s$ and e', if $e' \subseteq e$, then $e' \in s$.*

From the basic semantic definitions, we can straightforwardly define derived predicate operators such as disjunction ($\vee$), implication ($\rightarrow$), and existential quantification ($\exists_C$ and $\exists_S$), which is deferred to the supplementary material.

$$[\![c : S]\!]^\sigma_{\mathcal{M}} \Leftrightarrow [\![c]\!]^\sigma_{\mathcal{M}} \in [\![S]\!]^\sigma_{\mathcal{M}}$$

$$[\![S_1 \sqsubseteq S_2]\!]^\sigma_{\mathcal{M}} \Leftrightarrow [\![S_1]\!]^\sigma_{\mathcal{M}} \subseteq [\![S_2]\!]^\sigma_{\mathcal{M}}$$

$$[\![\mathsf{Assertional}\,(S)]\!]^\sigma_{\mathcal{M}} \Leftrightarrow [\![S]\!]^\sigma_{\mathcal{M}} \text{ is downward closed}$$

$$[\![\forall_C\, q.\, P]\!]^\sigma_{\mathcal{M}} \Leftrightarrow \text{for all subsets } s \text{ of } \Omega,\; [\![P]\!]^{\sigma[q \mapsto s]}_{\mathcal{M}}$$

$$[\![\forall_S\, V.\, P]\!]^\sigma_{\mathcal{M}} \Leftrightarrow \text{for all subsets } s \text{ of } \mathcal{P}(\Omega),\; [\![P]\!]^{\sigma[V \mapsto s]}_{\mathcal{M}}$$

$$[\![P_1 \wedge P_2]\!]^\sigma_{\mathcal{M}} \Leftrightarrow [\![P_1]\!]^\sigma_{\mathcal{M}} \text{ and } [\![P_2]\!]^\sigma_{\mathcal{M}}$$

$$[\![\neg P]\!]^\sigma_{\mathcal{M}} \Leftrightarrow \text{not } [\![P]\!]^\sigma_{\mathcal{M}}$$

$$[\![c_1 =_C c_2]\!]^\sigma_{\mathcal{M}} \Leftrightarrow [\![c_1]\!]^\sigma_{\mathcal{M}} = [\![c_2]\!]^\sigma_{\mathcal{M}}$$

$$[\![S_1 =_S S_2]\!]^\sigma_{\mathcal{M}} \Leftrightarrow [\![S_1]\!]^\sigma_{\mathcal{M}} = [\![S_2]\!]^\sigma_{\mathcal{M}}$$

Fig. 5. Semantics of predicates.

Example 2. The predicate $c_1 \times c_2 : (A \sqcap \copyright, G \sqcap \copyright)$ from Example 1 is true precisely when, for every behavior $B \neq \emptyset$ that is allowed by A, the intersection of B and the behaviors of c_1 and c_2 are allowed by nonempty behaviors in G. Or more formally, the predicate is true for $\mathcal{M}$ and σ when for every $B \in [\![A]\!]^\sigma_{\mathcal{M}}$ such that $B \neq \emptyset$, it holds that $[\![c_1]\!]^\sigma_{\mathcal{M}} \cap [\![c_2]\!]^\sigma_{\mathcal{M}} \cap B \in [\![G \sqcap \copyright]\!]^\sigma_{\mathcal{M}}$.

3.3   Translation to First-Order Logic

Our translation of the specification language to first-order logic (FOL) is intuitively based on first interpreting predicates as formulas in two-sorted FOL and then leveraging the standard translation of sorts to obtain unsorted formulas [4]. Our first sort is $\mathcal{C}$, the sort of components, whose domain is $\mathcal{P}(\Omega)$, and the second sort is $\mathcal{S}$, the sort of specifications, whose domain is $\mathcal{P}(\mathcal{P}(\Omega))$. The translation from specification language predicates to unsorted FOL formulas was not explicitly defined in the work of Nyberg et al. [9]; here, we briefly sketch the translation and its correctness, and defer the full details to the supplementary material, where we use Harrison's formalized theory of FOL inside HOL4 [5].

Given a specification language model $\mathcal{M}$ and substitution σ, we construct a corresponding FOL model $L(\mathcal{M})$ and FOL substitution $L(\sigma)$, whose domain is the disjoint union of $\mathcal{P}(\Omega)$ and $\mathcal{P}(\mathcal{P}(\Omega))$. In this construction, we consider component and specification syntax as FOL function symbols, and predicate syntax as FOL predicate symbols, defining functions $c2t$ and $S2t$ that convert components and specifications to FOL terms, and a function $P2f$ (using $c2t$ and $S2t$) that translates predicates to FOL formulas. Quantification in predicates is handled by adding an implication using the additional predicate symbols isc and isS, which express that a term is a component or specification, respectively. Using this translation, Theorem 1 expresses how specification language predicates are interpreted in FOL.

Theorem 1 (Soundness of predicate translation to FOL). *For every model $\mathcal{M}$, substitution σ, and specification language predicate P, $[\![P]\!]_{\mathcal{M}}^{\sigma}$ holds precisely when $L(\mathcal{M}), L(\sigma) \models P2f(P)$, where $\models$ is the first order satisfaction relation.*

The proof is deferred to supplementary material [10], so we give an example that highlights the general idea of the translation.

Example 3. Consider a quantified version of the predicate from Example 1:

$$\forall_{\mathcal{C}}\, q. \forall_{\mathcal{S}}\, V_1. \forall_{\mathcal{S}}\, V_2.\, q : (V_1 \sqcap \text{©}, V_2 \sqcap \text{©})$$

The corresponding unsorted FOL formula obtained by $P2f$ is

$$\forall q.\, isc(q) \rightarrow \forall V_1.\, isS(V_1) \rightarrow \forall V_2.\, isS(V_2) \rightarrow$$
$$impl(q, ag(conj(V_1, compat), conj(V_2, compat)))$$

where $impl$ is a predicate symbol corresponding to the implementation operator ":", and ag, $conj$, and $compat$ are function symbols corresponding to the assume-guarantee, conjunction, and compatibility specification operators, respectively.

3.4 Specification Language Metatheory

In this section, we state some key formalized meta-theoretic results about the specification language, which are mostly reformulations of results from the work of Nyberg et al. [9]. The first three properties are useful for rewriting when performing proofs in the system in Sect. 3.5.

Property 1. Component composition is idempotent, associative, and commutative. That is, for all $\mathcal{M}$ and σ, $[\![c \times c =_{\mathcal{C}} c]\!]_{\mathcal{M}}^{\sigma}$, $[\![c_1 \times (c_2 \times c_3) =_{\mathcal{C}} (c_1 \times c_2) \times c_3]\!]_{\mathcal{M}}^{\sigma}$, and $[\![c_1 \times c_2 =_{\mathcal{C}} c_2 \times c_1]\!]_{\mathcal{M}}^{\sigma}$.

Property 2. Specification conjunction is idempotent, associative, and commutative. That is, for all $\mathcal{M}$ and σ, we have $[\![S \sqcap S =_{\mathcal{S}} S]\!]_{\mathcal{M}}^{\sigma}$, $[\![S_1 \sqcap (S_2 \sqcap S_3) =_{\mathcal{S}} (S_1 \sqcap S_2) \sqcap S_3]\!]_{\mathcal{M}}^{\sigma}$, and $[\![S_1 \sqcap S_2 =_{\mathcal{S}} S_2 \sqcap S_1]\!]_{\mathcal{M}}^{\sigma}$.

Property 3. Parallel composition of specifications is associative and commutative. That is, for all $\mathcal{M}$ and σ, it holds that $[\![S_1 \parallel (S_2 \parallel S_3) =_S (S_1 \parallel S_2) \parallel S_3]\!]^\sigma_\mathcal{M}$ and $[\![S_1 \parallel S_2 =_S S_2 \parallel S_1]\!]^\sigma_\mathcal{M}$. Idempotency does not hold.

The following five properties are the basis (in the form of introduction and elimination rules) for the proof system in Sect. 3.5.

Property 4 (Refinement/REF introduction/elimination). For all $\mathcal{M}$ and σ, if $[\![\forall_C q . q : S_1 \to q : S_2]\!]^\sigma_\mathcal{M}$, then $[\![S_1 \sqsubseteq S_2]\!]^\sigma_\mathcal{M}$ (intro); if $[\![c : S_1]\!]^\sigma_\mathcal{M}$ and $[\![S_1 \sqsubseteq S_2]\!]^\sigma_\mathcal{M}$, then $[\![c : S_2]\!]^\sigma_\mathcal{M}$ (elim).

Property 5 (Assertional/ASSN introduction/elimination). For all $\mathcal{M}$ and σ, if $q_1 \neq q_2$ and $[\![\forall_C q_1 . \forall_C q_2 . q_1 : S \to q_1 \times q_2 : S]\!]^\sigma_\mathcal{M}$, then $[\![\mathsf{Assertional}(S)]\!]^\sigma_\mathcal{M}$ (intro); if $[\![\mathsf{Assertional}(S)]\!]^\sigma_\mathcal{M}$ and $[\![c_1 : S]\!]^\sigma_\mathcal{M}$, then $[\![c_1 \times c_2 : S]\!]^\sigma_\mathcal{M}$ (elim).

Property 6 (Conjunction/CONJ introduction/elimination). For all $\mathcal{M}$ and σ, if $[\![c : S_1]\!]^\sigma_\mathcal{M}$ and $[\![c : S_2]\!]^\sigma_\mathcal{M}$, then $[\![c : S_1 \sqcap S_2]\!]^\sigma_\mathcal{M}$ (intro); if $[\![c : S_1 \sqcap S_2]\!]^\sigma_\mathcal{M}$, then $[\![c : S_1]\!]^\sigma_\mathcal{M}$ and $[\![c : S_2]\!]^\sigma_\mathcal{M}$ (elim).

Property 7 (Parallel/PAR introduction/elimination). For all $\mathcal{M}$ and σ, if $[\![c_1 : S_1]\!]^\sigma_\mathcal{M}$ and $[\![c_2 : S_2]\!]^\sigma_\mathcal{M}$, then $[\![c_1 \times c_2 : S_1 \parallel S_2]\!]^\sigma_\mathcal{M}$ (intro); if variables q_1, q_2 do not occur in c for $q_1 \neq q_2$, and $[\![c : S_1 \parallel S_2]\!]^\sigma_\mathcal{M}$, then $[\![\exists_C q_1 . \exists_C q_2 . q_1 : S_1 \wedge q_2 : S_2 \wedge c =_C q_1 \times q_2]\!]^\sigma_\mathcal{M}$ (elim).

Property 8 (Contract/CONT introduction/elimination). For all $\mathcal{M}$ and σ, if q_1 does not occur in c_2 and $[\![\forall_C q_1 . q_1 : S_1 \to q_1 \times c_2 : S_2]\!]^\sigma_\mathcal{M}$, then $[\![c_2 : (S_1, S_2)]\!]^\sigma_\mathcal{M}$ (intro); if $[\![c_1 : S_1]\!]^\sigma_\mathcal{M}$ and $[\![c_2 : (S_1, S_2)]\!]^\sigma_\mathcal{M}$, then $[\![c_1 \times c_2 : S_2]\!]^\sigma_\mathcal{M}$ (elim).

Finally, the two properties below shed some light on specifications, in particular conjunction, the top specification and assertional contracts.

Property 9 (Conjunction vs. parallel composition). For all $\mathcal{M}$ and σ, $[\![S_1 \sqcap S_2 \sqsubseteq S_1 \parallel S_2]\!]^\sigma_\mathcal{M}$; if $[\![\mathsf{Assertional}(S_1)]\!]^\sigma_\mathcal{M}$ and $[\![\mathsf{Assertional}(S_2)]\!]^\sigma_\mathcal{M}$, then $[\![S_1 \parallel S_2 \sqsubseteq S_1 \sqcap S_2]\!]^\sigma_\mathcal{M}$.

Property 10 (Generality, assertional contracts). For all $\mathcal{M}$ and σ, $[\![S =_S (T_{\parallel}, S)]\!]^\sigma_\mathcal{M}$ holds, and if $[\![\mathsf{Assertional}(S_2)]\!]^\sigma_\mathcal{M}$, then $[\![\mathsf{Assertional}((S_1, S_2))]\!]^\sigma_\mathcal{M}$.

3.5   Proof System

We define a proof system for the specification language as an inductive relation $\Gamma \vdash P$, where Γ is a set of predicates used as premises. The proof system rules are shown in Fig. 6, where we use the notation $vars(c)$ for the set of variables in a component c, and $P[c/q]$ for the capture-avoiding substitution of the component c for the variable q in P (and $P[S/V]$ analogously for specifications).

Theorem 2 (Proof system soundness). *The proof system in Fig. 6 is sound with respect to the predicate semantics in Fig. 4. That is, whenever $\Gamma \vdash P$, then for all $\mathcal{M}$ and σ, if $[\![P']\!]^\sigma_\mathcal{M}$ for all $P' \in \Gamma$, then $[\![P]\!]^\sigma_\mathcal{M}$.*

$$\frac{\Gamma \vdash \forall_c\, q.\, P}{\Gamma \vdash P[c/q]}\ \text{ALL\_EL\_C} \qquad \frac{}{\Gamma, P \vdash P}\ \text{AX} \qquad \frac{\Gamma \vdash \forall_c\, q.\, q : S_1 \to q : S_2}{\Gamma \vdash S_1 \sqsubseteq S_2}\ \text{REF\_IN}$$

$$\frac{\begin{array}{c}\Gamma \vdash c : S_1\\ \Gamma \vdash S_1 \sqsubseteq S_2\end{array}}{\Gamma \vdash c : S_2}\ \text{REF\_EL} \qquad \frac{\begin{array}{c}\Gamma \vdash c_1 : S_1\\ \Gamma \vdash c_2 : S_2\end{array}}{\Gamma \vdash c_1 \times c_2 : S_1 \| S_2}\ \text{PAR\_IN} \qquad \frac{\Gamma \vdash c : S_1 \sqcap S_2}{\Gamma \vdash c : S_1}\ \text{CONJ\_EL1}$$

$$\frac{\begin{array}{c}q_1 \neq q_2\\ \Gamma \vdash \forall_c\, q_1.\, \forall_c\, q_2.\, q_1 : S \to q_1 \times q_2 : S\end{array}}{\Gamma \vdash \text{Assertional}\,(S)}\ \text{ASSN\_IN} \qquad \frac{\Gamma \vdash c : S_1 \sqcap S_2}{\Gamma \vdash c : S_2}\ \text{CONJ\_EL2}$$

$$\frac{\begin{array}{c}\Gamma \vdash \text{Assertional}\,(S)\\ \Gamma \vdash c_1 : S\end{array}}{\Gamma \vdash c_1 \times c_2 : S}\ \text{ASSN\_EL} \qquad \frac{\begin{array}{c}q \notin vars\,(c)\\ \Gamma \vdash \forall_c\, q.\, q : S_1 \to q \times c : S_2\end{array}}{\Gamma \vdash c : (S_1, S_2)}\ \text{CONT\_IN}$$

$$\frac{\begin{array}{c}\Gamma \vdash c : S_1\\ \Gamma \vdash c : S_2\end{array}}{\Gamma \vdash c : S_1 \sqcap S_2}\ \text{CONJ\_IN} \qquad \frac{\begin{array}{c}\Gamma \vdash c : S_1 \sqcap S_3\\ \Gamma \vdash S_1 \sqsubseteq S_2\end{array}}{\Gamma \vdash c : S_2 \sqcap S_3}\ \text{CR} \qquad \frac{\begin{array}{c}\Gamma \vdash c_1 : S_1\\ \Gamma \vdash c_2 : (S_1, S_2)\end{array}}{\Gamma \vdash c_1 \times c_2 : S_2}\ \text{CONT\_EL}$$

$$\frac{\begin{array}{c}q' \notin fcvars\,(P)\\ q' \notin fcvars\,(\Gamma)\\ \Gamma \vdash P[q'/q]\end{array}}{\Gamma \vdash \forall_c\, q.\, P}\ \text{ALL\_IN\_C} \qquad \frac{\begin{array}{c}\Gamma \vdash c =_c c'\\ \Gamma \vdash P[c/q]\end{array}}{\Gamma \vdash P[c'/q]}\ \text{EQ\_EL\_C} \qquad \frac{\begin{array}{c}\Gamma \vdash S =_\mathcal{S} S'\\ \Gamma \vdash P[S/V]\end{array}}{\Gamma \vdash P[S'/V]}\ \text{EQ\_EL\_S}$$

$$\frac{\begin{array}{c}q_1 \neq q_2\\ q_1 \notin vars\,(c)\\ q_2 \notin vars\,(c)\\ \Gamma \vdash c : S_1 \| S_2\end{array}}{\Gamma \vdash \exists_c\, q_1.\, \exists_c\, q_2.\, q_1 : S_1 \wedge q_2 : S_2 \wedge c =_c q_1 \times q_2}\ \text{PAR\_EL}$$

Fig. 6. Proof system rules.

Compared to the original proof system by Nyberg et al. [9], we define and prove sound rules for the sorted quantifiers and other standard FOL operators as part of the supplementary material, and also add equality elimination rules for rewriting, which were previously used implicitly.

Example 4. Let A, A_1, A_2, G, G_1, G_2 be specifications in the set

$$\Gamma_{ex} = \{\text{Assertional}(A), A \sqsubseteq A_1, A \sqsubseteq G_1 \sqcap A_2, G_2 \sqcap G\}$$

and also

$$\Delta_{ex} = \{\forall_c\, q.\, \forall_c\, q'.\, \forall_c\, q''.\, (q \times q') \times q'' =_c q \times (q' \times q''),$$
$$G_1 \sqcap A =_\mathcal{S} A \sqcap G_1,\ G_1 \sqcap (A \sqcap \textcircled{c}) =_\mathcal{S} (A \sqcap G_1) \sqcap \textcircled{c}\}$$

Define the predicate P_{ex} as

$$\forall_c\, q_1.\, q_1 : (A_1 \sqcap \textcircled{c}, G_1 \sqcap \textcircled{c}) \to$$
$$\forall_c\, q_2.\, q_2 : (A_2 \sqcap \textcircled{c}, G_2 \sqcap \textcircled{c}) \to q_1 \times q_2 : (A \sqcap \textcircled{c}, G \sqcap \textcircled{c})$$

As shown formally in HOL4 in the supplementary material, it holds that $\Gamma_{ex} \cup \Delta_{ex} \vdash P_{ex}$; this corrects the previous non-mechanized proof [9]. Since the premises in Δ_{ex} are true for any $\mathcal{M}$ and σ, we can conclude using Theorem 2 that $[\![P_{ex}]\!]^\sigma_{\mathcal{M}}$ whenever $[\![P]\!]^\sigma_{\mathcal{M}}$ for every $P \in \{\mathsf{Assertional}(A), A \sqsubseteq A_1, A \sqsubseteq G_1 \sqcap A_2, G_2 \sqcap G\}$.

Finally, using proof system soundness we can obtain decomposition corollaries such as the following:

Corollary 1. *For all $\mathcal{M}$ and σ, whenever it holds that*

- *$[\![S_1 \| S_2 \| S_3 \sqsubseteq S]\!]^\sigma_{\mathcal{M}}$,*
- *$[\![P]\!]^\sigma_{\mathcal{M}}$ for every $P \in \Gamma$,*
- *$\Gamma \vdash c_1 : S_1$, $\Gamma \vdash c_2 : S_2$, and $\Gamma \vdash c_3 : S_3$,*

then $[\![c_1 \times c_2 \times c_3 : S]\!]^\sigma_{\mathcal{M}}$.

In other words, to establish that the composed system $c_1 \times c_2 \times c_3$ satisfies the specification S, it is sufficient to establish that some "component" specifications S_1, S_2, and S_3 together refine S, and then use the proof system to establish that each component satisfies its corresponding specification.

4   Specifications on Timed Words

The specification language of Sect. 2 is parameterized on an abstract set of system runs Ω, intuitively representing all possible executions of systems in the domain being modeled. As a first step towards reasoning about the FLD system (Fig. 1), we instantiate Ω as an (abstract) set Ω_{TW} of *timed words*, where each element may be viewed as an infinite sequence of samples of system states from a real-valued timeline, as made precise below. We also extend the specification language to include Metric Interval Temporal Logic (MITL) formulas [1,8]. In contrast to proof systems based simply on sets of runs (or traces) for temporal logics, the instantiation allows relational properties over timed words.

4.1   Specification Language Extension

To allow expressing properties at the level of individual timed words, we enrich the specification language with MITL formulas as shown in Fig. 7. Specifically, we add MITL formulas as a form of specification language constant $\mathbb{S}$, using the notation $\widehat{\phi}$ to indicate that the MITL formula ϕ is used as a specification. Formulas may contain closed or open intervals I, bounded by non-negative integers a and b. The MITL syntax is parameterized on "atomic" formulas p that may express properties of individual system states in runs.

Intuitively, a formula $\phi_1 \mathsf{U}_I \phi_2$ states that ϕ_1 is true *until* ϕ_2 becomes true inside the interval I (measured from the current point in time). Conversely, for $\phi_1 \mathsf{S}_I \phi_2$, ϕ_1 is true *since* ϕ_2 was true in the past.

Following this pattern, $\square_I \phi$ and $\boxminus_I \phi$ state that ϕ is always true inside the interval I, forward and backward in time, respectively. $\lozenge_I \phi$ and $\lozenge_I \phi$ state that ϕ is true at some point inside I, again forward and backward in time.

$$I ::= [a,b] \mid (a,b] \mid [a,b) \mid [a,\infty) \mid (a,b) \mid (a,\infty)$$
$$\phi ::= p \mid \neg\phi \mid \phi \wedge \phi \mid \phi \, \mathsf{U}_I \, \phi' \mid \phi \, \mathsf{S}_I \, \phi'$$
$$\mid \Box_I \, \phi \mid \Diamond_I \, \phi \mid \boxminus_I \, \phi \mid \ominus_I \, \phi$$
$$\mathbb{S} ::= \mathsf{S} \mid \copyright \mid T_{\|} \mid \widehat{\phi}$$

Fig. 7. Extended specification syntax for timed words.

4.2 Semantics of MITL Formulas and Extended Specifications

This section describes our semantics of the specification language extension from above, which assigns sets of timed words to MITL formulas. This can be viewed as an adaptation of MITL from previous work [8] to our setting.

Definition 3 (Timed words). *Let $\mathcal{A}$ be a set of* system states, *and let τ be a function from natural numbers $\mathbb{N}$ to tuples $\mathcal{A} \times \mathbb{R}_{\geq 0}$. We call τ a* timed word, *and for $k \in \mathbb{N}$, we write $aval(\tau(k))$ for the first component of the tuple, the system state at k, and $tval(\tau(k))$ for the second component, representing the state's moment in time.*

Our intention is intuitively for a timed word τ to describe a (countable) set of samples of a system's state over real-valued time, and for this intuition to make sense, we must have $tval(\tau(i)) < tval(\tau(j))$ whenever $i < j$.

Before defining the semantics of MITL formulas, we define operations on intervals, following previous work using MITL.

Definition 4 (Positive and negative shift). *The* positive shift operator $\oplus$ *takes a real number t and an interval I and returns sets of non-negative real numbers, as defined below. The* negative shift operator $\ominus$ *is defined analogously.*

$$t \oplus [a,b] = \{\, r \in \mathbb{R}_{\geq 0} \mid t + a \leq r \leq t + b \,\}$$
$$t \oplus (a,b] = \{\, r \in \mathbb{R}_{\geq 0} \mid t + a < r \leq t + b \,\}$$
$$t \oplus [a,b) = \{\, r \in \mathbb{R}_{\geq 0} \mid t + a \leq r < t + b \,\}$$
$$t \oplus [a,\infty] = \{\, r \in \mathbb{R}_{\geq 0} \mid t + a \leq r \,\}$$
$$t \oplus (a,b) = \{\, r \in \mathbb{R}_{\geq 0} \mid t + a < r < t + b \,\}$$
$$t \oplus (a,\infty) = \{\, r \in \mathbb{R}_{\geq 0} \mid t + a < r \,\}$$

Using shifts, we define the semantics of a MITL formula ϕ by mapping the formula and a natural number i (indicating the word position) to a set of timed words in Ω_{TW}, as shown in Fig. 8. The semantics is parameterized on a relation $\models$ which defines which MITL atomic propositions are true in a system state. Finally, we define the semantics of the extended specifications from Fig. 7 following the definitions in Fig. 3 (instantiating Ω to Ω_{TW}) by adding $[\![\widehat{\phi}]\!]_{\mathcal{M}}^{\sigma} = \mathcal{P}([\![\phi]\!]^0)$. Intuitively, this means that MITL formulas in specifications denote the set of sets of timed words that satisfy the formula.

$$[\![\, p \,]\!]^i = \{\, \tau \in \Omega_{TW} \mid aval(\tau(i)) \models p \,\}$$

$$[\![\, \neg \phi \,]\!]^i = \Omega_{TW} \setminus [\![\, \phi \,]\!]^i$$

$$[\![\, \phi \wedge \phi' \,]\!]^i = [\![\, \phi \,]\!]^i \cap [\![\, \phi' \,]\!]^i$$

$$[\![\, \phi\, \mathsf{S}_I\, \phi' \,]\!]^i = \{\, \tau \in \Omega_{TW} \mid \exists\, j.\; tval(\tau(j)) \in tval(\tau(i)) \ominus I \wedge \tau \in [\![\, \phi' \,]\!]^j \,\wedge$$
$$\forall\, k.\; tval(\tau(k)) \in \{\, r \in \mathbb{R} \mid tval(\tau(j)) \leq r \leq tval(\tau(i)) \,\} \rightarrow \tau \in [\![\, \phi \,]\!]^k \,\}$$

$$[\![\, \phi\, \mathsf{U}_I\, \phi' \,]\!]^i = \{\, \tau \in \Omega_{TW} \mid \exists\, j.\; tval(\tau(j)) \in tval(\tau(i)) \oplus I \wedge \tau \in [\![\, \phi' \,]\!]^j \,\wedge$$
$$\forall\, k.\; tval(\tau(k)) \in \{\, r \in \mathbb{R} \mid tval(\tau(i)) \leq r \leq tval(\tau(j)) \,\} \rightarrow \tau \in [\![\, \phi \,]\!]^k \,\}$$

$$[\![\, \boxminus_I\, \phi \,]\!]^i = \{\, \tau \in \Omega_{TW} \mid \forall\, j.\; tval(\tau(j)) \in tval(\tau(i)) \ominus I \rightarrow \tau \in [\![\, \phi \,]\!]^j \,\}$$

$$[\![\, \diamondsuit_I\, \phi \,]\!]^i = \{\, \tau \in \Omega_{TW} \mid \exists\, j.\; tval(\tau(j)) \in tval(\tau(i)) \ominus I \wedge \tau \in [\![\, \phi \,]\!]^j \,\}$$

$$[\![\, \Box_I\, \phi \,]\!]^i = \{\, \tau \in \Omega_{TW} \mid \forall\, j.\; tval(\tau(j)) \in tval(\tau(i)) \oplus I \rightarrow \tau \in [\![\, \phi \,]\!]^j \,\}$$

$$[\![\, \Diamond_I\, \phi \,]\!]^i = \{\, \tau \in \Omega_{TW} \mid \exists\, j.\; tval(\tau(j)) \in tval(\tau(i)) \oplus I \wedge \tau \in [\![\, \phi \,]\!]^j \,\}$$

Fig. 8. MITL semantics

4.3 Proof System Extension

Rather than extending our proof system from Fig. 6 with rules for general reasoning about MITL, we introduce the rule below to allow proofs to use MITL formulas as premises. We expect that MITL formula premises in proofs could be discharged in many ways, such as via semantic reasoning in a theorem prover or using a model checker.

$$\frac{\phi_1 \rightarrow \phi_2}{\Gamma \vdash \widehat{\phi_1} \sqsubseteq \widehat{\phi_2}}\; \text{MITL}$$

5 Fuel Level Display Verification Decomposition

In this section, we describe the application of specifications on timed words from Sect. 4 to the Fuel Level Display (FLD) system outlined in Sect. 2.

5.1 System Runs and Variables

To enable reasoning about the FLD system, we restrict the set of runs Ω_{TW} per Definition 3 to obtain the set Ω_{FLD}, where atomic propositions p_{FLD} express properties of individual FLD system states inside timed words. More specifically, we let p_{FLD} contain all propositions of the form $x = v$, $x < v$ and $x > v$ (and conjunctions of them) in the expected way, where x is an FLD variable and v a value, e.g., between 0 and 100. Moreover, we define an FLD system state as a mapping of all FLD variables to corresponding values.

Definition 5. *The set of possible runs of the FLD system is a set Ω_{FLD} of timed words τ such that:*

- *for all $i, j \in \mathbb{N}$ and all $\tau \in \Omega_{FLD}$, if $i < j$ then $tval(\tau(i)) < tval(\tau(j))$.*
- *for all $i \in \mathbb{N}$ and all $\tau \in \Omega_{FLD}$, $aval(\tau(i))$ maps variables to allowed values.*

5.2   Specification

The top-level FLD specification intuitively says that if the display level Dl shows r (a percentage), then at some recent point in the past, the actual level Al was also approximately r (a percentage). Using a MITL formula we call ϕ_{FLD}, we express this intuition more formally as follows:

$$\square_{[0,\infty)} (Dl = r \rightarrow \diamondsuit_{[0,t]} (Al \approx_m r)).$$

Here, $x \approx_m v$ is a shorthand for the absolute difference of x and v being less or equal to a predetermined margin of error m, e.g., 3% points. Further, t is a positive integer that is similarly a predetermined margin of error, expressed in units of time (e.g., milliseconds) that gives an upper bound on the reaction time of the system. We then define the specification term S_{FLD} as $\hat{\phi}_{FLD}$.

   This means that if we consider the FLD system abstractly as a component c_{FLD}, to *verify* FLD, we need to establish that $c_{FLD} : S_{FLD}$.

5.3   Decomposition

Based on the system structure, the FLD system can be viewed as a composition of three components c_{meter}, c_{ctrl}, and c_{tank}, i.e.,

$$c_{FLD} = c_{meter} \times c_{ctrl} \times c_{tank}.$$

We can then give MITL formulas for each major component with corresponding intervals t_1, t_2, and t_3 (that together must add up to t or less):

$$\phi_{meter} : \square_{[0,\infty)} (Dl = f(v) \rightarrow \diamondsuit_{[0,t_1]} (A_{v_{in}} \approx_m v))$$
$$\phi_{ctrl} : \square_{[0,\infty)} (A_{v_{in}} \approx_m v \rightarrow \diamondsuit_{[0,t_2]} (A_{v_{out}} \approx_m v))$$
$$\phi_{tank} : \square_{[0,\infty)} (A_{v_{out}} \approx_m v \rightarrow \diamondsuit_{[0,t_3]} (Al \approx_m f(v)))$$

where we assume f is a function translating analog voltages to percentage points.

   To enable trustworthy compositional verification of the whole FLD system, we would like to reduce the verification of $c_{FLD} : S_{FLD}$ to verification of its components. Using Corollary 1, we therefore reduce verification of $c_{FLD} : S_{FLD}$ to obtaining proofs of the following:

– $S_{meter} \| S_{ctrl} \| S_{tank} \sqsubseteq S_{FLD}$, which reduces to reasoning on the semantics of MITL formulas—specifically, showing inclusion in the FLD specification timed word set for the intersection of the three component specification timed word sets.
– $c_{meter} : S_{meter}$ where $S_{meter} = \hat{\phi}_{meter}$, whose proof can use the proof system.
– $c_{ctrl} : S_{ctrl}$ where $S_{ctrl} = \hat{\phi}_{ctrl}$, whose proof can use the proof system.
– $c_{tank} : S_{tank}$ where $S_{tank} = \hat{\phi}_{tank}$, whose proof can use the proof system.

6   Formalization in the HOL4 Theorem Prover

The HOL4 formalization of the specification language and its metatheory and instantiation for timed words is around 6000 lines of code and is available as supplementary material to the paper [10]. We used the Ott tool [12] to define the specification language and proof system and exported them to HOL4. We mainly chose HOL4 due to its easily accessible and trustworthy formalization of first-order logic and corresponding model theory, translated from the HOL Light system [5,6]. For convenience, we defined a syntax and semantics of FOL which uses strings for symbols such as atomic propositions rather than natural numbers as used by Harrison. However, we prove this string-based semantics equivalent to the numbers-based semantics that is part of the examples distributed with HOL4, release trindemossen-1.

7   Limitations and Challenges for Applications

The formalized specification language and metatheory (and its instantiation for timed words) aims provide a foundation for sound decomposition of correctness proofs for embedded systems consisting of many components to correctness proofs about individual components. We believe the specification language is sufficiently general to account for many practically relevant notions of "system runs" in addition to timed words, and also capture common idioms for contract based specifications of components in embedded systems, e.g., as expressed by Cimatti and Tonetta [3] or Benveniste et al. [2].

However, while the specification language and proof system can already be practically used in a sound way inside the HOL4 theorem prover, we do not believe this mode of use is feasible for large-scale applications due to the considerable training and expertise required for using interactive theorem provers. Instead, the HOL4 formalization can be viewed as a guide and ground truth for standalone practical tools for specification decomposition and proof search. For example, the HOL4 formalization could be used to provide a certified checker of proof system proofs encoded in some intermediate textual format. Such intermediate textual format proofs could be produced by actual users through some untrusted graphical manual proof tool, or by an untrusted automated proof tool using unverified heuristics. By having text-format proofs certified by a checker directly connected to the formalized theory, trust in such proofs is reduced to trust in HOL4, which uses the so-called *LCF approach* of a small trusted proof kernel [13]. Another option is to directly exploit the connection to FOL by using automated FOL solvers such as Vampire [7] to prove specification predicates, but we expect this approach to be less trustworthy unless the FOL proofs can also be reconstructed in HOL4, which may be difficult.

The specification language and proof system is meant to abstract from details about real-world embedded system components by allowing them to be represented by opaque constants, e.g., c_{meter}. We expect that during practical application, users will *assume* (by adding to the set of premises) that component constants satisfy a certain specification, and possibly later establish this fact using some independent appropriate method such as model checking. Another way to control the complexity is by representing some (real-world) composed components by a single component constant. In this way, usage of the specification language and proof system can scale to large systems with many components. Nevertheless, to preserve trustworthiness, the metatheory of language should ideally be instantiated to the required notion of system run, which requires interactive theorem prover expertise. In addition, applications should validate that the formal definition of system run (given by the set Ω) corresponds to what is meant by run in practice, which might only be feasible to do experimentally.

8   Conclusions

We presented a general theory of compositional specifications which we formalized, along with its metatheory and proof system, in the HOL4 theorem prover. We also instantiated the general system to decompose verification for a fuel level display system.

Previous work on the specification language did not explicitly consider variables and substitutions, or explicitly elaborate the connection to FOL [9]. Most of our corrections to the language and proof system are related to variable management, but we also add predicates and rules for (sorted) equality and demonstrate that they are crucial for practical use, in particular for rewriting specification terms to assume the proper shape.

Following this abstract validation of the language, several tool-related developments become possible that enable practical use of the language and system in a trustworthy way. Most directly, it becomes possible to perform automatic proof search (inside or outside HOL4), e.g., using proof search strategies to automatically perform decomposition of a top-level specification. Thanks to the translation to first-order logic, automated semantic reasoning could also be performed using existing automated solvers.

References

1. Alur, R., Feder, T., Henzinger, T.A.: The benefits of relaxing punctuality. J. ACM **43**(1), 116–146 (1996). https://doi.org/10.1145/227595.227602
2. Benveniste, A., et al.: Contracts for system design. Found. Trends Electron. Des. Autom. **12**(2–3), 124–400 (2018). https://doi.org/10.1561/1000000053
3. Cimatti, A., Tonetta, S.: Contracts-refinement proof system for component-based embedded systems. Sci. Comput. Program. **97**, 333–348 (2015). https://doi.org/10.1016/j.scico.2014.06.011
4. Enderton, H.B.: A Mathematical Introduction to Logic, 2nd edn. Academic Press (2001)
5. Harrison, J.: Formalizing basic first order model theory. In: Grundy, J., Newey, M. (eds.) TPHOLs 1998. LNCS, vol. 1479, pp. 153–170. Springer, Heidelberg (1998). https://doi.org/10.1007/BFb0055135
6. Harrison, J.: Compendium of old work on formalizing metatheory of first-order logic and proof procedures (2019). https://github.com/jrh13/hol-light/commit/013324af7ff715346383fb963d323138

7. Kovács, L., Voronkov, A.: First-order theorem proving and Vampire. In: Computer Aided Verification, pp. 1–35. Springer, Heidelberg (2013)

8. Maler, O., Nickovic, D., Pnueli, A.: From MITL to timed automata. In: Asarin, E., Bouyer, P. (eds.) FORMATS 2006. LNCS, vol. 4202, pp. 274–289. Springer, Heidelberg (2006). https://doi.org/10.1007/11867340_20

9. Nyberg, M., Westman, J., Gurov, D.: Formally proving compositionality in industrial systems with informal specifications. In: Margaria, T., Steffen, B. (eds.) ISoLA 2020. LNCS, vol. 12478, pp. 348–365. Springer, Cham (2020). https://doi.org/10.1007/978-3-030-61467-6_22

10. Palmskog, K.: A theory of specifications, components, contracts, and compositionality formalized in HOL4 (2025). https://doi.org/10.5281/zenodo.15321668. https://zenodo.org/records/15321668

11. Roever, W.-P.: The need for compositional proof systems: a survey. In: de Roever, W.-P., Langmaack, H., Pnueli, A. (eds.) COMPOS 1997. LNCS, vol. 1536, pp. 1–22. Springer, Heidelberg (1998). https://doi.org/10.1007/3-540-49213-5_1

12. Sewell, P., et al.: Ott: effective tool support for the working semanticist. J. Funct. Program. **20**(1), 71–122 (2010). https://doi.org/10.1017/S0956796809990293

13. Slind, K., Norrish, M.: A brief overview of HOL4. In: Mohamed, O.A., Muñoz, C., Tahar, S. (eds.) TPHOLs 2008. LNCS, vol. 5170, pp. 28–32. Springer, Heidelberg (2008). https://doi.org/10.1007/978-3-540-71067-7_6

Verification and Concurrency

Failure Divergence Refinement for Event-B

Sebastian Stock[1], Michael Leuschel[2]([⊠]), and Atif Mashkoor[1]

[1] Institute for Software Systems Engineering, Johannes Kepler University Linz, Linz, Austria
{sebastian.stock,atif.mashkoor}@jku.at
[2] Institut für Informatik, Universität Düsseldorf, Düsseldorf, Germany
leuschel@uni-duesseldorf.de

Abstract. When validating formal models, sizable effort goes into ensuring two types of properties: safety properties (nothing bad happens) and liveness properties (something good occurs eventually. Event-B supports checking safety properties all through the refinement chain. The same is not valid for liveness properties. Liveness properties are commonly validated with additional techniques like animation, and results do not transfer quickly, leading to re-doing the validation process at every refinement stage. This paper promotes early validation by providing failure divergence refinement semantics for Event-B. We show that failure divergence refinement preserves trace properties, which comprise many liveness properties, under certain natural conditions. Consequently, revalidation of those properties becomes unnecessary. Our result benefits data refinements, where no abstract behavior should be removed during refinement. Furthermore, we lay out an algorithm and provide a tool for automatic failure divergence refinement checking, significantly decreasing the modeler's workload. The tool is compared and evaluated in the context of sizable case studies.

Keywords: Refinement · Failure traces · Event-B · Divergence · Liveness

1 Introduction

Formal models are used to ensure the consistency of requirements. While creating a formal model, the modeler is concerned with two fundamental tasks: verification and validation. Verification checks for internal consistency, e.g., the preservation of invariants and the well-definedness of expressions. Validation checks whether the desired behavior is part of the model. For validation, we can distinguish between showing the absence of bad states, i.e., safety properties, and the presence of desirable behavior, i.e., liveness properties [19].

The research presented in this paper has been partially conducted within the IVOIRE project, which is funded by "Deutsche Forschungsgemeinschaft" (DFG) and the Austrian Science Fund (FWF) grant # I 4744-N.

P. Rümmer and Z. Wu (Eds.): TASE 2025, LNCS 15841, pp. 85–103, 2026.
https://doi.org/10.1007/978-3-031-98208-8_6

Event-B's [1] standard proof obligations (PO) are aimed at verifying safety properties even during refinement, as pointed out by Hoang and Abrial [10]. Validation obligations (VO) [17], on the other hand, provide support for validation. However, POs and VOs face challenges for checking liveness properties.

The drawback is significant: Assumptions about the abstract model's behavior do not automatically apply to the refining model. Consequently, the modeler confronts a dilemma: either redo sizable parts of the validation work for each refinement step, which can be time-consuming, or defer complete validation until the model is more concrete, risking project integrity if errors are too late.

We introduce a technique to address these issues by establishing failure divergence refinement for Event-B models. This approach extends standard Event-B refinement, enabling reasoning about preserving traces, a part of liveness properties. Failure divergence refinement ensures that every abstract trace corresponds to a concrete trace, keeping the representation of desirable traces. Once a failure divergence refinement relationship is established, trace-based validation results from a refined Event-B model can be applied to the refining model without requiring re-validation, thereby promoting early validation. It is thus also helpful to check that a data refinement does not accidentally remove behavior. By providing a fully automatic tool within the ProB [14] environment, we make this process fully automatic and avoid the complexity of adding new proof obligations (POs). We can also provide the modeler with counterexamples where no refinement relationship can be established. Thus, we additionally enable targeted debugging of faulty refinement relationships.

The paper proceeds as follows: In Sect. 2, we provide an overview of Event-B, its refinement calculus, and the notion of traces. Section 3 will tailor the known notions of trace refinement, failure traces, divergence, and failure divergence refinement to Event-B. Section 4 then provides the first main contribution by showing that, given a natural condition, traces are preserved if two machines are in failure divergence refinement to each other. Section 5 discusses our second contribution, an implementation to check Event-B machines for failure divergence refinement. Section 6 presents an evaluation of this implementation on existing case studies. We explore the complementarity of our approach with existing techniques in Sect. 7 and conclude with future directions in Sect. 8.

2   Background

Event-B is a formal modeling language based on set theory and first-order logic. Modelers create so-called `machines`, which can be seen as state machines. Typically, such machines are created and maintained with the help of the Rodin [2] platform, which helps discharge and track POs. Listing 1.1 shows a basic example of a vending machine. There are two `variables`[1], `stock` and `coin`, and with

---

[1] In practice, an `invariant` clause defines the variables, and many POs rely on these invariants. However, we assume the presence of invariants implicit as indicated by inlining them in the `variables` clause. For the rest of this paper, we solely focus on the state space induced by variables and invariants, assuming there are no invariant violations, which is enforced via POs.

the help of the events, we can insert coins, vend some beverages, or restock the system if it runs empty.

Refinement. Refinement in Event-B is a way to extend an existing machine rigorously. Refining an abstract machine aims to make it more concrete by gradually adding complexity[2]. One or more concrete events can refine abstract events. Furthermore, the modeler can introduce new events, refining the virtual skip event, which is invisible at the abstract level. The Rodin tool generates additional POs to ensure a correct refinement.

A refinement for Listing 1.1 can be seen in Listing 1.2, where we partitioned the generic stock of beverages into specific stocks for soda and water. As previously discussed, concrete events can refine abstract events in various ways. insert_coin is refined by just one event. The vend event is refined by vend_soda and vend_water. select_drink refines the invisible abstract event skip.

Formalization. A B machine induces a state space, as formalized in Definition 1, similar to Zhu et al. [30].

Definition 1. *(State Space of a machine) The state space of an Event-B machine M is a quadruple (S, E, δ, I) where S is the set of all possible states, $I \subseteq S$ the initial states, E is the set of events, and $\delta \in E \rightarrow (S \leftrightarrow S)$ describes the transitions. To denote an individual transition, we write $s \xrightarrow{e}_M s'$ if $(s \mapsto s') \in \delta(e)$.*

A state itself consists of a mapping from variables and constants to values. Note that later some propositions will require finite state spaces.[3]

Example. *For our machine in Listing 1.1, the state space is the quadruple (S, E, δ, I) with $S = \{\{soda = 3, coin = 0\}, \{soda = 3, coin = 1\}, ...\}$, $I = \{\{soda = 3, coin = 0\}\}$, $E = \{insert\_coin, vend, restock\}$, and $\delta = \{insert\_coin \mapsto \{(\{soda = 3, c = 0\}, \{soda = 3, coin = 1\}), ...\}, ...\}$. We have, e.g., $\{soda = 3, coin = 0\} \xrightarrow{insert\_coin}_M \{soda = 3, coin = 1\}$.*

Definition 2. *(Event-B refinement) Let $(S_A, E_A, \delta_A, I_A{}^4)$ and $(S_C, E_C, \delta_C, I_C)$ be the state space of two machines A and C. We write $A \sqsubseteq_{ref} C$ if C is an Event-B refinement [1] of A. During refinement, new events can be introduced in C, which refines the invisible skip. We denote the set of these events as $\mathcal{N}_C$. If no new events are introduced, $\mathcal{N}_C = \varnothing$. Event-B also allows renaming events. We capture this renaming in the mapping $\psi_{C,A} \in E_C \setminus \mathcal{N}_C \twoheadrightarrow E_A$ from concrete to abstract events.[5] This means that every event, minus the events introduced via skip, is assigned to an abstract event.*

---

[2] A detailed overview is given by Hoang [9].
[3] Propositions 1 and 2 will rely on this.
[4] For the following we assume $|I_A| = 1$.
[5] $\twoheadrightarrow$ is the total surjection.

```
1   machine m0
2   variables
3     stock ∈ N ∧ coin ∈ N
4
5   events
6     INITIALISATION ≜ then
7         stock :=  3
8         coin := 0
9     end
10
11    insert_coin ≜ when
12    stock > 0 ∧ coin + 1 ≤ stock
13    then
14        coin := coin + 1
15    end
16
17    vend ≜ when
18      coin > 0 ∧ stock > 0
19    then
20        stock :=  stock - 1
21        coin := coin - 1
22    end
23
24    restock ≜ when
25      stock = 0
26    then
27        stock := 3
28    end
29  end
```

Listing 1.1. Vending machine

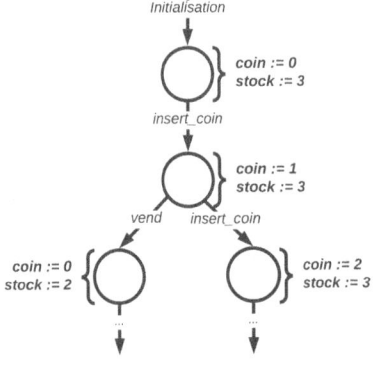

Fig. 1. Visualization of the state space of Listing 1.1

```
1   machine m1 refines m0
2   variables
3   soda ∈ N ∧ water ∈ N ∧
4   soda + water = stock ∧
5   selectedDrink ∈ {soda, water, none}
6
7   events
8     INITIALISATION   then
9         soda := 2 || water := 1 ||
10        coin := 0 || selectedDrink := none
11    end
12
13    insert_coin refines insert_coin ≜ when
14      soda + water > 0 ∧
15      coin + 1 ≤ soda + water ∧
16      selectedDrink = none
17    then
18        coin := coin + 1
19    end
20
21    select_drink ≜ any drink
22    where
23      selectedDrink = none ∧ coin > 0 ∧
24      drink ∈ {soda, water} ∧
25      (drink = soda ⇒ soda > 0) ∧
26      (drink = water ⇒ water > 0)
27    then
28        selectedDrink := drink
29    end
30
31    vend_soda refines vend ≜ when
32      selectedDrink = soda
33    then
34        soda :=  soda - 1 ||
35        selectedDrink := none ||
36        coin := coin - 1
37    end
38
39    vend_water refines vend ≜ when
40      selectedDrink = water
41    then
42        water :=  water - 1 ||
43        selectedDrink := none ||
44        coin := coin - 1
45    end
46
47    restock refines restock ≜ when
48      soda + water = 0
49    then
50        soda :=  2 ||
51        water :=  1
52    end
```

Listing 1.2. Vending machine refining Listing 1.1

Note that the definition of $\psi_{C,A}$ as a function above has subtle consequences. If an abstract event has parameters that do not exist at the concrete level, Event-B stipulates the definition of a witness predicate (see Sect. 5.1.7 of [1]). To make $\psi_{C,A}$ unambiguous (i.e., a function), we require that the witness predicate is *deterministic*, i.e., it has a single solution for every concrete event. This requirement will play an important role later in our main Proposition 2. In practice, most witnesses are deterministic, so our requirement is reasonable.

We can use the relational image operator [ ] to apply $\psi_{C,A}$ to sets, i.e., $\psi_{C,A}[E] = \{e_c \in E \mid \psi_{C,A}(e_c)\}$.

Traces in Event-B. Another view on Event-B machines is from the perspective of traces, which consist of states and events. Definition 3 is aligned with the definition of Zhu et al. [30].

Definition 3. *(Finite trace) Let the state space of a machine M be $(S_M, E_M, \delta_M, I_M)$. We define the transitive closure of $s \xrightarrow{e} s'$ as follows: $s_0 \xrightarrow{e_0, e_1, \ldots, e_n} s_n$ if $s_0 \xrightarrow{e_0} s_1 \xrightarrow{e_1} .. \xrightarrow{e_n} s_n$. Let E_M^* be the set of finite sequences over E_M. We denote the set of all traces of M as follows: $traces(M) = \{\sigma \in E_M^* \mid s_0 \in I_M \wedge s_n \in S_M\}$. Finally, we denote the last state reached by a trace σ by $last(\sigma)$.*

Example. *Consider Fig. 1, where we see a visualization of the beginning of the state space of Listing 1.1. This part of the state space has the following traces: $\langle \rangle$, $\langle insert\_coin \rangle$, $\langle insert\_coin, insert\_coin \rangle$, $\langle insert\_coin, vend \rangle$, etc. Note that we do not explicitly write the* **INITIALISATION** *event, rather assuming it has been performed implicitly at the beginning of a trace to reach the initial state.*

3   Traces and Failure Traces in Event-B

3.1   Trace Refinement

Trace refinement is usually defined via the subset relation over the set of traces [19] ($A \sqsubseteq_t C$ iff $traces(C) \subseteq traces(A)$). However, due to the renaming $\psi_{C,A}$ and new events $\mathcal{N}_C$, we cannot apply this definition as is. In the following Definition 4, we take these particularities into account to be able to compare the traces of A and C:

Definition 4. *(Concealment & renaming in traces) Let two machines, A and C, be in a refinement relationship $A \sqsubseteq_t C$. For $\sigma = e_1, \ldots, e_n \in traces(C)$ we define:*

1. *$\tau_{C,A}(\sigma) = \langle \rangle$ if $n = 0$*
2. *$\tau_{C,A}(\sigma) = \tau_{C,A}(e_2, \ldots, e_n)$ if $e_1 \in \mathcal{N}_C$*
3. *$\tau_{C,A}(\sigma) = \psi_{C,A}(e_1) \frown \tau_{C,A}(e_2, \ldots, e_n)$ otherwise.*

The $\tau_{C,A}$ operator removes the skip events from the trace and renames the remaining events to their counterparts in A.

τ is also applicable to a set of traces as follows $\tau_{C,A}(T) = \{t \in T \mid \tau_{C,A}(t)\}$.

With the help of τ we can give a notion of trace refinement based on our definition of trace Definition 3.

Definition 5. *(Trace refinement)* *A is a trace refinement of C, denoted by A* $\sqsubseteq_t C$, *iff* $\tau_{C,A}(traces(C)) \subseteq traces(A)$.

Example. *Consider Fig. 2, which shows a part of the state space of Listing 1.2. The traces of this machine would be the following:* $\langle\rangle, \langle insert\_coin\rangle, \langle insert\_coin, select\_drink\rangle$, *etc. Concealing and renaming yields:* $\tau_{m1,m0}(\langle insert\_coin, select\_drink\rangle) = \langle insert\_coin\rangle$.

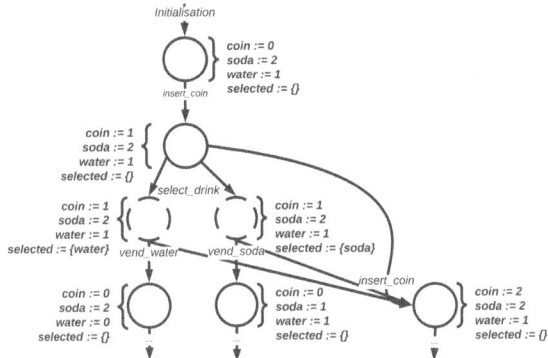

Fig. 2. Visualization of the state space of Listing 1.2

Finally, we know from Derrick and Boiten [5] that trace refinement is strong enough to mimic forward-backward simulation (it is more strict than pure forward simulation and, consequently, stricter than standard Event-B POs). This insight has multiple consequences for us: 1) A refinement relationship built on top of trace refinement will be, at minimum, as strong as forward-backward simulation, and 2) all Event-B POs will be preserved. Every concrete trace thus has an abstract equivalent in trace refinement. However, in our general aim to preserve liveness properties, it also becomes clear that we need a more powerful refinement notion to show that every abstract trace has a concrete equivalent.

3.2   Failure Traces in Event-B

Failure traces [5,13] extend regular traces by recording additional information about their last state, namely which events are refused at the end.

Definition 6. *(Enabled & refused events)* *Let* $s \in S_M$ *be a state of M. The enabled events of s are defined by* $enabled(s) = \{e \mid (s \mapsto s') \in \delta_M(e)\}$. *The refused events are the complement:* $refusal(s) = E_M \setminus enabled(s)$.

Now, we additionally need a notion of stable states to only compare the proper states in a refinement check, i.e., those concrete states that do not allow the execution of events introduced by `skip`

Definition 7. *(Stable states)* *Let* $A \sqsubseteq_t C$. *We define* $stable_C = \{s \in S_C \mid \nexists e \cdot e \in \mathcal{N}_C \wedge (s \mapsto s') \in \delta_C(e)\}$, *where* S_C *are the states of* C. *This means a state has no outgoing transitions introduced by refining* `skip`. *A state* s *is stable iff* $s \in stable_C$. *If* C *is not a refining machine, then all states of* C *would be stable.*

We use the notion of traces, refused events, and stable states to create the notion of failure trace in Definition 8.

Definition 8. *(Failure trace)* *The set of failure traces for a machine* M *are defined as* $failure(M) = \{(\sigma, X) \mid \sigma \in traces(M) \wedge last(\sigma) \in stable_M \wedge X = refusal(last(\sigma))\}$

Example. *Again, we consider Fig. 1 and Listing 1.1. From the visible state space, we have the following failure traces:* $(\langle\rangle, \{vend, restock\}), (\langle insert\_coin \rangle, \{restock\})$, *etc.*

3.3 Failure Divergence Refinement

Definition 8 is stronger than Definition 3 – we store trace plus additional information. The next goal is to define refinement for failure traces. For this, we must translate failure sets while accounting for Event-B particularities. We introduce a particular translation operator in Definition 9. Note that this function not only takes a set of events and renames them but also ensures that all refining events are present for each refined event. This is necessary so as not to wrongly discard intuitively correct failure refinements. We give an example for this case with the notion of Definition 10.

Definition 9. *Let* X *be a refusal set within the context of two machines* $A \sqsubseteq_t C$. *The set of abstract refusals is defined as:* $AbsRefusal(X) = \{y \in \psi_{C,A}[X] \mid \psi_{C,A}^{-1}[y] \subseteq X\}$. *Furthermore, as the last state is stable* $X \cap \mathcal{N}_C = \varnothing$.

With this, we define the failure trace refinement in Definition 10.

Definition 10. *(Failure trace refinement)* *We define failure trace refinement as* $\forall(\sigma, X) \cdot (\sigma, X) \in failure(C) \Rightarrow (\tau_{C,A}(\sigma), AbsRefusal(X)) \in failure(A)$ *and write* $A \sqsubseteq_f C$.

Example. *Consider Fig. 2, which shows a part of the state space of Listing 1.2. The failure traces of this machine would be the following* $(\langle\rangle, \{vend\_water, vend\_soda, restock\})$ *with AbsRefusal being* $\{vend, restock\}$, $(\langle insert\_coin, select\_drink \rangle, \{restock, vend\_soda\})$ *with AbsRefusal* $\{restock\}$. *Applying* τ *to the trace part yields the traces from Sect. 3.2.* $(\langle insert\_coin \rangle, \{vend, restock\})$ *is not a valid failure trace, as the last state is unstable. Elaborating on the necessity of stable states for failure traces, we consider the following example: In Fig. 2, a trace* $\pi = \langle insert\_coin \rangle$ *would have the* $refusal(last(\pi)) = \{vend\_water, vend\_soda, restock\}$. *However,* $refusal(last(\tau(\pi))) = \{restock\}$ *misses the vend transition. Thus by only using this weak definition, Listing 1.2 would not refine Listing 1.1.*

Motivating Definition 7 consider $\sigma = \langle insert\_coin \rangle$. *If we do not force stable states, Listing 1.2 would not refine Listing 1.1, as the failure sets are different.*

For Definition 9, consider $\sigma = \langle insert\_coin, select\_drink \rangle$ *with* $refusal(last(\sigma)) = \{\text{restock}, \text{vend\_water}\}$. *Consequently,* $\tau(\sigma) = \langle insert\_coin \rangle$ *with* $refusal(last(\tau(\sigma))) = \{\text{restock}\}$. *Both traces would refine each other but not failure refine each other, even though they represent the same (abstract) behavior.*

Event-B can introduce divergence during refinement by presenting events that refine skip. Usually, divergence is prevented by marking events with the keywords `convergent` or `anticipated`, which induce POs that must be discharged to establish that these events do not introduce divergence. We check for this property without relying on these keywords, as shown in Definition 11.

Definition 11. *(Divergence and failure divergences refinement) Let* $A \sqsubseteq_t C$ *and* C *have a finite state space. We define the set of divergent states of* C *by* $divergence_C = \{s \mid \exists \sigma \in \mathcal{N}_C^{*6} \;.\; s \overset{\sigma}{\Longrightarrow} s\}$. *I.e., such states from which we find a sequence of skip refining events such that they form a loop. A trace refinement free of divergence is a trace divergence refinement* $A \sqsubseteq_{td} C$ *iff* $A \sqsubseteq_t C \wedge divergence_C = \varnothing$. *A failure trace refinement free of divergence is a failure divergence refinement* $A \sqsubseteq_{fd} C$ *iff* $A \sqsubseteq_f C \wedge divergence_C = \varnothing$.

It could happen that a refining machine only consists of unstable states, and thus, we could not make statements about failure (divergence) refinement. To rule out this phenomenon, we introduce a guarantee for stable states in machines.

Proposition 1 (Divergence freeness guarantees the existence of stable states). *Let* $A \sqsubseteq_{td} C$ *and the state spaces be finite. Further, let* $\sigma \in traces(A)$ *and let* $\Pi = \{\pi \in traces(C) \mid \tau_{C,A}(\pi) = \sigma\}$. *If* $\Pi \neq \varnothing$ *then* $\exists \pi \cdot \pi \in \Pi$ *such that* $last(\pi) \in stable_C$.

With these tools, we can now show that, under some conditions, abstract traces have a concrete counterpart under failure divergence refinement.

4   Trace Equivalence

As a failure trace also records disabled events, failure refinement cannot simply remove choices that are present in the abstract machine. Another observation is that failure divergence refinement in Event-B works differently from the CSP version. In CSP, failure divergence refinement does not imply trace equivalence:

Example. *Let* $C = a \rightarrow STOP$ *and* $A = a \rightarrow STOP \sqcap b \rightarrow STOP$ *be two CSP processes.*[7] *We have the following failure traces*

---

[6] Similar to E_M^* back in Definition 3.

[7] Observe that $\sqcap$ is the internal choice operator that induces an invisible skip (aka τ) action in CSP.

1. $failures(C) = \{(\langle\rangle, \{b\}), (\langle a\rangle, \{a, b\})\}$,
2. $failures(A) = \{(\langle\rangle, \{b\}), (\langle a\rangle, \{a, b\})\} \cup \{(\langle\rangle, \{a\}), (\langle b\rangle, \{a, b\})\}$.

Hence C failure refines A, i.e., $A \sqsubseteq_{fd} C$, but the trace $\langle b\rangle \in traces(A)$ has no counterpart in C. So, in this case, failure refinement does not ensure the preservation of traces. This counter-example does not carry over to our Event-B setting. Indeed, a major difference is that in our setting, skip events can only occur in the refined model, not in the abstract one.

Unfortunately, the above example using the internal choice operator in the abstraction is not the only problem, as the following example shows.

Example. *Let $C = a \to STOP$ and $A = a \to b \to STOP \square a \to STOP$ be two CSP processes (where $\square$ is the external choice operator).*

1. $failures(C) = \{(\langle\rangle, \{b\}), (\langle a\rangle, \{a, b\})\}$,
2. $failures(A) = \{(\langle\rangle, \{b\}), (\langle a\rangle, \{a, b\})\} \cup \{(\langle a\rangle, \{a\}), (\langle a, b\rangle, \{a, b\})\}$.

Again C failure refines A, i.e., $A \sqsubseteq_{fd} C$, but the trace $\langle a, b\rangle \in traces(A)$ has no counterpart in C. This time, though, the example does translate to Event-B. Listing 1.3 shows the Event-B encoding of A, and Listing 1.4 shows C. The fundamental problem is that A is not a deterministic event (see Definition 12 below). Indeed, in our proof later, we need to map a failure trace in C to a single failure trace in A. Our solution is to disallow machines like the one in Listing 1.3. Luckily, every Event-B machine can be rewritten into an event-deterministic one, possibly by adding parameters. This is done in Listing 1.5. Note that if the concrete machine does not also have this parameter, Event-B requires the addition of a witness predicate. Here, we also require that the witness predicate produces a single solution.[8]

The above insight leads to the following definition:

Definition 12. *An Event-B machine M is **event deterministic** if $\forall \sigma, X_1, X_2$ we have $\{(\sigma, X_1), (\sigma, X_2)\} \subseteq failure(M) \Rightarrow X_1 = X_2$.*

This is guaranteed in Event-B if we only use deterministic assignments. Note that one can always rewrite an Event-B model into such a form. E.g., for $x :: E$ we add a parameter x' with $x' \in E$ in the guard and use the assignment $x := x'$. This was done in Listing 1.5.

As discussed in Definition 2 above, we require $\psi_{C,A}$ to consider the witness predicates, and we require the witness predicates to be deterministic. Together with Definition 12, we can thus map any concrete trace to a single abstract trace with a single failure set, which allows us to prove our main result in Proposition 2.

To extend the power of our primary contribution, we extend our definition of traces one last time to infinite traces in Definition 13.

---

[8] This is usually the practice case; witness predicates are always equalities.

```
1  machine A
2  variables
3    pc ∈ 0..3
4  events
5    INITIALISATION then
6      pc := 0
7    end
8
9  a ≙ when
10     pc=0
11   then
12     pc :: {1,2}
13   end
14
15  b ≙ when
16     pc=2
17   then
18     pc := 3
19   end
```

Listing 1.3. Non-deterministic abstract machine

```
1  machine C refines A
2  variables
3    pc ∈ 0..3
4  events
5    INITIALISATION then
6      pc := 0
7    end
8
9  a ≙ when
10     pc=0
11   then
12     pc := 1
13   end
14
15  b ≙ when
16     pc=2
17   then
18     pc := 3
19   end
```

Listing 1.4. Concrete refinement

```
1  machine ADet
2  variables
3    pc ∈ 0..3
4  events
5    INITIALISATION then
6      pc := 0
7    end
8
9  a ≙ any npc where
10     pc=0  ∧
11     npc ∈ {1,2}
12   then
13     pc := npc
14   end
15
16  b ≙ when
17     pc=2
18   then
19     pc := 3
20   end
```

Listing 1.5. An event-deterministic machine

Definition 13. *(Infinite traces) Let the state space of a machine M be* $(S_M, E_M, \delta_M, I_M)$. *Let* E_M^{Δ} *the set of infinite sequences, i.e.,* $s_0 \overset{e_0,e_1,\cdots}{\Longrightarrow}$. *We denote the infinite traces starting from an initial state as* $traces(M)_{\Delta}$.

With the notion of failure divergence refinement, traces, and infinite traces, we can now reason whether a refinement preserves finite and infinite traces.

Proposition 2 (Failure divergence refinement implies trace equivalence). *Let A and C be two machines with finite state spaces and with* $A \sqsubseteq_{fd} C$. *Let A be event deterministic. Then* $traces(A) \subseteq \tau_{C,A}(traces(C))$, *and* $traces(A)_{\Delta} \subseteq \tau_{C,A}(traces(C)_{\Delta})$[9]. *I.e., failure divergence refinement guarantees that every abstract trace has a concrete equivalent.*

This proposition implies that all arguments and reasoning for trace properties in the abstract machine carry over to later refinements[10]. This simplifies the validation process, allowing us to validate trace properties in their abstract forms, facilitating early validation, and reducing development overhead.

5 Failure Divergence Checking in Practice

We build on existing tools to realize failure divergence refinement for Event-B. ProB [14] is an animator and model checker for formal modeling languages like Event-B. We will use ProB as a base for our algorithm as it can understand

---

[9] $\tau_{C,A}$ is the renaming and concealment operator from Definition 4.

[10] The backward direction of the proven inclusion is enforced by trace refinement/forward-backward simulation.

and interact with Event-B models, helping us focus more on implementing the approach than handling the models.

Before we implemented our approach, ProB could already deal with trace refinement, as shown in the previously cited contribution by Leuschel and Butler [15]. For this, the user must first model-check the abstract model, export the state space, and import the abstract state space and concrete machine into the algorithm for trace refinement check. Our work will use this existing infrastructure as it is reliable and robust enough to handle the extension to Event-B failure divergence refinement.

5.1 Algorithm

Setup. The failure divergence algorithm is shown in Algorithm 1. The algorithm's input is the $\psi_{C,A}$, and $\mathcal{N}_C$, which we must synthesize beforehand. Furthermore, we expect both machines' state space to be available to access them with the $trans(s_1, e, s_2)$ predicate. This predicate works via unification[11], e.g., we provide it with two states, and it will infer the possible events that satisfy the predicate.

For the output, we expect the evaluation's result to be either true or false. If both machines are not valid failure divergence refinements, we expect an abstract and concrete trace that serves as a counterexample.

Computation. The core idea is to uncover all reachable pairs of abstract and concrete states (lines 7 and 16) while checking for every pair of states that the failures are the same (lines 5 ndd 27). The function in line 27 also checks for divergence[12]. Algorithm 8 checks whether the current state is unstable, and if this is the case, we skip the computation of the abstract trace. The algorithm recursively iterates over all reachable transitions (lines 10 and 19) and stores the encountered pairs (line 4), thus achieving complete coverage. Should the algorithm find that a pair of states is not a failure refinement of each other, it will terminate with a `false`. If the algorithm can visit all reachable states in both machines without finding any nonmatching pairs, the algorithm terminates with a `true`.

Limitations. The algorithm works on finite state spaces, and as the set of seen states increases in every recursion, eventually, the algorithm terminates. Practically, the modeler is limited by available memory as all possible computable transitions are used.

The problem of failure/divergence is generally seen as a PSPACE-hard problem (see Appendix C.1 in Roscoe [19]). Currently supported are only deterministic choices in the initial state, i.e., cases where $|I_a| = 1$ and $|I_c| = 1$. Furthermore, the algorithm expects both machines to have some refinement relationship as it has to calculate the $\psi_{C,A}$ function and the $\mathcal{N}_C$ set.

---

[11] Like the Prolog programming language.

[12] We abstracted the simpler divergence check for the sake of readability and space usage. In practice, the divergence check is part of the algorithm.

Algorithm 1: Failure divergence refinement checking

Input: The state space of the abstract machine accessible via $trans_a(s_1, e, s_2)$ and the state space of the concrete machine via $trans_c(s_1, e, s_2)$, furthermore the relation $\psi_{C,A}$ and a set of $\mathcal{N}_C$ events. Finally, we have a set of seen states S_s that is empty at the start

1 isFailureRefinement := failLoop($s_c, s_a, \langle\rangle, \langle\rangle$)
2 **function** failLoop(s_c, s_a, t_c, t_a)
3   **if** $(s_c, s_a) \notin S_s$ **then**
4        $S_s := S_s \cup \{(s_c, s_a)\}$
5   **if** $failureRefines(s_c, s_a)$ **then**
6   nexCon := $\{(e_c, s_c') \mid trans_a(s_c, e_c, s_c')\}$
7   **forall the** $(e_c, s_c') \in nexCon$ **do**
8   **if** $e_c \in \mathcal{N}_C$ **then**
9                 $t_c^{tp} := t_c + (e_c, s_c')$
10   res := failLoop(s_c', s_a, t_c^{tp}, t_a)
11   **if** $(false, t_c', t_a') = res$ **then**
12   **return** $(false, t_c', t_a')$

13   **else**
14   nexAbs := $\{(e_a, s_a') \mid trans_a(s_a, e_a, s_a')\}$
15   res := $\varnothing$
16   **forall the** $(e_a, s_a') \in nexAbs \wedge e_a = \psi_{C,A}(e_c)$ **do**
17                   $t_c^{tp} := t_c + (e_c, s_c')$
18                   $t_a^{tp} := t_a + (e_a, s_a')$
19   res := res $\cup$ failLoop($s_c', s_a', t_c^{tp}, t_a^{tp}$)
20   **if** $\forall(b, t_c', t_a') \cdot (b, t_c', t_a') \in res \wedge b = false$ **then**
21   **return** $any\ (false, t_c', t_a') \in res$

22   **return** $(true, t_c, t_a)$
23   **else**
24   **return** $(false, t_c, t_a)$

25   **else**
26   **return** $(true, t_c, t_a)$

27 **function** failureRefines(s_c, s_a)
28   **if** $\nexists e \cdot e \in \mathcal{N}_C \wedge trans_c(s_c, e, \_s_c')$ **then**
29   absFailure := $\{e_a \mid trans_a(s_a, e_a, \_s_a')\}$
30   conFailure := $\{e_c \mid trans_c(s_c, e_c, \_s_c')\}$
31   **return** $absFailure = AbsRefusals(conFailure)$
32   **else**
33   **return** $s_c \in divergence_C$

Another limitation is that we have set δ as a total function back in Definition 1. This means we do not allow multiple transitions between two states. Finally, we currently restrict ourselves to refinement that uses the *extends* keyword for our implementation. For full support for the *refines* keyword, we lack support for reordering, redefinition, renaming, or removing parameters. However, it is a technical problem to draw this information out of the AST of the Event-B machine and preprocess it to make it available.

6 Evaluation

For evaluating our algorithm, we have two aims[13]. First, we want to show that the algorithm works and can provide an advantage by establishing a failure divergence refinement relationship or pointing out mistakes. Second, we want to do this within a reasonable time compared to other similar operating validation methods. We consider methods similar if they also explicitly traverse the entire state space. This paper used basic model checking, i.e., checking for invariant violations and trace refinement checking, a contribution of Leuschel and Butler [15]. We extended the provided algorithm to handle Event-B particularities as discussed in Sect. 2. Model checking and trace refinement are provided within ProB[14].

As a model to evaluate, we choose our example model from Listings 1.1 and 1.2 a version of the interlocking Event-B model introduced by Stock et al. [24] and a version of the hemodialysis machine (HD machine) Event-B model introduced by Hoang et al. [12].

6.1 Case Studies

Interlocking. Interlocking describes a system managing trains and train tracks in a rail yard. Routes through the rail yard are divided into blocks they share with other routes. The peculiarity is that trains should not collide and should be on a valid track configuration. The model here was initially introduced by Abrial [1], and the authors in Stock et al. [24] extend it to demonstrate the so-called abstraction approach.

Hemodialysis Machine. Hemodialysis purifies a patient's blood if the patient's body cannot do it by itself, e.g., in case of kidney failure. For the hemodialysis process, a machine controls parameters such as heart rate and blood pressure and adjusts the treatment accordingly. The case study was proposed by Mashkoor [16], and we use the implementation of Hoang et al. [12].

6.2 Experiment Setup

We ran all models through the ProB [14] model checker. We used an Intel Core i7-10700 2.90GHz × 8 CPU with 16GB RAM running Linux Mint for the benchmarks. Each measurement was run ten times, and the mean was taken. We restricted the search space to make it finite for our evaluation of the HD machine. The model-checking results are shown in Table 1. We measured the time spent and the number of states and transitions to give insight into the model's size.

---

[13] A replication package can be found at: https://zenodo.org/doi/10.5281/zenodo. 10377564. It contains a stand-alone version of the tool and the files used in the case study.

[14] FDR3, as the prominent refinement checker for CSP does not support Event-B; therefore, we cannot perform a direct comparison.

Seven machines were investigated, the two vending machines from the beginning (vend_abst & vend_conc) with abstract and concrete machines, respectively. There are three versions of the interlocking (inter_abst & inter_conc & inter_fixed), with inter_fixed being a corrected version of inter_abst. We found a bug during failure divergence refinement checking and provided a fix. Finally, we selected sizable models from the HD machines (hd_abst & hd_conc), again with the first being the abstract and the second being the refinement.

Table 1. Baseline performance of model checking on the models

Project	Model checking	Number of States	Number of Transitions
vend_abst	26 ms	10	14
vend_conc	38 ms	29	47
inter_abst	41 ms	81	325
inter_fixed	33 ms	56	186
inter_conc	3666 ms	3508	11714
hd_abst	484 ms	484	3282
hd_conc	11218 ms	16968	94738

6.3   Results

Vending Machine. For the vending machine model, we could successfully establish failure divergence refinement. The runtime is short, as shown in Table 2. The individual runs had high fluctuations, and one reason for this may be the small size and internal optimization strategies. Therefore, we could not see a clear trend in which technique is faster or slower.

Interlocking. Initially, the interlocking model failed the failure divergence refinement check (see Table 2). Using counterexamples provided by our tool, we identified a divergence issue caused by an event refining `skip` while being enabled infinitely without altering the state. As we saw no good reason for this behavior, we prohibited it by strengthening the event guards.

Additionally, we observed that the refinement was stricter concerning allowed route combinations, concluding that block abstraction was too liberal. To rectify this, we reintroduced a restriction on route exclusivity without relying on blocks, successfully validating our fixed model.

The latter fix shrinks the state space significantly, as several route combinations are now invalid. This can be seen in Table 2. Compared to Table 1 the refinement checking is faster than model checking for the fixed version.

Hemodialysis Machine. Learning from the interlocking, we did a brief pre-check for divergence for the HD machine. One event to set the patient's values introduced divergence by being enabled constantly. We altered the model so that the event could only be used once. With this modified model, we established failure divergence refinement. The statistics can be seen in Table 2.

The trace refinement is significantly faster than failure divergence refinement. We explain this by the fact that the model has the following three new events: PM_SetsPressure, CS_LowLevel_Abnormal, and CS_TopLevel_RaisesAlarm. For those events, divergence must be checked in nearly every state, as almost every state is stable. The divergence check is expensive as it uses set operations internally. This might be a direction for future improvement.

General Observations. Sometimes, model checking is slower than trace and failure divergence refinement checking. The internal mechanism of ProB and the nature of the models explain this. Calculating a specific transition can be more expensive than other transitions, depending on the complexity of the constraints describing the transitions. Similarly, during refinement checking, the exploration process is guided by the already explored abstract state space, which can reduce the calculation cost.

Table 2. Comparison trace refinement and failure divergence refinement

Project	Trace refinement	Failure divergence refinement
Vending Machine	51 ms	46 ms
Interlocking	4077 ms	19 ms[a]
Interlocking (fixed)	934 ms	1008 ms
HD machine	560 ms	4147 ms

[a] Results in a fail (divergence).

6.4   Lessons Learned

From our experiments, we could learn multiple things. **First**, failure divergence refinement is often slower than trace refinement checking as divergence and failure sets need to be calculated. The divergence and refusal sets calculations can be expensive, as we can see with the HD machine. **Second**, counterexamples provided helpful information in cases where failure divergence refinement failed. We could spot subtle undetected issues, e.g., divergence, which many case study implementations do not explicitly treat.

6.5   Threats to Validity

Based on the categories provided by Wright et al. [29]. We want to highlight a threat to internal validity. As we relied on ProB, we only used those models we knew ProB could handle in the first place (i.e., those that can be fully explored). Furthermore, we only choose those models that have a deterministic initial state. Those factors are also a threat to external validity as we cannot make any guarantee for models outside this scope.

7   Related Work

CSP Influences. Failure traces are usually defined regarding linear transition systems (LTS). However, significant focus and practical development is on the CSP [13] language. Many works by Wehrheim [25–28] cover the effect trace and failure divergence refinement has on behavioral properties within the context of CSP. Our work draws inspiration from this, as reasoning about traces can be more appealing than reasoning about POs (which is an alternative, as shown later). Traces represent what a system can do, so when Algorithm 1 produces counterexamples, those may be easier to comprehend than failing proof.

As B is the direct predecessor of Event-B, the contribution of Dunne and Conroy [6] is noteworthy as it provides POs for B such that CSP semantics like failure-divergence hold. Hallerstede [8], in his work, describes how CSP failure divergence refinement corresponds to deadlock freeness proofs of Event-B. In four contributions, Schneider et al. [20–23] describe how CSP semantics relate to Event-B refinement. The main contribution here is a coupling of Event-B ∥ CSP, allowing us to observe Event-B behavior regarding CSP traces. From this, the authors make further observations of the relationship between the Event-B refinement strategy and traces in CSP.

These contributions aim to relate trace semantics to (Event-)B POs. Our contribution differs as we aim to add failure divergences semantics to Event-B without relating it to POs. This nonrelation, for now, is by choice, as we focus on getting a push-button tool ready that can directly assist in modeling chores like validating (trace) liveness properties for refinements without having to think about any proofs. Furthermore, in contrast to proofs, we can produce counter-examples, thus helping to debug models.

LT Properties in Event-B. Several significant related works aim to preserve LT(L) properties during Event-B refinement. Hoang and Abrial [10] relate liveness properties in the context of LTL with new Event-B proof obligations, i.e., one could formulate LTL properties for the price of additional proofs to be discharged for every new property. Integrating LTL properties this way makes them accessible to the refinement mechanism. However, not all LTL property types are covered, and the new POs never became part of the standard Event-B POs or the Rodin toolset. Hoang et al. [11] and Zhu et al. [31] extend the findings to all LTL properties and their preservation during refinement. Rivière et al. [18] proposed reasoning of liveness properties for reflexive Event-B; however, to our knowledge, it did not yet tackle the challenge of refinement.

8   Conclusion and Future Work

This work introduces failure divergence refinement for Event-B, enabling preservation assumptions about behavioral properties during refinement. Modelers can conduct the refinement check push-button through the algorithm and tool presented, contrasting previous methods requiring additional proofs. This offers swift, early feedback, facilitating the trickle-down of validation results along refinement chains without redoing validation.

In the future, we aim to integrate the tool into ProB2-Ui [3] for accessibility. As discussed in Sect. 4, an extension to LTL (or even CTL) is possible, and we plan to explore this. Furthermore, investigating readiness refinement/bisimulation (cf. [4]) is an intriguing avenue. Eshuis and Fokkinga [7] have observed a strong resemblance between failure divergence refinement and bisimulation for LTS, which warrants further exploration.

References

1. Abrial, J.R.: Modeling in Event-B: System and Software Engineering. Cambridge University Press, Cambridge (2010)
2. Abrial, J.R., Butler, M., Hallerstede, S., Hoang, T.S., Mehta, F., Voisin, L.: Rodin: an open toolset for modelling and reasoning in Event-B. Int. J. Softw. Tools Technol. Transfer **12**(6), 447–466 (2010)
3. Bendisposto, J., et al.: ProB2-UI: a Java-based user interface for ProB. In: Lluch Lafuente, A., Mavridou, A. (eds.) Formal Methods for Industrial Critical Systems, pp. 193–201. Springer, Cham (2021)
4. De Roever, W.P., Engelhardt, K.: Data Refinement: Model-Oriented Proof Methods and Their Comparison. Cambridge University Press, Cambridge (1998)
5. Derrick, J., Boiten, E.: Refinement: Semantics, Languages and Applications. Springer, Cham (2018)
6. Dunne, S., Conroy, S.: Process refinement in B. In: Treharne, H., King, S., Henson, M., Schneider, S. (eds.) ZB 2005: Formal Specification and Development in Z and B, pp. 45–64. Springer, Heidelberg (2005)
7. Eshuis, R., Fokkinga, M.M.: Comparing refinements for failure and bisimulation semantics. Fund. Inform. **52**(4), 297–321 (2002)
8. Hallerstede, S.: On the purpose of Event-B proof obligations. Formal Aspects Comput. **23**, 133–150 (2011)
9. Hoang, T.S.: An introduction to the Event-B modelling method, pp. 211–236. Springer, Heidelberg (2013)
10. Hoang, T.S., Abrial, J.R.: Reasoning about liveness properties in Event-B. In: Qin, S., Qiu, Z. (eds.) Formal Methods and Software Engineering, pp. 456–471. Springer, Heidelberg (2011)
11. Hoang, T.S., Schneider, S., Treharne, H., Williams, D.M.: Foundations for using linear temporal logic in Event-B refinement. Formal Aspects Comput. **28**, 909–935 (2016)
12. Hoang, T.S., Snook, C., Ladenberger, L., Butler, M.: Validating the requirements and design of a hemodialysis machine using iUML-B, BMotion studio, and co-simulation. In: Butler, M., Schewe, K.D., Mashkoor, A., Biro, M. (eds.) Abstract State Machines, Alloy, B, TLA, VDM, and Z, pp. 360–375. Springer, Cham (2016)

13. Hoare, C.A.R., et al.: Communicating Sequential Processes, vol. 178. Prentice-Hall, Englewood Cliffs (1985)
14. Leuschel, M., Butler, M.: ProB: a model checker for B. In: Araki, K., Gnesi, S., Mandrioli, D. (eds.) FME 2003. LNCS, vol. 2805, pp. 855–874. Springer, Heidelberg (2003). https://doi.org/10.1007/978-3-540-45236-2_46
15. Leuschel, M., Butler, M.: Automatic refinement checking for B. In: Lau, K.K., Banach, R. (eds.) Formal Methods and Software Engineering, pp. 345–359. Springer, Heidelberg (2005)
16. Mashkoor, A.: The hemodialysis machine case study. In: Butler, M., Schewe, K.D., Mashkoor, A., Biro, M. (eds.) Abstract State Machines, Alloy, B, TLA, VDM, and Z, pp. 329–343. Springer, Cham (2016)
17. Mashkoor, A., Leuschel, M., Egyed, A.: Validation obligations: a novel approach to check compliance between requirements and their formal specification. In: 43rd IEEE/ACM International Conference on Software Engineering: New Ideas and Emerging Results, ICSE (NIER) 2021, Madrid, Spain, 25–28 May 2021, pp. 1–5. IEEE (2021). https://doi.org/10.1109/ICSE-NIER52604.2021.00009
18. Rivière, P., Singh, N.K., Aït-Ameur, Y., Dupont, G.: Formalising liveness properties in Event-B with the reflexive EB4EB framework. In: Rozier, K.Y., Chaudhuri, S. (eds.) NASA Formal Methods, pp. 312–331. Springer, Cham (2023)
19. Roscoe, A.: The theory and practice of concurrency (1998)
20. Schneider, S., Treharne, H., Wehrheim, H.: A CSP approach to control in Event-B. In: Méry, D., Merz, S. (eds.) Integrated Formal Methods, pp. 260–274. Springer, Heidelberg (2010)
21. Schneider, S., Treharne, H., Wehrheim, H.: Bounded retransmission in Event-B—CSP: a case study. Electron. Notes Theor. Comput. Sci. **280**, 69–80 (2011). https://doi.org/10.1016/j.entcs.2011.11.019. https://www.sciencedirect.com/science/article/pii/S157106611100168X. Proceedings of the B 2011 Workshop, a satellite event of the 17th International Symposium on Formal Methods (FM 2011)
22. Schneider, S., Treharne, H., Wehrheim, H.: A CSP account of Event-B refinement (2011)
23. Schneider, S., Treharne, H., Wehrheim, H.: The behavioural semantics of Event-B refinement. Formal Aspects Comput. **26**, 251–280 (2014)
24. Stock, S., Vu, F., Geleßus, D., Leuschel, M., Mashkoor, A., Egyed, A.: Validation by abstraction and refinement. In: Glässer, U., Creissac Campos, J., Méry, D., Palanque, P. (eds.) Rigorous State-Based Methods, pp. 160–178. Springer, Cham (2023)
25. Wehrheim, H.: Behavioural subtyping and property preservation. In: Smith, S.F., Talcott, C.L. (eds.) Formal Methods for Open Object-Based Distributed Systems IV, pp. 213–231. Springer, Boston (2000)
26. Wehrheim, H.: Behavioral subtyping relations for active objects. Formal Methods Syst. Des. **23**, 143–170 (2003)
27. Wehrheim, H.: Refinement and consistency in multiview models. In: Bezivin, J., Heckel, R. (eds.) Language Engineering for Model-Driven Software Development. Dagstuhl Seminar Proceedings (DagSemProc), vol. 4101, pp. 1–11. Schloss Dagstuhl – Leibniz-Zentrum für Informatik (2005). https://doi.org/10.4230/DagSemProc.04101.13. https://drops.dagstuhl.de/opus/volltexte/2005/19
28. Wehrheim, H.: Refinement and consistency in component models with multiple views. In: Reussner, R.H., Stafford, J.A., Szyperski, C.A. (eds.) Architecting Systems with Trustworthy Components, pp. 84–102. Springer, Cham (2006)

29. Wright, H.K., Kim, M., Perry, D.E.: Validity concerns in software engineering research. In: Proceedings of the FSE/SDP Workshop on Future of Software Engineering Research, FoSER 2010, pp. 411–414. ACM (2010). https://doi.org/10.1145/1882362.1882446

30. Zhu, C., Butler, M., Cirstea, C.: Towards refinement semantics of real-time trigger-response properties in Event-B. In: 2019 International Symposium on Theoretical Aspects of Software Engineering (TASE), pp. 1–8. IEEE (2019). https://doi.org/10.1109/TASE.2019.00-26

31. Zhu, C., Butler, M., Cirstea, C., Hoang, T.S.: A fairness-based refinement strategy to transform liveness properties in Event-B models. Sci. Comput. Program. **225**, 102907 (2023). https://doi.org/10.1016/j.scico.2022.102907. https://www.sciencedirect.com/science/article/pii/S016764232200140X

Mining Diamonds in Labelled Transition Systems

P. H. M. van Spaendonck[(✉)] and K. H. J. Jilissen

Eindhoven University of Technology, Eindhoven, The Netherlands
{p.h.m.v.spaendonck,k.h.j.jilissen}@tue.nl

Abstract. Labelled transition systems can be a great way to visualise the complex behaviour of parallel and communicating systems. However, if, during a particular time frame, no synchronisation or communication between processes occurs, then multiple parallel sequences of actions are able to interleave arbitrarily, and the resulting graph quickly becomes too complex for the human eye to understand easily.

With that in mind, we propose an exact formalisation of these arbitrary interleavings, and an algorithm to find all said interleavings in any arbitrary finite LTS, to reduce the visual complexity of labelled transition systems.

Keywords: Labelled Transition Systems · State Space Reduction · Concurrent Systems · State Space Visualisation

1 Introduction

Parallel and communicating systems are often difficult to understand due to the divergence that arises from asynchronicity. Toward this end, labelled transition systems (LTSs) are a common way to visualise the divergent behaviour of such systems. As with many visualisation techniques, keeping the visual complexity of a given LTS at a minimum is important for its effectiveness as a communication tool between model-based engineers and software engineers. Techniques for reducing this visual complexity are not a novel field and have been studied extensively, e.g. reduction through equivalence relations or pre-orders.

We identify a pattern that can occur easily in communication systems and which introduces large amounts of visual clutter. That is, if, during a particular time frame, no synchronisation or communication between processes occurs, then multiple parallel sequences of actions can interleave arbitrarily, and the resulting graph quickly becomes too complex for the human eye to understand easily. In particular, we argue that while the fact that no synchronisation or communication occurs is useful information for an engineer, given that the result of each

This publication is part of the PVSR project (with project number 17933) of the MasCot research programme which is financed by the Dutch Research Council (NWO).

interleaving is always the same, explicitly labelling each possible interleaving is merely an exercise in combinatorics.

This pattern, dubbed a *diamond pattern* due to its structure, occurs when we have a set of asynchronous sequential actions that must all fully execute before any further progress can occur. For example, work is divided up over multiple threads and calculations can only continue after all threads have calculated their results. Given n parallel processes, the pattern itself becomes a n-dimensional hypercube that consists of all possible interleavings of these sequences, cf. the two LTSs in Example (1a) and (1b). The aforementioned example is still relatively easy to understand, but with the number of parallel processes increasing, this is no longer the case.

Example 1. The two LTSs (1a) and (1b) both contain all possible interleavings of the sequences $a_1 \cdot a_2$ and b, starting from state $\hat{q}$. The LTS (1c) contains a single "macro"-transition denoting that the sequence $a_1 \cdot a_2$ occurs in parallel to the sequence b.

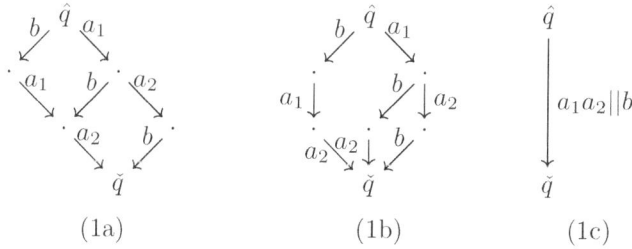

(1a)   (1b)   (1c)

The difficulty in noticing these patterns is not only limited to cases with a large number of parallel processes. In Example 2, the two LTSs have near identical structures. The LTS (2a) can be summarised as the interleaving $ba||ca$, but the LTS (2b) cannot. Note also that all interleavings end in the state $\check{q}$, yet the grid-like structure often associated with such congruences ends in the state right before it.

Example 2. The two LTSs below have near identical structures, the only difference being the label of the final transitions to $\check{q}$ and $\check{p}$. However, only the LTS (2a) contains all (and only all) interleaving of the two sequences $b \cdot a$ and $c \cdot a$, while in the LTS (2b) a second action a is never enabled.

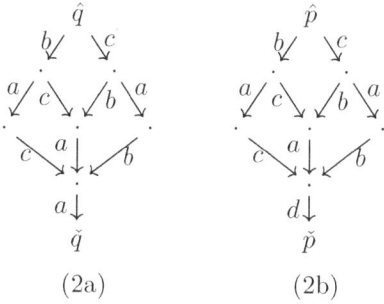

(2a)   (2b)

As such, this paper aims to find these *diamond patterns* in arbitrary (non-deterministic) LTSs without any prior knowledge about the relation between its action labels, and replacing them with a single transition that captures the precise parallelisation that occurs, e.g. see the LTS in Example (1c). Especially towards reducing the visual complexity of arbitrary LTSs, finding the specific parallelised sequences can be useful to highlight aspects of the modelled system.

Specifically, the contributions of this paper are as follows: We present a formalisation of the diamond pattern, including proofs on the correctness of the formalisation. We investigate the relationship between diamond convergences and equivalence relations on LTSs and prove that strong bisimilarity is the exact relation that preserves diamond convergences for arbitrary LTSs. Last, we present an algorithm for finding all diamonds in any arbitrary LTS.

In Sect. 2, we briefly discuss the closely related body on partial order refinement and other techniques aimed at simplifying the visualisation of complex communicating systems. In Sect. 3, we give the definitions of and related to LTSs that are used throughout the rest of the paper. In Sect. 4 we formalise what diamonds are and when a diamond occurs in an LTS and prove some rudimentary properties aimed at the completeness and soundness of our definitions. In Sect. 5 we prove that strong bisimilarity is the precise equivalence relation that preserves diamond convergence. In Sect. 6 we outline our novel algorithm for finding all diamonds in any LTS and outline its correctness proof. In Sect. 7 we conclude and discuss some possible directions for future work related to diamond patterns.

2   Related Work

The work presented here is closely related to partial order reduction (POR) methods, e.g. [1,4,19,22], in which the commutativity of parallel and independent operations is used to bundle together functionally equivalent traces. These POR methods are used during state space exploration and model checking to avoid having to consider multiple functionally equivalent traces, and thus accelerate said algorithms. To achieve this speedup, POR methods have to consider only a strict subset of all traces/transitions. Which subset is considered influences the set of properties that is preserved, e.g. LTL for ample sets [19], $CTL^*_{\setminus \circ}$ for ample sets with stuttering [1], or deadlock for stubborn sets [22]. As we show later, reduction modulo diamond convergence is equivalent to reduction modulo strong bisimulation. It is thus much stronger in preserving behaviour than the aforementioned POR techniques by preserving all properties in CTL^* [7], and only matched when strong assumptions are made a-priori about the parallelisation of the system, e.g. in [11].

As noted by Groote et al. in [5], these convergences are inherent to any parallel systems. However, POR techniques have to consider only a strict subset of these convergences to gain any potential speedup during state space exploration. More-so, they can only consider outgoing transitions to find these, whereas the reduction algorithm introduced here finds all diamond convergences by traversing incoming transitions.

We now discuss some other methods for reducing the visual complexity of LTSs, since our work is aimed towards doing the same. In [26], van Ieperen presents layout and rendering techniques aimed at improving the visual readability of LTSs with over 10000 states. These techniques are applied to various large pre-existing formal models. Of particular interest are the presented Alma, leader election protocol [3], and Twilight models, which contain large degrees of asynchronous behaviour, and thus contain many diamond patterns and/or patterns similar to diamond patterns. However, as the authors themselves note, a survey with a statistically significant sample size is still required to properly assess the effectiveness of these techniques.

In [8], Herman et al. conduct a significantly large survey on various visualisation techniques for graphs. These visualisation techniques are specific to visualising parts of a graph as a tree with a single begin- and multiple endpoints. However, we note that communicating systems can often be cyclic, such as the aforementioned Alma and Twilight models in [26], and thus these techniques can only be applied to specific, non-cyclic, parts of particular models.

In [6], Groote and van Ham present the LTSView tool. This tool, aimed at providing insight into the global structure of significantly large statespaces, clusters together similar states into discs and arranges these discs into a 3-dimensional treelike structure. The authors use the tool to provide information on various real world models, including a model with just over 10^6 states.

The visual complexity of an LTS can also be improved by reducing the size of a given LTS. This can be done by reducing modulo some equivalence relation, e.q. trace equivalence, strong bisimulation [17], or branching bisimulation [24], or modulo some preorder relation, e.g. the simulation preorder [2].

It should also be noted that LTSs are not the only way to visualise complex parallel systems. Other visualisation/formalisation techniques include, in no particular order, Kripke Structures [13], Petri Nets [20], and state transition graphs [21,25], and variations of all these. Each technique focuses on different aspects of communicating behaviour, and thus each has its own respective advantages and disadvantages.

3   Preliminaries

A *labelled Transition System* is a simple way to formalise the behaviour of a non-deterministic (parallel) system as a directed graph [15]. Edges are labelled with actions taken from some action-alphabet A, representing some atomic event occuring, and lead to a (possibly new) state. For this paper, we only consider LTSs with a finite set of states and action labels.

Definition 1. *A labelled Transition System (LTS) is defined as a tuple* $\langle Q, q_0, A, \rightarrow \rangle$ *where:*

- Q *is the finite set of states;*
- $q_0 \in Q$ *is the initial state;*
- A *is a finite set of action labels;*

- $\to \subseteq Q \times A \times Q$ *is the transition relation where* $\langle q, a, q' \rangle \in \to$ *is usually written as* $q \xrightarrow{a} q'$.

Additionally, given any LTS $\langle Q, q_0, A, \to \rangle$, *state* $q \in Q$, *and label* $a \in A$, *we have* $q \xrightarrow{a} \overset{def}{=} \exists_{q' \in Q}[q \xrightarrow{a} q']$.

Throughout the paper, we make use of *action sequences*, sometimes referred to as words or strings in automata theory [9,10], which are concatenations of zero or more actions.

Definition 2. *Given a set of actions* A, *the set* A^* *denotes the set of action sequences. We use* $\varepsilon \in A^*$ *to denote the empty sequence. Additionally, given any action* $a \in A$ *and action sequences* $s \in A^*$, *we have:*

- $hd(as) = a$, $tl(as) = s$,
- *the length* $| \ | : A^* \to \mathbb{N}$ *is defined s.t.* $|\varepsilon| = 0$ *and* $|as| = 1 + |s|$, *and*
- *the minimal alphabet* $A^- : A^* \to \mathcal{P}(A)$ *is defined s.t.* $A^-(\varepsilon) = \emptyset$ *and* $A^-(as) = \{a\} \cup A^-(s)$.

Additionally, we generalise the $\to$ *relation for LTSs s.t. given any LTS* $\langle Q, q_0, A, \to \rangle$, *we have* $q \xrightarrow{\varepsilon} q$ *for all* $q \in Q$, *we have* $q \xrightarrow{as} q''$ *for all* $q, q'' \in Q, a \in A, s \in A^*$ *iff there is some state* $q' \in Q$ *with* $q \xrightarrow{a} q' \xrightarrow{s} q''$, *and we have* $q \xrightarrow{s}$ *for all* $q \in Q, s \in A^*$ *iff there is some state* $q' \in Q$ *with* $q \xrightarrow{s} q'$.

As noted earlier, notions of equivalences of different LTSs have been studied extensively, e.g. the work by Van Glabbeek [23] on the linear time-branching time spectrum gives a nice overview on various equivalence relations. Two common equivalence relations, of which we discuss their relation to the diamond patterns later, are *trace equivalence* [16], and *strong bisimilarity* [14,18].

Definition 3. *Given two LTSs* $l = \langle Q, q_0, A, \to \rangle$, *and* $l' = \langle Q', q_0', A, \to' \rangle$, *we say that* l *and* l' *are trace equivalent, denoted as* $l =_{tr} l'$, *iff* $traces(q_0) = traces(q_0')$, *where for any state* $q \in Q$, $traces(q) = \{s \in A^* | q \xrightarrow{s} \}$.

Definition 4. *Given an LTS* $\langle Q, q_0, A, \to \rangle$ *and some relation* $R \subseteq Q \times Q$, *we say that* R *is a bisimulation iff:*

- R *is symmetric;*
- *Given states* $q, q', q_{to} \in Q$ *and action* $a \in A$ *such that* $q \xrightarrow{a} q_{to}$ *and* qRq' *then there is some state* $q_{to}' \in Q$ *with* $q' \xrightarrow{a} q_{to}'$ *and* $q_{to}Rq_{to}'$.

We say two states $q, q' \in Q$ *are (strongly) bisimilar, denoted as* $q \underline{\leftrightarrow} q'$, *iff there is a bisimulation* R *with* qRq'.

We say two LTSs $l = \langle Q, q_0, A, \to \rangle$ *and* $l' = \langle Q', q_0, A, \to' \rangle$ *are (strongly) bisimilar iff there is bisimulation* R *s.t.* $q_0 R q_0'$ *in* $\langle Q \uplus Q', q_0, A \cup A', \to \cup \to' \rangle$.

Particularly useful when reducing the complexity of an LTS is the notion of some LTS that is minimal modulo a given equivalence relation to describe an LTS in a given equivalence class of LTSs, i.e. all LTSs that are equivalent modulo said equivalence relation, that cannot be reduced to have fewer states. Note that it is not important to us that the number of transitions cannot be further reduced.

Definition 5. *Given any equivalence relation $=_x$ on LTSs, and an LTS $l = \langle Q, q_0, A, \rightarrow \rangle$. We say that l is minimal modulo $=_x$ iff given states $q, q' \in Q$ if $q =_x q'$ then $q = q'$.*

Example 3. The following three LTSs, with initial states p, q, and r, are all trace equivalent. However the states q and r are not strongly bisimilar, since after the taking the left a transition in q, the c action, which is always enabled after taking the a transition in r, cannot be simulated. The LTS with intial state q is minimal modulo strong bisimulation, and the LTS with initial state r is minimal modulo trace equivalence.

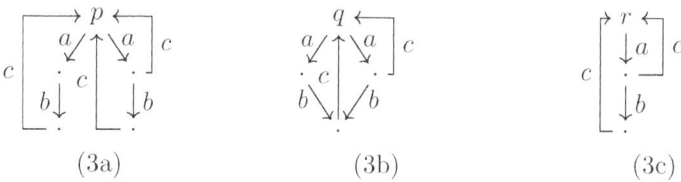

(3a)   (3b)   (3c)

4   Diamond Patterns

Before we proceed to define what a diamond pattern is, we note a particular oddity, shown in Example 4, that arises with monotone sequences, i.e. a sequence consisting only of the repetition of a single action, e.g. a, bbb. In such instances, the particular parallel composition leading to the diamond pattern in question, has to be arbitrated post reduction modulo strong bisimulation. Since reduction modulo some equivalence relation weaker than isomorphism is a commonly applied technique when working with LTSs, we opt to group such monotone (sub-)patterns together in our definition.

Example 4. The two LTSs below, (4a) and (4b), are strongly bisimilar. Starting in their initial states $\hat{q}$ and $\hat{p}$, it is possible to perform any interleaving of the sequences aa and a. However, it is also possible to perform any interleaving of the three identical sequences a, or simply perform the sequence aaa. After reduction modulo strong bisimulation, the parallel characterisation is ambiguous.

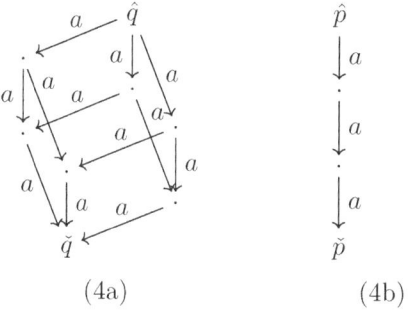

(4a)   (4b)

In Definition 6, we define what a *diamond pattern* is. Simply put, a diamond consists of interleaving actions, representing monotone sequences, and non-monotone action sequences of arbitrary positive lengths.

Definition 6. *A diamond pattern* $\diamond = \langle C_a, C_s \rangle$ *is a tuple of two mappings:* $C_a \colon A \to \mathbb{N}$ *denoting the cardinality of actions in the diamond, and* $C_s \colon A^*_{\backslash m} \to$ $\mathbb{N}$ *denoting the cardinality of non-monotone sequences in the diamond, where* $A^*_{\backslash m} \subset A^*$ *is defined as* $A^*_{\backslash m} = \{s \in A^* \mid |A^-(s)| \geq 2\}$. *The set of all diamond patterns over A is* $\Diamond(A)$.
Additionally, we have:

- *we denote the empty diamond, i.e. the diamond with cardinality 0 for all actions and actions sequences, as* $\varnothing$,
- $hd(\langle C_a, C_s \rangle) = \{a \in A \mid C_a(a) \neq 0\} \cup \{a \in A \mid \exists s \in A^*_{\backslash m}.hd(s) = a \wedge C_s(s) \neq 0\}$, *and*
- *the size of a diamond* $|\ | \colon \Diamond(A) \to \mathbb{N}$ *is defined s.t.* $|\langle C_a, C_s \rangle| = \sum_{a \in A} C_a(a) + \sum_{s \in A^*_{\backslash m}} |s| * C_s(s)$.

We often forgo writing down the mappings and instead write down the explicit actions and action sequences that are not mapped to 0, e.g. given $A = \{a, b, c\}$ we write the diamond $\langle C_a, C_s \rangle$ where $C_a = \{a \mapsto 3, b \mapsto 0, c \mapsto 1\}$, and $C_s(ab) = 2, C_s(bcc) = 1$, and $C_s(s) = 0$ for any $s \notin \{ab, bcc\}$ as:

$$a^3 || c^1 || (ab)^2 || (bcc)^1$$

The diamond above describes the interleaving of 3 a actions, 1 c action, 2 ab sequences, and 1 bcc sequence. We later define when such a diamond pattern actually occurs in an LTS.

The *tail* operations, see Definition 7, give all possible resulting diamonds after taking a single action, an action sequence, or a diamond. If the action, action sequence, or diamond is not contained in the diamond, then an empty set is returned. The *tail* operation for removing a single action is best understood as distinguishing 3 cases: the action a is present one or more times as a single action, the diamond contains one or more sequences as where s is not monotone, and/or the diamond contains one more sequences as, where s is monotone. We show the results of different tail operations on various diamonds in Example 5.

Definition 7. *We define the tail operation on diamonds and single actions as* $tl \colon \Diamond(A) \times A \to \mathcal{P}(\Diamond(A))$ *s.t. given any action $a \in A$ and diamond* $\diamond = \langle C_a, C_s \rangle \in \Diamond(A)$ *we have:*

$$tl(\langle C_a, C_s \rangle, a) = \{\langle C_a[a \mapsto C_a(a) - 1)], C_s \rangle \mid C_a(a) > 0\}$$
$$\cup \{\langle C_a, C_s[as \mapsto C_s(as) - 1, s \mapsto C_s(s) + 1] \rangle \mid$$
$$\exists s \in A^*_{\backslash m}.C_s(as) > 0\}$$
$$\cup \{\langle C_a[b \mapsto C_a(b) + k], C_s[ab^k \mapsto C_s(ab^k) - 1] \rangle \mid$$
$$\exists b \in A, k \in \mathbb{N}_{>0}.C_s(ab^k) > 0\}$$

Similarly, we define the tail operation on diamonds and action sequences such that for all diamonds $\diamond \in \Diamond(A)$, actions $a \in A$ and action sequences $s \in A^*$, we have:

$$tl(\diamond, \varepsilon) = \{\diamond\}, \quad and \quad tl(\diamond, as) = \bigcup_{\diamond' \in tl(\diamond, a)} tl(\diamond', s).$$

Lastly, we define the tail operation on two diamonds, such that given two diamonds $\diamond, \diamond_{pf} \in \Diamond(A)$, we have:

$$tl(\diamond, \diamond_{pf}) = \begin{cases} \{\diamond\} & \textbf{if } \diamond_{pf} = \varnothing \\ \bigcup_{\substack{a \,\in\, hd(\diamond_{pf}), \\ \diamond' \,\in\, tl(\diamond,\, a), \\ \diamond'_{pf} \,\in\, tl(\diamond_{pf},\, a)}} tl(\diamond', \diamond'_{pf}) & \textbf{otherwise} \end{cases}$$

Example 5. Below are examples of the *tail* mapping respectively using actions, sequences and diamonds as the second argument.

actions:

$tl((ab)^1||(cd)^1, a) = \{b^1||(cd)^1\} \quad tl((ab)^1||(cd)^1, e) \qquad = \emptyset$

$tl((ab)^1||(ac)^1, a) = \{b^1||(ac)^1, c^1||(ab)^1\}$

action sequences:

$tl((ab)^1||(cd)^1, ab) = \{(cd)^1\} \qquad tl((ab)^1||(cd)^1, ac) \qquad = \{b^1||d^1\}$

diamonds:

$tl(a^4, a^2) \qquad = \{a^2\} \qquad tl((ab)^1||(cd)^1, a^1||c^1) \qquad = \{b^1||d^1\}$

$tl(a^1||b^1, a^1||b^1) = \{\varnothing\} \qquad tl((abb)^1||(abd)^1, a^1||(ab)^1) = \{b^1||(bd)^1, b^2||d^1\}$

In Definition 8 we define the *sequence-of* relation which indicates if a given sequence is an interleaving of the actions and sequences of a given diamond. The relation does not enforce that all actions and the complete sequences are contained in the interleaving sequence. For example, we have $acb \sqsubseteq ab||cd$, and $c \sqsubseteq ab||cd$, but not $ad \sqsubseteq ab||cd$.

Definition 8. *We define the sequence-of relation* $(\sqsubseteq) : A^* \times \Diamond(A)$ *such that:*

- $\varepsilon \sqsubseteq \diamond$ *for any diamond* $\diamond \in \Diamond(A)$*, and*
- *for any action* $a \in A$*, sequence* $s \in A^*$*, and diamond* $\diamond \in \Diamond(A)$ *if* $s \sqsubseteq tl(\diamond, a)$ *then* $as \sqsubseteq \diamond$*.*

In Definition 9 we define when a diamond is considered to be the prefix of another diamond.

Definition 9. *We define the prefix relation on diamonds* $\sqsubseteq \,\subseteq \Diamond(A) \times \Diamond(A)$*, s.t. given any two diamonds* $\diamond, \diamond' \in \Diamond(A)$*, we have* $\diamond \sqsubseteq \diamond'$ *iff* $tl(\diamond, \diamond') \neq \emptyset$*.*

In Definition 10, we inductively define the precise condition for when we consider a diamond pattern to occur within an LTS. Informally, we say that a state diamond converges in another state iff every *head*-action of the diamond is enabled, and after taking said action, only the remaining diamond is possible.

This is repeated until the diamond is empty and we have arrived in the target state. After taking the first transition, the requirement on what actions can be enabled is strengthened (from $\xrightarrow{\diamond}$ to $\xRightarrow{\diamond}$) to ensure that only actions pertaining to the current diamond are enabled. As such, multiple diamonds can be enabled in a given state, but we still enforce exclusivity during the execution of a given diamond. Unless otherwise specified when talking about diamond convergence, the equivalence relation $=_x$ is assumed to be the standard identity equivalence on states ($=$). We list some examples of the diamond convergence relations in Example 6.

Definition 10. *Given an LTS* $\langle Q, q_0, A, \rightarrow \rangle$, *an equivalence relation* $=_x$ *on states, states* $\hat{q}, \check{q} \in Q$, *and diamond pattern* $\diamond \in \Diamond(A)$ *we say that* $\hat{q}$ *strictly* $\diamond$-*converges up to* $=_x$ *in* $\check{q}$, *denoted as* $\hat{q} \xRightarrow{\diamond} [\check{q}]_{=_x}$, *iff:*

1. *if* $\diamond = \varnothing$ *then* $\hat{q} =_x \check{q}$,
2. *if* $\diamond \neq \varnothing$ *then for any action* $a \in hd(\diamond)$ *and diamond* $\diamond' \in tl(\diamond, a)$ *there exists state* $q \in Q$ *with* $\hat{q} \xrightarrow{a} q$ *and* $q \xRightarrow{\diamond'} [\check{q}]_{=_x}$, *and*
3. *if* $\diamond \neq \varnothing$ *then for any outgoing transition* $\hat{q} \xrightarrow{a} q$ *there exists diamond* $\diamond' \in tl(\diamond, a)$ *with* $q \xRightarrow{\diamond'} [\check{q}]_{=_x}$.

We say that $\hat{q}$ $\diamond$-*converges up to* $=_x$ *in* $\check{q}$, *denoted* $\hat{q} \xrightarrow{\diamond} [\check{q}]_{=_x}$, *if at least the conditions 1 and 2 hold.*

If $=_x$ *is the standard identity equivalence on states* ($=$), *we use the simpler notations* $\hat{q} \xRightarrow{\diamond} \check{q}$ *and* $\hat{q} \xrightarrow{\diamond} \check{q}$

Example 6. In the LTSs below we have $\hat{q} \xrightarrow{a^1 || b^1} \check{q}$ and $\hat{q} \xrightarrow{b^1 || c^1} \check{q}'$. We do not have $\hat{p} \xrightarrow{a^1 || b^1} \check{p}$, because in p we do not have $p \xRightarrow{a} \check{p}$ due to the transition $p \xrightarrow{a} \check{p}'$. If we were to have some equivalence relation $=_x$ with $\check{p} =_x \check{p}'$, then the weaker diamond convergence $\hat{p} \xRightarrow{a^1 || b^1} [\check{p}]_{=_x}$ would hold.

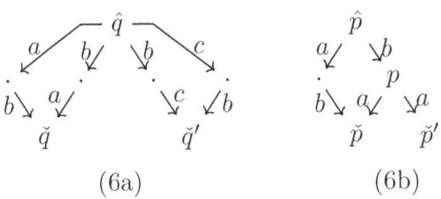

(6a)   (6b)

With diamond convergence now properly defined, we proceed to prove some properties that one might prefer to follow from diamond convergence. In Theorem 1, we prove that diamond convergences are complete, i.e. all interleavings of the diamond can occur.

Theorem 1. *Given an LTS* $\langle Q, q_0, A, \rightarrow \rangle$, *states* $\hat{q}, \check{q} \in Q$ *and diamond* $\diamond \in \Diamond(A)$ *with* $\hat{q} \xrightarrow{\diamond} \check{q}$, *we have that for all non-empty sequences* $s \in A^*$ *with* $s \Subset \diamond$, *there exist some state* $q' \in Q$ *and diamond* $\diamond_{tl} \in tl(\diamond, s)$ *such that* $\hat{q} \xrightarrow{s} q' \xRightarrow{\diamond_{tl}} \check{q}$.

Proof. Let $\hat{q}, \check{q}$ and $\diamond \in \Diamond(A)$ with $\hat{q} \xrightarrow{\diamond} \check{q}$. We prove using strong induction over $|s|$ that for all non-empty sequences $s \in A^*$ if $s \sqsubseteq \diamond$ then there is some state $q' \in Q$ and diamond $\diamond_{tl}$ such that $\hat{q} \xrightarrow{s} q' \xrightarrow{\diamond_{tl}} \check{q}$. As such, let $k \in \mathbb{N}$ s.t. for all $s' \sqsubseteq \diamond$ with $0 < |s'| < k$ there exists state $q' \in Q$ and diamond $\diamond' \in tl(\diamond, s')$ with $\hat{q} \xrightarrow{s'} q' \xrightarrow{\diamond'} \check{q}$, and let $s \in A^*$ with $s \sqsubseteq \diamond$ and $|s| = k$. We make a case distinction on $|s|$.

Case $|s| = 1$, we have $s = a$ for some action $a \in A$. Since $a \in hd(\diamond)$, there exists diamond $\diamond_{tl} \in tl(\diamond, a)$. Since $\hat{q} \xrightarrow{\diamond} \check{q}$, there exists state $q \in Q$ such that $\hat{q} \xrightarrow{a} q \xrightarrow{\diamond_{tl}} \check{q}$.

Case $|s| > 1$, there exist $a \in A, s' \in A^*$ with $s = s'a$. Since $|s'| < k$, there exist $q' \in Q, \diamond' \in \Diamond(A)$ with $\hat{q} \xrightarrow{s} q' \xrightarrow{\diamond'} \check{q}$. Since $q' \xrightarrow{\diamond'} \check{q}$ and $a \in hd(\diamond')$, we have $q'' \in Q, \diamond'' \in tl(\diamond, s'a)$ with $\hat{q} \xrightarrow{s'} q' \xrightarrow{a} q'' \xrightarrow{\diamond''} \check{q}$. $\square$

Within the context of finding and replacing diamonds in a given LTS, it is important that diamonds cannot overlap. If this were possible, and a particular diamond and its transitions and states were replaced with a single diamond transition, then any other diamond that shares transition with the replaced diamond would no longer be enabled since part of its transitions are now gone, as is illustrated in Example 7. Towards ensuring that the above does not happen, in Theorem 2 we state that if two strict diamond convergences occur from a given state, then one of the two diamonds is a prefix of the other diamond. As such, as long as only the biggest diamond is taken, no information is lost when replacing diamonds.

Example 7. In the LTS below, the distinct diamonds $\diamond_1$ and $\diamond_2$ share an overlap in states, i.e. q_{pf} and all other states belonging to the action sequence s_{pf}. If the transitions and states belonging to $\diamond_1$ were replaced with a single diamond transition, the part of the behaviour also belonging to $\diamond_2$, i.e. the s_{pf} transition, would disappear, and $\hat{q} \xrightarrow{\diamond_2} q_2$ would no longer hold.

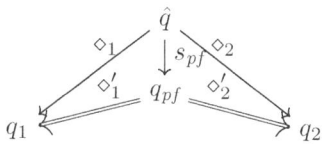

Theorem 2. *Given any LTS $\langle Q, q_0, A, \rightarrow \rangle$, states $q, q_1, q_2 \in Q$, and diamonds $\diamond_1, \diamond_2 \in \Diamond(A)$, we have that if $q \xrightarrow{\diamond_1} q_1$ and $q \xrightarrow{\diamond_2} q_2$ then either $\diamond_1 \sqsubseteq \diamond_2$ or $\diamond_2 \sqsubseteq \diamond_1$.*

Proof. We prove this using strong induction on $|\diamond_1|$. Let $k \in \mathbb{N}$ and let us assume, as our induction hypothesis, that for all states $q, q_1, q_2 \in Q$ and diamonds $\diamond_1, \diamond_2 \in \Diamond(A)$ with $q \xrightarrow{\diamond_1} q_1, q \xrightarrow{\diamond_2} q_2$, and $|\diamond_1| < k$ we have that either $\diamond_1 \sqsubseteq \diamond_2$ or $\diamond_2 \sqsubseteq \diamond_1$. Now, let us assume states $q, q_1, q_2 \in Q$, and diamonds $\diamond_1, \diamond_2 \in \Diamond(A)$ with $q \xrightarrow{\diamond_1} q_1, q \xrightarrow{\diamond_2} q_2$, and $|\diamond_1| = k$. We proceed with case distinction on $|\diamond_1|$.

Case $|\diamond_1| = 0$. As such $\diamond_1 = \emptyset \sqsubseteq \diamond_2$.

Case $|\diamond_1| > 0$. Thus there exist some action $a \in hd(\diamond_1)$ and diamond $\diamond_1' \in tl(\diamond_1, a)$. It follows that there exists some state $q' \in Q$ with $q \xrightarrow{a} q' \xrightarrow{\diamond_1'} q_1$. Since $q \xRightarrow{\diamond_2} q_2$, we have that $a \in hd(\diamond_2)$ and there exists diamond $\diamond_2' \in tl(\diamond_2, a)$ with $q' \xRightarrow{\diamond_2'} q_2$. Since $|\diamond_1'| < k$, we have, as per our induction hypothesis, that either $\diamond_1' \sqsubseteq \diamond_2'$ or $\diamond_2' \sqsubseteq \diamond_1'$.

If $\diamond_1' \sqsubseteq \diamond_2'$, then $tl(\diamond_2', \diamond_1') \neq \emptyset$. Consequently, since $a \in hd(\diamond_1)$, $\diamond_2' \in tl(\diamond_2, a)$, and $\diamond_1' \in tl(\diamond_1, a)$, we have that $tl(\diamond_2, \diamond_1) \neq \emptyset$, and thus $\diamond_1 \sqsubseteq \diamond_2$. In the same manner, we have that if $\diamond_2' \sqsubseteq \diamond_1'$ then $\diamond_2 \sqsubseteq \diamond_1'$.   □

5   Diamond Preservation Under Equivalence Relations

As we have remarked before, reduction modulo some equivalence relation is a useful tool when it comes to reducing the complexity of state spaces. In Definition 11, we define the notion of *diamond equivalence*, i.e. two states are diamond equivalent iff the same diamond convergences are possible in both states. A desirable property would be for diamond equivalence to be preserved by a given equivalence reduction, e.g. reduction modulo some equivalence relation neither adds nor removes diamond convergences. What we find, is that diamond-equivalence and strong bisimulation are in fact equivalent. In Theorem 3 we show that a diamond equivalence relation is a bisimulation, and conversely, in Theorem 4 we show that a bisimulation relation is a diamond equivalence relation.

Definition 11. *Given an LTS $\langle Q, q_0, A, \rightarrow \rangle$, and some equivalence relation $R \subseteq Q \times Q$, we say that R is a diamond equivalence relation iff: For all states $\hat{q}, \check{q}, \hat{q}' \in Q$ and diamonds $\diamond \in \Diamond(A)$ if $\hat{q}R\hat{q}'$ and $\hat{q} \xrightarrow{\diamond} \check{q}$ then $\hat{q}' \xrightarrow{\diamond} [\check{q}]_R$.*

Corollary 1. *Given any diamond equivalence relation $=_\diamond$, LTSs $l = \langle Q, q_0, A, \rightarrow \rangle$, and $l' = \langle Q', q_0', A \rightarrow' \rangle$ s.t. $q_0 =_\diamond q_0'$ and l' is minimal modulo $=_\diamond$. Then for all states $\hat{q}, \check{q} \in Q, \hat{q}', \check{q}' \in Q'$ with $\hat{q} =_\diamond \hat{q}'$ and $\check{q} =_\diamond \check{q}'$ we have if $\hat{q}$ $\diamond$-converges to $\check{q}$ for some diamond $\diamond \in \Diamond(A)$, then $\hat{q}'$ $\diamond$-converges to $\check{q}'$.*

Theorem 3. *Any diamond equivalence relation is a bisimulation.*

Proof. Let $\langle Q, q_0, A, \rightarrow \rangle$ be some LTS, $\hat{q}, \hat{q}', \check{q}' \in Q$ be states, $=_\diamond$ some diamond equivalence relation, and $a \in A$ be some action such that $\hat{q} =_\diamond \hat{q}'$ and $\hat{q} \xrightarrow{a} \check{q}$. We now prove that there is some $\check{q}' \in Q$ such that $\hat{q}' \xrightarrow{a} \check{q}'$ and $\check{q} =_\diamond \check{q}'$. We note that $a^1 \in \Diamond(A)$ and since $\hat{q} \xrightarrow{a} \check{q}$, we have that $\hat{q}$ a^1-converges in $\check{q}$. As per the $=_\diamond$ equivalence relation, there exists state $\check{q}' \in Q$ such that $\hat{q}'$ a^1-converges up to $=_\diamond$ in $\check{q}'$. Or in other words, there exists a state $\check{q}' \in Q$ with $\hat{q} \xrightarrow{a} \check{q}$ and $\check{q} =_\diamond \check{q}'$.   □

Theorem 4. *Any strong bisimulation relation is a diamond-equivalence relation.*

Proof. Let us assume some LTS $l = \langle Q, q_0, A, \rightarrow \rangle$, and strong bisimulation relation $\underleftrightarrow{}$. We prove that for all states $\hat{q}, \hat{q}', \check{q} \in Q$ and $\diamond \in \Diamond(A)$ with $\hat{q} \underleftrightarrow{} \hat{q}'$ we have that if $\hat{q} \xrightarrow{\diamond} \check{q}$ then $\hat{q}' \xrightarrow{\diamond} [\check{q}]_{\underleftrightarrow{}}$, and if $\hat{q} \xRightarrow{\diamond} \check{q}$ then $\hat{q}' \xRightarrow{\diamond} [\check{q}]_{\underleftrightarrow{}}$ using strong induction on $|\diamond|$. We note that diamond equivalence follows from the first implication.

Let us thus assume some $k \in \mathbb{N}$ s.t. the above holds for all states $\hat{q}, \hat{q}', \check{q} \in Q$ and diamond $\diamond \in \Diamond(A)$ with $|\diamond| < k$. We now prove that given states $\hat{q}, \hat{q}', \check{q} \in Q$ with $\hat{q} \underleftrightarrow{} \hat{q}'$ and diamond $\diamond \in \Diamond(A)$ with $|\diamond| = k$ and $\hat{q} \xrightarrow{\diamond} \check{q}$, we have that if $\hat{q} \xrightarrow{\diamond} \check{q}$ then $\hat{q}' \xrightarrow{\diamond} [\check{q}]_{\underleftrightarrow{}}$, and if $\hat{q} \xRightarrow{\diamond} \check{q}$ then $\hat{q}' \xRightarrow{\diamond} [\check{q}]_{\underleftrightarrow{}}$.

Case $k = 0$, i.e. $\diamond = \emptyset$. Thus we have that $\hat{q} = \check{q}$, and consequently $\check{q} \underleftrightarrow{} \hat{q}'$. Since $\diamond = \emptyset$, we have that $\hat{q}' \xrightarrow{\diamond} \hat{q}'$ and $\hat{q}' \xRightarrow{\diamond} \hat{q}'$, and thus $\hat{q}' \xrightarrow{\diamond} [\check{q}]_{\underleftrightarrow{}}$ and $\hat{q}' \xRightarrow{\diamond} [\check{q}]_{\underleftrightarrow{}}$.

Case $k > 0$. Let us assume that $\hat{q} \xrightarrow{\diamond} \check{q}$, and let $a \in hd(\diamond)$ and $\diamond_{tl} \in tl(\diamond, a)$. It follows that there exists a state $q \in Q$ with $\hat{q} \xrightarrow{a} q \xrightarrow{\diamond_{tl}} \check{q}$. Since $\hat{q} \underleftrightarrow{} \hat{q}'$, there exists a state $q' \in Q$ with $\hat{q}' \xrightarrow{a} q'$ and $q \underleftrightarrow{} q'$. Since $|\diamond_{tl}| < k$, we have that $q' \xrightarrow{\diamond_{tl}} [\check{q}]_{\underleftrightarrow{}}$, and consequently $\hat{q}' \xrightarrow{\diamond} [\check{q}]_{\underleftrightarrow{}}$

Now let us make the stronger assumption that $\hat{q} \xRightarrow{\diamond} \check{q}$, and let $q \in Q$ and $a \in A$ s.t. $\hat{q} \xrightarrow{a} q$. Since $\hat{q} \underleftrightarrow{} \hat{q}'$, there exists a state $q' \in Q$ with $\hat{q}' \xrightarrow{a} q'$ and $q \underleftrightarrow{} q'$. Since $\hat{q} \xRightarrow{\diamond} \check{q}$, we have $\diamond_{tl} \in tl(\diamond, a)$ s.t. $q \xRightarrow{\diamond_{tl}} \check{q}$. Since $|\diamond_{tl}| < k$, we have that $q' \xRightarrow{\diamond_{tl}} [\check{q}]_{\underleftrightarrow{}}$, and consequently $\hat{q}' \xRightarrow{\diamond} [\check{q}]_{\underleftrightarrow{}}$

It thus follows that any strong bisimulation relation is also a diamond-equivalence relation.   □

Unlike strong bisimilarity, the weaker equivalence relation of trace-equivalence is not diamond-preserving, as showcased by Example 8. Since trace equivalence and bisimulation are equivalent for deterministic systems, it follows that trace equivalence does preserve diamonds given that the LTS is deterministic.

Example 8. Consider the LTSs below, we have that states p and q are trace equivalent, as $traces(p) = traces(q) = \{ba_1a_2, a_1ba_2, a_1a_2b\}$, however the diamond $b^1 || (a_1a_2)^1$ is not preserved, since the actions a_1 and a_2 are not enabled in the state q'.

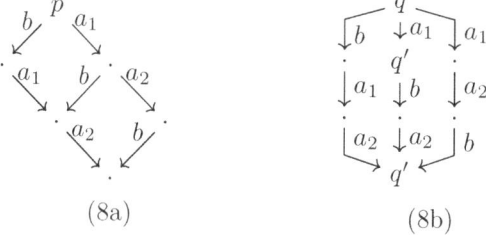

(8a)   (8b)

6   Finding Diamonds

We now outline our algorithm, shown in Algorithm 1, for finding all diamonds in a given LTS. Our algorithm navigates backwards across incoming transitions from a particular origin state $\check{q}$ to find all diamonds converging in $\check{q}$. The *todo* list of states contains states that have a strict diamond-convergence in $\check{q}$. States are added to this list in a breadth-first manner, and removed in FIFO order. Starting with only diamonds consisting of a single action, by repeatedly executing the Step algorithm, shown in Algorithm 2, we check to see if a larger diamond, consisting of one additional action, converging in $\check{q}$ exists. When a larger strict diamond convergence is found, the source state is added to the *todo* list. When the list is empty, the algorithm terminates.

During execution, both algorithms update two mappings. The convergence mapping $\Diamond$, keeps track of any found diamond convergence, i.e. the diamond and resulting state. The strictness mapping x is used to keep track of whether or not the outgoing diamond convergence is a strict diamond convergence. Since multiple strict diamond convergences from a single state cannot occur unless one diamond is a prefix of the other, as a result of Theorem 2, it is sufficient to keep track of this per state, instead of per diamond-convergence. When the algorithm terminates, the mappings $\Diamond$ and x will have been fully populated. When used on every state in the LTS, the $\Diamond$ mapping can subsequently be used to construct an LTS containing precisely all diamond convergences.

Algorithm 1: This algorithm finds all non-empty diamond converging in the state $\check{q}$.

Data: An LTS $\langle Q, q_0, A, \rightarrow \rangle$, and a state $\check{q} \in Q$.

1   $todo \leftarrow [\,]$;

2   **for** $\langle q_{src}, a, \check{q} \rangle \in \rightarrow$ **do**

3   add $\langle a, \check{q} \rangle$ **to** $\Diamond(q_{src})$;

4   **if** $|\{\langle a', q' \rangle \mid q_{src} \xrightarrow{a'} q'\}| = 1$ **then**

5         $x(q_{src}) \leftarrow true$;

6   **add** q_{src} **to** *todo*;

7   **end**

8   **end**

9   **for** $q \in todo$ **do**

10   **pick** $\langle \Diamond_{tl}, q' \rangle \in \Diamond(q)$ *with* $q' = \check{q}$;

11   **for** $\langle \hat{q}, a, q \rangle \in \rightarrow$ **with** $\hat{q} \notin todo$ **do**

12   **if** $Step(\hat{q}, a, q, \Diamond_{tl}, \check{q}) = strict, \Diamond_H$ **then**

13   **add** $\hat{q}$ **to** *todo*;

14   **end**

15   **end**

16 **end**

We now discuss Algorithm 1 in more detail. First, for each incoming transition $q_{src} \xrightarrow{a} \check{q}$, we test to see if this transition is the only outgoing state of the source state. If so, we have that $q_{src} \xRightarrow{a^1} \check{q}$ and q_{src} is added to *todo*, so that we can look for any larger diamond converging in $\check{q}$. Second, the *Step* algorithm, outlined in Algorithm 2, is repeatedly executed to answer the following question: given states

$\hat{q}, q, \check{q} \in Q$, action $a \in A$, and non-empty diamond $\diamond \in \Diamond(A)$ with $\hat{q} \xrightarrow{a} q \overset{\diamond}{\Longrightarrow} \check{q}$, is there some diamond $\diamond_H \in \Diamond(A)$ with $\diamond \in tl(\diamond_H, a)$ and $\hat{q} \xrightarrow{\diamond_H} \check{q}$, and if so is it a strict diamond-convergence. This is also formalised as Theorem 5. If a strict diamond convergence $\hat{q} \overset{\diamond_H}{\Longrightarrow} \check{q}$ is found through the Step algorithm, the source state is added to the *todo* list, so that we can look for an even larger diamond converging in $\check{q}$.

The *Step* algorithm works as follows: First, all hypothesis diamonds are constructed in the set $\Diamond_H$, and tested for diamond convergence in lines 3 through 12. Here, for all $a \in hd(\diamond_H)$, the tail diamonds $tl(\diamond_H, a)$, are added to *todo*. Then all matching outgoing transitions are checked to test if the resulting state has a diamond convergence to $\check{q}$. If *todo* is not empty afterwards, then there is some action $a \in hd(\diamond_H)$ and tail diamond $diamond_{tl} \in tl(\diamond_H, a)$ for which there is no state $q' \in Q$ with $\hat{q} \xrightarrow{a} q' \overset{\diamond_{tl}}{\Longrightarrow}$, and thus $\hat{q} \xrightarrow{\diamond_H} \check{q}$ does not hold.

If b remained *true*, we proceed to lines 14 through 21 to test if the convergence is strict or not. This is done by testing each outgoing transition to see if it has a corresponding tail diamond in the resulting state. Since the algorithm is executed breadth-first, we always have that $\Diamond(q')$ and $x(q')$ have been populated if it does diamond converge in $\check{q}$ with the remaining diamond.

In Theorem 5, we prove that given that the algorithm is executed breadth-first, i.e. $\Diamond$ and x are populated with all smaller diamonds, then the *Step* algorithm will always update $\Diamond$ and x accordingly.

Theorem 5. *Given any LTS $\langle Q, \_, A, \rightarrow \rangle$, states $\hat{q}, q, \check{q} \in Q$, action $a \in A$, and diamond $\diamond \in \Diamond(A)$, s.t. $\hat{q} \xrightarrow{a} q \overset{\diamond}{\Longrightarrow} \check{q}$, and mappings $\Diamond : Q \rightarrow \mathcal{P}(\Diamond(A) \times Q), x : Q \rightarrow \mathbb{B}$, and we have that $\Diamond$ and x are populated with precisely all diamonds originating in q' smaller than $\diamond$, i.e.*

$$\forall_{\diamond' \in \Diamond(A), q' \in Q}. |\diamond'| \leq |\diamond| \Rightarrow (q' \xrightarrow{\diamond'} \check{q} \Leftrightarrow \langle \diamond', \check{q} \rangle \in \Diamond(\hat{q})) \wedge (q' \overset{\diamond'}{\Longrightarrow} \check{q} \Leftrightarrow x(q')), then$$

the following predicate is an invariant for calling the Step$(\hat{q}, a, q, \diamond, \check{q})$ function shown in Algorithm 2: for all states $\hat{q}' \in Q$ we have

$$\forall \langle \diamond', \check{q}' \rangle \in \Diamond(\hat{q}'). \hat{q}' \xrightarrow{\diamond} \check{q}'$$
$$\wedge x(\hat{q}') \Leftrightarrow \exists \langle \diamond', \check{q}' \rangle \in \Diamond(\hat{q}'). \hat{q}' \overset{\diamond'}{\Longrightarrow} \check{q}'.$$

Proof. Let us assume that the invariant holds initially. We note the following predicate is an invariant for the **for**-loops on lines 4 and 6:

$$\neg b \Rightarrow \exists a \in hd(\diamond_H), \diamond_{tl} \in tl(\diamond_H, a). \neg \exists q' \in Q. \hat{q} \xrightarrow{a} q' \overset{\diamond_{tl}}{\Longrightarrow} \check{q}$$

We now prove that when $\langle \diamond_H, \check{q} \rangle$ is added to $\Diamond(\check{q})$ on line 14, we have $\hat{q} \xrightarrow{\diamond_H} \check{q}$. Towards this, let us assume some action $a_i \in hd(\diamond_H)$ and diamond $\diamond_i \in tl(\diamond, a_i)$. Since b is still *true* and we have iterated over all $a \in hd(\diamond_H)$, it follows from the aforementioned loop invariant that $\hat{q} \xrightarrow{\diamond_H} \check{q}$, and thus the first part of the invariant for calling Step$(\hat{q}, a, q, \diamond, \check{q})$ holds.

Second, we prove that when $x(\check{q})$ is set to *true*, we also have $\hat{q} \overset{\diamond_H}{\Longrightarrow} \check{q}$. We note that when the **for**-loop on line 15 completes successfully, i.e. *non-strict* is never returned, we have for any $a' \in A, q' \in Q$ with $\hat{q} \overset{a'}{\to}$ that $a' \in hd(\diamond_H)$ and $q' \overset{\diamond_{tl}}{\Longrightarrow} \check{q}$ with $\diamond_{tl} \in tl(\diamond_H, a')$, and thus we have $\hat{q} \overset{\diamond_H}{\Longrightarrow} \check{q}$.

Lastly, we prove that if *non-strict*, $\diamond_H$ is returned, and $x(\hat{q})$ is not changed, then we have that $\neg(\hat{q} \overset{\diamond_H}{\Longrightarrow} \check{q})$. Since *non-strict* is returned, there exists $a \in A, q' \in Q$ with $\hat{q} \overset{a}{\to} q'$ and either $a' \notin \diamond_H$, $\neg x(q')$, or $\Diamond(q') \cap \{\langle \diamond_{tl}, \check{q} \rangle \mid \diamond_{tl} \in tl(\diamond_H, a')\}$, let a, q' be as such. If $a' \in hd(\diamond_H)$, then $\neg(\hat{q} \overset{\diamond_H}{\Longrightarrow} \check{q})$ trivially follows. Let us thus assume that $a' \in hd(\diamond_H)$ and let us assume towards contradiction, that $\hat{q} \overset{\diamond_H}{\Longrightarrow} \check{q}$. From this assumption it follows that there exists some diamond $\diamond_{tl} \in tl(\diamond_H, a')$ with $q' \overset{\diamond_{tl}}{\Longrightarrow} \check{q}$. Since $|\diamond_{tl}| = |\diamond|$, we have that $\langle \diamond_{tl}, \check{q} \rangle \in \Diamond(q')$ and $x(q')$. This contradicts the **if**-condition evaluating to *true*, and thus we have $\neg(\hat{q} \overset{\diamond_H}{\Longrightarrow} \check{q})$. $\qquad \square$

Algorithm 2: The Step algorithm finds the possible (exclusive) diamond in a given state, given that only said diamond is available in the given state.

Data: An LTS $\langle Q, q_0, A, \to \rangle$, a state $q_i \in Q$, states $\hat{q}, q, \check{q} \in Q$, action $a \in A$, and non-empty diamond $\diamond \in \Diamond(A)_{\backslash \varnothing}$, s.t. $\hat{q} \overset{a}{\to} q \overset{\diamond}{\Longrightarrow} \check{q}$, and mappings $\Diamond : Q \to \mathcal{P}(\Diamond(A) \times Q), x : Q \to \mathbb{B}$

1   $\diamond_H \leftarrow \{\diamond_H \in \Diamond(A) \mid \diamond \in tl(\diamond_H, a)\}$;
2   **for** $\diamond_H \in \diamond_H$ **do**
3 | $b \leftarrow true$;
4 | **for** $a \in hd(\diamond_H)$ **do**
5 | | $todo \leftarrow tl(\diamond_H, a)$;
6 | | **for** $q' \in Q$ **where** $\hat{q} \overset{a_i}{\to} q' \wedge x(q')$ **do**
7 | | | $todo \leftarrow todo \setminus \{\diamond \in \Diamond(A) \mid \langle \diamond, \check{q} \rangle \in \Diamond(q')\}$
8 | | **end**
9 | | **if** $todo \neq \emptyset$ **then**
10 | | | $b \leftarrow false$;
11 | | **end**
12 | **end**
13 | **if** b **then**
14 | | add $\langle \diamond_H, \check{q} \rangle$ to $\Diamond(\hat{q})$;
15 | | **for** $\langle \hat{q}, a', q' \rangle \in \to$ **do**
16 | | | **if** $a' \notin hd(\diamond_H) \vee \neg x(q') \vee \Diamond(q') \cap \{\langle \diamond_{tl}, \check{q} \rangle \mid \diamond_{tl} \in tl(\diamond_H, a')\} = \emptyset$ **then**
17 | | | | **return** *non-strict*, $\diamond_H$;
18 | | | **end**
19 | | **end**
20 | | $x(\hat{q}) \leftarrow true$;
21 | | **return** *strict*, $\diamond_H$;
22 | **end**
23 **end**
24 **return** *false*;

A simple proof-of-concept implementation of the algorithm in python is available together with some examples on [12]. In Fig. 1 we showcase a small toy LTS before applying our algorithm, which finds the given diamond and replaces it with a single transition. The algorithm was also used on a model of Sliding window protocol, this reduced the number of transitions in the model from 57k transitions to 50k transitions.

Whilst further work towards both space and time complexity of said algorithms is required, we believe the time complexity of the *Step* to be $\mathcal{O}(\lambda^3)$, and the time complexity of the traversal algorithm to be $\mathcal{O}(m * \lambda^3 + n)$, where m is the number of transitions, n the number of states, and λ is the largest diamond width in the given LTS. Since λ is generally insignificant compared to m, the algorithm has a general runtime of $\mathcal{O}(m + n)$.

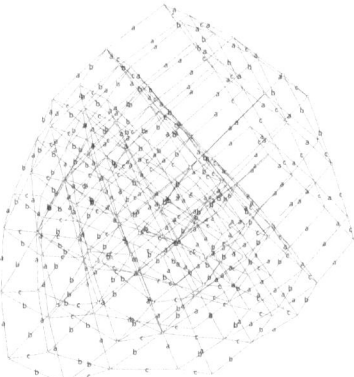

Fig. 1. The diamond $a^3||c^1||(ab)^2||(bcc)^1$ before reduction.

7   Conclusion and Future Work

We have formally defined the notion of a diamond and when a diamond occurs in a given LTS. We have proven important properties related to what we desire of the diamond-convergence relation, i.e. we have shown that diamonds contain all possible interleavings of their sequences and that a maximal diamond in a given state can safely be replaced with a single diamond transition. Additionally, we have proven that strong bisimulation is the precise equivalence relation that preserves diamonds for arbitrary LTSs. Lastly, we have introduced a novel algorithm, with correctness proof, for finding all maximal diamonds in any LTS.

The algorithm and techniques introduced in this paper capture precisely all diamond convergences in any arbitrary LTS. We stress that capturing precisely all such convergences is a novel part of this work that is not covered by partial order reduction techniques, which present the state-of-the-art techniques for dealing with such patterns. In particular, not only the presence of a diamond convergence but also the lack thereof can provide additional insight to the user.

We believe the following continuations to be of particular interest for future work: In model-based techniques, it is convenient to abstract away internal operations using the τ action. It would be intuitive to further refine the theory surrounding diamonds in relation to the special τ action and equivalence relations associated with it. Other future work exists in further analysis of the time and space complexity of the introduced algorithm, and further optimizations. In particular, when calculating the diamond convergences for every state, transitions are often considered multiple times. Reducing repeated work could be a prime candidate for optimization.

References

1. Baier, C., Katoen, J.P.: Principles of Model Checking. MIT Press (2008)
2. Cleaveland, R., Sokolsky, O.: Equivalence and preorder checking for finite-state systems. In: Handbook of Process Algebra, pp. 391–424 (2001)
3. Gallager, R.G., Humblet, P.A., Spira, P.M.: A distributed algorithm for minimum-weight spanning trees. ACM Trans. Program. Lang. Syst. **5**(1), 66–77 (1983). https://doi.org/10.1145/357195.357200
4. Godefroid, P.: Partial-Order Methods for the Verification of Concurrent Systems: An Approach to the State-Explosion Problem. Springer (1996)
5. Groote, J.F., van der Hofstad, R., Raffelsieper, M.: On the random structure of behavioural transition systems. Sci. Comput. Program. **128**, 51–67 (2016)
6. Groote, J.F., Van Ham, F.: Interactive visualization of large state spaces. Int. J. Softw. Tools Technol. Transf. **8**, 77–91 (2006)
7. Grumberg, O., Clarke, E., Peled, D.: Model checking. In: International Conference on Foundations of Software Technology and Theoretical Computer Science. Springer, Heidelberg (1999)
8. Herman, I., Melançon, G., Marshall, M.S.: Graph visualization and navigation in information visualization: a survey. IEEE Trans. Visual Comput. Graphics **6**(1), 24–43 (2000)
9. Hopcroft, J.E., Motwani, R., Ullman, J.D.: Introduction to automata theory, languages, and computation. ACM SIGACT News **32**(1), 60–65 (2001)
10. Hopcroft, J.E., Ullman, J.D.: Formal Languages and Their Relation to Automata. Addison-Wesley Longman Publishing Co., Inc., USA (1969)
11. Huhn, M., Niebert, P., Wehrheim, H.: Partial order reductions for bisimulation checking. In: Foundations of Software Technology and Theoretical Computer Science: 18th Conference, Chennai, India, 17–19 December 1998, Proceedings 18, pp. 271–282. Springer (1998)
12. Jilissen, K., van Spaendonck, F.: LTS diamond reduction algorithm (2025). https://doi.org/10.5281/zenodo.14980765
13. Kripke, S.A.: Semantical considerations on modal logic. Acta Philos. Fennica **16** (1963)
14. Milner, R.: Functions as processes. Math. Struct. Comput. Sci. **2**(2) (1992)
15. Milner, R.: Communicating and Mobile Systems: The Pi Calculus. Cambridge University Press (1999)
16. Olderog, E.R., Hoare, C.: Specification-oriented semantics for communicating processes. Acta Inform. **23**, 9–66 (1986)

17. Park, D.: Concurrency and automata on infinite sequences. In: Deussen, P. (ed.) Theoretical Computer Science, pp. 167–183. Springer, Heidelberg (1981)
18. Park, D.: Concurrency and automata on infinite sequences. In: Theoretical Computer Science: 5th GI-Conference, Karlsruhe, 23–25 March 1981, pp. 167–183. Springer (2005)
19. Peled, D.: All from one, one for all: on model checking using representatives. In: Courcoubetis, C. (ed.) Computer Aided Verification, pp. 409–423. Springer, Heidelberg (1993)
20. Peterson, J.L.: Petri nets. ACM Comput. Surv. (CSUR) 9(3), 223–252 (1977)
21. Pretorius, A.J., Van Wijk, J.J.: Visual analysis of multivariate state transition graphs. IEEE Trans. Visual Comput. Graphics 12(5), 685–692 (2006)
22. Valmari, A.: Stubborn sets for reduced state space generation. In: Advances in Petri Nets 1990 10, pp. 491–515. Springer (1991)
23. Van Glabbeek, R.J.: The linear time-branching time spectrum I. The semantics of concrete, sequential processes. In: Handbook of Process Algebra, pp. 3–99. Elsevier (2001)
24. Van Glabbeek, R.J., Weijland, W.P.: Branching time and abstraction in bisimulation semantics. J. ACM (JACM) 43(3), 555–600 (1996)
25. Van Ham, F., Van De Wetering, H., Van Wijk, J.J.: Visualization of state transition graphs. In: IEEE Symposium on Information Visualization, INFOVIS 2001, pp. 59–66. IEEE (2001)
26. Van Ieperen, G.: Visualisation of large labelled transition systems. Master thesis, Eindhoven University of Technology (2021)

Portability of Optimizations from SC to TSO

Akshay Gopalakrishnan$^{(\boxtimes)}$ [iD] and Clark Verbrugge [iD]

McGill University, Montreal, Canada
akshay.akshay@mail.mcgill.ca, clump@cs.mcgill.ca

Abstract. It is well recognized that the safety of compiler optimizations is at risk in a concurrent context. Existing approaches primarily rely on context-free thread-local guarantees, and prohibit optimizations that introduce a *data-race*. However, compilers utilize global context-specific information, exposing safe optimizations that may violate such guarantees as well as introduce a race. Such optimizations need to individually be proven safe for each language model. An alternate approach to this would be proving them safe for an intuitive model (like interleaving semantics), and then determine their portability across other concurrent models. In this paper, we address this problem of porting across models of concurrency. We first identify a global guarantee on optimizations portable from *Sequential Consistency (SC)* to *Total Store Order (TSO)*. Our guarantee is in the form of constraints specifying the syntactic changes an optimization must not incur. We then show these constraints correlate to prohibiting the introduction of *triangular races*, a subset of data-race relevant to TSO. We conclude by showing how such race-inducing optimizations relate to porting across *Strong Release Acquire (SRA)*, a known causally consistent memory model.

Keywords: Memory Consistency · Compiler Optimizations · Correctness · Sequential Consistency · Total Store Order

1 Introduction

Compilers today are primarily responsible for the performance of any program. This is mainly due to plethora of optimizations they perform, which help reduce computation and memory costs significantly. However, performing them on concurrent programs has greatly been restricted due to safety concerns. The core reason for this is the underlying concurrent semantics (memory model), which break the guarantees of functional behavior of programs assumed by compilers [1].

Existing efforts have no doubt addressed this up to some extent [18]. Optimizations which can be performed are subject to the underlying thread-local guarantees provided by the model. For instance, any code motion involving shared memory accesses are prohibited under Sequential Consistency (*SC*).

© The Author(s), under exclusive license to Springer Nature Switzerland AG 2026
P. Rümmer and Z. Wu (Eds.): TASE 2025, LNCS 15841, pp. 122–140, 2026.
https://doi.org/10.1007/978-3-031-98208-8_8

Whereas any motion involving only write-read reordering is permitted under Total Store Order (*TSO*). Optimizations are also prohibited from introducing data-races, and programs are often required to be *data-race-free*.

However, writing race-free programs is hard, and locating data-race errors in a program is often difficult, let alone debug. To add, the race-free restriction may be too strict for compilers, and weaker guarantees are shown to suffice [16,20]. Moreover, thread-local restrictions can be overly conservative, and may prove detrimental when designing optimizations leveraging aspects of concurrency.

As an example, consider the program P as described in Fig. 1, where y is shared memory initialized to 0, and c is thread-local. ... represent any thread-local computation in each thread. First thread writes to y, whereas the second spins until it observes the updated value.

Fig. 1. Optimizations leveraging thread/memory fairness and value range analysis.

From the compiler's perspective, the following observation can be made, subject to a fair scheduler

- The second thread will eventually see the updated value of y (memory fairness [12]).
- The second thread will only see the updated value of y as 1 (value range analysis over y).
- Thus, $while(!c)$ will eventually fail to hold (thread fairness).

With this, the compiler can assert spinning on the loop may not be required if the updated value of y is guaranteed to be in memory before it is read. To do this, it can simply sequence (inline) the write $y = 1$ to take place before both the threads[1]. This is shown as P' in Fig. 1. Further, it can perform simple store-to-load forwarding, which results in the loop condition to be false from the start. This gives us the optimized program P'' in Fig. 1. Such an optimization is safe under both *SC* and *TSO* semantics, the original and the optimized program both terminate with the same state of memory $c = 1$.

However, the situation is slightly different if the optimization is done in the presence of another concurrent context. In Fig. 2 left, the original program cannot

---

[1] As a C code, this would translate to creating a thread which does $y = 1$ followed by creating two threads which do the other computations.

terminate with $a = 1 \wedge b = 0 \wedge c = 1 \wedge d = 0$, both under *TSO* and *SC* semantics. The thread-local state $c = 1 \wedge d = 0$ implies $y = 1$ is visible to all threads before $x = 1$. Hence, the reads to x and y done after loop termination cannot observe the stale value of y (as $b = 0$ shows).

$$\begin{array}{l} a = x; \\ b = y; \\ \dots \end{array} \;\Big\|\; \begin{array}{l} x = 1; \\ \dots \end{array} \;\Big\|\; \mathbf{P} \quad \longmapsto \quad \begin{array}{l} a = x; \\ b = y; \\ \dots \end{array} \;\Big\|\; \begin{array}{l} x = 1; \\ \dots \end{array} \;\Big\|\; \mathbf{P'} \quad \longmapsto \quad \begin{array}{l} a = x; \\ b = y; \\ \dots \end{array} \;\Big\|\; \begin{array}{l} x = 1; \\ \dots \end{array} \;\Big\|\; \mathbf{P''}$$

$(i) \qquad\qquad (ii) \qquad\qquad (iii)$

Fig. 2. Under different program context, optimization to P'' is unsafe under *TSO*.

The same above reasoning is true for both the optimized programs (middle and right) under *SC* semantics, thereby disallowing the outcome in question. However, the situation is different under *TSO*: the program in Fig. 2 middle can exhibit the outcome [21]. Reading $c = 1$ from $y = 1$ does not enforce a global ordering between the writes $x = 1$ and $y = 1$[2]. The same reasoning applies for the final optimized program (Fig. 2 right). Thus, the same optimization is unsafe when considered under a different program context.

Examples like above represent the kind of global optimizations that can be permitted for *TSO*. However, as we see, doing them depends on the right program context. Identifying a precise constraint over *all possible* program contexts specific to *TSO* may be non-trivial.

We adopt an alternate approach that may be more suitable to put into practice. We instead determine constraints on optimizations which are portable from *SC* to *TSO*. Working towards identifying such a constraint has led to the following contributions

1. We find a suitable thread-global syntactic constraint on optimizations that do not eliminate/introduce writes.
2. We show that our constraint correlates to disallowing optimizations resulting in a new *triangular-race*, a subset of *data-races*.
3. We discover that porting *SC* optimizations that introduce such *triangular races* in addition translates to porting across a Causally Consistent memory model known as Strong Release Acquire (SRA) [11].

The associated proofs and auxiliary results of our contributions are provided in the extended version [8].

[2] Operationally, the read value can be fetched from the FIFO write buffer where $y = 1$ is first committed. The buffer can be flushed at any latter time, and only then would imply a global memory ordering with $x = 1$.

2   Preliminaries

We give a brief overview of the formal elements involved in this work. Section 2.1 introduces the pre-trace model, and Sect. 2.2 the representation of optimizations, both from our previous work [10]. Section 2.3 introduces the axiomatic models for *SC* and *TSO* we use.

The language is given in Fig. 3. A program *prog* is a parallel composition of individual sequential programs *sp*, each of which are associated with a thread id t and a sequence of actions p. An action is either a memory event *st* or a conditional branch code block (for simplicity, loops are not included). Memory events can be a read from $(a = x)$, write to $(x = e)$, or read-modify-write $(rmw(x, a, v))$ to some shared memory x. Write events are also associated with a value v or some thread-local variable a (for simplicity we keep it as integers). Let *tid* be a mapping from memory events to their associated thread-id.

$$prog := sp\|prog \mid sp$$
$$sp := t : p$$
$$p := st \mid p;p; \mid \text{if}(cond) \text{ then } \{p\} \text{ else } \{p\}$$
$$st := a = x; \mid x = v; \mid rmw(x, a, v);$$

$$e := a \mid v$$
$$cond := \text{true} \mid \text{false} \mid a == v \mid a! = v$$
$$domains := v \in \mathbb{Z} \mid t \in (\mathbb{N} \cup \{0\})$$

Fig. 3. Programs - Adapted from [10]

2.1   Pre-trace Model

The pre-trace model at its core, reflects the compiler's perspective of a program (see [10] for full formal details). Programs are viewed in their abstract forms, with syntactic order (po) and conditional dependencies (Fig. 4 middle). As opposed to traditional mapping of abstract programs to concurrent executions, they are first mapped to a set of pre-traces instead (Fig. 4 left and right).

A pre-trace is a sub-program without conditionals that contains a possible execution path of the actual program. In Fig. 4, pre-trace $P1$ (left) is derived by taking the left conditional branch path, whereas $P2$ (right) is derived by choosing the right. Notice that both $P1$, $P2$ do not have the read values restricted, and thus, represent an over-approximation of the actual program behavior[3].

Notations. Let po(P) represent the syntactic order in P. Let $st(P), w(P)$, $r(P), u(P)$ represent the set of events/write/read/read-modify-write events respectively of pre-trace P ($u(P) = r(P) \cap w(P)$). The above can be filtered via an optional subscript *loc*, giving the set of events operating on the same shared memory *loc*.

---

[3] Synthesizing pre-traces for a given language from abstract programs would also require the language's appropriate sequential semantics. The results in this paper are independent of the choice of such semantics.

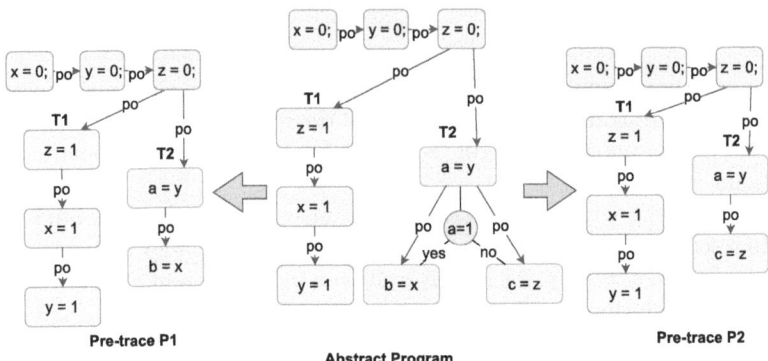

Fig. 4. Abstract program (middle) mapped to its possible pre-traces P1 (left) and P2 (right) (Adapted from Fig 11 of [10]).

Outcome. To represent executions E, each pre-trace P is associated with a reads-from set rf $(w_{loc}(P) \times r_{loc}(P))$, denoting the source (write event) of the read value, and memory order set mo $(w(P) \times w(P))$, denoting the order in which writes are propagated to main memory. Let $p(E)$ give the pre-trace of E and $\mathrm{rf}(E), \mathrm{mo}(E)$ give the rf, mo relations of E respectively. A candidate execution E (like Fig. 5 $E1, E2$) of a pre-trace is one where

- Each read has some value - $\forall r \in r(p(E))$. $\exists w \in w(p(E))$. $(w,r) \in \mathrm{rf}(E)$.
- Each read has exactly one source write - $(w,r) \in \mathrm{rf}(E) \wedge (w',r) \in \mathrm{rf}(E) \implies w = w'$.
- Propagation order is total - $\mathrm{mo}(E)$ total order.
- Propagation order per-shared location is strict $\forall loc$. $\mathrm{mo}_{loc}(E)$ strict.

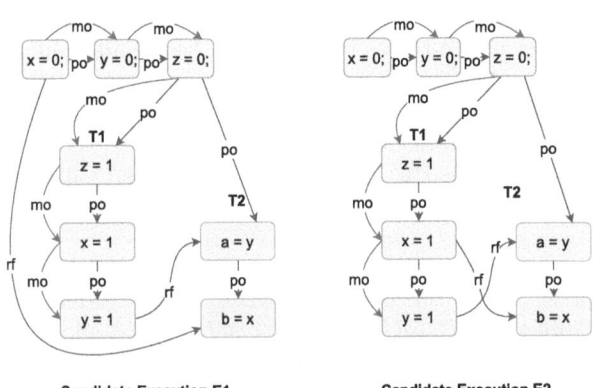

Fig. 5. Pre-trace $P1$ from Fig. 4 annotated with rf and mo edges to represent a two possible candidate execution $E1$ and $E2$ (Adapted from Fig 12 of [10]).

An *observable-behavior* of a candidate execution is the final state of memory (rf relation(s) and mo maximal per-location). $\langle P \rangle$ represents the set of all candidate executions of pre-trace P.

Memory Model. The concurrency semantics or memory model are a set of constraints (consistency rules) on these candidate executions. They are typically in the form of acyclic/irreflexivity constraints on the relations between memory events in the execution. Executions that adhere to the rules are deemed *consistent*, whereas those which do not are *inconsistent*. For example, consider the candidate executions $E1, E2$ from Fig. 5. $E1$ indicates a clear 'message passing' violation: on seeing $a = 1$, $b = 0$ should not be possible. A memory model prohibiting such message passing violations can be '$(\text{rf}^{-1} \cup \text{mo}_{loc} \cup \text{po} \cup \text{rf})$ *acyclic*'[4]. With this constraint, $E1$ is inconsistent, however, $E2$ is consistent.

Notations $[\![P]\!]_M$ represents the set of candidate executions of pre-trace P consistent under memory model M. $I\langle P \rangle_M$ represents the inconsistent set. A memory model M is weaker than B (weak$\langle M, B \rangle$) if the set of consistent executions under B is lesser than those under M ($\forall P . [\![P]\!]_B \subseteq [\![P]\!]_M$).

2.2 Optimization as Transformation-Effects

Pre-traces are useful in decomposing an optimization into several *transformation-effects*, each on a different pre-trace of the source program. These effects are defined as syntactic changes, involving a set of program orders removed/added (po$^-$, po$^+$) and set of memory events removed/added (st^-, st^+). A transformation effect tr modifying P to P' is denoted as $P \mapsto_{tr} P'$. Recalling the example from Fig. 1, the optimizations have at least the following effects for each pre-trace[5].

1. $P \mapsto_{tr1} P'$ - $(st^- = st^+ = \text{po}^- = \phi) \wedge (\text{po}^- = \{(y = 1, c = y), (y = 1, a = x)\})$.
2. $P' \mapsto_{tr2} P''$ - $(st^- = \{c = y\}) \wedge (st^+ = \text{po}^+ = \phi) \wedge (\text{po}^- = \{(y = 1, c = y), (c = y, a = x)\})$.

Safety. An optimization is considered *safe* for a program under a memory model M if the set of consistent observable behaviors do not increase. At the level of pre-traces, an effect $P \mapsto_{tr} P'$ is safe if the *set of behaviors* specified by $[\![P]\!]_M$ does not increase. Two executions $E1, E2$ have the *same observable behavior* ($E1 \sim E2$) if the set of shared memory read/write(s) common to both have same rf/mo relations respectively[6]. This is used to compare set of behaviors: $A \sqsubseteq B$ denotes a set of executions A are contained in B. Thus, a transformation-effect $P1 \mapsto_{tr} P2$ is safe under memory model M ($psafe(M, tr, P)$), if $[\![P']\!]_M \sqsubseteq [\![P]\!]_M$.

---

[4] Note that this is not indicative of the precise constraint for message passing violations; it prohibits all executions as rf $\cup$ rf^{-1} is cyclic. See Definition 1(d) for the correct one.

[5] At least is used to denote that a loop results in multiple pre-traces, one for every number of iteration.

[6] Note that we relate the entire mo relation, not just the maximal elements.

2.3   Axiomatic Version of SC and TSO

We adopt the declarative (axiomatic) style of both *SC* and *TSO* described using irreflexivity constraints [13].

Relational notations. Given a binary relation R, let R^{-1}, $R^?$, R^+ and $[E]$ represent inverse, reflexive, transitive closure and identity relation over a set E respectively. Let $R1; R2$ represent sequential composition of two binary relations. A relation $R1; R2$ *forms a cycle* (or simply $R1; R2$ *cycle*) if there exists a cyclic path $[a]; R1; [b]; R2; [a]$ which is non-empty (reflexive). Lastly, we say 'we have $[a]; R1; [b]$' if the relation is non-empty.

Additional Relations. Let *read-from-internal* (rfi) represent the subset of rf such that both the write and read are of the same thread. Let *reads-from-external* (rfe) be the rest. Let *happens-before* (hb) be $(\text{po} \cup \text{rf})^+$. Let *memory-order-loc* (mo_{loc}) represent the memory order between writes to same memory, and $\text{mo}_{!loc}$ the rest. Further, let *memory-order-ext* (mo_{ext}) represent the memory order between writes not ordered by any hb relation ($\text{mo} \setminus (\text{mo} \cap \text{hb})$). Finally, let *reads-before* (rb) represent the sequential composition $\text{rf}^{-1}; \text{mo}_{loc}$.

Using the above elements, *SC* has the following set of constraints [13].

Definition 1. *An execution E is consistent under SC if the following rules hold*

a) *mo strict total order.*	b) *hb irreflexive.*	c) *mo; hb irreflexive.*
d) *rb; hb irreflexive.*	e) *rb; mo irreflexive.*	f) *rb; mo; hb irreflexive.*

and the fragment of *TSO* not involving fences have the following set of constraints.

Definition 2. *An execution E is consistent under TSO if the following rules hold*

a) *mo strict total order.*	b) *hb irreflexive.*
c) *mo; hb irreflexive.*	d) *rb; hb irreflexive.*
e) *rb; mo irreflexive.*	f) *rb; mo; rfe; po irreflexive.*
g) *rb; mo; [u]; po irreflexive.*	

We can, for *TSO*, consider fences equivalent to a read-modify-write to a shared location not used [11,13]. Note that *TSO* and *SC* have Rules (a) through (e) the same, with Rule (f) of *SC* being divided into two rules (f) and (g).

3   Optimizations: From SC to TSO

We now address the porting problem using transformation effects over pre-traces. Section 3.1 states our desired property to be proven over effects. Section 3.2 goes over identifying the constraints over optimizations that enable proving said property. Section 3.3 states our main result, with examples giving intuition behind the proof. Section 3.4 relates our result to triangular races and causal consistency.

3.1   From Optimizations to Effects

Our objective of identifying a set of optimizations portable to TSO can instead be viewed at the level of effects. An optimization of a program is portable from memory model B to M if all its constituent safe effects under B are also safe in M. Lifting this notion to any program, we converge to the following property between models defined in [10][7].

Definition 3. *Memory model M is* complete w.r.t. B (comp$\langle M, B \rangle$) *if*

$$\forall \, P \mapsto_{tr} P' \; . \; psafe(B, tr, P) \implies psafe(M, tr, P).$$

Proving comp$\langle M, B \rangle$ between models is infeasible by enumerating the set of effects and pre-traces, as both are unbounded. Proving the contrapositive however, can be done using the constraints specific to B and M. At its core, it requires showing $psafe(B, tr, P)$ to be false for any tr such that $\neg psafe(M, tr, P)$. The following lemma quantifies all such tr[8].

Lemma 1. *Consider memory models M, B with weak$\langle M, B \rangle$ and a transformation-effect $P \mapsto_{tr} P'$ with $\langle P' \rangle \sqsubseteq \langle P \rangle$. Then tr is unsafe under M but safe under B if for every $E' \in \langle P' \rangle$ such that*

$$E' \in [\![P']\!]_M \wedge \nexists E \in [\![P]\!]_M \; . \; E \sim E'.$$

we have

a) $\forall \, E \in \langle P \rangle \, . \, E \sim E' \implies E \in I\langle P \rangle_M.$ b) $E' \in I\langle P' \rangle_B.$

Requirements for M, B, tr. Lemma 1 relies on two conditions. First, M must be weaker than B. This is true when $M = TSO$ and $B = SC$ [21]. Second, we require $\langle P' \rangle \sqsubseteq \langle P \rangle$. Intuitively, it means that any behavior P', without any memory model constraints must also be observable in P. This disallows write-introduction effects: wi $(st^+ \cap w(P') = \phi)$, forming our first constraint over tr[9]. We believe this to be a reasonable constraint, given that any write introduced may be read, leading to an unobservable outcome in the original program.

3.2   Identifying Constraint over Effects

The example from Fig. 2 shows global SC optimizations are portable to TSO only under appropriate program context. Instead of identifying such contexts, we can identify constraints on the set of effects that make it unsafe to port. These constraints will be a mixture of the original program context and the effects.

We start by viewing the same optimization at the level of pre-traces in Fig. 6. The optimizations $tr1$ and $tr2$ have the following constraints over their corresponding effects.

---

[7] The origins behind Def 3 stem from preserving safety of optimizations across memory models that are incrementally built by adding desired optimizations.

[8] While Theorem 4.4 [10] addresses the same issue, its core proof relies on our formulated lemma.

[9] This can be inferred simply by using the $\sim$ relation used to compare two executions having the same observable behavior.

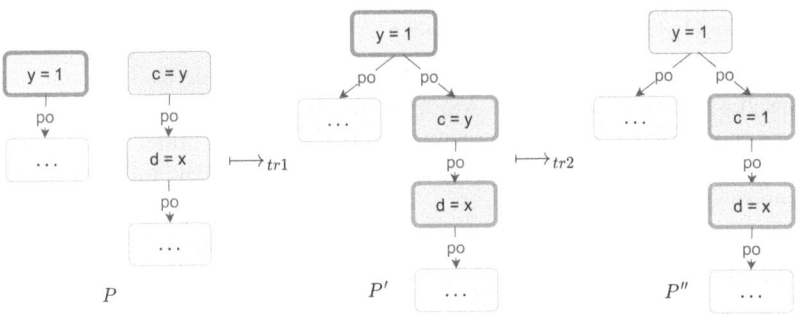

Fig. 6. Example optimization of Fig. 1 revisited as effects over pre-traces.

1. $P \mapsto_{tr1} P'$ - $(y = 1, c = y), (y = 1, d = x) \in po^+$.
2. $P' \mapsto_{tr2} P''$ - $(c = y \in st^-) \wedge ((y = 1, c = y), (c = y, d = x) \in po^-)$.

We observe that the effect $tr2$ is a form of *read-after-write elimination*, which is safe under *TSO* irrespective of program context [21]. Thus, the constraint is relevant over $tr1$.

Constraint 1. *The effect $P \mapsto P'$ may be unsafe under TSO if the following hold*

    a) $(w_y, r_y), (w_y, r_x) \in po^+$.   *b)* $(r_y, r_x) \notin po^-$.

We can further refine this constraint, noting that without the concurrent context in Fig. 2, $tr1$ is safe under *TSO*. Specifically, we note the context $x = 1$, and two candidate executions $E \sim E'$ of the pre-traces as in Fig. 7. Notice that E is inconsistent under *TSO* as $[d = x]$; rb; mo; rfe; po forms a cycle. On the other hand E' is consistent as $[d = x]$; rb; mo; po cycles are permitted under *TSO*. This implies the subset of $P \mapsto_{tr1} P'$, having a write $w_x \in st(P)$ is unsafe under *TSO*.

Constraint 2. *The effect $P \mapsto P'$ may be unsafe under TSO if the following hold*

    a) $w_x, w_y, r_x \notin st^-$.   *b)* $(w_x, r_x), (r_x, w_x) \notin po^+$.
    c) $(w_x, w_y), (w_y, w_x) \notin po^+$.

Constraints 1,2 together are still not precise enough to categorize the effect we desire. This can be seen in the following variation of P' in Fig. 8. Since $x = 2$ is in between $y = 1$ and $a = x$, the execution is inconsistent under *TSO*. We either have mo; hb cycle ($E1'$) or rb; hb cycle ($E2'$), both of which violate the constraints of *TSO*. Similar is the case if the write $x = 2$ is replaced by a read-modify-write u instead, giving us rb; mo; $[u]$; po cycle for $E2'$. This leaves us with the effect $tr1$

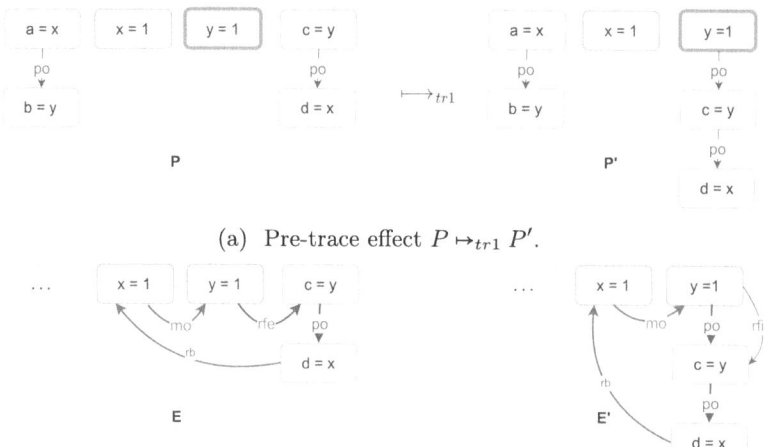

(a) Pre-trace effect $P \mapsto_{tr1} P'$.

(b) Candidate executions of P and P' for the outcome $a = 1 \wedge b = 0 \wedge c = 1 \wedge d = 0$.

Fig. 7. Example optimization of Fig. 2 revisited as effects over pre-traces.

being safe under TSO^{10}. Thus, an additional constraint is needed to ensure the effect should not cause any $w'_x(P) \cup u(P)$ to be in syntactic order between w_y and r_x.

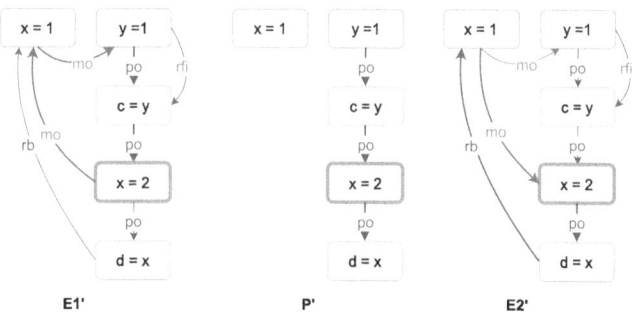

Fig. 8. A variation of effect $tr1$ which is safe under TSO.

Constraint 3. *The effect* $P \mapsto P'$ *may be unsafe under TSO if the following hold*

a) $\forall e \in (w_x(P) \cup u(P)) \,.\, (w_y, e), (e, r_x) \in po(P) \implies (e, r_x) \in po^-$.

b) $\nexists e \in (w_x(P) \cup u(P) \cup st^+) \,.\, (w_y, e), (e, r_x) \in po^+$.

---

[10] It is easy to see the other candidate executions of P and P' support this claim.

We finally have our constraint on effects, which we combine to define the effects unsafe under *TSO* as per program context.

Definition 4. *A transformation-effect $P \mapsto P'$ involves* tso *unsafe write-read inlining (tuwri) if it satisfies Constraints 1,2,3 for P having $w_y, r_y, w_x, r_x \in st(P)$ with*

a) $(w_y, r_y), (r_y, w_y) \notin po(P)$.   b) $(w_y, w_x), (w_x, w_y) \notin po(P)$.
c) $(w_x, r_x), (r_x, w_x) \notin po(P)$.   d) $(w_x, r_y), (r_y, w_x) \notin po(P)$.
e) $(r_y, r_x) \in po(P)$.

or Constraints 2, 3 for P having $w_x, r_x, w_y, e \in st(P)$ with

a) $(w_y, r_x) \in po(P)$.   b) $(w_x, w_y), (w_y, w_x) \notin po(P)$.
c) $(w_x, r_x), (r_x, w_x) \notin po(P)$.   d) $(w_y, e), (e, r_x) \in po(P)$.
e) $e \in (w_x(P) \cup u(P))$.

3.3   Main Result

We now formally state our result, followed by explaining the steps taken to prove it. For simplicity, we consider *tr* to have no write-elimination effects: we $(st^- \cap w(P) = \phi)$, deferring it to future work.

Theorem 1. *For transformation-effects $P \mapsto_{tr} P'$ not involving we, wi and tuwri, we have $comp\langle TSO, SC \rangle$.*

Identifying Cycles in E, E' The proof involves relying on the following lemma, which lists the minimal cycles that must exist to violate any constraint of *SC*

Lemma 2. *For any execution E inconsistent under SC, at least one of the following is true.*

a) *mo non-strict.*   b) *mo; po cycle.*
c) *rfi; po cycle.*   d) *rb; po cycle.*
e) *rb; rfe; po cycle.*   f) *mo; rfe; po cycle.*
g) *rb; hb; rfe; po cycle.*   h) *rb; mo cycle.*
i) *mo; rf cycle.*   j) *rb; mo_{ext}; rfe; po cycle.*
k) *rb; mo; po cycle.*

Proposition 1. *Any execution E' consistent under TSO but inconsistent under SC has $rb; mo_{ext}; po$ cycle.*

Next, since E must be inconsistent under *TSO*, every cycle except a subset of (k) from Lemma 2 can be true. Specifically, (k), from Def 2, reduces to $rb; mo; [u]; po$ cycle in E.

We now proceed with the proof using Lemma 1 where $B = SC$ and $M = TSO$. We go case-wise over each cycle possible in E, comparing them with those in $E' \sim E$, and showing that it is possible to derive an $E'_t \in \llbracket P' \rrbracket_{SC}$ such that $\forall E_t \in \langle P \rangle . E_t \sim E'_t \implies E_t \in I\langle P \rangle_{SC}$. This simply implies $\neg psafe(SC, tr, P)$, thereby proving our result by contradiction.

Cases of Same Memory Deordering. For example Fig. 9 is a case where $[a = x]$; rb; po is a cycle in E, whereas $[a = x]$; rb; mo_{ext}; po is a cycle in E'. We can extract the information about po from both E and E', to identify an effect which we can instead prove to be unsafe under SC. Since we have $st^- \cap w(P)$, we can infer that $P \mapsto_{tr} P'$ incurs same memory write-read de-ordering $(x = 1, a = x) \in \text{po}^-$. Such a de-ordering we show to be unsafe under SC independent of the whole program context, thus, addressing such cycles in general.

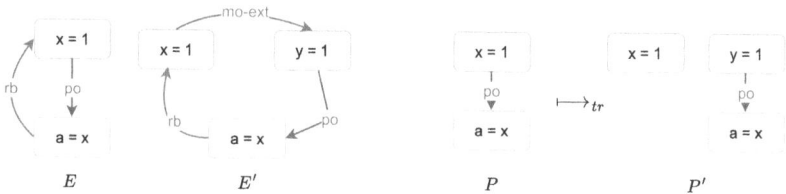

Fig. 9. Executions E, E' imply same memory write-read de-ordering effect (right).

Deriving Alternate E, E'. Other cases can be more involved, and may require extracting information on mo and rf in addition to po from E and E'. For instance, take the case where $[a = x]$; rb; rfe; $[b = x]$; po cycle in E as in Fig. 10 middle. If $P \mapsto_{tr} P'$ has $\{a = x, b = x\} \in st^-$, then we can show there will always exist some $E_t \in [\![P]\!]_{TSO}$ such that $E_t \sim E'$. This violates our premise, thereby addressing all three cases[11].

For the case where both reads exist in P', we have same memory read-read de-ordering $(b = x, a = x) \in \text{po}^-$. To prove this is unsafe under SC, we use information from rf and mo relations in E'. We show it is always possible to manipulate $\text{mo}(E')$ and $\text{rf}(E')$ relations to derive some $E'_t \in [\![P']\!]_{SC}$ for which there does not exist another $E_t \in [\![P]\!]_{SC}$ such that $E_t \sim E'_t$. This by definition implies $\neg psafe(SC, tr, P)$[12]. An example manipulating $\text{mo}(E')$ is shown in Fig. 10 E' (left) and corresponding E'_t (right) derived by changing $[x = 1]$; mo_{ext}; $[y = 1]$ to $[y = 1]$; mo_{ext}; $[x = 1]$ instead. We show that *reversing* such mo_{ext} relations does not alter the cycle involving $a = x$ in E, yet removing it from E'.

Usage of Constraint tnwri. An example where the constraint Definition 4 is required is shown in Fig. 11(a). We just have $[a=x]$; rb; $[x=2]$; mo_{ext}; $[y=1]$; rfe; $[a=y]$; po; $[b = x]$ cycle in E and $[a = x]$; rb; $[x = 2]$; mo_{ext}; $[w]$; po cycle in E'. Using constraint tnwri, we can infer w is not '$y = 1$' in P'. This permits manipulating $[x = 2]$; mo; $[w]$ to $[w]$; mo; $[x = 2]$ to remove the cycle with $a = x$ in E', while also preserving the cycle mentioned in E. This gives us our desired E'_t and E_t.

---

[11] These cases of read elimination can represent some form of load/store forwarding as well as unused read elimination done by the compiler.

[12] De-ordering of same memory reads can be safe under SC if there is no same memory concurrent write. However, such a case will also imply rb; po cycle in E', violating the premise.

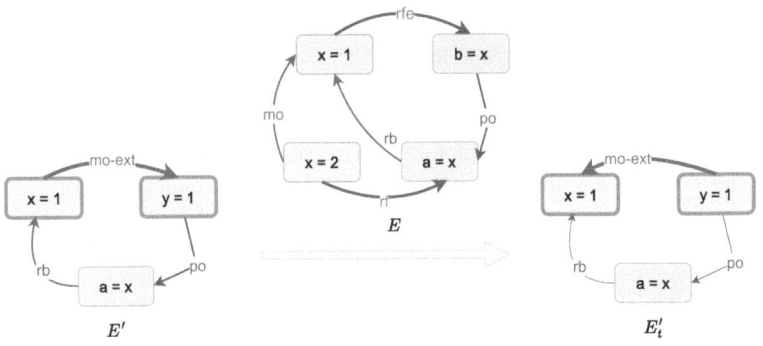

Fig. 10. Execution E (middle) implies same memory read-read de-ordering effect.

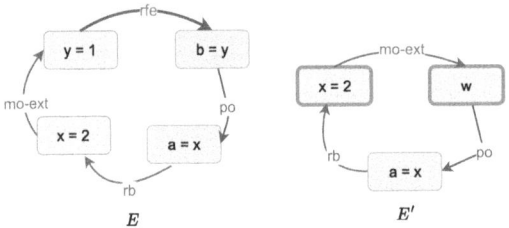

Fig. 11. Example where the constraint tuwri is used to infer $\neg psafe(SC, tr, P)$.

For other cases, we show that in general manipulating $\text{mo}_{ext}(E')$ and $\text{rf}(E')$ relations will give similarly our desired E'_t as described above.

3.4 Correlation with Races

Typically, safety of program optimizations are with the assumption that the source program is data-race-free, a semantic constraint that must be verified given source program. To add, optimizations are considered safe only if they do not introduce data-races. This prohibits optimizing programs unless we can verify data-race-freedom, something which is very hard to determine, let alone program. Our result w.r.t. TSO shows that such a constraint may be too strict, and that it is possible to have constraints weaker than data-race-freedom, at the level of syntactic constraints over optimizations instead.

$$ x = 1; \ \left\| \begin{array}{l} y = 1; \\ a = x; \ (0) \end{array} \right\| \left\| \begin{array}{l} b = x; \ (1) \\ c = y; \ (0) \end{array} \right. $$

Fig. 12. Example of a triangular race. Adapted from [20]

An interesting correlation exists between our constraint and a subset of race inducing optimizations. To understand this, we refer to the example in Fig. 12.

Observe that, under *TSO* or *SC* semantics, $b = 1$ and $c = 0$ implies $x = 1$ must be visible to all processors before $y = 1$. This would imply, observing $a = 0$ would not be possible under *SC*. However, for *TSO*, it is an acceptable outcome. If $y = 1$ remains in the write buffer, the read to x can be done before $x = 1$ is flushed to main memory. Such an execution is called to exhibit a *triangular race* (TR), a data race that occurs between $x = 1$ and $a = x$ along with a preceding write $y = 1$ to it [20].

Adapting the axiomatic definition from [20], we define triangular race as follows

Definition 5. *A candidate execution E has an* Axiomatic TR *if there exists events w_x, r_x, w_y such that*

a) $x \neq y$.

b) $tid(w_x) \neq tid(r_x)$.

c) $tid(w_y) = tid(r_x)$.

d) $[w_y]; po; [r_x]$.

e) $[w_x]; mo; [w_y]$.

f) $\exists w'_x \neq w_x . [w'_x]; rf; [r_x]$.

g) $\forall w'_x \in st(p(E)) . [w'_x]; po; [w_y] \implies [w'_x]; mo; [w_x]$.

Definition 5 constraints (a), (b), (c), (d) gives us a shape of pre-traces whose executions can exhibit an Axiomatic TR. We can further refine this shape, using the following lemma below.

Lemma 3. *Any execution E consistent under TSO that has an Axiomatic TR with events $w_x, r_x, w_y \in st(P)$ will have the following additional constraint on $p(E)$.*

a) $\nexists w'_x . [w_y]; po; [w'_x]; po; [r_x] \in po(P)$.

b) $\nexists u(z, a, v2) \in u(P) . [w_y]; po; [u]; po; [r_x] \in po(P)$.

Finally, we can use the constraint on pre-traces to link triangular races to our constraint over transformation-effects portable from *SC* to *TSO*

Lemma 4. *If $P \mapsto_{tuwri} P'$ then $\exists E' \in [\![P']\!]_{TSO} . E'$ has an Axiomatic TR.*

The proof is straightforward: the constraints over P' can easily be implied using the Constraints 1, 2, 3 that constitute the effect tuwri.

Lemma 4 allow us to finally claim the following from Theorem 1, correlating triangular races to our result[13].

Corollary 1. *For $P \mapsto_{tr} P'$ with no wc, wi and not introducing an Axiomatic TR, we have $comp\langle TSO, SC \rangle$.*

---

[13] Notice that our original constraint is weaker, in that certain triangular races are permitted to be introduced.

3.5 From Triangular Races to Causal Consistency

Just like tuwri relates to triangular races, an interesting correlation exists with Causal Consistency. We discovered that tuwri had an interesting correlation with Strong Release Acquire (SRA). SRA is known to be strictly weaker than TSO, and for two threaded programs with no updates/fences, the behaviors permitted by both models coincide [11]. We instead provide an alternative description, one that establishes a relation with optimizations and races. First, SRA can be viewed equivalent to allowing optimizations of Definition 4 over TSO. The following theorem shows that in the absence of two specific constraints present in *TSO*, the constraint tuwri is not required

Theorem 2. *Considering constraints* $a1 = rb; mo; rfe; po$ *irreflexive and* $a2 = rb; mo; [u]; po$ *irreflexive we have* $comp\langle TSO \smallsetminus \{a1 \cup a2\}, SC\rangle$ *for tr not involving* ui *and* we.

$TSO \smallsetminus \{a1 \cup a2\}$, to our surprise, turns out to be precisely SRA.

Lemma 5. *The memory model M is equivalent to strong release acquire SRA.*

Proof. The equivalence follows directly from the alternative formulation of SRA in Def 10, Sect. 3.2 of [11].

Since tuwri relates to triangular races (Lemma 4), SRA can instead be described as the model that permits optimizations introducing triangular races over *TSO*. Further, for programs which are write-write race free, we also know that behaviors permitted by both SRA and Release Acquire (RA)[14] coincide [11]. This implies, for WW-race free programs, Theorem 2 holds even when $M = RA$.

4 Discussion

Theorem 1 places 3 global constraints on possible syntactic changes involving shared memory events. More generally, any optimization designed relying on SC is applicable for TSO provided they adhere to the 3 syntactic constraints specified. To recap, these constraints are the prohibition of write introduction, write elimination and the introduction of particular *triangular-races* in the optimized program. The complexity of detecting triangular races will be the same as data races; both require identifying *conflicting* memory accesses. However, the former enables incorporating thread-local (excluding write-elimination) as well as global optimizations like those of Fig. 1. The 3 constraints are also sound, accurately prohibiting optimizations under program contexts as those in Fig. 2. Out of these, we *conjecture* the exclusion of write elimination we is conservative (excluding it has simplified our proofs). For now, we can port optimizations involving redundant write-before-write elimination effects; they are safe for TSO irrespective of program context [18]. An immediate future work would be to include other forms of write elimination.

---

[14] RA forms a significant part of concurrency models used for programming languages like C++, Rust, Java, etc.

Porting Program Analyses. Aggressive compiler optimizations are almost always backed by some program (data flow) analyses. Although several have been designed for concurrent programs, they rely on sequentially consistent semantics [14,27], and may be unsound for weaker models like TSO [3]. While this may require significant changes to existing analyses, our result can help ameliorate this problem to some extent. For instance, the *delay set analysis* [27] used to enable safe code motion under SC can also be used for TSO. This is because our constraint over effects do not prohibit any form of thread-local reordering effects, thereby enabling their portability across TSO. The same can be said for analyses that enable redundant/dead-code eliminations (provided they are of read or a form of write-before-write as stated). However, for analyses that are used to optimize programs beyond such syntactic changes, our result gives no guarantee. An example for this is the *octagon range analysis*, a form of range analysis that can be used to identify redundant control dependencies in the program [17]. Such analyses however, can be modified to be used for weaker models like TSO, SRA, etc. [3].

4.1   Related Work

The impact of memory consistency on program transformations can be traced back to when hardware optimizations were being introduced [1,21,25]. However, compiler optimizations are much more complex and varied than those performed by hardware [2,14,27], and one of the earliest known impacts on them was seen designing memory model for Java [23]. Optimizations like bytecode reordering, copy propagation, thread-inlining, redundant read/write eliminations, etc. performed on Java Programs violated the specifications [15,22,26]. C11 faces a similar problem: optimizations involving non-atomics, eliminating redundancies, strengthening, thread-inlining, etc. were unsafe [19,28]. Not to mention that permitting optimizations also birthed the famed out-of-thin-air problem among language memory models [4].

The general problem of identifying which compiler optimizations are allowed by a memory model can be resolved conservatively by identifying which thread-local optimizations were safe under any program context [18,28,29]. These can be broadly categorized as adjacent reordering/elimination and introduction of redundant memory accesses, which can be inferred using trace semantic guarantees [29]. However, designing/verifying optimizations using these sound fragments for given language still requires reasoning with the associated weak memory model [5,7]. Some progress has been made in this direction, showing when it is adequate to rely on simple sequential reasoning to design optimizations for complex memory models [6]. However, they are primarily for non-atomic optimizations that can be divided into these sound fragments.

Optimizations can also be performed using context-specific information obtained from a varied analysis on a multi-threaded program [3,14,24,27]. A direction towards incorporating such optimizations can be to identify if analyses proven safe under a model be reused in another [3]. Our work is exactly in this direction, albeit in a syntactic sense [9,10]. Safety of transformation-effects over pre-traces are context specific, and proving Complete between two models allow us to gain context-specific transformations from one model to the other. The added advantage is that such an approach also encompasses all the sound (context-free) optimizations. For instance, [11] show that all thread-local optimizations sound in RA are preserved in SRA. Our result on comp$\langle TSO, SC \rangle$ also provides the same conclusion for SC and TSO, albeit in the opposite direction.

5   Conclusion

In this paper, we identify syntactic constraints that enable porting SC optimizations across TSO. These also include optimizations leveraging concurrency, which may not be thread-local. We identify the correlation of our constraint with triangular races, followed by identifying syntactic constraints to port across SRA, a causally consistent memory model. Future work involves porting other variants of write-eliminations, as well as porting across Release Acquire, a significant subset of concurrent language models (C++20, Java) used today.

Acknowledgments. We thank the reviewers for their detailed and insightful feedback. This research is supported by NSERC Discovery Grant RGPIN-2019-05213.

References

1. Adve, S.V., Gharachorloo, K.: Shared memory consistency models: a tutorial. Computer **29**(12), 66–76 (1996). https://doi.org/10.1109/2.546611
2. Aho, A., Monica, Sethi, R., Ullman, J.: Compilers: Principles, Techniques and Tools (1986)
3. Alglave, J., Kroening, D., Lugton, J., Nimal, V., Tautschnig, M.: Soundness of data flow analyses for weak memory models. In: Yang, H. (ed.) APLAS 2011. LNCS, vol. 7078, pp. 272–288. Springer, Heidelberg (2011). https://doi.org/10.1007/978-3-642-25318-8_21
4. Batty, M., Memarian, K., Nienhuis, K., Pichon-Pharabod, J., Sewell, P.: The problem of programming language concurrency semantics. In: Vitek, J. (ed.) ESOP 2015. LNCS, vol. 9032, pp. 283–307. Springer, Heidelberg (2015). https://doi.org/10.1007/978-3-662-46669-8_12
5. Chakraborty, S., Vafeiadis, V.: Validating optimizations of concurrent C/C++ programs. In: Proceedings of the 2016 International Symposium on Code Generation and Optimization, CGO 2016, pp. 216–226. Association for Computing Machinery, New York (2016). https://doi.org/10.1145/2854038.2854051
6. Cho, M., Lee, S.H., Lee, D., Hur, C.K., Lahav, O.: Sequential reasoning for optimizing compilers under weak memory concurrency. In: Proceedings of the 43rd ACM SIGPLAN International Conference on Programming Language Design and Implementation, PLDI 2022, pp. 213–228. Association for Computing Machinery, New York (2022). https://doi.org/10.1145/3519939.3523718

7. Dodds, M., Batty, M., Gotsman, A.: Compositional verification of compiler optimisations on relaxed memory. In: Ahmed, A. (ed.) ESOP 2018. LNCS, vol. 10801, pp. 1027–1055. Springer, Cham (2018). https://doi.org/10.1007/978-3-319-89884-1_36

8. Gopalakrishnan, A., Verbrugge, C.: Portability of optimizations from SC to TSO (2025). https://arxiv.org/abs/2504.17646

9. Gopalakrishnan, A., Verbrugge, C., Batty, M.: Memory consistency models for program transformations: an intellectual abstract. In: Proceedings of the 2023 ACM SIGPLAN International Symposium on Memory Management, ISMM 2023, pp. 30–42. Association for Computing Machinery, New York (2023). https://doi.org/10.1145/3591195.3595274

10. Gopalakrishnan, A., Verbrugge, C., Batty, M.: Memory consistency and program transformations. Form. Asp. Comput. (2025). https://doi.org/10.1145/3721143

11. Lahav, O., Giannarakis, N., Vafeiadis, V.: Taming release-acquire consistency. In: Proceedings of the 43rd Annual ACM SIGPLAN-SIGACT Symposium on Principles of Programming Languages, POPL 2016, pp. 649–662. Association for Computing Machinery, New York (2016). https://doi.org/10.1145/2837614.2837643

12. Lahav, O., Namakonov, E., Oberhauser, J., Podkopaev, A., Vafeiadis, V.: Making weak memory models fair. Proc. ACM Program. Lang. **5**(OOPSLA), 1–27 (2021). https://doi.org/10.1145/3485475

13. Lahav, O., Vafeiadis, V.: Explaining relaxed memory models with program transformations. In: Fitzgerald, J., Heitmeyer, C., Gnesi, S., Philippou, A. (eds.) FM 2016. LNCS, vol. 9995, pp. 479–495. Springer, Cham (2016). https://doi.org/10.1007/978-3-319-48989-6_29

14. Lee, J., Padua, D.A., Midkiff, S.P.: Basic compiler algorithms for parallel programs. In: Snir, M., Chien, A.A. (eds.) Proceedings of the 1999 ACM SIGPLAN Symposium on Principles and Practice of Parallel Programming (PPOPP 1999), Atlanta, Georgia, USA, 4–6 May 1999, pp. 1–12. ACM (1999). https://doi.org/10.1145/301104.301105

15. Manson, J., Pugh, W.W., Adve, S.V.: The java memory model. In: Palsberg, J., Abadi, M. (eds.) Proceedings of the 32nd ACM SIGPLAN-SIGACT Symposium on Principles of Programming Languages, POPL 2005, Long Beach, California, USA, 12–14 January 2005, pp. 378–391. ACM (2005). https://doi.org/10.1145/1040305.1040336

16. Marino, D., Singh, A., Millstein, T.D., Musuvathi, M., Narayanasamy, S.: DRFX: a simple and efficient memory model for concurrent programming languages. In: Zorn, B.G., Aiken, A. (eds.) Proceedings of the 2010 ACM SIGPLAN Conference on Programming Language Design and Implementation, PLDI 2010, Toronto, Ontario, Canada, 5–10 June 2010, pp. 351–362. ACM (2010). https://doi.org/10.1145/1806596.1806636

17. Miné, A.: The octagon abstract domain. High. Order Symb. Comput. **19**(1), 31–100 (2006). https://doi.org/10.1007/s10990-006-8609-1

18. Moiseenko, E., Podkopaev, A., Koznov, D.V.: A survey of programming language memory models. Program. Comput. Softw. **47**(6), 439–456 (2021). https://doi.org/10.1134/S0361768821060050

19. Morisset, R., Pawan, P., Nardelli, F.Z.: Compiler testing via a theory of sound optimisations in the C11/C++11 memory model. In: Boehm, H., Flanagan, C. (eds.) ACM SIGPLAN Conference on Programming Language Design and Implementation, PLDI 2013, Seattle, WA, USA, 16–19 June 2013, pp. 187–196. ACM (2013). https://doi.org/10.1145/2491956.2491967

20. Owens, S.: Reasoning about the implementation of concurrency abstractions on x86-TSO. In: D'Hondt, T. (ed.) ECOOP 2010. LNCS, vol. 6183, pp. 478–503. Springer, Heidelberg (2010). https://doi.org/10.1007/978-3-642-14107-2_23

21. Owens, S., Sarkar, S., Sewell, P.: A better x86 memory model: x86-TSO. In: Berghofer, S., Nipkow, T., Urban, C., Wenzel, M. (eds.) TPHOLs 2009. LNCS, vol. 5674, pp. 391–407. Springer, Heidelberg (2009). https://doi.org/10.1007/978-3-642-03359-9_27

22. Pugh, W.W.: Fixing the java memory model. In: Fox, G.C., Schauser, K.E., Snir, M. (eds.) Proceedings of the ACM 1999 Conference on Java Grande, JAVA 1999, San Francisco, CA, USA, 12–14 June 1999, pp. 89–98. ACM (1999). https://doi.org/10.1145/304065.304106

23. Pugh, W.W.: The java memory model is fatally flawed. Concurr. Pract. Exp. **12**(6), 445–455 (2000)

24. Rinard, M.: Analysis of multithreaded programs. In: Cousot, P. (ed.) Static Analysis, pp. 1–19. Springer, Heidelberg (2001). https://doi.org/10.1007/3-540-47764-0_1

25. Sarkar, S., Sewell, P., Alglave, J., Maranget, L., Williams, D.: Understanding power multiprocessors. In: Proceedings of the 32nd ACM SIGPLAN Conference on Programming Language Design and Implementation, PLDI 2011, pp. 175–186. Association for Computing Machinery, New York (2011). https://doi.org/10.1145/1993498.1993520

26. Ševčík, J., Aspinall, D.: On validity of program transformations in the java memory model. In: Vitek, J. (ed.) ECOOP 2008. LNCS, vol. 5142, pp. 27–51. Springer, Heidelberg (2008). https://doi.org/10.1007/978-3-540-70592-5_3

27. Shasha, D.E., Snir, M.: Efficient and correct execution of parallel programs that share memory. ACM Trans. Program. Lang. Syst. **10**(2), 282–312 (1988). https://doi.org/10.1145/42190.42277

28. Vafeiadis, V., Balabonski, T., Chakraborty, S., Morisset, R., Nardelli, F.Z.: Common compiler optimisations are invalid in the C11 memory model and what we can do about it. In: Rajamani, S.K., Walker, D. (eds.) Proceedings of the 42nd Annual ACM SIGPLAN-SIGACT Symposium on Principles of Programming Languages, POPL 2015, Mumbai, India, 15–17 January 2015, pp. 209–220. ACM (2015). https://doi.org/10.1145/2676726.2676995

29. Ševčík, J.: Safe optimisations for shared-memory concurrent programs. SIGPLAN Not. **46**(6), 306–316 (2011). https://doi.org/10.1145/1993316.1993534

SAT and SMT Solving

Adaptive Clause Management in SMT Solvers: A Dynamic Weighting Framework for Formal Verification

Wenda Leng[1], Meihua Liu[2(✉)], and Yufeng Jin[1(✉)]

[1] School of Electronic and Computer Engineering, Peking University Shenzhen Graduate School, Peking University, Shenzhen, China
2301212964@stu.pku.edu.cn, yfjin@pku.edu.cn
[2] Shenzhen GWX Technology Co., Ltd., Shenzhen, China
amo_jane@outlook.com

Abstract. This paper introduces a novel dynamic weighting framework for clause management in Satisfiability Modulo Theories (SMT) solvers. By employing real-time metric adaptation, the proposed framework circumvents the limitations of conventional evaluation criteria. The core contribution lies in a phase-aware weight calibration strategy that dynamically aligns conflict pattern characteristics with optimal combinations of evaluation metrics. Experimental evaluations, including integration with Yices2, demonstrate solving speed enhancements of up to 97.67% and 119.80% compared to conventional approaches in Yices2 across three SMT-COMP benchmark sets. Furthermore, the proposed framework exhibits exceptional performance in real-world scenarios, particularly for the formal verification of circuit designs. Overall, this dynamic weighting framework significantly improves solver adaptability to evolving search space characteristics, thereby offering substantial benefits for formal circuit verification.

Keywords: Dynamic clause weighting · Formal verification · Satisfiability modulo theories · Literal block distance · Clause activity

1 Introduction

Model checking is a widely adopted technique in formal verification for validating circuit properties. By modeling the circuit, these properties are represented as a Satisfiability Modulo Theories (SMT) problem, which is then analyzed using an SMT solver. However, as the circuit scale increases, the number of variables and constraints in the SMT formulation escalates, leading to significantly increased complexity in the verification process [23].

Early SMT solvers, such as Chaff [19] and Minisat [11], were originally based on the Davis-Putnam-Logemann-Loveland (DPLL) algorithms [8]. Since then, researchers have introduced various enhancements to SMT solvers, including restart strategies [13,15], activity-based branching heuristics [16], and clause

© The Author(s), under exclusive license to Springer Nature Switzerland AG 2026
P. Rümmer and Z. Wu (Eds.): TASE 2025, LNCS 15841, pp. 143–160, 2026.
https://doi.org/10.1007/978-3-031-98208-8_9

learning [24]. Clause learning has emerged as one of the most critical components in modern SMT solvers. Its key idea is to derive a clause that succinctly represents the underlying cause of a conflict encountered during the search. This clause is then added to the Conjunctive Normal Form (CNF) representation of the problem to prune the search space more effectively, a process commonly referred to as Conflict-Driven Clause Learning (CDCL). Currently, CDCL is widely acknowledged as the most efficient algorithm for solving SMT problems and serves as the basis for most state-of-the-art solvers [20, 26]. However, as SMT problems grow in complexity, conflicts tend to arise more frequently, which leads to an overaccumulation of learned clauses that can consume considerable memory resources. This proliferation of clauses may cause the search space to expand exponentially and reduce the efficiency of Boolean Constraint Propagation (BCP).

The management of learned clauses has received significant attention in the literature [11, 12, 18, 19]. These strategies typically follow a scheduled cleanup sequence, specifically deleting lower-quality learned clauses after a fixed number of conflicts. Consequently, it becomes essential to periodically discard learned clauses, particularly those that are less relevant or do not significantly aid future searches, in order to maintain solver performance. Between deletion steps, an *activity* (i.e., clause activity, a metric used to measure SMT clauses) is assigned to each learned clause as it is generated to evaluate its quality [11]. Additionally, the activity is updated each time a conflict occurs, based on the clause's relevance to the subsequent search. Although these approaches have proven effective in practice, establishing a criterion for identifying the most relevant clauses remains a challenging task [14].

This work is motivated by the observation that most existing evaluation criteria for learned clauses are restricted to a narrow set of features. Two commonly adopted metrics, namely Literal Block Distance (LBD) and clause activity, exemplify this situation, as both are extensively employed in state-of-the-art SMT solvers yet each accounts for only one facet of clause quality. For example, while clauses with low LBD values risk becoming irrelevant over time, clauses with high activity frequently grow lengthy and complex, thereby undermining solver performance. In response to these constraints, this paper introduces a dynamic weighting framework that combines LBD and clause activity. By integrating multiple dimensions of clause quality, the proposed approach aims to maintain solver efficiency and facilitate more nuanced oversight of learned clauses.

To the best of our knowledge, Yices2 achieves superior performance compared with many conventional solvers in the formal verification of digital circuits. Accordingly, we integrated our framework into Yices2 by incorporating two additional strategies, the BerkMin Strategy (BMS) [12] and the Relevance Based Strategy (RBS) [19]. Our experimental results on two integrated approaches, one of which is based on Yices2, reveal speedups of 97.67% and 119.80% over conventional strategies across three SMT-COMP benchmark sets. Furthermore, these solver variants exhibit exceptional effectiveness in real-world circuit formal verification scenarios. The primary contributions of this paper are summarized as follows:

- This paper proposes a dynamic weighting framework for clause management that integrates LBD and activity metrics, capturing both dynamic and structural characteristics of learned clauses to guide clause management.
- This paper incorporates the BerkMin strategy and the relevance-based strategy into the proposed framework, thereby demonstrating its flexibility and extensibility.
- This paper implements two integrated approaches in the Yices2 solver, and comprehensive experimental evaluations demonstrate significant improvements in their solution performance.

2 Background

This section provides a formal exposition of two commonly adopted clause quality metrics in SMT solving: Literal Block Distance (LBD) and activity.

2.1 Literal Block Distance

The evaluation metric based on LBD is an effective method to assess the quality of the learned clauses, proposed by Audemard and Simon [2]. This measure was subsequently employed in a clause deletion strategy for the Glucose solver [4], which achieved a championship in the Application Track of the 2011 SAT Competition. LBD is specifically defined as follows:

Definition 1 (Literal Block Distance). *The literal block distance constitutes a quantitative measure for evaluating learned clause quality in conflict-driven clause learning solvers. The formal computation of literal block distance comprises two phases:*

$$DL(C) = \{DecisionLevel(l) \mid l \in C\} \tag{1}$$

$$LBD(C) = |DL(C)| = \left| \bigcup_{l \in C} DecisionLevel(l) \right| \tag{2}$$

where $DecisionLevel(l) \in \mathbb{N}^+$ specifies the decision level assignment for literal l, and $DL(C)$ denotes the decision level set abstraction operation. The metric is grounded in the following two principles:

$$\Psi_1 : Corr(V_C) \propto \frac{1}{LBD(C)} \tag{3}$$

$$\Psi_2 : Q(C) \propto \frac{1}{LBD(C)} \tag{4}$$

where $Q(C)$ denotes clause quality and $Corr(V_C)$ represents variable correlation within clause C. In other words, a smaller number of decision layers indicates stronger variable correlation and a higher likelihood that the learned clause will be useful in conflict resolution. Consequently, the quality of a learned clause is inversely proportional to the number of decision layers it contains.

Example 1. Consider the learned clause C_1, shown as follows.

$$C_1 = P_1 \vee \neg P_2 \vee \neg P_3 \vee P_4 \tag{5}$$

The decision level assignments for literals are formally defined as:

$$\begin{aligned} \mathrm{DL}(P_1) = 1, \quad \mathrm{DL}(\neg P_2) = 2, \\ \mathrm{DL}(\neg P_3) = 2, \quad \mathrm{DL}(P_4) = 3 \end{aligned} \tag{6}$$

The Literal Block Distance is computed through set cardinality measurement:

$$\mathrm{LBD}(C_1) = \left| \bigcup_{l \in C_1} \{\mathrm{DL}(l)\} \right| = |\{1, 2, 3\}| = 3 \tag{7}$$

Additionally, clauses whose LBD value equals 2 are frequently referred to as glue clauses [7]. Variables within these clauses exhibit strong interdependencies, which often leads to more efficient BCP with fewer decision steps, thereby reducing the overall search space. Consequently, most modern CDCL solvers preserve glue clauses permanently.

In general, the LBD value of a learned clause remains fixed after its initial assignment. However, subsequent clause deletion strategies have introduced refinements that permit dynamic adjustment. Specifically, whenever a learned clause plays a role in conflict analysis, it is deemed to be of higher quality, prompting a decrease and update of its LBD value. In addition, this metric is leveraged to optimize other components of the solving process, such as influencing the restart strategy in the Glucose solver.

2.2   Activity

The concept of *activity* was first proposed in the MiniSAT solver as a means of evaluating learned clause quality by assigning an activity value to each clause [11]. The determination of this activity proceeds in two steps. First, each newly generated learned clause is an uniform initial activity. Subsequently, whenever a learned clause participates in a conflict, its activity is increased. A formal definition is provided as follows:

Definition 2 (Activity). *Let $C_{learned}$ denote the set of learned clauses and κ a conflict event. The activity metric $A : C \to \mathbb{R}^+$ is determined by:*

$$A(c) \leftarrow a_{init}, \quad \forall c \in C_{learned} \tag{8}$$

where $a_{init} \in \mathbb{R}^+$ specifies the initial activity value. When conflict occurs, the activity update rule is defined as:

$$A(c) \leftarrow A(c) + \gamma \cdot \underbrace{\mathcal{P}(c,\kappa)}_{conflict\ factor} \cdot \underbrace{Decay^{-N(c)}}_{aging\ factor} \tag{9}$$

where $\mathcal{P}(c,\kappa) = 1$ if clause c participates in ConflictAnalysis(κ), otherwise $\mathcal{P}(c,\kappa) = 0$; $\gamma \in \mathbb{R}^+$ controls the learning rate, Decay $\in (0,1)$ is the aging coefficient, and $N(c)$ counts the number of conflicts since clause c's creation.

The core concept behind using activity to guide the deletion strategy is to retain as much relevant information as possible for solving the SMT problem, while maintaining an optimal number of learned clauses. In practice, once the number of conflicts exceeds a specified threshold, the learned clauses are sorted based on their activity, and those with lower activity values are removed. For instance, at each scheduled deletion phase, MiniSAT prunes the half of clauses exhibiting the lowest activity levels. To prevent keeping clauses that start with high activity but later lose relevance, their activity is periodically reduced by multiplying it by a factor less than 1 after a fixed number of conflicts. Currently, advanced SMT solvers such as Z3 [9] and Yices2 [10] employ this activity-based deletion strategy.

3   Dynamic Weighting Framework

The section introduces the dynamic weighting framework, which integrates both LBD and activity metrics. We then propose two solver variants that incorporate the BerkMin strategy and the relevance-based strategy, respectively.

3.1   Hybrid LBD-Activity Integration Framework

The number and timing of learned clause deletions are among the most critical factors in clause deletion strategies [14]. However, these factors are challenging to address in many studies, primarily due to the NP-hard nature of the satisfiability problem, which introduces substantial uncertainty into the solution process. Currently, LBD and activity are widely accepted as core evaluation criteria respectively measuring the number of decision layers in clause blocks and the degree of conflict participation. Although these metrics have significantly enhanced solver performance, their simplicity limits the exhaustive use of conflict information. To achieve more fine grained management of learned clauses, we comprehensively consider structural and dynamic attributes by integrating the LBD and activity metrics into a unified framework named the Hybrid LBD Activity Integration Framework (HLAIF). In the early phases of conflict resolution, clause activity remains inherently unstable and relying exclusively on it for deletion decisions may result in many false deletions. Therefore, we initially prioritize LBD when removing clauses. After a predetermined number of conflicts has taken place, the remaining learned clauses are evaluated according to their

---

Algorithm 1. Hybrid LBD-Activity Integration Framework

Input:
    C_{learned}: Set of learned clauses
    $N(c)$: Current conflict count
    T: Base conflict threshold ($T \in \mathbb{Z}^+$, default 2000)
    λ: Interval scaling factor ($\lambda \in \mathbb{R}^+$)
Output: Updated clause database C_{learned}

1: **if** $N_c < T(1 + \lambda)$ **then**   ▷ Adaptive threshold condition
2:     **for** each clause $c_i \in C_{\text{learned}}$ **do**
3:         $\text{LBD}(c_i) \leftarrow \left| \bigcup_{l \in C} \text{DecisionLevel}(l) \right|$
4:         **if** $\text{LBD}(c_i) > \theta$ **then**   ▷ $\theta = 6$ by empirical study
5:             $C_{\text{learned}} \leftarrow C_{\text{learned}} \setminus \{c_i\}$
6:             $\delta_{\text{del}} \leftarrow \delta_{\text{del}} + 1$ ▷ Deletion counter update
7:         **end if**
8:     **end for**
9: **else**
10:     **if** $\delta_{\text{del}} < 0.1 \cdot N_c$ **then**   ▷ Clause maintenance condition
11:         $\text{SORT}(C_{\text{learned}}, A(c_i) \downarrow)$ ▷ Descending sort by activity
12:         $k \leftarrow \lfloor \frac{|C_{\text{learned}}|}{2} \rfloor$
13:         $C_{\text{high}} \leftarrow c_j | j < k$ ▷ Higher-activity subset
14:         $C_{\text{low}} \leftarrow c_j | j \geq k$ ▷ Lower-activity subset
15:         $C_{\text{low}} \leftarrow \text{PROCESSCLAUSES}(C_{\text{low}})$ ▷ Dynamic elimination strategy
16:         $C_{\text{learned}} \leftarrow C_{\text{high}} \cup C_{\text{low}}$ ▷ Update clause database
17:     **end if**
18: **end if**
19: **return** C_{learned}

---

activity, and those with lower activity are removed alongside additional considerations that include clause length, clause age, and relevance. This framework curbs the likelihood of excessive deletions while drawing on both structural and dynamic information.

Algorithm 1 formalizes the dynamic clause management protocol within the HLAIF framework. For each learned clause $c_i \in C_{\text{learned}}$, the LBD metric is computed as $\text{LBD}(c_i) = \left| \bigcup_{l \in C} \text{DecisionLevel}(l) \right|$, thereby initiating the procedure.

Empirical studies [7] indicate that clauses satisfying $\text{LBD}(c_i) > \theta$ (where $\theta = 6$) exhibit exponentially decreasing returns for conflict resolution. Consequently, such clauses are immediately removed from the learned set, i.e., $C_{\text{learned}} \leftarrow C_{\text{learned}} \setminus \{c_i\}$.

The adaptive threshold strategy triggers when $N_c \geq T(1 + \lambda)$, activating two-phase deletion control:

- **Effectiveness validation.** The inequality $\delta_{\text{del}} < 0.1 N_c$ is enforced to maintain at least a 10% deletion ratio.

– **Activity-based pruning.** For underperforming cycles, the lower half of the learned clauses $\lfloor \frac{|C_{\text{learned}}|}{2} \rfloor \leq j < |C_{\text{learned}}|$ is strategically removed based on the following activity measure:

$$A(c) = a_{\text{init}} + \sum_{i=1}^{n(c)} \left[\gamma \cdot P(c, \kappa_i) \cdot \text{Decay}^{-N_i(c)} \right], \quad \forall c \in C_{\text{learned}} \quad (10)$$

It is important to note that the number of deleted clauses exerts a pivotal influence on solver performance. Overly aggressive deletion can remove valuable clauses prematurely, whereas insufficient deletion can inflate memory consumption and slow down BCP.

The HLAIF framework is designed to enable fine-grained management of learned clauses, preventing the premature removal of valuable clauses while improving the overall efficiency and effectiveness of clause deletion strategies. Unlike the Glucose solver, which triggers clause deletions only after reaching a predefined conflict threshold, HLAIF incorporates a dynamic decision-making strategy. Specifically, after each conflict, the framework evaluates whether to delete clauses with LBD values exceeding 6, allowing for a more flexible and adaptive deletion process.

3.2 Framework-Embedded BerkMin Strategy

The BerkMin strategy selects learned clauses for deletion based on multiple criteria, including clause length, clause age, and activity evaluation. Algorithm 2 outlines the operational framework of the BerkMin clause management strategy. During the initialization phase, the algorithm examines three fundamental metrics for each clause. The literal count $L(c)$ indicates the clause length, the activity $A(c)$ reveals its relevance in the solving process, and the age parameter $\alpha(c)$ is derived from its birthtime. To establish a temporal reference, the algorithm determines the maximum clause age, denoted as α_{max}. Following initialization, clauses are categorized into two subsets, newly learned clauses (C_{new}) and older clauses (C_{old}), using an age threshold set at $\frac{1}{16}\alpha_{\text{max}}$. This classification enables distinct removal criteria. Clauses in C_{old} that fulfill $L(c) \geq 9$ and $A(c) \leq \theta_{\text{old}}$ are removed, whereas clauses in C_{new} are removed if they satisfy $L(c) \geq 43$ and $A(c) \leq 7$. The updated clause database is then constructed by merging the filtered subsets ($C_{\text{new}} \cup C_{\text{old}}$). This dual-threshold strategy, incorporating age-dependent constraints, ensures the retention of clauses that exhibit both structural compactness and high relevance to the current problem-solving context.

The BerkMin strategy is integrated into the proposed HLAIF framework to validate its effectiveness and is referred to as BMS. The strategy is activated when the proportion of learned clauses removed based solely on the LBD value falls below 10% of the total learned clauses. Under this condition, BMS selectively processes 50% of the learned clauses exhibiting lower activity. BMS employs a multi-faceted evaluation approach, concurrently considering LBD value, clause

---

Algorithm 2. BerkMin Strategy

Input: Set of learned clauses C_{learned}
Output: Updated clause database C_{learned}

1: **for all** clauses $c \in C$ **do**   ▷ Initialize
2:     $L(c) \triangleq |\text{literals}(c)|$ ▷ clause length
3:     $A(c) = a_{\text{init}} + \sum_{i=1}^{n(c)} \left[\gamma \cdot P(c, \kappa_i) \cdot \text{Decay}^{-N_i(c)} \right]$ ▷ clause activity
4:     $\alpha(c) \triangleq t$ ▷ clause age
5:     $\alpha_{\text{max}} \leftarrow \max_{c \in C} \alpha(c)$
6: **end for**
7: **for all** clauses $c \in C$ **do**   ▷ Partition clauses
8:     **if** $\alpha(c) < \frac{1}{16}\alpha_{\text{max}}$ **then**
9:         $C_{\text{new}} \leftarrow C_{\text{new}} \cup \{c\}$
10:     **else if** $\alpha(c) \geq \frac{1}{16}\alpha_{\text{max}}$ **then**
11:         $C_{\text{old}} \leftarrow C_{\text{old}} \cup \{c\}$
12:     **end if**
13: **end for**
14: **for all** clauses $c \in C_{\text{old}}$ **do**   ▷ Filter old clauses
15:     **if** $(L(c) \geq 9) \vee (A(c) \leq \theta_{\text{old}})$ **then**
16:         $C_{\text{old}} \leftarrow C_{\text{old}} \setminus \{c\}$
17:     **end if**
18: **end for**
19: **for all** clauses $c \in C_{\text{new}}$ **do**   ▷ Filter new clauses
20:     **if** $(L(c) \geq 43) \wedge (A(c) \leq 7)$ **then**
21:         $C_{\text{new}} \leftarrow C_{\text{new}} \setminus \{c\}$
22:     **end if**
23: **end for**
24: $C_{\text{learned}} \leftarrow C_{\text{new}} \cup C_{\text{old}}$ ▷ **Update clause database**
25: **return** C_{learned}

---

activity, clause age, and clause length to dynamically adjust the deletion strategy. This adaptive strategy enables the solver to more effectively distinguish and eliminate low-quality clauses, thereby enhancing both the efficiency and robustness of the SMT solving process.

3.3 Framework-Embedded Relevance-Based Strategy

It is important to note that BMS introduces substantial computational overhead in both time and space due to its reliance on multiple evaluation metrics. This additional complexity can impact solver performance and exacerbate the challenges associated with debugging and maintenance. Therefore, we introduce a classical and computationally lightweight relevance-based deletion strategy within the HLAIF framework, referred to as RBS. The relevance evaluation criterion, originally proposed in the Chaff solver [19], assesses learned clauses by analyzing the number of unassigned literals they contain during subsequent conflict analysis. A clause with a higher number of unassigned literals exhibits a lower likelihood of being involved in future conflicts, thereby indicating reduced relevance.

Algorithm 3. Relevance-Based Strategy

Input: Set of learned clauses C_{learned}
Output: Updated clause database C_{learned}
1: **for all** clause $c \in C_{\text{learned}}$ **do**
2:      $R(c) \leftarrow \sum_{\ell \in c} \mathbb{I}\ell$ unassigned   ▷ Number of unassigned literals
3:      **if** $R(c) \geq \theta_{rbs}$ **then**
4:           $C_{\text{learned}} \leftarrow C_{\text{learned}} \setminus c$
5:           $\theta_{rbs} \leftarrow \alpha \cdot \theta_{rbs}$ ▷ Adaptive threshold decay
6:      **end if**
7: **end for**
8: **return** C_{learned}

Algorithm 3 iteratively manage the learned clause database C_{learned} by evaluating the relevance of each clause c. Specifically, for each clause $c \in C$, the relevance metric $R(c)$ is calculated by the formula:

$$R(c) = \sum_{\ell \in c} \mathbb{I}(\ell \text{ is unassigned}) \tag{11}$$

where $\mathbb{I}(\cdot)$ is an indicator function that returns 1 if the literal ℓ is unassigned and 0 otherwise.

Clauses satisfying $R(c) \geq \theta_{rbs}$, where θ_{rbs} is a dynamically adjusted threshold, are retained in C_{learned}, while the remaining clauses are eliminated. To achieve a balance between exploration and exploitation in clause management, the threshold θ_{rbs} is adaptively scaled by a factor α. This adaptive strategy facilitates the efficient pruning of less relevant clauses, thereby improving solver performance by prioritizing clauses that are critical to the current search state. The refined clause database C_{learned} is then returned as the updated set.

The implementation of RBS serves dual objectives of validating the HLAIF framework's effectiveness and investigating how deletion strategy complexity impacts framework efficiency and generalization. The strategy becomes active when the LBD measure does not eliminate at least 10% of the learned clauses, and clause refinement is subsequently carried out through an unassigned literal analysis. Specifically, the number of unassigned literals is computed for the lower-activity half of the learned clauses, and a deletion threshold of 10 unassigned literals is applied. This multi-stage filtering process establishes quantifiable complexity constraints while ensuring framework adaptability through dynamic parameter interaction.

4   Implementation and Experimental Evaluation

4.1   Experimental Setup

To validate the effectiveness of the proposed HLAIF framework, the Yices2 implementation is extended and optimized, producing two solver variants:

– *Y-BMS*: A Yices2-based solver variant that integrates the BerkMin strategy within the HLAIF framework.
– *Y-RBS*: A Yices2-based solver variant that integrates a relevance-based strategy within the HLAIF framework.

For comparative evaluation, the default clause management strategies of Z3 and Yices2 serve as baseline solvers.

To achieve comprehensive and robust validation, a benchmark suite was constructed with 1,099 benchmarks, drawn from SMT-LIB v2.6 and selected SMT-COMP benchmarks. The suite includes *bench_ab* with 255 benchmarks from SMT-LIB v2.6, along with *2018-Goel-hwbench* containing 791 benchmarks and *brummayerbiere* comprising 76 benchmarks from the SMT-COMP. These benchmarks, widely recognized for their comprehensiveness and credibility, were preprocessed to maintain consistency in evaluation. Numerous studies have employed these benchmarks to examine clause deletion and selection strategies. In addition, to investigate the efficacy of the proposed framework in formal verification, the suite also comprises 7 benchmarks derived from real circuit designs.

The experimental setup adheres to the standard protocol of the international SMT competition, imposing a 1200-second timeout per benchmark. The performance of each solver variant is primarily evaluated based on the number of successfully solved benchmarks. If two solvers solve an identical number of benchmarks, total solving time serves as a secondary ranking criterion, with the solver achieving a shorter cumulative solving time deemed superior. To minimize potential fluctuations in execution time due to CPU resource contention, each benchmark is processed by only one solver at a time. All experiments are conducted on a Linux system equipped with an Intel® Core™ i5-1135G7 @ 2.40 GHz processor, with the solver code compiled using GCC version 11.4.0.

4.2   Experimental Results

Experimental results indicate that Y-BMS achieves runtime improvements over Yices2 in 62.94% of the evaluated benchmarks, with particularly large gains in medium difficulty problems, as demonstrated by an 81.07% advantage in the 1 to 10 s range. This outcome underscores the efficacy of Y-BMS in accelerating the solving process. However, the performance advantage declines to 68.25% in the 10 to 100 s range, suggesting diminishing returns as problem complexity increases.

Figure 2 extends this analysis to Y-RBS, highlighting the broader optimization capabilities of the proposed framework. Y-RBS achieves an overall superiority of 78.27%, surpassing the performance gains observed with Y-BMS. A positive correlation between time complexity and the superiority margin emerges. While a 78.94% advantage is observed for benchmarks with runtimes between 0.1 and 1 s, this margin increases to 90% for bechmarks exceeding 100 s. This counterintuitive trend indicates that Y-RBS yields relatively greater performance gains on more challenging benchmarks, reflecting the effectiveness of learned clause deletion strategies that accumulate benefits over extended search periods.

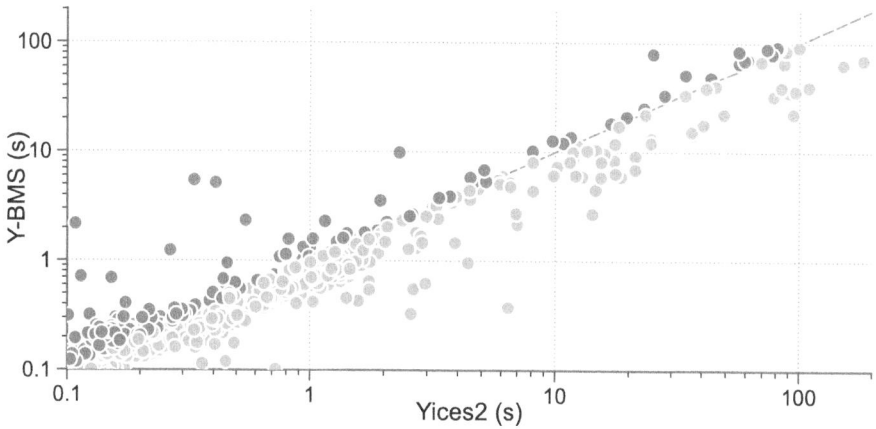

Fig. 1. Comparison of solving time between Y-BMS and Yices2

Finally, the direct comparison in Fig. 3 contrasts Y-BMS and Y-RBS. In this analysis, Y-RBS outperforms Y-BMS in 60.55% of the benchmarks. For benchmarks with runtimes exceeding 10 s, 92.31% exhibit a tenfold speedup. These results underscore the enhanced acceleration performance of Y-RBS on complex problem benchmarks.

Synthesizing these observations, Y-RBS establishes itself as the more versatile optimizer with broad-spectrum improvements, particularly excelling in complex problem domains. Meanwhile, Y-BMS remains relevant for time-sensitive medium-complexity scenarios. This performance difference highlights the potential value of implementing adaptive solver selection strategies on HLAIF, informed by preliminary problem characterization.

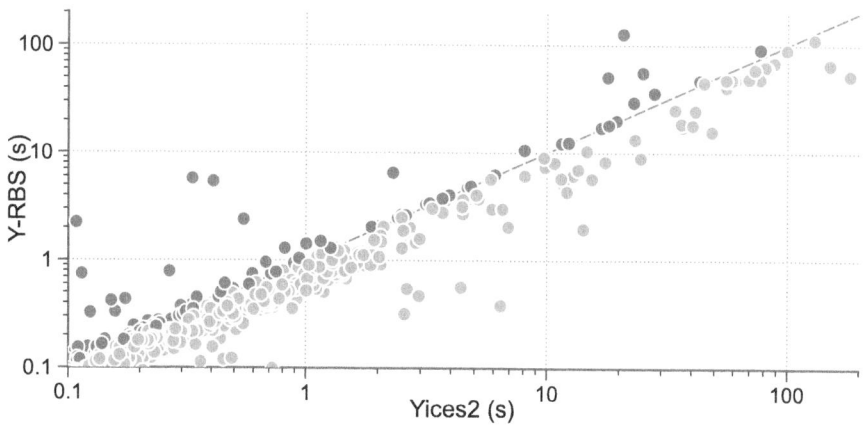

Fig. 2. Comparison of solving time between Y-RBS and Yices2

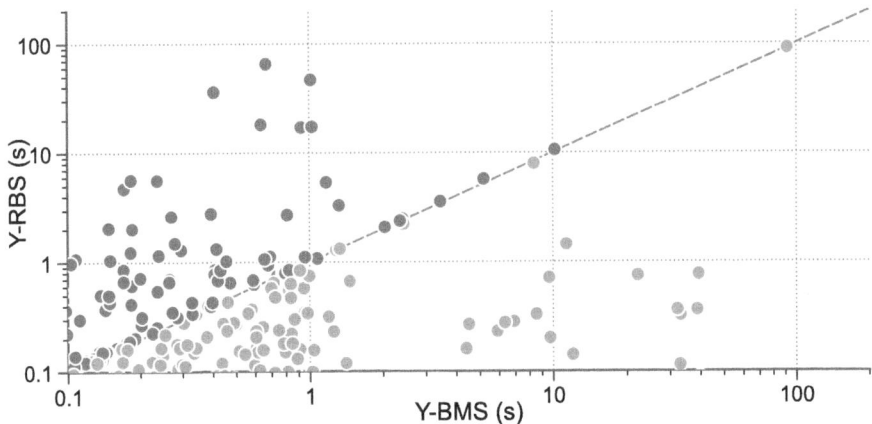

Fig. 3. Comparison of solving time between Y-RBS and Y-BMS

Table 1. Solvers' Outcomes on Various Benchmark Subsets

Benchmark	Solver	Result Breakdown				
		Solved	SAT	UNSAT	UNKNOWN	Time (s)
bench_ab	Z3	285	285	0	0	2.850
	Yices2	285	284	1	0	0.578
	Y-BMS	285	285	0	0	0.355
	Y-RBS	285	285	0	0	0.321
2018-Goel-hwbench	Z3	791	421	370	0	730.420
	Yices2	791	420	371	0	470.214
	Y-BMS	791	420	371	0	158.897
	Y-RBS	791	420	371	0	136.321
brummayerbiere	Z3	76	31	32	13	23593.3
	Yices2	76	31	33	12	19707.1
	Y-BMS	76	32	34	10	14760.5
	Y-RBS	76	32	34	10	14617.3

To conduct a more extensive evaluation of the proposed framework, four different solvers (Z3, Yices2, Y-BMS, and Y-RBS) were assessed on three benchmark subsets. As summarized in Table 1, the recorded results include the overall solving time, the total number of solved benchmarks, and the numbers of SAT, UNSAT, and UNKNOWN solutions. Simultaneous observation of these metrics provides a more nuanced view of each solver's capabilities and limitations. Performance evaluations indicate that Y-BMS and Y-RBS achieve average solving speed improvements of up to 97.67% and 119.80% respectively over conventional Yices2 strategies, highlighting the efficiency gains facilitated by the proposed framework.

In the *bench_ab* benchmark subset, both Y-BMS and Y-RBS successfully solved all benchmarks, matching the number solved by Yices2, while demonstrating faster solving times. Yices2 required 0.578 s to address 285 benchmarks, whereas Y-BMS and Y-RBS needed approximately 0.355 and 0.321 s, respectively. Moreover, both Y-BMS and Y-RBS solved one additional benchmark compared to Yices2, indicating a marginally higher success rate in this subset.

For the *2018-Goel-hwbench* benchmark subset, all four solvers successfully processed 791 benchmarks. Z3 required more than 730 s, whereas Yices2 and Y-BMS completed their tasks in approximately 470 s and 159 s, respectively. Y-RBS further reduced the total runtime to about 136 s. Y-BMS and Y-RBS solved the same benchmarks as Yices2 while substantially lowering the total solving time. This outcome highlights their ability to handle complex tasks with considerably lower latency.

Finally, the more challenging *brummayerbiere* benchmark subset reveals that Y-RBS and Y-BMS not only outperform Z3 and Yices2 by solving an additional benchmark. Their average solving times are markedly lower. Z3 required more than 23,593.3 s and Yices2 around 19,707 s, while Y-BMS and Y-RBS completed in 14,760 s and 14,617 s, respectively. These improvements suggest that the dynamic weighting framework in Y-BMS and Y-RBS is robust to deliver notable efficiency gains even in competition-level scenarios.

Overall, experimental results conclusively demonstrate that the advanced variants Y-BMS and Y-RBS, developed within the proposed framework, provide substantial performance improvements. These solvers achieve markedly reduced overall solving times across varied benchmarks, coupled with a notably lower incidence of unresolved outcomes. Altogether, these findings underscore the framework's effectiveness in addressing complex SMT problems with enhanced efficiency and higher success rate.

In order to evaluate the performance of Y-BMS and Y-RBS in real-world circuit property verification tasks, we applied these solvers to seven open-source circuits of varying complexity. Initially, each circuit's RTL description was annotated with relevant assertions, converted into a CSV format, and then processed using Yosys tools [25] for parsing, synthesis and transformation, followed by the execution of experiments. As illustrated in Fig. 4, the first three circuits (*src_add*, *yhud580*, and *wz_al*) required less than one second to solve. Consequently, the performance gains observed for Y-BMS and Y-RBS are moderate, with average runtime reductions of 13.69% and 14.68%, respectively. In contrast, the remaining four benchmarks (*ac91_ale*, *ac92_ale*, *add_bx_ale*, and *add_tree_sv*) presented substantially higher complexity. Under these more demanding conditions, both solvers outperformed the baseline Yices2 by a greater margin, achieving runtime reductions of approximately 36.77% for Y-BMS and 37.02% for Y-RBS. These results provide compelling evidence that the novel solver variants developed within HLAIF consistently accelerate property verification, with their advantages becoming increasingly pronounced as circuit complexity grows. By resolving constraints more efficiently, Y-BMS and Y-RBS achieve substantial speedups across verification scenarios.

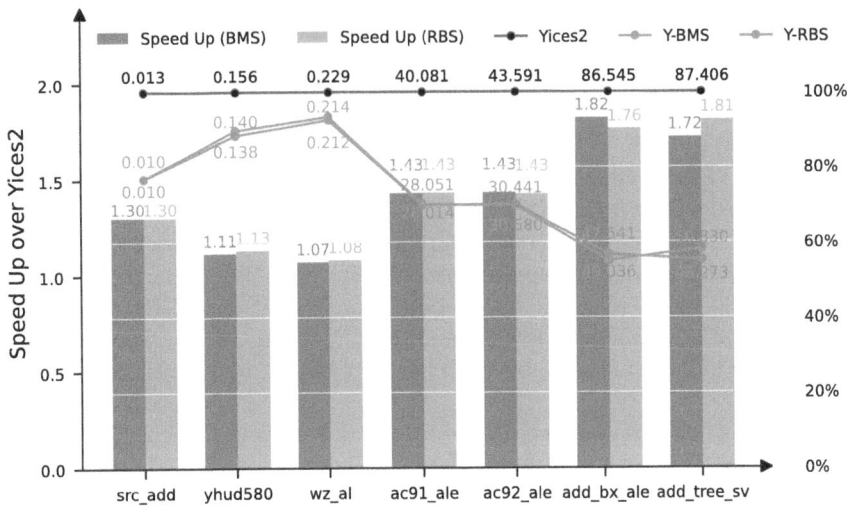

Fig. 4. Performance Improvement of Y-BMS and Y-RBS in Real-World Circuit Verification.

4.3   Result Analysis

In the first half of Figs. 1 and 2, Yices2, Y-BMS, and Y-RBS complete the tasks with high speed, and Yices2 exhibits a slight performance advantage due to the tasks' inherent simplicity and relatively few conflicts. In particular, rather than following Yices2's default strategy, HLAIF computes additional evaluation metrics such as the LBD value, activity, clause length, and clause relevance to guide the removal of learned clauses. The computational overhead introduced by these extra calculations reduces efficiency in smaller benchmarks. However, when SMT problem complexity increases, the proposed framework achieves significant performance gains. These observations indicate that the HLAIF framework integrates multiple deletion strategies by accounting for diverse factors that influence clause quality, thereby enhancing overall solver performance.

Table 2. Performance Comparison of Solvers on CPA-Ind

Solver	Performance Metrics			
	Solved	Time (s)	Decisions	Restarts
Yices2	622	37.268	1.224×10^7	13.188
Y-BMS	622	21.047	6.306×10^6	8.209
Y-RBS	622	23.680	6.824×10^6	8.934

An analysis of Table 1 indicates that incorporating the HLAIF framework with the BerkMin strategy and the relevance-based strategy significantly enhances solver search efficiency and overall problem-solving capability. Furthermore, the experiments show that Y-RBS achieves a slight performance advantage over Y-BMS for certain problem benchmarks. This suggests that the combined evaluation strategy incorporating relevance, LBD value, and clause activity provides more precise guidance in clause management.

To further evaluate the impact of these strategies, the proposed method was applied to a subset of 622 benchmarks from the SMT-COMP benchmarks CPAchecker-kInduction-Sos_Lab (CPA Ind), with the results summarized in Table 2. Both Y-BMS and Y-RBS successfully solved all benchmarks and achieved significant reductions in average solving time, decision counts, and restarts counts compared with the baseline solver Yices2. For example, Y-BMS decreased the solving time from 37 s to 21 s, nearly halved the number of decisions, and lowered the restart count by more than one third. Y-RBS exhibited a similar trend, although its solving times and decision counts were slightly higher than those of Y-BMS on this subset. These findings illustrate that incorporating HLAIF and adaptive criteria can markedly strengthen the solver's ability to identify critical clauses. Moreover, different clause-deletion strategies appear to offer varying degrees of benefit depending on the specific characteristics of the input problems. This underscores the importance of tailoring solver heuristics to the unique demands of diverse tasks.

5   Related Work

Early research in propositional satisfiability (SAT) [5] laid the foundation for the development of Satisfiability Modulo Theories (SMT) solvers [6], which extend SAT based reasoning by incorporating background theories such as arithmetic, bit vectors, and arrays. Two principal SMT frameworks have emerged, namely the Eager and the Lazy frameworks. In the Eager framework, the solving and proving processes operate concurrently, often employing preprocessing techniques to accelerate the entire procedure. In contrast, the Lazy framework separates these processes to prevent the generation of redundant information and thereby reduce memory usage [22]. Despite this architectural distinction, both frameworks depend on effective clause management strategies, particularly clause learning and deletion, to sustain scalability and efficiency.

Research on clause management has evolved considerably. Early investigations explored the relationships among unassigned variables, clause length, clause age, and other metrics to assess their impact on solver performance. For instance, the Chaff solver [19] introduced a deletion strategy based on relevance, positing that clauses with a greater number of unassigned variables exhibit lower utility. Subsequently, MiniSAT [11] incorporated deletion strategies based on clause activity, whereby the activity of a clause increases when it participates in conflicts. Similarly, the ZChaff [18] and BerkMin [12] solvers applied deletion strategies that considered clause length, age, and activity.

More recent approaches have further refined these strategies. The Glucose solver [1,3] introduced the Literal Block Distance (LBD) metric, which quantifies the effectiveness of clause learning by evaluating the number of distinct assignment levels present in a clause. Fewer assignment levels imply a higher correlation among variables, while a greater number of levels suggest a lower correlation. Building on this, the COMiniSatPS solver [21] improved upon the aggressive deletion strategy of MiniSAT and Glucose—which typically removes half of the learned clauses at each step—by classifying clauses into three levels based on their LBD values and applying differentiated deletion strategies accordingly. Additionally, Jabbour et al. [14] introduced the Size-Bounded Random (SBR) strategy, which retains all clauses shorter than or equal to a predefined threshold k while randomly deleting clauses that exceed this size, while combining clause length considerations with stochastic deletion to enhance solver performance on complex benchmarks.

Building on these advancements, Lonlac et al. [17] proposed a novel deletion strategy called dominance-based deletion. They highlighted that selecting an appropriate evaluation criterion for learned clauses remains an open challenge, as different criteria yield varying results. To address this, they proposed a composite approach that combines multiple evaluation criteria to assess clause quality more robustly. Specifically, they developed a formula to calculate the degree of dominance of a learned clause by averaging metrics such as the LBD value, clause length, and clause activity. To prevent any single criterion from disproportionately influencing the result, each metric is normalized prior to averaging. Learned clauses are then ranked based on their average evaluation score, which determines the deletion order.

6   Conclusions

In this paper, we introduce a dynamic weighting framework that leverages both LBD and clause activity to capture the structural characteristics of learned clauses as well as their conflict participation frequency. By integrating the Berk-Min strategy and the relevance-based strategy, the proposed framework facilitates a multidimensional evaluation of learned clauses, enabling their fine-grained management to enhance search efficiency and overall solver performance. Experimental results demonstrate that our approach significantly improves Yices2's performance, achieving average speed enhancements of 97.67% and 119.80% on benchmark suite while increasing the number of solved benchmarks. Moreover, the practical applicability of HLAIF is further validated on real-world circuit benchmarks, underscoring its robustness and effectiveness.

Acknowledgments. This work is supported by Shenzhen Science and Technology Program under Grant No. KJZD20230923115005009. It is also supported by the project under Grant No. KQTD20200820113105004.

References

1. Audemard, G., Simon, L.: Glucose: a solver that predicts learnt clauses quality. SAT Compet. 7–8 (2009)
2. Audemard, G., Simon, L.: Refining restarts strategies for SAT and UNSAT. In: Principles and Practice of Constraint Programming: 18th International Conference, CP 2012, Québec City, QC, Canada, 8–12 October 2012, pp. 118–126. Springer (2012)
3. Audemard, G., Simon, L.: Glucose in the SAT 2014 competition. In: Proceedings of SAT Competition, vol. 2014, p. 31 (2014)
4. Audemard, G., Simon, L.: On the glucose sat solver. Int. J. Artif. Intell. Tools **27**(01), 1840001 (2018)
5. Barrett, C.: From sat to SMT: successes and challenges. In: ACL2 Workshop, Northeastern University, 11–12 May 2009, pp. 1–71 (2009)
6. Barrett, C., Sebastiani, R., Seshia, S.A., Tinelli, C.: Satisfiability modulo theories. In: Handbook of Satisfiability, pp. 1267–1329. IOS Press (2021)
7. Chowdhury, M.S., Müller, M., You, J.H.: Exploiting glue clauses to design effective CDCL branching heuristics. In: Principles and Practice of Constraint Programming: 25th International Conference, CP 2019, Stamford, CT, USA, 30 September–4 October 2019, Proceedings 25, pp. 126–143. Springer (2019)
8. Davis, M., Logemann, G., Loveland, D.: A machine program for theorem-proving. Commun. ACM **5**(7), 394–397 (1962)
9. De Moura, L., Bjørner, N.: Z3: An efficient SMT solver. In: International conference on Tools and Algorithms for the Construction and Analysis of Systems, pp. 337–340. Springer (2008)
10. Dutertre, B.: Yices 2.2. In: International Conference on Computer Aided Verification, pp. 737–744. Springer (2014)
11. Eén, N., Sörensson, N.: An extensible sat-solver. In: International Conference on Theory and Applications of Satisfiability Testing, pp. 502–518. Springer (2003)
12. Goldberg, E., Novikov, Y.: BerkMin: a fast and robust sat-solver. Discret. Appl. Math. **155**(12), 1549–1561 (2007)
13. Gomes, C.P., Selman, B., Kautz, H., et al.: Boosting combinatorial search through randomization. In: AAAI/IAAI, vol. 98, no. 1998, pp. 431–437 (1998)
14. Jabbour, S., Lonlac, J., Sais, L., Salhi, Y.: Revisiting the learned clauses database reduction strategies. Int. J. Artif. Intell. Tools **27**(08), 1850033 (2018)
15. Kautz, H., Horvitz, E., Ruan, Y., Gomes, C., Selman, B.: Dynamic restart policies. In: AAAI/IAAI, vol. 97, pp. 674–681 (2002)
16. Liang, J.H., Ganesh, V., Zulkoski, E., Zaman, A., Czarnecki, K.: Understanding VSIDS branching heuristics in conflict-driven clause-learning SAT solvers. In: Hardware and Software: verification and Testing: 11th International Haifa Verification Conference, HVC 2015, Haifa, Israel, 17–19 November 2015, Proceedings 11, pp. 225–241. Springer (2015)
17. Lonlac, J., Nguifo, E.M.: Top-k learned clauses for modern sat solvers. Int. J. Artif. Intell. Tools **32**(01), 2350003 (2023)
18. Mahajan, Y.S., Fu, Z., Malik, S.: Zchaff2004: an efficient sat solver. In: International Conference on Theory and Applications of Satisfiability Testing, pp. 360–375. Springer (2004)
19. Moskewicz, M.W., Madigan, C.F., Zhao, Y., Zhang, L., Malik, S.: Chaff: engineering an efficient sat solver. In: Proceedings of the 38th annual Design Automation Conference, pp. 530–535 (2001)

20. Oh, C.: Between SAT and UNSAT: the fundamental difference in CDCL SAT. In: International Conference on Theory and Applications of Satisfiability Testing, pp. 307–323. Springer (2015)
21. Oh, C.: Cominisatps pulsar and ghackcomsps. SAT Compet. **2017**, 1 (2017)
22. Sebastiani, R.: Lazy satisfiability modulo theories. J. Satisfiabil. Boolean Model. Comput. **3**(3–4), 141–224 (2007)
23. Shim, C., Bae, J., Kim, B.: 30.3 VIP-Sat: a Boolean satisfiability solver featuring 5×12 variable in-memory processing elements with 98% solvability for 50-variables 218-clauses 3-sat problems. In: 2024 IEEE International Solid-State Circuits Conference (ISSCC), vol. 67, pp. 486–488. IEEE (2024)
24. Silva, J.M., Sakallah, K.A.: GRASP-a new search algorithm for satisfiability. In: Proceedings of International Conference on Computer Aided Design, pp. 220–227. IEEE (1996)
25. Wolf, C.: Yosys manual. Retrieved January **16**, 2021 (2021)
26. Zhang, L., Madigan, C.F., Moskewicz, M.H., Malik, S.: Efficient conflict driven learning in a Boolean satisfiability solver. In: IEEE/ACM International Conference on Computer Aided Design, ICCAD 2001. IEEE/ACM Digest of Technical Papers (Cat. No. 01CH37281), pp. 279–285. IEEE (2001)

SNRWLS: Improve (W)PMS Solver with Weighting Strategies Related to Number of Soft Clauses

Shuhao Chen[1], Menghua Jiang[1], and Yin Chen[1,2(✉)]

[1] School of Computer Science, South China Normal University, Guangzhou, China
1182198326@qq.com, jiangmenghua@m.scnu.edu.cn
[2] School of Artificial Intelligence, South China Normal University, Foshan, China
ychen@scnu.edu.cn

Abstract. Maximum Satisfiability Problem (MaxSAT) is a fundamental constraint optimization problem that plays a critical role in various real-world applications. (Weighted) Partial MaxSAT problem, denoted as (W)PMS, is the practical generalization of MaxSAT, and stochastic local search (SLS) algorithms are commonly used to solve (W)PMS problems. In this work, we study the deficiencies in the previous SLS solver and improve some of its strategies to obtain a new SLS solver, named SNRWLS, which includes three new strategies. First, we propose a strategy of parameter adjustment, which tunes some parameters of the solver when the search reaches a fixed time point. Second, we propose an initialization method that utilizes the assignment information of variables in obtained solutions to produce an initial assignment. Third, we propose a new weighting strategy and determine whether to apply its methods based on the number of soft clauses. Experimental results show that SNRWLS significantly outperforms state-of-the-art SLS solvers.

Keywords: maximum satisfiability · local search · initial assignment · clause weighting · number of clauses

1 Introduction

The Maximum Satisfiability Problem (MaxSAT) is one of the fundamental problems in artificial intelligence and theoretical computer science, and it is an extension of the Boolean Satisfiability Problem (SAT). MaxSAT is a fundamental constraint optimization problem, which involves finding an optimal solution that maximizes the objective function value while satisfying a series of constraints, that is, to find an assignment for a given set of Boolean variables and Boolean expressions that maximizes the number of satisfied clauses. Partial MaxSAT (PMS) and Weighted Partial MaxSAT (WPMS) are two generalized forms of MaxSAT. In the PMS, clauses are classified into hard and soft clauses, and the aim of the problem is to find an assignment that satisfies all of the hard clauses while maximizing the number of satisfied soft clauses. WPMS is an extension

P. Rümmer and Z. Wu (Eds.): TASE 2025, LNCS 15841, pp. 161–176, 2026.
https://doi.org/10.1007/978-3-031-98208-8_10

of PMS, in which each soft clause is associated with a positive integer as the weight of the clause, and the aim of the problem becomes to find an assignment such that all hard clauses are satisfied while the sum of the satisfied soft clause weights is as large as possible. In (W)PMS, hard and soft clause can correspond to the constraint (i.e., hard constraint) and the optimization objective (i.e., soft constraint) of the optimization problem respectively when coding the practical problem. This distinction makes (W)PMS more flexible and adaptable to a wider range of practical applications.

The research of MaxSAT solving algorithm has always been one of the hot topics in the fields of artificial intelligence and computer science. MaxSAT has a wide range of applications across various domains. Many optimization problems can be encoded as (W)PMS, which can then be solved using (W)PMS solvers. In earlier studies, (W)PMS has been proven to be applicable to many real-world problem-solving scenarios, such as finding error sources in electronic design automation [1], group testing [2], optimal partial order planning problem [3], and set covering problems [4].

Stochastic local search (SLS) is an incomplete algorithm based on local search, which is widely used to find approximate solutions for large-scale test cases. It performs a random walk iteratively in the solution space, selecting variables and flipping their values to satisfy all hard clauses while maximizing the sum of weights of satisfied soft clauses. In recent years, with the efforts of related researchers, many numerous SLS solvers with remarkable effectiveness have been developed, such as SatLike3.0 [16], BandMaxSAT [17], and NuWLS [18], etc. These solvers incorporate many creative strategies, mainly falling into three categories: weighting mechanisms for adjusting the importance between clauses, algorithms for assigning initial values to variables, and algorithms for selecting variables to flip.

Although these solvers have achieved significant success in solving (W)PMS problems, they still have shortcomings and room for improvement. For example, they lack corresponding measures when they stop outputting better solutions far before reaching the cutoff time, resulting in a waste of solution time; during the search process, when reassigning initial values to variables, they fail to fully utilize the valuable information contained in the previous variable values; the designed clause weight adjustment strategy cannot be flexibly adjusted according to the characteristics of clauses in different instances. To address these issues, in this paper, we propose a new (W)PMS local search algorithm based on NuWLS.

The main contributions of this work are as follows:

- We propose a strategy of parameter adjustment, which tunes some parameters of the solver when the search reaches a fixed time point. This strategy aims to reactivate the solver by tuning the parameters at a time point when the solver shows low efficiency, so that the solver can better utilize the whole cutoff time.
- We propose a new strategy for providing initial variable assignment, named Vote-Assn. Vote-Assn saves the assignments of each variable each time the

solver obtains a solution, and uses the information contained in these assignments to produce high-quality initial assignments.

- We propose a new weighting strategy, named SNR-Weighting. The new strategy in SNR-Weighting consists of three parts: (1) increasing the weight of hard clauses more significantly when the solver has not found a feasible solution yet; (2) delaying the smoothing process for clauses that have just had their weights increased; and (3) advancing the weighting of soft clauses under certain conditions. For all these new strategies, their adoption during the search process is determined by the number of soft clauses in the current instance, which can improve the performance of the weighting strategy.
- Based on these three ideas, we propose a new SLS solver, named SNRWLS. SNRWLS significantly outperforms the state-of-the-art SLS solvers Band-MaxSAT and NuWLS on all standard benchmarks in the incomplete tracks of MaxSAT Evaluations (MSEs).

2   Related Work

In recent years, with the application value of MaxSAT in industrial and other practical fields being continuously discovered, solving algorithms for MaxSAT have garnered growing attention. The algorithms for solving MaxSAT problems are mainly divided into two categories: complete algorithms and incomplete algorithms. Complete algorithms guarantee that an optimal solution can be found at the end of the algorithm execution, and their optimality can be proven, which mainly includes branch-and-bound algorithms [5,6] and SAT-based algorithms [7-9]. Incomplete algorithms cannot guarantee that the solution found is optimal, but they can find a solution that is as good as possible within a given time.

SLS is a representative incomplete algorithm. The early SLS usually starts from a random assignment and uses the greedy strategy to flip variables to achieve better assignment [10]. Cha et al. and Thornton et al. further refined the weighting mechanism by addressing the issue that the weight of hard clauses may be too large [11], and dynamically adjusted the clause weights during the process of finding better solutions to more effectively determine the direction for further search [12,13]. On the other hand, to avoid the problem of low-quality random initial assignments, Cai et al. introduced a unit propagation technique that provides SLS with a more feasible initial solution [14].

Cai et al. proposed the well-known SATLike solver, which has the ability to compare with complete solvers in dealing with large problem instances in practical engineering and industrial fields [15]. Then, the authors of SATLike further introduced two improved versions: SATLike2.0 and SATLike3.0 [16]. Up to SATLike3.0, the new strategies added mainly include: a new weighting mechanism Weighting-MS, which assigns different weights to soft clauses and hard clauses to help the solver better prioritize between them; a probabilistic sampling strategy BMS, which significantly reduces the time spent on selecting the next variable to flip; a reduction algorithm UP-Deci, which generates an initial solution for the solver; and soft construction score of variables, which helps the solver identify the potentially more advantageous side when unit propagation encounters a conflict.

Due to the outstanding performance of SATLike3.0 in incomplete solving of (W)PMS, many related researchers have chosen to make further improvements based on it. Among these, BandMaxSAT and NuWLS are particularly notable examples. BandMaxSAT, proposed by Zheng et al., incorporates the basic model of Multi-Armed Bandit (MAB) from reinforcement learning [17,18]. It makes the arms in MAB correspond to soft clauses in (W)PMS, effectively evaluating the benefit of satisfying a soft clause and using this evaluation to determine which soft clause to satisfy next. Additionally, the introduction of the hybrid decimation method, HyDeci, also enhances the original unit propagation strategy. NuWLS, proposed by Chu et al., incorporates a novel clause weighting strategy called Dist-Weighting that updates the weights of hard and soft clauses using different conditions [19]. It is worth noting that, unlike SATLike3.0 and BandMaxSAT, NuWLS restarts after a certain number of steps in the local search phase. Each restart applies a new initialization method for clause weights proposed by the authors, which significantly impacts the solver's performance.

3   Preliminaries

The MaxSAT problem is typically defined on propositional logic Conjunctive Normal Form (CNF). Consider a set of Boolean variables $V = \{v_1, v_2, \ldots, v_n\}$, each variable x_i and its negation $\neg x_i$ is defined as a literal l. A clause is a disjunction of literals, i.e., $c_i = l_1 \vee l_2 \vee \ldots \vee l_m$, and a CNF formula F is a conjunction of clauses, i.e., $F = c_1 \wedge c_2 \wedge \ldots \wedge c_k$. A literal x_i is satisfied if the current assignment assigns the Boolean value True to x_i, while a literal $\neg x_i$ is satisfied if $\neg x_i$ is assigned False. A clause is said to be satisfied when at least one literal in the clause has been assigned the corresponding value; otherwise, it is falsified.

$V(F)$ represents the set of all variables in formula F. The variable x_i will be assigned a value of 1 or 0 during the search for a solution, representing the Boolean value True and False, respectively. A mapping $\alpha: V(F) \rightarrow \{0, 1\}$ is said to be a complete assignment of F if it maps all variables x to a Boolean value. Given a CNF formula F, the aim of MaxSAT is to find a complete assignment of $V(F)$ that satisfies as many clauses in F as possible. For the generalized form of MaxSAT, (W)PMS, when an assignment α satisfies all hard clauses, it is referred to as a feasible solution for (W)PMS, and the cost of α is denoted as $cost(\alpha)$. The aim of (W)PMS is to find a feasible solution α with the lowest $cost(\alpha)$. The feasible solution with the lowest $cost(\alpha)$ is also referred to as the optimal solution for a (W)PMS instance. For PMS, the lowest $cost(\alpha)$ means satisfying as many soft clauses as possible; for WPMS, the lowest $cost(\alpha)$ is achieved by minimizing the sum of the weights of unsatisfied soft clauses.

The solving process of the local search algorithm for MaxSAT involves a large number of operations that change the current assignments of variables, referred to as flipping. Flipping means to change the value of a variable from 1 to 0, or vice versa. In local search algorithms, a $score(x)$ is often introduced for variable x to assist the algorithm in selecting the variable to be flipped. The value of $score(x)$ is equal to the sum of the weights of the satisfied clauses increased by flipping variable x. If the score of a variable is greater than 0, it is called a good variable. During the solving process of the algorithm, if there is no good variable currently, it is said that the solution has fallen into a local optimum, meaning that flipping any single variable will not reduce the sum of the weights of the currently unsatisfied soft clauses.

4   Methodology

4.1   Bottleneck Time Parameter Adjustment for (W)PMS

As an incomplete algorithm, the local search algorithm will be set with a cutoff time for its execution. However, this cutoff time is often not fully utilized by local search algorithms when solving MaxSAT instances. In other words, when dealing with different instances, the algorithm may stop producing better solutions before a same time point, which we call the bottleneck time. Taking a cutoff time of 300 s as an example, and assuming a bottleneck time of 200 s, the proportion of SATLike3.0, BandMaxSAT and NuWLS getting better solutions after the bottleneck time is shown in Table 1. The proportions shown in Table 1 are the averages of the results obtained by the solver on five PMS and WPMS instances, respectively.

It can be observed from Table 1 that, on average, when facing instances of PMS, all three solvers have further solutions only on less than 15% of instances after reaching the bottleneck time, while this proportion is about 25% when facing instances of WPMS. This result indicates that these solvers have very low solving efficiency after the bottleneck time. To solve this problem, we tune part of the parameters of the solver when the solver run reaches the bottleneck time, in order to guide the solver to explore more directions different from the previous one. The parameters changed include the number of sampling k in the BMS strategy, which is changed from a fixed value to be related to the number of clauses in the instance; and the value h_inc in the weighting strategy, which represents the change in weights applied to hard clauses each time. In particular, if the solver is continuously outputting better solutions when it reaches the bottleneck time, this indicates that the solver has a high solving efficiency at that moment, and the solver should be kept in the current parameter settings to continue searching. Therefore, in addition to reaching the bottleneck time, the solver's parameters should only be tuned if it does not output a solution within 10 s.

Table 1. Proportion of Solutions Obtained after Bottleneck Time

	SATLike3.0	BandMaxSAT	NuWLS
PMS	0.147	0.140	0.114
WPMS	0.241	0.242	0.261

[a]Results keep three decimal places.

4.2   Vote-Assn for (W)PMS

NuWLS restarts and initializes the assignment of variables several times during the local search [19], it means that after a number of steps, the solver will discard the previously obtained variable assignments. However, these assignment results may contain some information that is beneficial to further search. That is, the assignment of some variables may be more suitable as a starting point for the next search.

Therefore, we propose a new initial complete assignment construction strategy called Vote-Assn. The pseudo-code of Vote-Assn is outlined in algorithm 1. Specifically, we save the assignment of each variable v in an array $initial\_value$ whenever the solver obtains a better feasible solution. In this way, when constructing the initial solution, we can use $initial\_value[v]$ to determine which value has been assigned to variable v more frequently in the already output solutions, and assign that value to variable v in current initialization (lines 7–10). In particular, to prevent the $initial\_value[v]$ of too many variables from reaching a large number that is difficult to reverse in sign, causing the solver to restart from the same or a similar initial assignment each time, the newly added part will be alternated with UP-Deci [16] (line 2). The new strategy will be executed only after at least one feasible solution has been obtained, and the parameter $temp$, which determines whether to execute the new strategy or UP-Deci, is set to 0 at the beginning of the entire SLS algorithm.

4.3   SNR-Weighting for (W)PMS

Weighting strategy is a popular strategy in SLS algorithm, used to escape local optima by adjusting the weights of clauses and changing their priority relationships. However, none of the previous weighting strategies attempt to discuss the effectiveness of the strategy in terms of the number of soft and hard clauses. Actually, the same weighting strategy may present different effects when facing different instances with different numbers of soft and hard clauses. For example, a weighting strategy may be highly efficient in the face of instances with a high number of soft clauses and perform poorly in the opposite case. Thus, we propose a new weighting strategy, named SNR-Weighting, which improves the weighting strategy Dist-Weighting in NuWLS, and the newly proposed strategy discusses the number of soft clauses.

Firstly, if the solver has not found a feasible solution, meaning there are still unsatisfied hard clauses, then the primary task of the solver should be to satisfy all the hard clauses. And the most direct way to make the solver more inclined to

---

Algorithm 1: Vote-Assn

Input: A (W)PMS instance F, number of instance variables $VarNum$
Output: A complete assignment A of variables in F

1 **if** $temp == 0$ **then**
2 | generate an initial complete assignment by Up-Deci(F);
3 | **if** A *feasible solution has been found* **then**
4 | | $temp := 1$;

5 **else if** $temp == 1$ **then**
6 | **for** *each* $v \in [0, VarNum - 1]$ **do**
7 | | **if** v *is assigned to 1 more frequently* **then**
8 | | | $v := 1$;
9 | | **else if** v *is assigned to 0 more frequently* **then**
10 | | | $v := 0$;
11 | | **else**
12 | | | assign v a random value;

13 | $temp := 0$;

14 **return** the resulting complete assignment A;

---

satisfy hard clauses is to increase the weight of the hard clauses. Therefore, each time the weight of a hard clause is increased, if the solver has not yet found a feasible solution, the increment is multiplied by a factor p greater than 1 (where $p = 2$ when solving WPMS; $p = 1.5$ when solving PMS) (lines 11–14). This strategy will be more effective when there are a large number of soft clauses, so it is set to only apply the strategy when the number of soft clauses is no less than λ.

Secondly, when the solver deems that a clause requires more attention in subsequent searches, it increases the clause's weight to make it a large-weight clause. The weight of a clause reflects its importance, and an appropriate weight relationship between clauses can guide the solver towards a reasonable search direction. However, previous weighting strategies do not consider the time when a clause becomes a large-weight clause during smoothing (i.e., reducing the weights of clauses). If some clauses are smoothed immediately after their weights are increased, it may cause the solver to miss a good search direction. To handle this issue, we propose a strategy of delayed smoothing, that is, skipping the first and second weight reduction operation of a large-weight clause. This strategy is also applied when the number of soft clauses is no less than δ (lines 5–6, lines 19–20).

Finally, in Dist-Weighting, the weight of soft clauses is increased only after all hard clauses are satisfied. This setting helps the solver better achieve the primary goal of the (W)PMS problem, which is to find a feasible solution. However, besides this goal, finding a solution with a lower cost is also an important criterion for evaluating the quality of a solver. In other words, the solver needs to find a balance between satisfying hard clauses and satisfying soft clauses, and should not be too inclined to hard clauses. Furthermore, if the number of hard clauses in an instance far exceeds the number of soft clauses, the interference of soft clauses with the goal of prioritizing hard clause satisfaction will be reduced. Therefore, we consider relaxing the restriction of satisfying all hard clauses when the proportion of soft clauses to the total number of clauses is low (less than γ), start weighting soft clauses earlier (lines 23–26).

Algorithm 2: SNR-Weighting

Input: The current assignment α, the best found solution so far α^*, number of soft clauses $SoftClauseNum$, number of clauses $ClauseNum$.

1 $prob :=$ A random real number between 0 and 1;
2 $p :=$ A fixed number greater than 1;
3 **if** $prob < h\_sp$ **and** *a solution has been found* **then**
4   **for** *each satisfied hard clause c* **do**
5   **if** $time\_large[c] \leq 1$ **and** $SoftClauseNum \geq \delta$ **then**
6              $time\_large[c] := time\_large[c] + 1;$
7   **else if** $w(c) > h\_inc$ **then**
8              $w(c) := w(c) - h\_inc;$
9 **else**
10   **for** *each falsified hard clause c* **do**
11   **if** *haven't found a solution yet* **and** $SoftClauseNum \geq \lambda$ **then**
12             $w(c) := w(c) + p * h\_inc;$
13   **else**
14             $w(c) := w(c) + h\_inc;$
15         $time\_large[c] := 0;$
16 **if** $cost(\alpha) \geq cost(\alpha^*)$ **then**
17   **if** $prob < s\_sp$ **then**
18   **for** *each satisfied soft clause c* **do**
19   **if** $time\_large[c] \leq 1$ **and** $SoftClauseNum \geq \delta$ **then**
20                 $time\_large[c] := time\_large[c] + 1;$
21   **else if** $w(c) > s\_inc$ **then**
22                 $w(c) := w(c) - s\_inc;$
23   **else if** *current assignment α is feasible* **or** (*number of unsatisfied clauses is less than 10%* **and** $SoftClauseNum / ClauseNum < \gamma$) **then**
24   **for** *each falsified soft clause c* **do**
25   **if** *w(c) does not exceed the upper weight limit of c* **then**
26                     $w(c) := w(c) + s\_inc; time\_large[c] := 0;$
27 **return;**

Here, λ, δ, and γ are all positive hyperparameters used to control whether to apply the corresponding sub-strategies in SNR-Weighting.

4.4   The SNRWLS Algorithm

Based on the three aforementioned ideas, we develop a new SLS algorithm named SNRWLS, an acronym for Soft Clauses Number Related Weighting based Local Search. The pseudo-code of SNRWLS is outlined in Algorithm 3.

Before the local search begins, set the found optimal solution α^* to empty and the lowest cost $cost^*$ to infinity. Then, the solver iteratively performs local search until the cutoff time is reached (lines 8–23). The search restarts after a certain number of steps, and when it starts or restarts, the solver utilizes Vote-Assn to obtain an initial complete assignment, from which the search is then conducted (line 5). During the search of the algorithm, whenever a better solution is found, α^* and $cost^*$ are updated accordingly.

In each round of the search, solver selects a variable and flips its value. The selection rule is as follows: if there are good variables (i.e., variables v with $score(v) > 0$), solver chooses a variable from the set D of good variables. In particular, if the number of variables in D exceeds a certain threshold, the solver switches to using the BMS strategy to sample from D, which ensures the quality of the selected variable while saving time on selection. Conversely, if D is empty, the solver first updates the weights of all clauses through SNR-Weighting. At this point, if there are any unsatisfied hard clauses, one is randomly chosen; otherwise, an unsatisfied soft clause is chosen, and then the variable with the highest score in that clause is selected for further flipping. After the search time reaches 200 s, if the solver does not find a solution within nearly 10 s, some parameters are tuned (lines 3–4).

Finally, when the cutoff time is reached, the solver reports α^* and $cost^*$. Otherwise, if no feasible solution has been found, it reports 'No solution found'.

5   Experiments

To validate the effectiveness of the proposed new strategy, we compare SNR-WLS with two state-of-the-art (W)PMS incomplete solvers from recent years: BandMaxSAT [18] and NuWLS [19]. Additionally, we conduct ablation studies to validate the new strategies proposed in SNRWLS.

5.1   Experimental Setup

All experiments are conducted on a server using an Intel(R) Xeon(R) Gold 5220R CPU with 2.20GHz and 256 GB RAM, running Ubuntu 22.04.3 Linux operation system on windows 10. SNRWLS is implemented in C++ and complied by g++ with "-O3" option. For SNR-Weighting, its hyperparameters λ, δ, and γ are set to 1000, 1000, and 0.4%, respectively. The influence of different hyperparameter settings on the performance of SNRWLS will be discussed in Sect. 5.4.

We evaluate SNRWLS on 12 benchmarks, i.e., PMS and WPMS benchmarks from the incomplete tracks of MaxSAT Evaluations (MSEs) 2019 to 2024, denoted by PMS_2019 to PMS_2024 and WPMS_2019 to WPMS_2024 respectively. The cutoff time is set to 300 s, consistent with the settings in MSEs and the

---

Algorithm 3: SNRWLS

Input: A (W)PMS instance F, cutoff time *cutoff*
Output: A feasible assignment α of F and its cost, or "No feasible solution found"

1 $\alpha^* := \emptyset; cost^* := +\infty$;
2 **while** *running time* < *cutoff* **do**
3   **if** *running time* $\geq$ 200 **and** *no solution was found within* 10 *seconds* **then**
4   tune parameters of the solver;
5      $\alpha :=$ an initial complete assignment by Vote-Assn(F);
6   initialize the clause weights;
7      $L = 10000000$;
8   **for** *step* = 0; *step* < L; *step* + + **do**
9   **if** α *is feasible* **and** $cost^* > cost(\alpha)$ **then**
10             $\alpha^* := \alpha; cost^* := cost(\alpha)$;
11             $L = step + 10000000$;
12   **if** $cost^* == 0$ **then**
13   **return** α^* and $cost^*$;
14   **if** $D := \{x | score(x) > 0\} \neq \emptyset$ **then**
15             $v :=$ a variable in D selected by BMS;
16   **else**
17   update clause weights by SNR-Weighting;
18   **if** $\exists$ *falsified hard clauses* **then**
19                 $c :=$ a random falsified hard clause;
20   **else**
21                 $c :=$ a random falsified soft clause;
22             $v :=$ the variable with highest score in c;
23         $\alpha := \alpha$ with v flipped;
24 **if** $\alpha^* \neq \emptyset$ **then return** α^* and $cost^*$;
25 **else return** No solution found;

---

two solvers used for comparison, each solver is executed once on each instance. We present the results of each benchmark by the number of times each solver achieves a lower cost, denoted as "#win". We also present the average time taken by the solver to achieve a lower cost on each benchmark, denoted as "#time", measured in seconds. The number of instances in each benchmark is indicated by "#inst". The best result for each benchmark is highlighted in bold.

5.2   Comparisons Against SLS Solvers

We respectively compared SNRWLS with the solvers used for comparison, Band-MaxSAT and NuWLS, on all test instances, and the results are shown in Table 2 and 3.

Table 2. Comparison of SNRWLS with BandMaxSAT

Benchmark	#inst.	SNRWLS		BandMaxSAT	
		#win.	time	#win.	time
PMS_2019	299	**213**	80.58	143	69.34
PMS_2020	258	**182**	80.85	123	78.37
PMS_2021	147	**104**	67.14	68	61.37
PMS_2022	168	**111**	76.85	77	70.02
PMS_2023	179	**121**	112.26	68	117.09
PMS_2024	216	**150**	80.29	100	82.64
WPMS_2019	292	**218**	121.56	99	85.33
WPMS_2020	249	**186**	120.54	80	95.95
WPMS_2021	147	**86**	137.87	55	118.55
WPMS_2022	191	**95**	171.57	84	120.58
WPMS_2023	155	**82**	153.54	61	123.77
WPMS_2024	224	**129**	148.16	99	132.51

Table 3. Comparison of SNRWLS with NuWLS

Benchmark	#inst.	SNRWLS		NuWLS	
		#win.	time	#win.	time
PMS_2019	299	**195**	82.62	189	66.72
PMS_2020	258	**172**	78.64	167	70.62
PMS_2021	147	**107**	75.25	91	43.58
PMS_2022	168	**125**	85.47	103	57.77
PMS_2023	179	**113**	111.11	102	87.53
PMS_2024	216	**150**	81.30	134	70.50
WPMS_2019	292	**196**	126.19	147	87.53
WPMS_2020	249	**166**	119.87	125	90.77
WPMS_2021	147	**92**	135.01	67	105.70
WPMS_2022	191	**127**	186.56	67	133.20
WPMS_2023	155	**108**	158.87	56	90.08
WPMS_2024	224	**153**	161.72	93	111.78

The data in Table 2 and 3 indicate that, across all benchmarks, SNRWLS obtains better solutions more times than BandMaxSAT and NuWLS. This indicates that SNRWLS has higher performance compared to these two solvers when solving (W)PMS problems.

Table 4. Comparison of SNRWLS with variant SNRWLS-abl1-3

Benchmark	#inst.	SNRWLS		SNRWLS-abl1		SNRWLS-abl2		SNRWLS-abl3	
		#win.	time	#win.	time	#win.	time	#win.	time
PMS_2019	299	**179**	76.51	163	66.76	177	75.95	167	70.67
PMS_2020	258	**155**	70.40	149	69.50	149	72.48	149	66.65
PMS_2021	147	**97**	62.56	89	48.78	90	63.94	94	68.64
PMS_2022	168	**110**	72.77	102	62.92	108	77.07	104	68.61
PMS_2023	179	**95**	102.94	89	95.84	85	91.54	88	87.85
PMS_2024	216	**138**	73.84	129	69.88	120	68.30	114	60.76
WPMS_2019	292	**176**	113.98	136	79.45	140	97.57	134	95.98
WPMS_2020	249	**153**	117.67	121	94.12	124	96.65	117	98.04
WPMS_2021	147	**84**	136.90	69	110.64	67	111.59	62	93.37
WPMS_2022	191	**86**	172.88	52	123.69	76	172.44	70	158.66
WPMS_2023	155	**79**	143.09	57	102.26	61	126.01	67	140.83
WPMS_2024	224	102	136.22	79	113.28	**110**	144.46	92	136.51

Table 5. Comparison of SNRWLS with SNRWLS-abl4 and SNRWLS-abl3

Benchmark	#inst.	SNRWLS		SNRWLS-abl4		SNRWLS-abl3	
		#win.	time	#win.	time	#win.	time
PMS_2019	299	175	78.00	**182**	73.87	166	71.58
PMS_2020	258	**155**	71.33	154	69.53	148	68.83
PMS_2021	147	**94**	66.34	91	50.83	90	71.63
PMS_2022	168	**109**	76.56	103	65.48	101	67.60
PMS_2023	179	**100**	107.84	80	99.13	94	91.04
PMS_2024	216	**133**	68.47	131	77.41	114	61.83
WPMS_2019	292	**170**	108.55	163	104.87	127	94.28
WPMS_2020	249	135	104.69	**136**	100.91	109	95.34
WPMS_2021	147	74	123.58	**81**	120.11	56	88.38
WPMS_2022	191	**85**	172.60	66	159.52	78	159.81
WPMS_2023	155	**77**	140.15	66	125.14	66	130.94
WPMS_2024	224	**113**	144.08	93	136.98	93	132.87

5.3   Ablation Study

Then, we conduct an ablation study to analyze the impact of the proposed new strategies on the overall performance of the solver. Based on SNRWLS, we design four variant solvers: SNRWLS-abl1, which removes parameter tuning for bottleneck time; SNRWLS-abl2, which removes Vote-Assn; SNRWLS-abl3, which removes SNR-Weighting; and SNRWLS-abl4, which does not discuss the number of soft clauses in SNR-Weighting. With these variant models, we constructed two groups of ablation experiments. The results are shown in Tables 4 and 5.

From Table 4, we can observe that, except for the 2024 WPMS benchmark where SNRWLS-abl2 has a slight advantage over SNRWLS, any solver lacking one of the new strategies performs worse than SNRWLS on all benchmarks, indicating that all three new strategies are effective and necessary. Meanwhile, it can be seen from the data of #time that the average time for SNRWLS-abl1 to obtain the optimal solution with lower cost is less than SNRWLS on all benchmarks. Combined with the fact that SNRWLS is superior to SNRWLS-abl1 on all benchmarks, it can be inferred that the measures we took at the bottleneck time successfully activated the solver. It makes the solver make full use of the whole cutoff time.

In addition, in order to explore the effectiveness of SNR-Weighting without discussing the number of soft clauses, we compared SNRWLS, SNRWLS-abl3 and SNRWLS-abl4. That is, we used three situations: using the complete SNR-Weighting, using SNR-Weighting without discussing the number of soft clauses, and not using SNR-Weighting at all. Table 5 shows that on most instances, the performance of SNRWLS-abl4 is better than that of SNRWLS-abl3, while the performance of SNRWLS is better than that of SNRWLS-abl4. This result indicates that even without discussing the number of soft clauses, SNR-Weighting remains effective, and its effectiveness is further enhanced when using the number of soft clauses as the division criterion. Meanwhile, we can also see that on a small number of benchmarks, without discussing the number of soft clauses can achieve better results. A potential reason is that the number of soft clauses is only one of the factors affecting whether the weighting strategy is suitable for the corresponding instances. Therefore, deciding whether to adopt the weighting strategy based on the number of soft clauses is not appropriate for some instances.

5.4   Effects of Hyperparameter Settings on SNR-Weighting

In SNR-Weighting, we introduce three hyperparameters, namely λ, δ, and γ, which are used to determine whether to apply the corresponding sub-strategies. To study the impact of different hyperparameter settings, we conducted an empirical evaluation to measure the performance of SNRWLS under various hyperparameter settings. Specifically, the values of λ and δ were set to $\{100, 1000, 10000\}$, and the values of γ were set to $\{0.2\%, 0.4\%, 0.8\%\}$. In this empirical evaluation, we selected two of the latest benchmarks, that is, the PMS and WPMS benchmarks from the incomplete track of MSEs 2024. Table 6 demonstrates the performance of SNRWLS under different hyperparameter settings. It can be seen from Table 6 that the parameter values selected in this paper $(1000,1000,0.4\%)$ have achieved the best results on both benchmarks. Additionally, variations in parameter settings had a significant impact on the performance of SNRWLS for WPMS instances, while their influence on PMS instances was relatively minor. This might also be one of the reasons why SNRWLS does not perform as outstandingly on PMS instances.

Table 6. Experimental Results of SNRWLS under Different Hyperparameter Settings

λ	δ	γ	WPMS_2024	PMS_2024
100	100	0.2%	97	148
100	1000	0.2%	94	150
100	10000	0.2%	90	146
100	100	0.4%	101	143
100	1000	0.4%	90	146
100	10000	0.4%	88	142
100	100	0.8%	98	147
100	1000	0.8%	89	149
100	10000	0.8%	84	147
1000	100	0.2%	95	149
1000	1000	0.2%	98	148
1000	10000	0.2%	89	145
1000	100	0.4%	100	140
1000	1000	0.4%	**108**	**151**
1000	10000	0.4%	93	143
1000	100	0.8%	95	150
1000	1000	0.8%	91	150
1000	10000	0.8%	86	146
10000	100	0.2%	88	150
10000	1000	0.2%	91	**151**
10000	10000	0.2%	99	141
10000	100	0.4%	88	140
10000	1000	0.4%	91	144
10000	10000	0.4%	94	143
10000	100	0.8%	92	147
10000	1000	0.8%	90	147
10000	10000	0.8%	92	146

6   Conclusion

The aim of this paper is to enhance the performance of a previous SLS solver by proposing several new strategies. Firstly, we introduce a parameter tuning strategy that modifies solver parameters at a predetermined point in time to guide the solver towards finding a new solution direction. Secondly, we propose a new initial solution generation strategy that uses the information of the obtained solutions to produce the initial assignment. Lastly, we introduce a new weighting strategy that utilizes the number of soft clauses to improve its performance. By integrating these three strategies, we propose a new SLS solver named SNRWLS. Extensive experiments have been conducted, demonstrating the effectiveness of SNRWLS.

In future work, we will continue to explore and improve these strategies. SNRWLS performs well on WPMS, but only slightly outperforms NuWLS on PMS. This will be a focus for our further improvement. We will also explore optimal hyperparameter settings, or reduce the use of hard-coding.

References

1. Chen, Y., Safarpour, S., Marques-Silva, J., Veneris, A.: Automated design debugging with maximum satisfiability. IEEE Trans. Comput.-Aided Des. Integr. Circ. Syst. **29**(11), 1804–1817 (2010)
2. Ciampiconi, L., Ghosh, B., Scarlett, J., Meel, K.S.: A MaxSAT-based framework for group testing. In: Proceedings of the AAAI Conference on Artificial Intelligence, New York, pp. 10144–10152 (2020)
3. Muise, C., McIlraith, S.A., Beck, J.C.: Optimization of partial-order plans via MaxSAT. In: ICAPS Workshop on Constraint Satisfaction Techniques for Planning and Scheduling Problems, COPLAS, Freiburg (2011)
4. Naji-Azimi, Z., Toth, P., Galli, L.: An electromagnetism metaheuristic for the unicost set covering problem. Eur. J. Oper. Res. **205**(2), 290–300 (2010)
5. Cherif, M.S., Habet, D., Abramé, A.: Understanding the power of Max-SAT resolution through UP-resilience. Artif. Intell. **289**, 103397 (2020)
6. Li, C.-M., Xu, Z., Coll, J., Manyà, F., Habet, D., He, K.: Combining clause learning and branch and bound for MaxSAT. In Proceedings of the 27th International Conference on Principles and Practice of Constraint Programming, Montpellier, vol. 210, pp. 38:1-38:18 (2021)
7. Fu, Z., Malik, S.: On solving the partial MAX-SAT problem. In: Biere, A., Gomes, C.P. (eds.) SAT 2006. LNCS, vol. 4121, pp. 252–265. Springer, Heidelberg (2006). https://doi.org/10.1007/11814948_25
8. Ansótegui, C., Bonet, M.L., Levy, J.: SAT-based MaxSAT algorithms. Artif. Intell. **196**, 77–105 (2013)
9. Nadel, A.: Anytime weighted MaxSAT with improved polarity selection and bitvector optimization. In: Proceedings of the 2019 Formal Methods in Computer Aided Design, San Jose, California, pp. 193–202 (2019)
10. Selman, B., Levesque, H.J., Mitchell, D.G.: A new method for solving hard satisfiability problems. In: Proceedings of the 10th National Conference on Artificial Intelligence, San Jose, California, pp. 440–446 (1992)
11. Cha, B., Iwama, K., Kambayashi, Y., Miyazaki, S.: Local search algorithms for partial MAXSAT. In: Proceedings of AAAI, Rhode Island, pp. 263–268 (1997)
12. Thornton, J., Bain, S., Sattar, A., Pham, D.N.: A two level local search for MAX-SAT problems with hard and soft constraints. In: Proceedings of Artificial Intelligence 2002, Heidelberg, pp. 603–614 (2002)
13. Thornton, J., Sattar, A.: Dynamic constraint weighting for over-constrained problems. In: Lee, H.-Y., Motoda, H. (eds.) PRICAI 1998. LNCS, vol. 1531, pp. 377–388. Springer, Heidelberg (1998). https://doi.org/10.1007/BFb0095285
14. Cai, S., Luo, C., Zhang, H.: From decimation to local search and back: a new approach to MaxSAT. In: Proceedings of the Twenty-Sixth International Joint Conference on Artificial Intelligence, Melbourne, pp. 571–577 (2017)

15. Lei, Z., Cai, S.: Solving (weighted) partial MaxSAT by dynamic local search for SAT. In: IJCAI, Stockholm, vol. 7, pp. 1346–1352 (2018)
16. Cai, S., Lei, Z.: Old techniques in new ways: clause weighting, unit propagation and hybridization for maximum satisfiability. Artif. Intell. **287**, 103354 (2020)
17. Slivkins, A.: Introduction to multiarmed bandits. Found. Trends Mach. Learn. **12**(1–2), 1–286 (2019)
18. Zheng, J., He, K., Zhou, J., Jin, Y., Li, C.-M., Manya, F.: BandMaxSAT: a local search MaxSAT solver with multi-armed bandit. In: Proceedings of the Thirty-First International Joint Conference on Artificial Intelligence, Vienna, pp. 1901–1907 (2022)
19. Chu, Y., Cai, S., Luo, C.: NuWLS: improving local search for (weighted) partial MaxSAT by new weighting techniques. In: The Thirty-Seventh AAAI Conference on Artificial Intelligence, Washington, DC, pp. 3915–3923 (2023)

Trustworthy AI and System Software

Robust Deep Reinforcement Learning Using Formal Verification

Avraham Raviv$^{(\boxtimes)}$, Shaiel Vistuch, Boaz Gurevich, Erel Dekel,
and Hillel Kugler

Bar-Ilan University, Ramat Gan, Israel
{ravivav1,hillelk}@biu.ac.il

Abstract. We propose a method to enhance the robustness and efficiency of deep reinforcement learning (DRL) by integrating formal verification techniques into the training loop. Our approach uses counterexamples generated by verification tools as corrective feedback to guide policy adjustments, enabling the agent to avoid unsafe actions and learn faster. Inspired by imitation learning, the verification tool acts as an expert that continuously refines the neural network when the agent's policy fails. Experiments in challenging environments such as Frozen Lake and Sokoban demonstrate that our method yields substantial improvements in success rates and reduces the number of training episodes by up to 70%, all while significantly enhancing policy safety. We release the code and full reproducibility instructions at https://github.com/AvrahamRaviv/Robust-DRL-FV.

1 Introduction

Over the past decade, Deep Neural Networks (DNNs) have significantly impacted machine learning, finding applications in computer vision [1,2], natural language processing [3–5], and autonomous systems [6]. DNNs are especially valued for their ability to model complex, high-dimensional data, achieving success in tasks from image recognition to speech synthesis and game playing [7]. Inspired by the human brain, these networks consist of multiple layers of interconnected neurons that learn to map inputs to outputs through large-scale supervised training.

The impressive capabilities of DNNs have motivated their integration into reinforcement learning (RL) frameworks, giving rise to deep reinforcement learning (DRL). In DRL, the expressive power of DNNs is harnessed to approximate policies or value functions, enabling RL algorithms to handle high-dimensional and complex environments. Unlike traditional RL, which often relies on hand-crafted features, DRL learns directly from raw inputs, thereby expanding its applicability to tasks such as robotic control, resource management, and game strategy development.

Despite its potential, RL still faces several challenges. The learning process can be slow and inefficient, especially in environments with sparse or delayed rewards. Agents often require extensive exploration to discover effective policies

P. Rümmer and Z. Wu (Eds.): TASE 2025, LNCS 15841, pp. 179–196, 2026.
https://doi.org/10.1007/978-3-031-98208-8_11

and can easily become trapped in suboptimal behaviors. Moreover, ensuring that an agent's decisions are both safe and reliable is critical, particularly in high-stakes applications like autonomous driving or healthcare. These issues motivate the search for methods that not only accelerate learning but also offer stronger guarantees regarding policy correctness.

Recent research has explored the integration of formal verification techniques with RL to address these challenges [8–11]. Formal verification, a method long used in software and hardware engineering, offers a rigorous way to ensure that systems meet specific correctness properties such as safety and liveness. By modeling an RL agent as a transition system, formal methods can verify that its policy adheres to desired criteria, potentially increasing both efficiency and reliability in critical settings.

In this work, we propose an approach that integrates formal verification into DRL by using verification tools as expert advisors. Our method leverages counterexamples provided by these tools to incrementally refine the agent's policy. When a policy violates a safety or performance property, the verification tool supplies a counterexample that guides targeted adjustments in the neural network. This feedback loop helps the agent converge more quickly while maintaining compliance with safety guarantees.

We validate our approach through experiments in two distinct environments: Frozen Lake and Sokoban. In these settings, we compare agents trained with and without formal verification feedback, and our results indicate improvements in both learning speed and policy robustness—especially in scenarios prone to non-terminal traps or adversarial conditions.

Our contributions are summarized as follows:

- We formalize the robustness of DRL as a verification problem, ensuring that policies avoid unsafe states and meet performance guarantees.
- We develop a verification-based backpropagation framework that integrates DRL with feedback from formal verification tools to enhance learning efficiency.
- We use counterexamples from formal verification as corrective signals to iteratively refine the agent's policy.
- We demonstrate the effectiveness of our approach through experiments in the Frozen Lake and Sokoban environments, showing notable improvements in success rates and learning efficiency compared to traditional methods.

The remainder of this paper is organized as follows. Section 2 reviews related work on integrating formal verification with DRL. Section 3 presents the necessary background and formalizes the robustness of RL and DRL as a verification problem. Section 4 details our experimental results in the Frozen Lake and Sokoban environments, and Sect. 5 concludes the paper with directions for future work.

2   Related Work

Several research efforts have begun to integrate formal verification techniques into DRL in order to guarantee safety and reliability. Broadly, these can be grouped into approaches based on (i) symbolic policies and safety shields, (ii) adversarial robustness and counterexample-guided repair, and (iii) verification-in-the-loop with abstraction.

Symbolic Policies and Safety Shields. One line of work couples RL with **runtime enforcement mechanisms** derived from formal specifications. *Shielding* methods synthesize a reactive filter that blocks any action which would violate a given safety property during training or deployment. Introduced by Alshiekh et al. [12], shielding uses temporal logic specifications to generate a safety monitor (or "shield") that overrides unsafe agent actions while otherwise allowing learning to proceed. Early shielding frameworks were demonstrated in discrete or symbolic state settings [12,13], and provided provable guarantees that the agent never enters forbidden states. Recent extensions have made shielding compatible with high-dimensional **continuous** state spaces and neural policies. Jansen et al. [14] proposed *probabilistic shields* that leverage model checking on Markov decision processes to compute the probability of failure for different actions, enabling the agent to adhere to safety constraints with high probability rather than absolute determinism. This is particularly important for environments with sensor noise or uncertainty, where a binary notion of safety is too restrictive. Carr et al. [15] further applied shielding to partially observable settings (POMDPs), showing that an appropriate shield can ensure safety under state uncertainty. In parallel, researchers have explored restricting the policy representation itself to a **verifiable form**. For example, Bastani et al. [13] train policies represented as compact decision trees, which can be exhaustively analyzed for safety properties post-training. Anderson et al. [16] extend this idea in the **REVEL** framework, which maintains a *neurosymbolic* policy: a combination of a neural network with a symbolic "shadow" policy that is formally verified to satisfy safety invariants. REVEL uses an iterative projection approach to ensure the learned policy remains within a safe subset of the policy space at all times, achieving provably safe exploration in continuous domains [16]. Another recent advance is to integrate logical constraints directly into the function approximator: Yang et al. [17] propose *probabilistic logic shields*, which encode the safety specification as a differentiable logic program layered within the policy network. This allows safety constraints to be enforced *directly through the policy's loss function*, so that the agent learns to satisfy the property by construction. Overall, approaches in this category use formal models (automata, logic programs, etc.) either alongside or within the policy to guarantee that safety requirements are respected **at runtime**, even as the agent learns.

Adversarial Robustness and Counterexample-Guided Repair. A complementary direction focuses on making DRL agents robust to adversarial inputs and using formal analysis to identify and fix potential failures. It is well known that neural policies can be vulnerable to subtle perturbations or unforeseen environment conditions. To address this, methods for *certified robustness* of DRL have emerged, drawing inspiration from adversarially robust deep learning. Chang et al. [18] focus on learning control policies and neural network Lyapunov functions for nonlinear control problems, with provable guarantee of stability. SMT solving over the reals [19] accelerates formal verification, enabling control robustness and faster convergence. Lütjens et al. [20] developed an online certified defense for deep RL, which computes guaranteed lower bounds on state-action values under worst-case input deviations. By choosing actions that maximize this worst-case value, their agent behaves safely even in the presence of sensor noise or adversarial observations, with formal assurance that small input perturbations will not cause catastrophic failures. In effect, such techniques provide **provable performance bounds** against a class of adversaries during policy execution. In addition to robust decision-making, researchers have investigated *formal fault detection and repair* for trained policies. One prominent approach is to adopt a **counterexample-guided refinement loop**, akin to the CEGAR paradigm in software verification, to iteratively improve a neural policy until it satisfies a given safety specification. Boetius and Leue [21] recently proposed an algorithm that uses a *safety critic* to search for counterexample trajectories where the agent violates a safety requirement; whenever a failure is found, they modify the policy (and concurrently retrain the critic) to eliminate that specific failure mode. This counterexample-guided repair process repeats until no further safety-violating behavior is discovered, yielding a repaired policy that is formally verified safe with respect to the specification. The repair procedure provides a way to achieve post hoc guarantees on black-box DRL agents without retraining from scratch. Similar ideas have been applied in simulation-based testing frameworks that falsify RL controllers by generating adversarial scenarios (e.g., via adaptive stress testing), although those typically provide empirical assurance rather than formal guarantees. By contrast, the adversarial robustness and repair approaches in recent literature aim to combine rigorous *verification* (to find corner-case failures or worst-case perturbations) with targeted *policy updates* that resolve those issues, thereby increasing the agent's reliability in safety-critical environments.

Verification-in-the-Loop and Abstraction Techniques. Rather than applying verification after training, another body of work tightly **couples formal verification with the learning process itself**. These approaches insert verification steps into the training loop so that the agent can proactively avoid unsafe behaviors and converge to a certified-safe policy. A key challenge here is the state and policy complexity of DRL, which makes direct verification intractable; hence, various *abstraction* methods are employed to simplify the problem. One representative example is the **Trainify** framework by Jin et al. [22], which uses a counterexample-guided abstraction refinement strategy during training. Trainify abstracts the continuous state space into a finite abstract model and uses a model checker to verify temporal safety properties on this abstraction at each iteration. If the model checker finds a counterexample (i.e., a possible policy execution leading to a violation of the property), the abstract state space is refined around that counterexample and the RL agent is retrained with the finer abstraction. This verify-train loop continues until the property is verified on the abstract model, at which point the corresponding concrete policy is guaranteed to satisfy the specification. By integrating the verifier into the learning loop, the agent is **constrained to explore safely** and does not need a separate repair phase. Abstraction-based training has shown promise in scaling verification to more complex DRL tasks: it limits the search space for the verifier and provides additional feedback to the learner. For instance, recent work demonstrates that training on an abstract state representation can yield tighter reachable set over-approximations, making safety verification more scalable, and can even facilitate analytical measures of robustness by analyzing state perturbations at the abstract level [22,23]. Beyond state abstraction, other forms of **runtime verification-in-the-loop** have been explored. Examples include learning with **control-theoretic certificates** (such as Lyapunov or barrier functions) that serve as safety envelopes during training [24], and synthesizing minimally invasive corrections to the policy whenever a formal monitor flags an impending violation. These techniques ensure that the learning algorithm remains within safe bounds at all times, effectively bridging the gap between formal methods and the exploratory nature of RL. As a result, the final policies are accompanied by formal guarantees (e.g., safety invariants or probabilistic bounds) derived from the verification component. An important ongoing direction is to extend verification-in-the-loop methods to stochastic and high-dimensional environments. Initial steps in this direction include combining DRL with **probabilistic verification** and statistical model-checking to handle uncertainties in the environment [14,23]. This will be crucial for deploying provably safe RL in real-world settings where transition dynamics or observations can be random. In summary, verification integrated into the training phase, aided by abstraction, enables agents to learn provably correct behaviors by design, rather than verifying and patching them after the fact.

Overall, the integration of formal verification with deep RL is rapidly advancing on multiple fronts. The approaches discussed above—safety shields and symbolic policy classes, adversarial robustness and repair, and training-time verification with abstraction—are complementary and can potentially be combined. For example, one might envision an RL framework that uses a symbolic shield for immediate safety, while periodically invoking a verifier to refine the policy against adversarial scenarios. The convergence of these ideas with techniques from probabilistic model checking, control theory, and neural network verification is steadily **increasing the trustworthiness of DRL** in safety-critical applications. As research from the last few years shows, incorporating formal correctness criteria into the reinforcement learning loop is a viable path toward agents that not only learn optimal behaviors but also come equipped with strong safety guarantees.

3   Robustness Formulation

This section introduces foundational concepts essential for understanding our approach. We first discuss fundamental ideas in RL, DRL, and Formal Verification, clearly establishing the necessary definitions and notations. Subsequently, we provide a rigorous formalization of robustness in RL and DRL agents as a verification problem.

3.1   Preliminaries

Reinforcement Learning. RL involves training an agent to maximize cumulative rewards through interactions with its environment. Formally, the environment is typically represented by a Markov Decision Process (MDP), defined as:

$$\mathcal{M} = (\mathcal{S}, \mathcal{A}, T, R, \gamma),$$

where:

- $\mathcal{S}$ is the set of states,
- $\mathcal{A}$ is the set of actions,
- $T : \mathcal{S} \times \mathcal{A} \to \Delta(\mathcal{S})$ is the transition function mapping each state-action pair to a probability distribution over the next states (here, $\Delta(\mathcal{S})$ denotes the set of all probability distributions over $\mathcal{S}$),
- $R : \mathcal{S} \times \mathcal{A} \to \mathbb{R}$ is the reward function, and
- $\gamma \in [0, 1)$ is the discount factor.

The agent's goal is to learn a policy $\pi(a \mid s)$ that maximizes the expected cumulative reward starting from time step t, formally expressed as:

$$G_t = \mathbb{E}_\pi \left[\sum_{k=0}^{\infty} \gamma^k r_{t+k} \right].$$

RL algorithms typically balance *exploration* (searching for potentially better actions) and *exploitation* (selecting known rewarding actions), and are categorized into *model-free* or *model-based* methods depending on whether they explicitly model environment dynamics.

Deep Reinforcement Learning. DRL leverages deep neural networks as function approximators for either policies or value functions, enabling effective operation within high-dimensional, complex environments. A prominent DRL method is the Deep Q-Network (DQN), which approximates the Q-value function $Q(s, a)$, representing the expected return when selecting action a in state s:

$$Q(s, a) = \mathbb{E} \left[r_t + \gamma \max_{a'} Q(s', a') \mid s, a \right].$$

In the above, s' and a' denote the state and action at the subsequent time step, respectively. To stabilize training, DQN incorporates techniques such as *experience replay buffers* and *target networks*. Double DQN (DDQN) further improves DQN by mitigating overestimation bias. Other notable DRL methods include policy-gradient and Actor-Critic approaches, particularly suitable for continuous action spaces.

Formal Verification. Formal verification employs rigorous mathematical techniques to ensure that systems adhere to specified correctness and safety properties. In the context of reinforcement learning, formal verification models the agent-environment interactions as a symbolic transition system. Such a system is defined as

$$\mathcal{T} = (\mathcal{V}, \Theta, \rho),$$

where:

- $\mathcal{V}$ is a set of state variables,
- $\Theta \subseteq \mathcal{S}$ is the set of initial states, and
- ρ is a Boolean formula over $\mathcal{V} \cup \mathcal{V}'$, with $\mathcal{V}'$ denoting the primed copy of $\mathcal{V}$, that characterizes the transition relation between the current and next states.

Properties such as safety (ensuring the system never enters unsafe states) and liveness (ensuring that certain desirable events eventually occur) are typically specified using temporal logics like Linear Temporal Logic (LTL) [25]. Moreover, LTL can be extended to capture optimality requirements by imposing bounded response properties, which enforce that the agent reaches its goals within a specified number of steps. This distinction allows us to differentiate between trajectories that are merely successful and those that are optimally efficient.

For example, a safety property may be expressed as:

$$\varphi_{\text{safety}} : \quad G(\neg unsafe),$$

meaning that the system must never enter any unsafe states.

A liveness property might require that the agent eventually reaches a goal state:

$$\varphi_{\text{liveness}} : \quad G\,(start \rightarrow F\,goal),$$

ensuring that if the goal is not immediately achieved, it will eventually be reached without becoming trapped in local loops.

To capture optimality, one may employ a bounded response property. For instance, one can specify that upon the initiation of an episode, the goal should be reached within k steps:

$$\varphi_{\text{optimality}} : \quad G\,(start \rightarrow F_{\leq k}\,goal),$$

where *start* is true at the beginning of an episode and $F_{\leq k}$ denotes that the goal must be reached within k steps. This property not only enforces eventual success but also promotes efficiency by distinguishing between suboptimal and optimal trajectories.

Violations of these specifications are used as counterexamples that illustrate scenarios where the property is breached, allowing the agent to avoid unsafe actions, choose actions that lead to the goal, and ultimately optimize its strategies.

3.2   Robustness as a Verification Problem

We define *robustness* as an agent's capability to consistently avoid unsafe states while achieving near-optimal performance under various conditions, including adversarial perturbations. For deep reinforcement learning (DRL) agents, this robustness is verified by analyzing their decision-making process through a symbolic transition system defined analogously as

$$\mathcal{T}_{\text{DRL}} = (\mathcal{V}_{\text{NN}}, \Theta_{\text{NN}}, \rho_{\text{NN}}),$$

where ρ_{NN} is a Boolean formula over the neural network's state variables and their primed copies, representing the network-induced transitions. Robustness verification requires that for all valid initial states $\mathcal{S}_{\text{valid}}$, the following safety property holds:

$$\forall t \geq 0 : \ s_t \in \mathcal{S}_{\text{valid}} \implies s_t \notin \mathcal{S}_{\text{unsafe}},$$

with $\mathcal{S}_{\text{unsafe}}$ denoting the set of unsafe states. In symbolic terms, we require:

$$\mathcal{T}_{\text{DRL}} \models (\forall s \in \mathcal{S}_{\text{valid}} : G \neg(s \in \mathcal{S}_{\text{unsafe}})).$$

To further ensure optimal performance, an optimality property can be incorporated to distinguish between merely successful and efficiently optimal trajectories. For instance, in the Frozen Lake environment, one may require that every episode starting from a valid state reaches a goal state within a bounded number of steps k. This bounded response property can be specified as:

$$\mathcal{T}_{\text{DRL}} \models (\forall s \in \mathcal{S}_{\text{valid}} : G \left(start(s) \rightarrow F_{\leq k} \, goal(s) \right)),$$

where $start(s)$ indicates the beginning of an episode and $F_{\leq k}$ denotes that the goal must be reached within k steps. This property not only guarantees safety but also drives the agent toward near-optimal trajectories.

Counterexample-Guided Policy Refinement. Central to our approach is the integration of verification-generated counterexamples into the DRL training process. Whenever the verification process identifies policy violations, these counterexamples serve as corrective feedback, iteratively refining neural network parameters to enhance overall robustness and reliability.

Verification-Based Backpropagation Algorithm. Our verification-driven algorithm integrates formal verification outcomes directly into the DRL training loop. In what follows, we assume that ALGO is a standard DRL algorithm (e.g., DQN) characterized by a learning rate α and a discount factor γ. The algorithm receives two sets of safety properties: (i) a set of single-step properties $PROPERTY_{GROUP1} = \{p_1, \ldots, p_i\}$ and (ii) a set of path-based properties $PROPERTY_{GROUP2} = \{p_{i+1}, \ldots, p_k\}$. Each property p_j is associated with a penalty reward r_j (with $r_j < 0$). An integer c specifies the number of iterations of property checks per episode, and the algorithm runs for a fixed number $MaxEpisodes$ of episodes.

Algorithm 1. Verification-Based Backpropagation

1: **Input:**
  – DRL algorithm ALGO (with learning rate α and discount factor γ).
  – Single-step safety properties $PROPERTY_{GROUP1} = \{p_1, \ldots, p_i\}$.
  – Path-based safety properties $PROPERTY_{GROUP2} = \{p_{i+1}, \ldots, p_k\}$.
  – Penalty rewards $\{r_1, \ldots, r_k\}$ corresponding to each property.
  – Trajectory check limit $c \in \mathbb{N}$.
  – Maximum number of episodes $MaxEpisodes \in \mathbb{N}$.
2: **for** $episode = 1$ to $MaxEpisodes$ **do**
3:   Execute one training episode using ALGO.
4:   Set $counter \leftarrow 0$.
5:   **while** $counter < c$ **do**
6:     $counter \leftarrow counter + 1$.
7:     /* **Phase 1: Single-step updates** */
8:     **for** each property $p_j \in PROPERTY_{GROUP1}$ **do**
9:       Identify (if exists) (s, a, r, s') where the current policy π violates p_j
10:      Compute loss:

$$L \leftarrow r_j + \gamma \max_{a'} Q(s', a') - Q(s, a)$$

11:      Update network weights by backpropagating L with step size α.
12:    /* **Phase 2: Trajectory-based updates** */
13:    Reset the environment.
14:    Execute the current policy for up to c^2 steps and record the trajectory $\tau = \{(s_1, a_1, r_1, s'_1), \ldots, (s_n, a_n, r_n, s'_n)\}$.
15:    **for** each property $p_j \in PROPERTY_{GROUP2}$ **do**
16:      **if** trajectory τ violates p_j **then**
17:        **if** p_j must be evaluated along the entire trajectory **then**
18:          **for** each transition $(s, a, r, s') \in \tau$ **do**
19:            Compute loss:

$$L \leftarrow r_j + \gamma \max_{a'} Q(s', a') - Q(s, a)$$

20:            Update network weights using loss L with step size α.
21:        **else**
22:          Identify the transition $(s^*, a^*, r^*, s'^*) \in \tau$ where the violation occurs.
23:          Compute loss:

$$L \leftarrow r_j + \gamma \max_{a'} Q(s'^*, a') - Q(s^*, a^*)$$

24:          Update network weights using loss L with step size α.

Algorithm Walkthrough: Initially, for each episode (up to $MaxEpisodes$), the algorithm runs a standard DRL episode via ALGO and checks each encountered state against all single-step properties in $PROPERTY_{GROUP1}$. When a violation is detected at a state s, a loss

$$L = r_j + \gamma \max_{a'} Q(s', a') - Q(s, a)$$

is computed and used to update the network weights via backpropagation with learning rate α. Next, the algorithm enters a secondary loop (repeated c times) in which the environment is reset and a complete trajectory τ is recorded over up to c^2 steps. For each path-based property in $PROPERTY_{GROUP2}$ that is violated along τ, the algorithm either updates all states in τ (if the property requires a full-trajectory evaluation) or only updates at the specific transition where the violation is detected. This integrated procedure guides the DRL agent to avoid unsafe actions both on a per-step basis and over longer trajectories.

3.3   Theoretical Analysis and Convergence Guarantees

To understand why our method improves both learning efficiency and safety, we provide several intuitive insights into how verification feedback interacts with the reinforcement learning process.

Safety Dynamics. Our algorithm introduces penalties to unsafe actions based on counterexamples identified during training. When a property violation is detected, the corresponding Q-value is reduced by applying a negative reward. Over time, these penalties make unsafe actions less likely to be selected, naturally guiding the policy toward safer behaviors. Since these updates are still grounded in the Q-learning framework, they integrate seamlessly without requiring structural changes to the learning algorithm.

Verification Effect. As training progresses and the policy improves, the number of property violations—and thus the number of penalties—tends to decrease. This gradual reduction of unsafe feedback contributes to learning stability and acts as an implicit regularization mechanism. In essence, verification serves as a safety-driven shaping signal: it is active early when needed most and fades as the agent converges toward a safe and effective policy.

Complexity Analysis. Integrating verification introduces an extra per-episode overhead of

$$\mathcal{O}(c \cdot T_{\text{verif}}),$$

where c is the number of repeated checks per episode and T_{verif} is the time required for a single check of all the properties. Although this additional computation might seem prohibitive at first glance, it is largely amortized by a significantly reduced number of training episodes. Specifically, if standard DRL converges in N_{std} episodes and our verification-enhanced method converges in N_{ver} episodes (with $N_{\text{ver}} \ll N_{\text{std}}$), the overall verification cost becomes negligible in comparison to the reduction in total training time. Therefore, while the worst-case per-episode cost is $\mathcal{O}(c \cdot T_{\text{verif}})$, the benefits of faster convergence and enhanced safety guarantees result in a net reduction of total computational effort, as we demonstrate empirically in the results section.

Convergence Discussion. Our method builds on the standard Q-learning update, which is proven to converge under conditions like a sufficiently small learning rate and adequate exploration. The extra verification-based updates are applied only when a counterexample is detected, and these updates work by reducing the Q-values associated with unsafe actions. This selective penalty ensures that the contraction properties of the Q-learning update are maintained, leading the algorithm to converge to a robust policy.

4   Results

In this section, we present a detailed account of our experimental evaluation of the proposed method that integrates formal verification feedback into deep reinforcement learning (DRL). We conducted experiments in two environments – Frozen Lake [26] and Sokoban [27] – to assess improvements in learning efficiency, robustness, and safety. For each environment, we compared agents trained with standard DRL methods to those that incorporate our verification-based backpropagation. In our framework, the formal verification component uses the Marabou framework [28] to check the neural network behavior and generate counterexamples, which then serve as corrective feedback during training.

Throughout our experiments, we enforce three types of formal specifications, as explained in Sect. 3.2:

- **Safety:** Ensuring the agent avoids undesirable terminal states (e.g., falling into holes or entering deadlock states).
- **Liveness:** Ensuring the agent eventually makes progress and does not get caught in loops.
- **Optimality:** Guiding the agent to achieve its goals efficiently, for example by reaching the target within a bounded number of steps.

The following subsections describe the experiments in detail.

4.1   Experiments in the Frozen Lake Environment

The Frozen Lake environment is a grid-based navigation challenge where the agent must move from a randomly chosen starting state to a predefined goal while avoiding holes. Movements are restricted to the four cardinal directions, and the success criterion is the percentage of starting states from which the goal is reached.

To rigorously evaluate robustness, we designed three levels of increasing difficulty (L1, L2, and L3), as illustrated in Fig. 1. Higher difficulty levels involve more intricate spatial configurations of holes and safe paths, demanding more cautious planning by the agent.

In this environment, we defined two property groups to enforce safety, liveness, and optimality:

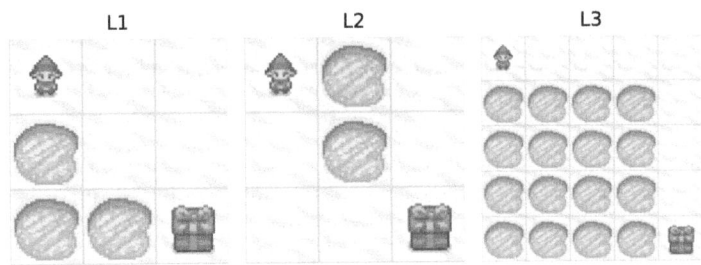

Fig. 1. Frozen Lake layouts for difficulty levels L1, L2, and L3. Different hole placements result in varying navigation challenges.

- $PROPERTY_{GROUP1}$: $\{p_1, p_2, p_3, p_4\}$ – These properties prevent the agent from moving into a hole from any of the four cardinal directions. They function as immediate, step-by-step safety checks.
- $PROPERTY_{GROUP2}$: $\{p_5, p_6, p_7\}$ – Here, p_5 is designed to avoid cycles or loops in the trajectory, p_6 ensures the agent remains within the board boundaries, and p_7 forces the agent to reach the goal within a bounded number of steps (for an $n \times n$ board, within $2n$ steps). These properties collectively encourage longer-term safety, liveness, and near-optimal performance.

Formally, the properties $\{p_1, p_2, p_3, p_4, p_6\}$ collectively enforce safety:

$$\forall s \in \mathcal{S}_{\text{valid}}, \quad G \neg (s \in \mathcal{S}_{\text{unsafe}}),$$

where $\mathcal{S}_{\text{unsafe}}$ consists of all holes and states outside the board. Meanwhile, property p_5 (preventing cycles) can be expressed as:

$$G (s \rightarrow X G \neg s),$$

and the bounded optimality (property p_7) is defined as:

$$G \left(start \rightarrow F_{\leq k}\ goal \right),$$

with *start* marking the episode's start, *goal* indicating success, and $k = 2n$ (where n is the board dimension). The choice of $k = 2n$ is justified by the board design—in our settings, the optimal path never requires backtracking.

The parameter c controlling the number of checks per episode is set equal to the board size, ensuring comprehensive safety evaluation each run. Violations of $PROPERTY_{GROUP1}$ as well as p_7 incur a penalty of -1, while violations of the remaining of $PROPERTY_{GROUP2}$ (i.e., p_5, p_6) incur a penalty of -0.5:

$$r_j = \begin{cases} -1, & \text{if } j \in \{1, 2, 3, 4, 7\}, \\ -0.5, & \text{if } j \in \{5, 6\}. \end{cases}$$

These penalties are incorporated into the loss function to steer the agent away from unsafe or inefficient decisions.

We performed three independent trials to account for randomness in network initialization and environmental dynamics. For each trial, two sets of experiments were conducted: one with a standard DRL algorithm and one using our verification-based backpropagation method (see Algorithm 1). All experimental conditions—including hyperparameters, network initialization, and total runtime—were held constant across experiments to ensure a fair comparison; specifically, we initialize ϵ at 1.0, set the discount factor γ to 0.8, use an ϵ_{min} of 0.01 with an exponential decay rate of 0.001, and set the batch size to 16.

Table 1 summarize performance metrics (runtime, success rate, average reward per episode, and episodes until convergence) with and without verification of properties p_1-p_6 for three DRL variants:

- **Algorithm 1 (DQL):** A simple deep Q-learning with a single network.
- **Algorithm 2 (DDQL):** Deep Q-learning with an added target network for stabilization.
- **Algorithm 3 (R-DDQL):** Revised Double Deep Q-learning designed to mitigate overestimation bias.

Table 1. Performance comparison in the Frozen Lake environment for three DRL algorithms, with and without formal verification.

Layout↓	Method→	Algorithm 1 (DQL)		Algorithm 2 (DDQL)		Algorithm 3 (R-DDQL)	
		With	Without	With	Without	With	Without
L1	Time (s)	20	20	20	20	20	20
	Success Rate	67%	0%	100%	0%	100%	13%
	Avg. Reward/Episode	−0.559	−7.709	0.220	−8.525	−0.597	−5.365
	# Episodes	278.67	9918	359.00	11190.67	188.33	15686.67
L2	Time (s)	20	20	20	20	20	20
	Success Rate	78%	22%	67%	11%	39%	11%
	Avg. Reward/Episode	−0.361	−3.528	−0.657	−6.036	−1.107	−5.842
	# Episodes	266.67	18886	263.33	12902.00	128.00	10273.00
L3	Time (s)	90	90	90	90	90	90
	Success Rate	33%	0%	67%	0%	54%	0%
	Avg. Reward/Episode	−3.098	−27.608	−1.833	−41.751	−1.333	−34.451
	# Episodes	376.33	25201.67	379.33	16775.33	365.67	20991.67

To further validate the scalability of our approach, we expanded the Frozen Lake environment to a 10×10 grid. In this larger setting, the state space is much larger and the arrangement of holes more complex. Standard DRL converged in only 4.34% of the trials after an average of approximately 25,000 episodes, while verification-enhanced agents converged in 56% of the trials, requiring on average only 7,000 episodes. This significant reduction in required episodes underscores the potential of formal verification feedback to guide the learning process in complex settings.

In addition, we tested the effect of p_7 on trajectory-based properties (group 2). We conducted experiments comparing settings that used only properties p_5 and p_6 with those incorporating p_7 as well on two new layouts, similar to L1 and L3. The experiments employed Algorithm 1 with DQN as the baseline ALGO, running five trials per layout, with all hyperparameters initialized as previously described. The results show that including p_7 improved success rates by more than 40% on average for the smaller layout and over 50% for the larger layout. These findings suggest that the verification process provides a practical enhancement by effectively steering agents toward more efficient behavior.

4.2   Experiments in the Sokoban Environment

The Sokoban environment poses a different kind of strategic challenge. In this puzzle, the agent must push boxes onto designated target positions while maneuvering around obstacles; a single inefficient move may lead to a deadlock, rendering the puzzle unsolvable.

For Sokoban, we adapted our formal specifications to the problem domain as follows. First, the **Safety Property** prevents moves that lead to deadlock, and is formally defined by

$$\forall s \in \mathcal{S}_{\text{valid}}, \quad G \neg \big(s \in \mathcal{S}_{\text{deadlock}} \big),$$

where $\mathcal{S}_{\text{deadlock}}$ is the set of unsolvable configurations. Second, the **Liveness Property** ensures that the agent eventually makes progress and inherently avoids cycles or repeated states (i.e., looping behavior), as expressed by

$$G \big(start \rightarrow F \, solved \big).$$

Finally, the **Optimality Property** encourages the agent to find efficient solutions by bounding the number of moves:

$$G \big(start \rightarrow F_{\leq k} \, solved \big),$$

where k depends on the board dimensions and the number of boxes.

In addition to these properties, we tested two distinct reward mechanisms:

1. **Simple Reward:** Penalizes every inefficient move (such as pushing a box in a nonproductive direction or moving into a wall), while rewarding successful puzzle completion.
2. **Hot Cold:** Provides nuanced feedback by rewarding moves that reduce the distance between boxes and targets, and penalizing moves that increase this distance.

A three-layer neural network with ReLU activations was used to capture spatial and strategic nuances, with additional improvements provided by prioritized experience replay and a target network. For all experiments, we initialize ϵ at 1.0, set the discount factor γ to 0.9, use an $\epsilon_{\min}$ of 0.01 with a decay rate of 0.001, and set the batch size to 16.

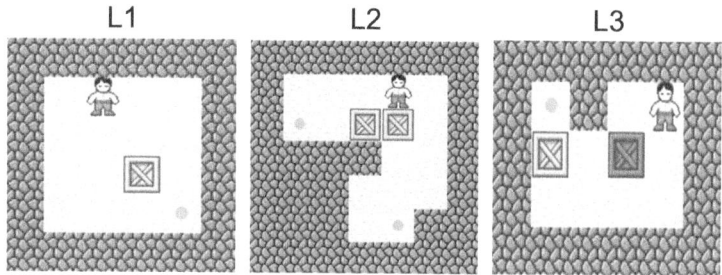

Fig. 2. Layouts of Sokoban environments at three levels of increasing difficulty (L1, L2, L3). The layouts illustrate varying puzzle complexities and obstacle arrangements that challenge the agent's planning abilities.

To systematically evaluate the impact of formal verification on strategic decision-making, we defined three difficulty levels (L1, L2, and L3) for Sokoban, as depicted in Fig. 2. These levels vary in board layout complexity, the number of boxes, and the arrangement of obstacles, thereby presenting progressively challenging scenarios. Table 2 reports the average number of episodes required to succeed for each level. The verification-based methods consistently improved both learning speed and success rate across all difficulty levels. Notably, using all properties together, learning was accelerated by approximately 45% in Level 1, 23% in Level 2, and 25% in Level 3 compared to the standard DRL approach.

Table 2. Summary of average number of episodes required to succeed in the Sokoban environment for three different layouts.

Difficulty	Baseline	With Safety+Liveness	With Safety+Liveness+K-step Verification
L1	494	355	274
L2	311	269	238
L3	281	239	211

Overall Conclusions

The experimental results in both the Frozen Lake and Sokoban environments demonstrate that incorporating formal verification feedback into DRL training significantly enhances performance:

1. **Learning Efficiency:** Verification-based feedback considerably reduces the number of episodes needed for convergence.
2. **Robustness and Safety:** Agents trained with verification feedback achieve higher success rates and more reliably avoid unsafe or inefficient actions.

3. **Scalability:** Consistent improvements across multiple difficulty levels and in larger or more complex settings highlight the method's scalability.

These findings validate our approach and suggest promising directions for future research, including exploring alternative DRL architectures, extending the framework to multi-agent settings, and applying the method in continuous control tasks. Further refinements in the verification process may yield even greater gains in efficiency and safety, broadening the applicability of our method in real-world scenarios.

5   Summary and Future Work

In this paper, we introduced a formal verification-based backpropagation method for DRL that provides corrective feedback during training, enabling agents to identify and rectify policy errors. This approach not only accelerates convergence but also enhances decision safety, as demonstrated by our experiments in Frozen Lake and Sokoban, where fewer training episodes were required and overall performance improved in terms of both safety and efficiency.

Our method incurs an additional computational overhead per episode – approximately $\mathcal{O}(c \cdot T_{\text{verif}})$ – due to verification checks. However, the reduction in the number of episodes needed for convergence compensates for the increased per-episode cost. Future work may focus on adaptive strategies for scheduling verification checks or parallelizing these operations to further optimize the overall training time.

Additionally, while our experiments show substantial gains, we observed that in challenging scenarios (e.g., environments with extremely sparse rewards or when counterexamples are less informative due to approximation limitations) the corrective feedback can be less effective. This highlights the critical role of the quality and relevance of counterexamples, suggesting that adaptive verification thresholds or hybrid approaches combining multiple robust learning techniques could be promising directions for future research.

In this work, we used three LTL properties – safety, liveness, and optimality-guided reachability – as a basis for integrating formal specifications into learning. Extending the property set to include more expressive or structured temporal logic formulas can further refine the learning process. For example, a property like $G(\textbf{start} \rightarrow (\textbf{ontrack } U \textbf{ goal}))$ could guide agents to remain on efficient paths step by step, rather than merely reaching the goal eventually. Exploring such richer LTL specifications is a natural next step for improving both the expressiveness and effectiveness of the verification signal.

Looking ahead, we plan to extend our method to more complex environments with larger state spaces and more intricate dynamics, as well as explore its application to other learning algorithms (e.g., actor-critic, policy gradient), multi-agent systems, and continuous control tasks. These efforts aim to further demonstrate the benefits of integrating formal verification into DRL for building more reliable and efficient learning agents.

References

1. Krizhevsky, A., Sutskever, I., Hinton, G.E.: Imagenet classification with deep convolutional neural networks. In: Pereira, F., Burges, C.J., Bottou, L., Weinberger, K.Q. (eds.) Advances in Neural Information Processing Systems, vol. 25. Curran Associates, Inc. (2012)
2. Dosovitskiy, A., et al.: An image is worth 16x16 words: transformers for image recognition at scale (2021)
3. Vaswani, A., et al.: Attention is all you need (2023)
4. Devlin, J., Chang, M.-W., Lee, K., Toutanova, K.: Bert: pre-training of deep bidirectional transformers for language understanding (2019)
5. Brown, T.B., et al.: Language models are few-shot learners (2020)
6. Kiran, B.R., et al.: Deep reinforcement learning for autonomous driving: a survey. IEEE Trans. Intell. Transp. Syst. **23**(6), 4909–4926 (2021)
7. Silver, D., et al.: Mastering the game of go with deep neural networks and tree search. Nature **529**(7587), 484–489 (2016)
8. Gross, D., Jansen, N., Junges, S., Pérez, G.A.: Cool-mc: a comprehensive tool for reinforcement learning and model checking. In: International Symposium on Dependable Software Engineering: Theories, Tools, and Applications, pp. 41–49. Springer (2022)
9. Akintunde, M.E., Botoeva, E., Kouvaros, P., Lomuscio, A.: Formal verification of neural agents in non-deterministic environments. Auton. Agents Multi-Agent Syst. **36**(1), 6 (2022)
10. Raviv, A., Bronshtein, E., Reginiano, O., Aluf-Medina, M., Kugler, H.: Learning through imitation by using formal verification. In: International Conference on Current Trends in Theory and Practice of Computer Science, pp. 342–355. Springer (2023)
11. Raviv, A., Gerber, Y., Benzinou, L., Aluf-Medina, M., Kugler, H.: Prediction and control of stochastic agents using formal methods. In: Narodytska, N., Amir, G., Katz, G., Isac, O. (eds.) Proceedings of the 6th Workshop on Formal Methods for ML-Enabled Autonomous Systems. Kalpa Publications in Computing, vol. 16, pp. 29–34. EasyChair (2023)
12. Alshiekh, M., Bloem, R., Ehlers, R., Könighofer, B., Niekum, S., Topcu, U.: Safe reinforcement learning via shielding. In: Proceedings of the 32nd AAAI Conference on Artificial Intelligence, pp. 2669–2678 (2018)
13. Bastani, O., Pu, Y., Solar-Lezama, A.: Verifiable reinforcement learning via policy extraction. In: Advances in Neural Information Processing Systems 31 (NeurIPS 2018), pp. 2499–2509 (2018)
14. Jansen, N., Könighofer, B., Junges, S., Serban, A., Bloem, R.: Safe reinforcement learning using probabilistic shields. In: 31st International Conference on Concurrency Theory (CONCUR). LIPIcs, vol. 171, pp. 3:1–3:16. Schloss Dagstuhl (2020)
15. Carr, S., Jansen, N., Junges, S., Topcu, U.: Safe reinforcement learning via shielding for POMDPs. CoRR, abs/2204.00755 (2022). arXiv:2204.00755
16. Anderson, G., Verma, A., Dillig, I., Chaudhuri, S.: Neurosymbolic reinforcement learning with formally verified exploration. In: Advances in Neural Information Processing Systems 33 (NeurIPS) (2020)
17. Yang, W.-C., Marra, G., Rens, G., De Raedt, L.: Safe reinforcement learning via probabilistic logic shields. In: Proceedings of the 32nd International Joint Conference on Artificial Intelligence (IJCAI) (2023)

18. Chang, Y.-C., Roohi, N., Gao, S.: Neural lyapunov control. In: Wallach, H., Larochelle, H., Beygelzimer, A., d'Alché-Buc, F., Fox, E., Garnett, R. (eds.) Advances in Neural Information Processing Systems, vol. 32. Curran Associates, Inc. (2019)

19. Gao, S., Avigad, J., Clarke, E.M.: δ-complete decision procedures for satisfiability over the reals. In: International Joint Conference on Automated Reasoning, pp. 286–300. Springer (2012)

20. Lütjens, B., Everett, M., How, J.P.: Certified adversarial robustness for deep reinforcement learning. In: Proceedings of the Conference on Robot Learning (CoRL). PMLR, vol. 100, pp. 1328–1337 (2020)

21. Boetius, D., Leue, S.: Counterexample-guided repair of reinforcement learning systems using safety critics. CoRR, abs/2405.15430 (2024). arXiv:2405.15430

22. Jin, P., Tian, J., Zhi, D., Wen, X., Zhang, M.: Trainify: a cegar-driven training and verification framework for safe deep reinforcement learning. In: Computer Aided Verification (CAV). LNCS, vol. 13371, pp. 193–218. Springer (2022)

23. Zhang, M.: Abstraction-based training and verification of safe deep reinforcement learning systems. Invited talk at SETTA Symposium, LNCS, vol. 13585 (2022). Extended abstract

24. Cheng, R., Orosz, G., Murray, R.M., Burdick, J.W.: End-to-end safe reinforcement learning through barrier functions for safety-critical continuous control tasks. In: Proceedings of the 33rd AAAI Conference on Artificial Intelligence (AAAI) (2019)

25. Pnueli, A.: The temporal logic of programs. In: Proceedings 18th IEEE Symposium on Foundations of Computer Science, pp. 46–57 (1977)

26. Brockman, G., et al.: Openai gym. arXiv preprint arXiv:1606.01578 (2016)

27. Junghanns, A., Schaeffer, J.: Sokoban: improving the search with relevance cuts. Theor. Comput. Sci. **252**(1), 151–175 (2001)

28. Wu, H., et al.: Marabou 2.0: a versatile formal analyzer of neural networks (2024)

A Formally Verified Neural Network Converter for the Interactive Theorem Prover COQ

Leo Alexander Gummersbach[1], Kim Völlinger[1(✉)],
and Andrei Aleksandrov[1,2]

[1] Technical University Berlin, Berlin, Germany
l.gummersbach@campus.tu-berlin.de, voellinger@tu-berlin.de
[2] Fraunhofer Institute FOKUS, Berlin, Germany
andrei.aleksandrov@fokus.fraunhofer.de

Abstract. For the formal verification of neural networks, a trained neural network is typically converted into a representation that a theorem prover can process. Since the verification results apply only to the converted network, the conversion is critical and must be trustworthy. This paper introduces the first formally verified neural network converter for a theorem prover, specifically the interactive theorem prover COQ. The verified converter contributes a reliable verification of neural networks within COQ by narrowing the gap between the execution and the verification environment of neural networks.

Keywords: Neural Networks · Formal Verification · COQ · ONNX

1 Introduction

The success of neural networks increases the demand for techniques and tools that ensure their safety, fairness or robustness [21]. To guarantee those properties, considerable efforts are dedicated to advancing the formal verification of neural networks. In the context of formal verification, it is common practice to convert an outside-trained neural network into a representation that can be processed by an external solver or a theorem prover [1]. Since the gained verification results are only valid for the converted network, an erroneous conversion could lead to the invalidation of these results. Consequently, the correctness of the conversion is critical to ensure a valid verification.

This paper presents the first formally verified neural network converter for a theorem prover, specifically the interactive theorem prover COQ. The converter processes neural networks in the Open Neural Network Exchange (ONNX) format[1], which is supported by all major machine learning frameworks. Then it generates representations of these neural networks employing a COQ model for

---

[1] https://onnx.ai/.

© The Author(s), under exclusive license to Springer Nature Switzerland AG 2026
P. Rümmer and Z. Wu (Eds.): TASE 2025, LNCS 15841, pp. 197–214, 2026.
https://doi.org/10.1007/978-3-031-98208-8_12

neural networks [2]. The converter is implemented in CoQ's functional programming language and is formally verified within CoQ. For usability, the CoQ converter has been trustfully extracted to the functional language OCaml. The advantage of the extraction is the ability to call the converter in one click, as a fast-running binary program.

To formally verify the conversion, we provide machine-checked proofs that establish the functional correctness of its individual components – similar to unit tests in traditional software testing. Furthermore, we ensure that the number of neurons is preserved during the conversion process. This property serves as a link between the converter's components – comparable to a system test in traditional software testing.

Contributions. To sum up, this paper makes the following contributions:

- a CoQ-based converter processing neural networks in the ONNX format and generating representations of these networks in CoQ (Sect. 4 and 5),
- a formal verification of the converter's correctness in CoQ, establishing trust in the conversion process (Sect. 4 and 5), and
- a demonstration of the converter's usage (Sect. 6).

The corresponding CoQ code is available on GITHUB.[2] The verified converter contributes to making neural network verification in CoQ more reliable by narrowing the gap between the execution environment and the verification framework of neural networks.

2 Related Work

A significant body of research focuses on the verification of neural networks using automated theorem provers [5,8,14,18–20,24], with a smaller but growing focus on interactive theorem provers [2–4,7,12,23,27]. Several tools aim to automate the import of neural networks from machine learning frameworks to an interactive theorem prover [4,7,24] with some using ONNX as the input format [12,20]. Notably, the International Verification of Neural Networks Competition [6] has standardized ONNX as the input format for all participating tools.

To the best of our knowledge, only two contributions specifically address the *trustworthy* conversion of trained neural networks [7,12]. In [7], the user is required to prove that the neural network's execution on test data is equivalent both inside and outside the ISABELLE prover, within an error margin. While this approach shares the mathematical rigor of this paper's approach, the key difference lies in our approach offering a static verification of the conversion, with the outcome of a verified tool that does not require user proofs for each imported network. In contrast, the approach in [12] uses hashing to improve the conversion's reliability, offering a practical checksum solution without the mathematical rigor of our approach.

---

[2] The CoQ code of this paper: https://github.com/verinncoq/converter.

3   Preliminaries

We briefly introduce neural networks and the ONNX format (Sect. 3.1), the interactive theorem prover Coq (Sect. 3.2), and the Coq model for neural networks (Sect. 3.3).

3.1   Neural Networks

Neural networks can approximate any function with arbitrary precision [11,15] by learning from sample points during training [9]. Structurally, a neural network is a graph with its nodes (neurons) grouped into layers where all neurons of a layer are designated the same function, usually called *activation function*. Each network has an arbitrary number of intermediate layers with an output layer at the end. Note that we do not consider inputs of a neural network to be a layer.

The ONNX Format. The converter's input is a neural network in the ONNX format, a universal exchange format, supported by the major machine learning frameworks. The ONNX format employs an acyclic graph model where nodes have attributes, e.g. input, output, an operation or a data type.

3.2   Interactive Theorem Prover Coq

The interactive theorem prover Coq [28] offers a functional programming language, a proof development system, and a rich collection of libraries. Additionally, through its extraction mechanism, Coq allows the generation of executable programs in widely-used functional languages such as OCaml. The extraction enables practical usability while preserving the verification results developed.

3.3   The Neural Network Model in Coq

For the converter's output, we employ a Coq library of neural networks [2] where a neural network is a recursive structure of layers, parameterized on the type of activation function and the dimensions of the layer's input and output. The library offers two verified activation functions: the generic summation function (Linear) and the rectified linear unit (ReLU) – one of the most popular activation functions in industry [22] and in formal verification [8]. To convert a neural network, its activation functions have to be supplied in Coq, ideally verified.

Example: Neural Network. To illustrate the Coq model, as an example, consider the neural network which is conceptually depicted in Fig. 1. This neural network consists of three layers: a linear layer, a ReLU layer and an output layer. In a linear layer, each neuron assigns *weights* to its incoming inputs and has a static *bias*. Mathematically, a linear layer represents an affine function $l(x) = Wx + b$ where W is a matrix of weights, x is a vector of inputs and b is a vector of biases. In our example, the linear layer is applied to the input vector $x = [x_1, x_2]^T$. The

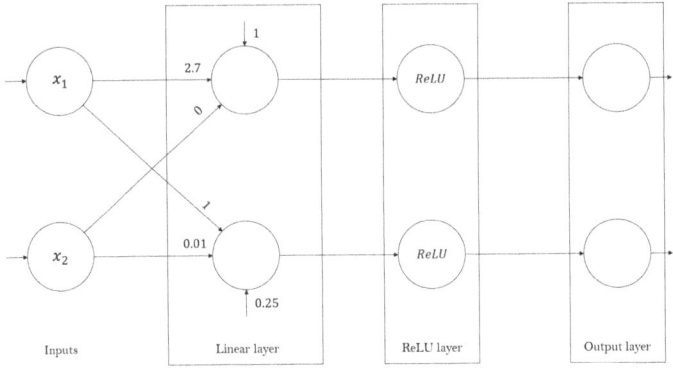

Fig. 1. The example neural network to illustrate the CoQ model.

weights and biases of a layer are determined during training. A ReLU layer consists of neurons that each apply the activation function $ReLU(x_i) = \max(0, x_i)$ to its input x_i. An output layer applies the identity function.

Example: Neural Network in CoQ . Within the CoQ model, the layers of a neural network are represented using functions that return a layer's internal representation. For the example neural network of Fig. 1, we consider the linear layer NNLinear and the ReLU layer NNReLU:

```
Definition NNLinear {input_dim hidden_dim output_dim: nat}
(W: matrix hidden_dim input_dim) (b: colvec hidden_dim)
(NNnext: NNSequential (input_dim:=hidden_dim) (output_dim:=output_dim))
  := NNPWALayer (LinearPWAF W b) NNnext.

Definition NNReLU {input_dim output_dim: nat}
(NNnext: NNSequential (input_dim:=input_dim) (output_dim:=output_dim))
  := NNPWALayer (input_dim:=input_dim) ReLU_PWAF NNnext.
```

Both layers expect the parameter NNnext which is the follow-up layer in the neural network. The layers make use of CoQ's dependent types to enforce matching input dimension and output dimensions (also called "hidden" dimension) between layers, as well as for the output dimension of the entire neural network.

The linear layer NNLinear additionally requires a weight matrix W and a bias vector b as parameters. For the example network, the CoQ representation of these parameters, example_weights and example_biases, where the type colvec is a column vector, is:

```
Definition example_weights: matrix 2 2 := [[2.7, 0 ], [1,    0.01]].
Definition example_biases: colvec 2 := [[1 ], [0.25]].
```

To sum up, the Coq representation of the example neural network is:

```
Definition example_nn := (NNLinear example_weights example_biases
  (NNReLU (NNOutput (output_dim:=2)))).
```

The example neural network `example_nn` is a recursive structure of layers: `NNLinear`, `NNReLU` and `NNOutput`, each embedded as a function parameter into the previous layer.

Piecewise Affine Activation Functions. The layers of the example neural network are piecewise affine layers, called `NNPWALayer` in the Coq representation. Typically verification techniques focus on piecewise affine activation functions, since they allow to encode the verification problem as an SMT or MILP problem [1]. The Coq library for neural networks is tailored to verification by defining a piecewise affine function through its polyhedral subdivisions [25]; many efficient verification algorithms are known in literature that work on polyhedra [26], with some being directly tailored to neural network verification [29].

Arithmetic Model. Neural networks are usually executed using floating-point numbers. In the Coq model, neural networks are defined on real numbers to enable verification using powerful decision procedures, e.g. the Coq-native decision procedure `lra` for linear real arithmetic or `nra` for non-linear arithmetic. Although the discrepancy between floating-point and real-valued neural networks can invalidate verification results [16,30], removing this discrepancy remains an open challenge in the neural network verification community [10], and is outside of the scope of this paper. In the converter, the transformation from floating-point into real numbers happens at a later stage of the conversion (see Sects. 5.4 and 6), implying that a change of the arithmetic model in the Coq model of neural networks can be easily reflected in the converter.

4   Overview of the Formally Verified Converter

We provide an overview of the converter by introducing its architecture (Sect. 4.1) and presenting the approach to its formal verification (Sect. 4.2).

In the following Sect. 5, we go through the converter's phases and formal verification in detail.

4.1   Architecture of the Converter

The converter's architecture is depicted in Fig. 2. The converter processes a neural network in the decoded[3] ONNX format, running through four *phases* to output a neural network in the chosen Coq model. During preprocessing, the converter handles the technicalities of the ONNX numbers. In the following

---

[3] ONNX files have to be decoded with `protoc`: https://github.com/onnx/onnx/blob/main/docs/IR.md.

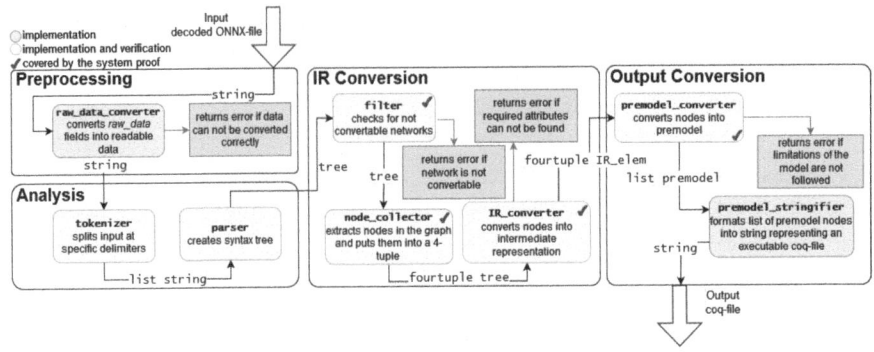

Fig. 2. The flowchart illustrates the converter's architecture. Its components are grouped in four phases: preprocessing, analysis, IR conversion, and output conversion.

analysis, a syntax tree is computed, which is then turned into an intermediate representation (IR) during the IR conversion phase. Finally, the converter generates the output network as an instance of the neural network model in CoQ during the output conversion. Each phase employs *components* which are CoQ functions that perform a specific role in a phase.

As verification techniques mostly target feedforward neural networks (i.e. no cycles in the network graph) [1], conversion for this class is offered. However, the converter is extendable to recurrent networks due to its modular architecture.

4.2   Formal Verification Approach

For the formal verification of the converter, we deliver *unit proofs*, machine-checked proofs that verify the functional correctness of the converter's components – similar to unit tests in classical software testing. Further, we prove that the number of neurons is preserved during the conversion. This property serves as a link between the converter's components – comparable to a *system test* in traditional software testing.

Unit Proofs. As indicated in Fig. 2, the functional correctness of each component is verified by a unit proof. The only unverified components are the `raw_data_converter` and the `premodel_stringifier`, which are handling technicalities of the ONNX numbers and generating an executable CoQ file, respectively. The unit proofs are discussed in the Sects. 5.2–5.4.

System Proof. As a system proof, we ensure that the conversion preserves the number of neurons of the neural network using the unit proofs. This verification is linking all the components indicated in Fig. 2 on the system level. This system proof is discussed in Sect. 5.5.

5 The Formally Verified Converter in Coq

We walk through the converter's phases where we present for each component, its functionality and its verification by a unit proof (Sect. 5.1–5.4). Finally, to complete the converter, we compose all components and discuss the verification of the composition by a system proof (Sect. 5.5).

5.1 Preprocessing Phase

The preprocessing consists of the component `raw_data_converter` handling the representation of ONNX numbers in Coq. The ONNX format stores the trained values, such as weights and biases, in binary form which requires conversion to reals in decimal form to fit the Coq model:

```
Definition raw_data_converter (s: list ascii) : error_option (list ascii)
```

The `raw_data_converter` converts these numbers from binary form into strings, and only later in the conversion process, these numbers become well-typed numbers inside Coq. Figure 3 exemplifies the raw data preprocessing. The `raw_data_converter` is one of the two unverified components.

```
initializer {
  dims: 4
  data_type: 1
  name: "net.0.bias"
  raw_data: "\207\3330?b\370-\276\333\210\370\275\337a\036?"
}
```

```
initializer {
  dims: 4
  data_type: 1
  name: ""net.0.bias""
  data_converted: 0.6908497214317322
  data_converted: -0.169892817735672
  data_converted: -0.12135478109121323
  data_converted: 0.6186808943748474
}
```

Fig. 3. Illustration of the preprocessing with the `raw_data_converter`. *Above:* a snippet from an ONNX file with a raw data field before preprocessing. *Below:* the according snippet of the preprocessed ONNX file with the raw data field replaced by decoded floating point values.

5.2 Analysis Phase

The analysis employs a `tokenizer` that splits the file into tokens, and a `parser` processing the tokens to build a syntax tree of the ONNX file.

```
attribute{
   name: "onnx::alpha"
   f: 1
   type: FLOAT
}
```

↓

attribute	{	name	:	"onnx::alpha"	f
:	1	type	:	FLOAT	}

Fig. 4. A tokenization example. *Above:* a snippet from an ONNX file. *Below:* tokens identified by the `tokenizer`.

Tokenizer. The `tokenizer` creates a list of tokens, as illustrated in Fig. 4:

```
Definition tokenizer (s: list ascii): list (list ascii)
```

For the formal verification, we prove that the `tokenizer` splits a string without adding or removing characters, except for whitespaces:

```
Theorem not_less_not_more: forall (s: list ascii),
filter isNotWhitespace s = filter isNotWhitespace (concat (tokenizer s)).
```

The proof relies on additional lemmas about the predicate `isNotWhitespace` filtering out white spaces, and its relation to the standard library function `concat`.

Parser. The `parser` generates a syntax tree out of the tokens, shown in Fig. 5:

```
Definition parser (l: list (list ascii)) : tree

Inductive tree :=
  | leaf (value : list ascii)
  | subtree (value: list ascii) (children : list tree).
```

At the core of the parser is the `append_at_end` function that receives a `tree`, a `depth` and a new token `value` to append:

```
Fixpoint append_at_end (t: tree) (depth: nat) (value: list ascii) : tree
```

Notably, the `append_at_end` function decides at which node in a layer the token will be attached, constructing the `tree` from left to right with new children added at the end of the child list. While limiting the function's flexibility, this restriction simplifies the verification. For the formal verification, we show that the parsed tree contains exactly all the tokens that are not delimiters (the characters "{", "}" and ":").

```
Theorem In_parser: forall (s: list ascii) (t: list (list ascii)),
Inb t s = true ∧ is_delimiter_string s = false
  → InTree s (parser t) = true.
```

The function `InTree` identifies if a given token is contained in the `tree`:

```
Fixpoint InTree (s: list ascii) (t: tree): bool
```

The proof relies on lemmas connecting the functions `append_at_end` and `InTree`:

```
Lemma InTree_eq: forall (s: list ascii) (t: tree) (d: nat),
  InTree s (append_at_end t d s) = true.
Lemma InTree_cons: forall (s r: list ascii) (t: tree) (d: nat),
  InTree s t = true → InTree s (append_at_end t d r) = true.
Lemma InTree_not_app: forall (s r: list ascii) (t: tree) (d: nat),
  InTree s (append_at_end t d r) = true ∧
  eqb (string_of_list_ascii r) (string_of_list_ascii s) = false →
  InTree s t = true ∨ s = (list_ascii_of_string "probably_misplaced_node").
```

The lemma `InTree_eq` states that appended strings are in the tree. The lemma `InTree_cons` ensures that appending a string does not remove present strings, while `InTree_not_app` reversely ensures that removing a string does not append strings.

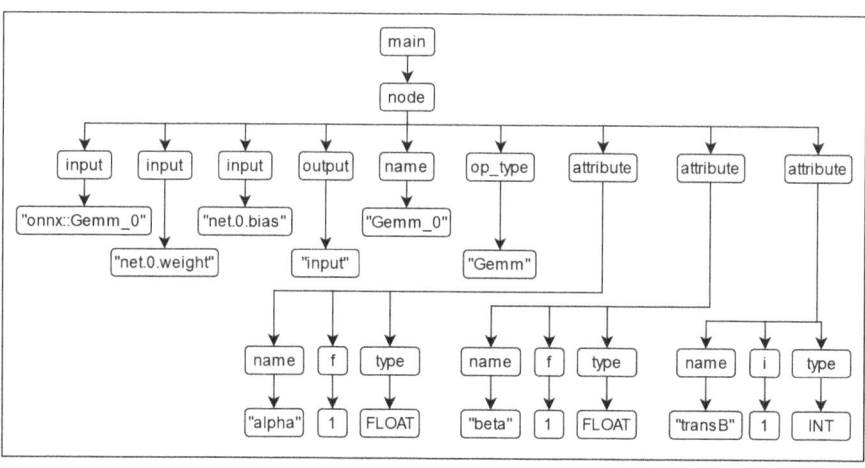

Fig. 5. A syntax tree of an ONNX file created by the `parser`.

5.3   Intermediate Representation Conversion Phase

The computed syntax tree is transformed into an intermediate representation during the phase of IR conversion. The components `filter`, `node_collector` and `IR_converter` belong to this phase.

Intermediate Representation. The IR serves as a bridge between the ONNX format and the resulting CoQ model by incorporating features from both. An element of the IR is represented by the type `IR_elem` in CoQ and can be one of the following: (1) `IR_input` – analog to an ONNX input node, (2) `IR_output` – analog to an ONNX output node, (3) `IR_node` – corresponding to an ONNX operator, or (4) `IR_initializer` – an ONNX node type containing static parameters of a neural network. Each `IR_elem` has a name which is the first `string` parameter and each `IR_node` references another node by using its name:

```
Inductive IR_elem :=
 | IR_input: string → IR_dim → IR_elem
 | IR_output: string → IR_dim → IR_elem
 | IR_node: string → list string → list string → IR_operation → IR_elem
 | IR_initializer: string → IR_fixedValue → IR_elem.
```

Filter. The `filter` ensures that tokens of the syntax tree are convertible to an IR, and aborts if a non-convertible token is found (e.g. an ONNX operator with no equal in the CoQ model):

```
Definition filter (t: tree): error_option tree
```

For the formal verification, we prove that if the `filter` does not return an error, the syntax tree remains unchanged:

```
Lemma no_error_same_tree: forall (t ft: tree),
 filter t = Success ft → eq_string_tree t ft.
```

Node collector. Each constructor of the `IR_elem` corresponds to an ONNX node type. The component `node_collector` processes the syntax tree, dividing it into four lists of trees, each containing one of the node types:

```
Definition node_collector (t: tree) : fourtuple tree

Inductive fourtuple (T: Type) :=
 | ft: (list T * list T * list T * list T) → fourtuple T.
```

A crucial aspect of the `node_collector` is its intrinsic understanding that each ONNX node, to be converted into an `IR_elem`, is a subtree of the syntax tree. For the formal verification, we prove that the `node_collector` divides nodes into four lists without adding or removing nodes:

```
Theorem same_node_count_node_collector: forall (t: tree),
  length (flatten_fourtuple (node_collector t)) = count_nodes t.
```

Intermediate Representation Converter. The final component in the IR conversion phase is the IR_converter that takes a fourtuple of trees and converts each tree to an IR_elem:

```
Definition IR_converter(t:fourtuple tree): error_option (fourtuple IR_elem)
```

Since the node_collector already categorizes the subtrees according to the ONNX node type, the IR_converter reuses this information to select the appropriate IR_elem constructor for each subtree. The IR_converter returns a fourtuple of IR_elem instances with each of the four lists created using the corresponding constructor. As a structural property on resulting neural networks, we verify that the IR_converter returns a fourtuple of the same size as the input fourtuple:

```
Theorem same_node_count_IR_converter: forall (ft: fourtuple tree)
  (tuple: fourtuple IR_elem), IR_converter ft = Success tuple →
  length (flatten_fourtuple_without_input tuple) =
    length (flatten_fourtuple_without_input ft).
```

5.4 Output Conversion Phase

The phase of the output conversion transforms the previously created IR instance into a Coq file holding the neural network as an instance of the Coq model.

Premodel. Central to this phase is the premodel, a type similar to the resulting Coq model, which is necessary as the converter's output is not an instance of a neural network in Coq, but a file that contains this instance. To generate an output in Coq, the Redirect Compute command is typically used, which leads to Coq unfolding the neural network as thoroughly as possible. However, due to the involved matrices and real numbers, the resulting output becomes difficult to read for humans. That is why we introduce the premodel NNPremodel.

Premodel Converter. The component premodel_converter transforms an instance in IR into the premodel:

```
Definition premodel_converter (ft: fourtuple IR_elem) :
  error_option (list NNPremodel)
```

A significant difference between NNPremodel and the output model is the premodel's non-recursiveness, simplifying the premodel_converter implementation by enabling a direct mapping from `IR_elem` to an element of `NNPremodel`. Consequently, the `premodel_converter` returns a list of premodel elements. This approach facilitates proving the number of nodes of the network being preserved in the premodel and the output:

```
Theorem same_node_count_premodel_converter: forall (ft: fourtuple IR_elem)
   (l: list NNPremodel), premodel_converter ft = Success l →
   length l = length (flatten_fourtuple_without_input ft).
```

Premodel Stringifier. The `premodel_stringifier` component generates a string saved in a COQ file that contains a valid instance of the neural network in the COQ model:

```
Definition premodel_stringifier (l: list NNPremodel) : string
```

The `premodel_stringifier` constructs a COQ file by (1) generating correct COQ imports, (2) printing correct instances of COQ's neural network model, and (3) creating a readable decimal representation for the network's weights and matrices. This component remains unverified, as it would require re-parsing the generated COQ file.

5.5 Composition of the Components

We present the final converter as a function composition of the outlined components. As we additionally support the option for error messages by using the return type `error_option`, we take usage of the specialized operator `|>` for the function composition.

Composed Converter. The composed converter generates either a COQ model of the input neural network or outputs an error description:

```
Definition convert_ONNX_to_Coq (s: string) : string :=
   let conversion :=
     ((fun raw_onnx ⇒ raw_data_converter (list_ascii_of_string raw_onnx)) |>
      (fun onnx ⇒ filter (parser (tokenizer onnx))) |>
      (fun token_tree ⇒ IR_converter (node_collector token_tree)) |>
      (fun ir ⇒ premodel_converter ir)) in
   match conversion s with
   | Success premodel ⇒ premodel_stringifier premodel
   | Error description ⇒ description
   end.
```

The Converter's System Proof. As a system proof, we ensure that the conversion preserves the number of neurons of the neural network using the outlined unit proofs. This verification links all the components used, indicated in Fig. 2, on the system level. Specifically, we verify that the number of ONNX nodes, minus all input nodes, is equal to the number of nodes (premodel elements) generated by the `premodel_converter`. Note that the Coq model does not have explicit input nodes.

The theorem's premise mimics the conversion by calling the components:

```
Theorem same_node_count:
  forall (t t_filtered: tree) (IR: fourtuple IR_elem) (p: list NNPremodel),
    filter t = Success t_filtered →
    IR_converter (node_collector t_filtered) = Success IR →
    premodel_converter IR = Success p →
    count_nodes_without_input t = List.length p.
```

The proof in Coq is a composition of the components' unit proofs. With this system proof, we set the foundation for a proof of structural equivalence between the original and converted networks. This theorem could be extended to stronger notions of equivalence, e.g. graph isomorphism.

As indicated in Fig. 2, the system proof covers most but not all components. To cover all components, we would need to reason about the resulting Coq code, which would involve formalizing the semantics of ONNX within Coq. While this presents a promising direction for future work, it is outside of the scope of this paper.

6 On How to Use the Converter

We demonstrate the converter's usage on the case study of the inverted pendulum – a neural network trained to balance an inverted pendulum on a moving cart (Sect. 6.1). We follow up with an discussion on the converter's extraction into a reliable OCaml version for practical usability (Sect. 6.2).

6.1 Demonstration of the Converter

We demonstrate the converter's usage on a neural network. The conversion process for this neural network can be repeated using the instructions in the GitHub repository of this paper.

Case Study. As illustrated on the left-hand side of Fig. 6, a neural network controls a moving cart in order to balance an inverted pendulum on the cart. This neural network is a popular example in reinforcement learning of controllers.[4]

---

[4] See https://gymnasium.farama.org/environments/classic_control/cart_pole/ for a discrete-time version of the inverted pendulum (called cart pole) in the context of reinforcement learning.

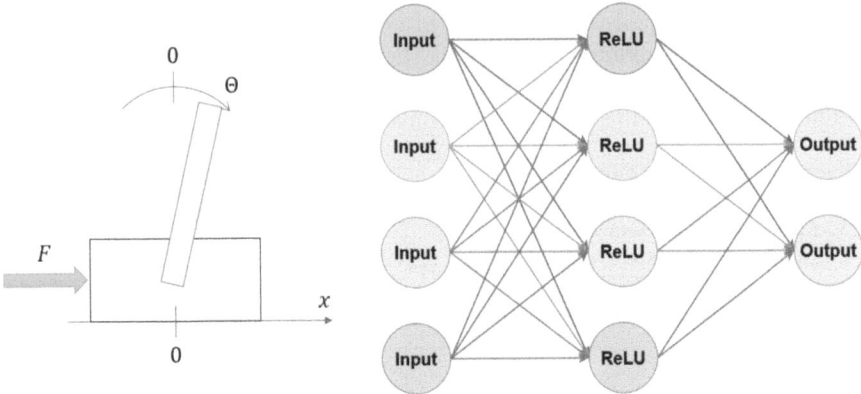

Fig. 6. *Left-hand side:* The neural network acts as a controller by regulating the force F applied to the cart in positive or negative direction on the x-axis, and thereby modifying the angle Θ of the balanced inverted pendulum. *Right-hand side:* A conceptual standard representation of the neural network trained to control the inverted pendulum.

Training of the Neural Network. We trained a neural network to balance the pendulum for 200 controller activations using the method described in [17]. The trained neural network is conceptually illustrated on the right-hand side of Fig. 6. It has four inputs, an output layer and an intermediate (or hidden) layer that applies the non-linear activation function ReLU.

Trained Neural Network in the COQ *Model.* After exporting the neural network from PyTorch to the ONNX format and decoding the ONNX file, the compiled converter can be used to create a COQ file containing the neural network in the COQ model. At the bottom of this resulting file, we find the neural network that consists of two linear layers, a ReLU layer and an output layer:

```
Definition onnxGemm__six_ := NNLinear
  (transpose net_two_weight)
  (scalar_mult (real_of_string "1") net_two_bias)
  (NNOutput (output_dim:=2)).
Definition input := NNReLU onnxGemm__six_.
Definition onnxGemm__zero_ := NNLinear
  (transpose net_zero_weight)
  (scalar_mult (real_of_string "1") net_zero_bias) input.
```

The names of each layer are copied from the original ONNX file.

Weights and Biases in the COQ *Model.* Each layer has weights and biases that are saved in the same file in the following format:

```
Definition net_two_bias := mk_colvec 2 (fun x: nat ⇒
  match x with
  | 1 ⇒ real_of_string "-0.5949365496635437011718750"%string
```

```
 | 0 ⇒ real_of_string "-0.18491101264953613281250000"%string
 | _ ⇒ real_of_string "0.0"%string
end)
```

The use of the premodel instead of `Redirect Compute` allows us to keep weights and biases as human-readable strings that will be converted to reals only after the COQ file is compiled.

6.2 Extraction of the Converter

For usability, the COQ converter has been extracted to OCAML. The advantage of the extraction is the ability to call the converter in one click, as a fast-running binary program. The extracted converter is reliable, as COQ's extraction mechanism preserves the verification results developed in COQ.

Handling Side Effects. COQ's extraction mechanism works straightforwardly for side-effect free programs. As the converter generates a COQ file, it has side effects. That is why we also use the library COQIO, designed to extract COQ programs with side effects to OCAML.[5]

Integration of the Converter into a Verification Framework. The converter takes a trained neural networks and generates a representation [2] that COQ can process and that is tailored to neural network verification. Hence, the converter allows the formal verification of outside-trained neural networks in COQ.

Since the verification results apply only to the converted network, the conversion is a critical step. The verified converter is trustworthy and thereby contributes to making neural network verification in COQ more reliable.

7   Discussion

We sum up our contributions (Sect. 7.1) and discuss future work (Sect. 7.2).

7.1   Summary

This paper presents the first formally verified converter of neural networks for a theorem prover. The converter processes neural networks in the ONNX format and generates a COQ file that holds an instance of the neural network in a COQ model tailored to verification. We implemented the converter in COQ's functional programming language and used its theorem proving system to formally establish its correctness.

---

[5] CoqIO library: https://github.com/coq-io/io This library is no longer maintained. In the future, it could be easily exchanged by a similar library to come, as only a few lines of code are affected.

The Verified Converter. In particular, we statically verified the functional correctness of the converter's individual components by machine checked unit proofs. While the converter's core functionality was verified, we excluded the initial and final components which are handling technicalities concerning the number representation in the ONNX format and the creation of a CoQ file, respectively. In addition, we ensure that the number of neurons is preserved during the conversion process. This system proof links the converter's components, and is a step toward proving the structural equivalence of the original and the converted networks with stronger equivalence notions such as isomorphism.

Usage of the Converter. The converter can be integrated into verification frameworks that use CoQ for neural network verification. For enhanced usability of the converter, a trustworthy OCAML version is available by CoQ's extraction mechanism. To demonstrate the converter's usage, we showcased the converter on a neural network that has been trained in PyTorch to balance an inverted pendulum. The verified converter contributes to making the verification of neural networks with CoQ reliable by narrowing the gap between the execution and the verification environment of neural networks.

7.2   Future Work

Extending the Supported Activation Functions. The activation function RELU is one of the most popular ones in industry [22] and in formal verification [8]. That is why the chosen CoQ model offers a verified version of the RELU function. Nevertheless, we plan to extend the converter's support to a broader range of activation functions.

Extending the Supported Architectures. As verification techniques mostly target feedforward neural networks (i.e. no cycles in the network graph) [1], conversion for this class is offered. However, the converter is extendable to recurrent networks due to its modular architecture.

Trustworthy Import of Data Sets. We aim to incorporate the conversion of data sets, as neural network verification often requires assessment of the training data. Finally, we intend to consider further file formats, such as NNEF[6].

Further Narrowing the Gap Between Execution and Verification. The focus of this paper is on establishing the converter's correctness by a static formal verification, relying on graph-theoretic properties. Future work entails considering the operational behavior by defining an error margin between the real-world execution and the numerical representation of neural networks in CoQ. One potential way to tackle the operational behavior is to formalize the execution semantics of a file format, in our case the ONNX semantics, in CoQ as done in [13].

---

[6] https://www.khronos.org/nnef.

References

1. Albarghouthi, A.: Introduction to neural network verification. Found. Trends Program. Lang. **7**(1–2), 1–157 (2021). https://doi.org/10.1561/2500000051
2. Aleksandrov, A., Völlinger, K.: Formalizing Piecewise Affine Activation Functions of Neural Networks in Coq. Nasa Formal Methods, Lecture Notes in Computer Science (2023)
3. Bentkamp, A., Blanchette, J.C., Klakow, D.: A formal proof of the expressiveness of deep learning. J. Autom. Reason. **63**(2), 347–368 (2018). https://doi.org/10.1007/s10817-018-9481-5
4. Bagnall, A., Stewart, G.: Certifying the true error: machine learning in Coq with verified generalization guarantees. In: AAAI Conference on Artificial Intelligence (2019)
5. Botoeva, E., Kouvaros, P., Kronqvist, J., Lomuscio, A., Misener, R.: Efficient verification of ReLU-based neural networks via dependency analysis. In: Proceedings of the AAAI Conference on Artificial Intelligence, vol. 34, pp. 3291–3299 (2020). https://doi.org/10.1609/aaai.v34i04.5729
6. Brix, C., Bak, S., Liu, C., Johnson, T.T.: The fourth international verification of neural networks competition (vnn-comp 2023): summary and results. arXiv preprint arXiv:2312.16760 (2023)
7. Brucker, A.D., Stell, A.: Verifying feedforward neural networks for classification in Isabelle/HOL. In: Formal Methods. FM 2023. Lecture Notes in Computer Science. Springer, Cham (2023)
8. Bunel, R., Turkaslan, I., Torr, P.H., Kohli, P., Kumar, M.P.: A unified view of piecewise linear neural network verification. In: Proceedings of the 32nd International Conference on Neural Information Processing Systems, NIPS 2018, pp. 4795–4804. Curran Associates Inc., Red Hook, NY, USA (2018)
9. Calin, O.: Deep Learning Architectures: A Mathematical Approach. Springer (2020)
10. Cordeiro, L.C., et al.: Neural network verification is a programming language challenge. arXiv preprint arXiv:2501.05867 (2025)
11. Cybenko, G.: Approximation by superpositions of a sigmoidal function. Math. Control Signals Syst. **2**(4), 303–314 (1989)
12. Daggitt, M.L., Kokke, W., Atkey, R., Arnaboldi, L., Komendantskya, E.: Vehicle: interfacing neural network verifiers with interactive theorem provers (2022)
13. Gauffriau, A., Pagetti, C.: Formal description of ml models for unambiguous implementation. arXiv preprint arXiv:2307.12713 (2023)
14. Tran, H.-D., Bak, S., Xiang, W., Johnson, T.T.: Verification of deep convolutional neural networks using ImageStars. In: Lahiri, S.K., Wang, C. (eds.) CAV 2020. LNCS, vol. 12224, pp. 18–42. Springer, Cham (2020). https://doi.org/10.1007/978-3-030-53288-8_2
15. Hornik, K.: Approximation capabilities of multilayer feedforward networks. Neural Netw. **4**(2), 251–257 (1991)
16. Jia, K., Rinard, M.: Exploiting verified neural networks via floating point numerical error. In: Drăgoi, C., Mukherjee, S., Namjoshi, K. (eds.) SAS 2021. LNCS, vol. 12913, pp. 191–205. Springer, Cham (2021). https://doi.org/10.1007/978-3-030-88806-0_9
17. Lapan, M.: Deep Reinforcement Learning Hands-On: Apply modern RL methods, with deep Q-networks, value iteration, policy gradients, TRPO, AlphaGo Zero and more. Packt Publishing Ltd. (2018)

18. Lin, W., et al.: Robustness Verification of Classification Deep Neural Networks via Linear Programming, pp. 11410–11419 (2019). https://doi.org/10.1109/CVPR. 2019.01168

19. Liu, C., Arnon, T., Lazarus, C., Strong, C., Barrett, C., Kochenderfer, M.J.: Algorithms for verifying deep neural networks. Found. Trends Optim. 4(3–4), 244–404 (2021). https://doi.org/10.1561/2400000035

20. Lopez, D.M., Choi, S.W., Tran, H.D., Johnson, T.T.: Nnv 2.0: the neural network verification tool. In: International Conference on Computer Aided Verification, pp. 397–412. Springer (2023)

21. Mäntymäki, M., Minkkinen, M., Birkstedt, T., Viljanen, M.: Defining organizational AI governance. AI Ethics 2(4), 603–609 (2022)

22. Montesinos López, O.A., Montesinos López, A., Crossa, J.: Fundamentals of artificial neural networks and deep learning. In: Multivariate Statistical Machine Learning Methods for Genomic Prediction. LNCS, pp. 379–425. Springer, Cham (2022). https://doi.org/10.1007/978-3-030-89010-0_10

23. Murphy, C., Gray, P., Stewart, G.: Verified perceptron convergence theorem. In: Proceedings of the 1st ACM SIGPLAN International Workshop on Machine Learning and Programming Languages, MAPL 2017, pp. 43–50. Association for Computing Machinery, New York (2017). https://doi.org/10.1145/3088525.3088673

24. Rossi, F., Bernardeschi, C., Cococcioni, M., Palmieri, M.: Towards formal verification of neural networks in cyber-physical systems. In: Benz, N., Gopinath, D., Shi, N. (eds.) NASA Formal Methods, pp. 207–222. Springer, Cham (2024)

25. Scholtes, S.: Introduction to Piecewise Differentiable Equations. Springer, New York (2012)

26. Schrijver, A.: Combinatorial Optimization: Polyhedra and Efficiency. Springer, Heidelberg (2002)

27. Selsam, D., Liang, P., Dill, D.L.: Developing bug-free machine learning systems with formal mathematics. In: Proceedings of the 34th International Conference on Machine Learning, ICML 2017, vol. 70, pp. 3047–3056. JMLR.org (2017)

28. The Coq Development Team: The Coq Proof Assistant (2022). https://doi.org/10. 5281/zenodo.7313584

29. Vincent, J.A., Schwager, M.: Reachable polyhedral marching (RPM): a safety verification algorithm for robotic systems with deep neural network components. In: 2021 IEEE International Conference on Robotics and Automation (ICRA), pp. 9029–9035 (2021). https://doi.org/10.1109/ICRA48506.2021.9561956

30. Zombori, D., Bánhelyi, B., Csendes, T., Megyeri, I., Jelasity, M.: Fooling a complete neural network verifier. In: International Conference on Learning Representations (2021)

COMPASS: An Agent for MLIR Compilation Pass Pipeline Generation

Hongbin Zhang[1,2], Shihao Gao[1,2], Yang Liu[1,2], Mingjie Xing[1(✉)], Yanjun Wu[1], and Chen Zhao[1]

[1] Institute of Software, Chinese Academy of Sciences, Beijing, China
{hongbin2019,gaoshihao2023,liuyang2023,mingjie,
yanjun,zhaochen}@iscas.ac.cn
[2] University of Chinese Academy of Sciences, Beijing, China

Abstract. MLIR is the state-of-the-art multi-level compilation infrastructure. It provides a reusable and extensible compiler intermediate representation (IR) framework that supports the collaboration of IRs across different levels. MLIR has been widely adopted in various compilers, forming a domain-specific compilation ecosystem. However, the features of MLIR also bring challenges to compilation pass pipeline arrangement. Managing mixed-level abstractions and diverse IR extensions requires significant expertise, which increases the complexity of developing MLIR compilation path.

COMPASS is proposed as an agent to generate MLIR pass pipelines, aiming to simplify the construction process and reduce reliance on manual expertise. Confronted with uncertain compilation passes and fragmented domain-specific knowledge, we address the problem by decomposing it into a unified compilation methodology and an extensible knowledge base. To achieve this, COMPASS combines an MLIR knowledge base with a compilation path generator to automate pass pipeline arrangement. The knowledge base is constructed using a large language model (LLM), while the generator performs backtracking over a pass-selection tree. Evaluation on a range of MLIR-based compilers shows that COMPASS achieves a success rate exceeding 90% across 1,256 test cases, successfully generating pass pipelines and compiling source files to their corresponding target abstraction levels. These results demonstrate that COMPASS enables the automatic generation of pass pipelines for MLIR-based compilers, reducing the human effort involved in the MLIR ecosystem.

Keywords: Compiler Pass Pipeline · Generative AI · MLIR

1 Introduction

As Moore's Law reaches its limits, domain-specific software and hardware stacks are becoming increasingly fragmented. MLIR [21] has emerged as a

This work was supported by the National Key R&D Program of China, Grant No. 2022YFB4401402.

solution by offering a unified compilation infrastructure that integrates diverse domain-specific representations. With the development of the MLIR ecosystem [3,5,6,8,9,28,31], its applications have covered multiple domains, including AI computing, programming languages, hardware development, and quantum computing. The core advantage of the MLIR infrastructure lies in its multi-level dialect system, which features syntactic uniformity, domain extensibility, and operation compatibility.

Although these MLIR features unify various domain-specific abstractions, they also bring challenges in arranging pass pipelines for MLIR-based compilers. Unlike traditional phase ordering problems, MLIR's high extensibility has created an open and continuously evolving ecosystem of dialects, operations, and passes. Compilation pass pipeline arrangement with mixed MLIR extensions becomes an expertise-driven problem. Currently, appropriate MLIR pass pipelines require manual arrangement by experts with rich domain knowledge, which increases the barrier to MLIR adoption and constrains the rapid development of its ecosystem.

To address these challenges, we propose COMPASS, an agent that generates MLIR pass pipelines. We decompose the problem into two key components: modeling a unified compilation methodology and acquiring extensible domain knowledge. Our implementation uses a tree-based backtracking algorithm to model the unified arrangement process of MLIR pass pipelines and employs an LLM [27] to construct the domain knowledge base of MLIR extensions. By integrating these two components, we design a learning and reasoning workflow that forms the foundation of the intelligent agent. As illustrated in Fig. 1, during the learning phase, COMPASS extracts domain knowledge from the source files of various MLIR-based compilers to construct a knowledge base. In the reasoning phase, it takes an input MLIR file and generates multiple feasible pass pipelines.

The evaluation of COMPASS is conducted on a range of mainstream MLIR-based compilers and extensions, including core MLIR [21], Torch-MLIR [6], StableHLO [8], and CIRCT [5]. COMPASS achieved over 90% automation success in pass pipeline arrangement across 1,256 compiler test cases. The experimental results confirm COMPASS's practical value in MLIR compilation path finalization.

The main contributions of this paper are summarized as follows:

1. We present the first systematic study on automating MLIR pass pipeline generation. By decomposing it into two dimensions, unified compilation methodology and extensible domain knowledge, we propose a complete solution.
2. We model the MLIR pass pipeline arrangement process as a tree-based backtracking algorithm and combine generative AI technology to support the MLIR's domain extensibility, developing an intelligent agent that can automatically generate pass pipelines.
3. We conduct experiments on mainstream MLIR compilers and provide analysis of the results, validating the effectiveness of our method.

The remainder of this paper is organized as follows: Sect. 2 presents the research background, providing a detailed introduction to the MLIR infrastructure and its pass pipeline arrangement methods; Sect. 3 elaborates the core ideas and design principles of COMPASS; Sect. 4 delves into the specific implementation details and technical solutions of COMPASS; Sect. 5 evaluates COMPASS's performance and analyzes its generated pass pipelines through multiple practical MLIR-based applications; Sect. 6 reviews related research work and provides a comparative analysis with our method; Sect. 7 concludes the paper.

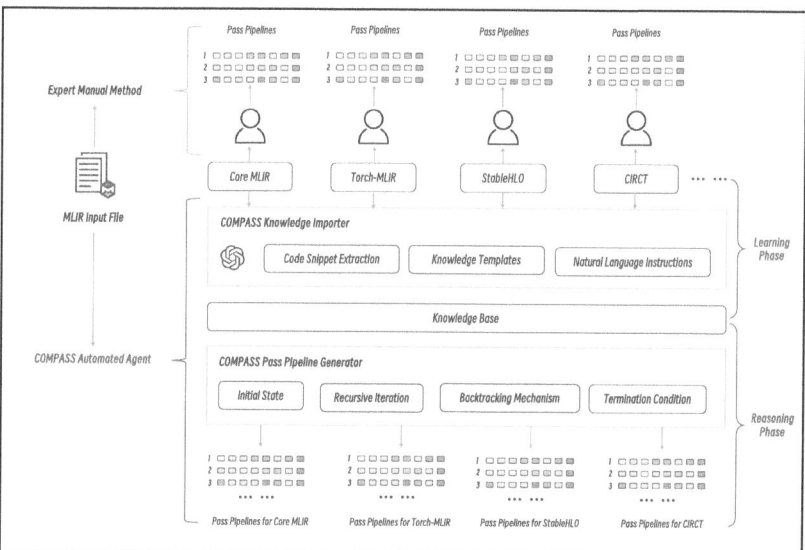

Fig. 1. COMPASS Overview - This figure compares the difference between COMPASS's automated approach and the manual expert method. The upper half of the figure shows how experts and maintainers of various MLIR compiler projects manually configure static compilation paths for their respective projects. When an MLIR file is input, the system uses these pre-made compilation paths for compilation lowering. The lower half of the figure shows COMPASS's approach: using an automated agent to learn and integrate knowledge and experience from various compilers. When an MLIR file is input, the COMPASS generator can dynamically generate multiple candidate pass pipeline solutions.

2   Background

This section provides an overview of the research background on MLIR infrastructure and ecosystem, focusing on analyzing the challenges in MLIR pass pipeline arrangement.

2.1   MLIR Infrastructure and Ecosystem

MLIR addresses the fragmentation of software and hardware stacks by providing a unified compiler infrastructure for efficient code representation and optimization. Its multi-level abstraction supports flexible transformations at various compilation stages, while its modular architecture enables easy extension with custom operations and types. Below, we provide explanations for key terms frequently referenced in this paper.

- **MLIR dialect**: A collection of domain-specific operations in MLIR that define computational abstractions, such as the Linalg, Vector, or LLVM dialects.
- **MLIR operation**: The fundamental computational unit in MLIR, where each operation belongs to a specific dialect, such as `linalg.matmul`.
- **MLIR pass**: A transformation or optimization unit in MLIR that performs pattern matching, rewriting, optimization, or code generation.
- **MLIR pass pipeline**: A compilation transformation process composed of multiple passes that progressively optimize and transform MLIR code.
- **MLIR infrastructure**: Includes IR definitions, pattern matching, optimizations, debugging tools, and backend support, providing a modular compiler toolchain.
- **MLIR dialect mixing feature**: This feature enables multiple dialects to coexist within the same MLIR code, facilitating the integration of different abstractions.
- **MLIR extensibility feature**: This feature supports the customization of dialects, operations, and passes for specific domains, enabling flexible adaptation to various computational scenarios and hardware architectures.

The MLIR ecosystem has rapidly expanded across various domains, with key contributions from projects like IREE [28], Torch-MLIR [6], StableHLO [8], Mojo [23], Triton [9], Buddy Compiler [3], and CIRCT [5]. These projects have introduced multiple dialects and optimization passes, which demonstrate MLIR's extensibility and adaptability. However, they introduce challenges in managing the increasing complexity of dialects and passes, requiring domain-specific expertise to organize efficient pass pipelines.

2.2 MLIR Pass Pipeline Arrangement

As shown in Fig. 1, pass pipelines in MLIR-based compilers are manually arranged, requiring developers to understand both MLIR's core concepts and domain-specific knowledge of compilers, dialects, and passes. Developers primarily rely on TableGen [4] definitions and test files to learn about dialects and passes. Due to the specialized expertise required, accurate pass pipelines are mostly designed by core maintainers. Even experienced users often struggle to construct efficient pass pipelines for unfamiliar MLIR projects in cross-project development. For beginners, arranging a feasible pipeline poses a considerable challenge.

Although various mechanisms have been proposed to support MLIR development [4,7,13], COMPASS is the first to address the problem of pass pipeline arrangement and offer a corresponding solution. Automating this process presents two key challenges:

Listing 1.1. An Example of MLIR Kernel Code Composed of Mixed Dialects

```
// Define an affine map with the given dimension.
#map = affine_map<(d0, d1, d2) -> (d0, d1, d2)>

func.func @kernel(%arg0: tensor<40x4096xf32>,
                  %arg1: tensor<4096x4096xf32>)
   -> tensor<1x40x4096xf32> {
   // Define a constant value with Arithmetic dialect.
   %cst = arith.constant dense<0.0> : tensor<40x4096xf32>
   // Perform a matrix multiplication with Linalg dialect.
   %0 = linalg.matmul
        ins(%arg0, %arg1 : tensor<40x4096xf32>, tensor<4096
             x4096xf32>)
        outs(%cst : tensor<40x4096xf32>) -> tensor<40x4096xf32>
   // Expand the shape of the result with Tensor dialect.
   %expanded = tensor.expand_shape %0 [[0, 1], [2]]
        output_shape [1, 40, 4096]
        : tensor<40x4096xf32> into tensor<1x40x4096xf32>
   // Define an empty tensor with Tensor dialect.
   %1 = tensor.empty() : tensor<1x40x4096xf32>
   // Define a constant value with Arithmetic dialect.
   %c2_i32 = arith.constant 2 : i32
   // Perform generic loops with Linalg dialect.
   %2 = linalg.generic
        {indexing_maps = [#map, #map],
         iterator_types = ["parallel", "parallel", "parallel"]}
        ins(%expanded : tensor<1x40x4096xf32>)
        outs(%1 : tensor<1x40x4096xf32>) {
   ^bb0(%in: f32, %out: f32):
      // Perform a power operation with Math dialect.
      %3 = math.fpowi %in, %c2_i32 : f32, i32
      linalg.yield %3 : f32
   } -> tensor<1x40x4096xf32>
   return %2 : tensor<1x40x4096xf32>
}
```

(1) The mixing nature of the input dialects in MLIR makes it difficult for a single fixed pass pipeline to support all MLIR programs. Listing 1.1 presents a kernel that uses mixed MLIR dialects, which is extracted from an AI model compilation process. In this example, the Linalg, Tensor, Arithmetic, and Math dialects each handle specific computations and form a mixed-dialect kernel. Different scenarios may involve different combinations of dialects. For instance, vector computations are represented via MemRef and Vector operations, combined with passes designed for vector-level transformations. This complexity of mixed dialect usage makes it difficult to derive a feasible compilation path through fixed rules.

(2) MLIR's extensibility leads to the emergence of extensive domain-specific knowledge. Arranging pass pipelines for various MLIR extensions requires learning the corresponding domain knowledge from Table-

Table 1. Number of Files and Lines of Code Required for Manually Arranging the Pass Pipeline

Statistical Items	Core MLIR	Torch-MLIR	StableHLO	CIRCT
Number of TableGen files	227	17	34	213
Lines of code in TableGen files	137,784	44,788	35,834	74,290
Number of test files	492	91	86	569
Lines of code in test files	245,438	52,660	144,266	196,486

Gen definitions and test files. Table 1 summarizes the number of files and lines of code in several extension projects discussed in this paper. It shows that understanding the domain knowledge and design concepts requires navigating a large number of files and code. Figure 2 illustrates the differences in domain knowledge between Core MLIR and the hardware-oriented extension CIRCT. A clear knowledge gap exists between the software compilation path on the left and the hardware compilation path on the right. Moreover, the arrangement process requires selecting and ordering the sequence of transformations from hundreds of candidates. As a result, the domain knowledge required to arrange pass pipelines for various MLIR extensions is diverse and substantial, making it challenging to handle.

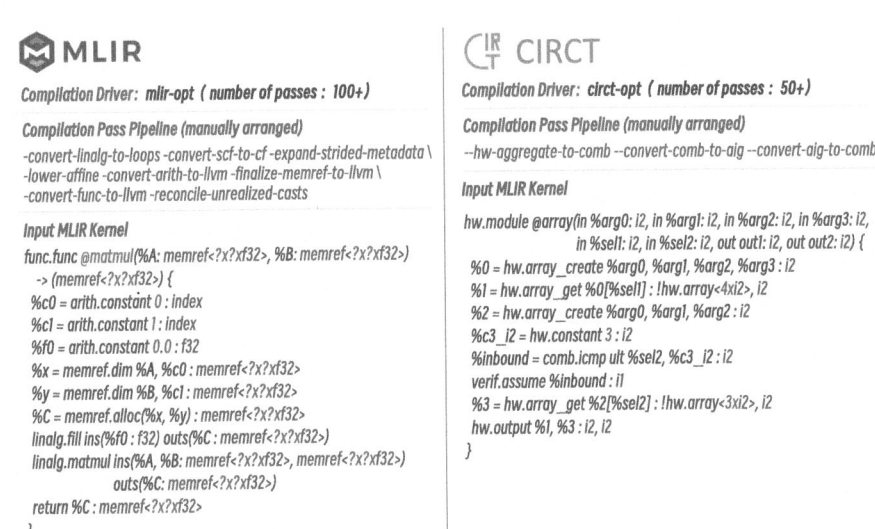

Fig. 2. Differences in Pass Pipeline and Domain Knowledge Between MLIR Extensions

3   COMPASS Overview

This section presents the core idea behind COMPASS and provides an overview of the agent's design methodology.

3.1   Core Idea

By identifying invariants and variables within MLIR's extensible ecosystem, we decompose the pass pipeline arrangement problem into two key components: **a unified compilation methodology** and **an extensible knowledge base**.

Unified Compilation Methodology: Tree-based Backtracking Algorithm. As an invariant of the problem, the unified compilation lowering method maintains consistency across all MLIR extensions. We use a tree-based backtracking algorithm to model the compilation process. In this structure, each node in the tree represents an intermediate compilation state and stores information about the current lowering phase. Each edge corresponds to a pass, transforming the MLIR kernel to the next state. If a pass results in an error or does not change the current state, the system backtracks and attempts an alternative pass for transformation. In the end, the system produces all feasible pass pipelines. This approach shifts pass pipeline arrangement from manual tasks to automated and reusable modeling processes.

Extensible Knowledge Base: Dynamic Knowledge Modeling. As a variable component of the problem, domain-specific knowledge reflects compilation requirements across different levels of abstraction. To effectively manage this knowledge, we designed a dynamic knowledge base as a modeling tool. This knowledge base aligns with the design characteristics of the target compiler. Specifically, the knowledge base covers dialect and operation information in each compiler pass while including hierarchical relationships between abstraction levels of different dialects. We leverage the capabilities of LLMs to automatically extract dialect, operation, and pass definitions from compiler source files and transform them into structured knowledge base formats, providing reliable knowledge support for the pass pipeline generator module.

3.2   COMPASS Agent

Based on the core ideas above, we designed the COMPASS agent to achieve automated pass pipeline arrangement for MLIR-based compilers. As shown in Fig. 1, this agent can be applied to multiple MLIR-based compilers. The COMPASS agent operates through two primary phases: learning and reasoning.

In the learning phase, the COMPASS agent takes the target compiler's source files as input, including the compiler's dialect and pass definition files and related test files. The COMPASS agent leverages LLM to analyze these files, extract the compiler's fundamental knowledge, and construct a formatted knowledge base.

The knowledge base provides the essential rules and structural information of the target compiler, forming the foundation for the agent to make effective decisions in the reasoning phase.

After the learning phase, the COMPASS agent connects its knowledge base with the pass-selection tree to prepare for the reasoning phase. The pass-selection tree serves as a model of the agent's state and action space, enabling dynamic state updates upon each pass selection. Each node in the tree represents a possible compilation state, while each branch represents the state change after selecting a specific pass. This approach enables the COMPASS agent to explore different pass arrangement strategies.

In the reasoning phase, the COMPASS agent receives MLIR input files and parses them into the root node of the pass-selection tree. Subsequently, COMPASS traverses and searches the tree guided by the knowledge base of the target compiler. The search process aims to find feasible pass pipelines. With the backtracking algorithm, COMPASS ensures that all input files can be compiled to the desired target abstraction level, such as LLVM dialect. COMPASS can generate various pass pipeline arrangement strategies, allowing users to select the most appropriate one based on their needs.

4   COMPASS Implementation

This section provides a detailed introduction to the three core components of the COMPASS agent: knowledge base architecture, knowledge importer implementation, and pass pipeline generator mechanism.

4.1   COMPASS Knowledge Base

In the design of COMPASS, the knowledge base stores and manages dialect and pass definitions from the target compiler, constructing a structured knowledge system. We define a knowledge base K, which consists of multiple dialects. Each dialect corresponds to one or more abstract levels and contains a set of associated passes. Specifically, the knowledge base K can be represented as:

$$K = \{(d_i, A_i, P_i) \mid d_i \in D, A_i \subseteq A(d_i), P_i \subseteq P(d_i)\}$$

Here, D is the set of dialects, and d_i is the target dialect. A is the set of abstract levels, and A_i represents the abstract levels corresponding to the dialect d_i. P is the set of passes. Each dialect d_i is associated with a set of passes P_i, which is a subset of $P(d_i)$.

Each pass p consists of three components: a name n, a type t, and a description $desc$, i.e.,

$$p = (n, t, desc)$$

Thus, the knowledge base K organizes the structure of each dialect, its associated abstract level, and its corresponding set of passes. The description of each pass can further be leveraged to infer its preconditions and subsequent transformations.

4.2   COMPASS Knowledge Importer

Based on the above knowledge base structure, the COMPASS knowledge importer needs to dynamically extract information from the compiler source files for each target compiler and update the knowledge base. The process of knowledge extraction requires three parts: code snippet extraction, knowledge template, and natural language instruction.

Code snippet extraction refers to the process of extracting actual code implementation from the target compiler's source files, including dialect definitions, pass registrations, operation implementations, unit tests, integration tests, and other related components. The COMPASS knowledge importer identifies these code snippets, which provide original implementation details for the knowledge base. These extracted snippets are integrated with the importer's formatting templates and natural language instructions to form the final knowledge base. For example, Listing 4.2 shows the definition of the **ConvertLinalgToLoopsPass** class. When the COMPASS knowledge importer locates a pass definition, it extracts the pass name **convert-linalg-to-loops** and the dialects required during compilation, such as Linalg, SCF, and Affine. Additionally, the **summary** and **description** sections often contain natural language cues that allow the inference of the pass's compilation stage, prerequisites, and successor phases. The LLM can process and interpret these textual descriptions to extract relevant information. All the information is then inserted into structured fields, forming part of the final knowledge base.

Listing 4.2. An Example of Code Snippet Extraction (the TableGen source code of *convert-linalg-to-loops* pass from Linalg dialect)

```
def ConvertLinalgToLoopsPass : Pass<"convert-linalg-to-loops">
{
  let summary = "Lower the operations from the linalg dialect
    into loops";
  let description = [{Lowers the 'linalg' ops to loop nests
    using 'scf.for'.Pre-condition: the operands used by the
    'linalg' ops have buffer semantics,i.e., tensor operands
    and results must be converted to memrefs via
    bufferization.}];
  let dependentDialects = [
    "linalg::LinalgDialect",
    "scf::SCFDialect",
    "affine::AffineDialect"
  ];
}
```

Listing 4.3. An Example of Knowledge Template (the information extracted by COM-PASS knowledge importer from *convert-linalg-to-loops* pass)

```
name: convert-linalg-to-loops
type: MODULE
dialect: linalg
required-dialects: {linalg, scf, affine}
compilation-phase: loop-structuring
predecessor-phase: bufferization
```

Knowledge templates provide a standardized and structured format for the knowledge base. The knowledge importer follows natural language instructions to extract necessary information from the target compiler's source code and then organizes this information according to the templates to form the knowledge base. The example in Listing 4.3 demonstrates how knowledge is summarized from code snippets and presented in the knowledge base. In this template, each pass is described in detail, listing the involved operation types and the corresponding transformation methods. The COMPASS knowledge importer utilizes LLM to learn and understand code snippets, and it will dynamically generate knowledge base entries based on these templates.

Listing 4.4. Built-In LLM Prompts for COMPASS Knowledge Importer

```
// Define the role of the LLM.
"You are a pass extraction expert..."
// Scope the range of input information.
"Only extract pass-related information, and exclude others
↪  ..."
// Extract pass-related information.
"Analyze the content and extract the pass name, type, and
↪ associated dialect information..."
// Infer the compilation phase of the pass.
"Determine at which compilation phase this pass is applied
↪  ..."
// Infer the compilation phase dependencies of the pass.
"Determine which compilation phase must be completed before
↪  this pass can be applied..."
```

Natural language instructions perform as a chain of thought in COMPASS that specifies the dialect and pass definition files, as well as guides the tasks for the knowledge importer. These instructions provide contextual information for the knowledge base construction task, helping the knowledge importer understand the compiler's design philosophy and operational steps. Listing 4.4 shows the natural language instructions for pass information collecting. The chain of thought defines the role of the LLM, which then extracts pass-related information from the specified source code scope and infers the compilation stage of each pass, along with its prerequisites and subsequent operations. Through these natural language instructions, the LLM within COMPASS can extract useful information from the code snippets and construct the knowledge base according to the formatting templates.

4.3   COMPASS Pass Pipeline Generator

COMPASS models the MLIR pass pipeline arrangement process as a backtracking search over a pass-selection tree. Let $OP = \{op_1, op_2, \ldots, op_N\}$ be the set of operations, and let $D = \{d_1, d_2, \ldots, d_N\}$ be the set of MLIR dialects. A transformation state at depth k as:

$$s_k = (D_k, P_k)$$

Here, $P_k = \langle p_0, p_1, \ldots, p_k \rangle$ is the ordered sequence of passes.

(1) Initial State Definition. The pass-selection tree backtracking algorithm begins with the initial state s_0, which indicates that all operations initially belong to multiple different dialects and no pass has been applied yet. Each operation op belongs to a corresponding initial dialect d_i, i.e., $op \in d_i$. The initial state can be represented as:

$$s_0 = (D_0, \emptyset)$$

Here, D_0 denotes the set of dialects that contain all operations op at the initial stage, representing the distribution of operations across different layers in the dialect hierarchy. Meanwhile, $\emptyset$ denotes that no pass has been selected yet, indicating that no compilation has occurred at this point.

(2) Recursive State Transitions. At each search step of the pass-selection tree, a pass p_k is selected, which will transfer some operations op from the current dialect to the target dialect and update the current state. The next state s_{k+1} after each iteration can be expressed as:

$$s_{k+1} = T(s_k, p_k) = (D_{k+1}, P_k \cup \{p_k\})$$

Here, $s_k = (D_k, P_k)$ represents the current state at the k-th step, which consists of the dialect set D_k for the operations and the sequence of passes P_k that have been selected up to this point. The selected pass p_k updates the dialect set for the operations. Some operations $op \in D_k$ are moved to a new dialect set D_{k+1}, and the sequence of executed passes is extended, forming the new state s_{k+1}.

(3) Backtracking Mechanism Application. In some cases, the selected pass p_k might fail to transfer the operation op from the current dialect to the target dialect. When this occurs, the backtracking mechanism is triggered, reverting to the previous state s_{k-1} and selecting an alternative pass p'_k. This backtracking process can be expressed by the following equation:

$$s_{k+1} = T(s_{k-1}, p'_k)$$

The backtracking mechanism ensures that even if a transformation step fails, alternative passes can be tried, until the correct path is found, ensuring that all operations op eventually lower to the target dialect.

(4) Termination Condition Check. The pass-selection tree search process will continue until all operations OP have been successfully lowered to the target dialect d_f. For example, compiling all dialects down to the LLVM dialect. This termination condition can be expressed as:

$$\forall op \in OP, \quad op \in d_f$$

Once all operations are lowered to the target dialect, the current pass pipeline is marked as feasible. The system then backtracks to explore other possible paths until all valid compilation passes have been fully explored.

5   Evaluation

This section evaluates COMPASS's capability to generate pass pipelines, estimates the human effort and maintenance costs that can be saved by the COMPASS agent, and discusses the experimental results.

5.1   Evaluation of the Pass Pipelines Generation Capability

In this experiment, COMPASS learns from multiple MLIR-based compilers and performs reasoning on different MLIR input files to evaluate its ability to generate pass pipelines. The experimental subjects include Core MLIR [21] (the upstream version of MLIR), Torch-MLIR [6], StableHLO [8], and CIRCT [5]. Except for Core MLIR, all other test subjects are domain-specific compilers built on top of MLIR and tailored for different application areas.

The experiment consists of learning and reasoning phases. During the learning phase, COMPASS extracts code snippets from the source code of the selected test subjects. Using the COMPASS knowledge importer, we construct a knowledge base for each test subject and summarize the learned dialects and passes in Table 2. In the reasoning phase, we use test files from target compilers as input. The COMPASS generator leverages the learned knowledge base to produce corresponding pass pipelines for each input file. These pipelines are then validated using the target compiler's tools to determine whether they correctly compile MLIR input files to the target abstraction level.

The experimental results presented in Table 2 demonstrates that COMPASS can generate pass pipelines and achieve a success rate of over 90%. The reasons behind the failed compilation cases can be summarized as follows: **(1) Unregistered dialects with no available transformation paths.** These dialects are used for compatibility testing in compilers and are not intended to be compilable. **(2) Syntax errors caused by duplicate function definitions.** MLIR test files often reuse the same function names for unit testing purposes, but these definitions are treated as syntax errors during end-to-end compilation. **(3) Missing transformations for some operations.** Some operations (e.g., `tosa.scatter`) only provide IR without corresponding lowering implementations, leading to search timeouts.

Table 2. Experimental Data of COMPASS Learning and Reasoning Phases

Experimental Items	Core MLIR	Torch-MLIR	StableHLO	CIRCT
Learned Dialects	18	3	3	29
Learned Passes	35	41	22	40
Test Cases	178	608	398	72
Success Pipelines	167	608	361	66
Failed Cases	11	0	37	6
Success Rate	93.8%	100%	90.7%	91.6%

Listing 4.5. The Pass Pipelines Generated by COMPASS for the Kernel in Listing 1.1

```
// Lowering from Linalg dialect to SCF dialect.
one-shot-bufferize{bufferize-function-boundaries},
↪ convert-linalg-to-loops, convert-scf-to-cf, convert-cf-to-llvm
↪ , convert-math-to-llvm, expand-strided-metadata, lower-
↪ affine, finalize-memref-to-llvm, convert-func-to-llvm,
↪ reconcile-unrealized-casts

// Lowering from Linalg dialect to Affine dialect.
one-shot-bufferize{bufferize-function-boundaries},
↪ convert-linalg-to-affine-loops, lower-affine, convert-math-to-
↪ llvm, arith-expand, convert-arith-to-llvm, convert-scf-to-
↪ cf, convert-cf-to-llvm, convert-func-to-llvm, expand-
↪ strided-metadata, finalize-memref-to-llvm, reconcile-
↪ unrealized-casts

// Lowering from Linalg dialect to Affine dialect and
// applying OpenMP parallel optimization.
one-shot-bufferize{bufferize-function-boundaries},
↪ convert-linalg-to-affine-loops, affine-parallelize, lower-affine,
↪ convert-scf-to-openmp, convert-openmp-to-llvm, convert-math-to-
↪ llvm, arith-expand, convert-arith-to-llvm, convert-scf-to-
↪ cf, convert-cf-to-llvm, convert-func-to-llvm, expand-
↪ strided-metadata, finalize-memref-to-llvm, reconcile-
↪ unrealized-casts
```

To demonstrate the capability of COMPASS, Listing 4.5 presents the pass pipeline generation results for the kernel in Listing 1.1. According to the results, COMPASS identified three feasible compilation paths for the given kernel. The first pipeline converts the Linalg dialect into the SCF dialect. The second pipeline converts the Linalg dialect into the Affine dialect. The third pipeline applies parallelization on top of the Affine dialect transformation. This example illustrates that COMPASS can generate multiple feasible compilation paths for a single input file, allowing users to choose the most suitable option or customize it as needed.

5.2   Evaluation of Human Effort and Maintenance Cost Savings

This experiment aims to evaluate the human effort and maintenance costs that the COMPASS agent can save. MLIR-based compilers and IR designs continue to evolve alongside domain requirements, and the dialects and passes of Core MLIR are also continuously developed. Interdependencies among MLIR-based projects often necessitate frequent adjustments to pass pipelines to ensure consistent compilation paths. Without COMPASS, these tasks impose considerable manual effort across development, maintenance, and knowledge transfer.

To quantify this human effort, we collected statistics on the modification frequency of test cases for each target compiler. According to the conventions of the MLIR ecosystem, whenever a dialect or pass is modified, the corresponding test cases must be updated to ensure coverage of the latest changes. Therefore, the frequency of test case modifications can be used to estimate the number of dialect and pass changes. This also allows us to evaluate the human effort required to maintain compilation pass pipelines.

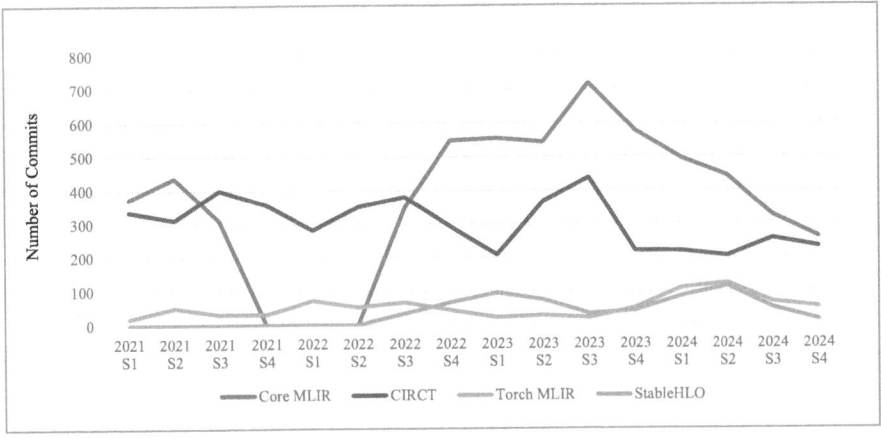

Fig. 3. Commits Modifying Dialect and Pass Test Cases Over the Past Four Years.

Figure 3 presents statistical data showing that the dialects and passes of MLIR-based compilers have been continuously evolving over the past three years. The update frequency ranges from 50 to 370 times per quarter, depending on the specific compiler. Maintaining a single MLIR extension project requires one to three synchronization updates per week. For projects that depend on core MLIR dialects, maintainers need to track upstream code changes and ensure consistency across the toolchain. COMPASS reduces this manual effort and maintenance burden by automatically generating pass pipelines. This enables developers and maintainers to keep compilation paths up to date without reviewing extensive commit histories.

5.3   Discussion

Based on the above experimental results and analysis, this section discusses COMPASS's advantages and potential directions for future work.

Advantages: COMPASS Reduces Pass Pipeline Arrangement and Maintenance Costs. Users can engage with MLIR-based compiler projects without deep expertise and arrange pass pipelines automatically. Moreover, COMPASS minimizes maintenance efforts by eliminating the need for maintainers to manually track dependencies between MLIR extensions.

Advantages: COMPASS Explores Diverse Compilation Paths. Unlike expert-driven manual arrangements that offer limited path options, COMPASS identifies multiple pass pipelines from source to target abstraction levels, thereby expanding the tuning search space for compiler designers.

Future Work: In the Learning Phase, Future Work Can Utilize Compiler Test Files to the Knowledge Base. Since this section uses test files as input for evaluation, we excluded them from the learning phase to avoid overlap between the training and test sets. However, this constraint led to the omission of some valuable knowledge. Incorporating test files could help infer potential relationships among passes, dialects, and operations, which can assist the tree-based search process through effective pruning.

Future Work: In the Reasoning Phase, Future Work can Incorporate a Cost Model to Select the Most Suitable Pass Pipeline for the Target Software and Hardware Environment. The contribution of this paper lies in the ability to arrange all possible pass pipelines. Building on this capability, future work can introduce a cost model to evaluate the generated code, thereby identifying the optimal pass pipeline that best satisfies specific requirements among all candidates.

6   Related Work

This section introduces the related work of this paper, focusing on two main aspects: LLM for compiler techniques and studies on compiler phase ordering problem.

6.1   LLM for Compiler Techniques

In recent years, LLMs have gained increasing attention in the field of compilers. Current research primarily focuses on compiler optimization, compiler verification, and compiler testing. In the field of compiler optimization, researchers have developed various LLM-based methods to improve code generation quality [10–12,14,15,17,29], including enhancing code execution speed and reducing target code size. In compiler verification, researchers utilize LLM technology to assist in compiler verification, ensuring the correctness and reliability of compiled programs [2,24]. In compiler testing, researchers use LLMs to generate test programs to detect potential deep logical errors in the compilation process [30].

Like the related work mentioned above, this paper also utilizes LLM to assist in compiler design and implementation. However, our work focuses on the pass pipeline arrangement and maintenance of MLIR-based compilers. Rather than optimizing or verifying generated code, we employ LLMs to facilitate understanding of the compiler architecture and its IRs. This enables us to construct a knowledge base for the target compiler, which can guide the pass pipeline generation process.

6.2   Compiler Phase Ordering Problem

The compiler phase ordering problem is a classic research topic that has received widespread attention for many years. We categorize the compiler phase ordering problem into iteration-based search methods [19,25,26] and learning-based methods [1,16,18,20,22]. Iteration-based search methods use multiple algorithms to gradually explore the space of compiler optimization phase combinations, seeking optimal or near-optimal solutions. Learning-based methods utilize various machine learning techniques, particularly reinforcement learning and supervised learning, to model the problem as a machine learning task, thereby automatically learning and determining the optimal ordering of compiler optimization phases. These two methods are not completely independent: search-based methods can incorporate machine learning techniques, while learning-based methods also include search processes.

The MLIR pass pipeline generation problem addressed in this paper is distinguished by its openness and extensibility, setting it apart from other related works. This task not only requires modeling the compilation lowering process but also demands coverage of extensible domain-specific knowledge and expertise. To address these challenges, we propose a combined approach that integrates machine learning and iterative search to build the COMPASS agent. Specifically, an LLM is used to construct the knowledge base during the learning phase, while tree-based iterative search methods are employed in the reasoning phase to generate the pass pipeline.

7   Conclusions

This paper introduces COMPASS, an agent for MLIR compilation pass pipeline generation. We propose a framework that combines LLM-derived knowledge with a tree-based backtracking algorithm. Based on this framework, we construct an automated agent capable of learning from compiler source code and reasoning about feasible compilation paths. Experiments across multiple MLIR-based compilers demonstrate that COMPASS can generate pass pipelines with high success rates, significantly reducing the development and maintenance burden associated with evolving MLIR ecosystems. In addition to practical effectiveness, our analysis reveals that COMPASS can aid in exploring the compiler design space and uncovering hidden pass dependencies. We believe that COMPASS offers a solid foundation for future research on compiler automation, particularly in scenarios requiring adaptability and extensibility.

References

1. Ashouri, A.H., Bignoli, A., Palermo, G., Silvano, C., Kulkarni, S., Cavazos, J.: Micomp: mitigating the compiler phase-ordering problem using optimization subsequences and machine learning. ACM Trans. Arch. Code Optim. (TACO) **14**(3), 1–28 (2017)
2. Chakraborty, S., et al.: Ranking llm-generated loop invariants for program verification. arXiv preprint arXiv:2310.09342 (2023)
3. Community, B.C.: Buddy compiler: an mlir-based compiler framework bridges dsls to dsas (2024). https://github.com/buddy-compiler/buddy-mlir. Accessed Dec 2024
4. Community, L.: Tablegen (2024). https://llvm.org/docs/TableGen/index.html. Accessed Dec 2024
5. Community, L.C.: Circt: Circuit ir compilers and tools (2024). https://github.com/llvm/circt. Accessed Dec 2024
6. Community, L.T.M.: The torch-mlir project (2024). https://github.com/llvm/torch-mlir. Accessed Dec 2024
7. Community, M.: Transform dialect (2024). https://mlir.llvm.org/docs/Dialects/Transform/. Accessed Dec 2024
8. Community, O.S.: Stablehlo (2024). https://github.com/openxla/stablehlo. Accessed Dec 2024
9. Community, T.L.: Triton (2024). https://github.com/triton-lang/triton. Accessed Dec 2024
10. Cummins, C., et al.: Large language models for compiler optimization. arXiv preprint arXiv:2309.07062 (2023)
11. Cummins, C., et al.: Meta large language model compiler: foundation models of compiler optimization. arXiv preprint arXiv:2407.02524 (2024)
12. Duan, S., Kanakaris, N., Xiao, X., Ping, H., Zhou, C., Ahmed, N.K., Ma, G., Capota, M., Willke, T.L., Nazarian, S., et al.: Leveraging reinforcement learning and large language models for code optimization. arXiv preprint arXiv:2312.05657 (2023)
13. Fehr, M., Niu, J., Riddle, R., Amini, M., Su, Z., Grosser, T.: Irdl: an ir definition language for ssa compilers. In: Proceedings of the 43rd ACM SIGPLAN International Conference on Programming Language Design and Implementation (2022). https://doi.org/10.1145/3519939.3523700
14. Grubisic, D., Cummins, C., Seeker, V., Leather, H.: Compiler generated feedback for large language models. arXiv preprint arXiv:2403.14714 (2024)
15. Grubisic, D., Seeker, V., Synnaeve, G., Leather, H., Mellor-Crummey, J., Cummins, C.: Priority sampling of large language models for compilers. In: Proceedings of the 4th Workshop on Machine Learning and Systems, pp. 91–97 (2024)

16. Huang, Q., et al.: Autophase: compiler phase-ordering for hls with deep reinforcement learning. In: 2019 IEEE 27th Annual International Symposium on Field-Programmable Custom Computing Machines (FCCM), pp. 308–308. IEEE (2019)

17. Hong, C., et al.: Llm-aided compilation for tensor accelerators. In: 2024 IEEE LLM Aided Design Workshop (LAD), pp. 1–14. IEEE (2024)

18. Jain, S., Andaluri, Y., VenkataKeerthy, S., Upadrasta, R.: Poset-rl: phase ordering for optimizing size and execution time using reinforcement learning. In: 2022 IEEE International Symposium on Performance Analysis of Systems and Software (ISPASS), pp. 121–131. IEEE (2022)

19. Jantz, M.R., Kulkarni, P.A.: Exploiting phase inter-dependencies for faster iterative compiler optimization phase order searches. In: 2013 International Conference on Compilers, Architecture and Synthesis for Embedded Systems (CASES), pp. 1–10. IEEE (2013)

20. Kulkarni, S., Cavazos, J.: Mitigating the compiler optimization phase-ordering problem using machine learning. In: Proceedings of the ACM International Conference on Object Oriented Programming Systems Languages and Applications, pp. 147–162 (2012)

21. Lattner, C., et al.: Mlir: scaling compiler infrastructure for domain specific computation. In: 2021 IEEE/ACM International Symposium on Code Generation and Optimization (CGO), pp. 2–14 (2021 https://doi.org/10.1109/CGO51591.2021.9370308

22. Liang, Y., et al.: Learning compiler pass orders using coreset and normalized value prediction. In: International Conference on Machine Learning, pp. 20746–20762. PMLR (2023)

23. Modular: Mojo : Programming language for all of ai (2024). https://github.com/modularml/mojo. Accessed Dec 2024

24. Munley, C., Jarmusch, A., Chandrasekaran, S.: Llm4vv: developing llm-driven test-suite for compiler validation. Future Gener. Comput. Syst. (2024)

25. Nobre, R., Bispo, J., Carvalho, T., Cardoso, J.M.: Nonio–modular automatic compiler phase selection and ordering specialization framework for modern compilers. SoftwareX **10**, 100238 (2019)

26. Nobre, R., Martins, L.G., Cardoso, J.M.: A graph-based iterative compiler pass selection and phase ordering approach. ACM SIGPLAN Not. **51**(5), 21–30 (2016)

27. OpenAI: Hello gpt-4o (2024). https://openai.com/index/hello-gpt-4o/. Accessed Dec 2024

28. Organization, I.: Iree: Intermediate representation execution environment (2024). https://github.com/iree-org/iree. Accessed Dec 2024

29. Taneja, J., Laird, A., Yan, C., Musuvathi, M., Lahiri, S.K.: Llm-vectorizer: Llm-based verified loop vectorizer. In: Proceedings of the 23rd ACM/IEEE International Symposium on Code Generation and Optimization, pp. 137–149 (2025)

30. Yang, C., et al.: Whitefox: white-box compiler fuzzing empowered by large language models. Proc. ACM Program. Lang. **8**(OOPSLA2), 709–735 (2024)

31. Zhang, H., Xing, M., Wu, Y., Zhao, C.: Compiler technologies in deep learning co-design: a survey. Intell. Comput. (2023)

A Coherent Index for Dichotomy in Version-Controlled Repositories

Laurent Bulteau[1,2], Pierre-Yves David[3], Florian Horn[1,4],
and Euxane Tran-Girard[2,3(✉)]

[1] Centre National de la Recherche Scientifique, Paris, France
[2] Université Gustave Eiffel, LIGM, 77454 Marne-la-Vallée, France
euxane.trangirard@univ-eiffel.fr
[3] Octobus, Paris, France
[4] Université Paris Cité, IRIF, 75013 Paris, France

Abstract. Version Control Systems such as Git and Mercurial model their repositories as collections of Merkle directed acyclic graphs. New versions of the code base are added as sources in local graphs and then shared with other agents in the lifetime of the project. In the largest graphs, which can grow to several millions of revisions, sub-linear algorithms become necessary for recurring tasks. A common solution is to use a precomputed index that can grow dynamically along with the graphs. In this paper, we propose a versatile and compact index (a few bytes per node in practice) for dichotomy operations on Merkle DAGs. Furthermore, our index is *coherent*, in the sense that all agents participating in a repository have the same information for each node they know about.

In order to define our index, we introduce the notion of *range*, a small-sized representation of a set of nodes which can easily be partitioned into smaller ranges. We show how it can be used for the problems of *reachability* and *label discovery*, and compare its performance with existing indices for reachability.

An implementation of our algorithms is available at https://doi.org/10.5281/zenodo.10715742.

Keywords: Merkle Graph · Reachability · Version-control systems

1 Introduction

Version-control systems are designed to help multiple developers work in parallel on a common project, sharing their progress seamlessly. In modern systems such as Mercurial or Git, this is achieved by using local *revision graphs* on a shared *repository*: each time a developer wants to save their progress, they add a new *revision*—a snapshot of their current version of the project—to their own local revision graph. These revisions are then shared among developers, often but not always through a server centralizing all data.

The data-structure for local revision graphs is a *Merkle DAG*, which is updated from the sources: new revisions are sources with outgoing arcs to the

P. Rümmer and Z. Wu (Eds.): TASE 2025, LNCS 15841, pp. 233–249, 2026.
https://doi.org/10.1007/978-3-031-98208-8_14

revision(s) from which they were derived. A global repository is a set of consistent revision graphs: if two revision graphs in the same repository share a common node u, they also share the nodes upon which u is based and, recursively, all nodes reachable from u.

Larger projects can involve hundreds of developers over many years with many sub-projects being developed in parallel. Such repositories can grow to millions of nodes, quickly leading to performance issues for complex operations even when the underlying algorithms are linear in time. In this paper, we propose a dichotomy framework which allows us to *split* sets of nodes to recursively explore subsets without having to enumerate the whole graph. We explore two concrete applications of this principle: the *reachability* test, which asks whether there is a dependency path between two revisions; and *label discovery*, which asks on which nodes two agents have added different *labels*, which are pieces of data associated to nodes after their creation.

It is possible to get sub-linear complexity for reachability testing on a specific graph by using a precomputed index, such as 2-hop. However, this is not enough for our purposes as such an index could be obsolete as soon as a new node is inserted. Furthermore, there is no guarantee in general that two agents reaching the same revision graph from different histories would get to the same index. Formally, we consider that an index is a function that gives a value for each revision in a graph, and we say that an index is *coherent* if the stored value for a specific node is constant over time and over all graphs in a given repository.

We also consider the label discovery problem as a test case for our dichotomy framework. The idea is to compute, exchange, and cache hash values for the labels of carefully chosen sets of nodes, so that only the modified sets need to be exchanged between two successive synchronisations. For this application the dichotomy algorithm must be able to pinpoint an edited label using as few cuts as possible, and conversely all cached sets containing any given node must be accessible easily in order to keep the cache up to date after label edits.

Previous Works. Representing the causal history of revisions using a DAG structure has been suggested and formalised by Plaice and Wadge [15] and implemented in current distributed version control systems (DVCS) such as Mercurial [14] and Git [10] as Merkle graphs. Several problems specific to DVCS have been studied in the literature. The problem of finding optimal search strategies using the graph structure for the purpose of regression testing has been implemented in Git and Mercurial and studied by Bendík et al. [2] and Courtiel et al. [8] using a dichotomy approach (unrelated to this paper). The problem of graph discovery, i.e. finding new nodes between two instances of a revision graph for the purpose of synchronisation, has been formulated and studied by Bulteau et al. [4].

The problem of label discovery, i.e. finding the differences between two labellings of a revision graph for the purpose of synchronisation, has not, to our knowledge, been extensively studied before. An experimental implementation of a restricted form of label discovery has been proposed in the *Evolve* extension of Mercurial [9] for synchronising obsolescence markers attached to nodes.

Label discovery can be seen as a graph generalization of the file synchronisation problem, cf. the rsync algorithm (Tridgell et al. [20]).

The problem of reachability (or path existence query) in unlabeled directed graphs (acyclic or not) has been extensively studied and iterated upon [11,23]. The main indexing approaches rely on chain cover (Jagadish [12], Chen and Chen [6], Bulteau et al. [5]), tree cover with interval labelling (Agrawal et al. [1], Yildirim et al. [22]), approximate transitive closure (Wei et al. [21], Su et al. [18]), and 2-hop (Cohen et al. [7], Zhu et al. [24], Lyu et al. [13]). These dynamic methods allow index updates under arbitrary node addition and deletion, without coherence restrictions. In practice, reachability tests for Merkle graphs have been implemented using chain cover in the Matrix communication protocol [19], and as pruned DFS in Mercurial [16] and Git [17], opportunistically using topological order, level and date information.

Our Results. We propose several algorithms leading to efficient solutions for reachability testing and label discovery through dichotomy. At the core of our approach lies the notion of *range*, i.e. a set of nodes that can be described concisely. Ranges are sets that can be defined as the first k nodes seen in a specific traversal of the reachable nodes from some node u, the *stable-tail sort* of u. We prove sublinear bounds on the depth of the dichotomy search tree, as well as other sublinear guarantees in specific cases (merge-free graphs). We evaluate the performances of our algorithms on a large dataset of revision graphs. In particular, for the reachability problem in a (single-agent) dynamic setting, we run comparisons against implementations of 2-Hop and BFL algorithms, where our algorithm is competitive on large graphs with the advantage of having a coherent index. Due to space constraints, proofs and detailed experimental results are deferred to the appendix.

2   Definitions, Notations, and General Properties

In this paper, we use the Python notation for lists to manipulate *ordered sets*: elements are written within brackets separated by commas; the cardinal of L is $|L|$; its $i+1$th element is $L[i]$; the concatenation of two disjoint lists K and L is $K + L$. We also use usual set notations: $x \in L$ means that x is an element of L and $L \setminus K$ is the ordered set obtained from L by removing each element of K.

Definition 1 (*Revision graph, repository, identifiers*). *A revision graph is a labeled directed acyclic graph $G = (V, E)$ with out-degree at most 2. Nodes of V are sometimes called* revisions. *If there is an arc $u \to v$ in E, we say that u is a parent of v and v is a child of u. If there is a path $u \to^* v$, possibly with $u = v$, we say that v is a descendant of u. We denote the set of descendant of a node u by $\overrightarrow{\mathcal{D}}(u)$. A node without parents is a source and a node without children is a sink. A node with two children is a merge.*

A repository (cf Fig. 1) is a collection of revision graphs where common nodes have the same children: if G and H are two revision graphs in the same repository that share a common node u and $u \to v \in E_G$, then $u \to v \in E_H$.

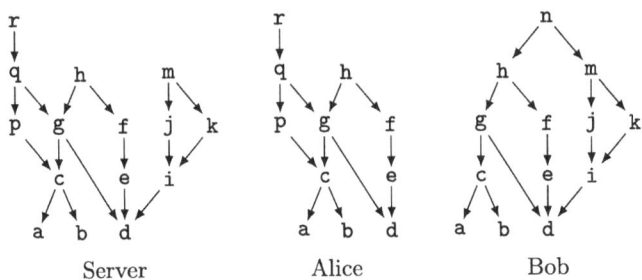

Fig. 1. A repository with three revision graphs corresponding to a scenario with a server centralizing data from Alice and Bob: nodes a to h are known by all three agents, p to r are known by the server and Alice, i to m are known by the server and Bob, and merge node n is known by Bob alone (it has not been sent to the server yet).

Revision graphs have two identifier functions: the hash identifier *of a node u, denoted #(u) depends on the contents of u and on the hash identifiers of its child(ren); the* local identifier *of u, denoted num(u) is an anti-topological bijection $V \to [1, \ldots, |V|]$ (i.e. num(u) > num(v) for each arc u → v). Note that a node has the same hash identifier in all revision graphs in a given repository, while this is not the case for the local identifier.*

Remark 1. A source of confusion in the study of Version Control Systems is that the graph terminology is opposite to the development terminology: graph-wise, a new revision is the parent of the revision it is based on, whereas in VCS-parlance, that revision would be considered its child. In this paper, we decided to use the graph terminology: the newest revisions are the ancestors of the oldest ones, rather than the other way around.

We introduce some technical concepts for nodes that give the necessary foundations for our dichotomy algorithms. These concepts are presented in Fig. 2.

Definition 2 (*Rank, tail child, exclusive child*). *The* rank *of a node u, denoted rank(u), is the number of its descendants: $\text{rank}(u) = |\overrightarrow{\mathcal{D}}(u)|$.*

If u is not a sink, the tail child *of u, denoted t(u) is its child with the larger rank. Its other child, if any, is the* exclusive child *of u and is denoted by x(u). If both children of u have the same rank, the tail child of u is the one with the lower hash identifier.*

The tail path *of u, denoted tail(u), is defined recursively as [u] if u is a sink and [u] + tail(t(u)) otherwise.*

Revision graphs grow by adding new sources to the graph, while existing nodes and arcs remain unchanged. In particular, the children (tail@tail child and exclusive@exclusive child) of a node, its hash identifier and rank are *coherent*: they stay constant after their creation, and are the same throughout all revision graphs in a given repository. These values are computed and stored when the

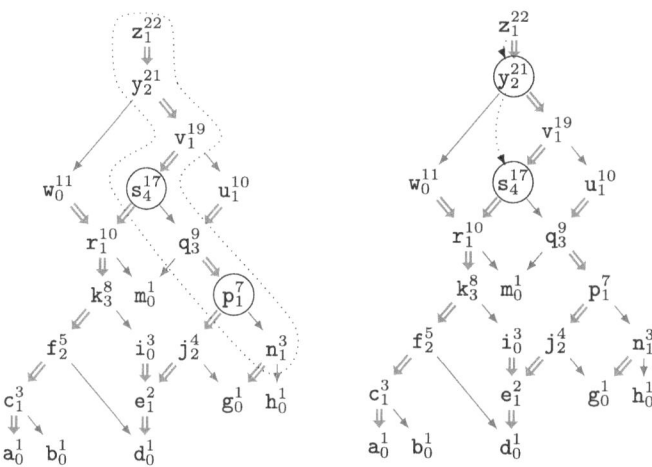

Fig. 2. Illustration for Definitions 2, 3 and 4. Super- and sub-scripts are respectively the rank and power of each node. Arcs to the tail child are doubled (red), others (blue) are to the exclusive child. Left: the switch list from z to n is $[s, p]$. Right: The anchor of z is y, the anchor of y is s, and s has no anchor. This yields the partition of $\overrightarrow{\mathcal{D}}(z)$ into canonical sets $\mathcal{C}(z) = \{z\}$, $\mathcal{C}(y) = \{y, w, v, u\}$ and $\mathcal{C}(s) = \overrightarrow{\mathcal{D}}(s)$. (Color figure online)

node is first created (*commit*) and do not need to be recomputed when the node is copied to another agent. Similarly, the notions introduced in the following definitions are also coherent since they are only built upon coherent data.

Definition 3 (*Power, anchor, canonical set*). *The* power *of a node u, denoted $\pi(u)$, is the highest bit that changes between the binary representations of $\mathrm{rank}(u)$ and $\mathrm{rank}(t(u))$. By convention, if u is a sink, $\pi(u) = 0$. Otherwise, $\pi(u)$ is the largest integer such that there exists an integer x with:*

$$\mathrm{rank}(u) \geq x \cdot 2^{\pi(u)} > \mathrm{rank}(t(u))$$

The anchor *of a node u, denoted $\mathrm{anc}(u)$, is the first node v of $\mathrm{tail}(u) \setminus \{u\}$ such that $\pi(v) \geq \pi(u)$; if no such node exists, we write $\mathrm{anc}(u) = \bot$.*

The canonical set *of a node u is the set $\mathcal{C}(u) = \overrightarrow{\mathcal{D}}(u) \setminus \overrightarrow{\mathcal{D}}(\mathrm{anc}(u))$ (using $\overrightarrow{\mathcal{D}}(\bot) = \emptyset$).*

The definition of power ensures that the canonical set is very small for most nodes, but grows exponentially as we follow chains of anchors (see Fig. 2):

Proposition 1. *If $\mathrm{anc}(u) \neq \bot$, then $\pi(\mathrm{anc}(u)) > \pi(u)$.*

Finally, we introduce the notion of switch list, which helps us bound the complexity of our enumeration algorithm and the depth of the dichotomy.

Definition 4 (*Switch list*). *Let u, v be a pair of nodes with $v \in \overrightarrow{\mathcal{D}}(u)$. The switch list* from u to v, *denoted $\sigma(u, v)$ is defined as follows:*

- *if $u = v$, $\sigma(u,v) = [\,]$;*
- *if $v \in \overrightarrow{\mathcal{D}}(\mathrm{t}(u))$, $\sigma(u,v) = \sigma(\mathrm{t}(u),v)$;*
- *otherwise, $\sigma(u,v) = [u] + \sigma(\mathrm{x}(u),v)$.*

The switch distance *from u to v, denoted $\mathrm{d}_S(u,v)$ is the length of $\sigma(u,v)$.*

The switch list can be seen as a short description of a specific path from u to v. That path follows the tail child whenever possible, and only chooses the exclusive child when v is not a descendant of the tail child of the current node. The switch list registers the nodes where the path needs to go to an exclusive child. The fact that the tail child has the larger rank allows us to bound the switch distance between any two nodes:

Lemma 1. *For any nodes u and v, $v \in \overrightarrow{\mathcal{D}}(u)$, the switch distance between u and v is at most $\sqrt{2\,\mathrm{rank}(u)}$.*

Proof. Let $\sigma(u,v) = [s_1, \ldots, s_k]$ be the switch list from u to v. As each s_i is a switch, it has both a tail child $\mathrm{t}(s_i)$ and an exclusive child $\mathrm{x}(s_i)$.

Furthermore, $u \notin \overrightarrow{\mathcal{D}}(\mathrm{t}(s_i))$, none of the $\{s_j\}_{j>i}$ is a descendant of $\mathrm{t}(i)$. It follows that s_i must have $(k+1-i)$ "new" descendants, which were not descendants of any lower switch.

We get $\mathrm{rank}(s_i) \geq \mathrm{rank}(s_{i+1}) + (k + 1 - i)$ and Lemma 1 follows.

The bound $d_S(u,v) \leq \sqrt{2\,\mathrm{rank}(u)}$ is tight: for any $k > 0$, one can build a graph with a pair of nodes u, v satisfying $d_S(u,v) = k$ and $\mathrm{rank}(u) = \binom{k+2}{2}$, as can be seen in Fig. 3.

3   Stable-Tail Sort and Ranges

3.1   STS Definition and Enumeration

In order to allow dichotomy algorithms on sets of nodes, we introduce linear orderings over nodes. We need these linear orderings to be coherent, i.e. that different agents have the same view on common nodes. In order to get good complexity properties, we also want them to be as *stable* as possible, i.e. node insertions in different revision graphs should not completely shuffle the permutation. We thus introduce the *stable-tail sort* below, defined as a coherent topological ordering of the reachable set of any node (in any repository, all revision graphs having the same node u have the same $\mathrm{STS}(u)$). See Fig. 4 for an illustration.

Definition 5 (STS: Stable-Tail Sort). *For a sink u we define $\mathrm{STS}(u) = [u]$. If u has only one child $\mathrm{t}(u)$, then $\mathrm{STS}(u) = [u] + \mathrm{STS}(\mathrm{t}(u))$. If u is a merge then we write $\mathrm{excl}(u) = \mathrm{STS}(\mathrm{x}(u)) \setminus \overrightarrow{\mathcal{D}}(\mathrm{t}(u))$ and $\mathrm{STS}(u) = [u] + \mathrm{excl}(u) + \mathrm{STS}(\mathrm{t}(u))$. The lists $\mathrm{excl}(u)$ and $\mathrm{STS}(\mathrm{t}(u))$ are respectively called the* exclusive *and* tail *parts of $\mathrm{STS}(u)$.*

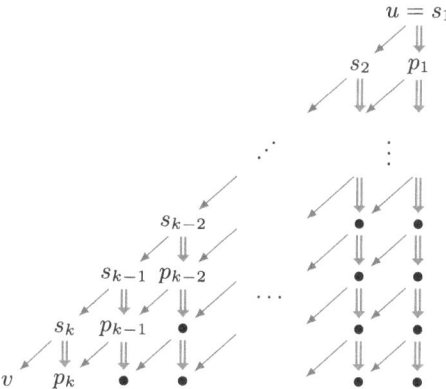

Fig. 3. Worst case for the number of switches between two revisions: the graph has $\binom{k+2}{2}$ vertices for a pair of nodes with switch distance k. We use notations u, v, s_i, p_i from the proof of Lemma 1; tail neighbour is directly below each node, and each exclusive neighbour is in diagonal to the left (the rank is equal for all pairs of neighbours, and we assume that the tie-breaking rule gives the desired property). Thus, the switch list is indeed $\sigma(u, v) = [s_1, \ldots, s_k]$ and $d_S(u, v) = k$. In other words, $d_S(u, v) = \Omega(\sqrt{\mathrm{rank}(u)})$ in this example.

Remark 2. A node's Stable-Tail Sort of its reachable set is *not* the projection of a graph-wide order on $\overrightarrow{\mathcal{D}}(u)$.

Intuitively the STS is a variation of the depth-first traversal of the reachable set, where instead of skipping nodes that have already been seen, one skips nodes that *will be seen again*. Indeed, switching the exclusive and tail parts in Definition 5 would define exactly the depth-first traversal. Our objective is, for any two nodes, to have a large common suffix. In particular for merges with a small exclusive part, a large suffix comes from $\mathrm{STS}(\mathrm{t}(u))$, which in turn has a large common suffix with its own tail child, etc.

Proposition 2. $\mathrm{STS}(u)$ *is a topological sort of* $\overrightarrow{\mathcal{D}}(u)$

Proof. By induction, this is clear for out-degree 0 and 1 nodes. For a degree-2 node u and any arc $x \to y$ with $x \in \overrightarrow{\mathcal{D}}(u)$, either $x = u$ (in which case x is the first node, so before y), either x and y are both in the exclusive or both in the tail parts (in which case x is before y by induction), either they are in different parts but then only y can be in the tail part (if $x \in \overrightarrow{\mathcal{D}}(\mathrm{t}(u))$, then $y \in \overrightarrow{\mathcal{D}}(\mathrm{t}(u))$), in which case x is before y by construction. □

Proposition 3. *For any u and $v \in \mathrm{tail}(u)$, $\mathrm{STS}(v)$ is a suffix of $\mathrm{STS}(u)$.*

Proof. By induction on u. This is trivial for $u = v$, and follows directly from the definition for $v = \mathrm{t}(u)$. For any other $v \in \mathrm{tail}(u)$, we have $v \in \mathrm{tail}(\mathrm{t}(u))$, so $\mathrm{STS}(v)$ is a suffix of $\mathrm{STS}(\mathrm{t}(u))$ and of $\mathrm{STS}(u)$. □

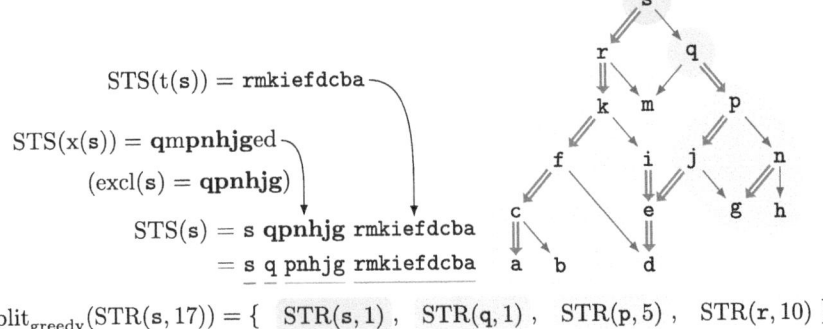

$$\mathrm{STS(t(s))} = \mathtt{rmkiefdcba}$$

$$\mathrm{STS(x(s))} = \mathtt{qmpnhjged}$$

$$(\mathrm{excl(s)} = \mathtt{qpnhjg})$$

$$\mathrm{STS(s)} = \mathtt{s\ qpnhjg\ rmkiefdcba}$$
$$= \mathtt{s\ q\ pnhjg\ rmkiefdcba}$$

$$\mathrm{split}_{\mathrm{greedy}}(\mathrm{STR(s,17)}) = \{\ \mathrm{STR(s,1)},\ \ \mathrm{STR(q,1)},\ \ \mathrm{STR(p,5)},\ \ \mathrm{STR(r,10)}\ \}$$

Fig. 4. Top: construction of STS(s) from its children: the whole STS(r) is used as a suffix, while the exclusive part (bold nodes) is listed according to STS(q). Bottom: when splitting the corresponding range, the exclusive part is greedily partitioned into $\mathrm{STR}(q,1) \cup \mathrm{STR}(p,5)$.

Proposition 4. *Let* $v \in \overrightarrow{\mathcal{D}}(u)$, $[w_1, \ldots, w_k]$ *be the list* $[\mathrm{x}(v), \mathrm{t}(v), \mathrm{t}(s_k), \ldots,$ $\mathrm{t}(s_1)]$ *(from which non-existing nodes are removed), and let* Z *be the suffix of* $\mathrm{STS}(u)$ *starting at* v. *Then* Z *can be written as a concatenation* $Z = [v] + Z_{w_1} + \ldots + Z_{w_k}$ *where each* Z_{w_i}, *if non empty, is a subsequence of* $\mathrm{STS}(w_i)$ *starting with* w_i. *Moreover, sets* Z_{w_i} *and* $\overrightarrow{\mathcal{D}}(w_j)$ *are disjoint for any* $i < j$.

Proof. By induction on v, starting with $v = u$. $\mathrm{STS}(u) = [u] + Z_{\mathrm{x}(u)} + Z_{\mathrm{t}(u)}$ where $Z_{\mathrm{x}(u)} = \mathrm{excl}(u)$ and $Z_{\mathrm{t}(u)} = \mathrm{STS}(\mathrm{t}(u))$. Also, $Z_{\mathrm{x}(u)}$ is disjoint from $\overrightarrow{\mathcal{D}}(\mathrm{t}(u))$.

For any $v \in \overrightarrow{\mathcal{D}}(\mathrm{t}(u))$, the suffix T of $\mathrm{STS}(u)$ starting at v is identical to the suffix of $\mathrm{STS}(\mathrm{t}(u))$ starting at v, and $\sigma(u, v) = \sigma(\mathrm{t}(u), v)$, so the same decomposition of Z holds for $\mathrm{t}(u)$ and u.

Otherwise, $v \in \overrightarrow{\mathcal{D}}(\mathrm{x}(u)) \setminus \overrightarrow{\mathcal{D}}(\mathrm{t}(u))$. Let Z' be the suffix of $\mathrm{STS}(\mathrm{x}(u))$ starting at v. By construction $Z = (Z' \setminus \overrightarrow{\mathcal{D}}(\mathrm{t}(u))) + \mathrm{STS}(\mathrm{t}(u))$. We have $\sigma(u, v) = [u] + \sigma(\mathrm{x}(u), v)$, so, writing $[w_1, \ldots, w_k]$ for the switch-successor list of v wrt. $\mathrm{x}(u)$, the switch-successor list of v wrt. u is $[w_1, \ldots, w_k, \mathrm{t}(u)]$. By induction $Z' = [v] + Z'_{w_1} + \ldots + Z'_{w_k}$. Write, for each $i \le k$, $Z_{w_i} = Z'_{w_i} \setminus \overrightarrow{\mathcal{D}}(\mathrm{t}(u))$. So Z_{w_i} is indeed a subsequence of $\mathrm{STS}(w_i)$. Moreover, if Z_{w_i} is not empty, then $\overrightarrow{\mathcal{D}}(w_i) \not\subseteq \overrightarrow{\mathcal{D}}(\mathrm{t}(u))$ and $w_i \notin \overrightarrow{\mathcal{D}}(\mathrm{t}(u))$. So since Z_{w_i} starts with w_i, Z'_{w_i} also starts with w_i. Overall $Z = [v] + Z_{w_1} + \ldots + Z_{w_k} + \mathrm{STS}(\mathrm{t}(u))$, which gives a correct decomposition. Disjunction follows by induction, except for Z_{w_i} and $\overrightarrow{\mathcal{D}}(\mathrm{t}(u))$ that are disjoint by definition of Z_{w_i}. $\square$

Although we precisely aim at avoiding any exhaustive enumeration of subsets of nodes, such enumeration is necessary in some cases, especially for short prefixes of STS(u), and needs to be as efficient as possible. A straightforward implementation would actually use a depth-first-search, remembering visited nodes and entering a node only if all its parents have been visited. However, the parents of a node are not stored explicitly in memory (they can be computed in $O(n)$, but this would be before the enumeration starts). Similarly, one could also run a regular DFS starting with the tail child and then swap the exclusive and tail parts for each merge node, but again, this strategy would require to visit the whole set $\overrightarrow{\mathcal{D}}(u)$ before starting the actual enumeration.

For a more efficient enumeration of prefixes of the STS of a node, and also to have a faster access to any node by index, we pre-compute the *leaps* of u. A leap of u is a maximal interval in $\mathrm{STS}(\mathrm{x}(u))$ such that all nodes in the interval also appear in $\overrightarrow{\mathcal{D}}(\mathrm{t}(u))$. Leaps can be stored concisely as pairs of integers, and we write $\mathcal{L}_u$ for the set of leaps of u. Then, $\mathrm{excl}(u)$ can be obtained by (1) enumerating $\mathrm{STS}(\mathrm{x}(u))$, (2) removing the positions contained in intervals of $\mathcal{L}_u$ (if any) and (3) applying a cut-off at the correct length: $|\mathrm{excl}(u)| = \mathrm{rank}(u) - \mathrm{rank}(\mathrm{t}(u)) - 1$ (see Algorithm 1 and Fig. 5). This straightforward algorithm can further be turned into an efficient enumeration algorithm.

Definition 6 (leap). *We say that u has an ℓ-leap at position p (with $\ell \geq 1$ and $2 \leq p \leq |\mathrm{excl}(u)|$) if, for some integer q, we have $\mathrm{excl}(u)[p-2] = \mathrm{STS}(\mathrm{x}(u))[q]$ and $\mathrm{excl}(u)[p-1] = \mathrm{STS}(\mathrm{x}(u))[q+1+\ell]$*

We use elements $\mathrm{excl}(u)[p-2]$ and $\mathrm{excl}(u)[p-1]$ since they correspond respectively to $\mathrm{STS}(u)[p-1]$ and $\mathrm{STS}(u)[p]$, and the leap modifies the "expected value" of $\mathrm{STS}(u)[p]$, that would have been $\mathrm{STS}(\mathrm{x}(u))[q+1]$ otherwise.

Theorem 1. *Let u be a node. There exists an enumeration algorithm for $\mathrm{STS}(u)$ using an index containing rank and leap data for all nodes, and taking time $O(1 + d_p(1 + \ell_p))$ for each position p, where (denoting $v = \mathrm{STS}(u)[p]$):*

- *$d_p = d_S(u, v)$ is the switch distance from u to v,*
- *$\ell_p = \max_{s \in \sigma(u,v)} |\mathcal{L}_u s|$ is the maximum number of leaps among switches of $\sigma(u, v)$*

Although in the worst case ℓ_p can be linear and d_p can grow in $\sqrt{n}$, most merges have no leaps at all. Indeed, if an agent creates a small chain of nodes locally and merges them back into a faster-growing graph, then the small chain will form the exclusive part of the merge: in this frequent scenario no leap at all is necessary. Thus, in most cases enumerating each position takes less than 2 look-ups.

Proof. The algorithm is based on the following observation: for any two successive nodes v, w in $\mathrm{STS}(u)$, i.e. with $v = \mathrm{STS}(u)[p]$ and $w = \mathrm{STS}(u)[p+1]$, we have $w \in \{\mathrm{x}(v), \mathrm{t}(v), \mathrm{t}(s_1), \ldots, \mathrm{t}(s_k)\}$ with the switch list $\sigma(u, v) = [s_1, \ldots, s_k]$. This is a direct corollary of Proposition 4. Thus, in addition to the current node v, the algorithm maintains the current switch list $\sigma(u, v)$, as well as the current position p_i of v in $\mathrm{STS}(p_i)$ for each *level* i.

In order to compute the next element w, we update p_i (to a new value denoted p_i') for each level. If $\mathrm{STS}(s_i)[p_i'] = \mathrm{t}(s_i)$, then the next element is $\mathrm{t}(s_i)$. This condition is easily verified using the rank, since for any node x, $\mathrm{t}(x)$ is at

```
1  def STS(u):
2  |   if u = ⊥ then
3  |   |   return []
4  |   X ← STS(x(u))
5  |   foreach interval I in leaps(u) do
6  |   |   remove elements with index in I from X
7  |   X ← X[0 : rank(u) − rank(t(u)) − 1]
8  |   return [u] + X + STS(t(u))
```

Algorithm 1: A recursive algorithm for STS, using rank and leap data to build the exclusive part $X = \text{excl}(u)$. We write $\text{x}(u) = \bot$ if u is not a merge, and $\text{t}(u) = \bot$ if u is a sink.

index $\text{rank}(x) - \text{rank}(\text{t}(x))$ in $\text{STS}(x)$. Otherwise, $w \in \text{excl}(s_i)$, and we move on to the next level with $s_{i+1} \in \text{STS}(\text{x}(s_i))$. By definition of leaps, $p'_{i+1} = p_{i+1} + (p'_i - p_i + L)$, where L is the sum of all leap lengths for leaps of s_i with positions between p_i (excluded) and p'_i (included). We repeat this step for all levels (i.e., all switches s_i), until either $w = \text{t}(s_i)$ for some i, or we reach the end of the switch list: then the computed value of p'_{k+1} corresponds to the index of w in $\text{STS}(v)$. This index is then sufficient to distinguish between $\text{x}(v)$ and $\text{t}(v)$. Finally, we update the switch list as follows: if $w = \text{t}(s_i)$ for some i, then s_i (and all subsequent nodes in the switch list) is no longer a switch to w, and $\sigma(u, w) = [s_1, \ldots s_{i-1}]$. Conversely, if $w = \text{x}(v)$, then v becomes an additional switch in the list, and $\sigma(u, w) = \sigma(u, v) + [v]$. Finally, if $w = \text{t}(v)$, then the switch list remains unchanged.

Remark 3. With small modifications, the above algorithm can be adapted to automatically skip subsets of the form $\overrightarrow{\mathcal{D}}(v)$ for any arbitrary node v (use a reachability query for each generated node, and truncate the pile whenever a node in $\overrightarrow{\mathcal{D}}(v)$ should have been output). We can moreover evaluate the number of skipped nodes, which allows to compute the rank and the leaps of any new merge node u in roughly $|\text{excl}(u)|$ steps.

3.2 Ranges and Splitting Rules

Using the Stable-Tail Sort, we can move on to defining *ranges* (i.e., distinguished subsets) of nodes, and subsequent splitting rules.

Definition 7 (STR: Stable-Tail Range). *The* stable-tail range *(or* range *for short) with head u and length $k > 0$, denoted $\text{STR}(u, k)$ is the set of nodes* $\{\text{STS}(u)[i] \mid 0 \leq i < k\}$. *A range is called* atomic *if $k = 1$,* full *if $k = |\overrightarrow{\mathcal{D}}(u)|$,* canonical *if $k = |\mathcal{C}(u)|$. It is* short *if $k \leq |\mathcal{C}(u)|$, and* long *otherwise (in particular, atomic and canonical ranges are short, full ranges are long unless* $\text{anc}(u) = \bot$*).*

We now present range-splitting algorithms, i.e. we aim at partitioning the nodes in a range into a (small) number of smaller ranges. We present below

Fig. 5. Illustration of Algorithm 1 for $u = $ s in the graph shown on the right. The top row is the final output STS(s), that also includes as suffixes STS(x) for each $x \in $ tail(s) $= [$s, r, k, f, c, a$]$, as illustrated with double red arcs. For each exclusive neighbor (blue arcs), the recursive call Line 4 computes a new STS X (shown in the row below). List X is then filtered to obtain the exclusive part (shaded blue areas) using two filters. The heavy orange line corresponds to the single leap of this graph (vertex m is in $\vec{\mathcal{D}}(\text{x}(\text{s})) \cap \vec{\mathcal{D}}(\text{t}(\text{s}))$), it is removed on Line 6. Heavy green lines are suffixes that can be removed using rank information (e.g. rank(k) $=$ rank(f) $+\,2$, so only the first 2 elements of STS(x(k)) are retained in excl(k)), they are removed on Line 7. Faster implementations of the algorithm directly skip over deleted subsequences (rather than enumerating and removing them): the complexity is driven by the number of rows (different STSs that needs to be enumerated in parallel), which corresponds to the maximum switch distance from u (e.g. $\sigma(\text{s}, \text{h}) = [\text{s}, \text{p}, \text{n}]$). (Color figure online)

two distinct *splitting rules*, combined into split$(S) =$ split$_{\text{anchor}}(S)$ if S is a long range, and split$(S) - $ split$_{\text{greedy}}(S)$ if S is short.

Splitting Rule 1 (Long ranges). *For any range S with head u, let* split$_{\text{anchor}}(S)$ $= \{S\}$ *if S is short, and* split$_{\text{anchor}}(S) = \{\mathcal{C}(u)\} \cup$ split$_{\text{anchor}}(S \cap \vec{\mathcal{D}}(\text{anc}(u)))$ *otherwise (cf Fig. 2).*

The second splitting rule, stated below, uses the notion of *longest range prefix* of some list L, which can be defined as the longest common prefix between L and STS($L[0]$) (it is indeed a range since it is a prefix of some STS).

Splitting Rule 2 (Short ranges). *For a range S with head u, let X be the prefix of* excl(u) *containing only nodes of S, and $T = S \cap \vec{\mathcal{D}}(\text{t}(u))$ (in particular, $X = $ excl(u) whenever T is not empty, and $S = \{u\} \cup$ set$(X) \cup T$). If X is not empty, we define successive ranges $X_1, \ldots, X_k$ such that X_i is the longest range prefix of $X \setminus (X_1 \cup \ldots \cup X_{i-1})$.*
Overall, split$_{\text{greedy}}(S) = \{\{u\}, X_1, \ldots, X_k, T\}$ *(cf Fig. 4).*

Intuitively, split$_{\text{anchor}}$ cuts long ranges at successive anchors to produce few ranges, all of them short (mostly even canonical). For short ranges, no anchor is available, and split$_{\text{greedy}}$ splits greedily to produce at least two ranges, short or long.

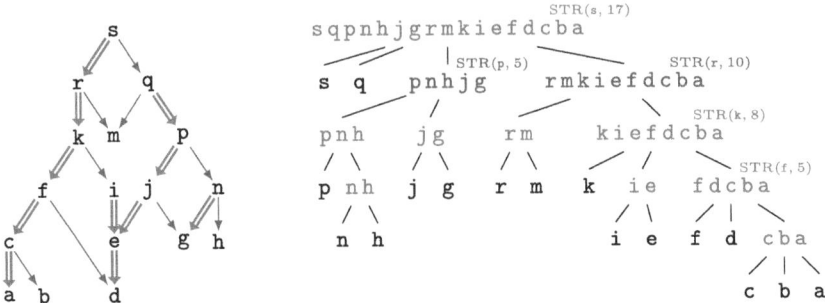

Fig. 6. Search tree (right) for the range $\overrightarrow{\mathcal{D}}(\mathbf{s}) = \mathrm{STR}(\mathbf{s}, 17)$ from the revision graph given on the left. Atomic ranges are shown in black, long ranges in blue and short ranges in red. The range content is enumerated explicitly (in STS order), and the notation as $\mathrm{STR}(x, i)$ is given as superscript for the longer ones. Here $T_{\overrightarrow{\mathcal{D}}(\mathbf{s})}$ has size 27, depth 6 and degree 4. (Color figure online)

3.3   Dichotomy Search with Ranges

Definition 8 (Search-Tree and Dichotomy search). *The* Search Tree *for a range* S, *denoted* T_S, *is the tree with root labelled with range* S *and, if* S *is not atomic, the subtree* T_{S_i} *for each* $S_i \in \mathrm{split}(S)$. *For a node* u, *we write* T_u *for the tree* $T_{\overrightarrow{\mathcal{D}}(u)}$.

A dichotomy search *for a node* $v \in S$ *is the path from the root* T_S *to the leaf* $T_{\mathrm{STR}(v,1)}$ *(such a path always exists since the splitting function on non-atomic ranges always yields a partition into strictly smaller ranges, so the leaves of* T_S *are exactly the nodes* $T_{\mathrm{STR}(v,1)}$ *for* $v \in S$).

Given a graph G, we are interested in the following metrics: the *worst-case depth* is the maximum depth (or height) of T_u for $u \in V$. The *worst-case degree* is the maximum number of sub-graphs of any node in these trees. The *total range count* is the overall number of distinct ranges seen in these trees. Both degree and depth need to be optimized, as the total time cost taken by a dichotomy search is typically the sum of all degrees along the path, which can be bounded in $O(\text{degree} \times \text{depth})$. The total range count needs also to be minimized, in order to optimize storage and caching: whenever meta-data needs to be stored for ranges in internal nodes of the tree (e.g. in label discovery, see Sect. 4.2), the number of cached ranges per node needs to be bounded on average in order to maintain a linear space requirement.

Theorem 2. *A graph with* n *nodes has worst-case depth* $O(\sqrt{n}\log(n))$

The worst-case degree can trivially be bounded by n. Function $\mathrm{split}_{\mathrm{anchor}}$ can be shown to have degree $\leq \log_2 n + 1$ but there is no theoretical bound for $\mathrm{split}_{\mathrm{greedy}}$.

4   Algorithms for Version-Control Systems

4.1   Range-Based Reachability Algorithm

The dichotomy framework defined in Sect. 3.3 can be used as a search-tree for reachability tests (determine if $x \in \overrightarrow{\mathcal{D}}(u)$). We use an approximate, constant-time oracle for range containment, i.e. a function that, given a node x and a range S returns yes ($x \in S$), no ($x \notin S$) or maybe. We run the oracle on range $S = \overrightarrow{\mathcal{D}}(u)$: we can have an answer if it returns yes or no. Otherwise, we continue recursively on each subrange in split(S) until either a yes is found, or no range remains (in which case the query is negative). For a range S with head u and candidate node x, the oracle applies the following rules in order, using pre-computed values for rank and minrank (where $\text{minrank}(u) = \min\{\text{rank}(v) \mid v \in \mathcal{C}(u)\}$):

1. If $u = x$, return yes;
2. If $\text{rank}(x) \geq \text{rank}(u)$ or $\text{num}(x) > \text{num}(u)$, return no[1]
3. If S is short and $\text{rank}(x) < \text{minrank}(u)$, return no;
4. Otherwise, return maybe.

The complexity of this reachability algorithm depends heavily on the shape of the graph. In the worst case, a large fraction of canonical ranges have nodes with ranks spanning an interval containing $\text{rank}(x)$, leads to a linear look-up time. We can however give a better bound on merge-free graphs. In practice, this latter behavior corresponds to our observations, even though the graphs are not merge-free.

Theorem 3. *The index of the range-based reachability algorithm is coherent. If G is a merge-free graph, then the index is linear and has query time $O(\log^2(n))$.*

Lemma 2. *A revision graph of size n with no merge node has worst-case degree $\leq \max(\log(n), 2)$ and worst-case depth $\leq 2\log(n) + 2$.*

Proof. We use n as an upper bound for $\text{rank}(u)$ for any u. Function $\text{split}_{\text{anchor}}$ has degree at most $\log(n)$, and $\text{split}_{\text{greedy}}$ has degree 2 for a non-merge node. For the depth, note that a dichotomy search never visits 2 long ranges consecutively, and that the value $\Pi(S)$ decreases strictly between successive short ranges. Since $0 \leq \Pi(S) \leq \log(|V|)$, we get a depth of $2\log(n) + 2$ overall.   □

4.2   Label Discovery

In the label discovery problem, two agents have revision graphs with the same set of nodes V, but not necessarily the same revision order. Furthermore, each agent has a label function, denoted respectively ℓ_1 and ℓ_2, assigning a label of some discrete type to each node. The goal is to determine the set $\Delta \subseteq V$ of nodes

---

[1] The second condition uses the non-coherent num function, although we do not count it as part of the index since it is already part of the input graph.

where ℓ_1 is different than ℓ_2. We want to minimize the number of exchanges between the agents as well at the total amount of information exchanged, as a function of $|\Delta|$, the number of differences between the two agents.

For each agent i we write $L_i(S)$ for a hash mixing all labels of all nodes in some range S^2; such values are assumed to be pre-computed whenever needed. We compute the deviations by maintaining a set of candidate ranges. Initially, the candidate ranges are the reachable sets of the sources of the graph. Then, we process the ranges in the candidate set successively as follows:

- If $L_1(S) = L_2(S)$, nothing (there are no differences in S);
- otherwise, if S is atomic, we add the single revision in S to Δ;
- otherwise, we add each range in split(S) to the set of candidate ranges.

Theorem 4. *Consider a single-source revision graph with worst-case depth H ($H = O(\sqrt{n}\log n)$ by Theorem 2) and worst-case degree D. The number of round-trips of the algorithm is at most H, and the total number of exchanged values is at most $DH|\Delta|$.*

In practice, computing the hashes of many different ranges is time-consuming, and we obtain a better balance between network exchanges and computation time with the two following modifications:

- long ranges are immediately split, to avoid computing and exchanging their hashes;
- for a short range S with head u, $S \subseteq \mathcal{C}(u)$, exchange $L(\mathcal{C}(u))$ instead of $L(S)$

The second modification leads to transient false positives (some ranges may have different exchanged hash value although the labels are identical): they are eliminated in subsequent rounds, when the partition is refined to smaller ranges. This allows us to use an index containing $L(S)$ for canonical and atomic ranges only, so $\leq 2n$ hashes in total.

5 Experimental Evaluation

We evaluate our algorithms in two phases. First, we run implementation-independent versions of our STS and STR algorithms in order to estimate, in real data, various statistics influencing our algorithms performances. Then, we compare running times and memory usage for our reachability algorithms with literature algorithms on largest graphs.

Our database consists of two collections of public repositories. The first (denoted DB_1) is an extraction of 18350 repositories from the Bitbucket public Mercurial archive [3]. We exclude repositories that have < 16 nodes or that are forks (smaller "subgraphs") of others. DB_1 has a total of 6 976 003 nodes. The second (denoted DB_2) is a set of 11 hand-picked repositories from large open-source projects (Mozilla, Netbeans, PyPy, Mercurial, Evolve, OpenJDK, NetBSD), for a total of 7 374 214 nodes.

---

[2] We assume that the hash values are large enough to ignore collisions: $L_1(S) = L_2(S)$ if and only if $\ell_1(u) = \ell_2(u)$ for all nodes $u \in S$.

Graph Statistics. Revision graphs are specific graphs in that they have a very high reachability ratio, i.e. a random pair of nodes has a high probability to be connected. The graph width (longest antichain) can however be surprisingly high, between $n/20$ and $n/10$ in many cases: this mostly occurs in graphs with many isolated sources that are "forgotten" and never merged with the rest of the graph.

Then, for our dichotomy algorithm, when visiting a search tree for $\overrightarrow{\mathcal{D}}(u)$, we have a typical height of $1.3\log(\operatorname{rank}(u))$, and each sub-range S has degree at most $2\log(|S|)$. This yields the desired sub-linear dichotomy framework that we aimed for in the first place.

Regarding cache performance, it is essential that the number of distinct ranges remains bounded: and indeed we use less than $2n$ distinct subranges in most graphs (even though an upper bound would be $O(n^2)$). Thus all range-related data can be cached linearly.

Reachability tests use an index containing typically less than $1.2n$ integers: we store the minrank of all canonical ranges and less than 0.3 leap per merge on average in most graphs (there are 2 integers per leap, and graphs have up to 30% merges). Half of random reachability queries require less than $2\log(n)$ oracle calls, but this value can be two orders of magnitude higher for the most complex graphs.

The statistics for Label Discovery follow directly from the dimensions of the search trees. A random edit is discovered with $1.3\log(n)$ round-trips on average. If the labels underwent more edits, only the total size of exchanged data increases significantly, the round-trips remain $\leq 2\log(n)$. Here, the linear caching capabilities allow an agent to perform label discoveries with an arbitrary number of peers without the need to recompute arbitrary hashes of label sets. Indeed, only $O(n)$ distinct ranges are ever exchanged, so the respective label hashes can easily be cached.

Reachability Algorithms. As noted in the Previous Works section, most known reachability algorithms use non-coherent indexes, which can be a major drawback in our context for external reasons (e.g. node insertion, but also data compression or cache management). We nonetheless compare our reachability algorithms with two literature algorithms that can be implemented to support node insertions in sublinear time: 2Hop (specifically the *TOL* algorithm [24]), and BFL [18].

We (re-)implemented each algorithm in Python for our benchmark and used random subgraphs of DB_2 to process. The processing step calls node insertions (in a random topological order), interleaved with reachability queries (corresponding to those required to compute the rank of each node).

The results are given in Fig. 7. A simple DFS gives optimal results for many instances, but some instances yield prohibitively high costs. BFL behaves similarly. Our range algorithm and 2Hop give comparable asymptotic behavior for processing the graph. However, this test only evaluates node insertions on a single graph. When synchronising nodes between agents, the coherent STR index can

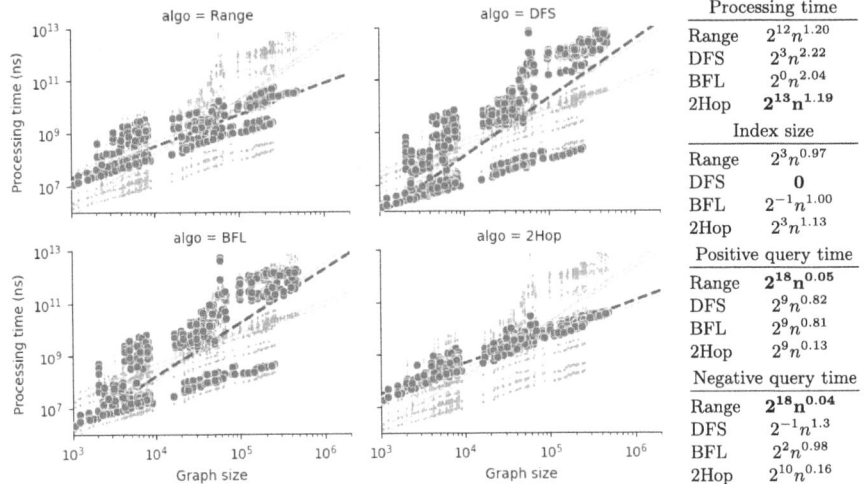

Fig. 7. Processing time for tested reachability algorithms as a function of the graph size. Each algorithm run is drawn as a red dot in the corresponding graph and as small gray dots for comparison in the other three graphs. Right: typical trends for time and memory over the whole benchmark, obtained using min-square linear regressions in log scale (drawn with dashed lines on the corresponding graphs for processing times). (Color figure online)

be shared along with node data without any additional computation, which is a major advantage (although hard to quantify) for this algorithm in our setting.

6   Conclusion

We presented a dichotomy framework tailored for revision graphs, based on stable orderings of reachable sets for each nodes. This framework requires only a light-weight, coherent index, and allows to perform several tasks in sub-linear time. In particular we obtain a competitive algorithm for reachability queries, even against state-of-the-art algorithms that are not bound by the coherence constraints.

In future works we aim at extending this framework to other applications, as well as investigating the many problems related to Version-Control Systems that remain mostly unexplored from a theoretical viewpoint, starting with efficient data-structures to store, retrieve or exchange any set of nodes.

References

1. Agrawal, R., Borgida, A., Jagadish, H.V.: Efficient management of transitive relationships in large data and knowledge bases. ACM SIGMOD Rec. **18**(2), 253–262 (1989)

2. Bendík, J., Benes, N., Cerna, I.: Finding regressions in projects under version control systems. arXiv preprint arXiv:1708.06623 (2017)
3. Bitbucket. Bitbucket public Mercurial archive (2020). https://bitbucket-archive.softwareheritage.org/
4. Bulteau, L., David, P.-Y., Horn, F.: The problem of discovery in version control systems. Procedia Comput. Sci. **223**, 209–216 (2023)
5. Bulteau, L., David, P.Y., Horn, F., Tran-Girard, E.: Incremental reachability. In: Proceedings of the 23rd Symposium on Experimental Algorithms (2025)
6. Chen, Y., Chen, Y.: An efficient algorithm for answering graph reachability queries. In: 2008 IEEE 24th International Conference on Data Engineering, pp. 893–902. IEEE (2008)
7. Cohen, E., Halperin, E., Kaplan, H., Zwick, U.: Reachability and distance queries via 2-hop labels. SIAM J. Comput. **32**(5), 1338–1355 (2003)
8. Courtiel, J., Dorbec, P., Lecoq, R.: Theoretical analysis of git bisect. Algorithmica 1–35 (2023)
9. David, P.-Y.: Hg evolve: obsolescence marker discovery implementation (2017). https://repo.mercurial-scm.org/evolve/file/11.1.1/hgext3rd/evolve/obsdiscovery.py
10. Hamano, J.C.: GIT-a stupid content tracker. Proc. Ottawa Linux Sympo. **1**, 385–394 (2006)
11. Hanauer, K., Henzinger, M., Schulz, C.: Recent advances in fully dynamic graph algorithms-a quick reference guide. ACM J. Exp. Algorithmics **27**, 1–45 (2022)
12. Jagadish, H.V.: A compression technique to materialize transitive closure. ACM Trans. Database Syst. (TODS) **15**(4), 558–598 (1990)
13. Lyu, Q., Li, Y., He, B., Gong, B.: DBL: efficient reachability queries on dynamic graphs. In: Jensen, C.S., et al. (eds.) DASFAA 2021. LNCS, vol. 12682, pp. 761–777. Springer, Cham (2021). https://doi.org/10.1007/978-3-030-73197-7_52
14. Mackall, O.: Towards a better SCM: Revlog and mercurial. Proc. Ottawa Linux Symp. **2**, 83–90 (2006)
15. Plaice, J., Wadge, W.W.: A new approach to version control. IEEE Trans. Softw. Eng. **19**(3), 268–276 (1993)
16. Racinet, G.: Mercurial lazy ancestor iterator Rust implementation (2018). https://repo.mercurial-scm.org/hg/file/6.6.3/rust/hg-core/src/ancestors.rs#l123
17. Stolee, D.: GIT mailing list: [RFC] generation number v2 (2018). https://lore.kernel.org/git/6367e30a-1b3a-4fe9-611b-d931f51effef@gmail.com/
18. Su, J., Zhu, Q., Wei, H., Yu, J.X.: Reachability querying: can it be even faster? IEEE Trans. Knowl. Data Eng. **29**(3), 683–697 (2016)
19. Synapse. Synapse internal docummentation: State resolution: the auth chain difference algorithm (2021). https://matrix-org.github.io/synapse/v1.98/auth_chain_difference_algorithm.html#chain-cover-index
20. Tridgell, A., Mackerras, P., et al.: The rsync algorithm (1996)
21. Wei, H., Yu, J.X., Lu, C., Jin, R.: Reachability querying: an independent permutation labeling approach. Proc. VLDB Endow. **7**(12), 1191–1202 (2014)
22. Yildirim, H., Chaoji, V., Zaki, M.J.: Dagger: a scalable index for reachability queries in large dynamic graphs. arXiv preprint arXiv:1301.0977 (2013)
23. Zhang, C., Bonifati, A., Özsu, M.T.: Indexing techniques for graph reachability queries. arXiv preprint arXiv:2311.03542 (2023)
24. Zhu, A.D., Lin, W., Wang, S., Xiao, X.: Reachability queries on large dynamic graphs: a total order approach. In: Proceedings of the 2014 ACM SIGMOD International Conference on Management of Data, pp. 1323–1334 (2014)

Program Analysis using Machine
Learning

CASTLE: Benchmarking Dataset for Static Code Analyzers and LLMs Towards CWE Detection

Richard A. Dubniczky[1](✉) [ID], Krisztofer Zoltan Horvát[1] [ID],
Tamás Bisztray[2,3] [ID], Mohamed Amine Ferrag[4] [ID], Lucas C. Cordeiro[5,6] [ID],
and Norbert Tihanyi[1,7] [ID]

[1] Eötvös Loránd University (ELTE), Budapest, Hungary
richard@dubniczky.com
[2] University of Oslo, Oslo, Norway
[3] Cyentific AS, Oslo, Norway
[4] Guelma University, Guelma, Algeria
[5] The University of Manchester, Manchester, UK
[6] Federal University of Amazonas, Manaus, Brazil
[7] Technology Innovation Institute (TII), Abu Dhabi, UAE

Abstract. Identifying vulnerabilities in source code is crucial, especially in critical software components. Existing methods such as static analysis, dynamic analysis, formal verification, and recently Large Language Models are widely used to detect security flaws. This paper introduces CASTLE (CWE Automated Security Testing and Low-Level Evaluation), a benchmarking framework for evaluating the vulnerability detection capabilities of different methods. We assess 13 static analysis tools, 10 LLMs, and fv formal verification tools using a hand-crafted dataset of 250 micro-benchmark programs covering 25 common CWEs. We propose the CASTLE Score, a novel evaluation metric for fair comparison. Our results reveal key differences: ESBMC (a formal verification tool) minimizes false positives but struggles with vulnerabilities beyond model checking, such as weak cryptography or SQL injection. Static analyzers suffer from high false positives, increasing manual validation efforts for developers. LLMs perform exceptionally well in the CASTLE dataset when identifying vulnerabilities in small code snippets. However, their accuracy declines, and hallucinations increase as the code size grows. These results suggest that LLMs could play a pivotal role in future security solutions, particularly within code completion frameworks, where they can provide real-time guidance to prevent vulnerabilities. The dataset is accessible at https://github.com/CASTLE-Benchmark

Keywords: Security · Static Code Analysis · Security Analysis · Generative AI · Large Language Models

1 Introduction

Rapid advancements in artificial intelligence (AI) have sparked both excitement and concern about the future of traditional software engineering. For instance,

© The Author(s), under exclusive license to Springer Nature Switzerland AG 2026
P. Rümmer and Z. Wu (Eds.): TASE 2025, LNCS 15841, pp. 253–272, 2026.
https://doi.org/10.1007/978-3-031-98208-8_15

Meta's recent announcement that AI could soon replace many software engineering roles highlights a shifting landscape in code development [1]. While AI-driven code generation offers remarkable efficiency, a study by Tihanyi et al. found that all examined *Large Language Models (LLMs)* produced vulnerable C code [2]. Similar conclusions have been reached in studies examining other programming languages, such as PHP and Python [3,4]. These large-scale studies consistently indicate that such vulnerabilities arise partly because LLMs lack contextual understanding during the generation process. x'Several studies highlight that once the code is generated, and a vulnerability is identified, LLMs are highly effective at resolving these issues [5,6]. The real challenge is: how do we identify the vulnerabilities? Numerous studies have explored methods for identifying vulnerabilities in large-scale codebases, and various static analysis tools are available on the market. Despite the growing importance of automated software verification, developers and security practitioners lack clear guidance on which tools are most reliable for detecting vulnerabilities in C code. Several interrelated issues contribute to this uncertainty, such as:

1. **Diverse vulnerability types.** Security flaws in C code range from classic memory management issues (e.g., buffer overflows) to subtler logical errors. We need to understand which detection methods can reliably detect different categories.
2. **Emergence of LLMs.** While LLMs exhibit promise in automated code generation, bug fixing, and vulnerability detection, their reliability in different vulnerabilities and coding scenarios is unclear.
3. **Lack of standardized benchmarks.** Existing datasets often contain too many samples with imbalanced CWE representations, and fail to represent the breadth of CWE vulnerabilities. Tools that rely on compilable code—particularly formal verification (FV) methods—are especially disadvantaged without realistic, fully functional programs. To gauge each tool's performance accurately, a benchmark must be rigorously validated, contain clearly labeled vulnerabilities, and support line-level detection granularity.

1.1   Motivation

Today, there are two major directions emerging in software engineering, which inspired us to design an entirely new benchmark. Existing benchmarks were no longer adequate to reflect or support these trends. First, code completion and real-time bug detection frameworks are becoming increasingly popular in many *Integrated Development Environments (IDEs)*, as they accelerate application development by automatically correcting common errors and suggesting relevant lines of code. In these scenarios, the focus is typically on small code snippets—usually between 20 and 100 lines—rather than scanning thousands of lines of code. Second, many developers are now utilizing LLMs to assist with various tasks during the software development process. In these cases, LLMs are often tasked with generating simple functions—such as creating a small prime number generator or reading user input to perform basic arithmetic—rather than producing complex systems like full-scale accounting software with tens of thousands of lines of code. In both scenarios, whether code is written by a human in an IDE or generated by an LLM, the result is typically a small code snippet, and our goal is to accurately identify potential vulnerabilities within that snippet. Given these challenges, a robust and compilable benchmark dataset that accurately captures major CWE vulnerabilities is paramount to answer the following research questions:

RQ1: How do state-of-the-art static analysis tools, formal verification methods, and LLM-based approaches compare to effectively detecting C code vulnerabilities?

RQ2: Are combinations of tools more effective than using a single tool?

RQ3: What metrics can reliably demonstrate these differences among various tools?

1.2 Main Contributions

Our study holds the following contributions:

- We introduce **CASTLE (CWE Automated Security Testing and Low-Level Evaluation)**, a curated collection of 250 compilable, compact C programs, each containing a single CWE. This benchmark is aimed at enabling direct comparisons among current and future vulnerability scanning tools, including traditional static analyzers, FV techniques, and LLM-based approaches. The small code snippets in the dataset resemble those typically produced by humans or LLMs during the software development lifecycle.
- We conduct a broad comparison of the most widely used static code analyzers and popular LLMs to assess their effectiveness in detecting important vulnerabilities in the C language, using a new metric called **CASTLE Score**, thereby providing crucial insights into their relative strengths and weaknesses.

The rest of this work is structured as follows: Sect. 2 reviews related literature and outlines the current state of vulnerability scanning tools and AI-based code analysis. Section 3 details the construction of the CASTLE benchmark, including the selection criteria for CWEs and the methodology for creating the curated C programs. Section 4 discusses the results, and presents the experimental setup and comparative analysis of the 13 static code analyzers, 12 format verification tools and 10 LLMs. Section 5 overviews limitations. Finally, Sect. 6 concludes the paper and outlines potential directions for further research.

2   Related Work

Ensuring software correctness, safety, and security is central to software engineering. Examining related literature on the role of AI in software development, most of the existing work and benchmarking approaches focused on testing LLMs' capabilities in producing functionally correct code. However, safety and security are just as important.

2.1   Datasets and Benchmarks

Existing vulnerability datasets are frequently used for fine-tuning machine learning models, yet they exhibit several shortcomings that make them unsuitable for comprehensive benchmarking. First, many datasets offer imbalanced representations of CWE categories, failing to provide adequate test coverage of certain vulnerability types. Second, an extreme or uneven distribution of vulnerable versus non-vulnerable samples either hinders accurate false-positive evaluation (when nearly all samples are vulnerable) or fails to capture diverse false-negative scenarios (when some vulnerability types remain underrepresented) (Table 1).

Table 1. C/C++ Datasets for Vulnerability Detection

Dataset	Size	#Multiple Vuln./File	Vuln. Snippets	Compilable	Granularity	Labelling	Source
Draper [7]	1274k	✔	5.62%	✘	function	Stat	mixed
Big-Vul [8]	264k	✘	100%	✘	function	Patch	real-world
DiverseVul [9]	349k	✘	7.02%	✘	function	Patch	real-world
FormAI-v2 [2]	331k	✔	62.07%	✔	file	FV	AI Gen.
PrimeVul [10]	235k	✘	3%	✘	function	Manual	real-world
SARD [11]	101k	✘	100%	✔	file	B/S/M	mixed
Juliet (C/C++) [12]	64k	✘	100%	✔	file	BDV	synthetic
Devign [13]	28k	✘	46.05%	✘	function	Manual	real-world
REVEAL [14]	23k	✘	9.85%	✘	function	Patch	real-world
CVEfixes [15]	20k	✘	100%	✘	commit	Patch	real-world

Legend:**Patch**: GitHub Commits Patching a Vulnerability, **Stat**: Static Analyzer, **BDV**: By Design Vulnerable, **FV**: Formal Verification with ESBMC, **Manual**: Manual Labeling by Human Experts

Furthermore, a key challenge is that many popular datasets lack compilable programs, making it impossible to meaningfully assess formal verification tools such as the *Efficient SMT-based Context-Bounded Model Checker* (ESBMC) [16]. In datasets like SARD [11], which includes the Juliet [12] test cases and 45,437 C samples mapped to CWE categories, many files exceed 3,000 lines of code. This introduces three key constraints:

1. Large token sizes impose high computational costs on LLM-based approaches and limit the use of smaller-parameter models;
2. The complexity and volume of large files can overwhelm formal verification tools, dramatically increasing runtime and impeding direct comparisons with other analyzers;
3. The code samples differ significantly from the small snippets typically generated by LLMs or written by humans within an IDE framework.

Another example is FormAI, a large-scale dataset labeled using ESBMC itself. As a result, it excludes crucial vulnerability classes, such as cross-site scripting (XSS), SQL injection or OS command injection, which exceed the capabilities of current FV tools. One more important point to highlight: most well-known datasets, such as SARD and Juliet, are widely used by tool developers and are also included in LLM training. To avoid bias and to accurately assess the true capabilities of current tools in identifying vulnerabilities, the creation of a new dataset is essential. This will provide an accurate snapshot of the current strengths and weaknesses of various tools.

2.2   The CASTLE Benchmark

CASTLE provides a collection of compilable code snippets, deliberately crafted to cover major CWEs while minimizing the number of queries required for effective analysis. This design enables the straightforward deployment of LLM-based methods and traditional static analyzers with specialized wrappers, facilitating rapid, automated evaluation across various tools. Additionally, the newly introduced *CASTLE score* provides a more detailed comparative metric than conventional pass/fail assessments, allowing for clearer differentiation of subtle performance variations among state-of-the-art tools. The CASTLE dataset balances vulnerable and non-vulnerable samples, permitting more robust evaluations of false positives and negatives.

2.3   Traditional Vulnerability Scanning Overview

Traditional approaches have long relied on static analysis methods, such as pattern matching, data flow analysis, and taint analysis, as well as dynamic analysis techniques like fuzz testing [17]. Likewise, *Formal Verification (FV)* methods [18], including *Bounded Model Checking (BMC)* [19] and theorem proving, are widely employed to detect security flaws such as buffer overflows. The NIST-led Static Analysis Tool Exposition (SATE) [20,21] provided large-scale evaluations on open-source code, confirming that while these scanners could spot certain weaknesses, no single method excelled across all vulnerability types.

Academic and industrial benchmarks reveal similar shortcomings. Early work by Wilander and Kamkar [22] showed that five tools missed most C function vulnerabilities and produced many false positives, a trend later echoed by Emanuelsson and Nilsson [23]. Johns and Jodeit [24] demonstrated synthetic benchmarks to distinguish genuine alerts from false alarms, while Bennett [25] reported detection rates of 11.2%–26.5% for standard SAST tools, improved to 44.7% by augmenting them with enhanced Semgrep rules.

2.4   LLM-Based Vulnerability Detection

Recent years have witnessed a growing interest in using LLMs for automated vulnerability detection [26–28]. Although these models are often praised for handling diverse code repositories, they primarily rely on pattern-based sequence learning rather than (neuro-)symbolic reasoning. As a result, LLMs can detect certain coding flaws effectively, yet they remain susceptible to overlooking complex or context-dependent vulnerabilities. Recent developments, particularly in decoder-only models such as OpenAI's ChatGPT and Meta's Code Llama, highlight a shift in how researchers and practitioners approach vulnerability detection. Their larger context window and on-demand text generation facilitate powerful few-shot or prompt-based strategies that, for specific benchmarks, surpass classical fine-tuned detectors. For instance, properly designed chain-of-thought prompts have been reported to increase F1 scores on real-world vulnerabilities by providing step-by-step guidance for analyzing the code [4]. Vulnerability detectors typically leverage transformer-based code models trained on massive code corpora spanning multiple languages. These training datasets frequently include insecure code, which can lead to biases or even issues such as *model collapse* [29]. Broadly, transformer models are categorized into three groups [30]:

1. **Encoder-Only**: Used for classification tasks. Early work on vulnerability detection often fine-tuned these models to label code snippets as "vulnerable" or "safe." They generally require full retraining for each new task.
2. **Encoder–Decoder**: Useful for sequence-to-sequence tasks, such as code summarization or refactoring, but they can also be adapted for classification.
3. **Decoder-Only**: Increasingly favored due to large context windows and flexible in-context learning. These models can be prompted to identify vulnerabilities (and sometimes even propose potential fixes) without parameter updates, relying on the knowledge captured during pre-training.

The trend toward decoder-only architectures aligns with industry practices, where state-of-the-art LLMs (e.g., GPT-4) are often served via specialized prompts rather than exhaustive retraining. This approach leverages *in-context learning*, enabling the model to understand and analyze security issues on demand. Carefully constructed prompts—such as chain-of-thought instructions—can improve detection accuracy by guiding the model's attention toward specific code patterns or CWE categories [4]. Existing work indicates that LLM-based solutions can outperform traditional static analyzers on well-defined benchmarks [26–28]. However, these improvements do not translate uniformly across all vulnerability types, and use cases: LLMs often fail at detecting nuanced, multi-function flaws or to interpret extensive code segments.

3   Methodology

This section overviews the dataset creation process and introduces our research's newly developed evaluation metrics. Figure 1 provides a visual overview of the dataset creation and testing framework.

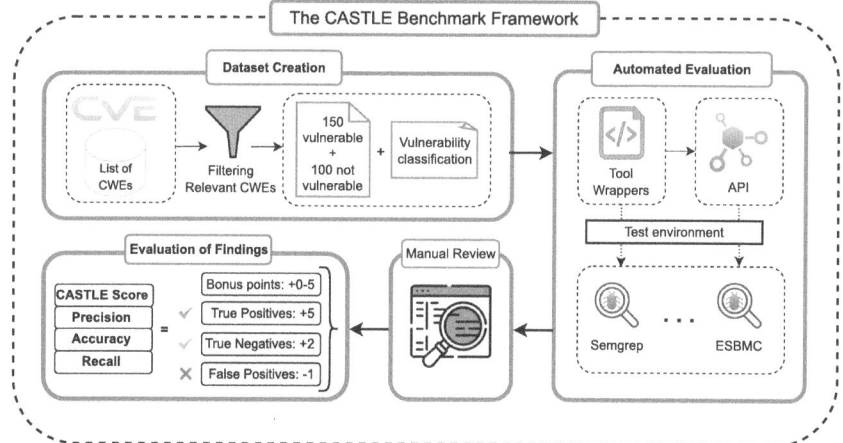

Fig. 1. The CASTLE Benchmark Framework.

3.1   Dataset

The CASTLE dataset comprises 250 small programs in C, each crafted manually by cybersecurity experts. It encompasses 25 distinct CWEs, with 10 test cases per CWE (6 vulnerable and 4 non-vulnerable). This balanced distribution facilitates focused assessments of each tool's vulnerability detection capabilities while accurately measuring false positives. In ambiguous cases, experts selected a higher-level CWE category or iteratively refined the test until only the most relevant CWE remained. Each program was required to compile without errors, although compiler warnings were permitted. All benchmarks were written in C and selected for their capacity to accommodate a wide range of vulnerability types, including intricate memory management issues. Furthermore, each test case was restricted to a single file (with optional external libraries) and designed to contain exactly one or zero vulnerabilities. This structure simplifies the identification of vulnerabilities and helps prevent confusion when validating false positives.

When incorporating the system prompt alongside the source code, the total input tokens across the dataset amount to approximately 115,620 tokens using the *cl100k_base* encoding scheme. This total reflects the resource considerations required when running evaluations with token-sensitive language models. The dataset was intentionally capped at 250 benchmarks to make thorough manual verification feasible. This rigorous verification process is indispensable for detecting false positives and confirming line-level detections. Moreover, this selective approach supports the cost-effective evaluation of computationally intensive tools, including advanced LLMs (e.g., GPT-o1, GPT-o3, DeepSeek R1).

The benchmarks exhibit substantial variability in complexity. Code lengths range from 7 to 164 lines, yielding 10,392 lines (an average of 42 lines). Each includes 1–8 functions (2.2 on average), with cyclomatic complexity values spanning 1–29 (mean 6.3). Halstead volumes range from approximately 89.9 to over 5,246.7, averaging 1,104.8. This breadth ensures the dataset covers a wide spectrum of vulnerabilities, from lower-level issues (e.g., memory management flaws, race conditions) to higher-level security risks (e.g., command injections, hard-coded credentials). Most CWEs were chosen based on their prevalence in the Top 25 CWEs of 2023–2024. Each test underwent iterative validation by human experts to ensure overall quality and reliability. Table 2 provides a comprehensive list of the included CWEs.

3.2 Test Format and Wrappers

Each test in the dataset comprises two components: a metadata block and the source code. Both are stored in a single file for streamlined development and validation, as illustrated in Listing 1.

Listing 1 An example of a micro-benchmark illustrating a buffer overflow

```
CASTLE-787-1.c Test Source Code

1   /*
2   =================================================
3   dataset: CASTLE-Benchmark
4   name: CASTLE-787-1.c
5   version: 1.1
6   compile: gcc CASTLE-787-1.c -o CASTLE-787-1
7   vulnerable: true
8   description: Buffer overflow in scanf function copying into a fixed length buffer.
9   cwe: 787
10  =================================================
11  */
12  #include <stdio.h>
13  int main(int argc, char *argv[])
14  {
15      char reg_name[12];
16      printf("Enter your username:");
17      scanf("%s", reg_name); // {!LINE}
18      printf("Hello %s.\n", reg_name);
19      return 0;
20  }
```

The metadata, formatted in YAML, precedes the source code and is removed during preprocessing. All lines containing vulnerabilities are marked using the

Table 2. CWEs in the benchmark mapped to MITRE's 2024 Top 25 list [31].

CWE	Top 25 Rank	Vulnerability Description
CWE-22	5	Improper Limitation of a Pathname to a Restricted Directory
CWE-78	7	Improper Neutralization of Special Elements used in an OS Command
CWE-89	3	Improper Neutralization of Special Elements used in an SQL Command
CWE-125	6	Out-of-bounds Read
CWE-134	12	Use of Externally-Controlled Format String
CWE-190	23	Integer Overflow or Wraparound
CWE-253	-	Incorrect Check of Function Return Value
CWE-327	-	Use of a Broken or Risky Cryptographic Algorithm
CWE-362	-	Concurrent Execution using Shared Resource with Improper Synchronization
CWE-369	23	Divide By Zero
CWE-401	-	Missing Release of Memory after Effective Lifetime
CWE-415	21	Double Free
CWE-416	8	Use After Free
CWE-476	21	NULL Pointer Dereference
CWE-522	14	Insufficiently Protected Credentials
CWE-617	-	Reachable Assertion
CWE-628	-	Function Call with Incorrectly Specified Arguments
CWE-674	24	Uncontrolled Recursion
CWE-761	20	Free of Pointer not at Start of Buffer
CWE-770	24	Allocation of Resources Without Limits or Throttling
CWE-787	2	Out-of-bounds Write
CWE-798	14	Use of Hard-coded Credentials
CWE-822	20	Untrusted Pointer Dereference
CWE-835	24	Loop with Unreachable Exit Condition
CWE-843	-	Access of Resource Using Incompatible Type

comment string // {!LINE}, ensuring consistent identification across different tools. We note that for LLM evaluation, all side-channel information that could introduce bias is removed during the analysis. Additionally, the metadata specifies the vulnerability's CWE classification and other contextual information. After processing, each test is converted into a JSON-formatted dictionary that includes the code, metadata, and computed software metrics (e.g., cyclomatic complexity, Halstead volume). This unified structure simplifies integration with the various wrappers, facilitating automated execution and standardized result reporting. To ensure a uniform and reproducible evaluation across all tools, we developed custom wrappers that automate installation, configuration, execution, and result retrieval. Each tool was containerized via Docker, alongside its dependencies for freely available static analyzers. We then used Python scripts to run each tool on all test cases, collecting and parsing the results into a standardized report format.

For closed-source solutions such as CodeThreat and Aikido, we uploaded the micro-benchmarks to secure repositories or dashboards accessible via proprietary APIs. The returned results were automatically parsed, and manual consistency checks were performed to verify alignment between reported findings and the tools' web interfaces.

LLM-based vulnerability detection was driven by a generic script that interacted with standard OpenAI APIs. Each model was prompted to return JSON-formatted detection results. Smaller models (fewer than 6B parameters) often struggled to generate well-structured JSON, suggesting limitations in handling detailed output formats. Additionally, models were sensitive to line-specific detections, occasionally identifying the correct vulnerability but offsetting the line number. We also prompted LLMs to provide the corresponding code lines to address minor positioning errors, allowing minimal adjustments during evaluation.

All wrappers developed for this research are publicly available in the main repository. However, intermediate analysis reports are not provided, as they may include proprietary information protected by the respective tool vendors. Each wrapper saves the results in a custom report format, which is later used to process the results and calculate the metrics for the tools.

3.3   The CASTLE Score

In this section, we introduce the *CASTLE* score, a new metric for evaluating the performance of vulnerability detection tools with the CASTLE-Benchmark. The CASTLE score integrates both true- and false-positive rates, awards bonus points for detecting high-impact vulnerabilities (based on the Top 25 CWEs), and rewards correct identification of non-vulnerable code. By incorporating these factors, the metric better captures a tool's overall reliability than standard pass/-fail evaluations.

Let $d^n = \{d_1, d_2, \ldots, d_n\}$ denote a dataset of $n \in \mathbb{N}^+$ micro-benchmark tests. Each test d_i targets a specific security weakness (e.g., buffer overflow) or contains no vulnerabilities. Let v_i denote the correct vulnerability label associated with d_i. If it does not contain a vulnerability, then $v_i = \emptyset$ For any given tool t, let $t(d_i)$ represent the set of vulnerabilities reported by t when analyzing d_i.

Bonus Formula: Following the Top 25 CWE list released by MITRE [31], let $S : \text{CWE} \rightarrow \{1, 2, \ldots, 25\} \cup \{\infty\}$ be a function that returns the rank of a given weakness if it appears in the top 25 list, with $S(c) = \infty$ assigned to any CWE not in the list. Define $b_{\max} = 5$ as the maximum bonus for detecting a Top-25 CWE.

For a found vulnerability labeled $cwe = t_{cwe}$, the bonus $B(t_{cwe})$ is computed as:

$$B(t_{cwe}) = \begin{cases} b_{\max} - \left\lfloor \frac{S(t_{cwe})-1}{b_{\max}} \right\rfloor, & \text{if } S(t_{cwe}) \leq 25 \\ 0, & \text{otherwise} \end{cases} \tag{1}$$

Thus, a tool detecting a highly ranked CWE (e.g., Top 5) receives the full bonus of 5 points, while lower-ranked CWEs yield a proportionally reduced bonus. CWEs outside the Top 25 list receive no bonus.

Scoring Formula: For each test d_i, a tool's performance is scored according to whether it correctly identifies the vulnerability or the true negative sample. The final CASTLE score for a tool t over the CASTLE benchmark is:

$$\text{CASTLE}(t, d^n) = \sum_{i=1}^{n} \begin{cases} 5 - (|t(d_i)| - 1) + B(t_{cwe}), & \text{if } v_i \neq \emptyset \wedge v_i \in t(d_i) \\ 2, & \text{if } v_i = \emptyset \wedge t(d_i) = \emptyset \\ -|t(d_i)|, & \text{otherwise} \end{cases} \tag{2}$$

Interpretation:

- *Correct Vulnerability Detection (True Positive):* If a sample (d_i) is vulnerable $(v_i \neq \emptyset)$ and the tool detects exactly that vulnerability, the tool scores 5 points plus an additional bonus $B(t_{cwe})$ depending on the CWE's standing in the top 25. However, multiple reported findings $(|t(d_i)| > 1)$ reduce the score by one for each, penalizing extraneous detections.
- *Correct Non-Vulnerability Detection (True Negative):* If the sample is non-vulnerable $(v_i = \emptyset)$ and the tool reports no vulnerabilities, it earns 2 points.
- *All Other Cases.* If the tool misses a vulnerability (failing to report v_i), or incorrectly flags any vulnerability (including false positives in a non-vulnerable test), the score is reduced by one for each false-positive finding $(-|t(d_i)|)$. Notably, it does not incur additional penalties if the tool reports nothing on a vulnerable benchmark.

We note that assigning zero points for false negatives does not mean the tool avoids penalty for missing a vulnerability. Instead, the absence of points itself acts as the penalty, indicating that no valid finding was made.

3.4 The CASTLE Combination Score

An additional feature of the CASTLE score is its applicability to tool combinations. Specifically, if two or more tools exhibit high overlap in detected CWEs, their combined false positives may outweigh any marginal gain from additional true positives, thus lowering the overall score. Conversely, if tools complement each other's coverage without substantially increasing false-positive rates, their combination can yield higher net performance. To compute the *CASTLE Combination Score*, one considers the union of reported vulnerabilities and awards true positives and true negatives once while aggregating penalties for all false positives. This ensures that overlapping detections do not artificially inflate the combined score and that the negative impact of extraneous findings remains cumulative. The combination score can be calculated for any number of tool combinations.

4   Discussion

We evaluated 13 static code analyzers, 12 formal verification tools, and 10 LLMs on the CASTLE benchmark. The results, including the CASTLE Scores, are presented in Table 3.

Tools and LLMs are distinctly separated, and the reasoning behind this will be discussed in this chapter. The CASTLE Score is designed to provide a balanced assessment of a tool's effectiveness by considering both true and false positives and the severity of vulnerabilities. Consequently, not finding a high-severity vulnerability leads to larger penalties than less impactful ones. A negative CASTLE Score could indicate that the volume of false positives generated by a tool imposes a significant triage burden on developers, outweighing its potential benefits. Overall, both the benchmark dataset and the introduced evaluation metric helped highlight various static analyzers' strengths and weaknesses.

4.1   Tool Evaluation on the CASTLE Benchmark

Figure 2 presents the results for tools without LLMs, along with their best-performing combinations.

The highest-performing individual tool in our analysis was ESBMC, a formal verification tool. Formal Verification methods have the main disadvantage of being unable to detect non-formal issues, such as SQL Injection, Path traversal, or hard-coded credentials. However, they compensate for this with their low false positive rate. Theoretically, bounded model checkers cannot produce false positives, as they always provide a counterexample to their findings, except in cases where the tool itself has bugs or reports esoteric scenarios. Both ESBMC and CBMC reported 12 similar but not identical false positives (see Fig. 3). These bugs in three categories, some of which we submitted as bug reports to the project [32–35], fixes are already available for some issues. While this dataset with its short code samples allowed relaxed setting for ESBMC with a longer timeout; `-overflow -no-unwinding-assertions -memory-leak-check -timeout 60 -multi-property -show-stacktrace`, with larger codebases formal verification tools could potentially struggle to finish the verification process in reasonable time, thereby limiting their thoroughness and reliability in giving accurate results. The best-performing SAST tool is CodeQL, which found 23% of the weaknesses in the code (35/150), the highest of the average of 17% among other SASTs. SonarQube found the most, around 30%, but it was dragged down by reporting 2.5 times as many false positives than CodeQL. Several tools, including Clang Analyzer and Cppcheck, displayed high precision (87% and 78%

Table 3. The results from 250 C tests and their CASTLE Scores.

| Name | Version | Results | | | | Evaluation Metrics | | | |
		TP	TN	FP	FN	P	R	A	CASTLE Score
ESBMC	7.8.1	53	99	12	97	82%	35%	58%	697
CodeQL	2.20.1	35	84	43	115	45%	23%	43%	600
Snyk	1.1295.4	30	86	28	120	52%	20%	44%	594
CBMC	5.95.1	41	97	12	109	77%	27%	53%	547
SonarQube	25.3.0	45	73	104	105	30%	30%	36%	542
GCC Fanalyzer	13.3.0	41	81	74	109	36%	27%	40%	523
Semgrep Code	1.110.0	26	76	76	124	26%	17%	34%	486
Aikido	N/A*	12	85	31	138	28%	8%	36%	484
Coverity	2024.12.1	31	87	61	119	34%	21%	40%	428
Jit	N/A*	13	85	58	137	18%	9%	33%	427
Cppcheck	2.13.0	18	100	5	132	78%	12%	46%	405
Clang Analyzer	18.1.3	13	99	2	137	87%	9%	45%	381
GitLab SAST	15.2.1	18	67	259	132	6%	12%	18%	215
Splint	3.1.2	23	36	1029	127	2%	15%	5%	-600
CodeThreat	N/A*	21	2	1104	129	2%	14%	2%	-710
GPT-o3 Mini	-	121	61	72	29	63%	81%	64%	955
GPT-o1	-	114	66	72	36	61%	76%	62%	930
DeepSeek R1	-	133	43	163	17	45%	89%	49%	888
GPT-4o	-	113	45	141	37	44%	75%	47%	814
QWEN 2.5CI (32B)	-	106	31	226	44	32%	71%	34%	666
GPT-4o Mini	-	117	27	276	33	30%	78%	32%	663
Falcon 3 (7B)	-	36	76	70	114	34%	24%	38%	557
Mistral Ins. (7B)	-	54	23	218	96	20%	36%	20%	344
Gemma 2 (9B)	-	42	42	288	108	13%	28%	18%	301
LLAMA 3.1 (8B)	-	56	22	374	94	13%	37%	14%	245

Legend: **TP** = True Positive; **TN** = True Negative; **FP** = False Positive; **FN** = False Negative; **P** = Precision; **R** = Recall; **A** = Accuracy;
* *Online API-based tools with unavailable version information (evaluation date: 02/2025)*

respectively) but struggled with low recall (9% and 12%). This trade-off implies they excel at correctly labeling the few issues they detect, yet they fail to identify a substantial portion of vulnerabilities. Conversely, CodeQL's more balanced approach (45% precision, 23% recall) often provides a more reliable day-to-day detection rate for developers. Splint and CodeThreat generated exceptionally high false positives (1,029 and 1,104, respectively). Their negative CASTLE Scores (−600 and −710) illustrate how overwhelmingly false alerts can erode a

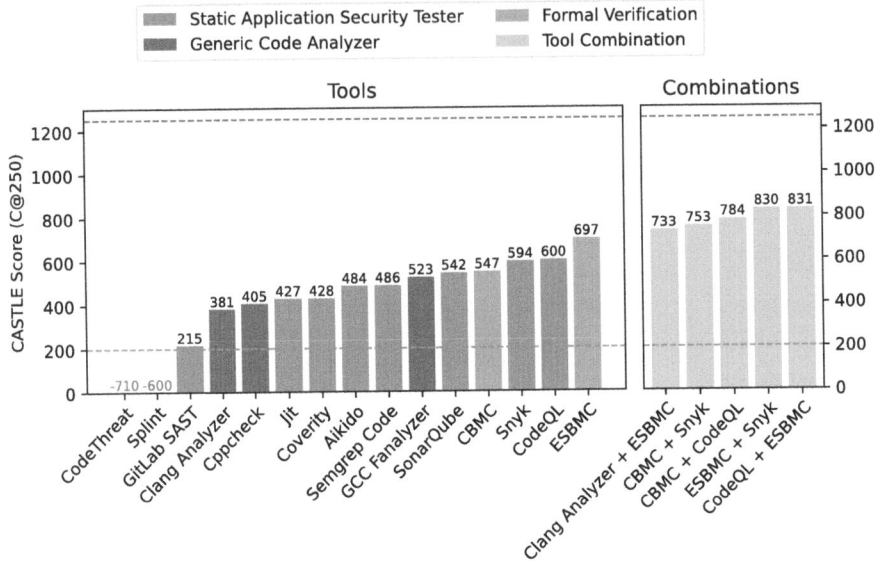

Fig. 2. CASTLE Scores for tools tested on 250 C programs, including the top five tool combinations. Tools reporting no issues score 200 points. The theoretical maximum of a perfect score is 1250 points.

tool's practical utility. Although both tools still produced a modest number of true positives, the excessive manual triage effort likely outweighs any marginal benefits for most real-world applications.

Another advantage of the CASTLE score over traditional metrics is that it provides a comparison between using tool combinations. If a pair of tools has a high overlap in the CWEs they can detect, the CASTLE Score of their combination will yield a lower result than the individual tools because of the oversized impact of increasing the rate of false positives. When looking at combination scores, the biggest increase happens with ESBMC and CodeQL, yielding 831 points. This is a 134 point increase over the higher performing ESBMC's base score of 697, and a 19% increase in the effectiveness of using both tools instead of just ESBMC, with a 39% increase above just using CodeQL. This shows that selecting tool combinations with different strengths significantly boosts the efficacy of the static analysis process.

4.2   LLM Evaluation on the CASTLE Benchmark

On the CASTLE dataset, LLMs exhibited notably strong performance. In particular, GPT-o3-mini achieved the highest overall score of 955 points, correctly identifying 121 out of the 150 known vulnerabilities. When examining the true positives across different LLM variants, we observed that GPT-4o and GPT-4o-mini generated a similar number of detections than GPT-o1 or GPT-o3-mini

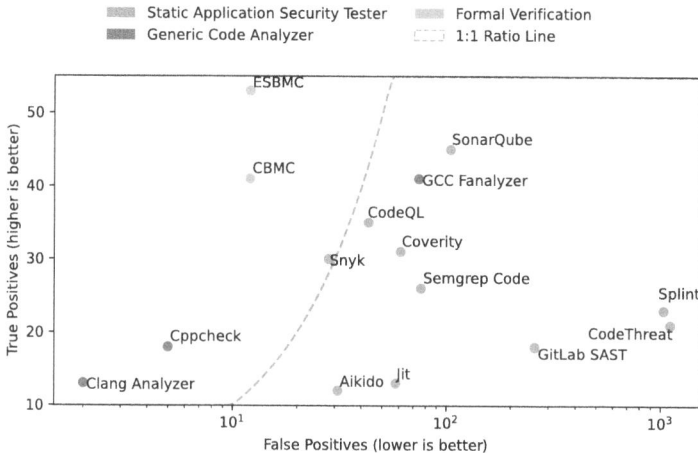

Fig. 3. True Positive vs False Positive rates across tools

for true positives. However, the *reasoning-oriented* models consistently produced fewer false positives, suggesting that their internal steps for "validating" potential vulnerabilities lead to more precise outcomes.

Our findings indicate that modern LLMs can pinpoint vulnerabilities in short, self-contained C programs. We conjecture that their neural architectures confer an inherent advantage in pattern recognition, whereas more advanced reasoning models are more effective at minimizing false detections. As a result, LLM-based approaches rival—and often surpass—several classical static analysis tools in detecting common software flaws within compact code segments. However, the next section highlights several limitations and issues for LLMs.

5   Limitations

Microbenchmark Scope: A fundamental concern with any microbenchmark-based study is its limited scope. Although the CASTLE dataset covers 25 distinct CWEs, each test typically focuses on a single vulnerability in an isolated context. Real-world software often exhibits multi-faceted security flaws spanning tens or hundreds of files. Consequently, tools optimized for detecting specific vulnerabilities may perform artificially well on microbenchmarks while missing complex, cross-file weaknesses that only arise in large-scale applications. Regardless, tools did not perform well on even this small test, indicating that their high false positive rates would be a problem for longer contexts.

Lack of Large Code Samples: Preliminary testing with a synthetic 400+ line C program created by merging multiple non-vulnerable test cases, revealed that LLMs tend to report false positives when dealing with larger codebases. Similarly, when one hidden vulnerability was introduced into this combined file, most

LLMs failed to detect it reliably, suggesting that these models' effectiveness may taper off with increasing code length. Formal verification approaches also suffer from scalability issues, such as state explosion, and may require lowered bounds that reduce their thoroughness. By contrast, classical static application security testers (SAST) can handle extensive projects more efficiently, yet their propensity for false positives undercuts overall usefulness in large-scale deployments.

Potential Overfitting: Because CASTLE test contents are fixed, tool vendors could theoretically fine-tune their analyzers to excel on known benchmarks, inflating reported accuracy while not generalizing to unseen software. Although this consideration does not impact the integrity of our current study, it underscores the importance of periodically refreshing the dataset or incorporating dynamic test-generation approaches for the future. Furthermore, while repeated evaluations of the same code typically yield consistent results (with observed deviations below 3%), the inherent stochasticity of model-based systems stands in contrast to the deterministic nature of many static analyzers.

6   Conclusion

In this study, we introduced the CASTLE benchmark, a curated collection of 250 compilable C micro-benchmarks covering 25 major CWEs. We proposed the CASTLE Score to evaluate diverse vulnerability detection tools, including static analyzers, formal verification methods, and Large Language Models (LLMs). Our work aimed to address the following research questions:

- **RQ1:** *How do state-of-the-art static analysis tools, formal verification methods, and LLM-based approaches compare in effectively detecting vulnerabilities in C code?*
  Answer: LLMs exhibit high effectiveness on compact code snippets, with GPT-o3-mini scoring the highest (955 points) by identifying 121 out of 150 vulnerabilities. However, their performance may decline on larger codebases, where false positives increase and hidden vulnerabilities often remain undetected. Static analyzers perform moderately but produce numerous false positives, creating substantial manual triage overhead. Formal verification tools yield minimal false positives within their supported classes (e.g., memory safety) but cannot detect certain higher-level vulnerabilities such as SQL injection, limiting their coverage.
- **RQ2:** *Are combinations of tools more effective than using a single tool?*
  Answer: Tool combinations frequently outperform individual tools, particularly when they offset each other's weaknesses. For instance, ESBMC (formal verification) combined with CodeQL achieved the highest two-tool CASTLE Score (831). Although overlapping detections can inflate false positives, well-chosen pairs leverage complementary detection strategies, enhancing overall reliability.

– **RQ3:** *What metrics can reliably demonstrate these differences among various tools?*
Answer: As shown in Table 3, neither precision, accuracy, nor recall could have produced the same results and insights. The CASTLE Score integrates true positives, false positives, and CWE frequency, providing a single, clear measure of tool performance. This setup enables transparent evaluation and straightforward comparisons across diverse methods, even for tool combinations.

Implications and Future Work. Although micro-benchmarks efficiently reveal how tools behave on targeted vulnerabilities, they may not reflect the full complexity of production-scale systems. Preliminary experiments indicate that LLMs and formal verification tools both face significant scalability barriers when analyzing large codebases. Ultimately, the insights gained through CAS-TLE underscore the importance of selecting and combining tools to fit specific project requirements rather than relying on any single method for comprehensive security assurance.

6.1 Conclusion Remark

Finally, we would like to highlight an important point regarding small code snippets. We received feedback from members of the research community expressing concerns that such snippets may not fully reflect real-world scenarios. While it's true that small code snippets may not represent complete, realistic applications, they are sufficient for evaluating the types of vulnerabilities a tool is capable of detecting.

If a tool fails to identify a buffer overflow in a five-line snippet, we cannot reasonably expect it to succeed in detecting the same issue within a larger and more complex codebase. In this sense, the CASTLE-Benchmark provides a valuable theoretical upper bound on a tool's detection capability.

We acknowledge that the rankings presented in Table 3 may vary if these tools are evaluated on larger programs. However, the ability—or inability—of a tool to detect certain vulnerability types will remain consistent. If a tool cannot detect a specific issue in a small snippet, it is unlikely to detect it in a larger context either. For this reason, the CASTLE benchmark is well suited for evaluating methods and tools to determine which are most appropriate for code completion frameworks, where small code snippets are typically analyzed.

Acknowledgement. This research is partially funded and supported by ZEISS Digital Innovation and the Technology Innovation Institute (TII). Additional support is provided by the TKP2021-NVA Funding Scheme under Project TKP2021-NVA-29, ELTE-OTP Cyberlab—a collaboration between Eötvös Loránd University (ELTE) and OTP Bank Plc—and the Research Council of Norway under Project No. 312122, 'Raksha: 5G Security for Critical Communications'.

Disclosure of Interests. The authors have no competing interests to declare that are relevant to the content of this article.

References

1. Marks, G.: Business tech news: Zuckerberg says ai will replace mid-level engineers soon. Forbes (2025). https://www.forbes.com/sites/quickerbettertech/2025/01/26/business-tech-news-zuckerberg-says-ai-will-replace-mid-level-engineers-soon/. Accessed 03 Feb 2025
2. Tihanyi, N., Bisztray, T., Ferrag, M.A., Jain, R., Cordeiro, L.C.: How secure is ai-generated code: a large-scale comparison of large language models. Empir. Softw. Eng. **30**(2), 47 (2024). https://doi.org/10.1007/s10664-024-10590-1
3. Tóth, R., Bisztray, T., Erdődi, L.: LLMs in web development: evaluating LLM-generated PHP code unveiling vulnerabilities and limitations. In: Ceccarelli, A., Trapp, M., Bondavalli, A., Schoitsch, E., Gallina, B., Bitsch, F. (eds.) Computer Safety, Reliability, and Security. SAFECOMP: Workshops, vol. 2024, pp. 425-437. Springer, Cham (2024)
4. Mechri, A., Ferrag, M.A., Debbah, M.: Secureqwen: leveraging llms for vulnerability detection in python codebases. Comput. Secur. **148**, 104151 (2025). https://www.sciencedirect.com/science/article/pii/S0167404824004565
5. Jin, M., Shahriar, S., Tufano, M., Shi, X., Lu, S., Sundaresan, N., Svyatkovskiy, A.: Inferfix: end-to-end program repair with llms. In: Proceedings of the 31st ACM Joint European Software Engineering Conference and Symposium on the Foundations of Software Engineering, ESEC/FSE 2023, pp. 1646-1656. Association for Computing Machinery, New York (2023). https://doi.org/10.1145/3611643.3613892
6. Tihanyi, N., Jain, R., Charalambous, Y., Ferrag, M.A., Sun, Y., Cordeiro, L.C.: A new era in software security: towards self-healing software via large language models and formal verification (2024). https://arxiv.org/abs/2305.14752
7. Russell, R., et al.: Automated vulnerability detection in source code using deep representation learning. In: 17th IEEE International Conference on Machine Learning and Applications (ICMLA), pp. 757-762. IEEE (2018)
8. Fan, J., Li, Y., Wang, S., Nguyen, T.N.: A c/c++ code vulnerability dataset with code changes and cve summaries. In: Proceedings of the 17th International Conference on Mining Software Repositories, MSR '20, pp. 508-512. Association for Computing Machinery, New York (2020)
9. Chen, Y., Ding, Z., Alowain, L., Chen, X., Wagner, D.: Diversevul: a new vulnerable source code dataset for deep learning based vulnerability detection. In: Proceedings of the 26th International Symposium on Research in Attacks, Intrusions and Defenses, RAID '23, pp. 654-668. Association for Computing Machinery, New York (2023)
10. Ding, Y., et al.: Vulnerability detection with code language models: how far are we?. In: 2025 IEEE/ACM 47th International Conference on Software Engineering (ICSE), pp. 469-481. IEEE Computer Society, Los Alamitos (2025). https://doi.ieeecomputersociety.org/10.1109/ICSE55347.2025.00038
11. National Institute of Standards and Technology. Software assurance reference dataset (sard) (2024). https://samate.nist.gov/SARD/. Accessed 10 Nov 2024
12. N. C. for Assured Software. Software assurance reference dataset (sard): Juliet c/c++ 1.3 (2024). https://samate.nist.gov/SARD/test-suites/112. Accessed 10 Nov 2024
13. Zhou, Y., Liu, S., Siow, J., Du, X., Liu, Y.: Devign: effective vulnerability identification by learning comprehensive program semantics via graph neural networks. Adv. Neural Inf. Process. Syst. **32**, 1-11 (2019)

14. Chakraborty, S., Krishna, R., Ding, Y., Ray, B.: Deep learning based vulnerability detection: are we there yet? IEEE Trans. Softw. Eng. **48**(9), 3280–3296 (2022)
15. Bhandari, G., Naseer, A., Moonen, L.: Cvefixes: automated collection of vulnerabilities and their fixes from open-source software. In: Proceedings of the 17th International Conference on Predictive Models and Data Analytics in Software Engineering, PROMISE 2021, pp. 30–39. Association for Computing Machinery, New York (2021)
16. Menezes, R.S., et al.: Esbmc v7.4: harnessing the power of intervals. In: Finkbeiner, B., Kovács, L. (eds.) Tools and Algorithms for the Construction and Analysis of Systems, pp. 376–380. Springer, Cham (2024)
17. Mallissery, S., Wu, Y.-S.: Demystify the fuzzing methods: a comprehensive survey. ACM Comput. Surv. **56**(3), 1–38 (2023). https://doi.org/10.1145/3623375
18. D'Silva, V., Kroening, D., Weissenbacher, G.: A survey of automated techniques for formal software verification. IEEE Trans. Comput. Aided Des. Integr. Circuits Syst. **27**(7), 1165–1178 (2008)
19. Biere, A., Cimatti, A., Clarke, E., Zhu, Y.: Symbolic model checking without BDDs. In: Cleaveland, W.R. (ed.) TACAS 1999. LNCS, vol. 1579, pp. 193–207. Springer, Heidelberg (1999). https://doi.org/10.1007/3-540-49059-0_14
20. Okun, V., Gaucher, R., Black, P.E.: Static analysis tool exposition (sate) 2008. NIST Spec. Publ. **500**, 279 (2009)
21. Delaitre, A., et al.: Sate vi report: Bug injection and collection (2023)
22. Wilander, J., Kamkar, M.: A comparison of publicly available tools for static intrusion prevention. In: Proceedings of the 7th Nordic Workshop on Secure IT Systems (NordSec), p. 108 (2002)
23. Emanuelsson, P., Nilsson, U.: A comparative study of industrial static analysis tools. Electron. Notes Theor. Comput. Sci. **217**, 5–21 (2008)
24. Johns, M., Jodeit, M.: Scanstud: a methodology for systematic, fine-grained evaluation of static analysis tools. In: IEEE Fourth International Conference on Software Testing, Verification and Validation Workshops, pp. 523–530. IEEE (2011)
25. Bennett, G., Hall, T., Winter, E., Counsell, S.: Semgrep*: improving the limited performance of static application security testing (sast) tools. In: Proceedings of the 28th International Conference on Evaluation and Assessment in Software Engineering, pp. 614–623 (2024)
26. Yang, Y., et al.: Dlap: a deep learning augmented large language model prompting framework for software vulnerability detection. J. Syst. Softw. **219**, 112234 (2025). https://www.sciencedirect.com/science/article/pii/S0164121224002784
27. Li, Z., Dutta, S., Naik, M.: Llm-assisted static analysis for detecting security vulnerabilities. arXiv preprint arXiv:2405.17238 (2024)
28. Lee, Y., Jeong, S., Kim, J.: Improving llm classification of logical errors by integrating error relationship into prompts. In: International Conference on Intelligent Tutoring Systems, pp. 91–103. Springer, Heidelberg (2024)
29. Shumailov, I., Shumaylov, Z., Zhao, Y., Papernot, N., Anderson, R., Gal, Y.: AI models collapse when trained on recursively generated data. Nature **631**(8022), 755–759 (2024). https://doi.org/10.1038/s41586-024-07566-y
30. Sheng, Z., et al.: Large language models in software security: a survey of vulnerability detection techniques and insights. arXiv preprint arXiv:2502.07049 (2025)
31. MITRE. 2024 CWE Top 25 Most Dangerous Software Weaknesses (2024). https://cwe.mitre.org/top25/archive/2024/2024_cwe_top25.html
32. Tihanyi, N.: ESBMC assumption on argv 2312 (2025). https://github.com/esbmc/esbmc/issues/2312. Accessed 8 Mar 2025

33. Tihanyi, N.: ESBMC 7.8 segmentation fault 2236 (2025). https://github.com/esbmc/esbmc/issues/2236. Accessed 8 Mar 2025
34. Tihanyi, N.: GCSE (segmentation fault -PART II) 2235 (2025). https://github.com/esbmc/esbmc/issues/2235. Accessed 8 Mar 2025
35. Tihanyi, N.: Discrepancy in GCSE (PART II) 2231 (2025). https://github.com/esbmc/esbmc/issues/2231. Accessed 8 Mar 2025

FAMIT: Mitigating False Alarms for Program Analysis Using Large Language Models

Jiabao Zeng[1], Yuanlin Li[1,2], Ran Zhang[1], Yuanmin Xie[1],
Kejia Li[3], and Min Zhou[1(✉)]

[1] KLISS, BNRist, School of Software, Tsinghua University, Beijing, China
{zengjb24,li-yl22,zhangr22,xieym23}@mails.tsinghua.edu.cn,
mzhou@tsinghua.edu.cn
[2] ValiantSec, Changsha, China
[3] Economics and Management School of Wuhan University, Wuhan 430072, China

Abstract. Static analysis tools are widely used in software engineering practice, but they suffer from a high false positive rate. In this paper, we propose an automated approach to mitigate false alarms based on large language models (LLMs). Our approach relies on the collaboration of three agents. The source code is sliced and incrementally provided to the agents on demand. By leveraging few-shot learning and beam search with self-reflection, our method effectively filters out false alarms. On an artificial test suite, it eliminates 91.9% of false alarms reported by traditional static analysis tools. The accuracy of bug reports (measured by the F1 score) is significantly improved from 0.575 to 0.913. Experimental results on real-world projects from GitHub show that false alarms are reduced by an average of 57.2% and up to 96.6%. Our approach is not a replacement for traditional static analysis tools but rather an enhancement. Therefore, it can be easily integrated with any static analysis tool to provide more accurate and efficient analysis reports.

Keywords: Static Analysis · False Alarm Mitigation · Large Language Model

1 Introduction

Static program analysis is pivotal in software engineering, providing in-depth inspections of source code vulnerabilities without executing the program. Despite their benefits, static analysis tools often suffer from a high rate of false alarms because they typically employ over-approximations of program states [9]. In practice, the proportion of false alarms may exceed 90% [11], which requires a substantial manual verification effort [10,28].

Large Language Models (LLMs), like GPT series [3,18,24,25], have demonstrated significant success in natural language processing. Pre-trained on extensive codebases, LLMs have shown promise in code understanding [4], but not yet

P. Rümmer and Z. Wu (Eds.): TASE 2025, LNCS 15841, pp. 273–281, 2026.
https://doi.org/10.1007/978-3-031-98208-8_16

fully comparable to human capabilities. Due to context length limit, LLMs cannot process an entire codebase at once. Although LLMs cannot directly eliminate false alarms, they can enhance specific code analysis tasks with proper guidance.

In this paper, an LLM-based approach is proposed to mitigate false alarms generated by static analysis tools. Our approach checks feasibility of bug reports represented as program paths and uses an LLM as the reasoning engine. It analyzes path conditions in source code and combines incremental code analysis and logical reasoning to assess both path feasibility and defect validation.

The major contributions of this paper are as follows. A novel LLM-based approach is proposed to automatically mitigate false alarms. An artificial test suite is designed for evaluation, consisting of 121 cases from common false alarm patterns. Our approach is implemented as the FAMIT (*F*alse *A*larm *Mi*tigation *T*ool) and compared with applying state-of-the-art LLMs such as OPENAI-o1 [20] and DEEPSEEK-R1 [6]. FAMIT is evaluated on both artificial test suite and real-world projects. On the artificial test suite, FAMIT eliminates over 90% of false alarms reported by static analysis tools and achieves the F1 score of 0.913 while the baseline achieves at most 0.870. On real-world projects from GitHub, FAMIT mitigates false alarms by 57.2% on average and up to 96.6%.

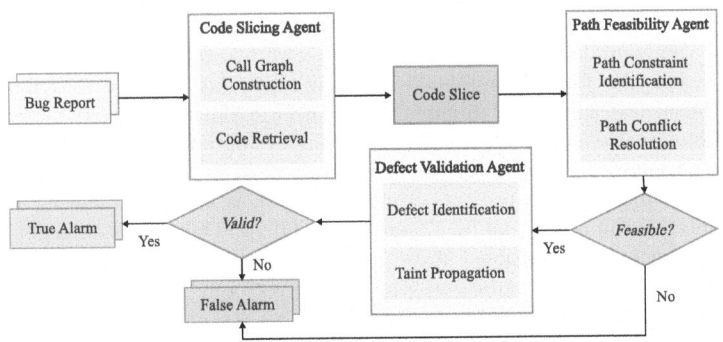

Fig. 1. Overview of FAMIT

2   The FAMIT Approach

Examples of false alarms are shown in Fig. 2, they are extracted from real bug reports. In the `infeasible_path` function, the formal parameter *tainted* is a tainted value and is assigned to a local variable t under the condition $x > 0$. Then it is passed to y under the condition $x < 0$, and the value of y is fed to a taint sink. The path is infeasible because it relies on the conflicting path conditions $x > 0 \land x < 0$. In the `broken_taint_path` function, the element $arr[1]$ is tainted but $arr[0]$ is not, thus the tainted value is not actually propagated to the `sink` function. Both examples can be eliminated using our approach.

An overview of our approach is shown in Fig. 1. For each bug report given as the program path, the *code slicing agent* retrieves the subset of related source code. This process is performed iteratively and only the necessary code is included. The *path feasibility agent* then checks for conflicts in the path conditions. An LLM is instructed to analyze path dependency conditions. For instance, the agent identifies conflicting conditions $x > 0$ and $x < 0$ in the `infeasible_path` function, thus dismissing the alert as a false alarm. Then, the *defect validation agent* analyzes the code slice and validates whether the given path is a witness of given defect type. For example, taint values should be properly propagated in a taint path (e.g., the `broken_taint_path` function). Only those paths that are feasible and valid are confirmed, others are regarded as false alarms.

```
1   def infeasible_path(tainted, x):       1   def broken_taint_path(tainted):
2       if x > 0:                          2       without_sanitize(tainted)
3           t = tainted                    3       arr = [1]
4       y = t if x < 0 else None           4       arr.append(tainted)
5       sink(y)                            5       sink(arr[0])
```

Fig. 2. Examples of false alarm

Incremental Code Analysis: LLMs have a limit on the context length. For example, DEEPSEEK-V3 [5] supports 64k tokens, while GPT-4O [19] and CLAUDE-3.5 SONNET [1] support 128k and 200k tokens respectively. An entire codebase may not be processed at once due to the limited context length. More importantly, irrelevant code can disrupt the LLM's reasoning process. Our approach, on the other hand, utilizes progressive prompting to avoid feeding the entire codebase at once. The source code is provided incrementally and dynamically based on the analytical requirements. Specifically, the LLM is provided an entry function as seed, then the relevant code is incrementally located under the help of call graph. In this way, the LLM focuses on the code slice of interest, thus accuracy and reliability is improved.

Few-Shot Learning: Currently, specialized code analysis tasks are still challenging for LLMs. Thus, few-shot learning is employed [30]. For instance, in the `broken_taint_path` function in Fig. 2, the LLM needs to recognize the difference between $arr[0]$ and $arr[1]$ through their indices, and subsequently determine that the taint propagation path is infeasible. Therefore, few-shot learning is employed to guide the LLM to notice some important aspects for code analysis. In all, nine instructions are proposed to the LLM, including those for handling array contents, branch statements, loops and iterations.

Beam Search with Self-Reflection: Due to the inherent randomness of LLMs, the results may vary with each run. Therefore, a multi-phase beam search is conducted as shown in Fig. 3. In each phase, the LLM will be asked to think differently and provide three responses while each response is based on refuting the previous one. Then majority voting is employed to determine the optimal response for each phase [23,29]. In this way, the model can improve the quality of its outputs through self-reflection and correct without external intervention.

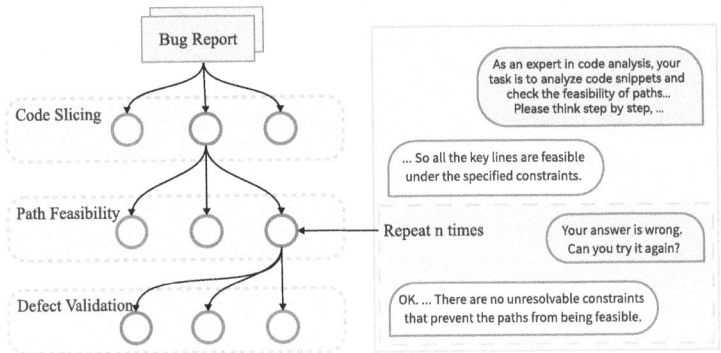

Fig. 3. Prompt strategy for beam search with self-reflection

Due to space limitation, technical details can not be explained in depth here, interested readers could find more details in the code as well as the data [1].

3   Experimental Evaluation

3.1   Experiment on Artificial Test Suite

An artificial test suite is constructed to evaluate our approach. It consists of 121 cases derived from common false alarm patterns, 52 of them are bad cases which contain real bugs while 69 are good cases (false alarms).

Our approach is not limited to a specific programming language or static analysis tool, like [2,7,22,26,27]. However, the experiment is conducted on Python because bug reports are produced by PYSA [7], a static analyzer designed for Python. Moreover, our approach is not restricted to any particular underlying LLM. Five LLMs are used in the experiment, including GPT-4o(donated by G_{4o}), CLAUDE-3.5 SONNET(C), DEEPSEEK-V3(D_{V3}), OPENAI-o1(G_{o1}) and DEEPSEEK-R1(D_{R1}). The last two are reasoning LLMs.

The experimental results are shown in Fig. 4 and Table 1. The number of bad/good cases in each category is listed in the first column. The bug reports refined by our approach (cols. 8–12) are compared with the original bug reports (col. 2) and those filtered by directly using above LLMs (cols. 3–7). Each cell contains a pair of numbers "α:β", representing the number of missing bad cases (α) and incorrectly reported good cases (β). Both α and β should be minimized.

---

[1] https://github.com/liyuanlintcl/FAMiT

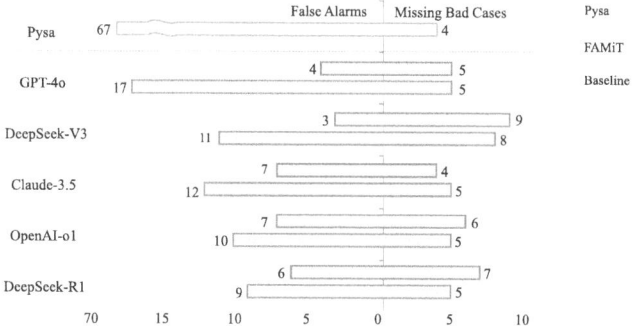

Fig. 4. Comparison results on the artificial test suite

On average, our approach filters out of 91.9% false alarms reported by PYSA. There is a significant improvement over baseline methods on general LLMs, the average number of false alarms is reduced by 63.6%. On reasoning LLMs, the improvement is slight. Overall, the F1 score of original bug reports is 0.575 and it is improved to 0.913 by our approach (using GPT-4o as the underlying engine), while the highest F1 score of baseline methods is 0.870.

While inspecting the performance on different false alarm patterns, FAMiT shows an improvement in the mathematical reasoning capabilities of the underlying LLM. For general LLMs, an average reduction of 83.3% errors is observed for the math pattern and 36.7% for the complex math pattern. Moreover, our approach eliminates all errors in the math pattern when reasoning model is used. This is due to the separation of path feasibility from defect validation, which allows for better handling of complex path conditions.

3.2   Experiment on Real-World Projects

Our method is also applied to real-world projects and the results are shown in Table 2. The table lists project names (the first column), true/false alarms of PYSA (the second column), and columns 3 to 12 indicate the number of true/false alarms that remain misidentified by the baseline methods and FAMiT. Specifically, each cell is formatted as "α/β" representing incorrectly reported true alarms (α) and false alarms (β), both of which should be minimized. We identify the ground truths of the alarms by manual analysis. Although the projects are public, the bug reports are not used in training LLMs.

The experimental results indicate that our approach reduces false alarms by 57.2% on average. In contrast to the artificial test suite above, the reasoning LLM DEEPSEEK-R1 outperforms other LLMs in mitigating false alarms, eliminating 96.6% of false alarms and achieving the highest F1 score of 0.867. Furthermore, FAMiT improves the F1 score by an average of 0.258 on reasoning LLMs and 0.099 on general LLMs. This is attributable to the more complex context of real-world projects. Due to more efficient training strategies, reasoning LLMs

Table 1. Detailed evaluation results on the artificial test suite

	PYSA	Baseline LLM					FAMIT				
		G_{4o}	D_{V3}	C	G_{o1}	D_{R1}	G_{4o}	D_{V3}	C	G_{o1}	D_{R1}
branch (5:6)	0:6	0:1	0:1	0:1	0:0	0:0	0:0	0:0	0:0	0:0	0:0
fields (9:13)	0:13	0:0	0:0	0:1	0:0	0:0	0:0	1:0	0:0	0:1	0:0
arrays (6:6)	0:6	0:0	0:0	0:0	0:0	0:0	0:0	0:0	0:0	0:0	0:0
cast (0:1)	0:1	0:1	0:1	0:0	0:1	0:1	0:0	0:0	0:1	0:0	0:0
exception (3:3)	0:3	0:2	0:0	0:0	0:0	0:0	0:0	0:0	0:0	0:0	0:0
polymorphism (5:5)	0:5	0:0	0:0	0:1	0:0	0:0	0:0	0:0	0:0	1:0	2:0
inter (6:7)	1:7	1:1	1:1	1:1	1:0	1:0	1:0	1:0	1:1	1:0	1:0
long function (5:5)	0:5	0:4	3:1	1:1	1:3	1:1	0:1	1:0	0:1	1:1	1:2
loop (4:4)	0:4	0:0	0:0	0:0	0:0	0:0	0:0	0:0	0:0	0:0	0:0
math (1:5)	0:5	0:4	1:3	0:3	0:2	0:3	1:0	1:0	0:0	0:0	0:0
complex math (0:5)	0:5	0:5	0:4	0:4	0:4	0:4	0:2	0:2	0:4	0:4	0:4
multi file (2:2)	2:0	2:0	2:0	2:0	2:0	2:0	2:0	2:0	2:0	2:0	2:0
recursion (2:2)	0:2	0:0	0:0	0:0	0:0	0:0	0:0	0:0	0:0	1:0	0:0
sensitivety (5:5)	1:5	1:0	1:0	1:0	1:0	1:0	1:1	3:1	1:0	1:0	1:0
Total (52:69)	4:67	5:17	8:11	5:12	5:10	5:9	5:4	9:**3**	**4**:7	6:7	7:6
F1 score	0.575	0.810	0.822	0.847	0.862	0.870	**0.913**	0.878	0.897	0.876	0.874

can accurately extract more complex path dependencies and propagation chains. However, FAMIT employing CLAUDE-3.5 SONNET as the underlying engine frequently misidentifies true alarms as false. We hypothesize that its code analysis capabilities may be less robust than its code generation strengths, warranting further investigation.

4   Related Works

Among all false alarm mitigation methods [9], the static program analysis method directly deals with the source code or intermediate representation, which is widely accepted by researchers with high confidence [8, 15–17]. Gao et al. [8] introduce BovInspector, a framework that automatically validates static buffer overflow warnings in C programs, and reduces false alarms through reachability analysis and symbolic execution, significantly improving the efficiency of static analysis. However, the symbolic execution of loops by BovInspector may encounter the path explosion problem, and FAMIT can utilize LLM to automatically and efficiently extract the conditional constraints in the loop.

LLMs have now been widely applied in code analysis [12, 14, 21, 31]. Khare et al. evaluate vulnerability detection performance across various datasets, languages and LLMs [12], which can accurately identify the sources, sinks and

Table 2. Evaluation results on the real-world projects

	P$_{YSA}$	Baseline LLM					FAM$_I$T				
		G_{4o}	D_{V3}	C	G_{o1}	D_{R1}	G_{4o}	D_{V3}	C	G_{o1}	D_{R1}
stable-diffusion-webui	2/2	0/2	0/2	1/2	0/2	0/2	1/2	0/2	2/1	2/1	2/0
linkding	0/10	0/9	0/10	0/9	0/8	0/7	0/7	0/1	0/2	0/2	0/0
mkdocs-material	0/10	0/9	0/10	0/10	0/7	0/6	0/9	0/5	0/6	0/4	0/0
OctoPrint	0/1	0/0	0/0	0/0	0/0	0/0	0/0	0/0	0/0	0/0	0/0
SeleniumBase	31/6	5/6	14/5	13/6	6/5	16/4	1/6	2/5	20/3	1/5	5/1
Total	33/29	5/26	14/27	14/27	6/22	16/19	**2/24**	**2/13**	22/12	3/12	7/**1**
F1 score	–	0.644	0.481	0.481	0.659	0.493	0.705	0.805	0.393	0.800	**0.867**

unsanitized paths. In addition to taint propagation, our work comprehensively checks for path condition conflicts. Li et al. propose the combination of static analysis and LLMs to identify *Use Before Initialization* in the Linux kernel for the first time [13,14]. While they focus on one single defect pattern, our work is more general and can mitigate various types of false alarms.

5   Conclusion

In this paper, an automatic and effective false alarm mitigation method is proposed. Our approach relies on the interaction of three carefully designed agents. In the future, we plan to investigate the possibility of fine-tuning LLMs with capable of code slicing, path feasibility checking, and defect validation, thereby basing every step on LLMs.

Acknowledgment. This research was supported by the Major Research Plan of the National Natural Science Foundation of China under Grant No. 92267203, National Key Research and Development Program of China (2022YFB43012).

References

1. Anthropic: Claude 3.5 Sonnet model card addendum (2024). https://www-cdn.anthropic.com/fed9cc193a14b84131812372d8d5857f8f304c52/Model_Card_Claude_3_Addendum.pdf
2. Baca, D.: Identifying security relevant warnings from static code analysis tools through code tainting. In: 2010 International Conference on Availability, Reliability and Security, pp. 386–390. IEEE (2010)
3. Brown, T., et al.: Language models are few-shot learners. In: Advances in Neural Information Processing Systems, pp. 1877–1901 (2020)
4. Chen, L., et al.: A survey on evaluating large language models in code generation tasks (2024). https://arxiv.org/abs/2408.16498
5. DeepSeek-AI: DeepSeek-V3 technical report (2024). https://arxiv.org/abs/2412.19437

6. DeepSeek-AI: DeepSeek-R1: Incentivizing reasoning capability in LLMs via reinforcement learning (2025). https://arxiv.org/abs/2501.12948
7. Facebook: Pysa (2025). https://github.com/facebook/pyre-check
8. Gao, F., Wang, Y., Wang, L., Yang, Z., Li, X.: Automatic buffer overflow warning validation. J. Comput. Sci. Technol. **35**(6), 1406–1427 (2020)
9. Guo, Z., et al.: Mitigating false positive static analysis warnings: progress, challenges, and opportunities. IEEE Trans. Softw. Eng. **49**(12), 5154–5188 (2023)
10. Johnson, B., Song, Y., Murphy-Hill, E., Bowdidge, R.: Why don't software developers use static analysis tools to find bugs? In: 2013 35th International Conference on Software Engineering, pp. 672–681. IEEE (2013)
11. Kang, H.J., Aw, K.L., Lo, D.: Detecting false alarms from automatic static analysis tools: how far are we? In: Proceedings of the 44th International Conference on Software Engineering, pp. 698–709. ACM (2022)
12. Khare, A., Dutta, S., Li, Z., Solko-Breslin, A., Alur, R., Naik, M.: Understanding the effectiveness of large language models in detecting security vulnerabilities (2024). https://arxiv.org/abs/2311.16169
13. Li, H., Hao, Y., Zhai, Y., Qian, Z.: Assisting static analysis with large language models: a chatgpt experiment. In: Proceedings of the 31st ACM Joint European Software Engineering Conference and Symposium on the Foundations of Software Engineering, pp. 2107–2111. ACM (2023)
14. Li, H., Hao, Y., Zhai, Y., Qian, Z.: Enhancing static analysis for practical bug detection: an LLM-integrated approach. Proc. ACM Program. Lang. **8**(OOPSLA1), 474–499 (2024)
15. Muske, T., Serebrenik, A.: Techniques for efficient automated elimination of false positives. In: 2020 IEEE 20th International Working Conference on Source Code Analysis and Manipulation, pp. 259–263. IEEE (2020)
16. Muske, T., Talluri, R., Serebrenik, A.: Reducing static analysis alarms based on non-impacting control dependencies. In: Lin, A.W. (ed.) APLAS 2019. LNCS, vol. 11893, pp. 115–135. Springer, Cham (2019). https://doi.org/10.1007/978-3-030-34175-6_7
17. Nguyen, T.T., Maleehuan, P., Aoki, T., Tomita, T., Yamada, I.: Reducing false positives of static analysis for SEI CERT C coding standard. In: 2019 IEEE/ACM Joint 7th International Workshop on Conducting Empirical Studies in Industry and 6th International Workshop on Software Engineering Research and Industrial Practice, pp. 41–48. IEEE (2019)
18. OpenAI: GPT-4 technical report (2023). https://arxiv.org/abs/2303.08774
19. OpenAI: Hello GPT-4o (2024). https://openai.com/index/hello-gpt-4o
20. OpenAI: Introducing OpenAI o1-preview (2024). https://openai.com/index/introducing-openai-o1-preview/
21. Pei, K., Bieber, D., Shi, K., Sutton, C., Yin, P.: Can large language models reason about program invariants? In: Proceedings of the 40th International Conference on Machine Learning, pp. 27496–27520. PMLR (2023)
22. Pylint contributors: Pylint (2025). https://github.com/pylint-dev/pylint
23. Qu, Y., Zhang, T., Garg, N., Kumar, A.: Recursive introspection: teaching language model agents how to self-improve (2024). https://arxiv.org/abs/2407.18219
24. Radford, A., Narasimhan, K., Salimans, T., Sutskever, I.: Improving language understanding by generative pre-training (2018). https://api.semanticscholar.org/CorpusID:49313245
25. Radford, A., Wu, J., Child, R., Luan, D., Amodei, D., Sutskever, I.: Language models are unsupervised multitask learners (2019). https://cdn.openai.com/better-language-models/language_models_are_unsupervised_multitask_learners.pdf

26. Ribeiro, A., Meirelles, P., Lago, N., Kon, F.: Ranking warnings from multiple source code static analyzers via ensemble learning. In: Proceedings of the 15th International Symposium on Open Collaboration, pp. 1–10. ACM (2019)

27. Ruohonen, J., Hjerppe, K., Rindell, K.: A large-scale security-oriented static analysis of Python packages in PyPI. In: 2021 18th International Conference on Privacy, Security and Trust, pp. 1–10 (2021)

28. Sadowski, C., Aftandilian, E., Eagle, A., Miller-Cushon, L., Jaspan, C.: Lessons from building static analysis tools at Google. Commun. ACM **61**(4), 58–66 (2018)

29. Snell, C., Lee, J., Xu, K., Kumar, A.: Scaling LLM test-time compute optimally can be more effective than scaling model parameters (2024). https://arxiv.org/abs/2408.03314

30. Song, Y., Wang, T., Cai, P., Mondal, S.K., Sahoo, J.P.: A comprehensive survey of few-shot learning: evolution, applications, challenges, and opportunities. ACM Comput. Surv. **55**(13s), 1–40 (2023)

31. Sun, Y., et al.: GPTScan: detecting logic vulnerabilities in smart contracts by combining GPT with program analysis. In: Proceedings of the IEEE/ACM 46th International Conference on Software Engineering, pp. 1–13. ACM (2024)

Security

A Cross-Domain Data Sharing Scheme Based on Federated Blockchain

Honglin Mao, Jie Zhang, Yao Zhang$^{(\boxtimes)}$, and Xiaohong Li$^{(\boxtimes)}$

College of Intelligence and Computing, Tianjin University, Tianjin 300350, China
{zzyy,xiaohongli}@tju.edu.cn

Abstract. Cross-domain data sharing involves exchanging or providing access to data between different systems or individuals, which is critical in domains such as healthcare, transportation, and data marketplaces. While blockchain technology addresses the single-point-of-failure issue inherent in cloud servers for cross-domain data sharing, existing blockchain-based methods face challenges such as complex permission management, high storage costs, and trust issues. To address these challenges, we propose a federated blockchain based cross-domain data sharing scheme that simplifies permission management by reducing the number of entities and specifying access rules, and decreases storage overhead through encrypted indexing. Our approach enhances trust by improving the ring signature algorithm to meet requirements for anonymity and accountability in sensitive data sharing. Specifically, the enhanced ring signature algorithm provides anonymous authentication and tamper-proof signatures while incorporating traceability features to balance privacy protection with security auditing. This scheme effectively resolves the challenges of privilege management, storage costs, trust crises, privacy protection, and security auditing in medical data sharing scenarios. Formal security proofs, performance analysis, and experimental results validate the scheme's security, efficiency, and feasibility. Experimental data shows a reduction in signing time by at least 30% and a 14% decrease in verification time.

Keywords: Ring signature · Cross-domain Data Sharing · Privacy protection · Signature traceability · Blockchain

1 Introduction

Cross-domain data sharing refers to the exchange and integration of data across various domains, departments, systems, or organizations. It has become an essential mechanism for collaboration and information exchange, particularly in fields such as healthcare [36]. By enabling the integration of data from diverse domains, cross-domain data sharing not only ensures data integrity but also enhances data utilization efficiency, prevents information silos, and improves system transparency and real-time capabilities [21]. Despite its benefits, security remains a

---

H. Mao and J. Zhang—Contributed equally to this work.

© The Author(s), under exclusive license to Springer Nature Switzerland AG 2026
P. Rümmer and Z. Wu (Eds.): TASE 2025, LNCS 15841, pp. 285–302, 2026.
https://doi.org/10.1007/978-3-031-98208-8_17

critical concern in cross-domain data sharing, as it is necessary to safeguard data integrity, ensure compliance, and protect user privacy. Specifically, inter-domain authentication plays a vital role in securing data exchanges [10].

While several studies have proposed cloud-based cross-domain data sharing schemes that provide centralized platforms for data exchange, these solutions often face significant challenges, such as trust crises. Specifically, issues such as inefficiency and privacy leakage have been highlighted in practical applications [4], which negatively affect system performance and resource utilization [29]. With the rise of cryptographic techniques, cloud-based data sharing solutions leveraging Public Key Infrastructure (PKI) have been introduced. However, these schemes encounter difficulties, including the complexity of certificate management [22] and vulnerability to a single point of failure [17]. As a result, innovative technological solutions are essential to address these limitations, and recent schemes have focused on mitigating the single point of failure issue through novel computing paradigms [9].

Blockchain-based cross-domain data-sharing schemes utilize decentralized networks, consensus mechanisms, and tamper-proof ledgers to enable trustless data verification without central authorities [5,28]. Smart contracts and transparency ensure data integrity, auditability, and secure exchange. However, challenges include: **Challenge 1:** complex decentralized privilege management due to conflicting multi-node authentication and access control needs; **Challenge 2:** scalability issues from ledger replication, increasing latency and storage costs; and **Challenge 3:** privacy-audit trade-offs, where transparency exposes sensitive metadata, risking anonymity [14]. These issues can lead to data leaks and affect healthcare data availability [20,31].

To address these issues, we propose a federated blockchain-based scheme using Hyperledger Fabric to simplify access control for **Challenge 1**, store encrypted data indices to address **Challenge 2**, and introduce a traceable ring signature (TRS) algorithm for **Challenge 3**, ensuring anonymity and traceability [16]. Our TRS algorithm reduces signing time by 30% and verification time by 14%, enhancing privacy and efficiency in medical data sharing.

This paper presents four key contributions: (1) We propose a federated blockchain-based cross-domain data sharing scheme that enhances interoperability and standardization. It ensures tamper-resistance, integrity, and transparency with traceable, auditable data flow and simplified rights management. (2) We design an improved traceable ring signature (TRS) algorithm, integrating it into the scheme to provide anonymity, unforgeability, and auditability. An authority node balances privacy and accountability by enabling signer tracing while preserving conditional anonymity. (3) We conduct rigorous security proofs, verifying anonymity, unforgeability, and traceability in medical data sharing scenarios. (4) Benchmark analysis shows our TRS achieves 30% faster signing and 14% lower verification latency compared to existing ring signatures, uniquely supporting authorized identity tracing for regulatory compliance.

2   Preliminaries

2.1   Ring Signature

Ring signatures (RS), pioneered by Rivest, Shamir, and Tauman [25], deliver cryptographic anonymity, unforgeability, and decentralized authentication [2] by eliminating centralized authorities through public key-based signing [7]. While foundational in systems like Monero [23] and enhanced via secure data-sharing variants [1,6,8,12,18,32,33,35], conventional RS suffers from accountability deficits due to untraceable signers. Fujisaki et al.'s traceable RS (TRS) [11] overcomes this through conditional anonymity—preserving privacy while embedding authorized traceability to resolve transaction ambiguity [27]—enabling auditable applications in healthcare, smart grids, and IoT [15,16,24,26] via privacy-audit equilibrium.

The basic structure of a ring signature scheme consists of three sub-algorithms: $Setup()$, $Sign()$, and $Verify()$. These sub-algorithms are detailed as follows:

- $Setup(1^\lambda) \rightarrow PP$: Initialization algorithm. Given the security parameter λ, this algorithm generates the public parameter PP along with the public-private key pair (pk, sk), where pk represents the user's public key and sk represents the user's private key.
- $Sign(m, sk, L) \rightarrow \sigma$: Signature algorithm. Given a message m, the signer uses their private key sk and the public key set L to generate the signature σ. Here, $L = \{PK_1, ..., PK_n\}$ denotes the set of public keys of the ring members, where n represents the number of users in the ring.
- $Verify(\sigma, m, L) \rightarrow True/False$: Signature verification algorithm. Given a message m, the verifier checks the validity of the signature σ against the public key set L, and outputs a boolean result indicating whether the verification succeeded $True$ or failed $False$.

Traceable ring signatures extend the basic scheme by adding an additional sub-algorithm:

- $Trace(\sigma, m, IDs, L) \rightarrow s$: Signature tracing algorithm. Given a message m, the verifier checks the signature σ against the public key set L and the identity set IDs, and outputs the index of the signer s.

2.2   Bilinear Mapping

Definition 1. *(Bilinear Mapping): Let q be a large prime. Consider a q-order additive cyclic group G_1, along with a q-order multiplicative cyclic group G_T. A mapping $e : G_1 \times G_1 \rightarrow G_T$ is said to be bilinear if it satisfies the following properties:*

1) Bilinearity: $\forall P_1, P_2, Q_1 \in G_1$ and $\forall \phi, \varphi \in Z_q^*$, it holds that:

$$e(P_1 + P_2, Q_1) = e(P_1, Q_1)e(P_2, Q_1) \ and \ e(\phi P_1, \varphi Q_1) = e(P_1, Q_1)^{\phi\varphi}$$

2) *Non-degeneracy:* $\exists P_1 \in G_1, \exists Q_1 \in G_1$ *such that* $e(P_1, Q_1) \neq 1_{G_T}$.

3) *Computability:* $\forall P_1 \in G_1, \forall Q_1 \in G_1$, *there exists an efficient algorithm to compute* $e(P_1, Q_1)$.

On elliptic curves, the bilinear mapping continues to meet these properties.

2.3   Computational Diffie-Hellman Problem

Definition 2. *(Computational Diffie-Hellman Problem, CDHP): Given a large prime* q, *suppose* $(P, aP, bP) \in G_1$, *where* G_1 *is a cyclic group of order* q *under addition, and* $a, b \in Z_q^*$ *are unknown, compute* abP. *The success probability of solving CDHP in is given by* $Adv_{\mathcal{A}}^{CDHP}(\lambda) = Pr[\mathcal{M}(P, aP, abP) = abP]$, *where* $\mathcal{M}$ *is a probabilistic polynomial-time algorithm. For any adversary* $\mathcal{A}$, *if* $Adv_{\mathcal{A}}^{CDHP}(\lambda)$ *is negligibly small in the probability polynomial time (PPT), then CDHP does not hold.*

3   Overview of Framework

In this section, we first give a framework description of a cross-domain data sharing scheme, including notation, entities, system architecture, and then give the security attribute conventions.

3.1   System Architecture

Table 1. Notations.

Symbol	Description
λ	Security Parameters
q	A Large Prime
G_1, G_T	Cyclic Groups of Order q
e	Bilinear Mapping $e : G_1 \times G_1 \to G_T$
P, Q	A Generator/Element in G_1
H_1, H_2	Secure Cryptographic Hash Functions
(y, S)	Private/Public Key Pairs of AN
z, P_{pub}	Master Key, Master Public Key
PP	System Parameters
$ABE.Enc, ABE.Dec$	CP-ABE Encryption/Decryption Indexing Operations
ID, k_{ID}	User Identification, Partial Private Key
v, Y_{ID}	User Secret Value, User Partial Public Key
(x, X)	User's Private/Public Key Pair
M	EHR Content
IDs	ID Collection
L	Public Key Collection
σ, M'	Signature, Short Encrypted Hash Index for EHR

We present the system architecture of the cross-domain data sharing scheme as illustrated in Fig. 1. The scheme involves five different types of entities:

1. **AN (Authority Node)**: AN is a distributed blockchain node responsible for system initialization, user identity management, signature traceability, and accountability for failed verifications.
2. **KGC (Key Generation Center)**: KGC is responsible for key distribution, generating a master key, public key, and providing partial private keys and identity IDs to users.
3. **DU (Data User)**: DU is an entity involved in generating, signing, uploading, and accessing Electronic Health Records (EHR), interacting with AN for authorization and permissions.
4. **EN (Entity Node)**: EN handles signature uploading and verification, storing data on the blockchain, generating EHR indexes, and comparing them to the blockchain for verification.
5. **Blockchain**: A platform that securely stores signatures, manages transactions, and records operations. Nodes like AN, KGC, and EN enable distributed key generation, data sharing, and auditing. All data access and modifications are logged, ensuring immutability and traceability of unauthorized actions, enhancing accountability.

This framework integrates Hyperledger Fabric's PBFT-based permissioned architecture with CP-ABE-enhanced encryption for Byzantine fault-tolerant EHR sharing. Fabric's modular design implements PBFT consensus to achieve 2/3 node integrity thresholds, coupled with multi-channel isolation for domain-specific transactional confidentiality. The v2.0+ private state databases enforce node authorization through smart contracts, while inspired by CP-ABE schemes [13,34] to bind EHRs with dynamic attribute policies—decryption requires both PBFT-validated ledger permissions and cryptographically proven credentials (Table 1). This dual-layer approach (PBFT for Byzantine resilience, CP-ABE for fine-grained access) guarantees tamper-evident auditability and policy-driven data sovereignty in federated healthcare ecosystems.

As illustrated in Fig. 1, to provide a clearer understanding of our proposed scheme, we detail the interaction process of each entity. Prior to these interactions, an initialization phase is required. This phase involves generating the system parameters PP, the master key and master public key, and the DU's identity ID along with its private/public key pair (x, X). The subsequent interaction processes are outlined as follows:

- **Publishing Access Rules**: To mitigate the complexity of permission management, all DUs negotiate and publish sharing rules and access policies—including DU identity, domain information, and data operations—on the blockchain platform, thereby enhancing transparency, preventing tampering, and streamlining permission allocation and management.
- **Data Sharing**: In sharing Electronic Health Records (EHRs), the solution uses traceable ring signature (TRS) technology to ensure data anonymity,

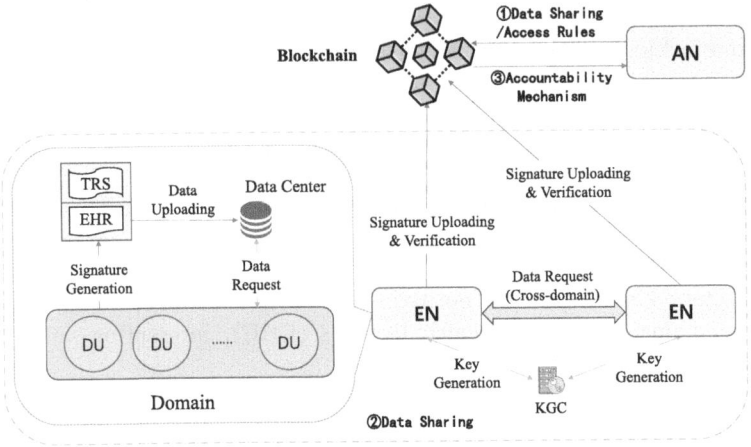

Fig. 1. Overview of Our Approach

while allowing traceability of the signer when needed, balancing privacy and security auditing. The EHR content is denoted as M, and DU generates a signature σ for M, which is verified by EN. To reduce blockchain storage and computation, EN stores M in a data center and uploads the encrypted index M' of the EHR and σ to the blockchain after validation. Access to the EHR is granted only after legitimate permission is verified. The data and signatures are standardized for inter-domain interoperability and compatibility.

– **Accountability Mechanism**: To ensure auditability, AN can identify the real signer from the signature σ. AN then generates an accountability report, which is sent to the relevant parties, holding the signer accountable. This mechanism not only ensures transparency of system operations but also enhances the security and trustworthiness of the system.

3.2 Security Attribute Convention

In this blockchain-based healthcare data sharing scenario, it is crucial to design traceable ring signature algorithms that enable accountability without requiring interaction between DUs during sensitive data generation. Additionally, AN should be able to identify the actual signer without interacting with the signer or the signature verifier. We analyze the security requirements of this scenario by defining 3 core properties: anonymity, non-tamperability, and traceability. We assume that the scheme adheres to the security guarantees provided by CDHP. To facilitate the proof of these security properties in subsequent sections, we introduce the following three types of oracles:

– **Oracle-Random(O_R)**: Outputs a random value.
– **Oracle-Corruption(O_C)**: Takes a public key pk_i as input and returns the corresponding private key sk_i.

- **Oracle-Signature(O_S):** Takes data m as input and returns a signature σ.

The scheme must satisfy the following security properties:

- **Anonymity:** The scheme satisfies anonymity if, for any adversary, given a set of identities $IDs = \{ID_1, ID_2, \ldots, ID_n\}$, with all DUs $ID_i \in IDs$, the probability of identifying the true signer from a signature σ is negligible, i.e., at most $1/n$.
- **Unforgeability:** The scheme satisfies unforgeability if, for any probabilistic polynomial-time (PPT) adversary $\mathcal{A}$, the probability of successfully tampering with a valid signature is negligible.
- **Traceability:** The scheme satisfies traceability if, for any $ID_i \in IDs$ within any ring, the probability of identifying the signer from the signature σ is negligible for any entity without AN privileges.
- **Auditability:** After obtaining the traceability results, AN checks and evaluates the signature behavior to ensure compliance with security and privacy policies, detect any violations, and confirm adherence to system standards.
- **Accountability:** After identifying the signer, AN reviews the signature behavior for compliance and enforces accountability according to regulations or system specifications, ensuring system security and transparency.

4 Methodology

In this section, we present the implementation of the proposed method based on the previously described framework. This includes defining access rules, data sharing processes with a detailed signature algorithm, and outlining the accountability mechanism. Before the implementation can proceed, the following initialization steps are required.

The cryptographic system initialization proceeds as follows: define security parameter λ and prime q, then instantiate hash functions $H_1 : \{0,1\}^* \to \mathbb{Z}_q^*$ and $H_2 : \{0,1\}^* \to G_1$. AN deploys blockchain-based consensus with traceability smart contracts, selecting private key $y \in \mathbb{Z}_q^*$ to compute public key $S = yP$. The KGC generates master key z and public key P_{pub}, while publishing system parameters $PP = \{\lambda, G_1, G_T, P, Q, e, H_1, H_2, S, P_{\text{pub}}\}$ on-chain. Private keys remain confidential through $ABE.Enc/Dec$ algorithms. For each user ID: (1) compute partial private key $k_{ID} = z + H_1(ID)$; (2) generate secret v to derive private key $x = vk_{ID}$; (3) calculate public key $X = vY_{ID}$ where $Y_{ID} = P_{\text{pub}} + H_1(ID)P$. Following initialization, all users possess certified key pairs (x, X), enabling execution of subsequent protocols (detailed in the next 3 subsections).

4.1 Publishing Access Rules

This subsection describes the process of defining and enforcing access rules for private data sharing, which consists of two main steps:

1. **Access Rules and Policy Definition**: All DUs define and publish access control rules and data-sharing policies on the blockchain. These policies specify the conditions under which specific private data can be accessed and by whom, thereby ensuring transparency and accountability.
2. **License Issuance**: AN checks if the user has permission to perform an operation on the data. If allowed, the EN issues a license, written as $lic = \{seq_l, X_s, op, t_r\}$. Here, seq_l is the license sequence number, X_s is the user identifier, op is the operation type, and t_r is the issuance timestamp. This license proves the user's access rights and allows secure data interaction.

4.2 Data Sharing

When a patient visits a doctor, medical data is generated, triggering DU (acting as both doctor and data owner) to sign the EHR. AN first verifies the license lic to authenticate DU's signing authority. Upon successful validation, DU generates the EHR and initiates the signature phase as follows: let s denote DU's serial number and n represent the ring length, then proceed with the steps outlined below:

1. Compute $HQ_s = H_2(ID_s)$, and randomly select $\phi \in \mathbb{Z}_q^*$ and compute $\Phi = \phi P$.
2. For each $j = 1, 2, \ldots, n$ with $j \neq s$, randomly select $u_j \leftarrow \mathbb{Z}_q^*$ and compute $U_j = u_j P$. Then compute $h_j = H_1(L, M, U_j, \Phi)$.
3. Compute $V = v_s Q$, $\tau = H_1(L, M, V)$, $a_s = H_1(L, \Phi)$. Finally, compute $\Theta = (\tau + a_s)Q$.
4. Randomly select $\forall T_1, T_2, \ldots, T_n \in G_1$ and compute $Y_s = v_s(S + HQ_s)$, $T_R = v_s \sum_{i=1}^{n} T_i$, and $T_s = (a_s + c_s)T_R$, where $c_s = H_1(ID_s)$. Then randomly select $\forall \delta \leftarrow \mathbb{Z}_q^*$ and compute $U_s = \delta X_s - \sum_{j \neq s}(U_j + h_j X_j)$, where $h_j = H_1(L, M, U_j, \Phi)$, $j = 1, 2, \ldots, n$. Finally, compute $W = (h_s + \delta)\Theta$ and $Z = x_s W$, where $h_s = H_1(L, M, U_s, \Phi)$.
5. The final generated signature is $\sigma = (V, U_1, U_2, \ldots, U_n, Z, \Phi, T_1, T_2, \ldots, T_n, T_s, Y_s)$.

After the signature is generated, the following operations are performed:

1. DU sends the tuple (M, σ) to AN for storage, and subsequently transmits (M, σ) to its EN, which verifies the validity of σ as follows:
   (a) Compute $\tau = H_1(L, M, V)$, $a_s = H_1(L, \Phi)$, and $\Theta = (\tau + a_s)Q$.
   (b) For each $j = 1, 2, \ldots, n$, compute $h_j = H_1(L, M, U_j, \Phi)$, and then verify the equation $e(P, Z) = e(\sum_{j=1}^{n}(U_j + h_j X_j), \Theta)$.
   (c) If the equation is valid, then the EHR content M and the signature σ are deemed valid, and the process continues. Otherwise, the result is notified to DU, and a traceability request is sent to AN.

2. EN stores M within the data center, generates a short cryptographic index $M' = \text{ABE.Enc}(M)$ for M, where M' can be decrypted by $ABE.Dec$, and uploads (M', σ) to the blockchain.

When DU sends a request to EN along with the associated EHR number, the request can pertain to two types of data sharing processes: intra-domain and cross-domain. These correspond to intra-domain data sharing and cross-domain data sharing, respectively. The permission verification and data sharing process is described as follows:

1. EN verifies whether DU possesses the necessary access rights to the requested data, as stipulated by the license lic. If DU has the appropriate privileges, the process continues to the next step. Otherwise, the process terminates.
2. EN retrieves the relevant EHR data from its local server. Let the EHR data be denoted as M and the corresponding blockchain-stored data as M'. If $M' = ABE.Enc(M)$, EN extracts the tuple (M', σ) and proceeds to the next step. If this condition is not met, EN reports a verification failure to DU and forwards an accountability request to AN, as detailed in Sect. 4.3. Upon successful verification, EN shares the EHR data M with DU.

This process ensures the secure and authorized sharing of medical data, safeguarding both intra-domain and cross-domain data exchanges.

4.3 Accountability Mechanism

In the event of a signature verification failure or other medical-related incidents, DU forwards a tuple (M, σ) and an accountability request to AN. AN subsequently invokes a smart contract to identify the specific signer responsible for the incident using a traceability algorithm, thereby ensuring accountability. The process is outlined as follows:

1. AN receives the tuple (M, σ), extracts the signature σ, and computes $\Gamma = \sum_{i=1}^{n} T_i$, where Γ represents the aggregation of the values T_i.
2. For each $i \in \{1, 2, \ldots, n\}$, AN performs the following computations:
   - Calculate $a_s = H_1(L, \Phi)$, and then compute $c_i = H_1(ID_i)$.
   - Determine $d_i = a_s + c_i$, and compute $\Omega = d_i Y_s$, where Y_s is a public value associated with the signer.
   - AN performs signature validation through verification of the pairing equation $e(T_s, S + HQ_i) = e(\Gamma, \Omega)$, enabling signer traceability by identifying the accountable signer s from valid cryptographic commitments.
3. Based on the outcome of the signature trace, AN generates an accountability report and forwards it to the identified signer s.

5 Security Proof

In this section, we prove the security of the 3 security properties of anonymity, non-tamperability, and traceability, using the random Oracle and CDHP assumptions. The proof results show that our scheme is secure.

5.1 Correctness of Signature

Theorem 1. *Correctness of the signature is satisfied if AN is completely trust-worthy and irreplaceable by any adversary $\mathcal{A}$, KGC is able to generate the master key and the master public key honestly, and DU as well as EN are able to execute the process correctly.*

Proof. Correctness needs to be satisfied for signature verification, as shown in the following proof process:

$$e\left(\sum_{j=1}^{n}(U_j + h_j X_j), \Theta\right) = e\left(\delta X_s - U_s + U_s + h_s X_s, \Theta\right) = e\left((\delta + h_s)X_s, \Theta\right)$$

$$= e\left(v_s(\delta + h_s)Y_s, \Theta\right) = e\left(v_s(\delta + h_s)(z + c_s)P, \Theta\right)$$

$$= e(x_s P, W) = e(P, x_s W) = e(P, Z)$$

As above, the signature correctness can be verified.   □

5.2 Anonymity

Theorem 2. *In our scheme, for any PPT adversary $\mathcal{A}$, the information and identities of DUs cannot be exposed.*

Proof. Assuming that DUs, EN, AN, and KGC behave honestly, they can be classified as follows. The challenger $\mathcal{C}$ initializes the system, computes the system's public parameters, and returns them to the adversary $\mathcal{A}$.

In the initialization phase, the following two scenarios need to be discussed:

1. **Master Key Generation**: The master key is a random number, and the master public key is a random point on the elliptic curve group G_1. The probability of a third party guessing the master key and the master public key is negligible.

2. **User Information Generation**: Each user's ID is represented as a randomly generated bit string, and the IDs of different doctors are unique. The probability of guessing a private key is negligible since c_i is a random number generated by the hash function, and v_i is a random number chosen by the doctor. The public key, similarly, is a random point on G_1.

During the signing phase, with n ring members, let V and $U_1, U_2, \ldots, U_n$ be random points on G_1, and δ, a_s random numbers generated by the signer. With H_1 as a hash function and Φ a random point on G_1, h_j (for $j = 1, 2, \ldots, n$) ensures U_s reveals no signer information. Per CDHP, these values are non-reversible. In the EHR acquisition phase, signature verification uses blockchain-stored data, with encrypted transaction data and addresses concealing the signer's identity.

In conclusion, given ring size n, the probability of adversary $\mathcal{A}$ guessing the signer is at most $1/n$. With large n, this probability is negligible, ensuring the anonymity of data users and participants.   □

5.3   Non-tamperability

Theorem 3. *For any PPT adversary $\mathcal{A}$, the probability of a signature being forged is negligible if CDHP holds.*

Proof. Let the adversary be denoted as $\mathcal{A}$ and the challenger as $\mathcal{C}$. The game is defined as solving CDHP. Given a random instance $(P, P_1 = aP, P_2 = bP) \in G_1^3$, where $a, b \in \mathbb{Z}_q^*$ are unknown to $\mathcal{C}$, $\mathcal{A}$ attempts to forge a valid signature. $\mathcal{C}$ will use $\mathcal{A}$'s forgery to compute abP. Assume there exists a user's public key that satisfies the relation $X_j = aP$, where j is the index of DU.

Initialization: The challenger $\mathcal{C}$ runs the algorithm to obtain the system parameters $PP = \{\lambda, G_1, G_T, P, Q, e, H_1, H_2, S\}$ and randomly chooses a value $z \in \mathbb{Z}_q^*$ as the master key, then computes the master public key $P_{\text{pub}} = zP$.

- O_C Query: If $i \neq j$, $\mathcal{C}$ answers the value $X_i \in G_1$ of $\mathcal{A}$'s public key. Otherwise, $\mathcal{C}$ returns $X_j = aP$ to the adversary $\mathcal{A}$.
- O_R Query: $\mathcal{C}$ generates a list L_h, which is initialized to be empty. Once $\mathcal{C}$ receives a query, it verifies the existence of the tuple (ID_i, c_i, v_i, X_i) in L_h, where ID_i is the identity, $c_i = H_1(ID_i)$, and v_i is the secret value. If present, $\mathcal{C}$ responds using such a record. Otherwise, $\mathcal{C}$ queries L_h to obtain a tuple (ID_i, c_i, v_i, X_i) and performs the following:
  - If $i = j$, $\mathcal{C}$ selects a value $v_i \in \mathbb{Z}_q^*$, computes the partial public key $Y_i = P_{\text{pub}} + H_1(ID_i)P$, and finally computes the public key $X_i = v_i Y_i$. $\mathcal{C}$ then adds the tuple (ID_i, c_i, v_i, X_i) to L_h.
  - Otherwise, $\mathcal{C}$ reselects a v_i value.
- O_C Query: If $i \neq j$, $\mathcal{C}$ returns the private key x_i to user i; otherwise, it terminates with $\perp$.
- Signature O_S Query:
  - Use O_C query: If $i \neq j$, $\mathcal{C}$ runs and knows the secret value v_i. Otherwise, $\mathcal{C}$ randomly chooses $\forall v \leftarrow \mathbb{Z}_q^*$ and computes $V = vQ$, where v represents the secret value.
  - Using O_R query: $\mathcal{C}$ computes $\tau = H_1(L, M, V)$ and $a_s = H_1(L, \Phi)$. Finally, $\mathcal{C}$ computes $\Theta = (\tau + a_s)Q$. Assume $\Theta = bP$. Then $\mathcal{C}$ randomly selects $\forall u_i \leftarrow \mathbb{Z}_q^*$ and computes $U_i = u_i P$. Subsequently, $\mathcal{C}$ computes $h_i = H_1(L, M, U_i, \Phi)$.
  - If $i = j$, $\mathcal{C}$ computes $HQ_i = H_2(ID_i)$.
  - For $i = j$, $\mathcal{C}$ randomly selects $\forall \delta \leftarrow \mathbb{Z}_q^*$ and computes $U_j = \delta X_j - \sum_{i \neq j}(U_i + h_i X_i)$, where $h_j = H_1(L, M, U_j, \Phi)$ and X_j is the public key of user j, $j = 1, 2, \ldots, n$. If the tuple $(L, M, U_j, \Phi, \hat{h}_j)$ exists in the list L_s (which is initialized to be empty) and j exists such that $h_j \neq \hat{h}_j$, return the signature O_S query, otherwise proceed to the next step.
  - $\mathcal{C}$ randomly selects $\forall T_1, T_2, \ldots, T_n \in G_1$, computes $Y_j = v_j(S + HQ_j)$, $T_R = v_j \sum_{i=1}^{n} T_i$, and finally computes $T_s = (a_s + c_j)T_R$, where $c_j = H_1(ID_j)$. Then $\mathcal{C}$ computes $W = (h_j + \delta)\Theta$, $Z = x_j W$, where $h_j = H_1(L, M, U_j, \Phi)$.

If $\mathcal{A}$ can effectively tamper with a valid signature

$$\sigma^* = (V^*, U_1, U_2, \ldots, U_n, Z^*, \Phi^*, T_1, T_2, \ldots, T_n, T_s^*, Y_s^*)$$

on the tuple (L^*, M^*, Φ^*), $\mathcal{A}$ forges another valid signature as follow:

$$\hat{\sigma}^* = (\hat{V}^*, U_1, U_2, \ldots, U_n, \hat{Z}^*, \hat{\Phi}^*, T_1, T_2, \ldots, T_n, \hat{T}_s^*, \hat{Y}_s^*)$$

According to the signature bifurcation theorem, the probability of the following events is non-negligible: if $i = j$, then $h_j^* \neq \hat{h}_j^*$; if $i \neq j$, then $h_i^* = \hat{h}_i^*$. Thus, the following equation is introduced:

$$e(P, Z^*) = e\left(\sum_{i=1}^{n}(U_i + h_i^* X_i), \Theta\right) \stackrel{?}{=} e(P, \hat{Z}^*) = e\left(\sum_{i=1}^{n}(U_i + \hat{h}_i^* X_i), \Theta\right) \quad (1)$$

Subtracting from Eq. (2) gives:

$$e(P, Z^* - \hat{Z}^*) = e(a(h_j^* - \hat{h}_j^*)P, \Theta) = e(P, a(h_j^* - \hat{h}_j^*)(\tau + a_s)Q) \quad (2)$$

Thus, $a(h_j^* - \hat{h}_j^*)bP = Z^* - \hat{Z}^*$.

This leads to $abP = (Z^* - \hat{Z}^*)(h_j^* - \hat{h}_j^*)^{-1}$.

Final Conclusion: $\mathcal{A}$ solves CDHP with non-negligible probability. Therefore, under the CDHP assumption, our scheme satisfies unforgeability. □

5.4   Auditability and Accountability

Theorem 4. *Our protocol enables tracing the real signer s by AN, which exclusively retains this capability. To verify a signature's authenticity, confirming the equation $e(T', Q + HQ_s) = e(\Gamma, \Omega)$ is essential.*

Proof. Once the actual signer s is identified, the following verification steps occur:

$$e(T', Q+HQ_s) = e((a_s+c_s)T_R, Q+HQ_s) = e(d_s T_R, Q+HQ_s)$$

$$= e\left(d_s v_s \sum_{i=1}^{n} T_i, Q+HQ_s\right) = e(d_s v_s \Gamma, Q+HQ_s)$$

$$= e(d_s \Gamma, v_s(Q+HQ_s)) = e(d_s \Gamma, Y') = e(\Gamma, d_s Y') = e(\Gamma, \Omega)$$

As above, the signature auditability and accountability can be verified. □

5.5   Other Security Features

- **Data integrity**: Maintaining data integrity is crucial. During signature verification, the equation $e(P, Z) = e(\sum_{j=1}^{n}(U_j + h_j X_j), \Theta)$ is pivotal. Any change in M alters h_j, invalidating the equation and causing verification to fail. Uploading the signature and hash index of EHR reduces the risk of tampering (Table 2).

- **Legitimacy of operation**: Ensuring user legitimacy is essential for secure data sharing. Signers must be authenticated, requiring appropriate licenses.
- **On-Blockchain traceability**: Traceability within the blockchain is crucial for accountability. Transactions must execute without interference, verified through unanimous agreement among network nodes. This decentralized validation mitigates the risk of a single point of failure.
- **Immutability**: The blockchain's immutability is integral to security. Consensus among nodes confirms block validity, making tampering difficult. Any modification disrupts the blockchain's integrity.
- **Verifiability**: Blockchain transparency allows comprehensive verification of transactions. Each transaction can be traced through the chain, facilitating signature validation using the ring signature mechanism.

6 Performance Analysis

6.1 Comparison of Ring Signature Schemes

Table 2. Comparison of different ring signature schemes, and "#" represents the baseline schemes

#	Architecture	Type of Ring Signature	ECC
[3]	Cloud Server	Certificateless, Untraceable	Pairing
[35]	Blockchain	Untraceable	Pairing
[30]	Blockchain	Untraceable	No Pairing
[15]	Blockchain	Certificateless, Traceable	Pairing
[19]	Web-based	Untraceable	Pairing
Ours	Federated Blockchain	Certificateless, Traceable	Pairing

We compared the ring signature scheme proposed in this paper with several existing schemes [3,15,19,30,35], highlighting the significant advantages of our approach. Our scheme leverages a federated blockchain architecture that offers superior security and control in restricted environments compared to cloud servers [3], web-based approaches [19], or other blockchains [30]; notably, its authentication-free, traceable ring signature type excels in data traceability. While the scheme in [15] also supports traceability, our approach—combined with the federated blockchain—significantly enhances data management and auditing efficiency, ensuring data integrity and transparency, and demonstrates superior performance (see Sect. 6.2 for details). In comparison to ring signature schemes lacking traceability [19,30], our scheme provides robust data traceability and auditing capabilities while maintaining privacy protection, and thus stands out in terms of architectural design, traceability, and bilinear pairing support, making it particularly suitable for applications requiring high security and strict regulatory compliance.

6.2   Experimental Design and Results

Table 3. Comparison of time overhead of different algorithms

#	Signing	Verification	Tracing
[15]	$(4n-1)T_{mp} + nT_h$	$nT_{mp}+2T_{bp}+3T_{pr}+nT_h$	$(3n-1)T_{mp}+(2+2n)T_{bp}$
[19]	$(2n+2)T_{mp}+2nT_h+2T_{pr}$	$2nT_{mp}+4T_{bp}+4T_{pr}+2nT_h$	—
Ours	$(n+8)T_{mp} + (n+3)T_h$	$(n+1)T_{mp}+2T_{bp}+T_{pr}+(n+2)T_h$	$nT_{mp}+(n+1)T_h+2nT_{bp}$

This section evaluates the computational overhead and performance of various bilinear pairing ring signature schemes, including those in [15] and [19], which involve two roles. We compare these schemes against our proposed method and also analyze blockchain performance. The key research questions explored in this section include:

- **RQ1:** How does the computational overhead of our ring signature algorithm compare to other schemes?
- **RQ2:** How does the overall performance of our ring signature algorithm compare to other schemes?
- **RQ3:** What are the blockchain platform's key performance metrics, such as CPU usage and memory?

Experimental Environment: To evaluate the performance of the signature algorithm, we set up a simulation environment on a Dell host running Ubuntu 22.04.3, equipped with an Intel Core i7-10700 processor and 40 GB of RAM. The environment was configured with Docker 24.0.5, Docker Compose 1.29.2, and Go 1.18.8 to deploy Hyperledger Fabric v2.2[1], utilizing the PBFT consensus protocol. Three peer nodes were deployed within the blockchain system. Additionally, we employed Hyperledger Caliper v0.4.2[2] to assess the blockchain's performance.

Comparison of Computational Overhead (RQ1): Table 3 compares the functionality and computational overhead of various ring signature schemes. Our proposed scheme shares similar signing and verification phases with others. The computational overhead for each phase is detailed in Table 3, with n representing the ring size. Assuming n users generate n individual signatures, the notations T_h, T_{mp}, T_{bp}, and T_{pr} represent the execution times for hash function mapping, scalar multiplication on G_1, bilinear pairing, and data processing (e.g., encryption/decryption), respectively.

Answer to RQ1: Our ring signature algorithm, as shown in Table 3, is generally more efficient than [19] in signing and verification time, requiring fewer computational operations. Compared to [15], it offers similar performance in signing and verification but with lower computational overhead in tracing operations.

---

[1] https://github.com/hyperledger/fabric.
[2] https://github.com/hyperledger/caliper.

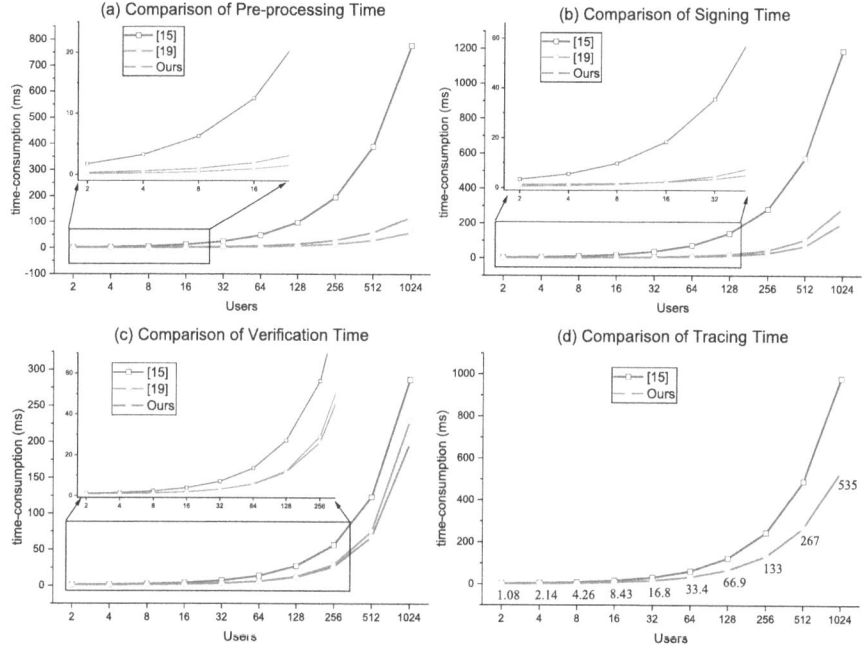

Fig. 2. Performance Comparison

Experimental Design and Results (RQ2): We evaluated our cryptographic framework by measuring the execution times of signature algorithms and encryption operations using Go's testing framework on 1,000 anonymized 1KB medical data entries[3] processed on the bn254 elliptic curve, ensuring 128-bit security with a 254-bit base domain size. The results in Figs. 2 show the time cost for preprocessing in (a), signature generation in (b), verification in (c), and tracing in (d) for ring sizes n from 2 to 1024.

Answer to RQ2: Our ring signature algorithm outperforms others, requiring master key computations during initialization, leading to a slightly longer setup time compared to [19]. However, it achieves 30% faster signature generation than [19] and an 83% reduction compared to [15]. Verification is 14% quicker than [15] and 31% quicker than [19], maintaining efficiency with added traceability through optimized hash functions, bilinear mappings, and data processing.

Blockchain Throughput Performance (RQ3): In our blockchain system, we deployed CA nodes within the AN, created a channel, and generated blocks. ENs were set up in Org0 and Org1, with DUs connected to peer0 and peer1. Smart contracts were installed on ENs and executed via CLI. We evaluated performance for signing, verification, and tracing, compared to BASIC. Averaged

---

[3] Due to privacy concerns and ethical considerations, the raw data cannot be shared publicly.

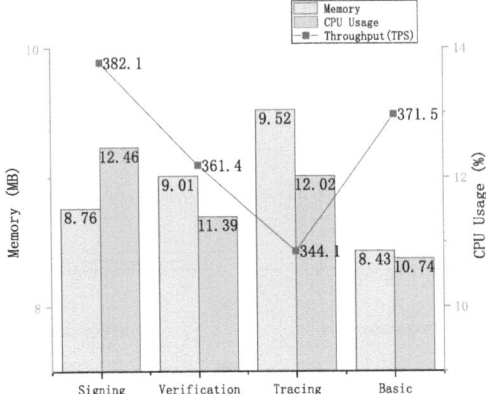

Fig. 3. Blockchain Performance

over 100 iterations, results show signing at 382.1 TPS (8.76 MB memory, 12.46% CPU), verification at 361.4 TPS (9.01 MB memory, 11.39% CPU), tracing at 344.1 TPS (9.52 MB memory, 12.02% CPU), and BASIC at 371.5 TPS (8.43 MB memory, 10.74% CPU), as in Fig. 3.

Answer to RQ3: Throughput is 382.1 TPS for signing, 361.4 TPS for verification, and 344.1 TPS for tracing, with 100% transaction success. Performance overhead increases minimally with ring signatures, showing efficiency.

7   Conclusion and Outlook

This paper presents a cross-domain data sharing scheme using federated blockchain and an enhanced ring signature algorithm. Unlike traditional ring signatures, our scheme offers data integrity, conditional anonymity, traceability, auditability, and privacy protection. By incorporating authority nodes, we improve traceability and accountability while ensuring conditional anonymity. Our scheme effectively protects medical data privacy and is validated through formal analyses for suitability in medical data sharing.

Funding Information. This work is supported by the National Key R&D Program of China under Grant 2021YFF1201102.

References

1. Au, M.H., Liu, J.K., Susilo, W., Yuen, T.H.: Secure id-based linkable and revocable-iff-linked ring signature with constant-size construction. Theoret. Comput. Sci. **469**, 1–14 (2013)
2. Bender, A., Katz, J., Morselli, R.: Ring signatures: stronger definitions, and constructions without random oracles. In: Halevi, S., Rabin, T. (eds.) TCC 2006. LNCS, vol. 3876, pp. 60–79. Springer, Heidelberg (2006). https://doi.org/10.1007/11681878_4

3. Bouakkaz, S., Semchedine, F.: A certificateless ring signature scheme with batch verification for applications in vanet. J. Inf. Secur. Appl. **55**, 102669 (2020)
4. Chandersekaran, C., Simpson, W., Trice, A.: Cross-domain solutions in an era of information sharing. In: The 1st International Multi-Conference on Engineering and Technological Innovation: IMET2008, Orlando, FL, vol. 1, pp. 313–318 (2008)
5. Chen, J., Zhan, Z., He, K., Du, R., Wang, D., Liu, F.: Xauth: efficient privacy-preserving cross-domain authentication. IEEE Trans. Dependable Secure Comput. **19**(5), 3301–3311 (2021)
6. Chow, S., Lui, R., Hui, L., Yiu, S.M.: Identity based ring signature: why, how and what next. In: Chadwick, D., Zhao, G. (eds.) EuroPKI 2005. LNCS, vol. 3545, pp. 144–161. Springer, Heidelberg (2005). https://doi.org/10.1007/11533733_10
7. Chow, S.S., Yap, W.S.: Certificateless ring signatures. Cryptology ePrint Archive (2007)
8. Deng, L., Li, S., Huang, H., Jiang, Y., Ning, B.: Certificateless ring signature scheme from elliptic curve group. J. Internet Technol. **21**(3), 723–731 (2020)
9. Ezawa, Y., Kakei, S., Shiraishi, Y., Mohri, M., Morii, M.: Blockchain-based cross-domain authorization system for user-centric resource sharing. Blockchain: Res. Appl. **4**(2), 100126 (2023)
10. Fan, K., Pan, Q., Wang, J., Liu, T., Li, H., Yang, Y.: Cross-domain based data sharing scheme in cooperative edge computing. In: 2018 IEEE International Conference on Edge Computing (EDGE), pp. 87–92. IEEE (2018)
11. Fujisaki, E., Suzuki, K.: Traceable ring signature. In: International Workshop on Public Key Cryptography, pp. 181–200. Springer (2007)
12. Garjan, M.S., Kılıç, N., Cenk, M.: Supersingular isogeny-based ring signature. Int. J. Inf. Secur. Sci. **12**(1), 32–57 (2023)
13. Hong, H., Chen, D., Sun, Z.: A practical application of CP-ABE for mobile PHR system: a study on the user accountability. Springerplus **5**, 1–8 (2016)
14. Khatoon, A.: A blockchain-based smart contract system for healthcare management. Electronics **9**(1), 94 (2020)
15. Lai, C., Ma, Z., Guo, R., Zheng, D.: Secure medical data sharing scheme based on traceable ring signature and blockchain. Peer-to-Peer Netw. Appl. **15**(3), 1562–1576 (2022)
16. Li, T., Wang, H., He, D., Yu, J.: Blockchain-based privacy-preserving and rewarding private data sharing for IoT. IEEE Internet Things J. **9**(16), 15138–15149 (2022)
17. Li, Y., Liu, Q.: A comprehensive review study of cyber-attacks and cyber security; emerging trends and recent developments. Energy Rep. **7**, 8176–8186 (2021)
18. Libert, B., Ling, S., Nguyen, K., Wang, H.: Zero-knowledge arguments for lattice-based accumulators: logarithmic-size ring signatures and group signatures without trapdoors. In: Fischlin, M., Coron, J.-S. (eds.) EUROCRYPT 2016. LNCS, vol. 9666, pp. 1–31. Springer, Heidelberg (2016). https://doi.org/10.1007/978-3-662-49896-5_1
19. Lin, C.C., Chang, C.C., Zheng, Y.Z.: A ring signature based anonymity authentication scheme for group medical consultation. Symmetry **12**(12), 2009 (2020)
20. Liu, J., Wang, L., Yu, Y.: Improved security of a pairing-free certificateless aggregate signature in healthcare wireless medical sensor networks. IEEE Internet Things J. **7**(6), 5256–5266 (2020)
21. Mavrogiorgou, A., et al.: A cross-domain data marketplace for data sharing. In: Proceedings of the 2022 European Symposium on Software Engineering, pp. 72–79 (2022)

22. Millán, G.L., Pérez, M.G., Pérez, G.M., Skarmeta, A.: PKI-based trust management in inter-domain scenarios. Comput. Secur. **29**(2), 278–290 (2010)

23. Möser, M., et al.: An empirical analysis of traceability in the monero blockchain. arXiv preprint arXiv:1704.04299 (2017)

24. Perera, M.N.S., Nakamura, T., Hashimoto, M., Yokoyama, H., Cheng, C.M., Sakurai, K.: A survey on group signatures and ring signatures: Traceability vs. anonymity. Cryptography **6**(1), 3 (2022)

25. Rivest, R.L., Shamir, A., Tauman, Y.: How to Leak a Secret. In: Boyd, C. (ed.) ASIACRYPT 2001. LNCS, vol. 2248, pp. 552–565. Springer, Heidelberg (2001). https://doi.org/10.1007/3-540-45682-1_32

26. Russo, A., Anta, A.F., Vasco, M.I.G., Romano, S.P.: Chirotonia: a scalable and secure e-voting framework based on blockchains and linkable ring signatures. In: 2021 IEEE International Conference on Blockchain (Blockchain), pp. 417–424. IEEE (2021)

27. Scafuro, A., Zhang, B.: One-time traceable ring signatures. In: Bertino, E., Shulman, H., Waidner, M. (eds.) ESORICS 2021. LNCS, vol. 12973, pp. 481–500. Springer, Cham (2021). https://doi.org/10.1007/978-3-030-88428-4_24

28. Shen, M., et al.: Blockchain-assisted secure device authentication for cross-domain industrial IoT. IEEE J. Sel. Areas Commun. **38**(5), 942–954 (2020)

29. Singh, P., Masud, M., Hossain, M.S., Kaur, A.: Cross-domain secure data sharing using blockchain for industrial IoT. J. Parallel Distrib. Comput. **156**, 176–184 (2021)

30. Singh, S., Satish, D., Lakshmi, S.R.: Ring signature and improved multi-transaction mode consortium blockchain-based private information retrieval for privacy-preserving smart parking system. Int. J. Commun Syst **34**(14), e4911 (2021)

31. Sun, J., Fang, Y.: Cross-domain data sharing in distributed electronic health record systems. IEEE Trans. Parallel Distrib. Syst. **21**(6), 754–764 (2009)

32. Sun, S.-F., Au, M.H., Liu, J.K., Yuen, T.H.: RingCT 2.0: a compact accumulator-based (linkable ring signature) protocol for blockchain cryptocurrency monero. In: Foley, S.N., Gollmann, D., Snekkenes, E. (eds.) ESORICS 2017. LNCS, vol. 10493, pp. 456–474. Springer, Cham (2017). https://doi.org/10.1007/978-3-319-66399-9_25

33. Tian, M., Zhang, Y., Zhu, Y., Wang, L., Xiang, Y.: DIVRS: data integrity verification based on ring signature in cloud storage. Comput. Secur. **124**, 103002 (2023)

34. Wang, S., et al.: A fast CP-ABE system for cyber-physical security and privacy in mobile healthcare network. IEEE Trans. Ind. Appl. **56**(4), 4467–4477 (2020)

35. Wang, Z., Fan, J.: Flexible threshold ring signature in chronological order for privacy protection in edge computing. IEEE Trans. Cloud Comput. **10**(2), 1253–1261 (2020)

36. Xiao, Z., et al.: Emrshare: a cross-organizational medical data sharing and management framework using permissioned blockchain. In: 2018 IEEE 24th International Conference on Parallel and Distributed Systems (ICPADS), pp. 998–1003. IEEE (2018)

Operational Semantics for Crystality: A Smart Contract Language for Parallel EVMs

Ziyun Xu[1], Hao Wang[2], and Meng Sun[1(✉)]

[1] School of Mathematical Sciences, Peking University, Beijing, China
{xuziyun,sunm}@pku.edu.cn
[2] International Digital Economy Academy (IDEA), Shenzhen, China
wanghao2020@idea.edu.cn

Abstract. The increasing demand for scalable blockchain has driven research into parallel execution models for smart contracts. Crystality is a novel smart contract programming language designed for parallel Ethereum Virtual Machines (EVMs), enabling fine-grained concurrency through Programmable Contract Scopes and Asynchronous Functional Relay. This paper presents the first formal structural operational semantics for Crystality, providing a rigorous framework to reason about its execution. We mechanize the syntax and semantics of Crystality in the theorem-proving assistant Coq, enabling formal verification of correctness properties. As a case study, we verify a simplified token transfer function, demonstrating the applicability of our semantics in ensuring smart contract correctness. Our work lays the foundation for formally verified parallel smart contracts, contributing to the security and scalability of blockchain systems.

Keywords: Operational Semantics · Blockchain · Smart Contract · Parallel Execution · Parallel EVMs · Coq · Formal Verification

1 Introduction

Blockchain technology has revolutionized decentralized computing by providing an immutable, transparent, and trustless execution environment [26]. At the heart of blockchain ecosystems are smart contracts-self-executing programs that automate decentralized agreements without relying on intermediaries. However, current mainstream blockchain platforms like Ethereum are built upon inherently sequential execution models, which severely limit transaction throughput and scalability [13]. As blockchain adoption grows, with increasing numbers of accounts, transactions, and decentralized applications (DApps), these execution inefficiencies create performance bottlenecks that hinder real-world usability [30].

This challenge has motivated extensive research into parallel execution mechanisms aimed at enhancing blockchain efficiency and scalability while preserving decentralization and security. Parallel Virtual Machine (Parallel VM) techniques [3,25,32,34,37] have emerged as a promising solution [2,6,11,12,16,29,

© The Author(s), under exclusive license to Springer Nature Switzerland AG 2026
P. Rümmer and Z. Wu (Eds.): TASE 2025, LNCS 15841, pp. 303–321, 2026.
https://doi.org/10.1007/978-3-031-98208-8_18

31], allowing concurrent execution of smart contracts across multiple virtual machines (VMs). While these approaches have achieved orders of magnitude improvements in transactions per second (TPS), they are constrained by three fundamental issues:

- Inefficient Concurrency Control: Optimistic concurrency control [3, 23, 25] suffers from excessive rollbacks due to contention on shared states, while pessimistic concurrency control [34, 37] incurs high overhead due to dependency analysis and locking.
- Failure to Exploit Commutativity: Most parallel execution frameworks strictly enforce block-defined transaction ordering, which disregards the commutativity of many smart contract operations, such as token transfers, voting [36], and airdrops [35], that could otherwise be executed in parallel. This limitation stems from their coarse-grained, transaction-level execution paradigm.
- Lack of Language-Level Parallelism Constructs: Smart contract languages like Solidity [9] and Move [5] operate under a shared-everything model without built-in mechanisms to express fine-grained concurrency at the state level. This limits their ability to fully exploit parallel execution opportunities.

In response to these challenges, Crystality, a novel smart contract programming model recently proposed by Wang et al. [38], introduces an approach to facilitate parallel execution across multiple EVMs. It provides a fine-grained state-level parallelism mechanism at the programming language level. Crystality introduces Programmable Contract Scopes as directives to partition contract states into independent, non-overlapping segments, and to decompose contract functions into smaller, parallelizable components based on state dependencies. This enables programmers to explicitly express state-level parallelism while allowing the underlying system to enforce asynchronous execution. Another key innovation in Crystality is Asynchronous Functional Relay, which orchestrates execution flow across multiple VMs based on data dependencies, thereby enabling non-blocking execution of commutative operations. Experimental evaluations have demonstrated that Crystality significantly improves blockchain throughput and scalability without compromising decentralization or security [38].

Despite its promising results, Crystality currently lacks a formal semantics [39], a critical prerequisite for rigorously defining program behavior, analyzing concurrency properties, and providing correctness guarantees [18], especially in high-assurance domains such as financial transactions, supply chain management, and decentralized governance. This is particularly important given its novel execution paradigm, where state partitioning, asynchronous relays, and cross-VM execution introduce intricate interactions that require precise formal treatment. A structural operational semantics [28] for Crystality would bridge the gap between its high-level programming constructs and their low-level execution semantics on parallel EVMs, ensuring Correctness-by-Construction.

While formal semantics for smart contract languages has received considerable attention, existing work has primarily focused on languages based on sequential execution models, particularly Solidity [8, 14, 15, 17, 20, 21, 24, 42, 43].

These semantics are not directly applicable to Crystality, as it introduces new execution paradigms and features that require novel formalization techniques.

In this paper, we present the first formal semantics for Crystality, making the following key contributions:

- **Structural Operational Semantics for Crystality:** We present a mathematically precise execution model for Crystality, including formal definitions of Programmable Contract Scopes and Asynchronous Functional Relay. To the best of our knowledge, this is the first formal semantics for a smart contract language explicitly designed for parallel EVMs.
- **Formalization and Verification in Coq:** We implement Crystality's core syntax and semantics in Coq, establishing a foundation for mechanized formal reasoning and verification. As a case study, we verify a simplified Crystality token transfer function, demonstrating the practical capabilities of our framework for verifying smart contract correctness.

The remainder of this paper is organized as follows: Sect. 2 provides an overview of Crystality, including its core constructs, syntax, and a motivating example. Section 3 introduces the structural operational semantics, detailing its formalization and execution rules. Section 4 presents our Coq-based formalization and verification case study. Section 5 briefly discusses related work. Section 6 concludes the paper and discusses future research directions.

2   A Primer on Crystality

Crystality is a novel parallel programming model designed for smart contracts on parallel EVMs. It allows each EVM to independently manage a portion of the ledger state and transactions, operate in parallel, and coordinate via a relay mechanism. The ledger state maps addresses to account states (key-value pairs), while transactions, as cryptographically signed messages, modify states via smart contract function calls.

Smart contracts are self-executing programs which maintain the ledger state that can be modified through function calls triggered by transactions. A smart contract comprises:

- State Variables: Key-value pairs storing contract data, such as account balances.
- Functions: Operations modifying state variables, such as transferring tokens.

Crystality facilitates fine-grained parallelism through two core mechanisms: Programmable Contract Scopes and Asynchronous Functional Relay.

2.1   Programmable Contract Scopes

Each contract variable and function is annotated with a @scope directive, defining its execution boundary. Scopes partition contract states into isolated execution units, minimizing conflicts and ensuring parallelism. This design enables concurrent state updates in Crystality.

For state variables, scopes are the storage regions in which the variables reside. The storage for state variables (the ledger state) is explicitly and deterministically partitioned into distinct, non-overlapping regions across multiple execution engines, ensuring balanced workload and efficient resource utilization. The scope of a state variable also defines how many instances of the variable exist on the blockchain.

There are three main types of scopes:

$$\langle scope \rangle ::= \texttt{@address} \mid \texttt{@engine} \mid \texttt{@global}$$

- Address Scope (`@address`): This scope partitions contract states based on user addresses, where each execution engine manages a subset of addresses. Each variable within this scope has one instance per valid address on each engine.
- Engine Scope (`@engine`): This scope is specific to each execution engine, representing local-shared states that can be immediately read or written by functions executed within the same engine. Each variable within this scope has a single instance per engine.
- Global Scope (`@global`): This is a logically singleton scope accessible by all execution engines. Variables in this scope are globally readable, but their updates require synchronization across all engines. It requires all execution engines to perform the same update operation in order to modify the value of the global state variable. Each variable within this scope has only one instance across the entire blockchain.

In Crystality, a function's scope determines its access to state variables. Unlike Solidity, function invocation requires specifying the current scope. A function can directly access variables and functions within its own scope and read state variables if their scope is equal to or broader than the function's. Write access follows the same rule, except `@global` state variables, which only `@global` functions can modify. Table 1 summarizes these rules, where 'R' denotes read permission, 'W' denotes write permission, and '-' indicates no access.

Table 1. Functions Access Permissions to State Variables

Func. Scope	State Var. Scope		
	`@address`	`@engine`	`@global`
`@address`	R W	R W	R
`@engine`	–	R W	R
`@global`	–	–	R W

In addition to state variables, Crystality supports temporary variables within functions. These are local to functions within specific scopes and stored in partitions corresponding to their scope. However, we can conceptualize temporary variables in the same manner as those in traditional programming languages, viewing them as existing in the function call stack.

2.2 Asynchronous Functional Relay

A fundamental challenge in parallel computing is managing code execution with respect to data dependencies. Since the required data for contract functions may reside in different scopes, Crystality adopts a unique execution model where functions can invoke one another asynchronously across scopes. In other words, functions can trigger relay calls. This model avoids the need to collect all relevant data into a single scope, enabling transaction routing directly to the scope that holds the relevant data. This approach allows inter-scope communication and facilitates complex workflows that span multiple scopes.

The relay mechanism decomposes transaction execution into multiple invocations of fine-grained, scope-narrowed functions. Functions in different scopes can execute in parallel without blocking each other. State updates are pipelined and concurrent across different execution engines.

A relay call is essentially a message containing the target scope, the identifier of the function to be invoked, and the associated arguments to pass.

$\langle relaycall \rangle$ ::= (relay @ $\langle exp \rangle$ | relay @engines | relay @global) $\langle identifier \rangle$ ($\langle exp \rangle^*$) ;

There are three types of relay target. The first type is used when relaying a function to a specific valid address. The value of *exp* is the target address. The second and third type broadcast to all engines. The difference between the second and third types lies in the scope of the function being relayed. The scope of the function must match the scope of the relay target. For instance, if the relay is directed to the @global scope, the function's scope must also be @global.

Crystality deliberately avoids relaying to a specific engine to maintain scalability and abstraction from blockchain implementation details.

The relay call is converted to a relay transaction by the execution engine and sent to the destination engine. While a transaction is being executed on the current engine, all dynamically generated relay calls are collected along with their invocation data, which are then packaged into relay transactions, and propagated to the target engine's broadcast network, where they reside in the mempool (the transaction pool that temporarily stores the transactions), awaiting inclusion, confirmation, and execution.

Unlike traditional function calls, where execution and state updates are immediate, a relay call returns instantly, with the actual execution taking place later, often in a different scope.

2.3 Syntax of Crystality

In the following, we introduce the syntax of Crystality, represented by a variant of Extended Backus-Naur Form (known as EBNF) where:

– Terminal symbols are written in `monospaced fonts`.
– Non-terminal productions are encapsulated in ⟨*angle brackets*⟩.
– Zero or one occurence is denoted by $^?$, zero or more occurences is denoted by $*$.

A contract takes the following syntactic form:

> ⟨*contractDecl*⟩ ::= `contract` ⟨*identifier*⟩ `{` ⟨*statevarDecl*⟩* ⟨*funcDecl*⟩* `}`

Identifier serves as a unique name for the contract. *StatevarDecl* defines the various state variables associated with the contract, and *funcDecl* specifies the functions within the contract.

> ⟨*statevarDecl*⟩ ::= ⟨*type*⟩ ⟨*scope*⟩ ⟨*identifier*⟩ `;`

StatevarDecl specifies both the type and the scope of the state variable. The abstract syntax tree of functions is as follows.

> ⟨*funcDecl*⟩ ::= `function` ⟨*identifier*⟩ ⟨*funcPara*⟩ ⟨*scope*⟩ `returns` ⟨*type*⟩$^?$ ⟨*funcBody*⟩
> ⟨*funcPara*⟩ ::= `(` `(` ⟨*type*⟩ ⟨*identifier*⟩ `,` `)`* ⟨*type*⟩ ⟨*identifier*⟩ `)` `|` `(` `)`
> ⟨*funcBody*⟩ ::= `{` ⟨*stmt*⟩ `}`
> ⟨*stmt*⟩ ::= ⟨*pstmt*⟩ `|` ⟨*stmt*⟩ ⟨*stmt*⟩ `|` `if` `(` ⟨*exp*⟩ `)` `then` `{` ⟨*stmt*⟩ `}` `else` `{` ⟨*stmt*⟩ `}`
> `|` `while` `(` ⟨*exp*⟩ `)` `{` ⟨*stmt*⟩ `}`
> ⟨*pstmt*⟩ ::= ⟨*type*⟩ ⟨*identifier*⟩ `;` `|` `skip` `|` ⟨*identifier*⟩ `:=` ⟨*exp*⟩ `;` `|` ⟨*relaycall*⟩
> `|` ⟨*returnstmt*⟩ `|` ⟨*identifier*⟩ `(` ⟨*exp*⟩* `)`
> ⟨*exp*⟩ ::= ⟨*identifier*⟩ `|` ⟨*identifier*⟩ `(` ⟨*exp*⟩* `)`

Basically, a function declaration consists of the following parts: its identifier, parameters along with their corresponding types, its scope, return type (if applicable), and the function body. The function body is enclosed within braces and consists of some statements. The statement may be primitive statement, sequential composition, conditional, or loop. A primitive statement may be temporary variable declaration, skip, assignment, relay call, return statement, or function call. The expression can be identifier or function call.

The following is an ERC20 token transfer contract in Crystality. The balance variable tracks user balances, and the transfer function moves tokens from the sender to a payee if the sender has sufficient funds.

```
contract MyToken {
    uint256 @address balance;
    function transfer(address payee, uint256 amount)
    @address returns
    {
        if (amount <= balance) then {
            balance := balance - amount;
            relay @ payee mint (amount);
        } else { skip }
```

```
        }
}
```

User balances are partitioned by address within the @address scope, ensuring each user has a unique balance instance. The transfer function, also scoped to @address, is invoked via a transaction specifying the sender's address. Execution occurs in the sender's partition, and if the payee's balance is in a different partition, a relay call handles the cross-partition update. This mechanism decouples payer and payee operations, reducing transaction contention.

To proceed with the deposit to the payee, a relay call is initiated with the payee's address as the target scope, directing execution to the engine managing the payee's state. The predefined mint function adds the specified amount to the balance.

3   Structural Operational Semantics of Crystality

In this section, we present the structural operational semantics of Crystality. We reveal the idea of the semantics from a general as well as abstract perspective, focusing on the theoretical underpinnings of the language rather than its specific implementation. Our semantics is independent of any particular realization of Crystality, aiming to capture the core behavior and rules governing the language in a formal and generalized manner.

First, we introduce the notations being used in the semantics and explain the necessity of these notations. Following this, we provide the semantics for statement execution, expression evaluation, and transaction execution respectively.

3.1   Notations

In the following, we use n to represent the number of engines and k to represent the number of addresses per engine. We use $\mathbb{A}$ to denote all memory addresses and $\mathbb{B}$ to denote bytes. Then a function $\mathbb{A} \to \mathbb{B}$ can represent storage, where it maps memory addresses to the corresponding byte values. We use $\mathbb{ID}$ to denote the set of all variable names (identifiers) and $\mathbb{IDF}$ the set of all function names (identifiers). Additionally, $\mathbb{T}$ is the set of all variable types.

We use $(\sigma_1, \Omega_1, Prog_1, \sigma_2, \Omega_2, Prog_2, ..., \sigma_n, \Omega_n, Prog_n, G)$ to represent the configuration of the entire blockchain system. Within this configuration, $G : \mathbb{A} \to \mathbb{B}$ represents the @global state variable storage. Each $\sigma_i = (\Psi_i, M_i)$ represents the state of the i-th engine. Ω_i represents the mempool of the i-th engine, which is an abstraction of the actual mempool maintained by every node that participates in the i-th engine. Nodes only store transactions for their own engine, so each Ω_i is different from one another. Relay calls, once packaged into relay transactions, are sent to Ω_i for storage. $Prog_i$ represents the program statements that is about to be executed on the i-th engine.

Specifically, $\Psi_i = (\Psi_{i,1}, \Psi_{i,2}, ..., \Psi_{i,k}, \Psi_{i,s})$ represents the state variable storage for the i-th engine, where $\Psi_{i,j} : \mathbb{A} \to \mathbb{B}$ denotes the storage for @address state variables at the j-th address in the i-th engine for all $1 \leq j \leq k$, and $\Psi_{i,s} : \mathbb{A} \to \mathbb{B}$ represents the storage for @engine state variables in the i-th engine.

M_i refers to the memory for temporary variables in the i-th engine, which contains a stack to model new scopes when calling a function. Each layer of the stack is a function $\mathbb{A} \to \mathbb{B}$, representing the memory for temporary variables within the current function scope. $top(M_i)$ returns the top layer of the stack, indicating the memory available in the current function scope. $X = pop(M_i)$ removes the top layer of the stack and returns the new stack. $Y = push(M_i, Z)$ pushes a new top Z to M_i, and the result is Y. Each layer of M_i is associated with two values: $scope$, which indicates the scope of the function, and rt, which represents the return value of the function (if the function has one). Both of these associated values must be defined when the layer is pushed onto the top of the stack. This ensures that, in addition to storing temporary variables, each function invocation layer maintains important contextual information including the current scope and, if applicable, its return value.

In addition, every storage or memory $f : \mathbb{A} \to \mathbb{B}$ is associated with a name space $N_f : \mathbb{ID} \to \mathbb{A} \cup None$ and a type space $T_f : \mathbb{ID} \to \mathbb{T} \cup None$, respectively mapping variable identifiers to memory addresses and types. When the identifier id is mapped to $None$ in the name space or type space, it means that id is not defined yet. To access locations in storage or memory, we use $[addr]_{store}^{size}$ to represent the value stored in position $addr$ of $size$ bytes in $store$. For example, given a variable identifier id allocated in f, the notation $[N_f(id)]_f^{size(T_f(id))}$ represents the value of id. The size of type t is given by $size(t)$.

For function identifiers, we define a set of auxiliary functions that retrieve relevant information about the function to make the semantics more concise:

- $\Lambda_{scope} : \mathbb{IDF} \to \{global, engine, address\}$ gives the scope of the function,
- $\Lambda_{paraname} : \mathbb{IDF} \to \mathbb{ID}^*$ gives the function's parameter list,
- $\Lambda_{paratype} : \mathbb{IDF} \to \mathbb{T}^*$ gives the function's parameter types,
- $\Lambda_{body} : \mathbb{IDF} \to Prog$ givens the function body, and
- $\Lambda_{rttype} : \mathbb{IDF} \to \mathbb{T} \cup None$ gives the function's return type (if applicable).

Now we introduce our notations for state modifications in the semantic rules. We use different forms of the same letter, such as with a prime, a hat or a bar, to indicate different modifications made to it. For a state σ, we use σ' to denote the state after we apply changes to σ. Sometimes we also use $\hat{\sigma}$, $\bar{\sigma}$, $\sigma^{(1)}$, $\sigma^{(2)}$ etc. to denote the intermediate state. For different letters with the same form, such as letters with primes, they represent the same modification stage.

It is important to note that since the name space and type space of a function are auxiliary information, changes to the name space or type space will also lead to changes in the function itself.

There is a 'zoom in and out' process here. For example, if $\Psi_{i,s}$ is modified to $\Psi'_{i,s}$, then σ_i is implicitly modified to σ'_i, with other parts remaining unchanged. This is because $\sigma_i = (\Psi_i, M_i)$ and $\Psi_i = (\Psi_{i,1}, \Psi_{i,2}, ..., \Psi_{i,k}, \Psi_{i,s})$. This convention is designed to make the formulas more concise and readable, without having to expand overly complex function definitions.

Consider the following semantic rule as an example:

$$\text{Ex} \frac{T_{\Psi'_{i,s}}(id) = Type \qquad [N_{\Psi'_{i,s}}(id)]^{size(Type)}_{\Psi'_{i,s}} = 10}{(..., \sigma_i, \Omega_i, Prog_i, ...) \to (..., \sigma'_i, \Omega_i, \cdot, ...)}$$

In this rule, the initial state of the i-th engine is σ_i and the code to be executed is $Prog_i$, which in this context is essentially a common assignment operation. After two changes above the line, the state of the i-th engine becomes σ'_i and the code to be executed becomes empty (denoted by $\cdot$). The two changes are 1) modifying the type space T of the storage $\Psi_{i,s}$ for the variable id to $Type$, and 2) setting the value of id in the storage $\Psi_{i,s}$ to 10. Aside from these two changes, state σ_i and σ'_i are the same. Additionally, the ellipsis (...) in the configuration under the line indicates that the other parts of the configuration remain unchanged.

In actual blockchain systems, all nodes in the same partition should ultimately execute the same code and have identical mempool. Therefore, in the following description, we will simplify the terminology. When we say the i-th engine executing certain code, it is actually the nodes in the i-th engine executing that code. Similarly, when we refer to the mempool of the i-th engine, we are actually referring to the mempools of the nodes in the i-th engine. Such simplification allows us to focus on the behavior at the engine level while abstracting away the details of individual node operations.

In the following we present the semantics of Crystality in rules of statements, expressions, and transactions. Common program constructs such as compositions, conditionals and loops are very similar to those in other high level languages. For space reasons, we focus on the semantics of Crystality's unique features, including variable declaration, assignment, evaluation, function calls, and relay calls. These core constructs capture the essence of Crystality's behavior, particularly its handling of different scopes and its asynchronous message passing via relay transactions.

3.2 Semantic Rules of Statements

The following three rules, SDa, SDs and SDg, correspond to state variable declaration statements in Crystality contracts. These statements are executed when the contract is deployed.

When a state variable is declared with the @address scope, an instance of the variable is created for each valid address within every engine. Appropriate storage space is allocated according to the variable's type.

In the rule SDa, the first formula indicates that initially the @address state variable named id is not defined in σ_i. The second represents the modification of the new type space of σ'_i, assigning the type of id to $Type$. The third shows that the new name space of σ'_i is updated by allocating memory space for id. The last one sets the value of id in the new σ'_i to the initial value of its specified $Type$. Since each valid address has its own instance of id, this operation must be applied to all k valid addresses within the engine.

$$N_{\Psi_{i,j}}(id) = None, \ 1 \le j \le k \qquad T_{\Psi'_{i,j}}(id) = Type, \ 1 \le j \le k$$
$$N_{\Psi'_{i,j}}(id) = allocate\_new(Type, \Psi_{i,j}), \ 1 \le j \le k$$
$$[N_{\Psi'_{i,j}}(id)]_{\Psi'_{i,j}}^{size(Type)} = init(Type), \ 1 \le j \le k$$

$$\text{SD}_A \ \frac{}{(..., \sigma_i, \Omega_i, Type \ @address \ id;, ...) \to (..., \sigma'_i, \Omega_i, \cdot, ...)}$$

When a state variable is declared with the @engine scope, an instance of the variable is created for each engine. State variable declarations are performed during contract deployment. Notably, each engine is required to execute the same statements to declare @engine state variables. The i-th engine is solely responsible for declaring its own instance of @engine variables.

$$N_{\Psi_{i,s}}(id) = None \qquad T_{\Psi'_{i,s}}(id) = Type$$
$$N_{\Psi'_{i,s}}(id) = allocate\_new(Type, \Psi_{i,s})$$
$$[N_{\Psi'_{i,s}}(id)]_{\Psi'_{i,s}}^{size(Type)} = init(Type)$$

$$\text{SD}_S \ \frac{}{(..., \sigma_i, \Omega_i, Type \ @engine \ id;, ...) \to (..., \sigma'_i, \Omega_i, \cdot, ...)}$$

When a state variable is declared with the @global scope, an instance of the variable is created in the @global variable storage space G. The declaration of @global state variables involves an implicit synchronization operation. For a @global state variable to be successfully created in G, all nodes across all engines must execute the declaration. This ensures that the @global state variable is consistently established and maintained across all engines.

We observe hereafter that all operations involving the @global scope are executed consistently across all engines (with the exception of relay calls). In the configuration below the line, the code to be executed for each engine $Prog_i$ must be identical, and these $Prog_i$ must be executed simultaneously. This requirement ensures that global operations, such as reading or modifying @global state variables, are synchronized across the entire system.

$$N_G(id) = None \qquad T_{G'}(id) = Type$$
$$\text{SD}_G \ \frac{N_{G'}(id) = allocate\_new(Type, G) \qquad [N_{G'}(id)_{G'}^{size(Type)}] = init(Type)}{(\sigma_1, \Omega_1, Type \ @global \ id;, ..., \sigma_n, \Omega_n, Type \ @global \ id;, G)}$$
$$\to (\sigma_1, \Omega_1, \cdot, ..., \sigma_n, \Omega_n, \cdot, G')$$

The next rule TD is for temporary variable declaration. The first formula in this rule indicates that the variable is not defined within the current function. The second specifies that the newly defined variable is of type $Type$. The third one allocates storage for the new variable and the fourth initializes the new variable. The configuration of the i-th engine changes accordingly.

$$\text{TD} \frac{\begin{array}{c} N_{top(M_i)}(id) = None \qquad T_{top(M_i)'}(id) = Type \\ N_{top(M_i)'}(id) = allocate\_new(Type, top(M_i)) \\ [N_{top(M_i)'}(id)]_{top(M_i)'}^{size(Type)} = init(Type) \end{array}}{(..., \sigma_i, \Omega_i, Type\ id;, ...) \rightarrow (..., \sigma_i', \Omega_i, \cdot, ...)}$$

The rule TA describes the behavior of temporary variable assignment statements within a function. First, the value of the expression exp is computed in the current configuration. If the corresponding temporary variable is already defined, its value in the top layer of M is updated to the value of exp. Note that the expression exp itself might also be a function call that returns a value, evaluating the value of exp could lead to a change in the state of the current engine. We use a symbol with a hat $\hat{\sigma}_i$ to record this change. During the evaluation of exp, relay transactions may be generated, causing changes in the mempool of other engines, which is reflected by Ω_l changing to Ω_l' for every l.

$$\text{TA} \frac{\begin{array}{c} top(M_i).scope \neq global \\ \mathcal{E}[\![(\sigma_1, \Omega_1, Prog_1, ..., \sigma_i, \Omega_i, exp, ..., \sigma_n, \Omega_n, Prog_n, G)]\!] \\ \rightarrow (\sigma_1, \Omega_1', Prog_1, ..., \hat{\sigma}_i, \Omega_i', v, ..., \sigma_n, \Omega_n', Prog_n, G) \\ N_{top(\hat{M}_i)}(id) \neq None \qquad [N_{top(\hat{M}_i')}(id)]_{top(\hat{M}_i')}^{size(T_{top(\hat{M}_i')}(id))} = v \end{array}}{\begin{array}{c} (\sigma_1, \Omega_1, Prog_1, ..., \sigma_i, \Omega_i, id := exp;, ..., \sigma_n, \Omega_n, Prog_n, G) \\ \rightarrow (\sigma_1, \Omega_1', Prog_1, ..., \hat{\sigma}_i', \Omega_i', \cdot, ..., \sigma_n, \Omega_n', Prog_n, G) \end{array}}$$

Another scenario for temporary variable assignment occurs when assigning a value to a temporary variable within an @global function. Since @global functions must be executed uniformly by all engines, guaranteeing that the same operation is applied globally, a different rule is required for this case.

$$\text{TAG} \frac{\begin{array}{c} top(M_i).scope = global,\ 1 \leq i \leq n \\ \mathcal{E}[\![(\sigma_1, \Omega_1, exp, ..., \sigma_n, \Omega_n, exp, G)]\!] \rightarrow (\sigma_1, \Omega_1', v, ..., \sigma_n, \Omega_n', v, G') \\ N_{top(M_i)}(id) \neq None,\ 1 \leq i \leq n \\ [N_{top(M_i')}(id)]_{top(M_i')}^{size(T_{top(M_i')}(id))} = v,\ 1 \leq i \leq n \end{array}}{(\sigma_1, \Omega_1, id := exp;, ..., \sigma_n, \Omega_n, id := exp;, G) \rightarrow (\sigma_1', \Omega_1', \cdot, ..., \sigma_n', \Omega_n', \cdot, G')}$$

We use the rule SAaa as an example for assignment statements of state variables across scopes. We need to classify the scope of the assignment statement and the scope of the involved state variables.

SAaa applies when both the function scope and the state variable scope are @address. In this case, the value of the expression exp is computed, and the state variable is updated with the new value. Here, σ_i and $\hat{\sigma}_i$ represent the state of the current engine before and after evaluating exp, respectively. Therefore, the two equations $top(...).scope$ indicate that before and after evaluating exp, the scopes are both address j.

The process involves first evaluating the expression exp to obtain its value in the current configuration. The rules for evaluating expressions are presented in Sect. 3.3. Depending on the scope classifications, the state variable's value is then updated in its respective scope.

$$\mathrm{SAAA} \frac{\begin{array}{c} \mathcal{E}[\![(\sigma_1, \Omega_1, Prog_1, ..., \sigma_i, \Omega_i, exp, ..., \sigma_n, \Omega_n, Prog_n, G)]\!] \\ \rightarrow (\sigma_1, \Omega_1', Prog_1, ..., \hat{\sigma}_i, \Omega_i', v, ..., \sigma_n, \Omega_n', Prog_n, G) \\ top(M_i).scope = (address, j) \quad top(\hat{M}_i).scope = (address, j) \\ N_{\Psi_{i,j}}(id) \neq None \quad [N_{\Psi_{i,j}'}(id)]_{\Psi_{i,j}'}^{size(T_{\Psi_{i,j}'}(id))} = v \end{array}}{\begin{array}{c} (\sigma_1, \Omega_1, Prog_1, ..., \sigma_i, \Omega_i, id := exp;, ..., \sigma_n, \Omega_n, Prog_n, G) \\ \rightarrow (\sigma_1, \Omega_1', Prog_1, ..., \hat{\sigma}_i', \Omega_i', \cdot, ..., \sigma_n, \Omega_n', Prog_n, G) \end{array}}$$

Return statements can be defined through assignment statements. Each layer of M is associated with a return value variable rt, which is a special identifier distinct from other variable names. The variable rt is declared immediately when the function is called, and its type is the return type of the function. Thus, the return value can be accessed through rt. The rules corresponding to functions with return values are presented in Sect. 3.3.

In the following, we use the rule IFaa as an example for function calls without return values. IFaa describes the scenario where a function with scope @address calls another function also with scope @address. During the execution of the function body, relay transactions may be generated, causing changes in the mempool of other engines, which is reflected by Ω_l changing to Ω_l' for every l.

$$\mathrm{IFAA} \frac{\begin{array}{c} \Lambda_{scope}(idf) = address \quad top(M_i).scope = (address, j) \\ \Lambda_{rettype}(idf) = None \quad \Lambda_{body}(idf) = Block \\ \Lambda_{paraname}(idf) = (id_1, ..., id_t) \quad \Lambda_{paratype}(idf) = (T_1, ..., T_t) \\ M_i^{(1)} = push(M_i, top(M_i)) \quad top(M_i^{(1)}).scope = (address, j) \\ top(M_i^{(1)}).rt = None \quad M_i^{(3)} = pop(M_i^{(2)}) \\ (\sigma_1, \Omega_1, Prog_1, ..., \sigma_i^{(1)}, \Omega_i, T_1 \ id_1 := exp_1; \\ ...; T_t \ id_t := exp_t; Block, ..., \sigma_n, \Omega_n, Prog_n, G) \\ \rightarrow (\sigma_1, \Omega_1', Prog_1, ..., \sigma_i^{(2)}, \Omega_i', \cdot, ..., \sigma_n, \Omega_n', Prog_n, G) \end{array}}{\begin{array}{c} (\sigma_1, \Omega_1, Prog_1, ..., \sigma_i, \Omega_i, idf(exp_1, ..., exp_t), ..., \sigma_n, \Omega_n, Prog_n, G) \\ \rightarrow (\sigma_1, \Omega_1', Prog_1, ..., \sigma_i^{(3)}, \Omega_i', \cdot, ..., \sigma_n, \Omega_n', Prog_n, G) \end{array}}$$

@global functions are executed on all nodes across all engines, ensuring that @global state variables remain consistent throughout the entire system. When a @global function is called, each node in every engine executes the function independently, and the result is a synchronized and uniform update to the @global state variables. The storage G may change, but the configuration of each engine cannot change because @global function is not allowed to modify @engine variables or @address variables of each engine.

The following rules (from RELa to RELg1) describe the behavior of relay calls. We formalize the rules for the packaging and propagation of the relay transactions.

A relay call is akin to a function call, but it is asynchronous. The call data is packaged into a relay transaction. The relay statement itself returns immediately. There are three types of relay targets, determining how the relay transaction is processed and executed on the target engine:

RELa specifies a specific target address. The evaluation of exp represents the corresponding address location. The result of the evaluation is (r, j), which denotes the j-th address of the r-th engine. The function idf with the given arguments is packaged into a relay transaction and sent to the engine responsible for the specific target address.

$$\Lambda_{scope}(idf) = address \qquad \mathcal{E}[\![(..., \sigma_i, \Omega_i, exp, ...)]\!] \to (..., \sigma_i, \Omega_i, (r, j), ...)$$

$$\text{REL}_A \frac{\begin{array}{c} \mathcal{E}[\![(..., \sigma_i, \Omega_i, exp_l, ...)]\!] \to (..., \sigma_i, \Omega_i, v_l, ...), \ 1 \le l \le t \\ \Omega'_r = \Omega_r \cup \{(address, j, idf(v_1, ..., v_t))\} \end{array}}{\begin{array}{c} (..., \sigma_i, \Omega_i, relay@exp \ idf(exp_1, ..., exp_t); , ..., \sigma_r, \Omega_r, Prog_r ...) \\ \to (..., \sigma_i, \Omega_i, \cdot, ..., \sigma_r, \Omega'_r, Prog_r, ...) \end{array}}$$

RELs acts like broadcast, relaying from one engine to all engines. Here the called function must have scope @engine. This statement adds a relay transaction to the mempool of every engine.

$$\Lambda_{scope}(idf) = engine$$

$$\text{REL}_S \frac{\begin{array}{c} \mathcal{E}[\![(..., \sigma_i, \Omega_i, exp_l, ...)]\!] \to (..., \sigma_i, \Omega_i, v_l, ...), \ 1 \le l \le t \\ \Omega'_i = \Omega_i \cup \{(engine, idf(v_1, ..., v_t))\}, \ 1 \le i \le n \end{array}}{\begin{array}{c} (\sigma_1, \Omega_1, Prog_1, ..., \sigma_i, \Omega_i, relay@engines \ idf(exp_1, ..., exp_t); , \\ ..., \sigma_n, \Omega_n, Prog_n, G) \\ \to (\sigma_1, \Omega'_1, Prog_1, ..., \sigma_i, \Omega'_i, \cdot, ..., \sigma_n, \Omega'_n, Prog_n, G) \end{array}}$$

The next rule also involves relaying to all engines, but it differ slightly from the previous one. Firstly, the functions invoked in this rules are @global functions. Secondly, the relay statements must be called from functions that have an @address or @engine scope, i.e. they cannot be invoked from a @global function. This restriction ensures that @global functions are only triggered by relay transactions initiated from more localized scopes.

$$\Lambda_{scope}(idf) = global \qquad top(M_i).scope = (address, j)$$

$$\text{REL}_{G1} \frac{\begin{array}{c} \mathcal{E}[\![(..., \sigma_i, \Omega_i, exp_l, ...)]\!] \to (..., \sigma_i, \Omega_i, v_l, ...), \ 1 \le l \le t \\ \Omega'_i = \Omega_i \cup \{(global, idf(v_1, ..., v_t))\}, \ 1 \le i \le n \end{array}}{\begin{array}{c} (\sigma_1, \Omega_1, Prog_1, ..., \sigma_i, \Omega_i, relay@global \ idf(exp_1, ..., exp_t); , \\ ..., \sigma_n, \Omega_n, Prog_n, G) \\ \to (\sigma_1, \Omega'_1, Prog_1, ..., \sigma_i, \Omega'_i, \cdot, ..., \sigma_n, \Omega'_n, Prog_n, G) \end{array}}$$

We formalize the execution rules governing Crystality's parallel execution paradigm. Specifically, the Para rule captures the parallel execution across multiple execution engines, allowing concurrent state updates in different engines. Additionally, we introduce the MemP rule to define mempool behavior in Crystality. This rule ensures that relay transactions in the mempool do not affect the execution of the current transaction, maintaining execution isolation from the mempool of each engine. These rules can be found at [41].

3.3   Semantic Rules of Evaluations

The semantics of accessing and reading of temporary variables is captured by the following rule TE. In any engine, the value of a temporary variable within the current function can be read as long as the variable is defined.

$$\text{TE} \frac{N_{top(M_i)}(id) \neq None \qquad [N_{top(M_i)}(id)]_{top(M_i)}^{size(T_{top(M_i)}(id))} = v}{\mathcal{E}[\![(..., \sigma_i, \Omega_i, id, ...)]\!] \to (..., \sigma_i, \Omega_i, v, ...)}$$

The following rules are related to reading state variables. Access to state variables must be determined based on the scope of the state variable and the scope of the current function. The permissions for functions to read state variables vary depending on their scope. For further details refer to Table 1. Here, we provide two rules, SEaa and SEgg, as examples for illustration.

At the j-th address in the i-th engine, the function can read the @address state variable of the j-th address in the i-th engine.

$$\text{SEAA} \frac{top(M_i).scope = (address, j)}{N_{\Psi_{i,j}}(id) \neq None \qquad [N_{\Psi_{i,j}}(id)]_{\Psi_{i,j}}^{size(T_{\Psi_{i,j}}(id))} = v}{\mathcal{E}[\![(..., \sigma_i, \Omega_i, id, ...)]\!] \to (..., \sigma_i, \Omega_i, v, ...)}$$

The evaluation within @global functions is performed on all nodes across all engines.

$$\text{SEGG} \frac{top(M_i).scope = global \qquad N_G(id) \neq None \qquad [N_G(id)]_G^{size(T_G(id))} = v}{\mathcal{E}[\![(\sigma_1, \Omega_1, id, ..., \sigma_n, \Omega_n, id, G)]\!] \to (\sigma_1, \Omega_1, v, ..., \sigma_n, \Omega_n, v, G)}$$

The rules about function calls with return values are similar to the previous rules for function calls without return values, but require the use of variable rt in each layer of M to record the return value. This ensures that the return value is captured properly and can be accessed after the function execution. Under normal circumstances, the return value of calls to @global functions should be the same across all engines. This consistency is ensured by the consensus mechanism. Additionally, since @global functions can only modify @global state variables, the configuration of each engine remains unchanged before and after the function call. However, because the function may contain relay statements, the mempool of each engine may change.

3.4   Semantic Rules of Transactions

Defining the semantics of transactions is fundamental to smart contract languages. We model a transaction as a function call, abstracting details such as gas and signatures while focusing on its functional behavior. To formalize this, we introduce T-functions, which encapsulate the essential execution logic of transactions. In the following, we outline the constraints that T-functions must satisfy and provide their precise mathematical definition.

Since a transaction is the outermost function, the current scope of the top layer of M must be *None*. The nodes can get the address of the sender of this transaction using function $get\_sender\_address()$ from the information attached to the transaction, and determine which engine the address is in. Then a new layer is built on top of stack M to denote the invocation of function, and records the scope. Upon function return, this layer is removed. We also need to record the changes of mempools of other engines because there may be relay statements in function body.

Crystality supports both user-initiated and relay transactions. The originating engine of a relay transaction is also identified via $get\_sender\_address()$, enabling a uniform handling mechanism for both types.

The impact of a transaction on the world state is reflected in each engine's storage Ψ_i, the storage space of @global state variables G, and each engine's mempool Ω_i, but not in each engine's memory M_i. This is because memory holds the values of temporary variables specific to the engine, which are created during function execution and deleted upon function return. Since the T-function invoked by the transaction is the outermost function, the memory stack of each engine is cleared when the transaction completes, ensuring memory is empty both before and after transaction execution.

The formal semantic rules are available at [41]. For instance, the IFta rule specifies the behavior when a transaction invokes a function with the scope @address within a contract.

4   Formalization and Verification of Crystality in Coq

Coq [19] is an interactive theorem prover based on higher-order logic, widely used for formal verification in programming languages, mathematics, and critical software systems. Unlike HOL4 [33], Isabelle/HOL [10], and PVS [27], Coq is built on the Calculus of Inductive Constructions, integrating higher-order logic with a richly typed functional programming language. It supports structural proof scripting and proof automation, making it effective for verifying properties like type soundness, program correctness, and compiler certification. Notable applications include CompCert [22], JavaCard security verification [1], and the Bedrock framework [7]. For a detailed introduction, see [4].

We formalize Crystality's core syntax and semantics in Coq and verify a simplified ERC20 token transfer function. Specifically, we prove that if the transfer amount does not exceed the sender's balance, the sender's balance decreases accordingly, and a relay transaction is created in the recipient's engine to increase the recipient's balance. If the transfer amount exceeds the sender's balance, the transaction fails, leaving the ledger state unchanged. Furthermore, using our semantic rules, we verify the refinement relationship between two token transfer functions. Due to space constraints, the full Coq formalization and verification are not provided here and available at [40].

While our current Coq formalization faithfully captures the core operational semantics of Crystality, it remains a foundational model with several limitations. In future work, we plan to significantly enrich the formalization to account for the full feature set of Crystality, particularly the semantics of parallelism and synchronization. We also intend to evaluate our semantics against more complex, real-world contracts to validate the expressiveness and applicability of our model.

5   Related Work

Although formal semantics for smart contract programming languages has garnered some attention, most of the existing research has concentrated on languages with sequential execution models, particularly Solidity. This includes a denotational semantics of Solidity proposed in [24], a big-step semantics of a subset of Solidity formalized in [43], an operational semantics for a subset of Solidity described in [8], an executable operational semantics of Solidity presented in [20,21], a formalization of Solidity in terms of a SMT-based intermediate language provided in [14,15], and a formal semantics for an intermediate specification language for the formal verification of Ethereum-based smart contracts in Coq, proposed in [42]. Additionally, [17] provides formal semantics for EVM using the K-framework. None of these are directly applicable to smart contract languages designed for parallel EVMs.

6   Conclusion

This paper presents the structural operational semantics for Crystality, a novel smart contract programming language designed for parallel EVMs. Our work provides a formal execution model that precisely captures Crystality's key features, including Programmable Contract Scopes and Asynchronous Functional Relay, which enable fine-grained state partitioning and efficient inter-scope communication. By formalizing the core syntax and semantics of Crystality in Coq, we establish a rigorous foundation for mechanized reasoning and verification of smart contracts. The verification of a simple token transfer function demonstrates the applicability of our framework in ensuring smart contract correctness.

Several avenues remain for future exploration. Extending the semantics to incorporate gas models and execution costs would enhance practical applicability. Strengthening security verification by formally proving protection against reentrancy attacks, front-running vulnerabilities, and state consistency violations in parallel execution settings is another key avenue. Additionally, establishing semantic correspondence with languages like Solidity would improve interoperability. Finally, developing a verified compiler that translates high-level Crystality code into optimized EVM bytecode would bridge the gap between formal semantics and real-world execution.

A complete version of this paper, including all formal semantic rules, is available at [41].

Acknowledgments. This work was supported by the National Key R&D Program of China under Grant 2022YFB2702200, and the NSFC under Grant 62172019.

References

1. Andronick, J., Chetali, B., Ly, O.: Using coq to verify java card^{TM} applet isolation properties. In: Basin, D., Wolff, B. (eds.) TPHOLs 2003. LNCS, vol. 2758, pp. 335–351. Springer, Heidelberg (2003). https://doi.org/10.1007/10930755_22
2. Anjana, P.S., Kumari, S., Peri, S., Rathor, S., Somani, A.: An efficient framework for optimistic concurrent execution of smart contracts. In: 2019 27th Euromicro International Conference on Parallel, Distributed and Network-Based Processing (PDP), pp. 83–92. IEEE (2019)
3. Aptos Foundation: The aptos blockchain: safe, scalable, and upgrade-able web3 infrastructure (2022). https://aptosfoundation.org/whitepaper/aptos-whitepaper_en.pdf
4. Bertot, Y., Castéran, P.: Interactive Theorem Proving and Program Development: Coq'Art: The Calculus of Inductive Constructions. Springer, Heidelberg (2013)
5. Blackshear, S., et al.: Rain, dario russi, stephane sezer, tim zakian, and runtian zhou. move: A language with programmable resources (2020)
6. Chen, Y., et al.: Forerunner: constraint-based speculative transaction execution for ethereum. In: Proceedings of the ACM SIGOPS 28th Symposium on Operating Systems Principles, pp. 570–587 (2021)
7. Chlipala, A.: The bedrock structured programming system: combining generative metaprogramming and hoare logic in an extensible program verifier. In: Proceedings of the 18th ACM SIGPLAN International Conference on Functional Programming, pp. 391–402 (2013)
8. Crosara, M., Centurino, G., Arceri, V.: Towards an operational semantics for solidity. In: VALID, pp. 1–6 (2019)
9. Ethereum Dev Team: Solidity documentation (2021). https://docs.soliditylang.org/en/latest/
10. Foster, S., Zeyda, F., Woodcock, J.: Isabelle/UTP: a mechanised theory engineering framework. In: Naumann, D. (ed.) UTP 2014. LNCS, vol. 8963, pp. 21–41. Springer, Cham (2015). https://doi.org/10.1007/978-3-319-14806-9_2
11. Garamvölgyi, P., Liu, Y., Zhou, D., Long, F., Wu, M.: Utilizing parallelism in smart contracts on decentralized blockchains by taming application-inherent conflicts. In: Proceedings of the 44th International Conference on Software Engineering, pp. 2315–2326 (2022)

12. Gelashvili, R., et al.: Block-stm: scaling blockchain execution by turning ordering curse to a performance blessing. In: Proceedings of the 28th ACM SIGPLAN Annual Symposium on Principles and Practice of Parallel Programming, pp. 232–244 (2023)

13. Georgiadis, E.: How many transactions per second can bitcoin really handle? Theoretically. IACR Cryptol. ePrint Arch., 416 (2019)

14. Hajdu, Á., Jovanović, D.: SOLC-VERIFY: a modular verifier for solidity smart contracts. In: Chakraborty, S., Navas, J.A. (eds.) VSTTE 2019. LNCS, vol. 12031, pp. 161–179. Springer, Cham (2020). https://doi.org/10.1007/978-3-030-41600-3_11

15. Hajdu, Á., Jovanović, D.: SMT-friendly formalization of the solidity memory model. In: ESOP 2020. LNCS, vol. 12075, pp. 224–250. Springer, Cham (2020). https://doi.org/10.1007/978-3-030-44914-8_9

16. Herlihy, M., Koskinen, E.: Transactional boosting: a methodology for highly-concurrent transactional objects. In: Proceedings of the 13th ACM SIGPLAN Symposium on Principles and Practice of Parallel Programming, pp. 207–216 (2008)

17. Hildenbrandt, E., et al.: KEVM: a complete formal semantics of the ethereum virtual machine. In: Proceedings of CSF 2018, pp. 204–217. IEEE Computer Society (2018)

18. Hoare, C., He, J.: Unifying Theories of Programming. Prentice Hall, Upper Saddle river (1998)

19. Huet, G., Kahn, G., Paulin-Mohring, C.: The coq proof assistant a tutorial. Rapport Techn. **178**, 113 (1997)

20. Jiao, J., Kan, S., Lin, S., Sanán, D., Liu, Y., Sun, J.: Executable operational semantics of solidity. CoRR arxiv:1804.01295 (2018)

21. Jiao, J., Kan, S., Lin, S., Sanán, D., Liu, Y., Sun, J.: Semantic understanding of smart contracts: executable operational semantics of solidity. In: Proceedings of SP 2020, pp. 1695–1712. IEEE (2020)

22. Krebbers, R., Leroy, X., Wiedijk, F.: Formal C semantics: compcert and the C standard. In: Klein, G., Gamboa, R. (eds.) ITP 2014. LNCS, vol. 8558, pp. 543–548. Springer, Cham (2014). https://doi.org/10.1007/978-3-319-08970-6_36

23. Kung, H.T., Robinson, J.T.: On optimistic methods for concurrency control. ACM Trans. Datab. Syst. (TODS) **6**(2), 213–226 (1981)

24. Marmsoler, D., Brucker, A.D.: A denotational semantics of solidity in isabelle/HOL. In: Calinescu, R., Păsăreanu, C.S. (eds.) SEFM 2021. LNCS, vol. 13085, pp. 403–422. Springer, Cham (2021). https://doi.org/10.1007/978-3-030-92124-8_23

25. Monad Pad: The monad white paper (2024). https://files.monadpad.xyz/whitepaper.pdf

26. Nakamoto, S.: Bitcoin: a peer-to-peer electronic cash system (2008). https://bitcoin.org/bitcoin.pdf

27. Owre, S., Rushby, J.M., Shankar, N.: PVS: a prototype verification system. In: Kapur, D. (ed.) CADE 1992. LNCS, vol. 607, pp. 748–752. Springer, Heidelberg (1992). https://doi.org/10.1007/3-540-55602-8_217

28. Plotkin, G.D.: A structural approach to operational semantics (1981)

29. Qi, X., Jiao, J., Li, Y.: Smart contract parallel execution with fine-grained state accesses. In: 2023 IEEE 43rd International Conference on Distributed Computing Systems (ICDCS), pp. 841–852. IEEE (2023)

30. Sanka, A.I., Cheung, R.: A systematic review of blockchain scalability: issues, solutions, analysis and future research. J. Netw. Comput. Appl. **195**, 103232 (2021)

31. Saraph, V., Herlihy, M.: An empirical study of speculative concurrency in ethereum smart contracts. arXiv preprint arXiv:1901.01376 (2019)

32. Sei Labs: Sei: The layer 1 for trading (2023). https://github.com/sei-protocol/sei-chain/blob/main/whitepaper/Sei_Whitepaper.pdf
33. Slind, K., Norrish, M.: A brief overview of HOL4. In: Mohamed, O.A., Muñoz, C., Tahar, S. (eds.) TPHOLs 2008. LNCS, vol. 5170, pp. 28–32. Springer, Heidelberg (2008). https://doi.org/10.1007/978-3-540-71067-7_6
34. Solana Foundation: 8 innovations that make solana the first web-scale blockchain (2019). https://solana.com/news/8-innovations-that-make-solana-the-first-web-scale-blockchain
35. Solidity airdrop smart contract (2018). https://github.com/SpringRole/smart-contracts/blob/master/contracts/AirDrop.sol
36. Solidity by example: Voting (2023). https://docs.soliditylang.org/en/v0.8.21/solidity-by-example.html
37. The MystanLabs Team: The sui smart contracts platform (2023). https://docs.sui.io/paper/sui.pdf
38. Wang, H., Pan, M., Wang, J.: Crystality: a programming model for smart contracts on parallel evms. In: Proceedings of the 30th ACM SIGPLAN Annual Symposium on Principles and Practice of Parallel Programming, PPoPP '25, pp. 412–425. Association for Computing Machinery (2025)
39. Winskel, G.: The Formal Semantics of Programming Languages - An Introduction. MIT Press, Cambridge (1993)
40. Xu, Z., Wang, H., Sun, M.: Coq formalization of crystality (2025). https://doi.org/10.5281/zenodo.14991761
41. Xu, Z., Wang, H., Sun, M.: Operational semantics for crystality: a smart contract language for parallel cvms (2025). https://arxiv.org/abs/2504.17336
42. Yang, Z., Lei, H.: Lolisa: formal syntax and semantics for a subset of the solidity programming language. CoRR arxiv:1803.09885 (2018)
43. Zakrzewski, J.: Towards verification of ethereum smart contracts: a formalization of core of solidity. In: Piskac, R., Rümmer, P. (eds.) VSTTE 2018. LNCS, vol. 11294, pp. 229–247. Springer, Cham (2018). https://doi.org/10.1007/978-3-030-03592-1_13

Detecting Speculative Data Flow Vulnerabilities Using Weakest Precondition Reasoning

Graeme Smith[1,2]([✉]) [iD]

[1] Defence Science and Technology Group, Brisbane, Australia
[2] School of Electrical Engineering and Computer Science,
The University of Queensland, Brisbane, Australia
g.smith1@uq.edu.au

Abstract. Speculative execution is a hardware optimisation technique where a processor, while waiting on the completion of a computation required for an instruction, continues to execute later instructions based on a predicted value of the pending computation. It came to the forefront of security research in 2018 with the disclosure of two related attacks, Spectre and Meltdown. Since then many similar attacks have been identified. While there has been much research on using formal methods to detect speculative execution vulnerabilities based on predicted control flow, there has been significantly less on vulnerabilities based on predicted data flow. In this paper, we introduce an approach for detecting the data flow vulnerabilities, Spectre-STL and Spectre-PSF, using weakest precondition reasoning. We validate our approach on a suite of litmus tests used to validate related approaches in the literature.

1 Introduction

Modern processors liberally employ speculative execution of instructions to optimise performance. Instructions can be executed before earlier instructions in a program based on predictions of the outcomes of the earlier instructions. The intention is to use latent processing cycles rather than waiting for the completion of computations required for the earlier instructions. When a prediction is found to be correct, the speculatively executed instructions are committed to memory. When a prediction is found to be incorrect, the speculatively executed instructions are rolled back, and execution restarted according to the actual outcome.

While the rollback of incorrect speculation maintains a program's functionality, traces of speculative execution are left in the processor's micro-architecture and can be exploited by an attacker to gain access to otherwise inaccessible (and hence potentially sensitive) data. The best known such attack, Spectre variant 1 (also known as Spectre-PHT) [22], takes advantage of the pattern history table (PHT), a micro-architectural component used to predict the outcome of a branch

P. Rümmer and Z. Wu (Eds.): TASE 2025, LNCS 15841, pp. 322–339, 2026.
https://doi.org/10.1007/978-3-031-98208-8_19

instruction. After finding a suitable *gadget* (i.e., code pattern) in a victim program, an attacker can train the PHT to expect a particular outcome and then
use this to exploit the gadget. For example, an attacker could train the PHT
to expect the following gadget to execute the body of the if statement. Then,
by providing a value of x greater than $array1\_size$, a value beyond the end of
$array1$ is accessed in the if statement's body. This value is subsequently used
to access a particular index of $array2$, reading the value at that index into the
cache. After rollback, this index can be deduced by a timing attack on the cache
[23]. Note that 512 corresponds to the cache line size in bits allowing the attacker
to determine, from the affected cache line, the value $array1[x]$.

$$r0 := x;$$
$$r1 := array1\_size;$$
$$\text{if}\,(r0 < r1)\{$$
$$\qquad r1 := array1[r0];$$
$$\qquad r2 := array2[r1 * 512];$$
$$\}$$

Since the disclosure of such attacks in 2018, a number of formal methods-
based approaches for detecting vulnerable gadgets have been developed [8]. These
have mostly focused on attacks exploiting speculation of control flow in a program, such as Spectre-PHT. Significantly less work exists on attacks exploiting
speculation of data flow such as Spectre variant 4 (Spectre-STL) [6][1]. This attack
exploits the incorrect prediction that a load is not dependent on an earlier store
and hence can be executed first, missing the Store-To-Load (STL) dependency.
A similar attack, Spectre-PSF [7,26], relies on the processor incorrectly predicting that a load *will* depend on an earlier store and speculatively executing the
load using the store's value, referred to as Predictive Store Forwarding (PSF).

In this paper, we provide a weakest precondition-based approach to detecting the data flow Spectre variants, Spectre-STL and Spectre-PSF, building on
a recent approach for Spectre-PHT [10]. The existing approach is detailed in
Sect. 2. In Sect. 3, we describe the data flow variants of Spectre with simple examples before presenting our formal approach to their detection in Sects. 4 and 5.
In Sect. 6 we discuss related formal approaches before concluding in Sect. 7.

2 Background

Winter et al. [31] present an information flow logic based on the weakest pre-
condition (wp) reasoning of Dijkstra [15,16]. The logic introduces additional
proof obligations to standard wp rules to ensure a form of *non-interference* [19]:
the proof obligations fail when sensitive information can be leaked to publicly
accessible variables or through observation of control flow.

This logic forms the basis of the approach to detecting Spectre-PHT vulnerable code by Coughlin et al. [10]. Following [9], that approach employs the

---

[1] Originally described by Jann Horn at https://project-zero.issues.chromium.org/
issues/42450580.

notion of a speculative context to track the effects of speculative execution. This is incorporated in a weakest precondition transformer wp_s which operates over *pairs* of predicates $\langle Q_s, Q \rangle$. The predicate Q_s represents the weakest precondition at that point in the program, assuming the processor is speculating, and Q the weakest precondition when it is not speculating. The security of a program ultimately depends on the non-speculative predicate Q holding in the program's initial state: proof obligations from the speculative state Q_s are taken into account by being transferred to the non-speculative state at points in the program where speculation can begin.

The rules of wp_s are defined over a high-level programming language representing assembly programs. The syntax of an instruction, α, and a program, p, is defined as follows.

$$\alpha ::= \text{skip}|r := e|r := x|x := e|\text{fence}|\text{leak } e$$
$$p ::= \alpha|p\,;p|\text{if } (b)\{p\}\text{else } \{p\}|\text{while } (b)\{p\}$$

where r is a register, x is a local or global variable (i.e., a memory location which in this paper can be an array access of the form $a[e]$), b a Boolean condition and e an expression. Both b and e are in terms of registers and literals only, as in assembly code. The language includes a fence instruction which prevents reordering of instructions (in the context of a processor's memory model) and also terminates current speculative execution. A special *ghost* instruction[2] leak e is inserted into a program to indicate that the following instruction(s) are part of a gadget that leaks the value e through a micro-architectural side channel when executed (speculatively, or otherwise).

Before analysing a program with the logic, leak instructions are inserted for each gadget of interest during a pre-pass over the code. Since typical gadgets can be detected syntactically, this is a straightforward task to mechanise. The expression e of the inserted leak instruction is based on what information leaks when the gadget is used in an attack. For the example of Sect. 1, leak $r1$ would be inserted immediately above the access to $array2$. After this pre-pass, the code is analysed using the logic to determine whether the information leaked is possibly sensitive and hence the gadget causes a security vulnerability. Since the pre-pass can be customised for different gadgets, the overall approach can be adapted to a variety of attacks, including new attacks as they are discovered.

2.1   Rules of wp_s

Skip. A skip instruction does not change the $\langle Q_s, Q \rangle$ tuple.

$$wp_s(\text{skip}, \langle Q_s, Q \rangle) = \langle Q_s, Q \rangle$$

Register Update. For each register or variable v in a program, the logic includes an expression Γ_v which evaluates to the *security level* of the information held by the variable. The possible values of security levels form a lattice

---

[2] A ghost instruction is not part of the actual code and is used for analysis purposes only.

$(L, \sqsubseteq)$ where each pair of elements $a, b \in L$ has a *join*, i.e., least upper bound, denoted by $a \sqcup b$, and a *meet*, i.e., greatest lower bound, denoted by $a \sqcap b$. The rule for updating a register r to the value of an expression e updates both r and Γ_r as follows, where $\Gamma_E(e) = \bigsqcup_{r \in regs(e)} \Gamma_r$ is the join of the security levels of the registers, $regs(e)$, to which e refers.

$$wp_s(r := e, \langle Q_s, Q \rangle) = \langle Q_s[r, \Gamma_r \backslash e, \Gamma_E(e)], Q[r, \Gamma_r \backslash e, \Gamma_E(e)] \rangle$$

where $Q[x_1, ..., x_n \backslash y_1, ..., y_n]$ replaces each free occurrence of x_i (for $1 \leq i \leq n$) in Q with y_i.

Load. Each variable x has a programmer-defined *security policy* $\mathcal{L}(x)$ denoting the highest security level that x may hold. This level may vary as the program executes [24,25] and hence $\mathcal{L}(x)$ is an expression in terms of other variables. For example, $\mathcal{L}(x) = $ (if $y = 0$ then *secret* else *public*), where *secret*, *public* $\in L$, captures that variable x may hold *secret* information when $y = 0$ and *public* information otherwise.

When loading the value of a variable x into a register r, it is possible that the security level of that value is undefined, e.g., when it has been set to an input value. Hence, Γ_r in the non-speculative state Q is updated to the meet of Γ_x and its maximum possible value, $\mathcal{L}(x)$.

In the speculative state Q_s, r and Γ_r are updated with values from memory (referred to as the *base state* and denoted with a $\flat$ superscript) when x is not defined in the speculative context, i.e., an earlier store to x has not occurred, and x and Γ_x otherwise. This is required to support concurrency since, during speculative execution, another thread may change a value in memory (the base state) but cannot change the corresponding value in the speculative state. Hence, values in the base state and speculative state can differ. The superscripts avoid the base state variables being affected by speculatively executed assignments.

Whether or not a variable x has been defined in the speculative context is captured by a Boolean ghost variable x_{def}.

$$
\begin{aligned}
wp_s(r := x, \langle Q_s, Q \rangle) = \ & \langle (x_{def} \implies Q_s[r, \Gamma_r \backslash x, \Gamma_x]) \wedge \\
& (\neg x_{def} \implies Q_s[r, \Gamma_r \backslash x^\flat, \Gamma_{x^\flat} \sqcap \mathcal{L}(x)[var \backslash var^\flat]]), \\
& Q[r, \Gamma_r \backslash x, \Gamma_x \sqcap \mathcal{L}(x)] \rangle
\end{aligned}
$$

where *var* is the list of program variables, and $var^\flat$ the same list with each element decorated with a $\flat$ superscript. Note that when x_{def} holds, we can use Γ_x directly, rather than the meet with $\mathcal{L}(x)$.

Store. A store to a variable, $x := e$, sets x_{def} to true and replaces each occurrence of variable x and Γ_x with expression e and security level $\Gamma_E(e)$, respectively, in both Q_s and Q. Additionally, in the non-speculative case non-interference is ensured by checking that

(i) the security level of e is not higher than the security classification of x, and

(ii) since x's value may affect the security classification of other variables, for each such variable y, y's current security level $\Gamma_y \sqcap \mathcal{L}(y)$ does not exceed its updated security classification when x is set to e.

Such checks are not required in the speculative case since, while speculating, values are not written to shared memory.

$$
\begin{aligned}
wp_s(x := e, \langle Q_s, Q \rangle) = \; & \langle Q_s[x, \Gamma_x, x_{def} \backslash e, \Gamma_E(e), true], \\
& Q[x, \Gamma_x \backslash e, \Gamma_E(e)] \wedge \Gamma_E(e) \sqsubseteq \mathcal{L}(x) \wedge \\
& (\forall y \cdot \Gamma_y \sqcap \mathcal{L}(y) \sqsubseteq \mathcal{L}(y)[x \backslash e]) \rangle
\end{aligned}
$$

Fence. The fence instruction terminates any current speculative execution. Hence, any proof obligations in the speculative state beyond the fence do not need to be considered at the point in the program where a fence occurs. Q_s is therefore replaced by $true$ and Q is unchanged.

$$
wp_s(\mathsf{fence}, \langle Q_s, Q \rangle) = \langle true, Q \rangle
$$

Leak. The instruction leak e leaks the value of expression e via a micro-architectural side channel, introducing a proof obligation into both Q_s and Q.

$$
wp_s(\mathsf{leak}\ e, \langle Q_s, Q \rangle) = \langle Q_s \wedge \Gamma_E(e) = \bot, Q \wedge \Gamma_E(e) = \bot \rangle
$$

where $\bot$ denotes the lowest value of the security lattice. Requiring that the leaked information is at this level ensures that the attacker cannot deduce anything new from the information, regardless of the level of information they can observe.

Sequential Composition. As in standard wp reasoning, sequentially composed instructions transform the tuple one at a time.

$$
wp_s(p_1 \mathbin{;} p_2, \langle Q_s, Q \rangle) = wp_s(p_1, wp_s(p_2, \langle Q_s, Q \rangle))
$$

If Statement. In the case of Spectre-PHT, speculation can begin at an if statement. Hence, it is at this point in the reasoning that the speculative proof obligation manifests itself as a proof obligation in the non-speculative state. For ease of presentation, we assume that the guard b does not change during speculation, hence the speculative proof obligation can be evaluated in the context of the guard.[3] The speculative proof obligation is from the opposite branch to the one that should be executed, with each variable x_{def} set to false (leaving just the predicates in terms of base variables) and all b subscripts removed (to identify these base variables with variables in the non-speculative state).

There is an additional proof obligation $\Gamma_E(b) = \bot$ on the non-speculative state since, in concurrent programs, the value of b can readily be deduced using

---

[3] An alternative rule that does not require this assumption is provided in [10].

timing attacks (even when the statement's branches do not change publicly accessible variables) [24,30]. An if statement might occur within a speculative context (when nested in or following an earlier if statement, for example). The branch that is followed speculatively is, in general, independent of that actually executed later. Hence, the speculative proof obligations from both branches are conjoined to form the speculative precondition.

Given $\langle Q_{s1}, Q_1 \rangle = wp_s(p_1, \langle Q_s, Q \rangle)$ and $\langle Q_{s2}, Q_2 \rangle = wp_s(p_2, \langle Q_s, Q \rangle)$, we have

$$wp_s(\text{if } (b)\{p_1\}\text{else } \{p_2\}, \langle Q_s, Q \rangle) =$$
$$\langle Q_{s1} \wedge Q_{s2}, (b \implies Q_1 \wedge Q_{s2}[var^b, d_1, ..., d_n \backslash var, false, ..., false]) \wedge$$
$$(\neg b \implies Q_2 \wedge Q_{s1}[var^b, d_1, ..., d_n \backslash var, false, ..., false]) \wedge$$
$$\Gamma_E(b) = \bot \rangle .$$

where $d_1, ..., d_n$ is the list of ghost variables of the form x_{def}.

While Loop. Speculation can also begin at each iteration of a while loop. Similarly to standard wp reasoning, we can soundly approximate the weakest precondition of a loop by finding invariants which imply our speculative and non-speculative postconditions. As with the if rule, a proof obligation $\Gamma_E(b) = \bot$ must hold in the non-speculative case.

$$wp_s(\text{while } (b)\{p\}, \langle Q_s, Q \rangle) = \langle Inv_s, Inv \rangle$$

where $Inv_s \implies Q_s$, $Inv \implies \Gamma_E(b) = \bot \wedge Inv_s[var^b, d_1, ..., d_n \backslash var, false, ...,$ $false]$ and $Inv \wedge \neg b \implies Q$, and given $wp_s(p, \langle Inv_s, Inv \rangle) = \langle P_s, P \rangle$, then $Inv_s \implies P_s$ and $Inv \wedge b \implies P$. Like the if rule, the while rule copies the proof obligations in the speculative precondition to the non-speculative precondition, and maintains those in the speculative precondition in case the loop is reached within an existing speculative context.

2.2   Using wp_s

The property that wp_s verifies, when the calculated weakest precondition of a program holds, is *value-dependent non-interference* based on the definition in [25]. This property states that, given two initial states s_1 and s_2 which agree on the values of variables which are non-sensitive, after executing a prefix of instructions t of the program on each state, the resulting states will continue to agree on the values of variables which are non-sensitive. In other words, the values of variables which are sensitive have no effect on those that are non-sensitive (and hence the sensitive values cannot be deduced from observations of the non-sensitive values). Formally, given a program c with precondition P and postcondition Q^4

$$P \implies wp_s(c, Q) \Rightarrow$$
$$\forall s_1, s_2 \in P, t \leqslant c \cdot \forall s_1' \cdot s_1 \sim s_2 \wedge s_1 \to_t s_1' \implies \exists s_2' \cdot s_2 \to_t s_2' \wedge s_1' \sim s_2'$$

---
[4] $\Rightarrow$ denotes logical entailment and binds less tightly then implication ($\implies$).

where $t \leqslant c$ denotes that t is a prefix of c, $s_1 \sim s_2$ denotes s_1 and s_2 agree on non-sensitive values, and $s_1 \rightarrow_t s_1'$ denotes s_1' is reached from s_1 by instructions t. Note that since the programming language is deterministic, the above property implies that all states reached from s_2 by t agree with the non-sensitive values of s_1'.

To support its use in a concurrent setting, wp_s also supports rely/guarantee reasoning [21,32]. To detect additional vulnerabilities that arise due to a processor's memory model, it is paired with a notion of reordering interference freedom (rif) [11,12]. These techniques (see [10] for details) are independent of the details of the logic's rules and can be equally applied to the extensions to wp_s in this paper.

3   Data Flow Spectre Variants

In addition to attacks related to speculation on control flow, such as Spectre-PHT of Sect. 1, attacks have been identified based on speculation on data flow; specifically speculation on dependencies between stores and subsequent loads. The most well-known of these is Spectre variant 4 (also known as Spectre-STL) [6]. This attack relies on a processor's memory disambiguator mispredicting that a load is independent of an earlier store, and hence executing the load with a stale value.

3.1   Spectre-STL

We illustrate Spectre-STL on Case 4 of the 13 litmus tests developed by Daniel et al. [13] and available at https://github.com/binsec/haunted_bench/blob/master/src/litmus-stl/programs/spectrev4.c. The test is reexpressed in the language from Sect. 2. In the code below, idx is an input provided by the user who may be an attacker, $secretarray$ is a publicly inaccessible array containing sensitive data and has length $array\_size$, and $publicarray2$ is a publicly accessible array which has length 512*256 (512 is the cache line size in bits, and 256 the number of integers representable using 8 bits).

$$r0 := idx;$$
$$r1 := array\_size;$$
$$r0 := r0 \ \& \ (r1 - 1);$$
$$secretarray[r0] := 0; \qquad // \text{ This store may be bypassed}$$
$$r1 := secretarray[r0];$$
$$r2 := publicarray2[r1 * 512];$$

The code begins by calculating the bitwise AND of idx and $array\_size - 1$ to obtain a valid index of $secretarray$. This avoids an array bounds bypass as in the Spectre-PHT attack. The value at the calculated index is set to 0, a non-sensitive value. This value is then read and used to read a value from $publicarray2$. The multiplication by 512 in the final step allows the value read from $secretarray$ to be deduced via a subsequent timing attack (by detecting the cache line affected by the read of *publicarray2*).

This code is secure provided the value used to read *publicarray2* is the non-sensitive value 0. However, if it is run and the memory disambiguator mispredicts that the load of *secretarray*[r0] is independent of the prior store then the load can be executed first. In this case, a sensitive value will be used in the read from *publicarray2*. To prevent bypassing the store in this way, a typical mitigation is to insert a fence instruction after the store to *secretarray* [26].

3.2   Spectre-PSF

Spectre-PSF is a variant of Spectre-STL where, rather than mispredicting that a dependency does not exist between a load and earlier store, the memory disambiguator mispredicts that a dependency *does* exist [7,26]. This behaviour has been confirmed as being possible on the AMD Zen 3 processor. We illustrate Spectre-PSF via an exploitable gadget from [26] (based on example code from AMD). The gadget is reexpressed in the language of Sect. 2. In the code below, *idx* is an input provided by the user, A is a public array of size 16, C is a public array of length $C\_size=2$ initialised to [0,0], and B is a public array of size 512*256.

```
r0 := idx;
r1 := C_size;
if (r0 < r1) {
    C[0] := 64;
    r1 := C[r0];        // Value 64 may be forwarded to r1
    r1 := A[r1 * r0];
    r2 := B[r1 * 512];
}
```

Ignoring speculation on the branch, the code is secure provided that the value loaded from $C[r0]$ is 64 only when *idx* (and hence r0) is 0: the value loaded from A will be the publicly accessible value at index 0 when *idx* is either 0 or 1. However, if the processor mispredicts a dependency between the store to $C[0]$ and the load from $C[r0]$ when *idx* is 1 then the value 64 can be (incorrectly) forwarded to the load. That is, r1 will be set to 64 and subsequently value $A[64]$ will be used in the index of B in the final load. This access of A will be out of bounds and hence to potentially sensitive data. Again, a fence after the store can be used to mitigate the vulnerability.

4   Detecting Spectre-STL

The wp_s logic in Sect. 2 assumes that speculation starts only at branching points (of if statements or while loops). To detect the data flow variants of Spectre, we need to also allow speculation to start at stores. For Spectre-STL, when a store is reached during execution, we can begin speculating that it is not required for the following code, and hence can be bypassed (the store executing later after the following code).

Given the code $s; c_1; c_2$ where s is a store and c_1 and c_2 are sequences of instructions, when the code of c_1 is not dependent on s, speculation over c_1 will lead to the execution $c_1; s; c_2$, where s has effectively been reordered after the instructions in c_1. When one or more instructions in c_1 are dependent on s, speculating over c_1 will lead to the execution $\mathbf{spec}(c_1); s; c_1; c_2$, where $\mathbf{spec}(c_1)$ includes rolling back the speculation's effects and hence has no affect on the program, but may alter the processor's microarchitecture.

In practice, the number of instructions in c_1 is limited by the processor's *speculation window*, i.e., the upper bound on the number of instructions that can execute speculatively. This bound will depend on the microarchitectural components involved in the speculation. For Spectre-STL, it will depend on the size of the store buffer where bypassed store instructions wait to be executed, i.e., committed to memory. The size of this buffer can be up to 106 stores[5] and hence, in general, beyond the size of the single procedures we are targeting in our work. Hence, as in wp_s we assume speculation can continue to the end of our code and do not explicitly model a speculation window. This results in a logic that is sound (as we check vulnerabilities within *any* sized speculation window), but can lead to false positives in cases where the actual speculation window is shorter than the code remaining to be executed.

To extend wp_s to detect Spectre-STL vulnerabilities, we modify the store rule as follows.

(i) The speculative postcondition Q_s is added to the non-speculative precondition. By transferring the speculative *post*condition, we effectively ignore the store, reflecting that it does not occur as part of the speculation. As in the if statement rule, all ghost variables y_{def} are replaced by false (to leave just the predicates in terms of the base variables) and each base variable y^b is replaced by y (to identify these variables with variables in the non-speculative predicate).

(ii) The speculative postcondition is also added to the speculative precondition. This reflects the case where the speculation on the store occurs in the context of an ongoing speculative execution. In this case, the store (being bypassed) will have no effect on the ongoing execution. For example, the rule will not cause a proof obligation $\Gamma_x = \bot$ to be resolved by a store $x := 0$ (where the literal 0 is a non-sensitive value).

The resulting rule is formalised below (where the additions to the original store rule from Sect. 2, corresponding to (i) and (ii) above, are underlined).

$$wp_{STL}(x := e, \langle Q_s, Q \rangle) = \langle \underline{Q_s \wedge} Q_s[x, \Gamma_x, x_{def} \backslash e, \Gamma_E(e), true],$$
$$Q[x, \Gamma_x \backslash e, \Gamma_E(e)] \wedge \Gamma_E(e) \sqsubseteq \mathcal{L}(x) \wedge$$
$$(\forall y \cdot \Gamma_y \sqcap \mathcal{L}(y) \sqsubseteq \mathcal{L}(y)[x \backslash e]) \wedge$$
$$\underline{Q_s[var^b, d_1, ..., d_n \backslash var, false, ..., false]} \rangle \qquad (1)$$

where $d_1, ..., d_n$ is the list of ghost variables of the form y_{def}.

---

[5] https://www.anandtech.com/show/16226/apple-silicon-m1-a14-deep-dive/2.

$\langle(idx_{def} \Rightarrow$
  $(secretarray[idx\&(array\_size - 1)]_{def} \Rightarrow \Gamma_{secretarray[idx\&(array\_size-1)]} = \bot) \wedge$
  $(\neg secretarray[idx\&(array\_size - 1)]_{def} \Rightarrow \Gamma_{secretarray[idx\&(array\_size-1)]^{\flat}} = \bot)) \wedge$
 $(\neg idx_{def} \Rightarrow$
  $(secretarray[idx^{\flat}\&(array\_size - 1)]_{def} \Rightarrow \Gamma_{secretarray[idx^{\flat}\&(array\_size-1)]} = \bot) \wedge$
  $(\neg secretarray[idx^{\flat}\&(array\_size - 1)]_{def} \Rightarrow \Gamma_{secretarray[idx^{\flat}\&(array\_size-1)]^{\flat}} = \bot)),$
 $\Gamma_{secretarray[idx\&(array\_size-1)]} = \bot\rangle$
 r0 := idx;
$\langle(secretarray[r0\&(array\_size - 1)]_{def} \Rightarrow \Gamma_{secretarray[r0\&(array\_size-1)]} = \bot) \wedge$
  $(\neg secretarray[r0\&(array\_size - 1)]_{def} \Rightarrow \Gamma_{secretarray[r0\&(array\_size-1)]^{\flat}} = \bot),$
 $\Gamma_{secretarray[r0\&(array\_size-1)]} = \bot\rangle$
 r1 := array_size;   // $array\_size = array\_size^{\flat}$ since $array\_size$ is a constant
$\langle(secretarray[r0\&(r1 - 1)]_{def} \Rightarrow \Gamma_{secretarray[r0\&(r1-1)]} = \bot) \wedge$
  $(\neg secretarray[r0\&(r1 - 1)]_{def} \Rightarrow \Gamma_{secretarray[r0\&(r1-1)]^{\flat}} = \bot),$
 $\Gamma_{secretarray[r0\&(r1-1)]} = \bot\rangle$
 r0 := r0 & (r1 -1);
$\langle(secretarray[r0]_{def} \Rightarrow \Gamma_{secretarray[r0]} = \bot) \wedge$
  $(\neg secretarray[r0]_{def} \Rightarrow \Gamma_{secretarray[r0]^{\flat}} = \bot), \Gamma_{secretarray[r0]} = \bot\rangle$
 secretarray[r0] := 0 ;   // This store may be bypassed
$\langle(secretarray[r0]_{def} \Rightarrow \Gamma_{secretarray[r0]} = \bot) \wedge$
  $(\neg secretarray[r0]_{def} \Rightarrow \Gamma_{secretarray[r0]^{\flat}} = \bot), \Gamma_{secretarray[r0]} = \bot\rangle$
 r1 := secretarray[r0];
$\langle\Gamma_{r1} = \bot, \Gamma_{r1} = \bot\rangle$
 leak r1;
$\langle true, true\rangle$
 r2 := publicarray2[r1*512];
$\langle true, true\rangle$

Fig. 1. Spectre-STL litmus test (code highlighted in gray).

To illustrate the utility of this rule, we apply it (along with other rules of wp_s) to the litmus test from Sect. 3.1 in Fig. 1, and to the same litmus test with a fence inserted to prevent speculation in Fig. 2. In both cases, a leak instruction is added before the access to *publicarray2*.

The introduced leak instruction adds proof obligations in both the speculative and non-speculative states that Γ_{r1} is $\bot$. Preceding backwards through the proof of Fig. 1, these obligations are transformed by the load to $r1$ to conditions on *secretarray*[r0]; in the speculative case this condition is dependent on whether *secretarray*[r0] is defined during the speculation.

The interesting step is the store to *secretarray*[0]. Since the value stored is non-sensitive, the proof obligation is satisfied in the non-speculative case (assuming *secretarray*[0] is not used in the security classification $\mathcal{L}$ of another variable). Hence, the non-speculative precondition of the store includes only the transferred condition from the speculative postcondition, i.e., $\Gamma_{secretarray[r0]} = \bot$. The spec-

$\langle true,\ true \rangle$
r0 := idx;
$\langle true,\ true \rangle$
r1 := array_size;
$\langle true,\ true \rangle$
r0 := r0 & (r1 -1);
$\langle true,\ true \rangle$
secretarray[r0] := 0;   // This store may no longer be bypassed
$\langle true, \Gamma_{secretarray[r0]} = \bot \rangle$
fence;
$\langle ((secretarray[r0]_{def} \Rightarrow \Gamma_{secretarray[r0]} = \bot) \wedge$
$(\neg secretarray[r0]_{def} \Rightarrow \Gamma_{secretarray^b[r0]} = \bot),\ \Gamma_{secretarray[r0]} = \bot \rangle$
r1 := secretarray[r0];
$\langle \Gamma_{r1} = \bot, \Gamma_{r1} = \bot \rangle$
leak r1;
$\langle true,\ true \rangle$
r2 := publicarray2[r1*512];
$\langle true,\ true \rangle$

Fig. 2. Spectre-STL litmus test with fence mitigation applied.

ulative precondition is equivalent to the speculative postcondition: the second conjunct of the precondition in rule (1) evaluates to true when $secretarray[r0]$ is defined and $secretarray[r0]$ is non-sensitive.

Proceding further backwards through the proof, the index used to access $secretarray$ is replaced with $idx\ \&\ (array\_size\ -\ 1)$. Thus, the final non-speculative precondition is $\Gamma_{secretarray[idx\ \&\ (array\_size-1)]} = \bot$, indicating that the code is secure provided that this condition holds initially. This is more precise than a simple syntactic analysis which identifies the gadget, but does not define the conditions under which it can be successfully exploited.

The proof in Fig. 2 is identical before the fence instruction is reached (i.e., below the fence instruction). At this point, the speculative predicate becomes true and hence no condition is transferred to the non-speculative precondition at the store instruction. The result is that the final non-speculative precondition is true, indicating that the code is always secure.

To further validate our rule, we applied it (along with other required rules from wp_s) to the remaining 12 litmus tests of Daniel et al. [13] (see Appendix A of [29]) and for each of the 9 litmus tests with a vulnerability, we applied it to a version of the litmus test with a fence added as a mitigation. All vulnerabilities were detected and all tests with mitigations showed the vulnerability could no longer occur. However, there is one test where we detect a vulnerability and Daniel et al. do not. This test, Case 9, is the same as Case 4 but includes a loop after the store which is intended to fill the reorder buffer[6], forcing the store to be evaluated and take effect in memory before the load from *publicarray2*. Since our logic supports detection of Spectre-PHT (as well as Spectre-STL), it allows the loop to speculatively exit early. In general, our logic detects multiple variants of Spectre including, as in this case, vulnerabilities that arise due to their combination.

5 Detecting Spectre-PSF

Store forwarding refers to using the value of a store instruction in a subsequent load instruction before the store has taken effect in memory. This can be done safely when the store and load are to the same address. On some processors, store forwarding can be done speculatively based on a prediction that a store and subsequent load are to the same address. This leads to the Spectre-PSF vulnerability described in Sect. 3.2.

Abstracting from how the prediction is made, our rule reflects that the value of a store instruction, can be used speculatively in *any* subsequent load. When there is no leak or a given load does not cause a leak, the misprediction is benign and does not manifest in our reasoning. When the load does cause a leak, the variable associated with the load will appear in the postcondition of the store. For each subset of such variables, we replicate the speculative proof obligation with the variables replaced by the value of the store. This captures all possible predictions including those in which the value of the store is forwarded to more than one subsequent load. These additional proof obligations are also transferred to the non-speculative precondition of the store, reflecting that speculation may have begun at the store. The rule is formalised below (with the additions to the Spectre-STL store rule from Sect. 4 underlined).

$$
\begin{aligned}
&wp_{PSF}(x := e, \langle Q_s, Q \rangle) = \\
&\quad \langle \underline{\forall \{y_1, ..., y_m\} \subseteq vars(Q_s)} \cdot \\
&\qquad \underline{(Q_s \land Q_s[x, \Gamma_x, x_{def} \backslash e, \Gamma_E(e), true])[y_1, ..., y_m \backslash e, ..., e]}, \\
&\quad Q[x, \Gamma_x \backslash e, \Gamma_E(e)] \land \Gamma_E(e) \sqsubseteq \mathcal{L}(x) \land \\
&\quad (\forall y \cdot \Gamma_y \sqcap \mathcal{L}(y) \sqsubseteq \mathcal{L}(y)[x \backslash e]) \land \\
&\quad \underline{\forall \{y_1, ..., y_m\} \subseteq vars(Q_s)} \cdot \\
&\qquad Q_s[var^\flat, d_1, ..., d_n \backslash var, false, ..., false]\underline{[y_1, ..., y_m \backslash e, ..., e]} \rangle \quad (2)
\end{aligned}
$$

where $vars(\mathcal{L}(x))$ denotes the list of variables occurring free in $\mathcal{L}(x)$, and $d_1, ..., d_n$ is the list of ghost variables of the form y_{def}. Note that when the set $\{y_1, ..., y_m\}$ is the empty set, the predicate in both the speculative and non-speculative preconditions are equivalent to those of the STL rule. Hence, this rule will detect vulnerabilities to both Spectre-STL and Spectre-PSF.

---

[6] The reorder buffer contains *all* speculated instructions and provides an upper limit on the number of instructions that can be speculatively executed.

$\langle ..., idx < C\_size \Rightarrow \Gamma_{A[C[idx]*idx]} = \bot \wedge \Gamma_{A[64*idx]} = \bot \wedge \Gamma_{C[idx]} = \bot \wedge$
$\qquad \Gamma_{A[C[0\mapsto 64][idx]*idx]} = \bot) \wedge (idx \geq C\_size \Rightarrow ...)\rangle$

r0 := idx;
$\langle ..., \Gamma_{r0} = \bot \wedge (r0 < C\_size \Rightarrow \Gamma_{A[C[r0]*r0]} = \bot \wedge \Gamma_{A[64*r0]} = \bot \wedge \Gamma_{C[r0]} = \bot \wedge$
$\qquad \Gamma_{A[C[0\mapsto 64][r0]*r0]} = \bot) \wedge (r0 \geq C\_size \Rightarrow ...)\rangle$

r1 := C_size;
$\langle ..., \Gamma_{r0} = \bot \wedge \Gamma_{r1} = \bot \wedge$
$\quad (r0 < r1 \Rightarrow \Gamma_{A[C[r0]*r0]} = \bot \wedge \Gamma_{A[64*r0]} = \bot \wedge \Gamma_{C[r0]} = \bot \wedge$
$\qquad \Gamma_{A[C[0\mapsto 64][r0]*r0]} = \bot) \wedge (r0 \geq r1 \Rightarrow ...)\rangle$

if (r0 < r1){

$\qquad \langle ..., \Gamma_{A[C[r0]*r0]} = \bot \wedge \Gamma_{A[64*r0]} = \bot \wedge \Gamma_{r0} = \bot \wedge \Gamma_{C[r0]} = \bot \wedge$
$\qquad \Gamma_{A[C[0\mapsto 64][r0]*r0]} = \bot\rangle$

$\qquad$ C[0] := 64;   // Value 64 may be forwarded to r1

$\qquad \langle as\ below\rangle$

$\qquad$ **leak** r0;

$\qquad \langle (A[C[r0]*r0]_{def} \wedge C[r0]_{def} \Rightarrow \Gamma_{A[C[r0]*r0]} = \bot \wedge \Gamma_{r0} = \bot \wedge \Gamma_{C[r0]} = \bot) \wedge$
$\qquad (A[C[r0]*r0]_{def} \wedge \neg C[r0]_{def} \Rightarrow \Gamma_{A[C[r0]^\flat*r0]} = \bot \wedge \Gamma_{r0} = \bot \wedge \Gamma_{C[r0]^\flat} = \bot) \wedge$
$\qquad (\neg A[C[r0]*r0]_{def} \wedge C[r0]_{def} \Rightarrow \Gamma_{A[C[r0]*r0]^\flat} = \bot \wedge \Gamma_{r0} = \bot \wedge \Gamma_{C[r0]} = \bot) \wedge$
$\qquad (\neg A[C[r0]*r0]_{def} \wedge \neg C[r0]_{def} \Rightarrow \Gamma_{A[C[r0]^\flat*r0]^\flat} = \bot \wedge \Gamma_{r0} = \bot \wedge \Gamma_{C[r0]^\flat} = \bot),$
$\qquad\quad \Gamma_{r0} = \bot \wedge \Gamma_{C[r0]} = \bot \wedge \Gamma_{A[C[r0]*r0]} = \bot\rangle$

$\qquad$ r1 := C[r0];

$\qquad \langle \Gamma_{r0} = \bot \wedge \Gamma_{r1} = \bot \wedge (A[r1*r0]_{def} \Rightarrow \Gamma_{A[r1*r0]} = \bot) \wedge$
$\qquad (\neg A[r1*r0]_{def} \Rightarrow \Gamma_{A[r1*r0]^\flat} = \bot), \Gamma_{r0} = \bot \wedge \Gamma_{r1} = \bot \wedge \Gamma_{A[r1*r0]} = \bot\rangle$

$\qquad$ **leak** r1*r0;

$\qquad \langle (A[r1*r0]_{def} \Rightarrow \Gamma_{A[r1*r0]} = \bot) \wedge (\neg A[r1*r0]_{def} \Rightarrow \Gamma_{A[r1*r0]^\flat} = \bot),$
$\qquad\quad \Gamma_{A[r1*r0]} = \bot\rangle$

$\qquad$ r1 := A[r1*r0];

$\qquad \langle \Gamma_{r1} = \bot, \Gamma_{r1} = \bot\rangle$

$\qquad$ **leak** r1;

$\qquad \langle true, true\rangle$

$\qquad$ r1 := B[r1];

$\qquad \langle true, true\rangle$

}

$\langle true, true\rangle$

Fig. 3. Spectre-PSF litmus test

To illustrate rule (2), we apply it to the litmus test from Sect. 3.2 in Fig. 3. Each load of an array value ($B[r1]$, $A[r1*r0]$ and $C[r0]$) introduces a potential leak. Note that the leak due to the load of $C[r0]$ does not change the state tuple $\langle Q_s, Q\rangle$ since both the non-speculative and speculative predicates already imply $\Gamma_{r0} = \bot$. For the non-speculative precondition of the store $C[0] := 64$, the postcondition $\Gamma_{r0} = \bot$ is unchanged, the postcondition $\Gamma_{C[r0]} = \bot$ is transformed to true, and the postcondition $\Gamma_{A[C[r0]*r0]} = \bot$ is transformed to $\Gamma_{A[C[0\mapsto64][r0]*r0]} = \bot$ where $C[0 \mapsto 64]$ is array C with element 0 equal to 64.

In addition, for each subset of global variables in the non-speculative post-condition, we need to transfer the required predicate to the non-speculative precondition. There are two global variables, $A[C[r0] * r0]$ and $C[r0]$, and hence four subsets including the empty set. The speculative postcondition with variables of the form y_{def} set to false, and variables of the form $y^\flat$ replaced by y is $\Gamma_{A[C[r0]*r0]} = \bot \wedge \Gamma_{r0} = \bot \wedge \Gamma_{C[r0]} = \bot$. Hence, the required predicates for each subset of global variables are as follows.

- For the empty set $\{\}$, we have $\Gamma_{A[C[r0]*r0]} = \bot \wedge \Gamma_{r0} = \bot \wedge \Gamma_{C[r0]} = \bot$.
- For $\{A[C[r0] * r0]\}$, we have $\Gamma_{r0} = \bot \wedge \Gamma_{C[r0]} = \bot$ since $\Gamma_{A[C[r0]*r0]} = \bot$ is true when $A[C[r0] * r0]$ is 64.
- For $\{C[r0]\}$, we have $\Gamma_{A[64*r0]} = \bot \wedge \Gamma_{r0} = \bot$ since $\Gamma_{C[r0]} = \bot$ is true when $C[r0]$ is 64.
- For $\{A[C[r0] * r0], C[r0]\}$, we have $\Gamma_{r0} = \bot$.

Conjoining the four predicates above gives us the condition required for the leaks not to be exploitable via either Spectre-STL (the empty-set case) or Spectre-PSF: $\Gamma_{A[C[r0]*r0]} = \bot \wedge \Gamma_{A[64*r0]} = \bot \wedge \Gamma_{r0} = \bot \wedge \Gamma_{C[r0]} = \bot$.

The overall non-speculative precondition for the program is derived under the assumptions that C_size and the input idx are non-sensitive, and that $idx \geq 0$ and all elements of arrays A and C are non-sensitive. To keep the presentation simple, we elide the speculative precondition above the store $C[0] := 64$ and the non-speculative proof obligation due to Spectre-PHT, i.e., the non-speculative proof obligation when $idx \geq C\_size$.

When $idx = 0$, the precondition simplifies to true since each array index evaluates to 0 which is in the range of the respective arrays (recall from Sect. 3.2 that C is of size 2 and A of size 16). When $idx = 1$, $A[64 * idx]$ accesses a memory location beyond the end of array A and hence data which is potentially sensitive. Hence, the code is not provably secure: the Spectre-PSF vulnerability discussed in Sect. 3.2 is detected.

Adding a fence instruction after the store will prevent speculative store forwarding. This situation is also correctly evaluated by our logic. The fence's speculative precondition is true and hence no proof obligations are transferred to the non-speculative precondition of the store. This results in the precondition of the program when idx is 0 or 1 evaluating to true.

The above litmus test (in both fenced and unfenced form) constitutes the only litmus test for Spectre-PSF in the literature. Other approaches for detecting Spectre-PSF are based on an explicit semantics of the microarchitectural features that give rise to the vulnerability [20] or, like us, rely on this single litmus test for validation [26].

6 Related Work

Cauligi et al. [8] provide a detailed comparison of 24 formal semantics and tools for detecting Spectre vulnerabilities. While all approaches support Spectre-PHT, only 5 out of 24 [5,7,13,20,26] support Spectre-STL (and only 2 of these [20,26] have support for Spectre-PSF). Three of the five are based on explicit models of a processor's microarchitecture [7,13,20] and two on more abstract semantics [5,26].

Of the former approaches, Cauligi et al. [7] and Guanciale et al. [20] model program instructions by translation to sequences of fetch, execute and commit microinstructions. Additional state information and associated microinstructions provide the prediction and rollback facilities required to model speculative execution. This level of detail has the potential to detect more vulnerabilities than abstract approaches, and in fact Guanciale et al. [20] independently discover Spectre-PSF (which they call Spectre-STL-D). However, such detailed models also add complexity to analysis.

Cauligi et al.'s approach [7] is supported by symbolic execution as is the approach of Daniel et al. [13]. The latter work addresses scalability issues inherent with symbolic execution by removing redundant execution paths, and representing aspects of the microarchitectural execution symbolically rather than explicitly. These optimisations are validated using a set of litmus tests including those for Spectre-STL that we adopt in this paper. Later work by the authors [14] looks at modelling and implementing a hardware taint-tracking mechanism to mitigate vulnerabilities to Spectre, including Spectre-STL.

Fabian et al. [17] (not included in the above comparison) also employ symbolic execution for detecting Spectre vulnerabilities, including Spectre-STL. They define a framework for composing semantics of different variants of Spectre allowing to detect leaks due to a combination of, for example, Spectre-PHT and Spectre-STL. Our approach also allows the detection of such vulnerabilities as the proof obligations for each of the different Spectre variants is checked. We have confirmed this by applying the approach to Listing 1 of [17] (see Appendix B of [29]).

Barthe et al. [5] provide a higher-level semantics of speculative execution for a simple while language (similar to the language in this paper). Rather than modelling speculation via microinstructions, the semantics includes high-level directives which, for example, force a particular branch to be taken, or indicate which store is to be used by a load. The approach is implemented in the Jasmin verification framework [2,3].

Ponce de León and Kinder [26] provide an axiomatic semantics for speculative execution (based on the work of Alglave et al. [1]) which is significantly less complex than the operational semantics of other approaches. The semantics defines which executions are valid via constraints on various relations between loads and stores in a program. Their approach is validated for Spectre-STL and Spectre-PSF using the same litmus tests as in this paper, and supported by bounded model checking.

Our work differs from the existing approaches by having its basis in weakest precondition (wp) reasoning. This opens the opportunity to adapt existing program analysis tools such as Boogie [4] or Why3 [18] which automate such reasoning (see [28] for work in this direction). Such tooling requires the user to provide annotations, particularly loop invariants, to programs but is able to handle greater nondeterminism than symbolic execution or model checking where nondeterminism can adversely affect scalability.

Our work is also based on an approach [10] which can be combined with rely/guarantee reasoning for analysis of concurrent programs [21,32] and the proof technique, reordering interference freedom (rif), for taking into account processor weak memory models [11]. Its underlying logic can also be extended to support controlled release of sensitive information via declassification [27].

7 Conclusion

This paper has presented a weakest precondition-based approach for detecting vulnerabilities to the major data flow variants of Spectre, Spectre-STL and Spectre-PSF. The approach extends an existing approach for Spectre-PHT and can detect vulnerabilities to all three attacks including when the attacks occur in combination. The approach has been validated with a set of litmus test used to validate related approaches and tools in the literature. A deeper evaluation of the approach, including its use on concurrent programs, requires automated tool support which is left to future work. Since it is based on weakest precondition reasoning, such support can be built on an existing auto-active program analyser such as Boogie or Why3.

Acknowledgements. Thanks to Kirsten Winter, Robert Colvin and Mark Beaumont for feedback on this paper.

References

1. Alglave, J., Maranget, L., Tautschnig, M.: Herding cats: modelling, simulation, testing, and data mining for weak memory. ACM Trans. Program. Lang. Syst. **36**(2), 7:1–7:74 (2014). https://doi.org/10.1145/2627752, http://doi.acm.org/10.1145/2627752

2. Almeida, J., et al.: Jasmin: high-assurance and high-speed cryptography. In: Thuraisingham, B., Evans, D., Malkin, T., Xu, D. (eds.) Proceedings of the 2017 ACM SIGSAC Conference on Computer and Communications Security, CCS 2017, pp. 1807–1823. ACM (2017). https://doi.org/10.1145/3133956.3134078

3. Almeida, J., et al.: The last mile: high-assurance and high-speed cryptographic implementations. In: 2020 IEEE Symposium on Security and Privacy, SP 2020, pp. 965–982. IEEE (2020). https://doi.org/10.1109/SP40000.2020.00028

4. Barnett, M., Chang, B.-Y.E., DeLine, R., Jacobs, B., Leino, K.: Boogie: a modular reusable verifier for object-oriented programs. In: de Boer, F.S., Bonsangue, M.M., Graf, S., de Roever, W.-P. (eds.) FMCO 2005. LNCS, vol. 4111, pp. 364–387. Springer, Heidelberg (2006). https://doi.org/10.1007/11804192_17

5. Barthe, G., et al.: High-assurance cryptography in the spectre era. In: 42nd IEEE Symposium on Security and Privacy, SP 2021, pp. 1884–1901. IEEE (2021). https://doi.org/10.1109/SP40001.2021.00046

6. Canella, C., et al.: A systematic evaluation of transient execution attacks and defenses. In: Heninger, N., Traynor, P. (eds.) 28th USENIX Security Symposium, USENIX Security 2019, Santa Clara, CA, USA, August 14-16, 2019, pp. 249–266. USENIX Association (2019)

7. Cauligi, S., et al.: Constant-time foundations for the new Spectre era. In: Donaldson, A.F., Torlak, E. (eds.) Proceedings of the 41st ACM SIGPLAN International Conference on Programming Language Design and Implementation, PLDI 2020, pp. 913–926. ACM (2020). https://doi.org/10.1145/3385412.3385970

8. Cauligi, S., Disselkoen, C., Moghimi, D., Barthe, G., Stefan, D.: SoK: practical foundations for software Spectre defenses. In: 43rd IEEE Symposium on Security and Privacy, SP 2022, pp. 666–680. IEEE (2022). https://doi.org/10.1109/SP46214.2022.9833707

9. Colvin, R.J., Winter, K.: An abstract semantics of speculative execution for reasoning about security vulnerabilities. In: Sekerinski, E., et al. (eds.) FM 2019. LNCS, vol. 12233, pp. 323–341. Springer, Cham (2020). https://doi.org/10.1007/978-3-030-54997-8_21

10. Coughlin, N., Lam, K., Smith, G., Winter, K.: Detecting speculative execution vulnerabilities on weak memory models. In: Platzer, A., Rozier, K.Y., Pradella, M., Rossi, M. (eds.) Formal Methods - 26th International Symposium, FM 2024. LNCS, vol. 14933, pp. 482–500. Springer, Cham (2024). https://doi.org/10.1007/978-3-031-71162-6_25

11. Coughlin, N., Winter, K., Smith, G.: Rely/guarantee reasoning for multicopy atomic weak memory models. In: Huisman, M., Păsăreanu, C., Zhan, N. (eds.) FM 2021. LNCS, vol. 13047, pp. 292–310. Springer, Cham (2021). https://doi.org/10.1007/978-3-030-90870-6_16

12. Coughlin, N., Winter, K., Smith, G.: Compositional reasoning for non-multicopy atomic architectures. Formal Aspects Comput. **35**(2), 8:1–8:30 (2023). https://doi.org/10.1145/3574137

13. Daniel, L., Bardin, S., Rezk, T.: Hunting the haunter - efficient relational symbolic execution for Spectre with Haunted RelSE. In: 28th Annual Network and Distributed System Security Symposium, NDSS 2021. The Internet Society (2021)

14. Daniel, L., Bognar, M., Noorman, J., Bardin, S., Rezk, T., Piessens, F.: Prospect: provably secure speculation for the constant-time policy. In: Calandrino, J.A., Troncoso, C. (eds.) 32nd USENIX Security Symposium, USENIX Security 2023, pp. 7161–7178. USENIX Association (2023)

15. Dijkstra, E.W.: A Discipline of Programming. Prentice-Hall (1976). https://www.worldcat.org/oclc/01958445

16. Dijkstra, E.W., Scholten, C.S.: Predicate Calculus and Program Semantics. Springer, Heidelberg (1990)

17. Fabian, X., Guarnieri, M., Patrignani, M.: Automatic detection of speculative execution combinations. In: Yin, H., Stavrou, A., Cremers, C., Shi, E. (eds.) Proceedings of the 2022 ACM SIGSAC Conference on Computer and Communications Security, CCS 2022, pp. 965–978. ACM (2022). https://doi.org/10.1145/3548606.3560555

18. Filliâtre, J.-C., Paskevich, A.: Why3 — where programs meet provers. In: Felleisen, M., Gardner, P. (eds.) ESOP 2013. LNCS, vol. 7792, pp. 125–128. Springer, Heidelberg (2013). https://doi.org/10.1007/978-3-642-37036-6_8

19. Goguen, J.A., Meseguer, J.: Security policies and security models. In: 1982 IEEE Symposium on Security and Privacy, 1982, pp. 11–20. IEEE Computer Society (1982). https://doi.org/10.1109/SP.1982.10014

20. Guanciale, R., Balliu, M., Dam, M.: InSpectre: breaking and fixing microarchitectural vulnerabilities by formal analysis. In: Ligatti, J., Ou, X., Katz, J., Vigna, G. (eds.) CCS 2020: 2020 ACM SIGSAC Conference on Computer and Communications Security, pp. 1853–1869. ACM (2020). https://doi.org/10.1145/3372297.3417246

21. Jones, C.B.: Specification and design of (parallel) programs. In: IFIP Congress, pp. 321–332 (1983)

22. Kocher, P., Horn, J., et al.: Spectre attacks: exploiting speculative execution. In: 2019 IEEE Symposium on Security and Privacy, SP 2019, pp. 1–19. IEEE (2019). https://doi.org/10.1109/SP.2019.00002

23. Liu, F., Yarom, Y., Ge, Q., Heiser, G., Lee, R.B.: Last-level cache side-channel attacks are practical. In: 2015 IEEE Symposium on Security and Privacy, SP 2015, pp. 605–622. IEEE Computer Society (2015). https://doi.org/10.1109/SP.2015.43

24. Murray, T.C., Sison, R., Engelhardt, K.: COVERN: A logic for compositional verification of information flow control. In: 2018 IEEE European Symposium on Security and Privacy, EuroS&P 2018, pp. 16–30. IEEE (2018). https://doi.org/10.1109/EuroSP.2018.00010

25. Murray, T.C., Sison, R., Pierzchalski, E., Rizkallah, C.: Compositional verification and refinement of concurrent value-dependent noninterference. In: IEEE 29th Computer Security Foundations Symposium, CSF 2016, pp. 417–431. IEEE Computer Society (2016). https://doi.org/10.1109/CSF.2016.36

26. Ponce de León, H., Kinder, J.: Cats vs. spectre: an axiomatic approach to modeling speculative execution attacks. In: 43rd IEEE Symposium on Security and Privacy, SP 2022, pp. 235–248. IEEE (2022). https://doi.org/10.1109/SP46214.2022.9833774

27. Smith, G.: Declassification predicates for controlled information release. In: Riesco, A., Zhang, M. (eds.) 23rd International Conference on Formal Engineering Methods (ICFEM 2022). LNCS. Springer, Cham (2022)

28. Smith, G.: A Dafny-based approach to thread-local information flow analysis. In: 11th IEEE/ACM International Conference on Formal Methods in Software Engineering, FormaliSE 2023, pp. 86–96. IEEE (2023). https://doi.org/10.1109/FormaliSE58978.2023.00017

29. Smith, G.: Detecting speculative data flow vulnerabilities using weakest precondition reasoning (2025). https://arxiv.org/abs/2504.19128

30. Smith, G., Coughlin, N., Murray, T.: Value-dependent information-flow security on weak memory models. In: ter Beek, M.H., McIver, A., Oliveira, J.N. (eds.) FM 2019. LNCS, vol. 11800, pp. 539–555. Springer, Cham (2019). https://doi.org/10.1007/978-3-030-30942-8_32

31. Winter, K., Coughlin, N., Smith, G.: Backwards-directed information flow analysis for concurrent programs. In: 34th IEEE Computer Security Foundations Symposium, CSF 2021, pp. 1–16. IEEE (2021). https://doi.org/10.1109/CSF51468.2021.00017

32. Xu, Q., de Roever, W.P., He, J.: The rely-guarantee method for verifying shared variable concurrent programs. Formal Aspects Comput. **9**(2), 149–174 (1997). https://doi.org/10.1007/BF01211617

Dynamic Analysis

Random Testing of Model Checkers for Timed Automata with Automated Oracle Generation

Andrea Manini$^{(\boxtimes)}$ [ID], Matteo Rossi [ID], and Pierluigi San Pietro [ID]

Politecnico di Milano, Milan, Italy
{andrea.manini,matteo.rossi,pierluigi.sanpietro}@polimi.it

Abstract. A key challenge in formal verification, particularly in Model Checking, is ensuring the correctness of the verification tools. Erroneous results on complex models can be difficult to detect, yet a high level of confidence in the outcome is expected. Indeed, these tools are frequently novel and may not have been thoroughly tested. When standard benchmarks may be insufficient or unavailable, random test case generation offers a promising approach. To scale up, random testing requires comparing actual versus expected results, i.e., solving the oracle problem.

To address this challenge, this work introduces a novel theoretical framework based on a modular variant of Timed Automata (TA), called Tiled Timed Automata (TTA), for testing model checkers operating with variations of TA, by building oracles based on Weighted Automata. The framework is initially applied to verify model checkers solving the emptiness problem for Parametric TA and it is validated, in this specific scenario, by our tool, TABEC, which randomly generates tests predicting their expected outcome through automated oracle generation. Furthermore, the general nature of TTA facilitates the framework adaptation to model checkers solving other decidable problems on TA, as detailed for the minimum-cost reachability problem of Priced TA.

1 Introduction

Ensuring the correctness of systems subject to vital temporal constraints is crucial to prevent considerable economic or human losses. To address this challenge, various formal techniques have been developed to rigorously verify such systems. Due to the intricacy and difficulty of correctness proofs based on mathematical logic, automated verification techniques, such as Model Checking, are now central to formal verification. Model Checking relies on a formal model of the system under study to check its behavior against relevant formal properties.

Timed Automata (TA) are a popular mathematical formalism used to model concurrent and real-time systems, which are among the most difficult to develop and test. Since the primary purpose of verification tools for TA is to ensure

---

The experimental results presented in this paper are reproducible using the artifact available at: 10.5281/zenodo.14871008.

© The Author(s), under exclusive license to Springer Nature Switzerland AG 2026
P. Rümmer and Z. Wu (Eds.): TASE 2025, LNCS 15841, pp. 343–360, 2026.
https://doi.org/10.1007/978-3-031-98208-8_20

the behavioral correctness of modeled systems, they must be as error-free as possible. However, ensuring the complete absence of errors in verification tools is challenging, since their intrinsic complexity hinders the rigorous proof of their correctness. Model checkers are software artifacts, hence traditional software engineering techniques for detecting errors—e.g., testing [24]—can be employed.

Testing formal verification tools usually consists in running a set of standard benchmarks, whose results are known and thus can be checked against the actual tool output. However, the number of benchmarks is often limited and they may fail to cover new features of the specification language if the latter is extended. The original motivation of this work was indeed introducing a new framework for rigorously testing the correctness of model checkers working with variations of TA. We developed a tool implementing this framework using a particular class of Parametric TA (PTA). A well-established way to be confident of the correctness both of the technique and of the tool is to run a very large set of tests. Hence, in our implementation, we validated the correctness of the framework and tool by applying random testing techniques [1], often used in software engineering for evaluating the robustness and performance of programs.

Automatically verifying the accuracy of testing results, particularly for randomly-generated, non-trivial test cases, is a daunting task, known as the *oracle testing problem* [14], still a significant research topic [5,6,16]. Contemporary research initiatives, particularly those aligned with formal methods, have dedicated significant attention to the problem of deriving test oracles from specifications expressed in different kinds of temporal logics [9–12,22]. Examples building TA-based oracles can be found in [4,23]. To the best of our knowledge, no existing techniques automatically generate test oracles for TA-based tools. The recent work [8] applies mutation testing to networks of TA, implementing new mutation operators and evaluating their effectiveness with Uppaal [15].

The idea behind the test oracle generation underpinning our framework consists in creating a set of *tiles*, i.e., TA whose behavior can be easily characterized by inspection, and then combining them in a randomly-generated automaton, called Tiled TA (TTA). A TTA can then be "flattened" into a TA analyzed by our verification tool, called TABEC (Timed Automata Builder and Emptiness Checker) [17]. By abstracting a TTA as a Weighted Automaton, it is possible to generate an oracle predicting a priori the correct result of the verification, e.g., the range of values (if any) admissible for the parameter (when considering PTA tiles). Although TABEC has been implemented with reference to PTA, the theoretical concepts presented in this paper are general and can be easily adapted to other variants of TA, as outlined for illustrative purposes with Priced TA.

The main contribution of this work is two-fold: (i) we introduce a novel theoretical framework based on TTA to facilitate the testing of model checkers for variations of TA. First, by using a decidable variant of PTA, we show how to use our framework to verify model checkers solving the language emptiness problem for PTA; then, we outline how to adapt the framework to the minimum-cost reachability problem of Priced TA; (ii) we developed TABEC to validate our theoretical results with respect to the emptiness problem. By generating test oracles, TABEC predicts the range of values (if any) for the unknown parameter.

The organization of this paper is as follows: Sect. 2 provides the theoretical foundations for this work. Section 3 presents an algorithm to solve the language emptiness problem of the considered decidable PTA variant. Section 4 derives the theoretical framework for model checkers solving the language emptiness problem of PTA. Section 5 details experimental results. Section 6 adapts the framework to Priced TA. Sect. 7 concludes and outlines future developments.

2   Theoretical Background

(Parametric) Timed Automata. Let Σ be a finite alphabet. An ω-*language* is the set of infinite words $\sigma = a_0 a_1 a_2 \ldots$ defined over Σ. A *time sequence* $\tau = \tau_0 \tau_1 \tau_2 \ldots$ is an infinite sequence of non-negative real numbers such that, for all $i \geqslant 0$, it holds that $\tau_i < \tau_{i+1}$ (strict monotonicity) and for all $t \in \mathbb{R}_{>0}$ there is $i \geqslant 0$ such that $\tau_i > t$ holds (progression). A *timed ω-word* (sometimes simply called *timed word*) is a pair (σ, τ), where σ is an infinite word and τ is a time sequence. Timed Automata are defined as follows [2]:

Definition 1 (Timed Automaton). *A* Timed Automaton $\mathcal{A}$ *(shortened as TA) is a tuple* $\mathcal{A} = (\Sigma, Q, q_0, B, X, T)$, *where* Σ *is a finite input alphabet,* Q *is a finite set of locations,* q_0 *is the initial location,* $B \subseteq Q$ *is a subset of locations, called accepting locations,* X *is a finite set of clocks, and* $T \subseteq Q \times Q \times \Gamma(X) \times \Sigma \times 2^X$ *is a transition relation.*

The input alphabet Σ does not affect the results presented in this paper, hence in the following we assume it to be the singleton $\Sigma = \{a\}$ or just omit it.

Clocks are special variables that can only be reset or checked against an integer constant. Their value grows linearly in time until a reset occurs. When a clock is reset, its value becomes 0, from which it starts increasing again. The set $\Gamma(X)$ contains *clock guards*—i.e., predicates over clocks that must be satisfied for a transition to fire; they are specified according to the following grammar: $\gamma := x < c \mid x = c \mid \neg\gamma \mid \gamma \wedge \gamma$, where $\gamma \in \Gamma(X)$, $x \in X$, and $c \in \mathbb{N}$. The powerset 2^X indicates that a transition may reset a subset of the clocks.

A pair (q, v) is called a *configuration* for a TA, where $q \in Q$ is a location and $v : X \to \mathbb{R}_{\geqslant 0}$ is called a *clock valuation*. A *run* ρ over a timed word (σ, τ) is an infinite sequence $\rho = (q_0, v_0)(q_1, v_1) \ldots$ of configurations starting in location q_0 such that $v_0(x) = 0$ for all $x \in X$ and, if $(q_i, v_i)(q_{i+1}, v_{i+1})$ is a pair of consecutive configurations in the run, then there is a transition $(q_i, q_{i+1}, \gamma_i, \sigma(i), Y_i) \in T$, with v_i satisfying γ_i, and v_{i+1} such that the clocks in Y_i are 0, while the others are incremented by $\tau_{i+1} - \tau_i$. Let $inf(\rho)$ denote the set of locations visited infinitely often in a run ρ. A run ρ is *accepting* according to a Büchi acceptance condition if, and only if, $inf(\rho) \cap B \neq \varnothing$ holds—i.e., ρ enters one or more accepting locations infinitely often. A timed ω-word is accepted if it has an accepting run.

TA can be enriched by adding a set P of parameters to Definition 1, obtaining Parametric TA (shortened as PTA) [3]. Parameters enable flexible system representation by describing characteristics unknown at modeling time. The value a

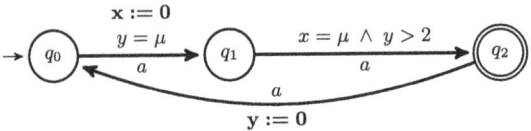

Fig. 1. Example of PnrtTA, where $\Sigma = \{a\}$, $X = \{x, y\}$, and $P = \{\mu\}$. Clock resets are represented in bold, while clock guards are represented in italic. The initial location is q_0, while the (only) accepting location is q_2.

parameter can assume is determined by a mapping $\mathcal{I} : P \to \mathbb{R}$, where $\mathcal{I}$ is called a *parameter valuation*. Clock guards in PTA include the following additional rules in their grammar: $x < \mu$ and $x = \mu$, where $\mu \in P$. The notion of run for a PTA can be trivially extended to consider parameter valuations. We call a run ρ of a PTA, with parameter valuation $\mathcal{I}$, a *parametric run*.

This work focuses on a particular version of TA, defined as follows [7]:

Definition 2 (Non-resetting test TA). *Let $\mathcal{A} = (\Sigma, Q, q_0, B, X, T)$ be a TA. For each transition $u \in T$ of $\mathcal{A}$ of the form $u = (q_u, q'_u, \gamma_u, a_u, Y_u)$, let $X(\gamma_u)$ be the set of clocks that appear in γ_u. Then, $\mathcal{A}$ is called a* non-resetting test Timed Automaton *(shortened as nrtTA) if, for all $u \in T$, $X(\gamma_u) \cap Y_u = \varnothing$.*

Basically, in an nrtTA a clock cannot be used both in guards and resets within the same transition. Definition 2 can trivially be extended by introducing a set P of parameters, obtaining *Parametric nrtTA* (shortened as PnrtTA). In the remainder of this work we focus on PnrtTA having two clocks and only one parameter, and refer to this variant simply as PnrtTA. An example of a PnrtTA satisfying these requirements is given in Fig. 1. This restriction enables the application of the theoretical results presented below.

Decidability of PnrtTA. The recent work [7] proves that the emptiness problem is decidable for PnrtTA. The result is summarized as follows:

Theorem 1. *Let $\mathcal{A}$ be a PnrtTA and C be the largest constant appearing in the guards of $\mathcal{A}$. Then:*

1. *There exists a constant value $\Xi > 2C$ such that, $\forall \bar{\mu} \in \mathbb{R} : \bar{\mu} > 2C$, with $\bar{\mu} \neq \Xi$, if there is a parametric run ρ for $\mathcal{A}$ having a parameter valuation equal to $\bar{\mu}$, then there is also a parametric run $\hat{\rho}$ for $\mathcal{A}$ having a parameter valuation equal to Ξ.*
2. *There exists a constant value $0 < \alpha < \frac{1}{2}$ such that, $\forall n \in \mathbb{N} : 0 < n < 4C$, if there is a parametric run ρ for $\mathcal{A}$ having a parameter valuation equal to $\bar{\mu}$, with $\frac{n}{2} < \bar{\mu} < \frac{n+1}{2}$, then there is also a parametric run $\hat{\rho}$ for $\mathcal{A}$ having a parameter valuation equal to $\hat{\mu} = \frac{n}{2} + \alpha$.*

The two values Ξ and α can be easily computed as a function of C and of the number of locations of $\mathcal{A}$ (denoted as $|Q|$) [7].[1]

---

[1] More precisely, Ξ is any value greater than $1 + C(1 + |Q|)$, while α is required to be any value less than $\frac{1}{4(1 + C \cdot max(|Q|, 4C))}$.

Weighted Automata. Weighted Automata are used in this paper to derive test oracles. Weights over a semiring facilitate the definition of test oracles that operate on different mathematical entities. The most appropriate semiring must be manually chosen to align with the specific operational context of the problem at hand. We follow the definitions of [20, Chapter 4], with minor differences.

A *semiring* $\check{S} = (S, \oplus, \otimes, 0_S, 1_S)$ is an algebraic structure such that: (i) S is a set, (ii) $\oplus$ (called sum) and $\otimes$ (called product) are associative binary operations over S, (iii) $\oplus$ is commutative, (iv) 0_S is the identity of $\oplus$, (v) 1_S is the identity of $\otimes$, (vi) $\otimes$ distributes over $\oplus$ both from the left and the right, and (vii) 0_S is an annihilator for $\otimes$ (i.e., for all $s \in S$, $s \otimes 0_S = 0_S \otimes s = 0_S$).

Example 1. For $k \geqslant 1$, let $\mathcal{B}_k$ be the set $\{0,1\}^k$ of Boolean words of length k, and OR, AND be the corresponding bitwise operations. Then, $W^{k-\text{bit}} = (\mathcal{B}_k, OR, AND, 0^k, 1^k)$ is a semiring, since (i) OR, AND have the required properties over Boolean words, (ii) 0^k, 1^k are the identity for the OR and AND respectively, and (iii) $s\,AND\,0^k = 0^k\,AND\,s = 0^k$ for every $s \in \mathcal{B}_k$.

Example 2. Another example of semiring is $W^{\text{price}} = (\mathbb{N} \cup \{+\infty\}, \min, +, +\infty, 0)$, often called the tropical, or min-plus, semiring. In this case, weights represent costs to be summed and minimized; the value $+\infty$ is the identity of the $\min$ operation since, e.g., $\min(x, +\infty) = x$ for every $x \in \mathbb{N}$.

Definition 3 (Weighted Automaton). *A* Weighted Automaton $\mathcal{W}$ *over a semiring* $(S, \oplus, \otimes, 0_S, 1_S)$ *is a tuple* $\mathcal{W} = (\Sigma, Q, q_0, F, w)$, *where* Σ *is a finite input alphabet,* Q *is a finite set of states,* $q_0 \in Q$ *is the initial state,* $F \subseteq Q$ *is a set of final states, and* $w = w_T \cup w_F$ *is a weight function, where* $w_T : Q \times \Sigma \times Q \to S$ *is the transition weight function and* $w_F : F \to S$ *is the final weight function.*

A *path* P of $\mathcal{W}$ is a *finite* sequence $q_0 y_1 q_1 y_2 \ldots y_n q_n$, for $n \geqslant 0$, where $q_i \in Q$ for all $i \geqslant 0$, q_0 is initial, and $y_i \in \Sigma$. The *label* of P is $l(P) = y_1 \ldots y_n$. It is possible to extend the weight function w to paths as follows: given a finite path $P = q_0 y_1 q_1 y_2 \ldots y_n q_n$, its weight is 0_S if q_n is not final, otherwise it is:

$$w(P) = \left(\prod_{1 \leqslant i \leqslant n} w_T(q_{i-1}, y_i, q_i) \right) \otimes w_F(q_n),$$

where $\prod$ uses the $\otimes$ operation for the product.

The *behavior* of $\mathcal{W}$ is the mapping $w_l : \Sigma^* \to S$ defined for all $y \in \Sigma^*$ as:

$$w_l(y) = \sum_{P:l(P)=y} w(P),$$

where $\sum$ uses the $\oplus$ operation for the sum.

For example, in a Weighted Automaton $\mathcal{W}$ defined over the min-plus semiring of Example 2, a weight may represent a cost (a price) to pay to traverse a transition of $\mathcal{W}$. Costs are summed up along a path, and the cost of a given word is defined as the minimum cost among all paths labeled with that word. Paths ending in a non-final state have weight $+\infty$. The behavior of $\mathcal{W}$ is just the mapping defining the cost of each word.

3   Checking PnrtTA Emptiness

We developed and implemented an algorithm based on Theorem 1 to determine, given a PnrtTA $\mathcal{A}$, whether its language is empty. The key idea consists in replacing the parameter with suitable constant values, so that checking the emptiness of $\mathcal{A}$ is reduced to checking the emptiness of several TA without parameters.

A pseudocode version of this algorithm is reported in Algorithm 1, called EmpCheck (we also refer to it as EmpCheckFast when *fastFlag* is true). Given a PnrtTA $\mathcal{A}$ as input, EmpCheck can find all parameter values that can lead to a Büchi acceptance condition in $\mathcal{A}$. In particular, line 2 checks the case in which $\mu > 2C$. A total of $4C + 1$ iterations are performed from line 6 to line 10 to check the case in which $\mu \leqslant 2C$ and μ is a multiple of $\frac{1}{2}$ holds. Lastly, if the condition on line 11 is not satisfied, a total of $4C$ iterations are performed from line 13 to line 17 to check the case in which $\mu < 2C$ holds. If any of the conditions on lines 3, 8, or 15 are satisfied, the algorithm halts immediately.

The CheckNonParEmptiness$(\mathcal{A}, \bar{\mu})$ procedure substitutes each parameter occurrence in $\mathcal{A}$ with a specific constant value $\bar{\mu}$ derived from Theorem 1, depending on the considered case; this substitution yields a usual TA without parameters. The resulting automaton is then checked by the same procedure, leveraging existing verification tools capable of detecting Büchi acceptance conditions in TA.

Algorithm 1: Checking the language emptiness of PnrtTA

Data: $\mathcal{A}$: a PnrtTA, *fastFlag*: a Boolean value.
Result: *true* if the language of $\mathcal{A}$ is not empty, *false* otherwise.

```
 1 begin
 2 │   isAccepting ← CheckNonParEmptiness(A, Ξ);
 3 │   if (fastFlag ∧ isAccepting) = true then
 4 │   └   return true;
 5 │   n ← 0;
 6 │   while n ⩽ 2C do
 7 │   │   isAccepting ← isAccepting ∨ CheckNonParEmptiness(A, n);
 8 │   │   if (fastFlag ∧ isAccepting) = true then
 9 │   │   └   return true;
10 │   └   n ← n + ½;
11 │   if isAccepting = false then
12 │   │   n ← 0;
13 │   │   while n < 4C do
14 │   │   │   isAccepting ← isAccepting ∨ CheckNonParEmptiness(A, n/2 + α);
15 │   │   │   if (fastFlag ∧ isAccepting) = true then
16 │   │   │   └   return true;
17 │   │   └   n ← n + 1;
18 │   return isAccepting;
```

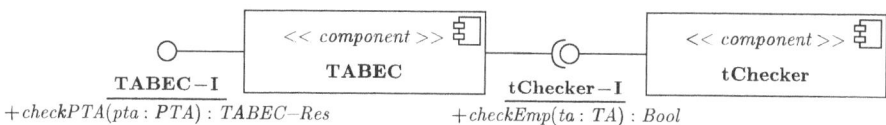

Fig. 2. Component diagram illustrating the interaction between TABEC and tChecker. As highlighted by the *tChecker-I* interface and its *checkEmp()* method, tChecker is only responsible for verifying the emptiness of a given TA $\mathcal{A}$ and returning the result (either true or false) to TABEC. The *TABEC-I* interface defines the functionalities provided by TABEC. The return type *TABEC-Res* of the *checkTA()* method represents a custom output type containing emptiness results, as well as possible values of the parameter leading to a Büchi acceptance condition in $\mathcal{A}$.

Since the `CheckNonParEmptiness`$(\mathcal{A}, \bar{\mu})$ procedure is PSPACE-complete, it follows that both EmpCheck and EmpCheckFast are PSPACE-complete as well.

The current implementation of TABEC uses tChecker [13] as the verification engine for emptiness checking of TA. The widely used tool Uppaal is not suitable for this task, as it does not support the detection of Büchi acceptance conditions in TA, unlike tChecker. The component diagram of Fig. 2 illustrates the interaction between TABEC and tChecker. The latter is responsible for analyzing the emptiness of a given TA and returning the results via the *tChecker-I* interface.

There is a slight difference between the nrtTA model used in this work and the one that is given to tChecker by TABEC. In tChecker, time sequences are only weakly monotonic (i.e., time may also not advance between two transitions), while in the nrtTA model they are strictly monotonic. To force strict monotonicity, the set of clocks of a given nrtTA $\mathcal{A}$ is enriched with an additional clock z. Since clock z is never compared with constants (other than 0) or parameters, it does not affect the language accepted by $\mathcal{A}$, thus preserving emptiness results before and after its addition. The new clock z is reset on every transition entering a location and introduces an additional condition $\gamma := z > 0$ to be added to preexisting guards on every transition exiting from a location. This process transforms $\mathcal{A}$ into an equivalent TA that no longer retains the non-resetting test property. The content of this paper is not affected, as this is only an implementation mechanism to achieve strict monotonicity in practice. A graphical example of this transformation is given in Fig. 3.

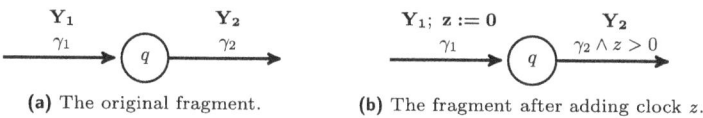

(a) The original fragment.   (b) The fragment after adding clock z.

Fig. 3. Illustrative transformation resulting from the addition of clock z to a nrtTA fragment consisting of a single location with one incoming and one outgoing transition. The symbols Y_1, Y_2 and γ_1, γ_2 denote, respectively, generic resets and guards.

4   Oracle Generation Framework

This section introduces tiles and Tiled TA, used to create the oracles needed to verify the correctness of model checkers for TA. We begin by providing general definitions and then focus on the emptiness problem for Parametric TA.

Tiled Timed Automata. Tiles are particular TA that can be considered as building blocks for creating more complex TA, having an effect which can be easily predicted. The latter varies based on the nature of the considered tiles, as will be shown later for parametric tiles and in Sect. 6 for priced tiles.

Definition 4 (Tile). *A tile T is a tuple $T = (\Sigma, Q, B, X, T, In, Out, \mathcal{F})$, where Σ, Q, B, X, T are as in Definition 1 and where $In \subseteq Q$ is the set of* input *locations, $Out \subseteq Q$ is the set of* output *locations, B may be empty, and $\mathcal{F}$ is a set containing the functions (called compatibility functions) $\mathcal{I}_{T,\gamma} : In \to \Gamma(X)$, $\mathcal{I}_{T,Y} : In \to 2^X$, $\mathcal{O}_{T,\gamma} : Out \to \Gamma(X)$, and $\mathcal{O}_{T,Y} : Out \to 2^X$.*

Let T be a tile. When needed, we use T as subscript to separate the elements of different tiles, e.g., In_T and Out_T indicate, respectively, the input and output sets of T. If T is such that both $B_T \neq \varnothing$ and $Out_T = \varnothing$ hold, then T it is called an *accepting tile*. Input and output locations, along with compatibility functions, are used to connect tiles together according to the following relation:

Definition 5 (Tile transition relation). *Given an alphabet Σ and a set Θ of tiles, let $X_\Theta = \bigcup_{T \in \Theta} X_T$ be the set of clocks of Θ. A tile transition relation Υ is a set of tuples included in $\bigcup_{T,T' \in \Theta} Out_T \times In_{T'} \times \Gamma(X_\Theta) \times \Sigma \times 2^{X_\Theta}$ such that, for all transitions $(q, q', \gamma, a, Y) \in \Upsilon$, the assume-guarantee constraint $\mathcal{O}_{T,\gamma}(q) \Rightarrow \mathcal{I}_{T',\gamma}(q')$ holds, $\gamma = \mathcal{O}_{T,\gamma}(q)$, and $Y = \mathcal{O}_{T,Y}(q) \cup \mathcal{I}_{T',Y}(q')$.*

Since accepting tiles have no output locations, a tile transition relation does not contain transitions exiting from them. Definition 5 specifies how different tiles are connected together, enabling the construction of arbitrarily large TA:

Definition 6 (Tiled TA). *A Tiled Timed Automaton $\mathcal{A}$ (shortened as TTA) is a tuple $\mathcal{A} = (\Theta, T_0, \Sigma, \mathbb{B}, X_\Theta, \Upsilon)$, where Θ is a set of tiles, $T_0 \in \Theta$ is the initial tile, Σ is a finite input alphabet, $\mathbb{B} \subseteq \Theta$ is a set of accepting tiles, X_Θ is a set of clocks defined as $X_\Theta = \bigcup_{T \in \Theta} X_T$, and Υ is a tile transition relation defined over Σ and Θ as in Definition 5.*

A Büchi acceptance condition for TTA is introduced by requiring that an accepting tile is reached and that one of its final locations is visited infinitely often. A TTA cannot exit an accepting tile; this allows it to accept infinite words while visiting its tiles only finitely many times.

The *flattening* of a TTA $\mathcal{A}$ results in a TA, denoted by $\mathcal{A}_{flat}$, obtained by substituting each tile within $\mathcal{A}$ with its corresponding TA. The ω-language accepted by $\mathcal{A}$, denoted by $\mathcal{L}(\mathcal{A})$, is defined as the ω-language accepted by $\mathcal{A}_{flat}$. For all runs $\rho = (q_0, v_0)(q_1, v_1) \ldots$ of $\mathcal{A}_{flat}$ it must hold that $q_0 \in In_{T_0}$ and $v_0(x) = 0$ for all $x \in X_\Theta$.

An example of TTA is shown in Fig. 4 where, for a Büchi acceptance condition to hold, it suffices to reach tile T_3 starting from tile T_0.

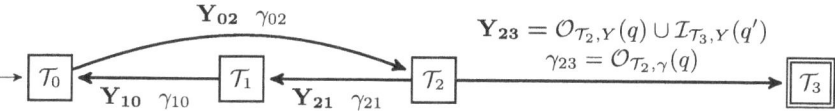

Fig. 4. TTA where tile T_0 is initial, tile T_3 is accepting, location $q \in Out_{T_2}$, and location $q' \in In_{T_3}$. Resets and guards of the tile transition relation are shown, respectively, in bold and italic; on the transition from tile T_2 to tile T_3 they are made explicit.

Underlying Weighted Automaton. Let $\mathcal{A} = (\Theta, T_0, \Sigma, \mathbb{B}, X_\Theta, \Upsilon)$ be a TTA. We can associate each non-accepting tile $T \in (\Theta \setminus \mathbb{B})$ with a weight function $w_T : Out_T \to S$, mapping each output location of T to a weight in the domain S of an appropriate semiring. The semiring and weights must be manually defined for each problem at hand. Since accepting tiles do not have output locations, we also define a weight function $w_\mathbb{B} : \mathbb{B} \to S$ associating a weight with each accepting tile. The weight function over Θ is defined as $w_\Theta = w_\mathbb{B} \cup \bigcup_{T \in (\Theta \setminus \mathbb{B})} w_T$. A particular Weighted Automaton is derived from $\mathcal{A}$ and w_Θ:

Definition 7 (Underlying Weighted Automaton). *Let $\mathcal{A} = (\Theta, T_0, \Sigma, \mathbb{B}, X_\Theta, \Upsilon)$ be a TTA and w_Θ be a weight function over Θ. The* Underlying Weighted Automaton *of $\mathcal{A}$ is the Weighted Automaton $\mathcal{W}_{\mathcal{A},w} = (\Sigma, Q, q_0, F, w)$, where $Q = \Theta$, $q_0 = T_0$, $F = \mathbb{B}$, and $w = w_T \cup w_F$ is such that, for all transitions $(q, q', \gamma, a, Y) \in \Upsilon$, where $q \in Out_T$ and $q' \in In_{T'}$, for $T \in (\Theta \setminus \mathbb{B})$ and $T' \in \Theta$, $w_T(T, a, T') = w_\Theta(q)$ holds and, for all $T \in \mathbb{B}$, $w_F(T) = w_\Theta(T)$ holds.*

For instance, consider the TTA $\mathcal{A}$ of Fig. 4: $\mathcal{W}_{\mathcal{A},w}$ is obtained by replacing guards and resets on each transition with weights. Then, the weight of the path $P = T_0 T_2 T_3$ in $\mathcal{W}_{\mathcal{A},w}$ is $w(P) = w_\Theta(q_0) \otimes w_\Theta(q) \otimes w_\Theta(T_3)$, where $q_0 \in Out_{T_0}$.

Notice that an Underlying Weighted Automaton is always defined on finite runs, while a TTA only accepts infinite words. Weights characterize the behavior of TTA, as shown later for PTTA and in Sect. 6 for Priced TA.

Parametric TTA. A *parametric tile* is a non-resetting test tile with one parameter (denoted by μ) and two clocks. Parametric tiles can force μ to be inside one or more intervals. Given the region characterization of [7], such intervals are of the form $\frac{a}{2} \sim_1 \mu \sim_2 \frac{b}{2}$, where $a \in \mathbb{N}$, $b \in (\mathbb{N} \cup \{+\infty\})$, $\sim_1, \sim_2 \in \{<, \leqslant\}$, and $a \leqslant b$; for ease, the case $a = b$ defines a single point, still treated as an interval. A non-accepting parametric tile T can force μ inside one or more intervals if there exists at least one path from In_T to Out_T. A set of intervals δ_q, also called *parameter set*, is forced for each reachable output location $q \in Out_T$. An accepting tile T has a parameter set δ_T, which is nonempty if there exists at least one infinite path from In_T visiting some location in B_T infinitely often.

Figure 5 shows an example of parametric tile T. For the transition from q_0 to q_1 to fire, clock y, reset to 0 upon entering T as imposed by $\mathcal{I}_{T,Y}(q_0) = \{y\}$, must have a value equal to μ. Next, for the transition from q_1 to q_2 to fire, clock x must be equal to μ (it was reset when entering q_1), while clock y, thanks to the

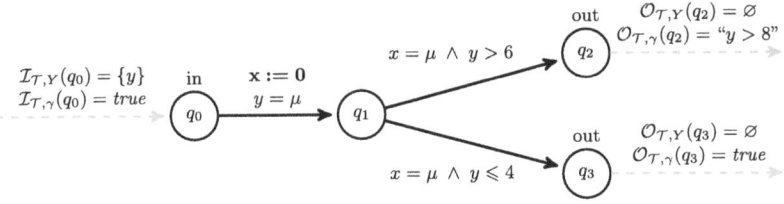

Fig. 5. Tile forcing the intervals $\delta_{q_2} = \{(3,+\infty)\}$ and $\delta_{q_3} = \{(0,2]\}$. The tile is neither initial nor accepting. Compatibility functions are reported over gray dashed arrows, which symbolically represent a tile transition relation.

constraint on clock x, must satisfy $6 < y = 2\mu$, implying $3 < \mu$ holds. A similar argument applies for the transition from q_1 to q_3, implying $0 < \mu \leqslant 2$ holds. Despite enforcing the interval $(3,+\infty)$ upon reaching q_2, constraint $\mathcal{O}_{T,\gamma}(q_2)$ requires that $y > 8$ must hold if T is connected via the transition exiting q_2.

A parametric tile T is *elementary* if the connection in sequence of two instances T_1, T_2 of T, i.e., $\Upsilon \subseteq Out_{T_1} \times In_{T_2} \times \Gamma(X_\Theta) \times \Sigma \times 2^{X_\Theta}$, for $\Theta = \{T_1, T_2\}$, can generate any interval in which to constrain μ. The tile T of Fig. 6 is elementary. Figure 7 shows a tile obtained by connecting in sequence two instances of T: T_1 with $n = 4$ and $\sim\ = >$, and T_2 with $n = 8$ and $\sim\ = \leqslant$.

A *Parametric TTA* $\mathcal{A}$ (shortened as PTTA) is a TTA containing at least one parametric tile. Tile transition relations are assumed to be non-resetting test. From now on, we use the term *tile* to refer to a parametric tile.

We require that, for every tile T of a PTTA $\mathcal{A}$, the compatibility function $\mathcal{I}_{T,\gamma}$ guarantees that each parameter set δ_q and δ_T remains unchanged for all clock values satisfying the guards specified by $\mathcal{I}_{T,\gamma}$. This condition and the assume-guarantee constraint of Definition 5 together ensure that, in a run, parameter sets do not depend on the values of the clocks upon entering a tile. Therefore, when verifying the non-emptiness of $\mathcal{A}$ using its Underlying Weighted Automaton, the actual values of the clocks upon entering or exiting a tile can be ignored.

Oracles for PTTA. We now introduce an *ad hoc* weight function for PTTA over the $W^{k-\mathrm{bit}} = (\mathcal{B}_k, OR, AND, 0^k, 1^k)$ semiring:

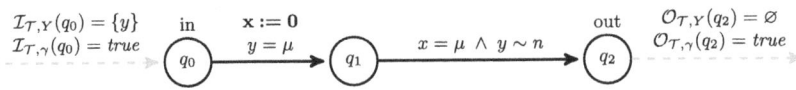

Fig. 6. Elementary tile T forcing the interval $\mu \sim \frac{n}{2}$, where $\sim\ \in \{<, \leqslant, \geqslant, >\}$. Here, n is a tile-specific integer constant which must be substituted to obtain the desired interval. T does not assume any constraint on clock x and resets clock y upon entrance.

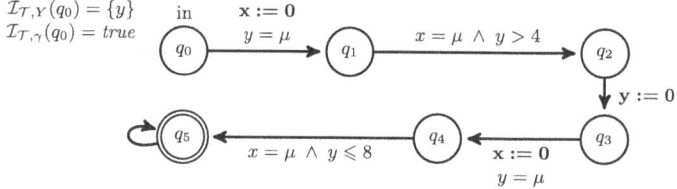

Fig. 7. Accepting tile $\mathcal{T}$ (obtained combining two elementary tiles in sequence) forcing the interval $(2, 4]$, hence $\delta_{\mathcal{T}} = \{(2, 4]\}$.

Definition 8 (PTTA weight function). *Let $\mathcal{A}$ be a PTTA with tile set Θ, C be the maximum constant appearing in the guards of $\mathcal{A}$, and $k = 8C+2$. A weight function for $\mathcal{A}$ over W^{k-bit} is a mapping $w_{\Theta} : (\mathbb{B} \cup \bigcup_{\mathcal{T} \in (\Theta \setminus \mathbb{B})} Out_{\mathcal{T}}) \to \mathcal{B}_k$.*

In fact, according to Theorem 1, a PnrtTA can be studied by picking one or more of the following $k = 8C + 2$ intervals:

$$\{0\}, (0, \tfrac{1}{2}), \{\tfrac{1}{2}\}, (\tfrac{1}{2}, 1), \{1\}, (1, \tfrac{3}{2}), \dots, (\tfrac{4C-1}{2}, 2C), \{2C\}, (2C, +\infty). \qquad (1)$$

We can define a bijection between $\mathcal{B}_k$ and the powerset of all intervals shown in Eq. 1 by uniquely associating each word in $\{0, 1\}^k$ with a set of intervals: a word $w \in \{0, 1\}^k$ has a 1 in position i if, and only if, the i-th interval is in the set. For instance, the word $01^3 0^{k-4}$ maps to the interval $(0, 1) = (0, \tfrac{1}{2}) \cup \{\tfrac{1}{2}\} \cup (\tfrac{1}{2}, 1)$; the word $0^6 1^{k-6}$ maps to $[\tfrac{3}{2}, +\infty)$, and the word $01^8 0^{k-9}$ maps to $(0, 2]$.

Definition 9 (Productivity). *Let $\mathcal{A} = (\Theta, \mathcal{T}_0, \Sigma, \mathbb{B}, X_{\Theta}, \Upsilon)$ be a PTTA and w_{Θ} be a weight function as in Definition 8. A tile $\mathcal{T} \in (\Theta \setminus \mathbb{B})$ is productive for w_{Θ} if, for each $q \in Out_{\mathcal{T}}$, $w_{\Theta}(q)$ is uniquely associated with δ_q and δ_q is not empty. Analogously, a tile $\mathcal{T} \in \mathbb{B}$ is productive for w_{Θ} if $w_{\Theta}(\mathcal{T})$ is uniquely associated with $\delta_{\mathcal{T}}$ and $\delta_{\mathcal{T}}$ is not empty.*

Theorem 2. *Let $\mathcal{A} = (\Theta, \mathcal{T}_0, \Sigma, \mathbb{B}, X_{\Theta}, \Upsilon)$ be a PTTA and w_{Θ} be a weight function as in Definition 8. If every tile in Θ is productive for w_{Θ}, checking the non-emptiness of $\mathcal{A}$ is equivalent to checking the existence of words with non-zero weight in $\mathcal{W}_{\mathcal{A}, w}$. In other words, $\mathcal{L}(\mathcal{A})$ is non-empty if, and only if, there exists $y \in \Sigma^*$ and a path P in $\mathcal{W}_{\mathcal{A}, w}$ with a non-zero weight in $\mathcal{B}_k$ such that $l(P) = y$.*

The proof of Theorem 2 can be found in [18]. By analyzing each tile individually, a weight can be assigned to ensure its productivity, enabling the application of the oracle verification procedure outlined in Algorithm 2. On line 2, a PTTA $\mathcal{A}$ is randomly generated by using a set Θ of productive tiles, weighted over the semiring W^{k-bit}. Next, on line 3, the tool T under test is run with $\mathcal{A}_{flat}$ as input, producing a pair of results: *isEmpty*, a Boolean indicating if T detects an empty language, and *witness*, a path leading to a Büchi acceptance condition in $\mathcal{A}_{flat}$, if it exists. If the condition on line 4 holds, a path P in $\mathcal{W}_{\mathcal{A}, w}$ corresponding to *witness* is constructed: $w(P)$ is then checked to actually be non-zero (regarding

---

Algorithm 2: Testing a PTA tool using oracles

Data: Θ: a set of productive tiles weighted over $W^{k-\text{bit}}$, T: a tool to test.
Result: *true* if T behaves correctly, *false* otherwise.

1 **begin**
2     $\mathcal{A} \leftarrow \texttt{GenerateRandomPTTA}(\Theta)$;
3     $\langle isEmpty, witness \rangle \leftarrow \texttt{RunTool}(T, \mathcal{A}_{flat})$;
4   **if** $isEmpty = false \wedge witness \neq \varnothing$ **then**
5       $P \leftarrow$ path in $\mathcal{W}_{\mathcal{A},w}$ corresponding to *witness*;
6   **return** $w(P) \neq 0_{\mathcal{B}_k}$;
7   **return** $\texttt{NonZeroWords}(\mathcal{W}_{\mathcal{A},w})$;

W^{k-bit}): if non-zero, then T passes the test, else it fails. If the condition on line 4 does not hold, the existence of words with non-zero weight (regarding W^{k-bit}) in $\mathcal{W}_{\mathcal{A},w}$ is verified: if none exist, then T passes the test, else it fails.

The decidability and complexity of checking the existence of words with a non-zero weight in a Weighted Automaton depend on the chosen semiring. The problem is decidable for the Boolean words semiring $W^{k-\text{bit}}$ and its complexity is in polynomial-time when the constant k is coded in unary, since it can be reduced to a generalization of the Floyd-Warshall algorithm for solving the shortest distance problem in a complete semiring [19].

5 Experimental Results

This section explains how oracle generation is implemented in practice in TABEC and presents the results of its experimental evaluation. To validate our theoretical results, an extensive testing phase was performed on a Linux machine having an AMD EPYC 7282 CPU, 16 cores, 32 threads, 2.8–3.2 GHz.

5.1 Forecasting Parameter Values with TABEC

TABEC allows users to generate PTTA (manually or automatically) as a composition of tiles, and subsequently test their emptiness. At the time of writing, TABEC is still a prototype; in particular, tiles must have only one input location and up to two output locations. Furthermore, the input location of a tile must have at most one incoming transition. For these reasons, the PTTA considered by the current version of TABEC have a *binary tree* structure, as shown for instance in Fig. 8. The binary tree structure cannot model all real-world systems; still, it acts as a reference scalability performance indicator: if performance is poor on binary tree-like PTTA, it will be poor on generic PTTA as well.

By Theorem 2, TABEC can predict the interval in which the parameter value may fall (if any exists) before performing the actual emptiness test, thus producing a test oracle. For practical reasons, TABEC operates using unions and intersections of intervals, which correspond to the *OR* and *AND* operations

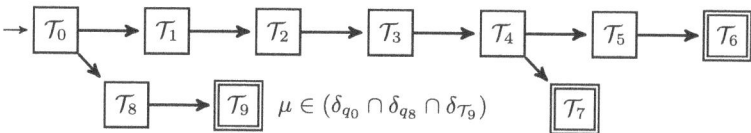

Fig. 8. Example of a binary tree-like PTTA. For simplicity, compatibility functions are omitted. A possible valid set of intervals for μ is shown on the right of tile $\mathcal{T}_9$. It is computed as the intersection of the parameter sets of the tiles traversed to reach $\mathcal{T}_9$. Here, $q_0 \in Out_{\mathcal{T}_0}$ (from which the transition from $\mathcal{T}_0$ to $\mathcal{T}_8$ originates) and $q_8 \in Out_{\mathcal{T}_8}$.

over Boolean words in the semiring $W^{k\text{-bit}}$ performed by Underlying Weighted Automata. In the case of binary trees, each path P from $\mathcal{T}_0$ to an accepting tile $\mathcal{T}$ is a sequence of tiles: the set of intervals in which the parameter value may fall upon reaching $\mathcal{T}$ over P is obtained by intersecting the parameter sets of the tiles in P, considering only those related to the output locations from which the transitions in P originate, along with the parameter set of $\mathcal{T}$. The complete set of admissible intervals is obtained by repeating this computation for each path from $\mathcal{T}_0$ to an accepting tile. Figure 8 provides an example of this computation when considering the path $P = \mathcal{T}_0 \mathcal{T}_8 \mathcal{T}_9$. The set of intervals obtained upon reaching tile $\mathcal{T}_9$ from $\mathcal{T}_0$ in P is computed as $\delta_{q_0} \cap \delta_{q_8} \cap \delta_{\mathcal{T}_9}$, where $q_0 \in Out_{\mathcal{T}_0}$ is the origin of the transition from $\mathcal{T}_0$ to $\mathcal{T}_8$ and $q_8 \in Out_{\mathcal{T}_8}$.

5.2   Scalability of TABEC

In the following, we refer to randomly generated PTTA simply as "TA". The *size* of a TA is the sum of its locations and transitions. Random generation enabled scalability testing, and no bugs were detected in either tChecker or TABEC.

A test suite evaluating the scalability of TABEC was initially conducted. These tests were performed on both EmpCheck and EmpCheckFast. Timeouts of 62 and 122 min were set to stop test execution when exceeding this time limit. A total of 367 tests were performed. The second row of Table 1 contains the biggest TA size obtained for both versions of the algorithm run by setting the aforementioned timeouts. EmpCheck revealed to be slower, since it was not able to check a larger TA before reaching the timeouts. This can be inferred from the first row of Table 1 showing that, considering the same timeouts, EmpCheck executed fewer tests than EmpCheckFast. The correctness of the results provided by tChecker was evaluated using TABEC's oracle capabilities. 129 out of 367 tests admitted a Büchi acceptance condition. For these tests, the parameter value interval was computed by the verification algorithm with 100% accuracy.

5.3   Resource Utilization Testing

A second test suite was conducted to measure tChecker resource utilization for each call made to the tool, i.e., each call to *checkEmp()* of Fig. 2, using the

Table 1. Scalability results of TABEC considering EmpCheck and EmpCheckFast.

Metric	EmpCheck	EmpCheck	EmpCheckFast	EmpCheckFast
#Tests	79	103	81	104
MaxSize	869	1172	911	1199
#NonEmpty	28	38	25	38
#Empty	51	65	56	66
Accuracy	100%	100%	100%	100%
Timeout[min]	62	122	62	122

EmpCheckFast algorithm and focusing on computation time and memory. A total of 18 tests of increasing complexity were generated, iteratively incrementing TA size at steps of 40 locations and 80 transitions each. The maximum constant appearing in the generated TA was 10. Measurements are shown in Fig. 9, where it is clear that the overall tChecker execution time does not increase linearly with the size of TA. The figure contains mean measurements derived by averaging results obtained during each test execution. In particular, each test is weighted by the number of times tChecker was invoked by EmpCheckFast within that test, in order to obtain a valid parameter value. The bars above individual columns represent the highest measured value for each specific test.

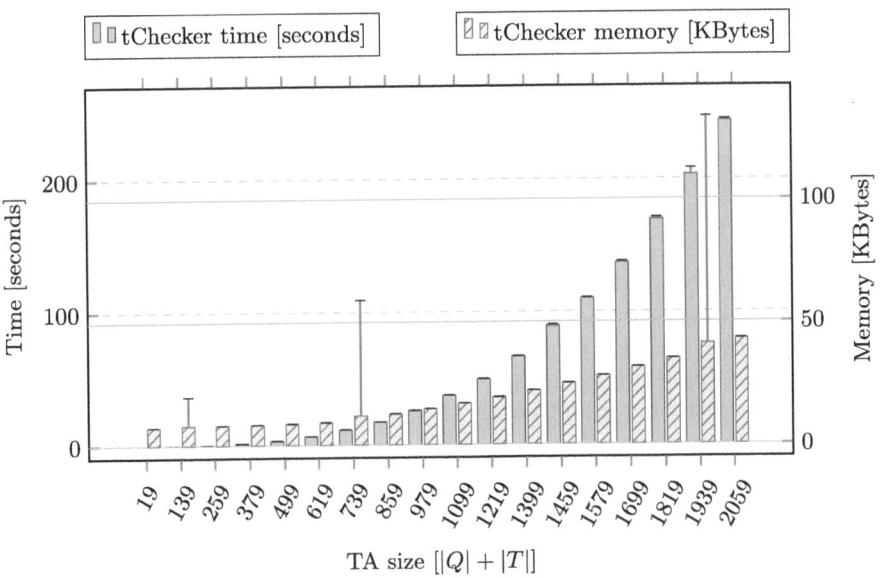

Fig. 9. Plot containing mean time and memory used by tChecker during tests.

6   Oracle Generation for Priced Timed Automata

In this section we extend the oracle generation framework introduced in Sect. 4 to another formalism, namely *Priced Timed Automata* (shortened as PriTA) [21].

Priced Timed Automata. A PriTA $\mathcal{A}$ is obtained by adding a *cost function* $c : (Q \cup T) \to \mathbb{N}$ to Definition 1 of TA, assigning costs to locations and transitions. The overall cost of a location $q \in Q$ equals the value specified by $c(q)$ multiplied by the total time $\mathcal{A}$ stays in q; for a transition $t \in T$, it corresponds to the value specified by $c(t)$. For convenience, we assume that given a pair of locations $\langle q, q' \rangle$, each transition from q to q' has the same cost, denoted by $c(\langle q, q' \rangle)$. As customary for PriTA, we refer to the set B of accepting locations as the set of *goal* locations. Let $\rho_n = (q_0, v_0)(q_1, v_1) \ldots (q_n, v_n)$ be a finite run of $\mathcal{A}$ over a timed word (σ, τ); its total cost, up to configuration n $(n \geqslant 1)$, is computed as:

$$Cost(\rho_n) = \sum_{k=0}^{n-1} c(q_k) \cdot (\tau_{k+1} - \tau_k) + c(\langle q_k, q_{k+1} \rangle).$$

Finite runs are used to solve the *minimum-cost reachability problem*, i.e., finding the minimum cost (often, a lower bound on the cost), denoted by $mc(B)$, to reach the set $B \subseteq Q$ of goal locations:

$$mc(B) = \inf\{ Cost(\rho_n) \mid \rho_n = (q_0, v_0)(q_1, v_1) \ldots (q_n, v_n) \wedge q_n \in B\}.$$

An example of PriTA $\mathcal{A}$ is given in Fig. 10. We assume that, before the execution starts from location q_0, the total cost of $\mathcal{A}$, denoted by $Cost_{\mathcal{A}}$, is equal to 0. The guard on transition t_0 imposes that exactly 2 time units must elapse for t_0 to fire. Thus, when entering location q_1, $Cost_{\mathcal{A}}$ has the following value: $Cost_{\mathcal{A}} = c(q_0) \cdot 2 + c(t_0) = 1 \cdot 2 + 4 = 6$. Applying the same reasoning to the run $\rho_3 = (q_0, v_0)(q_1, v_1)(q_2, v_2)(q_3, v_3)$ gives a total cost of $Cost_{\mathcal{A}}(\rho_3) = c(q_0) \cdot 2 + c(t_0) + c(q_1) \cdot 3 + c(t_1) + c(q_2) \cdot 1 + c(t_2) = 14$.

Tiled PriTA. A cost function c can be added to Definition 4 of tiles, obtaining so-called *PriTA tiles*. Figure 11 provides an example of a PriTA tile $\mathcal{T}$. Since the compatibility function $\mathcal{I}_{\mathcal{T}, Y}$ resets clock x upon entering location q_0 and time is strictly monotonic, the guard on transition t_0 requires a value of $0 < x < \alpha$ time units to elapse before exiting q_0. The compatibility function $\mathcal{O}_{\mathcal{T}, \gamma}$ imposes a constraint requiring that clock x is exactly equal to α when exiting $\mathcal{T}$. The

Fig. 10. Example of PriTA. The cost function c is shown on each location and transition.

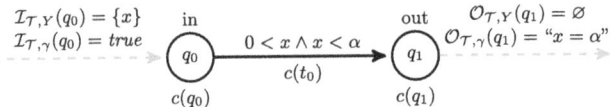

Fig. 11. Example of a PriTA tile, where $\alpha \in \mathbb{N}_{>0}$ is a tile-specific constant. The function c assigns costs to the locations q_0 and q_1 and to the transition t_0.

lower bound on the cost accrued upon exiting $\mathcal{T}$ from location q_1 is equal to $Cost_{out} = \alpha \cdot p + c(t_0)$, where $p = \min(c(q_0), c(q_1))$.

In general, given a tile $\mathcal{T}$, the value $Cost_{out} \in \mathbb{N}$ is computed as the lower bound on the cost required to traverse $\mathcal{T}$ and exiting from an output location $q \in Out_{\mathcal{T}}$. This value is called the *weight* of the tile at the output location q.

A *Tiled PriTA* $\mathcal{A}$ is a TTA $\mathcal{A} = (\Theta, \mathcal{T}_0, \Sigma, \mathbb{B}, X_\Theta, \Upsilon)$ as in Definition 6, where Θ contains only PriTA tiles. We now derive an oracle for testing model checkers solving the min-cost reachability problem. Let $w_\Theta : (\mathbb{B} \cup \bigcup_{\mathcal{T} \in (\Theta \setminus \mathbb{B})} Out_{\mathcal{T}}) \to \mathbb{N}$ be a weight function mapping accepting tiles and output locations of non-accepting tiles to their corresponding weight, and $w_\Upsilon : \Upsilon \to \mathbb{N}$ be a weight function mapping each transition of $\mathcal{A}$ to its cost. The definition of the Underlying Weighted Automaton of $\mathcal{A}$ over the min-plus semiring $W^{\text{price}} = (\mathbb{N} \cup \{+\infty\}, min, +, +\infty, 0)$ can be easily obtained by adapting w_Υ to Definition 7. Solving min-cost reachability for $\mathcal{A}$ is equivalent to solving the same problem for $\mathcal{W}_{\mathcal{A},w}$. Indeed, also in the case of W^{price}, this problem can be reduced to solving a shortest distance problem by applying the polynomial-time algorithm of [19].

7   Conclusion and Future Works

This work presented a novel theoretical framework for rigorously testing the correctness of model checkers solving verification problems for variations of Timed Automata. Our framework generates a Tiled Timed Automaton (i.e., a modular Timed Automaton) and reduces it to a Weighted Automaton used as an oracle. A tool, called TABEC, was developed to validate the framework in the context of the emptiness problem by using parametric non-resetting test Timed Automata.

Empirical results underscore the robustness of our framework, providing a solid foundation for future developments and improvements. The current implementation of TABEC restricts tile composition to binary trees. However, our framework supports more general structures for tile composition (e.g., cycles between different tiles), therefore we plan to extend TABEC in this direction.

We also described how to build oracles for model checkers solving the min-cost reachability problem for Priced TA. Our framework, however, is not confined to PnrtTA and Priced TA; we plan to adapt it to other TA variants, expanding the spectrum of model checkers and their corresponding solvable problems eligible for oracle testing. This would require a suitable definition of tiles, along with a careful identification of the appropriate semiring for each problem at hand.

References

1. Agrawal, P., Agrawal, V.: Probabilistic analysis of random test generation method for irredundant combinational logic networks. IEEE Trans. Comput. **C-24**(7), 691–695 (1975). https://doi.org/10.1109/T-C.1975.224289
2. Alur, R., Dill, D.L.: A theory of timed automata. Theor. Comput. Sci. **126**(2) (1994)
3. Alur, R., Henzinger, T.A., Vardi, M.Y.: Parametric real-time reasoning. In: Proceedings of the Twenty-Fifth Annual ACM Symposium on Theory of Computing. Association for Computing Machinery (1993)
4. André, É., Arcaini, P., Gargantini, A., Radavelli, M.: Repairing timed automata clock guards through abstraction and testing. In: Beyer, D., Keller, C. (eds.) Tests and Proofs, pp. 129–146. Springer (2019)
5. Barr, E.T., Harman, M., McMinn, P., Shahbaz, M., Yoo, S.: The oracle problem in software testing: a survey. IEEE Trans. Softw. Eng. **41**(5), 507–525 (2015)
6. Bernot, G., Gaudel, M.C., Marre, B.: Software testing based on formal specifications: a theory and a tool. Softw. Eng. J. **6**(6), 387–405 (1991)
7. Bersani, M.M., Rossi, M., San Pietro, P.: On decidability timed automata with 2 parametric clocks (2025). https://arxiv.org/abs/2503.04374
8. Cortés, D., Ortiz, J., Basile, D., Aranda, J., Perrouin, G., Schobbens, P.Y.: Time for networks: mutation testing for timed automata networks. In: Proceedings of the 2024 IEEE/ACM 12th International Conference on Formal Methods in Software Engineering (FormaliSE), FormaliSE 2024, pp. 44–54. Association for Computing Machinery (2024)
9. Dillon, L.K., Ramakrishna, Y.S.: Generating oracles from your favorite temporal logic specifications. SIGSOFT Softw. Eng. Notes **21**(6), 106–117 (1996)
10. Dillon, L.K., Yu, Q.: Oracles for checking temporal properties of concurrent systems. SIGSOFT Softw. Eng. Notes **19**(5), 140–153 (1994)
11. Drusinsky, D.: The temporal rover and the ATG rover. In: Havelund, K., Penix, J., Visser, W. (eds.) SPIN Model Checking and Software Verification, pp. 323–330. Springer, Heidelberg (2000)
12. Geilen, M.: On the construction of monitors for temporal logic properties. Electron. Notes Theor. Comput. Sci. **55**(2), 181–199 (2001)
13. Herbreteau, F., Srivathsan, B., Tran, T.T., Walukiewicz, I.: Why liveness for timed automata is hard, and what we can do about it. ACM Trans. Comput. Logic **21**(3) (2020)
14. Howden, W.E.: Theoretical and empirical studies of program testing. IEEE Trans. Softw. Eng. **SE-4**(4) (1978)
15. Larsen, K.G., Pettersson, P., Yi, W.: UPPAAL in a nutshell. Int. J. Softw. Tools Technol. Transf. **1**(1–2), 134–152 (1997)
16. Liu, Z., Liu, K., Xia, X., Yang, X.: Towards more realistic evaluation for neural test oracle generation. In: Proceedings of the 32nd ACM SIGSOFT International Symposium on Software Testing and Analysis, ISSTA 2023, pp. 589–600. Association for Computing Machinery, New York (2023)
17. Manini, A.: https://github.com/andreamanini98/TABEC
18. Manini, A., Rossi, M., San Pietro, P.: Random testing of model checkers for timed automata with automated oracle generation (2025). https://arxiv.org/abs/2503.04589. Extended version
19. Mohri, M.: Weighted Automata Algorithms, pp. 213–254. Springer, Heidelberg (2009)

20. Pin, J. (ed.): Handbook of Automata Theory. European Mathematical Society Publishing House, Zürich, Switzerland (2021). Chapter 4
21. Rasmussen, J.I., Larsen, K.G., Subramani, K.: On using priced timed automata to achieve optimal scheduling. Formal Methods Syst. Des. **29** (2006)
22. Richardson, D.J., Aha, S.L., O'Malley, T.O.: Specification-based test oracles for reactive systems. In: Proceedings of the 14th International Conference on Software Engineering, ICSE 1992, pp. 105–118. Association for Computing Machinery (1992)
23. Wang, X., Wang, J., Qi, Z.C.: Automatic generation of run-time test oracles for distributed real-time systems. In: de Frutos-Escrig, D., Núñez, M. (eds.) Formal Techniques for Networked and Distributed Systems - FORTE 2004, pp. 199–212. Springer, Heidelberg (2004)
24. Young, M., Pezze, M.: Software Testing and Analysis: Process, Principles and Techniques. Wiley (2005)

State Significance-Guided Fuzzing for Stateful Protocol Program

Kunpeng Jian[1,2,3,4], Yanyan Zou[1,2,3,4](✉), Chen Wang[5], Ning Li[1,2,3,4],
Menghao Li[1,2,3,4], and Wei Huo[1,2,3,4](✉)

[1] Institute of Information Engineering, Chinese Academy of Sciences, Beijing, China
{jiankunpeng,zouyanyan,lining0820,limenghao,huowei}@iie.ac.cn
[2] School of Cyber Security, University of Chinese Academy of Sciences,
Beijing, China
[3] Key Laboratory of Network Assessment Technology, Chinese Academy of Sciences,
Beijing, China
[4] Beijing Key Laboratory of Network Security and Protection Technology,
Beijing, China
[5] Academy of Cyber, Beijing, China

Abstract. Stateful protocols are fundamental to network, yet their vulnerabilities can lead to severe security risks. Fuzzing, an effective testing technique, is widely used to uncover vulnerabilities in stateful protocol programs, enhancing their robustness and security. Existing fuzzers for stateful protocols typically employ state-guided strategies, selecting a state for testing in each iteration. However, these approaches often struggle with inaccurate state identification, failing to align with the actual protocol states of the program. Additionally, not all states carry equal risk; some are more likely to harbor vulnerabilities. Current methods overlook this variation in state significance during state selection, which diminishes the overall efficiency of fuzzing. To overcome these limitations, we propose a state importance-based fuzzing approach for stateful protocols and implement a prototype tool, SSGFuzz. SSGFuzz identifies state variables and states from the program by leveraging the characteristics of stateful protocols and evaluates the importance of each state across multiple dimensions. During the fuzzing process, SSGFuzz prioritizes state selection and test case mutation based on state importance, focusing on those states most likely to contain vulnerabilities. We conducted comparative experiments between SSGFuzz and existing fuzzers. The results show that SSGFuzz achieves an average increase of 36.4% in state coverage and 4.8% in code coverage, while also triggering more crashes, which facilitates the discovery of additional vulnerabilities.

Keywords: Fuzzing · Stateful protocol · Vulnerability revealing ·
Security and privacy

1 Introduction

Stateful protocol programs form the cornerstone of modern network infrastructure, enabling complex interactions through persistent state management during

P. Rümmer and Z. Wu (Eds.): TASE 2025, LNCS 15841, pp. 361–379, 2026.
https://doi.org/10.1007/978-3-031-98208-8_21

communication sessions. Their operational integrity and security constitute critical requirements, given their role in supporting essential services and ensuring reliable data exchange across distributed systems. Vulnerabilities in these protocols can yield severe consequences, as exemplified by the Heartbleed vulnerability [26] in OpenSSL's TLS implementation, which enabled potential leakage of sensitive data through memory corruption. Such incidents underscore the necessity of rigorous testing methodologies to ensure protocol reliability. Among these methodologies, fuzzing has emerged as a prominent technique for vulnerability discovery, employing automated input generation to identify security flaws and enhance system robustness.

Traditional approaches to stateful protocol fuzzing relied on manually constructed templates derived from protocol specifications. These templates typically encoded two elements: (1) message formats governing message content generation, and (2) state machines dictating valid message sequences. Prominent implementations of this paradigm include Peach [4] and Boofuzz [21]. While effective for well-documented protocols, template-based methodologies impose substantial manual effort, demanding domain expertise in protocol specifications and significant engineering resources to develop program-specific templates. This requirement inherently limits scalability across diverse protocol implementations.

Contemporary research has shifted toward mutation-based techniques that obviate template creation, instead leveraging initial seed inputs to autonomously generate test cases. This transition demonstrates superior generalizability, enabling broader applicability and accelerated testing workflows for stateful protocols. AFLNet [22] exemplifies modern state-guided fuzzers, employing state coverage metrics to prioritize seed selection and mutation strategies. These fuzzers approximate protocol states during execution, typically through response codes or program variables, and prioritize seeds that traverse new state transitions. The fuzzing cycle iteratively selects a target state, identifies associated seeds, and applies mutations to explore state-dependent behaviors. Recent advancements, including Nyx-Net [24], further address performance bottlenecks by transforming asynchronous network interactions into optimized execution modes. However, these solutions frequently require target-specific adaptations, limiting their generalizability across protocol implementations.

However, existing state abstraction mechanisms exhibit critical limitations. First, state identification often relies on superficial protocol outputs (e.g., HTTP status codes) rather than internal program state, creating a semantic gap between observed behaviors and actual implementation states. This imprecision misdirects exploration toward spurious states, yielding ineffective seed prioritization and test cases that fail to exercise meaningful protocol logic. Second, current approaches treat all states uniformly despite substantial variations in their security-criticality and code complexity. Existing fuzzers lack prioritization frameworks to allocate testing resources accordingly. These deficiencies result in suboptimal vulnerability detection.

To address these limitations in existing approaches, we propose a state significance-guided fuzzing approach for stateful protocol programs and presents a prototype tool, SSGFuzz. SSGFuzz identifies state variables based on their characteristics in stateful protocol programs and determines their concrete states during execution, assuming independence between variables to avoid exponential state-space complexity. Based on this information, it measures the significance of each state. SSGFuzz utilizes instrumentation to track state coverage through the identified state variables. During fuzzing, seed selection and mutation are conducted according to the significance of the states, focusing on testing the most critical states.

The primary contributions of this paper are as follows:

(1) We propose a method for identifying state variables and concrete states in stateful protocol programs. This method employs context-sensitive data-flow analysis, leveraging the characteristics of stateful protocol programs to identify state variables and their concrete states within the program.
(2) We introduce a method for measuring the significance of states. The significance of a state is assessed from three dimensions: its capacity to transition to other states, the complexity of the code controlled by the state, and its impact on other states.
(3) We implement the prototype tool SSGFuzz. SSGFuzz prioritizes testing significance states during fuzzing to improve the overall effectiveness. We conducted experiments with SSGFuzz, and the results demonstrate that SSG-Fuzz exceeds existing fuzzers like AFLNet in terms of state coverage, code coverage, and vulnerability discovery.

2   Background and Motivation

In this section, we introduce the foundational concepts of stateful protocol programs and present motivating example that exposes the limitations of existing fuzzing methodologies. Thereby justifying the need for our approach. Stateful protocol programs process temporally ordered input sequences governed by two dimensions: syntactic validity of individual messages and state-dependent sequence validity. Syntactic constraints derive from protocol message specifications, while temporal validity is dictated by a finite state machine (FSM) defining the program's operational semantics. The program's execution can be characterized as a discrete state transition process. Specifically, the program selects the appropriate message processing logic based on its current state, and the protocol state is dynamically updated according to the results of message parsing. This state-dependent behavior introduces unique challenges for stateful protocol fuzzing: test case generation must not only ensure syntactic validity but also construct message sequences compliant with state machine. Traditional fuzzing techniques, which primarily focus on input format mutation, struggle to address this state dependency. Stateful protocol fuzzing approaches mitigate this by incorporating protocol state machines or runtime state tracking to generate effective test cases.

The behavior of such programs can be formally modeled using finite state machine theory as a triple (S, Σ, δ), where S denotes the finite state set, Σ

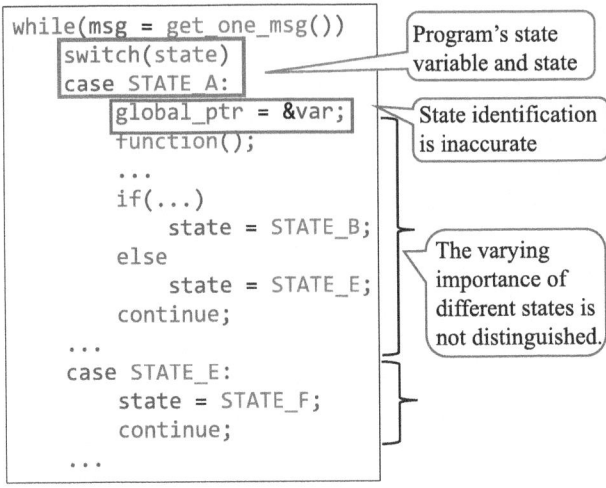

Fig. 1. Code Pattern in Stateful Protocol Program

represents the input alphabet, and $\delta : S \times \Sigma \rightarrow S$ defines the state transition function. For any state $s \in S$, the set of valid input messages is $\Sigma_s \subseteq \Sigma$. This state-dependent validity imposes formal constraints on fuzzing strategies. Given a seed message sequence $M = (m_1, m_2, \ldots, m_k)$, the mathematical expectation of valid mutant sequences M' expressed as:

$$E[valid(M')] = \prod_{i=1}^{k} \left[P(m'_i \in \Sigma_{s_{i-1}}) \times P(\delta(s_{i-1}, m'_i) = s_i) \right] \qquad (1)$$

Equation 1 reveals two essential constraints: (1) each mutant message m'_i must belong to the valid input set $\Sigma_{s_{i-1}}$ of the preceding state, and (2) the state transition induced by m'_i must produce a valid s_i. The multiplicative probability collapse creates an exponential reduction in valid test cases as sequence length increases, a manifestation of the *curse of dimensionality* in stateful protocol fuzzing. Consequently, the single-message mutation strategy emerges as a practical solution for ensuring $P(M' \in ValidPath) > 0$. Mutation position selection thus directly governs code path exploration efficiency and vulnerability discovery ability.

Prior code coverage-guided fuzzers (e.g., AFL and libFuzzer) predominantly utilize basic code coverage metrics to evaluate test case efficacy. During execution, these fuzzers preserve test cases that trigger previously unexplored code paths as seeds and prioritize them through energy scheduling algorithms. However, this approach exhibits significant limitations: it fails to identify semantic constraints inherent in protocol state transitions, nor can it determine optimal positions for modification during mutation operations. In stateful protocol testing, random selection of mutation positions frequently violates the necessary conditions for valid state transitions, resulting in generated test cases that fail to satisfy the protocol's fundamental semantic requirements.

Stateful protocol fuzzers like AFLNet [22] employ state-guided testing strategies through three-phase process: (1) select target state s_{target} from covered states in previous fuzzing iteration, (2) select seed sequences containing message patterns that satisfy $\delta(s_i, m_j) = s_{target}$ for some (s_i, m_j) pair, and (3) apply single-message mutation strategy exclusively to messages m_k that operate within s_{target}'s syntactic constraints ($m_k \in \Sigma_{s_{target}}$). While this methodology enhances test validity by preserving state transition integrity, its efficacy fundamentally depends on two requirements: state fidelity (precise alignment between inferred and actual implementation states) and state criticality (prioritization of states governing security-critical behaviors).

In real-world fuzzing environments, abstract protocol states must be mapped to their concrete program implementations. Through analysis of stateful protocol programs and established software engineering practices, we have identified that protocol state machines are typically implemented through the evolution of specific variable values within program code. These variables, which we designate as **state variables**, encapsulate the current protocol state through discrete values. During program execution, control flow is determined by these state variable values, which are subsequently updated under well-defined conditions. The discrete values of these variables constitute what we define as **states**. Figure 1 demonstrates a representative code pattern in stateful protocol implementations, wherein `state` serves as a state variable, and the program executes distinct logical paths through conditional structures based on `state` values (e.g., `STATE_A`, `STATE_E`), updating the `state` variable during these operations.

Our formulation provides advantages in fuzzing contexts as it establishes a direct correspondence between internal program logic and protocol states. Existing tools employ state acquisition mechanisms with notable limitations. Fuzzers such as AFLNet [22] infer states from server responses, which often lack direct correspondence with the program's internal implementation. While StateAFL [19] addresses this issue by monitoring long-lived program variables during I/O processing, it introduces system noise by treating all persistent variables (e.g., `global_ptr`) as state indicators through hash values, as illustrated in Fig. 1.

Furthermore, existing techniques employ uniform state prioritization, disregarding variations in code complexity and vulnerability likelihood. For instance, Fig. 1 demonstrates that `STATE_A` governs a significantly larger and more complex code region than `STATE_E`, implying a higher likelihood of vulnerabilities. Existing approaches passively collect state coverage data without distinguishing such disparities, resulting in suboptimal resource allocation during fuzzing.

To overcome these limitations, our methodology comprises three phases. First, we identify variables that explicitly encode protocol states and enumerate their valid values (concrete states). Second, we develop a multi-dimensional metric to quantify the significance of each state. Third, during fuzzing, we dynamically prioritize target states based on their computed significance, focusing testing efforts on states with higher significance. This strategy enhances testing efficiency by preferentially targeting states with greater potential to expose vulnerabilities or expand code coverage.

3   Methodology

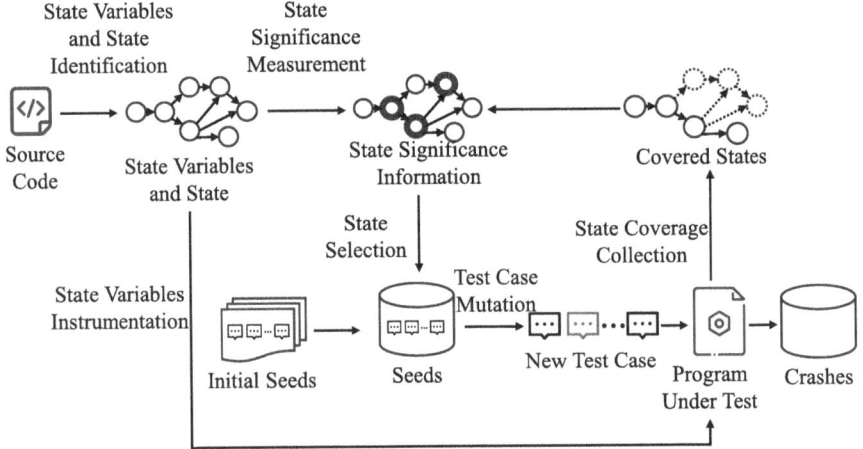

Fig. 2. Overview of SSGFuzz

In this section, we present our proposed methodology for state significance-guided fuzzing of stateful protocol programs, as implemented in our prototype tool, SSGFuzz. The approach addresses three core challenges: (1) accurate identification of states, (2) quantitative assessment of state significance, and (3) dynamic prioritization of testing targets.

Figure 2 presents an overview of SSGFuzz[1]. The process begins with a static analysis of the source code to identify state variables and their possible values, which correspond to distinct states. This phase employs context-sensitive data-flow analysis to filter non-state variables while preserving transition relationships between states. SSGFuzz quantifies state significance through three metrics: (1) the state's ability to transition to other states, (2) the complexity of the code controlled by the state, and (3) the state's influence on other states. The instrumentation phase embeds monitoring probes at state variable access points to track state coverage during fuzzing. During each fuzzing cycle, a stochastic multi-objective strategy selects target states using a probability distribution that prioritizes states with higher metric valuations while maintaining exploration diversity. Mutation operations focus exclusively on messages $m_k \in \Sigma_{s_{target}}$ within sequences that transition to s_{target}.

---

[1] https://github.com/flysoar/SSGFuzz.

The following sections provide comprehensive descriptions of our state identification algorithm, significance metric formulation, and adaptive scheduling mechanism.

3.1   State Variables and State Identification

There are three characteristics of state variables. First, state variables manifest as global variables or persistent object fields, maintaining value persistence across message-handling procedures. Second, state variables play a critical role in determining the program's control flow, as the program must execute appropriate logic based on its current state. Third, state variables exhibit a finite set of possible values (states), with transitions between them explicitly codified via assignments within state-controlling code segments.

We formalize the state space as follows. Let SV denote the set of state variables in the program. For each variable $v \in SV$, let S_v represent its finite set of possible states. The overall program state space S and transition set T are defined as:

$$S = \bigcup_{v \in SV} S_v, \quad T = \{(s_{\text{src}}, s_{\text{dst}}) \in S \times S \mid s_{\text{src}} \rightarrow s_{\text{dst}}\} \tag{2}$$

In practice, the program's state space could theoretically be modeled as the Cartesian product $\prod_{v \in SV} S_v$, leading to exponential growth. However, protocol implementations often exhibit independence between state variables (e.g., a connection status variable and a cryptographic nonce variable are updated in separate control flows). We leverage this observation to define S as the union of per-variable states, significantly reducing analysis complexity while retaining practical fidelity for vulnerability discovery.

Based on the three characteristics of state variables, we propose an effective method for identifying state variables within the program. Algorithm 1 details this procedure, outlining steps to identify state variables, their corresponding states, and the transition relationships between states.

The algorithm begins by identifying candidate state variables based on the first two characteristics described earlier (Line 3). It then analyzes their assignment and usage statements to determine candidate values ((e.g., if (state == s1)) and if (state == s2))) (Line 7–12). To resolve runtime-dependent values (e.g., variables influenced by input messages), we employ context-sensitive, interprocedural data-flow analysis. In stateful protocol implementations, abstract protocol states are distributed across multiple state variables. Consequently, message-handling routines commonly utilize conditional checks involving these variables. The analysis context is restricted to execution paths activated by message processing events, as value expressions originate from stateful protocol workflows. Specifically, control flow paths extending from conditional statements involving candidate state variables to value expressions are utilized as analytical contexts (Line 9). During the value resolution phase (Line 10), the algorithm traces these control flow paths to identify deterministic constant. A

Algorithm 1: State Variables and States Identification

Input: Program code P

Output: Set of state variables SV, Set of states S, Set of transitions T

1   $SV, PSV, S, T \leftarrow \emptyset$;

2   **foreach** variable v in P **do**

3   **if** IsGlobalOrObjectFieldVar(v) **and** IsAffectControlFlow(v) **then**

4         $PSV \leftarrow PSV \cup \{v\}$

5   **foreach** variable v in PSV **do**

6      $Values_v \leftarrow \emptyset$;

7      $ExpressionList \leftarrow$ CollectExpressionsFromConditionalsAndAssignments(v, P) ;

8   **foreach** Expression e in $ExpressionList$ **do**

9   **foreach** context c in CollectPathsFromConditionalsToExpressions(e, V) **do**

10            $value \leftarrow$ EvaluateExpression(e, c);

11   **if** $value$ is concrete **then**

12               $Values_v \leftarrow Values_v \cup \{value\}$;

13   **if** IsMostExprDeterminate($ExpressionList$) **then**

14         $T_v \leftarrow \emptyset$;

15   **foreach** pair ($value_1$, $value_2$) in $Value_v \times Value_v$ **do**

16            $stmt_1 \leftarrow$ GetConrrespondExprStmt($value_1$) ;

17            $stmt_2 \leftarrow$ GetConrrespondExprStmt($value_2$) ;

18   **if** $stmt_1$ is AssignmentStmt **and** $stmt_2$ is ConditionStmt **and** $stmt_1$ is control-dependent on $stmt_2$ **then**

19               $T_v \leftarrow T_v \cup \{(value_1, value_2)\}$;

20   **if** Values of v are interconnected in T_v **then**

21            $SV \leftarrow SV \cup \{v\}$, $S \leftarrow S \cup \{Values_v\}$, $T \leftarrow T \cup \{T_v\}$

22   **foreach** pair ($value_1$, $value_2$) in $S \times S$ **do**

23      $stmt_1 \leftarrow$ GetConrrespondExprStmt($value_1$) ;

24      $stmt_2 \leftarrow$ GetConrrespondExprStmt($value_2$) ;

25   **if** $stmt_1$ is AssignmentStmt **and** $stmt_2$ is ConditionStmt **and** $stmt_1$ is control-dependent on $stmt_2$ **then**

26         $T \leftarrow T \cup \{(value_1, value_2)\}$;

27   **return** SV, S, T

---

value expression may have multiple contexts, and if a constant is determined in any context, that value is considered valid. If most of a candidate state variable's values remain indeterminate, the variable is excluded from further consideration (Line 13).

Next, we infer the transition relationships between the states of the candidate state variables. Transition relationships are inferred via control dependence analysis. If an assignment to state variable v_2 is control-dependent on a conditional statement involving state variable v_1, a transition from v_1's state to v_2's state is recorded. For example, in Fig. 1, transitions from STATE_A to STATE_B and STATE_E are captured. Variables with interconnected state graphs are classified as state variables (Lines 19–21). We then identify cross-variable transition relationships, transitions between states of distinct state variables, as one dimension for our significance measurement (Lines 22–26). These cross-variable transitions represent higher-order interactions (e.g., coordination between subsystems), which may reflect critical program logic.

3.2   State Significance Measurement

Having identified the program's states, we proceed to evaluate their significance through three dimensions: (1) state transition potential, (2) code complexity of state-controlling code, and (3) inter-state influence. Each dimension is formalized below to prioritize states for vulnerability discovery.

State Transition Potential. Prior work establishes that increased state transition coverage improves fuzzing efficacy in vulnerability detection [9]. We quantify this potential for a state $s \in S$ as its number of immediate successors:

$$TO(s) = |\{s' \in S \mid (s, s') \in T\}| \tag{3}$$

where T is the state transition set. States with higher $TO(s)$ values are prioritized, as they enable broader exploration of the protocol's behavioral space.

State-Controlling Code's Complexity. Complex code is more likely to contain vulnerabilities, especially within code segments that are executed only under specific states. Therefore, assessing the complexity of the code controlled by each state is essential for prioritizing testing efforts. We operationalize complexity using the Maintainability Index (MI) [29], which synthesizes three established metrics: (1) Cyclomatic Complexity [16] quantifies control flow intricacy via $E - N + 2P$, where E, N, and P represent edges, nodes, and independent paths, respectively; (2) Lines of Code (LOC) correlates code size with maintainability challenges; (3) Halstead Metrics Measure computational logic complexity through operator/operand counts [8]. The Halstead Volume is computed as $(N_1 + N_2) \times log_2(n_1 + n_2)$, where N_1/n_1 and N_2/n_2 denote total/distinct operators and operands. The MI for state s is calculated as:

$$MI(s) = 171 - 5.2 \times ln((N_1 + N_2) \times log_2(n_1 + n_2))$$
$$- 0.23 \times (E - N + 2P) - 16.2 \times ln(LoC) \tag{4}$$
$$CC(s) = 100 - max(0, (MI(s)) * 100/171)$$

Lower MI values indicate higher complexity. To align with our priority framework (higher values for critical states), we normalize and invert MI using Microsoft's scaling method [18]. Higher $CC(s)$ values indicate greater complexity, prioritizing states governing intricate code structures during testing. For cases where state-controlling code cannot be unambiguously identified (e.g., if (state != A) goto fail_process;), we assign a default minimal MI value to maintain consistency.

Inter-State Influence. Vulnerabilities in stateful protocols often manifest through multi-state interactions [9]. For example, a use-after-free vulnerability typically involves two states: one in which an object is freed and another in which the same object is subsequently reused. Therefore, conducting data flow analysis on state-controlling code to assess how a state influences other states through shared variables can facilitate vulnerability detection. Based on the characteristics of stateful protocol program, we collect global variables and object fields from state-controlling code to determine whether they influence other states. We then quantify the number of states affected by a given state s to evaluate its influence. Specifically, the number of states influenced by state s is calculated as:

$$IO(s) = |\{s' \in S \mid s' \neq s \land W(s) \cap R(s') \neq \emptyset\}| \tag{5}$$

where s' is a state influenced by s, $W(s)$ represents the set of assigned variables in the code controlled by state s, and $R(s')$ is the set of used variables in the code controlled by state s'. States impacting more peers (higher $IO(s)$) are prioritized, as their interactions may propagate erroneous behaviors.

3.3   State Selection and Test Case Mutation

Having quantified state significance through our established metrics, we now operationalize these measurements to direct fuzzing activities via guided state selection and test case mutation strategies. This section details SSGFuzz's integration of state significance metrics into its fuzzing framework, enhancing vulnerability discovery efficacy.

SSGFuzz employs instrumentation to track state coverage through the identified state variables. Each message in seed test cases may cover multiple states across distinct variables, collectively defining protocol state. Our fuzzing workflow begins with probabilistic selection of target states based on significance metrics. The fuzzer retrieves seed test cases capable of reaching these states, then applies mutations only to messages operating within the target state's syntactic constraints. This preserves preceding message integrity, maintaining valid state transition sequences. New test cases execute in instrumented environments, with coverage feedback updating the seed corpus and crashes logging in crash databases.

State selection operates via weighted sampling from covered states, denoted as *CoveredStates*, where weights derive from four dimensions: the number of transitions to other states (TO), the maintainability index of the state-controlling code (CC), the number of states influenced by the state (IO), and the number of paths discovered by the state (PA). The first three metrics represent the dimensions of state significance previously defined, while the fourth metric reflects the historical performance of the state during fuzzing. Incorporating the fourth metric ensures that states with strong historical performance are prioritized, compensating for the limitations of static analysis and preventing potentially valuable states from being overlooked. To compute the selection probability for each state, we apply the softmax function to the metric values, converting them into probabilities within a multinomial distribution. Specifically, the probability $P(s)$ of selecting state s is calculated as:

$$d \sim \{TO, CC, IO, PA\}, \quad P(s) = \frac{e^{d(s)}}{\sum_{s' \in CoveredStates} e^{d(s')}} \tag{6}$$

where d is a randomly selected metric dimension, and $d(s)$ is the score of state s in that dimension.

During the mutation process, in addition to utilizing AFL's [5] existing methods, message sequences are also mutated. Previous approaches would randomly insert or delete messages from the sequence. When inserting messages, SSG-Fuzz prioritizes those associated with states influenced by the target state. This strategy exploits protocol context similarities between the target state and its influenced states, increasing the probability of generating syntactically valid and semantically relevant test cases compared to random insertion.

4   Evaluation

4.1   Experiment Setup

To comprehensively evaluate SSGFuzz, we conducted experiments across four dimensions: state identification effectiveness, state coverage, branch coverage, and vulnerability discovery effectiveness.

We selected AFLNet, AFLNWE [6], StateAFL, and AFLNetLegion [11] as baselines for our evaluation. AFLNet is a widely used stateful protocol fuzzer that extracts states from the program's responses. AFLNWE extends AFL with support for network programs. StateAFL is a representative stateful protocol fuzzer that obtains state information from program variables. AFLNetLegion improves upon AFLNet's state extraction by attempting to distinguish states with finer granularity. We chose eight stateful protocol programs, including Live555, ProFTPD, Dcmtk, Kamailio, OpenSSH, OpenSSL, Dnsmasq, and TinyDTLS, as the benchmark, which covers a wide range of network protocols.

The experiments were conducted on an Ubuntu 20.04 LTS system with an Intel Xeon Gold 6242R processor and 128 GB of memory. To mitigate the randomness inherent in fuzzing, each approach was repeated 5 times, with each experiment lasting 24 h.

4.2   State Identification Effectiveness

Our state identification experiments with Kamailio revealed the system's extensive use of callback functions for SIP message processing, resulting in numerous indirect calls that complicate state transition identification. For Kamailio, we supplemented our automated techniques with manual analysis, labeling state

Table 1. State Identification Results

Benchmark	# of States/% of States					Time (s)
	Identified	Actual	Direct	Indirect	Non-Identified	
Live555	39	34/87.2%	0/0.0%	34/100.0%	2/5.6%	112.5
ProFTPD	39	39/100.0%	25/64.1%	14/35.9%	7/15.2%	319.3
Dcmtk	433	433/100.0%	421/97.2%	12/2.8%	3/0.7%	385.2
Kamailio	148	142/95.9%	73/51.4%	69/48.6%	15/9.6%	29239.9
OpenSSH	41	31/75.6%	18/58.1%	13/41.9%	9/22.5%	347.5
OpenSSL	237	231/97.5%	170/73.6%	61/26.4%	50/17.8%	3591.1
Dnsmasq	78	66/84.6%	0/0.0%	66/100.0%	2/0.0%	75.6
TinyDTLS	15	15/100.0%	15/100.0%	0/0.0%	0/0.0%	34.6
Average	128.8	123.9/92.6%	90.3/55.5%	33.6/44.5%	11.0/9.3%	4263.2

Identified presents the total states identified by SSGFuzz. Actual indicates valid states and their percentage of identified states. Direct and Indirect denote states directly related to protocol definitions versus implementation-specific states (e.g., system signal states, IO operations), with their respective proportions of valid states. Non-Identified represents undetected state values within identified state variables and their percentage of total states (identified plus non-identified). Time measures execution duration in seconds.

variables based on previously identified discrete-valued variables influencing control flow. Precise identification of indirect jumps remains a fundamental challenge in static analysis. When confronted with complex program structures, our algorithm requires specialized processing methods or supplementary manual analysis to maintain accuracy.

Table 1 presents the state identification results of SSGFuzz across multiple target programs. The experimental evaluation demonstrates that SSGFuzz achieves 92.6% accuracy in state identification, with seven of eight target programs exhibiting accuracy rates of 84.6% or higher. Analysis of false positives reveals two primary categories: (1) configuration-related values that exhibit state-like transition patterns during runtime but remain static during fuzzing operations, and (2) continuous variables incorrectly identified as discrete states when compared against threshold constants. These misidentifications have minimal impact on testing efficacy due to their static nature and low prevalence. Additionally, for the identified state variables, we analyzed unrecognized state values and found an average false negative rate of 9.3%. They primarily result from implicit states lacking explicit conditional control statements, thereby evading SSGFuzz's static analysis capabilities.

The valid identified states can be classified into two distinct categories based on their relationship with protocol specifications: directly related states (55.5%), which explicitly correspond to protocol definitions (e.g., error codes, handshake phase identifiers), and indirectly related states (44.5%), which pertain to implementation details rather than protocol specifications (e.g., system signals, media codecs). Prior fuzzers, such as AFLNet, often neglect the latter category despite its critical role in protocol implementation. Notably, Live555, Dnsmasq, and TinyDTLS exhibit distinctive state architectures: Live555 implements RTSP state handling through media codec operations rather than dedicated protocol state variables; Dnsmasq introduces internal states to manage record types within the inherently stateless DNS protocol; and TinyDTLS employs a single state variable to track handshake phases due to its minimalist codebase.

Performance analysis indicates that SSGFuzz's state identification process requires an average of 4263.2 s, with processing time primarily dependent on codebase scale and complexity (maximum: 29239.9 s for Kamailio). Given that static analysis is a one-time operation per program in practical fuzzing scenarios, this computational overhead is acceptable.

4.3   State Coverage

Using the identified states by SSGFuzz as a baseline, we conduct a statistical analysis of the state transition coverage achieved by various fuzzers in the experiment. Table 2 presents the state transition coverage of each fuzzer on the benchmark, with percentage values indicating the improvement or degradation relative to AFLNet. The experimental results show that SSGFuzz achieves the highest state transition coverage across all programs. In contrast, AFLNWE, due to its lack of an effective state guidance mechanism, performs the least effectively. Specifically, compared to AFLNet, SSGFuzz achieves a maximum improvement of 70.7% in state transition coverage, with an average improvement of 32.0%.

Table 2. State Transition Coverage Result

Benchmark	AFLNet	AFLNWE	StateAFL	AFLNetLegion	SSGFuzz	Improvement
Live555	51	38	72	68	**72**	41.1%
ProFTPD	55	36	68	48	**77**	40.0%
Dcmtk	82	67	72	61	**140**	70.7%
Kamailio	54	7	39	54	**62**	14.9%
OpenSSH	27	22	27	28	**44**	63.0%
OpenSSL	144	120	147	122	**154**	6.9%
Dnsmasq	11	11	11	11	**17**	54.5%
TinyDTLS	**21**	2	16	17	**21**	0.0%
Average	55.6	37.8	56.5	51.1	**73.4**	36.4%

The Improvement column shows the increase in state transition coverage achieved by SSGFuzz compared to AFLNet.

Further analysis reveals that SSGFuzz does not exhibit a significant improvement in state transition coverage on TinyDTLS. This limitation primarily stems from TinyDTLS's limited code complexity, which inherently restricts the diversity of discernible protocol states and thus the potential for state transition exploration. Similarly, improvements on OpenSSL remain modest despite its larger codebase and richer state space. We attribute this to OpenSSL's implementation of TLS, a cryptographically intensive authentication protocol. TLS sessions follow a highly deterministic state machine with rigid transition pathways, from handshake initialization to cryptographic verification, leaving minimal room for fuzzers to discover novel state path. This structural constraint inherently limits coverage improvements, even for state-guided fuzzers like SSGFuzz.

4.4 Branch Coverage

Table 3. Branch Coverage Result

Benchmark	AFLNet	AFLNWE	StateAFL	AFLNetLegion	SSGFuzz
Live555	2,908.2	−15.2%	−1.7%	−2.3%	**+4.1%**
ProFTPD	5,084.8	−2.6%	+0.2%	−1.4%	**+9.2%**
Dcmtk	2,402.8	−2.8%	−1.2%	−0.6%	**+8.1%**
Kamailio	10,504.2	−11.2%	−14.2%	+4.4%	**+7.3%**
OpenSSH	3,602.8	−1.2%	−2.4%	−4.9%	**+0.8%**
OpenSSL	9,589.2	−25.3%	−6.6%	−4.4%	**+1.7%**
Dnsmasq	1,126.2	−2.4%	−9.4%	+1.4%	**+1.9%**
TinyDTLS	459.8	−40.2%	−8.8%	−12.5%	**+5.6%**
Average	4,459.7	−12.6%	−5.5%	−2.5%	**+4.8%**

To save space, the AFLNet column displays the absolute number of branch coverage, all other columns denote the changes compared to AFLNet.

Table 3 presents the code branch coverage of fuzzers on the benchmark. We used the gcov tool to obtain code branch coverage numbers by replaying valuable test cases. The experimental results demonstrate that SSGFuzz consistently outperforms the other fuzzers across all programs, achieving a maximum improvement of 9.2% in code branch coverage compared to AFLNet, with an average improvement of 4.1%.

Specifically, SSGFuzz exhibits particularly significant performance advantages on programs such as ProFTPD, Dcmtk, and Kamailio. This can be attributed to the following factors: (1) these applications feature larger codebases and more complex system architectures, providing SSGFuzz with more opportunities to identify program states and state variables, thereby allowing the proposed method to fully leverage its strengths; and (2) the protocol message formats implemented by these programs are relatively simple, facilitating the generation of diverse test cases by SSGFuzz. However, SSGFuzz's performance is comparatively weaker on programs such as OpenSSH, OpenSSL, and Dnsmasq. This is primarily due to the strong constraints imposed by these programs on message types not present in the initial seed set, making it difficult to generate novel message types through mutation. This limitation restricts the exploratory capabilities of any fuzzer in message mutation, thereby hindering further improvements in code coverage for SSGFuzz.

4.5   Vulnerability Finding Effectiveness

Table 4 presents the number of crashes triggered and vulnerabilities discovered by each fuzzer on the benchmark. Crashes are clustered based on the crash addresses reported by AddressSanitizer, while vulnerabilities are confirmed through manual analysis. The experimental results demonstrate that SSGFuzz triggers the same or a greater number of crashes and discovers more vulnerabilities across all programs compared to other fuzzers.

Table 4. Number of Triggered Crashes and Vulnerabilities in Benchmark

Benchmark	# of Crashes/# of Vulnerabilities				
	AFLNet	AFLNWE	StateAFL	AFLNetLegion	SSGFuzz
Live555	**4/4**	1/1	3/3	**4/4**	**4/4**
Dcmtk	2/1	1/1	1/1	1/1	**5/2**
Dnsmasq	6/1	6/1	4/1	6/1	**14/1**
TinyDTLS	4/4	3/2	3/3	3/3	**8/6**
Total	16/10	11/5	11/8	14/9	**31/13**

The crashes are clustered by the crash address reported by AddressSanitizer, and the vulnerabilities are manually analyzed. The promgrams where no fuzzers can reveal bugs are excluded.

From the experimental results and table data, SSGFuzz demonstrates disproportionate effectiveness on Dcmtk, where its superior state transition coverage (Table 2) and branch coverage (Table 3) positively correlate with triggering of more crashes and discovery of more vulnerabilities. This phenomenon indicates that the optimization strategies of SSGFuzz enhance its vulnerability detection capabilities. However, on TinyDTLS, SSGFuzz achieves comparable state coverage to AFLNet but discovers more vulnerabilities located in deeper states. We attribute this to SSGFuzz's targeted state prioritization strategy, which focuses testing effort on states containing security-critical logic, a capability absent in baseline fuzzers.

5   Related Work

Template-Based Fuzzers. Early stateful protocol fuzzing [1,3,4,7,10,14,20, 21,27,28,31] techniques primarily employ template-based methods, where the core idea is to guide test case generation through predefined protocol specifications. The SNOOZE [3] framework introduces an XML-based descriptive language, allowing users to formally define protocol message formats and state machine models by writing templates. Similarly, the commercial fuzzer Peach [4] adopts a template-based design philosophy, supporting the testing of multiple protocols. In the open-source domain, Sulley [20] and its successor Boo-Fuzz [20] provide a flexible application programming interface, enabling users to customize fuzzing workflows and implement complex protocol interactions. To further enhance testing effectiveness, subsequent research integrates code coverage feedback mechanisms into the template-based approach. For instance, SGPFuzzer [30], PAVFuzz [32], and SulleyEx [15] incorporate coverage feedback algorithms into the architectures of BooFuzz, Peach, and Sulley, respectively, to optimize test case generation efficiency. Additionally, some studies propose automatically generating test sequences that conform to protocol state transition logic based on user-provided finite state machines, thereby increasing the automation level of template-based methods.

Mutation-Based Fuzzers. With the advancement of fuzzing technology, mutation-based generation strategies gradually become the mainstream approach for stateful protocol testing, with the core challenge being how to dynamically perceive protocol states. AFLNet [22] is the first to propose extracting state identifiers from server responses and guiding the fuzzing through state coverage. AFLNetLegion [11] improves upon this by refining the state differentiation mechanism, achieving finer-grained state partitioning through the distinction of state paths. LABRADOR [12] also infers states from responses and tests stateful protocol programs in a black-box manner. StateAFL [19] identifies long-lived variables in programs as state variables through static analysis and dynamic instrumentation, while NSFuzz [23] proposes an I/O loop boundary detection method to infer state transition points by locating network interaction loop structures. SGFuzz [2] treats all enumerated type variables as state variables. IoTInfer [25] employs an active learning framework, dynamically constructing protocol state machine models based on the L* algorithm, while Bleem [13] intercepts protocol interaction traffic through a man-in-the-middle (MitM) proxy to fuzz stateful protocols. ChatAFL [17] introduces large language models to generate semantically valid test cases capable of triggering specific state transitions through semantic understanding. Furthermore, some studies conduct specialized optimizations for specific protocols (e.g., the TCP/IP protocol stack) or complex state systems (e.g., operating system kernels, device drivers), demonstrating domain-specific adaptability.

6   Conclusion

In this paper, we analyze two key limitations in current fuzzing for stateful protocol programs: inaccurate state identification and the lack of state prioritization in targeted state selection. To address these limitations, we propose state significance-guided fuzzing for stateful protocol programs and develop a prototype tool, SSGFuzz. SSGFuzz first identifies state variables and states in the program based on their characteristics, then measures the significance of each state. During fuzzing, SSGFuzz selects states for each test iteration based on their significance. We evaluated SSGFuzz on eight stateful protocol programs. Experimental results demonstrate that, compared to other fuzzers, SSGFuzz improves state coverage by an average of 36.4%, and code coverage by 4.8%. Additionally, SSGFuzz triggers more crashes, leading to the discovery of more vulnerabilities.

Acknowledgment. The authors would like to thank the anonymous reviewers for their valuable feedback. This work is partly supported by the National Key R&D Program of China under Grant #2022YFB3103900, Strategic Priority Research Program of the CAS under Grant #XDCO2030200, and Chinese National Natural Science Foundation (Grants #62032010, #62202462).

References

1. Aschermann, C., Frassetto, T., Holz, T., Jauernig, P., Sadeghi, A., Teuchert, D.: NAUTILUS: fishing for deep bugs with grammars. In: 26th Annual Network and Distributed System Security Symposium, NDSS 2019, 24–27 February 2019. The Internet Society, San Diego, California, USA (2019)
2. Ba, J., Böhme, M., Mirzamomen, Z., Roychoudhury, A.: Stateful greybox fuzzing. In: 31st USENIX Security Symposium (USENIX Security 2022), pp. 3255–3272. USENIX Association, Boston, MA (2022)
3. Banks, G., Cova, M., Felmetsger, V., Almeroth, K.C., Kemmerer, R.A., Vigna, G.: SNOOZE: toward a stateful network protocol fuzzer. In: Information Security, 9th International Conference, ISC 2006, 30 August–2 September 2006, Proceedings. Lecture Notes in Computer Science, vol. 4176, pp. 343–358. Springer, Samos Island, Greece (2006)
4. GitLab: peach-fuzzer-community (2024). https://gitlab.com/peachtech/peach-fuzzer-community
5. Google: AFL (2021). https://github.com/google/AFL
6. Google: AFLNWE (2021). https://github.com/thuanpv/aflnwe
7. Gorbunov, S., Rosenbloom, A.: Autofuzz: automated network protocol fuzzing framework. IJCSNS **10**(8), 239 (2010)
8. Halstead, M.H.: Elements of Software Science (Operating and Programming Systems Series). Elsevier Science Inc. (1977)
9. Jian, K., et al.: Fuzzing for stateful protocol implementations: are we there yet? In: Chin, W., Xu, Z. (eds.) Theoretical Aspects of Software Engineering - 18th International Symposium, TASE 2024, Guiyang, China, 29 July–1 August 2024, Proceedings. Lecture Notes in Computer Science, vol. 14777, pp. 186–204. Springer (2024)
10. Kitagawa, T., Hanaoka, M., Kono, K.: Aspfuzz: a state-aware protocol fuzzer based on application-layer protocols. In: Proceedings of the 15th IEEE Symposium on Computers and Communications, ISCC 2010, 22–25 June 2010, pp. 202–208. IEEE Computer Society, Riccione, Italy (2010)
11. Liu, D., Ernst, G., Murray, T., Rubinstein, B.I.P.: Legion: best-first concolic testing (competition contribution). In: Fundamental Approaches to Software Engineering - 23rd International Conference, FASE 2020, 25–30 April 2020, Proceedings, vol. 12076, pp. 545–549. Springer, Dublin, Ireland (2020)

12. Liu, H., et al.: Labrador: response guided directed fuzzing for black-box IoT devices. In: 2024 IEEE Symposium on Security and Privacy (SP), p. 126. IEEE Computer Society, Los Alamitos, CA, USA (2024)

13. Luo, Z., et al.: Bleem: packet sequence oriented fuzzing for protocol implementations. In: 32st USENIX Security Symposium, USENIX Security 2023, 9–11 August 2023. USENIX Association, Anaheim, CA, USA (2023)

14. Ma, R., Wang, D., Hu, C., Ji, W., Xue, J.: Test data generation for stateful network protocol fuzzing using a rule-based state machine. Tsinghua Sci. Technol. **21**(3), 352–360 (2016)

15. Ma, R., Zhu, T., Hu, C., Shan, C., Zhao, X.: Sulleyex: a fuzzer for stateful network protocol. In: Network and System Security - 11th International Conference, NSS 2017, 21–23 August 2017, Proceedings. Lecture Notes in Computer Science, vol. 10394, pp. 359–372. Springer, Helsinki, Finland (2017)

16. McCabe, T.J.: A complexity measure. IEEE Trans. Softw. Eng. 308–320 (1976)

17. Meng, R., Mirchev, M., Böhme, M., Roychoudhury, A.: Large language model guided protocol fuzzing. In: Proceedings of the 31st Annual Network and Distributed System Security Symposium (NDSS) (2024)

18. Microsoft: Maintainability index range and meaning (2024). https://learn.microsoft.com/en-us/visualstudio/code-quality/code-metrics-maintainability-index-range-and-meaning?view=vs-2022

19. Natella, R.: Stateafl: greybox fuzzing for stateful network servers. Empir. Softw. Eng. **27**(7), 191 (2022)

20. OpenRCE: Sulley (2019). https://github.com/llvm/llvm-project

21. Pereyda, J.: boofuzz (2024). https://github.com/jtpereyda/boofuzz

22. Pham, V., Böhme, M., Roychoudhury, A.: AFLNET: a greybox fuzzer for network protocols. In: 13th IEEE International Conference on Software Testing, Validation and Verification, ICST 2020, 24–28 October 2020, pp. 460–465. IEEE, Porto, Portugal (2020)

23. Qin, S., Hu, F., Zhao, B., Yin, T., Zhang, C.: Registered report: nsfuzz: towards efficient and state-aware network service fuzzing. In: International Fuzzing Workshop (FUZZING) 2022, San Diego, CA, USA (2022)

24. Schumilo, S., Aschermann, C., Jemmett, A., Abbasi, A., Holz, T.: Nyx-net: network fuzzing with incremental snapshots. In: Bromberg, Y., Kermarrec, A., Kozyrakis, C. (eds.) EuroSys 2022: Seventeenth European Conference on Computer Systems, 5–8 April 2022, pp. 166–180. ACM, Rennes, France (2022)

25. Shu, Z., Yan, G.: Iotinfer: automated blackbox fuzz testing of IoT network protocols guided by finite state machine inference. IEEE Internet Things J. **9**(22), 22737–22751 (2022)

26. Synopsys: The Heartbleed Bug (2024). https://heartbleed.com/

27. Wang, H., Wen, Q., Zhang, Z.: Improvement of peach platform to support GUI-based protocol state modeling. In: 2013 IEEE International Conference on Green Computing and Communications (GreenCom) and IEEE Internet of Things (iThings) and IEEE Cyber, Physical and Social Computing (CPSCom), 20–23 August 2013, pp. 1094–1097. IEEE, Beijing, China (2013)

28. Wang, J., Guo, T., Zhang, P., Xiao, Q.: A model-based behavioral fuzzing approach for network service. In: 2013 Third International Conference on Instrumentation, Measurement, Computer, Communication and Control, pp. 1129–1134. IEEE, NW Washington, DC, USA (2013)

29. Welker, K.D., Oman, P.W., Atkinson, G.G.: Development and application of an automated source code maintainability index. J. Softw. Maint. Res. Pract. **9**(3), 127–159 (1997)

30. Yu, Y., Chen, Z., Gan, S., Wang, X.: Sgpfuzzer: a state-driven smart graybox protocol fuzzer for network protocol implementations. IEEE Access **8**, 198668–198678 (2020)
31. Zhao, J., Chen, S., Liang, S., Cui, B., Song, X.: Rfsm-fuzzing a smart fuzzing algorithm based on regression FSM. In: 2013 Eighth International Conference on P2P, Parallel, Grid, Cloud and Internet Computing, pp. 380–386. Compiegne, France (2013)
32. Zuo, F., Luo, Z., Yu, J., Liu, Z., Jiang, Y.: Pavfuzz: state-sensitive fuzz testing of protocols in autonomous vehicles. In: 58th ACM/IEEE Design Automation Conference, DAC 2021, 5–9 December 2021, pp. 823–828. IEEE, San Francisco, CA, USA (2021)

Unleash the Hidden Power of CAR-Based Model Checking Through Dynamic Traversal

Yibo Dong[1], Yu Chen[2], Jianwen Li[1(✉)], and Geguang Pu[1]

[1] Software Engineering Institute, East China Normal University, Shanghai, China
lijwen2748@gmail.com
[2] The School of Computer and Information Engineering, Chuzhou University, Chuzhou, China

Abstract. Complementary Approximate Reachability (CAR) is a leading SAT-based model checking algorithm that combines under- and over-approximating state sequences to verify safety properties. However, its performance is hindered by redundant computations caused by the fixed-order traversal of the under-approximating sequence. To address such a limit, in this paper, we propose a dynamic traversal strategy to optimize CAR. By identifying common inefficiency patterns, we introduce heuristic methods and a scoring mechanism to prioritize states that are more likely to advance verification. We also prove that the correctness of the CAR algorithm can be preserved while exploring only a subset of the U-sequence, enabling partial traversal strategies that significantly reduce computational overhead. Experimental results demonstrate that our approach could solve 10% more cases than the previous best CAR implementation [17] and outperform state-of-the-art IC3 model checkers, e.g., `IC3-REF` [4,11]. Our method bridges the gap between CAR's theoretical potential and practical scalability, offering a more efficient solution for industrial-scale verification.

Keywords: Model Checking · Formal Verification · Complementary Approximate Reachability

1 Introduction

Model checking has long been a cornerstone of formal verification, offering rigorous guarantees for the correctness of both hardware and software systems. Given a system model M and a temporal property P, model checking automatically verifies whether all behaviors of M satisfy P. Despite its widespread adoption, scalability remains a critical challenge, particularly for large, industrial-scale systems where the state space grows exponentially. In these settings, traditional methods often struggle to meet the time and memory constraints required for

J. Li—We thank the anonymous reviewers for their insightful feedback. This work is supported by NSFC Grant #62372178 and #U21B2015.

P. Rümmer and Z. Wu (Eds.): TASE 2025, LNCS 15841, pp. 380–397, 2026.
https://doi.org/10.1007/978-3-031-98208-8_22

practical use, making the quest for scalable, efficient model checking methods a vital area of research.

State-of-the-art safety model checking techniques, including Bounded Model Checking (BMC) [2,3], Property Directed Reachability (PDR/IC3) [4,9], and Complementary Approximate Reachability (CAR) [15], rely fundamentally on SAT solvers but adopt divergent strategies. BMC prioritizes shallow bug detection through bounded path exploration, offering speed at the cost of incompleteness. In contrast, PDR and CAR provide completeness but are generally slower for shallow bug-finding. Therefore, a combination of techniques is often used depending on the verification task.

Among these, the CAR framework uniquely combines over-approximation (O-sequence) and under-approximation (U-sequence), efficiently narrowing the search space and accelerating the verification process through a balance of bug-finding and proof capabilities. However, its practical scalability remains constrained by a rigid traversal of the U-sequence. This fixed-order strategy forces CAR to process states sequentially, irrespective of their individual utility, This results in two predominant inefficiency patterns: (1) *redundant states*, where multiple states generate identical unsatisfiable cores (UCs), and (2) *misleading states*, where a number of states repeatedly fail to transition into deeper O-frames, yet still consuming computational cycles due to their position in the traversal order. Consequently, even state-of-the-art implementations struggle with large-scale systems.

While prior optimizations like clause generalization [17] and assumption ordering [6–8] have sought to mitigate some of CAR's inefficiencies, they fail to address the core issue, i.e., the inflexible traversal order. In this paper, we propose a dynamic traversal strategy to improve CAR's performance by addressing these inefficiencies. Our approach introduces two key heuristics: *PickUC*, which prioritizes states that contribute more to narrowing the O-sequence, and *PickChildren*, which favors states with higher branching factors to avoid unproductive paths. Both heuristics are integrated into a unified scoring mechanism that ranks states based on their potential to advance the verification process. These strategies are part of a broader optimization we term *Dynamic Traversal (DT)*, which refines the traversal of the U-sequence.

While reordering improves state prioritization, it still involves full traversal of the U-sequence, meaning that even lower-priority states are still explored. However, we demonstrate that full traversal is not necessary for correctness. Specifically, we prove that CAR can retain its correctness while exploring only a subset of the U-sequence. Building on this insight, we propose a further optimization of dynamic traversal: instead of fully traversing, we selectively explore only a subset of states. This approach, which we call CAR-DT (CAR with the dynamic traversal optimization), focuses on the most promising states and therefore reduces unnecessary exploration and accelerating convergence, especially for large-scale verification tasks.

We implement our approaches on the best variant of CAR and conduct an extensive evaluation using all the 318 benchmarks from the HWMCC'24 competition [10] to assess its performance. The experimental results demonstrate that CAR-DT outperforms the original CAR, solving 13 more out of 145 cases. In comparison to state-of-the-art tools like IC3-REF [4,11], CAR-DT also demonstrates superior performance. These improvements bridge the gap between CAR's theoretical potential and its practical applicability, offering a scalable and efficient solution for industrial-scale verification tasks.

Our contributions can be summarized as follows:

- **Prioritized Traversal Strategy:** We propose a prioritized traversal strategy that optimizes U-sequence processing by prioritizing states based on their potential to refine O-frames or explore new transitions.
- **Theoretical Insight:** We prove that CAR's correctness is maintained while exploring only a subset of the U-sequence. This insight challenges the conventional wisdom that full traversal is necessary for correctness and lays the foundation for more efficient exploration strategies.
- **Dynamic Traversal:** Based on the theoretical insight, we introduce the *Dynamic Traversal* optimization, which focuses on high-potential states, reducing computation and accelerating convergence.
- **Empirical Validation:** We implement CAR-DT on the best variant of CAR and validate it on 318 benchmarks from the HWMCC'24 competition. Our results show that CAR-DT outperforms the original CAR and state-of-the-art tools like IC3-REF, offering a scalable solution for large-scale verification.

The remainder of this paper is organized as follows: In Sect. 3, we provide motivating examples. Section 4 then outlines our methodology, followed by the experimental results presented in Sect. 5.

2   Preliminaries

2.1   Boolean Transition System

A *Boolean transition system Sys* is defined as a tuple (V, I, T), where V is a set of Boolean variables, and each state s is a truth assignment to variables in V. I is a Boolean formula corresponding to the set of initial states. The transition relation T is a Boolean formula over $V \cup V'$, where V' is the set of primed variables. A state s_2 is a *successor* of state s_1 iff $s_1 \cup s_2' \models T$, which is also denoted by $(s_1, s_2) \in T$. A *path* of length k in Sys is a sequence $s_1, s_2, \ldots, s_k$ of states connected by transitions. A state t is reachable from s in k steps if there is a path of length k from s to t. Let S be a set of states in Sys. We denote the set of successors of states in S as $R(S) = \{t \mid (s, t) \in T, s \in S\}$. Conversely, we define the set of predecessors of states in S as $R^{-1}(S) = \{s \mid (s, t) \in T, t \in X\}$. Recursively, we define $R^0(S) = S$ and $R^i(S) = R(R^{i-1}(S))$ where $i \geq 0$, and the notation $R^{-i}(S)$ is defined analogously. In short, $R^i(S)$ denotes the states that are reachable from S in i steps, and $R^{-i}(S)$ denotes the states that can reach S in i steps.

2.2 Safety Model Checking and Reachability Analysis

Given a transition system $Sys = (V, I, T)$ and a safety property P, which is a Boolean formula over V, a model checker either proves that P holds for any state reachable from an initial state in I, or disproves P by producing a *counterexample*. In the former case, we say that the system is safe, while in the latter case, it is unsafe. A counterexample is a finite path from an initial state s to a state t violating P, i.e., $t \in \neg P$, and such a state is called a *bad* state. In symbolic model checking, safety checking is reduced to symbolic reachability analysis [2]. Reachability analysis can be performed in forward or backward search. Forward search starts from initial states I and searches for reachable states of I by computing $R^i(S)$ with increasing values of i, while backward search begins with states in $\neg P$ and computes $R^{-i}(S)$ with increasing values of i to search for states reaching I. Table 1 gives the corresponding formal definitions.

Table 1. Standard reachability analysis.

	Forward	Backward
Base	$F_0 = I$	$B_0 = \neg P$
Induction	$F_{i+1} = R(F_i)$	$B_{i+1} = R^{-1}(B_i)$
Safe Check	$F_{i+1} \subseteq \bigcup_{0 \leq j \leq i} F_j$	$B_{i+1} \subseteq \bigcup_{0 \leq j \leq i} B_j$
Unsafe Check	$F_i \cap \neg P \neq \emptyset$	$B_i \cap I \neq \emptyset$

For forward search, F_i denotes the set of states that are reachable from I within i steps, which is computed by iteratively applying R. At each iteration, we first compute a new F_i, and then perform safe checking and unsafe checking. If the condition in the safe/unsafe checking is satisfied, the search process terminates. Intuitively, unsafe checking $F_i \cap \neg P \neq \emptyset$ indicates that some bad states are within F_i and safe checking $F_{i+1} \subseteq \bigcup_{0 \leq j \leq i} F_j$ indicates that all the reachable states from I have been checked and none of them violate P. For backward search, the set B_i is the set of states that can reach $\neg P$ in i steps, and the search procedure is analogous to the forward one.

2.3 Complementary Approximate Reachability (CAR)

CAR is a recently proposed SAT-based model checking algorithm inspired by IC3/PDR [4,9]. CAR performs reachability analysis in both forward and backward directions by maintaining over- and under- approximate state sequences, which is defined as follows:

Definition 1 (Over/Under Approximating State Sequences). *Given a transition system $Sys = (V, I, T)$ and a safety property P, the over-approximating state sequence $O \equiv O_0, O_1, \ldots, O_i$ $(i \geq 0)$, and the under-approximating state sequence $U \equiv U_0, U_1, \ldots, U_j$ $(j \geq 0)$ are finite sequences*

Table 2. Definition of over-/under-approximate state sequences in CAR

	O-sequence	U-sequence
Base:	$O_0 = \neg P$	$U_0 = I$
Induction:	$O_{k+1} \supseteq R^{-1}(O_k)$	$U_{k+1} \subseteq R(U_k)$
Constraint:	$O_k \cap I = \emptyset$	$-\,-$

Algorithm 1: Complementary Approximate Reachability (CAR).

Input: A transition system $Sys = (V, I, T)$ and a safety property P
Output: 'Safe' or ('Unsafe' + a counterexample)

1 **if** SAT $(I \wedge \neg P)$ **then return** Unsafe
2 $U_0 := I$, $O_0 := \neg P$
3 **while** True **do**
4      $O_{tmp} := \neg I$
5   **while** state :=pickState *(U) is successful* **do**
6   stack $:= \emptyset$
7   stack.push (state, $|O| - 1$)
8   **while** stack.size $\neq 0$ **do**
9   (s,l) := stack.top()   // Assume $s \in U_j$
10   **if** l < 0 **then return** Unsafe
11   **if** isBlockedAt *(s, l)* **then**
12   backtrack (s,l)
13   Continue
14   **if** SAT $(s, T \wedge O'_l)$ **then**
15   t := getModel()
16              $U_{j+1} := U_{j+1} \cup$ t   // Widening U
17   stack.push (t,l-1)
18   **else**
19   stack.pop()
20   uc := getUC()
21   **if** $l + 1 < |O|$ **then** $O_{l+1} := O_{l+1} \wedge (\neg uc)$
22   **else** $O_{tmp} := O_{tmp} \wedge (\neg uc)$
23   backtrack (s,l)
24   **if** $\exists i \geq 1$ *s.t.* $(\bigcup_{0 \leq j \leq i} O_j) \supseteq O_{i+1}$ **then return** Safe
25   Add a new state-set to O and initialize it to O_{tmp}

---

of state sets, defined as shown in Table 2, where k denotes the frame index in the induction process, and $k \geq 0$.
These sequences determine the termination of CAR as follows:

- *Return 'Unsafe' if $\exists i \cdot U_i \cap \neg P \neq \emptyset$.*
- *Return 'Safe' if $\exists i \geq 1 \cdot (\bigcup_{j=0}^{i} O_j) \supseteq O_{i+1}$.*

CAR can be implemented in both forward (ForwardCAR) and backward (BackwardCAR) modes. BackwardCAR is advantageous for finding unsafe bugs, while ForwardCAR is effective for proving safety [14,15].

As shown in Algorithm 1, CAR works by progressively widening the U sets and narrowing the O sets. These sets are initialized at Line 2 with U set to the state I and O set to $\neg P$. The algorithm maintains a stack of pairs $\langle state, level \rangle$, where each state is associated with an index corresponding to an O frame. The temporary frame O_{tmp}, initialized to $\neg I$ at Line 4, is updated during the process to represent the next frame to be created.

In each iteration, CAR picks a state from the U-sequence, by default from the beginning to the end, as shown in Line 5, and pushes it to the stack. Then, for the state s at the top of the stack, CAR first checks if it is already blocked at this frame (Line 11). If so, CAR backtracks this state to a higher level (Line 12), skipping over frames that already block this state. Otherwise, CAR goes on to check if it can reach the O_l frame by checking whether $s \wedge T \wedge O_l'$ (Line 14) is satisfiable. If yes, a new state $t \in O_l$ is extracted from the model and added to the U-sequence, thereby widening it (Lines 15–17). Otherwise, the algorithm uses the unsatisfiable core (denoted as UC) to constrain the O frame for the next level, narrowing it (Lines 19–21), and pushes s back onto the stack. Afterward, CAR backtracks this state at Line 23.

Finally, CAR terminates the checking procedure with either 'Safe' or 'Unsafe'. The unsafe check attempts to find a path from I to $\neg P$ while the working level l is less than 0 (Line 10) and provides a counterexample. The safe check propagates clauses from O_i to O_{i+1}, checking for a fixpoint. If reached, the algorithm returns 'Safe' based on the check in line 24.

3   Motivating Examples

Before delving into the examples, let us briefly review how CAR operates. The CAR algorithm relies on SAT queries as its core mechanism to advance its search process (see Line 14 of Algorithm 1). The SAT query checks whether a state s from the U-sequence can transition to a particular O-frame O_i. If the query is successful (lines 15–17), a new reachable state is identified, and CAR uses this state to expand the U-sequence. Conversely, if the query fails, CAR refines the O-sequence by incorporating the negation of the identified UC. The search process of CAR is illustrated in Fig. 1.

CAR enhances search efficiency by retaining the reachable states in the U sequence for future reuse, distinguishing it from the PDR algorithm. However, an overabundance of remembered states could occasionally pose challenges. In practice, we have observed that the CAR algorithm can sometimes be stuck during the search process in certain situations, causing timeouts. Specifically, the search process can get stuck within a subspace, consuming a significant amount of time during a single iteration. This prompted us to investigate these occurrences further, where we identified two recurring patterns that frequently contribute to inefficient search progress.

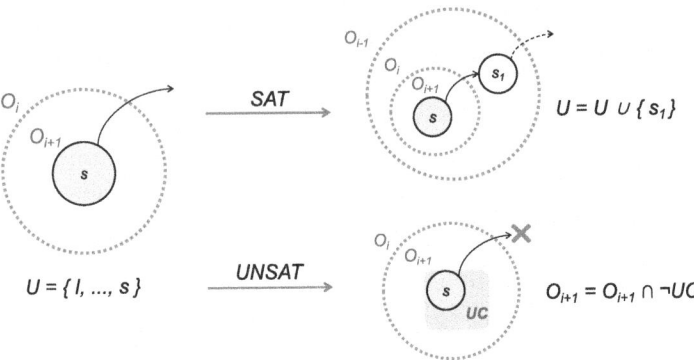

Fig. 1. The CAR algorithm searches for reachable states by leveraging SAT queries. When a state s in the U-sequence can transition to an O-frame O_i, it expands the U-sequence. Otherwise, it refines the O-sequence.

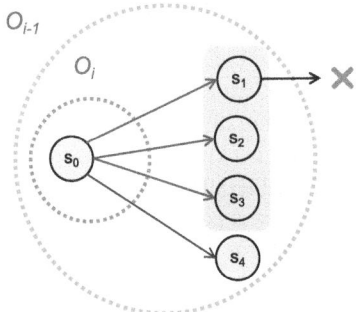

Fig. 2. Redundant states in the same subspace could generate identical UCs when attempting to reach O_{i-1}. Only one state (e.g., s_1) needs to be explored, while others (e.g., s_2, s_3) are redundant.

Redundant States. During the execution of the CAR algorithm, we observed that when multiple states in the U-sequence attempt to reach a specific O-frame, the UC generated by one state often blocks the others. For instance, as depicted in Fig. 2, state s_0 has four successor states in O_i. The shaded area indicates that s_1, s_2, and s_3 are within the same state space. When these states attempt to transition to a specific O-frame O_{i-1}, the UC generated by one of them (e.g., s_1) blocks the others (e.g., s_2 and s_3). This means that searching for s_2 and s_3 is redundant because their outcomes are already determined by s_1.

The root cause of this redundancy lies in the nature of SAT queries and the behavior of SAT solvers. When a SAT query is satisfiable, there may be multiple distinct assignments that satisfy the query. However, the SAT solver only returns one of these assignments. Often, some variables in the query are free, meaning their values do not affect the satisfiability of the query. Different assignments of these free variables can lead to multiple distinct states being generated. For example, if the SAT solver returns a state s_1 with a specific assignment of free variables, other states s_2 and s_3 that differ only in the assignments of these free variables will also be generated. When these states later attempt to transition to O_{i-1}, they are all blocked by the same UC generated for s_1, making their search redundant. Although CAR has a pre-check (Line 11 of Algorithm 1), the overhead is not negligible, especially when with a large amount of accumulated UCs.

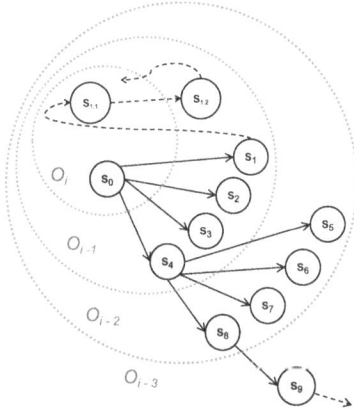

Fig. 3. Misleading states(e.g. s_1, s_2, s_3) cannot transition to lower frames, leading to the inefficient search.

Misleading States. We also observed an inefficiency in the search process when a state attempts to transition multiple steps. Some states returned by the SAT solver are not part of the actual transition trail and are added to the U-sequence after being accessed once. These states may repeatedly fail when revisited in the future. As shown in Fig. 3, s_0 in O_i can transition to O_{i-3} in 3 steps. During the search process, s_0 first reaches s_1 but fails to progress further and backtracks to $s_{1.1}$. Subsequently, s_0 reaches s_2 and s_3, each of which also fails to go further. After multiple SAT queries, s_0 finally reaches s_4, and through the trail $s_0 \rightarrow s_4 \rightarrow s_8 \rightarrow s_9$, it reaches O_{i-3}.

   This pattern is caused by the nature of SAT solver encoding. The SAT solver encodes single-step transition relations, so the states it returns for each step may not be the intermediate states required for a multi-step transition. For example, even though s_0 can reach s_9 in 3 steps; when we ask the SAT solver whether s_0 can reach O_{i-1}, it returns SAT but provides a state (s_1) that cannot reach O_{i-2}. Only after several rounds of queries is s_4 found, allowing the transition to proceed. This results in misleading states such as $s_1 - s_3$ and $s_5 - s_7$ in the figure, which are products of the SAT solver's single-step encoding and the different possible assignments to the constraints. Moreover, the presence of the backtracking mechanism in the CAR algorithm exacerbates the issue, as s_1 can introduce even more spurious states through backtracking, such as $s_{1.1} - s_{1.2}$.

4   Implementing Dynamic Traversal in CAR

Motivated by the observations in Sect. 3, we first introduce heuristic methods to optimize the traversal order of the U-sequence in CAR. These methods aim to address the inefficient search patterns in the original algorithm. Then, we propose the algorithm of CAR-DT (CAR with the dynamic traversal optimization), which can be regarded as a more flexible variant of CAR. Finally, we explore dynamic traversal approaches based on CAR to further enhance the efficiency.

4.1   Heuristic Methods for Optimizing U-Sequence Traversal

By recognizing the patterns observed in the CAR algorithm, we propose strategies to prioritize states more intelligently. Given that CAR is highly performance-sensitive, it is crucial to identify these patterns using methods that do not introduce additional computational costs. Fortunately, feasible approaches exist for both patterns. We introduce two heuristic methods, **PickUC** and **PickChildren**, corresponding to Redundant States and Misleading States, respectively. Additionally, we propose a combined scoring mechanism to dynamically prioritize states based on their potential to advance the search process.

PickUC: Distinct States First. For Redundant States, the number of UCs generated by a state can serve as an indicator. In the CAR algorithm, if a state is blocked by existing UCs, it will not generate a new UC despite consuming some checking time (the 'isBlockedAt' check, which can be generally understood as a subsumption test). Consequently, states that are 'always blocked by UCs generated by other states' will have a low number of generated UCs. This characteristic can be leveraged to efficiently identify Redundant States.

To address this, PickUC prioritizes states that generate more UCs in the previous round, as they are more likely to contribute to refining the O-sequence. Conversely, states blocked by existing UCs – therefore generating no new UCs – are deprioritized, reducing redundant computations.

PickChildren: Branching States First. For Misleading States, the number of children states can be used as a criterion. Misleading states, which repeatedly fail to transition further, tend to have a small number of children states (often zero). In contrast, correct states that can continue the transition process have more children (at least one). This difference in the number of children states can be used to distinguish between misleading and correct states.

To mitigate this issue, PickChildren prioritizes states with more successors (i.e., higher branching factors). These branching states are more likely to lead to productive transitions and help advance the search. By focusing on such states, the algorithm reduces time spent on unproductive leaf nodes.

Scoring Mechanism: Combination of Both Criterions. The generation of UCs relies on the SAT solver returning 'UNSAT', while the generation of successors depends on 'SAT' queries. Although these processes may initially seem contradictory, they are actually complementary. Specifically, the same $(state, level)$

Algorithm 2: The CAR algorithm with Dynamic Traversal

    Input: A transition system $Sys = (V, I, T)$ and a safety property P
    Output: 'Safe' or ('Unsafe' + a counterexample)
1 **if** SAT $(I \wedge \neg P)$ **then return** Unsafe
2 $U_0 := I,\ O_0 := \neg P$
3 **while** True **do**
4      $O_{tmp} := \neg I$
5   **while** state := pickStateDynamically *(U) is successful* **do**
6   stack := $\emptyset$
7   stack.push (state, $|O| - 1$)
8   **while** stack.size $\neq 0$ **do**
9   (s,l) := stack.top()   `// Assume s ` $\in U_j$
10   ...
11   ...
12   **if** $\exists i \geq 1$ *s.t.* $(\bigcup_{0 \leq j \leq i} O_j) \supseteq O_{i+1}$ **then return** Safe
13   Add a new state-set to O and initialize it to O_{tmp}

---

pair (see Line 9 of Algorithm 1) could be queried multiple times, yielding one or more SAT results, but ultimately resulting in a single UNSAT result (since the updated UCs prevent further successors from being found). For a specific state, the number of UCs reflects its ability to refine the O-sequence by eliminating redundant paths, while the number of successors indicates its potential to explore diverse transitions.

Building on these insights, we introduce a scoring mechanism that ranks states within the U-sequence. By balancing the factors, we can prioritizes states that efficiently prune the search space and explore deeper levels.

Specifically, each state is assigned a score based on a weighted sum of its UC count and number of successors:

$$score = w \cdot \mathrm{num(UCs)} + (1 - w) \cdot \mathrm{num(successors)} \qquad (1)$$

where w is a tunable weight balancing the contributions of these two factors. States are sorted in descending order of their scores in each iteration, with the initial state always preserved to ensure correctness. This mechanism directs the traversal toward states that either block redundant explorations through UCs or offer diverse transitions through high branching factors, thereby enhancing the efficiency of the CAR algorithm.

4.2 CAR with Partial Traversal

Prioritized traversal reduces the priority of low-value states, yet these states can still be visited. To avoid unnecessary exploration of less promising states, we propose the **Partial Traversal** strategy to enhance dynamic traversal. This strategy explores only a selected portion of the U-sequence to improve efficiency.

Algorithm 2 shows the implementation of the updated CAR-DT. The only difference between CAR-DT and the original CAR algorithm lies in the state selection
process (see Line 5). Specifically, CAR-DT only visits a subset of U-sequence. We
then prove that as long as the initial state is not excluded by the partial traversal,
the completeness of CAR-DT is maintained, as stated in the following theorem:

Theorem 1 (Completeness). *Given a Boolean transition system Sys and a
safety property P, CAR-DT terminates with UNSAFE if $Sys \not\models P$ and terminates
with SAFE if $Sys \models P$.*

Before proving the theorem, we first prove two lemmas separately.[1]

Lemma 1 (Completeness-UNSAFE). *Given a Boolean transition system
Sys and a safety property P, CAR-DT terminates with UNSAFE if $Sys \not\models P$.*

Proof. If the given problem is UNSAFE, there exists a finite path ρ from I to
$\neg P$. Let the length of ρ be $n + 1$, and label the states on the path as $\rho[j]$ for
$0 \le j \le n$, where $\rho[n] = I$ and $\rho[0] \in \neg P$.

Assume the O-sequence has grown to size $n + 1$[2], i.e., we have $O_0, O_1, \ldots, O_n$.
Since ρ is a valid path, for each j from 0 to $n - 1$, $\rho[j + 1] \wedge T \wedge O'_j$ is SAT, where
O'_j is the predicate for the next frame.

In CAR-DT, when the initial state I is selected (guaranteed not to be missed
by **pickStateDynamically**), the algorithm checks if $I \wedge T \wedge O'_n$ is SAT. Since
I can reach $\rho[n - 1]$ in one step, this query will be SAT. And with finite steps[3],
$\rho[n - 1]$ will be found and added to the working stack.

By induction, assume that $\rho[k]$ has been found and pushed to the working
stack for some $k < n$. When $\rho[k]$ is selected, the algorithm checks if $\rho[k] \wedge T \wedge O'_{k-1}$
is SAT. Similarly, this query will be SAT, and $\rho[k - 1]$ will be pushed to the stack.

Finally, $\rho[0] \in \neg P$ will be found, and the algorithm will terminate with
UNSAFE, returning the counterexample ρ.   □

Lemma 2 (Completeness-SAFE). *Given a Boolean transition system Sys
and a safety property P, CAR-DT terminates with SAFE if $Sys \models P$.*

Proof. By the design of CAR-DT, the O-sequence is monotonically increasing,
i.e., once the negation of a UC is added to an O-frame, it will never be removed.
With this continuous refinement, the O-sequence becomes increasingly precise,
and will eventually converge to the real reachable set R.

Since the system is SAFE, there exists no path from I to $\neg P$. As a result,
the O-sequence will eventually reach a fixpoint where no further states can be
added to the over-approximation. Formally, there exists a minimal k such that:
$\left(\bigcup_{0 \le j \le k} O_j \right) \supseteq O_{k+1}$ This implies that the O-sequence has stabilized and no
new states can be reached beyond this point.

---

[1] Due to space constraints, we only demonstrate the correctness of backward-CAR,
which involves a forward search. Forward-CAR can be proved similarly.

[2] This is guaranteed to happen within finite time. The proof is the same as the original
CAR algorithm.

[3] This is guaranteed by the termination of the original CAR algorithm.

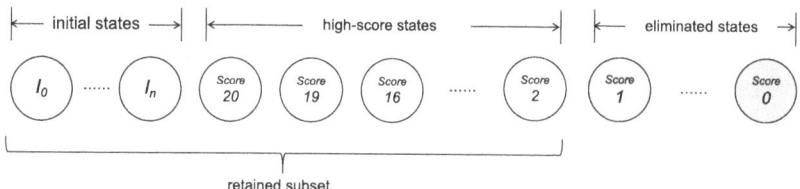

Fig. 4. Reordered U-sequence after scoring and truncation.

In CAR-DT, once the O-sequence reaches this fixpoint, the algorithm checks whether the condition $\exists i \geq 1$ such that $\left(\bigcup_{0 \leq j \leq i} O_j\right) \supseteq O_{i+1}$ holds. If this condition is satisfied, the algorithm terminates and returns 'Safe'.

Since the O-sequence is guaranteed to converge to the true reachable set R, the algorithm will eventually detect this fixpoint and correctly terminate with 'Safe'.   □

And finally, we prove Theorem 1:

Proof. An input problem could either be SAFE or UNSAFE. With the proved lemmas Lemma 1 and Lemma 2, the completeness of CAR-DT is proved.   ■

Building on the insight that full traversal of the U-sequence is not necessary for correctness, we now present the details of the CAR-DT implementation. The partial traversal focuses on the initial state and the most promising states in the U-sequence, identified by their scores from Eq. 1. Figure 4 illustrates the reordered U-sequence when applying partial traversal in CAR-DT. The traversal begins with the initial state, followed by states sorted according to their scores. States beyond the retained subset are excluded from further traversal. This approach reduces computational overhead by focusing on high-potential states while ensuring algorithm correctness by always preserving the initial states.

A special case of the partial traversal strategy retains only the initial state in the U-sequence. This is motivated by the fact that initial states typically exhibit high scores due to their lack of blocking constraints and high branching potential. By focusing exclusively on the initial states, this variant prevents the accumulation of redundant or misleading states and eliminates the need to manage a large U-sequence, resulting in $U = \{I\}$.

5   Evaluation

We implemented the proposed method on the state-of-the-art CAR-based single-core model checker SimpleCAR[4] [17], which incorporates the latest optimization of the CAR algorithm.[5]

---

[4] It is a core component of the SuperCAR model checker [16], which received the bronze award in recent HWMCC competition [10].

[5] All the artifacts are available at [1].

Table 3. Comparison of solved cases with different picking strategies. 'Basic' refers to the default traversal setting of the CAR algorithm. 'Par-2 Score' refers to the calculation of the average time consumption across all cases, where the run time of timed-out cases is counted as double. 'VirtualBest' refers to taking the best result of each checker.

Method	Safe			Unsafe			Total	Par-2 Score
	Gain	Loss	Solved	Gain	Loss	Solved		
Basic	-	-	106	-	-	26	132	4299.81
PickUC	7	1	**112**	0	0	26	**138**	**4204.39**
PickChildren	6	1	111	1	2	25	136	4249.70
VirtualBest	-	-	115	-	-	27	142	-

Table 4. Performance of CAR with the scoring mechanism. VBS refers to Virtual Best.

Strategies	PickChildren $(w = 0)$	Scoring with different w				PickUC $(w = 1)$	VBS
		$w = 0.3$	$w = 0.5$	$w = 0.7$	$w = 0.9$		
Cases Solved	136	131	136	**139**	134	138	146
Safe Solved	111	107	111	**112**	109	112	118
Unsafe Solved	25	24	25	**27**	25	26	28
Par-2 Score	4249.70	4326.27	4247.25	**4184.82**	4266.53	4204.39	-

5.1 Evaluation Setup

We conducted the experiments on a cluster, consisting of 240 nodes with 6720 processor cores altogether (14 processor cores per node) and running at 2.6GHz with 96GB of RAM per node. The operating system is RedHat 4.8.5-16.

We evaluated our method using all 318 AIGER-format benchmarks from the HWMCC 2024 competition, including both safe and unsafe cases, to show the effectiveness of CAR-DT in proving safety and finding counterexamples. For each running instance, the memory was limited to 8 GB; if not otherwise specified, the time was limited to 1 h.

5.2 Evaluation Results

RQ1: How Effective is the Prioritized Traversal Strategy? To compare the effectiveness of different picking methods on the CAR algorithm, we first evaluated the performance of SimpleCAR under different state prioritizations, the corresponding results are shown in Table 3.

The data reveals that both the PickUC and PickChildren strategies outperform the Basic traversal method. Specifically, PickUC gains 7 additional cases compared to Basic, despite incurring 1 loss. PickChildren gains 7 cases, which also contributes to the virtual best. Interestingly, virtual best solves 142 cases, with an increase of 10 cases, which is equivalent to the combined improvements of PickUC (6 cases) and PickChildren(4 cases) over Basic. This suggests that the

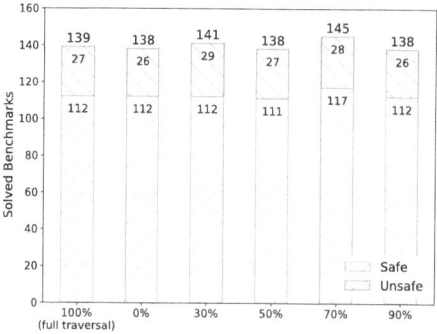

Fig. 5. The impact of different portion settings on the performance of the `CAR-DT` algorithm. The X-axis represents the portion setting. All variants are with the best Scoring strategy where $w = 0.7$.

Table 5. Par2-Score of `CAR-DT` with different configurations.

Strategies	Scoring method	CAR-DT (x)				
		$x = 0$	$x = 0.3$	$x = 0.5$	$x = 0.7$	$x = 0.9$
Par2-Score	4184.82	4190.66	4179.08	4201.00	**4074.68**	4212.43

strategies are complementary, indicating that integrating them into the scoring mechanism could further enhance the results.

To further explore the effects of combining the two picking strategies, we conducted experiments using various values of w, which represents the weight that balances the preference for avoiding either Redundant States or Misleading States. When $w = 1$, the method defaults to PickUC, while $w = 0$ corresponds to PickChildren. The experimental results, shown in Table 4, indicate that the optimal performance occurred when $w = 0.7$, which solved 112 safe cases and 27 unsafe cases. The virtual best of these scoring strategies reaches a total of 146 solved cases, showing that balancing the two patterns during the search process uncovers additional potential for solving even more cases.

Thus, the superior performance compared to the Basic method highlights the potential of **prioritized traversal** for advancing the verification process.

RQ2: Can CAR with Partial Traversal Achieve Better Performance?

To evaluate whether searching on a subset of the U-sequence can further enhance performance, we conducted experiments based on partial traversal. Specifically, in each iteration, we eliminated a certain proportion of states from the end of the ordered U-sequence, which corresponded to the least promising states. We denote this approach as `CAR-DT` (x), where only the top x states are retained. For example, `CAR-DT` (0%) reduces to the case where only the initial state is preserved, while `CAR-DT` (100%) retains all states, equivalent to the scoring method.

Table 6. The number of instances solved with a 1-hour timeout by different model checkers. 'Gain' and 'Loss' refers to the comparison with `CAR-DT`. 'VBS' means the virtual best.

	Safe			Unsafe			Total
	Gain	Loss	Solved	Gain	Loss	Solved	
CAR-DT	-	-	117	-	-	28	145
ABC-PDR	15	3	129	0	11	17	146
IIMC-PDR	8	24	101	2	8	22	123
IC3-REF	2	12	107	11	12	27	134
AVY	11	13	115	12	6	34	149
VBS	-	-	137	-	-	47	184

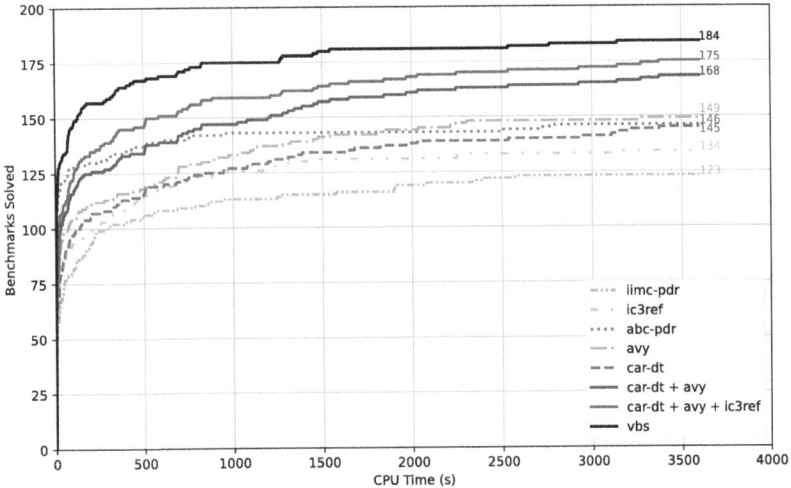

Fig. 6. Comparison of run-time performance among different model checkers.

Building upon the optimal scoring strategy identified in RQ1, we conducted experiments with several portion settings. The corresponding results are presented in Fig. 5. `CAR-DT` outperforms the optimal scoring method when the portion is set to 30% and 70%, whereas for other values, `CAR-DT` remains comparable to the scoring method. `CAR-DT` (70%) achieves a peak value of 145, yielding an improvement of 10% compared to the unoptimized Basic traversal strategy of CAR, representing a significant enhancement.

Table 5 compares the Par-2 score of `CAR-DT` across different portion settings. The results show that some variants achieves lower Par-2 scores compared to the scoring strategy. This indicates that dynamically discarding an appropriate proportion of states from the U-sequence can significantly reduce the computational overhead and improve the overall efficiency of the CAR algorithm. For instance, CAR-DT (70%) achieved a Par-2 score of 4074.68, which is much lower than the score of 4184.82 obtained by the optimal weight of the scoring method, demonstrating a notable improvement in verification efficiency.

RQ3: How Does CAR-DT Perform When Compared to the State-of-the-Art Model Checking Algorithms? To evaluate the performance of CAR-DT against state-of-the-art model checking algorithms, we conducted a comprehensive comparison with several leading tools, including ABC-PDR [5], IIMC-PDR [12], IC3-REF [11] and AVY [13].

As shown in Table 6, CAR-DT outperforms IC3-REF and IIMC-PDR, solving more instances within the given time limit. When compared to ABC-PDR and AVY, CAR-DT exhibits competitive performance, with a slight difference in the number of solved instances. It should also be noted that CAR-DT can solve more safe cases (117) than AVY (115). This indicates that our approach is particularly effective in proving safety properties, which is a crucial aspect of model checking.

Moreover, CAR-DT demonstrates notable complementarity with other algorithms. For example, it can solve 14 instances that ABC-PDR cannot, while ABC-PDR can solve 15 instances that CAR-DT cannot. Similarly, CAR-DT has a gain of 32 instances over IIMC-PDR and a gain of 24 instances over IC3-REF. These results highlight the unique strengths of CAR-DT in certain types of verification tasks. The virtual best solver of all these tools can resolve a total of 184 cases, which underscores the potential for further improvement through the combination of different algorithms. The high complementarity among these tools suggests that integrating CAR-DT with other state-of-the-art model checkers could lead to a more comprehensive and efficient verification framework. For instance, combining CAR-DT and AVY could leverage the strengths of both tools to solve a broader range of benchmarks more effectively.

Figure 6 provides a more detailed comparison of the run-time performance of these model checkers. It shows that CAR-DT consistently solves a significant number of benchmarks faster than IC3-REF and IIMC-PDR. The performance gap between CAR-DT and ABC-PDR is relatively small, indicating that both tools are effective for a wide range of verification tasks. AVY, while having the highest overall performance, does not exhibit a clear dominance over our approach in terms of run-time efficiency for individual benchmarks.[6]

In conclusion, CAR-DT demonstrates strong performance compared to state-of-the-art model checking algorithms. It outperforms some leading tools and shows competitive performance with others, while also exhibiting notable complementarity. These results highlight the effectiveness of our proposed dynamic traversal approach in enhancing the efficiency and scalability of CAR-based model checking.

---

[6] Notably, with only 3 cores (CAR-DT, AVY and IC3-REF), the combined performance already surpasses that of many candidates with 16 cores in HWMCC 2024.

6   Conclusion

In this paper, we proposed a dynamic traversal strategy for optimizing CAR-based model checking. By implementing prioritized traversal on a subset of U-sequence, we introduced an efficient approach that reduces redundant computations and improves scalability. The experimental results show that the application of our method, `CAR-DT`, significantly outperforms the original CAR algorithm and achieves competitive performance compared to state-of-the-art model checkers.

This work enhances CAR's practical applicability, offering a more efficient solution for large-scale verification tasks. In future work, we will focus on developing more intelligent methods to dynamically adjust the balance between these components.

References

1. CAR-DT artifact. https://doi.org/10.5281/zenodo.15165732
2. Biere, A., Cimatti, A., Clarke, E.M., Fujita, M., Zhu, Y.: Symbolic model checking using SAT procedures instead of BDDs. In: Proceedings of Design Automation Conference (DAC), pp. 317–320 (1999)
3. Biere, A., Cimatti, A., Clarke, E., Zhu, Y.: Symbolic model checking without BDDs. In: Cleaveland, W.R. (ed.) TACAS 1999. LNCS, vol. 1579, pp. 193–207. Springer, Heidelberg (1999). https://doi.org/10.1007/3-540-49059-0_14
4. Bradley, A.R.: SAT-based model checking without unrolling. In: Jhala, R., Schmidt, D. (eds.) VMCAI 2011. LNCS, vol. 6538, pp. 70–87. Springer, Heidelberg (2011). https://doi.org/10.1007/978-3-642-18275-4_7
5. Brayton, R., Mishchenko, A.: ABC: an academic industrial-strength verification tool. In: Touili, T., Cook, B., Jackson, P. (eds.) CAV 2010. LNCS, vol. 6174, pp. 24–40. Springer, Heidelberg (2010). https://doi.org/10.1007/978-3-642-14295-6_5
6. Dong, Y., Chen, Y., Li, J., Pu, G., Strichman, O.: Revisiting assumptions ordering in CAR-based model checking (long version). Technical report, arXiv (2024)
7. Dong, Y., Chen, Y., Li, J., Pu, G., Strichman, O.: Revisiting assumptions ordering in car-based model checking. IEEE Trans. Comput.-Aided Des. Integr. Circ. Syst. (2025)
8. Dureja, R., Li, J., Pu, G., Vardi, M.Y., Rozier, K.Y.: Intersection and rotation of assumption literals boosts bug-finding. In: Chakraborty, S., Navas, J.A. (eds.) VSTTE 2019. LNCS, vol. 12031, pp. 180–192. Springer, Cham (2020). https://doi.org/10.1007/978-3-030-41600-3_12
9. Eén, N., Mishchenko, A., Brayton, R.: Efficient implementation of property directed reachability. In: Proceedings of the International Conference on Formal Methods in Computer-Aided Design, FMCAD 2011, Austin, Texas, pp. 125–134. FMCAD Inc. (2011)
10. HWMCC (2024). https://hwmcc.github.io/2024/
11. IC3Ref. https://github.com/arbrad/IC3ref
12. IIMC. https://github.com/mgudemann/iimc
13. Ivrii, A., Gurfinkel, A.: Pushing to the top. In: Proceedings of the 15th Conference on Formal Methods in Computer-Aided Design, FMCAD 2015, Austin, Texas, pp. 65–72. FMCAD Inc. (2015)

14. Li, J., Dureja, R., Pu, G., Rozier, K.Y., Vardi, M.Y.: SimpleCAR: an efficient bug-finding tool based on approximate reachability. In: Chockler, H., Weissenbacher, G. (eds.) CAV 2018. LNCS, vol. 10982, pp. 37–44. Springer, Cham (2018). https://doi.org/10.1007/978-3-319-96142-2_5
15. Li, J., Zhu, S., Zhang, Y., Pu, G., Vardi, M.Y.: Safety model checking with complementary approximations. In: Proceedings of the 36th International Conference on Computer-Aided Design, ICCAD 2017, pp. 95–100. IEEE Press (2017)
16. Supercar. https://github.com/lijwen2748/hwmcc24
17. Xia, Y., Becchi, A., Cimatti, A., Griggio, A., Li, J., Pu, G.: Searching for i-good lemmas to accelerate safety model checking. In: Enea, C., Lal, A. (eds.) Computer Aided Verification, pp. 288–308. Springer, Cham (2023)

Author Index

© The Editor(s) (if applicable) and The Author(s), under exclusive license
to Springer Nature Switzerland AG 2026
P. Rümmer and Z. Wu (Eds.): TASE 2025, LNCS 15841, pp. 399–400, 2026.
https://doi.org/10.1007/978-3-031-98208-8

The manufacturer's authorised representative in the EU is Springer
Nature Customer Service Centre GmbH, Europaplatz 3, 69115 Heidelberg,
Germany. If you have any concerns regarding our products, please
contact ProductSafety@springernature.com

Printed and bound by CPI Group (UK) Ltd, Croydon, CR0 4YY

29/04/2026

02099458-0010